MAJOR TRENDS IN
Jewish Mysticism

GERSHOM G. SCHOLEM

SCHOCKEN BOOKS · NEW YORK

MAJOR TRENDS IN JEWISH MYSTICISM is based
on the Hilda Strook Lectures delivered by
Professor Scholem at the Jewish Institute of
Religion, New York

First SCHOCKEN PAPERBACK edition 1961
Reprinted from the Third Revised Edition

Eighth Printing, 1974

MORE THAN TWENTY YEARS have passed since I began to devote myself to the study of Jewish mysticism and especially of Kabbalism. It was a beginning in more than one sense, for the task which confronted me necessitated a vast amount of spade-work in a field strewn with ruins and by no means ripe as yet for the constructive labors of the builder of a system. Both as to historical fact and philological analysis there was pioneer work to be done, often of the most primitive and elementary kind. Rapid bird's-eye syntheses and elaborate speculations on shaky premises had to give way to the more modest work of laying the secure foundations of valid generalization. Where others had either disdained close acquaintance with the sources of what they frequently rejected and condemned, or erected some lofty edifice of speculation, I found myself constrained by circumstance and by inclination to perform the modest but necessary task of clearing the ground of much scattered debris and laying bare the outlines of a great and significant chapter in the history of Jewish religion. Needless to say, like all spade-work, the task gradually imposed on my mind a certain conception of the subject-matter as a whole. As the innumerable and often laborious investigations of detailed points neared completion, the outlines became less blurred, and presently there emerged from the confusing welter of fact and fiction a picture, more or less definite though not at all points complete, of the development of Jewish mysticism, its inner significance, its problems and its meaning for the history of Judaism in general. In many details this gradually unfolding conception differed not inconsiderably from the views hitherto current in the literature published on the subject. I owe a debt of gratitude to those among my predecessors in this field whose footsteps I have followed, but honesty compels me to add that on most points my later views have very little in common with their own.

Having arrived at this stage of research, nothing could have been more welcome to me than the invitation to serve as Stroock lecturer at the Jewish Institute of Religion in New York for the year 1938. Of the nine lectures contained in this volume, in which I have attempted to sum up some of the principal results of my investigations, seven were delivered there, six in English and one, the fifth, in Hebrew. The remaining two, namely the second and third, dealing with two additional important aspects of the development of Jewish mysticism which could not be included in the schedule of the original seven, were given upon other occasions.

All the lectures included in this volume are published in a considerably enlarged version, with the exception of the last which is reprinted almost in the original form. To have expanded the brief account of Hasidism given here by a closer examination of specific phenomena would have necessitated writing a new book. I have therefore contented myself with an exposition of my general views on the subject. All in all, it may be said that the purpose of this book is not to give a complete historical account of Jewish mysticism but an outline of its principal features in the form of an analysis of some of its most important phases. A comprehensive critical history of Jewish mysticism, with special reference to all the various currents and cross-currents of Kabbalism, would require several volumes. Since these lectures were not intended exclusively for re-search students in this field but for the much wider circle of those who take an interest in questions of Jewish history and religion, I have laid greater stress on the analysis and interpretation of mystical thought than on the historical links between the various systems. Where it was possible without introducing too much philo-logical detail I have nevertheless sketched the historical connections at least in outline. Only in the lecture on the Book Zohar and its author have I departed from this rule and attempted a more thorough philological analysis. I have considered it my obligation to do so both in view of the generally acknowledged importance of the matter for the history of Judaism and because of the unfortu-nate state of the discussion to date. Readers who take only slight interest in such questions of literary and historical criticism will miss little by skipping the fifth lecture. For similar reasons I have placed the notes at the end of the book, in order not to burden the text too much with references which have little meaning for those outside the circle of students of Judaism familiar with the reading of Hebrew texts.

This book challenges in some of its major theses not a few notions about Jewish history and religion which are more or less generally accepted by both Jews and non-Jews. If the great task of Jewish scholarship in our generation, the task of rewriting Jewish history with a deeper understanding of the interplay of religious, political and social forces, is to be successfully carried out, there is urgent need for a new elucidation of the function which Jewish mysticism has had at varying periods, of its ideals, and of its approach to the various problems arising from the actual conditions at such times. I have endeavored to present my views on this subject as concisely and at the same time as clearly as possible, in the hope of making a serious contribution to a very important and very much needed discussion. Among Hebrew writers, this discussion has now pro-ceeded for a number of years; in the corresponding English litera-ture on the subject it has been reopened by Salo Baron's "A Re-ligious and Social History of the Jews," the publication of which coincided with the delivery of these lectures. I, for one, sincerely believe that such a discussion of our past has something to do with our future.

I wish to take this opportunity to thank all those who have placed me under an obligation by their assistance and advice. My greatest debt is due to Mr. George Lichtheim, Jerusalem, for his translation of the bulk of the manuscript. Professor Henry Slonimsky and Professor Ralph Marcus, of the Jewish Institute of Religion, went through the first draft; Dr. J. L. Magnes, President of the Hebrew University, and Mr. Morton Smith, S.T.B. (Harvard), a research student at the University, have read the final manuscript. To them all I am more than obliged for their kind help and many valuable suggestions as to the correct wording of these lectures. Mr. Hayim Wirszubski, M.A., has assisted in the compilation of the Index.

I owe an especial debt of gratitude to Dr. Stephen S. Wise, President of the Jewish Institute of Religion, not only for the invitation to deliver these lectures, but also for his generous consent to their publication in the present form, and to Mr. Salman Schocken whose constant interest and help has made it possible to publish them in this enlarged version. I should equally like to mention the valuable suggestions I owe to discussions of many points of detail with friends and colleagues, especially with Prof. I. F. Baer.

Finally, I wish to express my thanks to all those who have shown me friendship and goodwill during my stay in America and made me feel at home in the great desert of New York; above all to Prof. Shalom Spiegel, of the Jewish Institute of Religion, for his unfailing friendship and readiness to give of his time and help. To Prof. Alexander Marx, of the Jewish Theological Seminary of America, to Mr. I. Mendelsohn and Dr. Abraham Halkin, of Columbia University Library, and to Dr. Walter Rothmann and Mr. Moses Marx, of the Library of the Hebrew Union College, I feel greatly indebted for the exceedingly liberal assistance they have extended to me during my work in these three great collections of Kabbalistical manuscripts in the United States. The many profitable hours I have spent there have left their imprint on the final text of this book, since I was able to make use of some important new material which had previously escaped my notice or which was not included in the collections of Europe and Palestine to which I had had access.

GERSHOM G. SCHOLEM

Jerusalem
The Hebrew University
    May 1941

PREFACE TO THE SECOND EDITION

THE KIND RECEPTION ACCORDED, in many circles, to this book, which deals with no easy subject indeed, has made necessary, after five years, a second edition. I have revised style and matter and have made some more substantial additions here and there, wherever the context allowed me to do so. I should have preferred very much to give an account of the beginnings of Kabbalism as from 1150 to 1250, all the more as it regards a problem having an extraordinary bearing on the history of Judaism. But it appeared in the course of the work that the subject needs a more thorough treatment than could possibly have been given within the framework of these lectures; I propose, therefore, to present the results of my studies in a special publication.

G. G. S.

Jerusalem, February 1946

PUBLISHER'S NOTE TO THE THIRD EDITION

THIS EDITION IS A REPRINT of the second, revised, edition. Misprints have been corrected. A number of studies which appeared after the second edition went to print have been added to the Bibliography.

October 1954

PUBLISHER'S NOTE TO THE PAPERBACK EDITION

THIS EDITION IS A REPRINT of the third edition. A selection of studies in the field which appeared after the third edition has been added to the Bibliography.

November 1960

CONTENTS

FIRST LECTURE: GENERAL CHARACTERISTICS OF JEWISH
MYSTICISM.   pp. 1—39.

> Purpose of these lectures. What is Mysticism? The paradoxical nature of
> mystical experience. Mysticism as an historical phenomenon. Mythology,
> Religion and Mysticism. Mystical interpretation of religious values. Jewish
> Mysticism influenced by the positive contents of Judaism. The Kabbalistic
> theory of the hidden God and His attributes. The Sefiroth. The Torah.
> Kabbalism and language. Mysticism and the historical world. Cosmogony
> and eschatology. Jewish Philosophy and Kabbalism. Allegorization and
> symbolism. Philosophical and mystical interpretation of Halakhah and
> Aggadah. Kabbalism and prayer. Mythical elements in Kabbalistic thought.
> The resurrection of myth in the heart of Judaism. The absence of the
> feminine element in Jewish Mysticism.

SECOND LECTURE: MERKABAH MYSTICISM AND JEWISH
GNOSTICISM   pp. 40—79

> The first period of Jewish Mysticism. Anonymity of the writings. Esoterism
> of the Mishnah teachers. Throne-mysticism. Apocalyptic and mysticism.
> The literature of the *Hekhaloth*-books. The *Yorde Merkabah* and their
> organization. Conditions of initiation. The ecstatic ascent of the soul and
> its technique. Magical elements. Dangers of the ascent. God as Holy King.
> The hymns of the Merkabah mystics. *Shiur Komah.* Enoch, Metatron and
> Yahoel. The cosmic curtain. Remains of Gnostic speculations on aeons.
> The "Book of Creation." Theurgy. Moral re-interpretation of the Merkabah.

THIRD LECTURE: HASIDISM IN MEDIAEVAL GERMANY   pp. 80—118

> The rise of Hasidism in Germany. Mystical tradition and German Jewry.
> The "Book of the Devout." Jehudah the Hasid and his disciples. Eschatolog-
> ical character of Hasidism. The new ideal of the Hasid: Ascetics, ataraxy
> and altruism. Love of God. A Judaized version of monkish Cynicism. The
> magic power of the Hasid. The Golem legend. Mysteries of Prayer. Oc-
> cultist practices. Hasidic conception of penitence. The conception of God in
> Hasidism. Immanence of God. *Kavod,* the Divine Glory. Traces of the
> Philonic doctrine of the *Logos.* The Cherub on the throne. Holiness and
> Greatness in God. The aim of prayer. The cosmic archetypes.

FOURTH LECTURE: ABRAHAM ABULAFIA AND THE
DOCTRINE OF PROPHETIC KABBALISM   pp. 119—155

Emergence of Kabbalism. Types of Kabbalists. Kabbalistic reticence and
censorship. Vision and, ecstasy. The conception of *Devekuth*—the Jewish
form of mystical union. Life and work of Abraham Abulafia. His theory of
ecstatical knowledge. The "science of combination." The music of pure
thought. The mystical nature of prophecy. Prophetic Kabbalism. Mystical
transfiguration as the essence of ecstasy. Mystical pragmatism. Practical
Kabbalism and magic. Later developments of Abulafia's doctrines. Translation of an autobiography written by a disciple of Abulafia.

FIFTH LECTURE: THE ZOHAR I. THE BOOK AND ITS
AUTHOR   pp. 156—204

The problem of the Zohar. Literary character and composition of the
Zohar. The whole of the Zoharic "literature" consists of two major parts:
the bulk of the Zohar and the *Raya Mehemna*. The bulk of the Zohar the
work of one author. Evidence of unity. The language and style of the
Zohar. Its stage-setting. Pseudo-realism. Principles of literary composition.
Sources of the Zohar: the real and fictitious ones. Treatment of the sources.
The author's predilection for certain Kabbalistic doctrines and dislike for
others. Absence of the doctrine of the *Shemitahs,* or units of cosmic development. Stages in the composition. The *Midrash Ha-Neelam* as the oldest
constituent of the Zohar. The *Midrash Ha-Neelam* written between 1275
and 1281; the bulk of the Zohar between 1281 and 1286; the *Raya Mehemna*
and *Tikkunim* about 1300. The question of the personality of the author.
Moses ben Shemtob de Leon. The old testimonial on his authorship. Moses
de Leon and Joseph Gikatila. Comparison of Moses de Leon's Hebrew writings with the bulk of the Zohar. Identity of the author of all these writings.
Other Kabbalistic pseudepigrapha written by Moses de Leon. Veiled references to his authorship of the Zohar in Moses' Hebrew writings. Moses de
Leon's spiritual development and his motives in writing the Zohar. Pseudepigraphy a legitimate category of religious literature.

SIXTH LECTURE: THE ZOHAR II. THE THEOSOPHIC
DOCTRINE OF THE ZOHAR   pp. 205—243

The difference between Merkabah Mysticism and Spanish Kabbalism. The
hidden God or *En-Sof*. The Sefiroth, the Realm of Divinity. Mystical conception of the Torah. Symbolical realization of the Sefiroth. Some instances
of Kabbalistic Symbolism. God as a mystical organism. Nothing and Being.

The first three stages of the Sefirotic development. Creation and its relation to God. Theogony and Cosmogony. Pantheistic leanings of the author of the Zohar. The original nature of Creation. Mythical imagery in Kabbalistic thought. The problem of sexual symbolism. The new idea of the Shekhinah as a feminine element in God and as the mystical Community of Israel. Man and his Fall. Kabbalistic ethics. The nature of evil. The Zohar and Jacob Boehme. Psychology of the Zohar. Unity of theosophy, cosmology and psychology.

SEVENTH LECTURE: ISAAC LURIA AND HIS SCHOOL   pp. 244—286

The Exodus from Spain and its religious consequences. Kabbalism on its way to Messianism. Apocalyptic propaganda by Kabbalists. The character and function of the new Kabbalism. Its center in Safed, Palestine. Moses Cordovero and Isaac Luria. Their personalities. Spread of Lurianic Kabbalism. Israel Sarug. Characteristics of the Lurianic doctrine. *Tsimtsum, Shevirah* and *Tikkun.* The twofold process of Creation. The withdrawal of God into Himself as the starting-point of Creation. Meaning of this doctrine. The primordial catastrophe, or Breaking of the Vessels. The origin of Evil. Two aspects of the theory of the *Tikkun,* or restoration of harmony. The mystical birth of the personal God and the mystical action of man. The emergence of theosophic worlds, and their relation to God. Theism and Pantheism in Luria's system. Mystical reinterpretation of Messianism. The doctrine of mystical prayer.*Kawwanah.* Man's role in the Universe. Luria's psychology and anthropology. The Exile of the Shekhinah. The uplifting of the holy sparks. Transmigration of the soul and its place in the Kabbalism of Safed. Influence of Lurianic Kabbalism. A great myth of Exile and Redemption.

EIGHTH LECTURE: SABBATIANISM AND MYSTICAL
HERESY   pp. 287—324

The Sabbatian movement of 1665—1666. Sabbatai Zevi, the Kabbalistic Messiah, and Nathan of Gaza, his prophet. Sabbatai Zevi's illness and its mystical interpretation by Nathan. Quasi-sacramental character of antinomian actions. Lurianism adapted to the personality of the new Messiah. Heretical turn of the movement after the apostasy of Sabbatai Zevi. Importance of Sabbatianism for Jewish history. A revolution of the Jewish consciousness. Connection between heretical Kabbalism and "Enlightenment." The Sabbatian ideology. A religion of paradoxes. Historical and mystical aspects of Redemption. Their clash after Sabbatai Zevi's apostasy.

Sabbatianism and Christianity. Influence of Marranic psychology on Sabbatianism. Doctrine of the necessary apostasy of the Messiah. The problem
of antinomianism. Moderate and radical forms of Sabbatianism. Mystical
nihilism and the doctrine of the Holiness of Sin. The new conception of
God: the first cause, or the God of Reason, and the first effect, or the God
of Revelation.

NINTH LECTURE: HASIDISM: THE LATEST PHASE   pp. 325—350

Polish and Ukrainian Hasidism of the eighteenth century and its problem.
Kabbalistic and Hasidic literature. The transformation of Kabbalism into
a popular movement. The alternatives of Kabbalistic development after the
collapse of Sabbatianism. Return to esoteric forms of worship: Rabbi Shalom Sharabi. Intensification of its popular aspects: Hasidism. Kabbalism
purged of its Messianic elements. Sabbatianism and Hasidism. Rabbi Adam
Baal Shem—a crypto-Sabbatian prophet. New type of leadership in Sabbatianism and Hasidism. Mystical revivalism. What is novel in Hasidism?
The essential originality of Hasidism not connected with mystical theosophy
but with mystical ethics. Zaddikism implied by the intrinsic nature of
Hasidism. Personality takes the place of doctrine. The figure of the Zaddik,
or Saint. The living Torah. The social function of the Saint as the center
of the community of men. Mysticism and magic in Hasidism. The Hasidic
story.

NOTES   pp. 351—424

BIBLIOGRAPHY   pp. 425—440

INDEX   pp. 441—456

TABLE OF TRANSLITERATION

In the text of the lectures, the use of Hebrew letters has been avoided throughout. The following is the transliteration of the Hebrew alphabet used, apart from the exceptions given below, in the present volume:

א	omitted	ל	l
בּ	b	מ	m
ב	v	נ	n
ג	g	ס	s
ד	d	ע	omitted
ה	h	פּ	p
ו	w	פ	f
ז	z	צ	ts
ח	h	ק	k
ט	t	ר	r
י	y	שׁ	sh
כּ	k	תּ	t
כ	kh	ת	th

Biblical names are given in the form used in the Authorized Version. Certain accepted terms are given in the transliterations generally current, e.g., Zaddik.

FIRST LECTURE

GENERAL CHARACTERISTICS OF JEWISH MYSTICISM

1

It is the purpose of these lectures to describe and to analyse some of the major trends of Jewish mysticism. I cannot of course hope to deal comprehensively in a few hours with a subject so vast and at the same time so intricate as the whole sweep and whirl of the mystical stream, as it runs its course through the movements which are known to the history of Jewish religion under the names of Kabbalah and Hasidism. Probably all of you have heard something about these aspects of Jewish religion. Their significance has been a matter of much dispute among Jewish scholars. Opinion has changed several times; it has fluctuated between the extremes of hostile criticism and condemnation on the one hand, and enthusiastic praise and defense on the other. It has not, however, greatly advanced our knowledge of what may be called the real nature of mystical lore, nor has it enabled us to form an unbiased judgment as to the part this lore has played and continues to play in Jewish history, or as to its importance for a true understanding of Judaism.

It is only fair to add that the exposition of Jewish mysticism, or that part of it which has so far been publicly discussed, abounds in misunderstandings and consequent misrepresentations of the subject matter under discussion. The great Jewish scholars of the past century whose conception of Jewish history is still dominant in our days, men like Graetz, Zunz, Geiger, Luzzatto and Steinschneider, had little sympathy—to put it mildly—for the Kabbalah. At once strange and repellent, it epitomised everything that was opposed to their own ideas and to the outlook which they hoped to make predominant in modern Judaism. Darkly it stood in their path, the ally of forces and tendencies in whose rejection pride was taken by a Jewry which, in Steinschneider's words, regarded it as its chief task to make a decent exit from the world. This fact may account for the negative opinions of these scholars regarding the function of mysticism in Jewish history. We are well aware that their attitude, so far from being that of the pure scholar, was rather that of the combatant actively grappling with a dangerous foe who is still full of strength and vitality; the foe in question being the Hasidic movement. Enmity can do a great deal. We should be thankful to those zealous early critics who, though their judgment and sense of values may have been affected and warped by their prejudices, nevertheless had their eyes open to see certain important factors with great distinctness. Often enough they were in the right, though not for the reasons they themselves gave. Truth to tell, the most astonishing thing in reading the works of these critics is their lack of adequate knowledge of the sources or the subjects on which in many cases they ventured to pass judgment.

It is not to the credit of Jewish scholarship that the works of the few writers who were really informed on the subject were never printed, and in some cases were not even recorded, since there was nobody to take an interest. Nor have we reason to be proud of the fact that the greater part of the ideas and views which show a real insight into the world of Kabbalism, closed as it was to the rationalism prevailing in the Judaism of the nineteenth century, were expressed by Christian scholars of a mystical bent, such as the Englishman Arthur Edward Waite[1] of our days and the German Franz Josef Molitor[2] a century ago. It is a pity that the fine philosophical intuition and natural grasp of such students lost their edge because they lacked all critical sense as to historical and philological data in this field, and therefore failed completely when they had to handle problems bearing on the facts.

The natural and obvious result of the antagonism of the great Jewish scholars was that, since the authorized guardians neglected this field, all manner of charlatans and dreamers came and treated it as their own property. From the brilliant misunderstandings and misrepresentations of Alphonse Louis Constant, who has won fame under the pseudonym of Eliphas Lévi, to the highly coloured humbug of Aleister Crowley and his followers, the most eccentric and fantastic statements have been produced purporting to be legitimate interpretations of Kabbalism. The time has come to reclaim this derelict area and to apply to it the strict standards of historical research. It is this task which I have set myself, and in the following lectures I should like to give some idea of the conclusions to which I have come in trying to light up this dark ground.

I do not have to point out that what I am going to say can in the nature of things be no more than a brief outline of the main structure of mystical thought, as it reveals itself in some of the classics of Jewish mysticism—more often than not in an obscure guise which makes it none too easy for modern minds to penetrate into its meaning. Obviously it is impossible to give a summary of the subject without at the same time attempting to interpret its meaning. It is a dangerous task to summarize in a few chapters a religious movement covering many centuries. In trying to explain so intricate a matter as Kabbalism the historian, too, must heed Byron's query: "Who will then explain the explanation?" For the rest, selection and abbreviation themselves constitute a kind of commentary, and to a certain extent even an appreciation of the subject. In other words, what I am going to present is a critical appreciation involving a certain philosophical outlook, as applied to the life texture of Jewish history, which in its fundamentals I believe to be active and alive to this day.

2

Since Jewish mysticism is to be the subject of these lectures, the first question bound to come up is this: what is Jewish mysticism? What precisely is meant by this term? Is there such a thing, and if so, what distinguishes it from other kinds of mystical experience? In order to be able to give an answer to this question, if only an incomplete one, it will be necessary to recall what we know about mysticism in general. I do not propose to add anything essentially new to the immense literature which has sprung up around this question during the past half-century. Some of you may have read the brilliant books written on this subject by Evelyn Underhill and Dr. Rufus Jones. I merely propose to rescue what appears to me important for our purpose from the welter of conflicting historical and metaphysical arguments which have been advanced and discussed in the course of the past century.

It is a curious fact that although doubt hardly exists as to what constitutes the phenomena to which history and philosophy have given the name of mysticism, there are almost as many definitions

of the term as there are writers on the subject. Some of these definitions, it is true, appear to have served more to obscure the nature
of the question than to clarify it. Some idea of the confusion engendered by these definitions can be gauged from the interesting
catalogue of "Definitions of Mysticism and Mystical Theology"
compiled by Dr. Inge as an appendix to his lectures on "Christian
Mysticism."

A good starting-point for our investigation can be obtained by
scrutinizing a few of these definitions which have won a certain
authority. Dr. Rufus Jones, in his excellent "Studies in Mystical
Religion" defines his subject as follows: "I shall use the word to
express the type of religion which puts the emphasis on immediate
awareness of relation with God, on direct and intimate consciousness of the Divine Presence. It is religion in its most acute, intense
and living stage."[4] Thomas Aquinas briefly defines mysticism as
cognitio dei experimentalis,[5] as the knowledge of God through experience. In using this term he leans heavily, like many mystics before and after him, on the words of the Psalmist (Psalm xxxiv, 9):
"Oh taste and see that the Lord is good." It is this tasting and
seeing, however spiritualized it may become, that the genuine mystic
desires. His attitude is determined by the fundamental experience
of the inner self which enters into immediate contact with God or
the metaphysical Reality. What forms the essence of this experience,
and how it is to be adequately described—that is the great riddle
which the mystics themselves, no less than the historians, have tried
to solve.

For it must be said that this act of personal experience, the systematic investigation and interpretation of which forms the task of
all mystical speculation, is of a highly contradictory and even paradoxical nature. Certainly this is true of all attempts to describe it
in words and perhaps, where there are no longer words, of the act
itself. What kind of direct relation can there be between the Creator
and His creature, between the finite and the infinite; and how can
words express an experience for which there is no adequate simile
in this finite world of man? Yet it would be wrong and superficial
to conclude that the contradiction implied by the nature of mystical
experience betokens an inherent absurdity. It will be wiser to
assume, as we shall often have occasion to do in the course of these
lectures, that the religious world of the mystic can be expressed in

terms applicable to rational knowledge only with the help of paradox. Among the psychologists G. Stratton, in his "Psychology of
Religious Life" (1911), has laid particular stress on this essential
conflict in religious life and thought, even in its non-mystical form.
It is well known that the descriptions given by the mystics of their
peculiar experiences and of the God whose presence they experience
are full of paradoxes of every kind. It is not the least baffling of
these paradoxes—to take an instance which is common to Jewish
and Christian mystics—that God is frequently described as the
mystical Nothing. I shall not try now to give an interpretation
of this term, to which we shall have to return; I only want to
stress the fact that the particular reality which the mystic sees or
tastes is of a very unusual kind.

To the general history of religion this fundamental experience
is known under the name of *unio mystica,* or mystical union with
God. The term, however, has no particular significance. Numerous
mystics, Jews as well as non-Jews, have by no means represented
the essence of their ecstatic experience, the tremendous uprush and
soaring of the soul to its highest plane, as a union with God. To
take an instance, the earliest Jewish mystics who formed an organized fraternity in Talmudic times and later, describe their experience in terms derived from the diction characteristic of their age.
They speak of the ascent of the soul to the Celestial Throne where
it obtains an ecstatic view of the majesty of God and the secrets
of His Realm. A great distance separates these old Jewish Gnostics
from the Hasidic mystics one of whom said:* "There are those
who serve God with their human intellect, and others whose gaze
is fixed on Nothing. . . . He who is granted this supreme experience
loses the reality of his intellect, but when he returns from such contemplation to the intellect, he finds it full of divine and inflowing
splendor." And yet it is the same experience which both are trying
to express in different ways.

This leads us to a further consideration: it would be a mistake
to assume that the whole of what we call mysticism is identical with
that personal experience which is realized in the state of ecstasy
or ecstatic meditation. Mysticism, as an historical phenomenon, comprises much more than this experience, which lies at its root. There
is a danger in relying too much on purely speculative definitions of
the term. The point I should like to make is this—that there is no

such thing as mysticism in the abstract, that is to say, a phenomenon or experience which has no particular relation to other religious phenomena. There is no mysticism as such, there is only the mysticism of a particular religious system, Christian, Islamic, Jewish mysticism and so on. That there remains a common characteristic it would be absurd to deny, and it is this element which is brought out in the comparative analysis of particular mystical experiences. But only in our days has the belief gained ground that there is such a thing as an abstract mystical religion. One reason for this widespread belief may be found in the pantheistic trend which, for the past century, has exercised a much greater influence on religious thought than ever before. Its influence can be traced in the manifold attempts to abandon the fixed forms of dogmatic and institutional religion in favour of some sort of universal religion. For the same reason the various historical aspects of religious mysticism are often treated as corrupted forms of an, as it were, chemically pure mysticism which is thought of as not bound to any particular religion. As it is our intention to treat of a certain definite kind of mysticism, namely Jewish, we should not dwell too much upon such abstractions. Moreover, as Evelyn Underhill has rightly pointed out, the prevailing conception of the mystic as a religious anarchist who owes no allegiance to his religion finds little support in fact. History rather shows that the great mystics were faithful adherents of the great religions.

Jewish mysticism, no less than its Greek or Christian counterparts, presents itself as a totality of concrete historical phenomena. Let us, therefore, pause to consider for a moment the conditions and circumstances under which mysticism arises in the historical development of religion and particularly in that of the great monotheistic systems. The definitions of the term *mysticism,* of which I have given a few instances, lead only too easily to the conclusion that all religion in the last resort is based on mysticism; a conclusion which, as we have seen, is drawn in so many words by Rufus Jones. For is not religion unthinkable without an "immediate awareness of relation with God"? That way lies an interminable dispute about words. The fact is that nobody seriously thinks of applying the term *mysticism* to the classic manifestations of the great religions. It would be absurd to call Moses, the man of God, a mystic, or to apply this term to the Prophets, on the strength of their immediate religious experience. I, for one, do not intend to employ a terminology which obscures the very real differences that are recognized by all, and thereby makes it even more difficult to get at the root of the problem.

3

The point which I would like to make first of all is this: Mysticism is a definite stage in the historical development of religion and makes its appearance under certain well-defined conditions. It is connected with, and inseparable from, a certain stage of the religious consciousness. It is also incompatible with certain other stages which leave no room for mysticism in the sense in which the term is commonly understood.

The first stage represents the world as being full of gods whom man encounters at every step and whose presence can be experienced without recourse to ecstatic meditation. In other words, there is no room for mysticism as long as the abyss between Man and God has not become a fact of the inner consciousness. That, however, is the case only while the childhood of mankind, its mythical epoch, lasts. The immediate consciousness of the interrelation and interdependence of things, their essential unity which precedes duality and in fact knows nothing of it, the truly monistic universe of man's mythical age, all this is alien to the spirit of mysticism. At the same time it will become clear why certain elements of this monistic consciousness recur on another plane and in different guise in the mystical consciousness. In this first stage, Nature is the scene of man's relation to God.

The second period which knows no real mysticism is the creative epoch in which the emergence, the break-through of religion occurs. Religion's supreme function is to destroy the dream-harmony of Man, Universe and God, to isolate man from the other elements of the dream stage of his mythical and primitive consciousness. For in its classical form, religion signifies the creation of a vast abyss, conceived as absolute, between God, the infinite and transcendental Being, and Man, the finite creature. For this reason alone, the rise of institutional religion, which is also the classical stage in the history of religion, is more widely removed than any other period from mysticism and all it implies. Man becomes aware of a fundamental duality, of a vast gulf which can be crossed by nothing but the *voice*;

the voice of God, directing and law-giving in His revelation, and the voice of man in prayer. The great monotheistic religions live and unfold in the ever-present consciousness of this bipolarity, of the existence of an abyss which can never be bridged. To them the scene of religion is no longer Nature, but the moral and religious action of man and the community of men, whose interplay brings about history as, in a sense, the stage on which the drama of man's relation to God unfolds.

And only now that religion has received, in history, its classical expression in a certain communal way of living and believing, only now do we witness the phenomenon called mysticism; its rise coincides with what may be called the romantic period of religion. Mysticism does not deny or overlook the abyss; on the contrary, it begins by realizing its existence, but from there it proceeds to a quest for the secret that will close it in, the hidden path that will span it. It strives to piece together the fragments broken by the religious cataclysm, to bring back the old unity which religion has destroyed, but on a new plane, where the world of mythology and that of revelation meet in the soul of man. Thus the soul becomes its scene and the soul's path through the abysmal multiplicity of things to the experience of the Divine Reality, now conceived as the primordial unity of all things, becomes its main preoccupation. To a certain extent, therefore, mysticism signifies a revival of mythical thought, although the difference must not be overlooked between the unity which is there before there is duality, and the unity that has to be won back in a new upsurge of the religious consciousness.

Historically, this appearance of mystical tendencies is also connected with another factor. The religious consciousness is not exhausted with the emergence of the classic systems of institutional religion. Its creative power endures, although the formative effect of a given religion may be sufficiently great to encompass all genuine religious feeling within its orbit for a long period. During this period the values which such a religious system has set up retain their original meaning and their appeal to the feelings of the believers. However, even so new religious impulses may and do arise which threaten to conflict with the scale of values established by historical religion. Above all, what encourages the emergence of mysticism is a situation in which these new impulses do not break through the shell of the old religious system and create a new one, but tend to remain confined within its borders. If and when such a situation arises, the longing for new religious values corresponding to the new religious experience finds its expression in a new interpretation of the old values which frequently acquire a much more profound and personal significance, although one which often differs entirely from the old and transforms their meaning. In this way Creation, Revelation and Redemption, to mention some of our most important religious conceptions, are given new and different meanings reflecting the characteristic feature of mystical experience, the direct contact between the individual and God.

Revelation, for instance, is to the mystic not only a definite historical occurrence which, at a given moment in history, puts an end to any further direct relation between mankind and God. With no thought of denying Revelation as a fact of history, the mystic still conceives the source of religious knowledge and experience which bursts forth from his own heart as being of equal importance for the conception of religious truth. In other words, instead of the one act of Revelation, there is a constant repetition of this act. This new Revelation, to himself or to his spiritual master, the mystic tries to link up with the sacred texts of the old; hence the new interpretation given to the canonical texts and sacred books of the great religions. To the mystic, the original act of Revelation to the community—the, as it were, public revelation of Mount Sinai, to take one instance—appears as something whose true meaning has yet to unfold itself; the secret revelation is to him the real and decisive one. And thus the substance of the canonical texts, like that of all other religious values, is melted down and given another form as it passes through the fiery stream of the mystical consciousness. It is hardly surprising that, hard as the mystic may try to remain within the confines of his religion, he often consciously or unconsciously approaches, or even transgresses, its limits.

It is not necessary for me to say anything further at this point about the reasons which have often transformed mystics into heretics. Such heresy does not always have to be fought with fire and sword by the religious community: it may even happen that its heretical nature is not understood and recognized. Particularly is this the case where the mystic succeeds in adapting himself to the 'orthodox' vocabulary and uses it as a wing or vehicle for his thoughts. As a matter of fact, this is what many Kabbalists have done. While Christianity and Islam, which had at their disposal more extensive means of repression and the apparatus of the State, have frequently and drastically suppressed the more extreme forms of mystical movements, few analogous events are to be found in the history of Judaism. Nevertheless, in the lectures on Sabbatianism and Hasidism, we shall have occasion to note that instances of this kind are not entirely lacking.

4

We have seen that mystical religion seeks to transform the God whom it encounters in the peculiar religious consciousness of its own social environment from an object of dogmatic knowledge into a novel and living experience and intuition. In addition, it also seeks to interpret this experience in a new way. Its practical side, the realization of God and the doctrine of the Quest for God, are therefore frequently, particularly in the more developed forms of the mystical consciousness, connected with a certain ideology. This ideology, this theory of mysticism, is a theory both of the mystical cognition of God and His revelation, and of the path which leads to Him.

It should now be clear why the outward forms of mystical religion within the orbit of a given religion are to a large extent shaped by the positive content and values recognized and glorified in that religion. We cannot, therefore, expect the physiognomy of Jewish mysticism to be the same as that of Catholic mysticism, Anabaptism or Moslem Sufism. The particular aspects of Christian mysticism, which are connected with the person of the Saviour and mediator between God and man, the mystical interpretation of the Passion of Christ, which is repeated in the personal experience of the individual—all this is foreign to Judaism, and also to its mystics. Their ideas proceed from the concepts and values peculiar to Judaism, that is to say, above all from the belief in the Unity of God and the meaning of His revelation as laid down in the Torah, the sacred law.

Jewish mysticism in its various forms represents an attempt to interpret the religious values of Judaism in terms of mystical values. It concentrates upon the idea of the living God who manifests himself in the acts of Creation, Revelation and Redemption. Pushed to its extreme, the mystical meditation on this idea gives birth to the conception of a sphere, a whole realm of divinity, which under-lies the world of our sense-data and which is present and active in all that exists. This is the meaning of what the Kabbalists call the *world of the 'Sefiroth'*. I should like to explain this a little more fully.

The attributes of the living God are conceived differently and undergo a peculiar transformation when compared with the mean-ing given to them by the philosophers of Judaism. Among the latter, Maimonides, in his "Guide of the Perplexed", felt bound to ask: How is it possible to say of God that He is living? Does that not imply a limitation of the infinite Being? The words "God is living", he argues, can only mean that he is not dead, that is to say, that he is the opposite of all that is negative. He is the negation of negation. A quite different reply is given by the Kabbalist, for whom the distinction, nay the conflict, between the known and the unknown God has a significance denied to it by the philosophers of Judaism.

No creature can take aim at the unknown, the hidden God. In the last resort, every cognition of God is based on a form of relation between Him and His creature, i.e. on a manifestation of God in something else, and not on a relation between Him and Himself. It has been argued that the difference between the *deus absconditus*, God in Himself, and God in His appearance is unknown to Kabba-lism.[7] This seems to me a wrong interpretation of the facts. On the contrary, the dualism embedded in these two aspects of the one God, both of which are, theologically speaking, possible ways of aiming at the divinity, has deeply preoccupied the Jewish mystics. It has occasionally led them to use formulas whose implied challenge to the religious consciousness of monotheism was fully revealed only in the subsequent development of Kabbalism. As a rule, the Kabba-lists were concerned to find a formula which should give as little offense as possible to the philosophers. For this reason the inherent contradiction between the two aspects of God is not always brought out as clearly as in the famous doctrine of an anonymous writer around 1300, according to whom God in Himself, as an absolute Being, and therefore by His very nature incapable of becoming the subject of a revelation to others, is not and cannot be meant in the documents of Revelation, in the canonical writings of the Bible, and in the rabbinical tradition.[8] He is not the subject of these writings and therefore also has no documented name, since every word of

the sacred writings refers after all to some aspect of His manifestation on the side of Creation. It follows that while the living God,
the God of religion of whom these writings bear witness, has innumerable names—which, according to the Kabbalists, belong to
Him by His very nature and not as a result of human convention—
the *deus absconditus,* the God who is hidden in His own self, can
only be named in a metaphorical sense and with the help of words
which, mystically speaking, are not real names at all. The favorite
formulae of the early Spanish Kabbalists are speculative paraphrases
like "Root of all Roots," "Great Reality," "Indifferent Unity,"⁹ and,
above all, *En-Sof.* The latter designation reveals the impersonal
character of this aspect of the hidden God from the standpoint of
man as clearly as, and perhaps even more clearly than, the others. It
signifies "the infinite" as such; not, as has been frequently suggested,
"He who is infinite" but "that which is infinite." Isaac the Blind
(one of the first Kabbalists of distinguishable personality) calls the
deus absconditus "that which is not conceivable by thinking", *not*
"He who is not etc."¹⁰ It is clear that with this postulate of an impersonal basic reality in God, which becomes a person—or appears
as a person—only in the process of Creation and Revelation,
Kabbalism abandons the personalistic basis of the Biblical conception of God. In this sense it is undeniable that the author of the
above-mentioned mystical aphorism is right in holding that *En-Sof*
(or what is meant by it) is not even mentioned in the Bible and the
Talmud. In the following lectures we shall see how the main schools
of Kabbalistic thought have dealt with this problem. It will not surprise us to find that speculation has run the whole gamut—from
attempts to re-transform the impersonal *En-Sof* into the personal
God of the Bible to the downright heretical doctrine of a genuine
dualism between the hidden *En-Sof* and the personal Demiurge of
Scripture. For the moment, however, we are more concerned with
the second aspect of the Godhead which, being of decisive importance for real religion, formed the main subject of theosophical
speculation in Kabbalism.

The mystic strives to assure himself of the living presence of God,
the God of the Bible, the God who is good, wise, just and merciful
and the embodiment of all other positive attributes. But at the
same time he is unwilling to renounce the idea of the hidden God
who remains eternally unknowable in the depths of His own Self,

or, to use the bold expression of the Kabbalists "in the depths of His nothingness."[11] This hidden God may be without special attributes — the living God of whom the Revelation speaks, with whom all religion is concerned, must have attributes, which on another plane represent also the mystic's own scale of moral values: God is good, God is severe, God is merciful and just, etc. As we shall have occasion to see, the mystic does not even recoil before the inference that in a higher sense there is a root of evil even in God. The benevolence of God is to the mystic not simply the negation of evil, but a whole sphere of divine light, in which God manifests Himself under this particular aspect of benevolence to the contemplation of the Kabbalist.

These spheres, which are often described with the aid of mythical metaphors and provide the key for a kind of mystical topography of the Divine realm, are themselves nothing but stages in the revelation of God's creative power. Every attribute represents a given stage, including the attribute of severity and stern judgment, which mystical speculation has connected with the source of evil in God. The mystic who sets out to grasp the meaning of God's absolute unity is thus faced at the outset with an infinite complexity of heavenly spheres and stages which are described in the Kabbalistic texts. From the contemplation of these 'Sefiroth' he proceeds to the conception of God as the union and the root of all these contradictions Generally speaking, the mystics do not seem to conceive of God as the absolute Being or absolute Becoming but as the union of both; much as the hidden God of whom nothing is known to us, and the living God of religious experience and revelation, are one and the same. Kabbalism in other words is not dualistic, although historically there exists a close connection between its way of thinking and that of the Gnostics, to whom the hidden God and the Creator are opposing principles. On the contrary, all the energy of 'orthodox' Kabbalistic speculation is bent to the task of escaping from dualistic consequences; otherwise they would not have been able to maintain themselves within the Jewish community.

I think it is possible to say that the mystical interpretation of the attributes and the unity of God, in the so-called doctrine of the 'Sefiroth', constituted a problem common to all Kabbalists, while the solutions given to it by and in the various schools often differ from one another. In the same way, all Jewish mystics, from the

Therapeutae, whose doctrine was described by Philo of Alexandria,[12] to the latest Hasid, are at one in giving a mystical interpretation to the Torah; the Torah is to them a living organism animated by a secret life which streams and pulsates below the crust of its literal meaning; every one of the innumerable strata of this hidden region corresponds to a new and profound meaning of the Torah. The Torah, in other words, does not consist merely of chapters, phrases and words; rather is it to be regarded as the living incarnation of the divine wisdom which eternally sends out new rays of light. It is not merely the historical law of the Chosen People, although it is that too; it is rather the cosmic law of the Universe, as God's wisdom conceived it. Each configuration of letters in it, whether it makes sense in human speech or not, symbolizes some aspect of God's creative power which is active in the universe. And just as the thoughts of God, in contrast to those of man, are of infinite profundity, so also no single interpretation of the Torah in human language is capable of taking in the whole of its meaning. It cannot be denied that this method of interpretation has proved almost barren for a plain understanding of the Holy Writ, but it is equally undeniable that viewed in this new light, the Sacred Books made a powerful appeal to the individual who discovered in their written words the secret of his life and of his God. It is the usual fate of sacred writings to become more or less divorced from the intentions of their authors. What may be called their after-life, those aspects which are discovered by later generations, frequently becomes of greater importance than their original meaning; and after all—who knows what their original meaning was?

5

Like all their spiritual kin among Christians or Moslems, the Jewish mystics cannot, of course, escape from the fact that the relation between mystical contemplation and the basic facts of human life and thought is highly paradoxical. But in the Kabbalah these paradoxes of the mystical mind frequently assume a peculiar form. Let us take as an instance their relation to the phenomenon of speech, one of the fundamental problems of mystical thought throughout the ages. How is it possible to give lingual expression to mystical knowledge, which by its very nature is related to a sphere where speech and expression are excluded? How is it possible to paraphrase adequately in mere words the most intimate act of all, the contact of the individual with the Divine? And yet the urge of the mystics for self-expression is well known.

They continuously and bitterly complain of the utter inadequacy of words to express their true feelings, but, for all that, they glory in them; they indulge in rhetoric and never weary of trying to express the inexpressible in words. All writers on mysticism have laid stress on this point.[13] Jewish mysticism is no exception, yet it is distinguished by two unusual characteristics which may in some way be interrelated. What I have in mind is, first of all, the striking restraint observed by the Kabbalists in referring to the supreme experience; and secondly, their metaphysically positive attitude towards language as God's own instrument.

If you compare the writings of Jewish mystics with the mystical literature of other religions you will notice a considerable difference, a difference which has, to some extent, made difficult and even prevented the understanding of the deeper meaning of Kabbalism. Nothing could be farther from the truth than the assumption that the religious experience of the Kabbalists is barren of that which, as we have seen, forms the essence of mystical experience, everywhere and at all times. The ecstatic experience, the encounter with the absolute Being in the depths of one's own soul, or whatever description one may prefer to give to the goal of the mystical nostalgia, has been shared by the heirs of rabbinical Judaism. How could it be otherwise with one of the original and fundamental impulses of man? At the same time, such differences as there are, are explained by the existence of an overwhelmingly strong disinclination to treat in express terms of these strictly mystical experiences. Not only is the form different in which these experiences are expressed, but the *will* to express them and to impart the knowledge of them is lacking, or is counteracted by other considerations.

It is well known that the autobiographies of great mystics, who have tried to give an account of their inner experiences in a direct and personal manner, are the glory of mystical literature. These mystical confessions, for all their abounding contradictions, not only provide some of the most important material for the understanding of mysticism, but many of them are also veritable pearls of literature. The Kabbalists, however, are no friends of mystical autobiography.

They aim at describing the realm of Divinity and the other objects of the contemplation in an impersonal way, by burning, as it were, their ships behind them. They glory in objective description and are deeply averse to letting their own personalities intrude into the picture. The wealth of expression at their disposal is not inferior to that of their autobiographical confrères. It is as though they were hampered by a sense of shame. Documents of an intimate and personal nature are not entirely lacking, but it is characteristic that they are to be found almost wholly in manuscripts which the Kabbalists themselves would hardly have allowed to be printed. There has even been a kind of voluntary censorship which the Kabbalists themselves exercised by deleting certain passages of a too intimate nature from the manuscripts, or at least by seeing to it that they were not printed. I shall return to this point at a later stage, when I shall give some remarkable instances of this censorship.[14] On the whole, I am inclined to believe that this dislike of a too personal indulgence in self-expression may have been caused by the fact among others that the Jews retained a particularly vivid sense of the incongruity between mystical experience and that idea of God which stresses the aspects of Creator, King and Law-giver. It is obvious that the absence of the autobiographical element is a serious obstacle to any psychological understanding of Jewish mysticism as the psychology of mysticism has to rely primarily on the study of such autobiographical material.

In general, it may be said that in the long history of Kabbalism, the number of Kabbalists whose teachings and writings bear the imprint of a strong personality is surprisingly small, one notable exception being the Hasidic movement and its leaders since 1750. This is partly due to personal reticence, which as we have seen was characteristic of all Jewish mystics. Equally important, however, is the fact that our sources leave us completely in the dark as regards the personalities of many Kabbalists, including writers whose influence was very great and whose teachings it would be worth while to study in the light of biographical material, were any available. Often enough such contemporary sources as there are do not even mention their names! Frequently, too, all that these writers have left us are their mystical tracts and books from which it is difficult, if not impossible, to form an impression of their personalities. There are very few exceptions to this rule. Among hundreds of Kabbalists whose writings are known to us, hardly ten would provide sufficient material for a biography containing more than a random collection of facts, with little or nothing to give us an insight into their personalities. This is true, for example, of Abraham Abulafia (13th century), of Isaac Luria (16th century) and, at a much later period, of the great mystic and poet Moses Hayim Luzzatto of Padua (died 1747), whose case is typical of the situation I have described. Although his mystical, moralizing and poetical works fill several volumes and many of them have been published, the true personality of the author remained so completely in the shadow as to be little more than a name until the discovery and publication, by Dr. Simon Ginzburg, of his correspondence with his teacher and his friends threw an abundance of light on this remarkable figure." It is to be hoped that the same will gradually be done for other great Jewish mystics of whom today we know very little.

My second point was that Kabbalism is distinguished by an attitude towards language which is quite unusually positive. Kabbalists who differ in almost everything else are at one in regarding language as something more precious than an inadequate instrument for contact between human beings. To them Hebrew, the holy tongue, is not simply a means of expressing certain thoughts, born out of a certain convention and having a purely conventional character, in accordance with the theory of language dominant in the Middle Ages. Language in its purest form, that is, Hebrew, according to the Kabbalists, reflects the fundamental spiritual nature of the world; in other words, it has a mystical value. Speech reaches God because it comes from God. Man's common language, whose prima facie function, indeed, is only of an intellectual nature, reflects the creative language of God. All creation—and this is an important principle of most Kabbalists—is, from the point of view of God, nothing but an expression of His hidden self that begins and ends by giving itself a name, the holy name of God, the perpetual act of creation. All that lives is an expression of God's language, — and what is it that Revelation can reveal in the last resort if not the name of God?

I shall have to return to this point at a latter stage. What I would like to emphasize is this peculiar interpretation, this enthusiastic appreciation of the faculty of speech which sees in it, and in its mystical analysis, a key to the deepest secrets of the Creator and His creation.

In this connection it may be of interest to ask ourselves what was the common attitude of the mystics toward certain other faculties and phenomena, such as intellectual knowledge, and more particularly rational philosophy; or, to take another instance, the problem of individual existence. For after all, mysticism, while beginning with the religion of the individual, proceeds to merge the self into a higher union. Mysticism postulates self-knowledge, to use a Platonic term, as the surest way to God who reveals Himself in the depths of the self. Mystical tendencies, in spite of their strictly personal character, have therefore frequently led to the formation of new social groupings and communities, a fact which is true also of Jewish mysticism; we shall have to return to this fact and to the problem it involves at the end of these lectures. At any rate, Joseph Bernhart, one of the explorers of the world of mysticism, was justified in saying "Have any done more to create historical movement than those who seek and proclaim the immovable?"[16]

6

It is precisely this question of history which brings us back to the problem from which we started: What is Jewish mysticism? For now the question is: What is to be regarded as the general characteristic of mysticism within the framework of Jewish tradition? Kabbalah, it must be remembered, is not the name of a certain dogma or system, but rather the general term applied to a whole religious movement. This movement, with some of whose stages and tendencies we shall have to acquaint ourselves, has been going on from Talmudic times to the present day; its development has been uninterrupted, though by no means uniform, and often dramatic. It leads from Rabbi Akiba, of whom the Talmud says that he left the 'Paradise' of mystical speculation safe and sane as he had entered it—something which cannot, indeed, be said of every Kabbalist—to the late Rabbi Abraham Isaac Kook, the religious leader of the Jewish community in Palestine and a splendid type of Jewish mystic.[17] I should like to mention here that we are in possession of a vast printed literature of mystical texts which I am inclined to estimate at 3,000.[18] In addition, there exists an even greater array of manuscripts not yet published.

Within this movement there exists a considerable variety of religious experience, to use William James' expression. There have been many different currents of thought, and various systems and forms of speculation. There is little resemblance between the earliest mystical texts in our possession, dating from Talmudic and post-Talmudic days, the writings of the ancient Spanish Kabbalists, those of the school which later flourished in Safed, the holy city of Kabbalism in the sixteenth century, and finally the Hasidic literature of the modern age. Yet the question must be asked whether there is not something more than a purely historical connection uniting these *disjecta membra,* something which also provides us with a hint as to what renders this mystical movement in Judaism different from non-Jewish mysticism. Such a common denominator can, perhaps, be discovered in certain unchanging fundamental ideas concerning God, creation and the part played by man in the universe. Two such ideas I have mentioned above, namely the attributes of God and the symbolic meaning of the Torah. But may it not also be that such a denominator is to be found in the attitude of the Jewish mystic towards those dominant spiritual forces which have conditioned and shaped the intellectual life of Jewry during the past two thousand years: the Halakhah, the Aggadah, the prayers and the philosophy of Judaism, to name the most important? It is this question which I shall now try to answer, though without going into detail.

As I have said before, the relation of mysticism to the world of history can serve as a useful starting-point for our investigation. It is generally believed that the attitude of mysticism toward history is one of aloofness, or even of contempt. The historical aspects of religion have a meaning for the mystic chiefly as symbols of acts which he conceives as being divorced from time, or constantly repeated in the soul of every man. Thus the exodus from Egypt, the fundamental event of our history, cannot, according to the mystic, have come to pass once only and in one place; it must correspond to an event which takes place in ourselves, an exodus from an inner Egypt in which we all are slaves. Only thus conceived does the Exodus cease to be an object of learning and acquire the dignity of immediate religious experience. In the same way, it will be remembered, the doctrine of "Christ in us" acquired so great an importance for the mystics of Christianity that the historical Jesus of Nazareth was quite often relegated to the background. If, however, the Absolute which the mystic seeks is not to be found in the varying occurrences of history, the conclusion suggests itself that it must either precede the course of mundane history or reveal itself at the end of time. In other words, knowledge both of the primary facts of creation and of its end, of eschatological salvation and bliss, can acquire a mystical significance.

"The Mystic," says Charles Bennett in a penetrating essay,[19] "as it were forestalls the processes of history by anticipating in his own life the enjoyment of the last age." This eschatological nature of mystical knowledge becomes of paramount importance in the writings of many Jewish mystics, from the anonymous authors of the early *Hekhaloth* tracts to Rabbi Nahman of Brazlav. And the importance of cosmogony for mystical speculation is equally exemplified by the case of Jewish mysticism. The consensus of Kabbalistic opinion regards the mystical way to God as a reversal of the procession by which we have emanated from God. To know the stages of the creative process is also to know the stages of one's own return to the root of all existence. In this sense, the interpretation of *Maaseh Bereshith*, the esoteric doctrine of creation, has always formed one of the main preoccupations of Kabbalism. It is here that Kabbalism comes nearest to Neoplatonic thought, of which it has been said with truth that "procession and reversion together constitute a single movement, the diastole-systole, which is the life of the universe."[20] Precisely this is also the belief of the Kabbalist.

But the cosmogonic and the eschatological trend of Kabbalistic speculation which we have tried to define, are in the last resort ways of escaping from history rather than instruments of historical understanding; that is to say, they do not help us to gauge the intrinsic meaning of history.

There is, however, a more striking instance of the link between the conceptions of Jewish mysticism and those of the historical world. It is a remarkable fact that the very term *Kabbalah* under which it has become best known, is derived from an historical concept. Kabbalah means literally "tradition", in itself an excellent example of the paradoxical nature of mysticism to which I have referred before. The very doctrine which centres about the immediate personal contact with the Divine, that is to say, a highly personal and intimate form of knowledge, is conceived as traditional wisdom.

The fact is, however, that the idea of Jewish mysticism from the start combined the conception of a knowledge which by its very nature is difficult to impart and therefore secret, with that of a knowledge which is the secret tradition of chosen spirits or adepts. Jewish mysticism, therefore, is a secret doctrine in a double sense, a characteristic which cannot be said to apply to all forms of mysticism. It is a secret doctrine because it treats of the most deeply hidden and fundamental matters of human life; but it is secret also because it is confined to a small élite of the chosen who impart the knowledge to their disciples. It is true that this picture never wholly corresponded to life. Against the doctrine of the chosen few who alone may participate in the mystery must be set the fact that, at least during certain periods of history, the Kabbalists themselves have tried to bring under their influence much wider circles, and even the whole nation. There is a certain analogy between this development and that of the mystery religions of the Hellenic period of antiquity, when secret doctrines of an essentially mystical nature were diffused among an ever-growing number of people.

It must be kept in mind that in the sense in which it is understood by the Kabbalist himself, mystical knowledge is not his private affair which has been revealed to him, and to him only, in his personal experience. On the contrary, the purer and more nearly perfect it is, the nearer it is to the original stock of knowledge common to mankind. To use the expression of the Kabbalist, the knowledge of things human and divine that Adam, the father of mankind, possessed is therefore also the property of the mystic. For this reason, the Kabbalah advanced what was at once a claim and an hypothesis, namely, that its function was to hand down to its own disciples the secret of God's revelation to Adam.[21] Little though this claim is grounded in fact—and I am even inclined to believe that many Kabbalists did not regard it seriously—the fact that such a claim was made appears to me highly characteristic of Jewish mysticism. Reverence for the traditional has always been deeply rooted in Judaism, and even the mystics, who in fact broke away from tradition, retained a reverent attitude towards it; it led them directly to their conception of the coincidence of true intuition and true tradition. This theory has made possible such a paradox as the Kabbalah of Isaac Luria, the most influential system of later Kabbalism, though the most difficult. Nearly all the important points and major theses in Luria's system are novel, one might even say excitingly novel—and yet they were accepted throughout as true Kabbalah, i.e. traditional wisdom. There was nobody to see a contradiction in this.

7

Considerations of a different kind will take us even deeper into the understanding of the problem. I have already said that the mystical sphere is the meeting-place of two worlds or stages in the development of the human consciousness: one primitive and one developed, the world of mythology and that of revelation. This fact cannot be left out of account in dealing with the Kabbalah. Whoever tries to gain a better understanding of its ideas, without attempting anything in the nature of an apology, cannot fail to notice that it contains, side by side with a deep and sensitive understanding of the essence of religious feeling, a certain mode of thought characteristic of primitive mythological thinking. The peculiar affinity of Kabbalist thought to the world of myth cannot well be doubted, and should certainly not be obscured or lightly passed over by those of us to whom the notion of a mythical domain within Judaism seems strange and paradoxical and who are accustomed to think of Jewish Monotheism as the classical example of a religion which has severed all links with the mythical. It is, indeed, surprising that in the very heart of Judaism ideas and notions sprang up which purported to interpret its meaning better than any others, and which yet represent a relapse into, or if you like a revival of, the mythical consciousness. This is particularly true of the Zohar and the Lurianic Kabbalah, that is to say, of those forms of Jewish mysticism which have exerted by far the greatest influence in Jewish history and which for centuries stood out in the popular mind as bearers of the final and deepest truth in Jewish thought.

It is no use getting indignant over these facts, as the great historian Graetz did; they should rather set us thinking. Their importance for the history of the Jewish people, particularly during the past four centuries, has been far too great to permit them to be ridiculed and treated as mere deviations. Perhaps, after all, there is something wrong with the popular conception of Monotheism as being opposed to the mythical; perhaps Monotheism contains room after all, on a deeper plane, for the development of mythical lore.

I do not believe that all those devoted and pious spirits, practically the vast majority of Ashkenazic and Sephardic Jewry, ceased, after the exodus from Spain, to be Jews also in the religious sense, only because their forms of belief appear to be in manifest contradiction with certain modern theories of Judaism. I, therefore, ask myself: What is the secret of this tremendous success of the Kabbalah among our people? Why did it succeed in becoming a decisive factor in our history, shaping the life of a large proportion of Jewry over a period of centuries, while its contemporary, rational Jewish philosophy, was incapable of achieving the spiritual hegemony after which it strove? This is a pressing question; I cannot accept the explanation that the facts I have described are solely due to external historical circumstances, that persecution and decline weakened the spirit of the people and made them seek refuge in the darkness of Mysticism because they could not bear the light of Reason. The matter appears to me to be more complicated, and I should like briefly to set out my answer to the question.

The secret of the success of the Kabbalah lies in the nature of its relation to the spiritual heritage of rabbinical Judaism. This relation differs from that of rationalist philosophy, in that it is more deeply and in a more vital sense connected with the main forces active in Judaism.

Undoubtedly both the mystics and the philosophers completely transform the structure of ancient Judaism; both have lost the simple relation to Judaism, that naiveté which speaks to us from the classical documents of Rabbinical literature. Classical Judaism expressed itself: it did not reflect upon itself. By contrast, to the mystics and the philosophers of a later stage of religious development Judaism itself has become problematical. Instead of simply speaking their minds, they tend to produce an ideology of Judaism, an ideology moreover which comes to the rescue of tradition by giving it a new interpretation. It is not as though the rise of Jewish philosophy and of Jewish mysticism took place in widely separated ages, or as though the Kabbalah, as Graetz saw it, was a reaction against a wave of rationalism. Rather the two movements are interrelated and interdependent. Neither were they from the start manifestly opposed to each other, a fact which is often overlooked. On the contrary, the rationalism of some of the philosophical *enlighteners* frequently betrays a mystical tendency; and conversely, the mystic

who has not yet learnt to speak in his own language often uses
and misuses the vocabulary of philosophy. Only very gradually did
the Kabbalists, rather than the philosophers, begin to perceive the
implications of their own ideas, the conflict between a purely philosophical interpretation of the world, and an attitude which progresses from rational thought to irrational meditation, and from
there to the mystical interpretation of the universe.

What many mystics felt towards philosophy was succinctly expressed by Rabbi Moses of Burgos (end of the 13th century). When
he heard the philosophers praised, he used to say angrily: "You
ought to know that these philosophers whose wisdom you are prais-
ing, end where we begin."[22] Actually this means two things: on the
one hand, it means that the Kabbalists are largely concerned with
the investigation of a sphere of religious reality which lies quite
outside the orbit of mediaeval Jewish philosophy; their purpose is
to discover a new stratum of the religious consciousness. On the
other hand, though R. Moses may not have intended to say this,
they stand on the shoulders of the philosophers and it is easier for
them to see a little farther than their rivals.

To repeat, the Kabbalah certainly did not *arise* as a reaction
against philosophical 'enlightenment,'[23] but once it was there it is
true that its function was that of an opposition to it. At the same
time, an intellectual dispute went on between the Kabbalah and the
forces of the philosophical movement which left deep marks upon
the former's structure. In my opinion, there is a direct connection
between Jehudah Halevi, the most Jewish of Jewish philosophers,
and the Kabbalists. For the legitimate trustees of his spiritual heritage have been the mystics, and not the succeeding generations of
Jewish philosophers.

The Kabbalists employed the ideas and conceptions of orthodox
theology, but the magic hand of mysticism opened up hidden
sources of new life in the heart of many scholastic ideas and abstractions. Philosophers may shake their heads at what must appear to
them a misunderstanding of the meaning of philosophical ideas.
But what from the philosopher's point of view represents a flaw
in the conception can constitute its greatness and dignity in the
religious sense. After all, a misunderstanding is often nothing but
the paradoxical abbreviation of an original line of thought. And

it is precisely such misunderstanding which has frequently become productive of new ideas in the mystical sphere.

Let us take, as an example of what I have said, the idea of "creation out of nothing." In the dogmatic disputations of Jewish philosophy, the question whether Judaism implies belief in this concept, and if so, in what precise sense, has played an important part. I shall not go into the difficulties with which the orthodox theologians found themselves faced whenever they tried to preserve the full meaning of this idea of creation out of nothing. Viewed in its simplest sense, it affirms the creation of the world by God out of something which is neither God Himself nor any kind of existence, but simply the non-existent. The mystics, too, speak of creation out of nothing; in fact, it is one of their favorite formulae. But in their case the orthodoxy of the term conceals a meaning which differs considerably from the original one. This *Nothing* from which everything has sprung is by no means a mere negation; only to us does it present no attributes because it is beyond the reach of intellectual knowledge. In truth, however, this Nothing—to quote one of the Kabbalists—is infinitely more real than all other reality.[24] Only when the soul has stripped itself of all limitation and, in mystical language, has descended into the depths of Nothing does it encounter the Divine. For this *Nothing* comprises a wealth of mystical reality although it cannot be defined. "Un Dieu défini serait un Dieu fini." In a word, it signifies the Divine itself, in its most impenetrable guise. And, in fact, *creation out of nothing* means to many mystics just *creation out of God*. Creation out of nothing thus becomes the symbol of emanation, that is to say, of an idea which, in the history of philosophy and theology, stands farthest removed from it.

8

Let us return to our original problem. As we have seen, the renaissance of Judaism on a new plane is the common concern of both the mystics and the philosophers. For all that, there remains a very considerable difference, a good example of which is afforded by the conception of *Sithre Torah*, or "Secrets of the Law". The philosophers no less than the mystics talk of discovering these secrets, using this esoteric phraseology with a profusion hardly distinguishable from the style of the real esoterics and Kabbalists. But what are these secrets according to the philosopher? They are the truths of philosophy, the truths of the metaphysics or ethics of Aristotle, or Alfarabi or Avicenna; truths, in other words, which were capable of being discovered outside the sphere of religion and which were projected into the old books by way of allegorical or typological interpretation. The documents of religion are therefore not conceived as expressing a separate and distinct world of religious truth and reality, but rather as giving a simplified description of the relations which exist between the ideas of philosophy. The story of Abraham and Sarah, of Lot and his wife, of the Twelve Tribes, etc., are simply descriptions of the relation between matter and form, spirit and matter, or the faculties of the mind. Even where allegorization was not pushed to such absurd extremes, the tendency was to regard the Torah as a mere vehicle of philosophic truth, though indeed one particularly exalted and perfect.

In other words, the philosopher can only proceed with his proper task after having successfully converted the concrete realities of Judaism into a bundle of abstractions. The individual phenomenon is to him no object of his philosophical speculation. By contrast, the mystic refrains from destroying the living texture of religious narrative by allegorizing it, although allegory plays an important part in the writings of a great many Kabbalists. His essential mode of thinking is what I should like to call symbolical in the strictest sense.

This point requires a little further explanation. Allegory consists of an infinite network of meanings and correlations in which everything can become a representation of everything else, but all within the limits of language and expression. To that extent it is possible to speak of allegorical immanence. That which is expressed by and in the allegorical sign is in the first instance something which has its own meaningful context, but by becoming allegorical this something loses its own meaning and becomes the vehicle of something else. Indeed the allegory arises, as it were, from the gap which at this point opens between the form and its meaning. The two are no longer indissolubly welded together; the meaning is no longer restricted to that particular form, nor the form any longer to that particular meaningful content. What appears in the allegory, in short, is the infinity of meaning which attaches to every representation. The "Mysteries of the Torah" which I just mentioned were for the philosophers the natural subject of an allegorical interpretation which gave expression to a new form of the mediaeval mind as much as it implied a veiled criticism of the old.

Allegorization was also, as I have said, a constant preoccupation of the Kabbalists, and it was not on this ground that they differed from the philosophers; nor was it the main constituent of their faith and their method. We must look for this in the attention they gave to the symbol—a form of expression which radically transcends the sphere of allegory. In the mystical symbol a reality which in itself has, for us, no form or shape becomes transparent and, as it were, visible, through the medium of another reality which clothes its content with visible and expressible meaning, as for example the cross for the Christian. The thing which becomes a symbol retains its original form and its original content. It does not become, so to speak, an empty shell into which another content is poured; in it-self, through its own existence, it makes another reality transparent which cannot appear in any other form. If allegory can be defined as the representation of an expressible something by another expressible something, the mystical symbol is an expressible representation of something which lies beyond the sphere of expression and communication, something which comes from a sphere whose face is, as it were, turned inward and away from us. A hidden and inexpressible reality finds its expression in the symbol. If the symbol is thus also a sign or representation it is nevertheless more than that.

For the Kabbalist, too, every existing thing is endlessly correlated with the whole of creation; for him, too, everything mirrors every-thing else. But beyond that he discovers something else which is not covered by the allegorical network: a reflection of the true transcendence. The symbol "signifies" nothing and communicates nothing, but makes something transparent which is beyond all expression. Where deeper insight into the structure of the allegory uncovers fresh layers of meaning, the symbol is intuitively under-stood all at once—or not at all. The symbol in which the life of the Creator and that of creation become one, is—to use Creuzer's words[25] —"a beam of light which, from the dark and abysmal depths of existence and cognition, falls into our eye and penetrates our whole being." It is a "momentary totality" which is perceived intuitively in a mystical *now*—the dimension of time proper to the symbol.

Of such symbols the world of Kabbalism is full, nay the whole world is to the Kabbalist such a *corpus symbolicum*. Out of the reality of creation, without the latter's existence being denied or annihilated, the inexpressible mystery of the Godhead becomes visible. In particular the religious acts commanded by the Torah, the *mitswoth*, are to the Kabbalist symbols in which a deeper and hidden sphere of reality becomes transparent. The infinite shines through the finite and makes it more and not less real. This brief summary gives us some idea of the profound difference between the philosophers' allegorical interpretation of religion and its symbolical understanding by the mystics. It may be of interest to note that in the comprehensive commentary on the Torah written by a great mystic of the thirteenth century, Moses Nahmanides, there are many symbolical interpretations as defined here, but not a single instance of allegory.

9

The difference becomes clear if we consider the attitude of philosophy and Kabbalah respectively to the two outstanding creative manifestations of Rabbinical Jewry: Halakhah and Aggadah, Law and Legend. It is a remarkable fact that the philosophers failed to establish a satisfactory and intimate relation to either. They showed themselves unable to make the spirit of Halakhah and Aggadah, both elements which expressed a fundamental urge of the Jewish soul, productive by transforming them into something new.

Let us begin with the Halakhah, the world of sacred law and, therefore, the most important factor in the actual life of ancient Jewry. Alexander Altmann, in raising the question: What is Jewish Theology? is quite justified in regarding as one of the decisive weaknesses of classical Jewish philosophy the fact that it ignored the problem presented by the Halakhah.[26] The whole world of religious law remained outside the orbit of philosophical inquiry, which means of course, too, that it was not subjected to philosophical criticism. It is not as if the philosopher denied or defied this world. He, too, lived in it and bowed to it, but it never became part and parcel of his work as a philosopher. It furnished no material for his thoughts. This fact, which is indeed undeniable, is particularly glaring in the case of thinkers like Maimonides and Saadia, in whom the converging streams meet. They fail entirely to establish a true synthesis of the two elements, Halakhah and philosophy, a fact which has already been pointed out by Samuel David Luzzatto. Maimonides, for instance, begins the *Mishneh Torah,* his great codification of the Halakhah, with a philosophical chapter which has no relation whatever to the Halakhah itself. The synthesis of the spheres remains sterile, and the genius of the man whose spirit moulded them into a semblence of union cannot obscure their intrinsic disparity.

For a purely historical understanding of religion, Maimonides' analysis of the origin of the *mitswoth,* the religious commandments, is of great importance,[27] but he would be a bold man who would maintain that his theory of the *mitswoth* was likely to increase the enthusiasm of the faithful for their actual practice, likely to augment their immediate appeal to religious feeling. If the prohibition against seething a kid in its mother's milk and many similar irrational commandments are explicable as polemics against long-forgotten pagan rites, if the offering of sacrifice is a concession to the primitive mind, if other *mitswoth* carry with them antiquated moral and philosophical ideas—how can one expect the community to remain faithful to practices of which the antecedents have long since disappeared or of which the aims can be attained directly through philosophical reasoning? To the philosopher, the Halakhah either had no significance at all, or one that was calculated to diminish rather than to enhance its prestige in his eyes.

Entirely different was the attitude of the Kabbalists. For them the Halakhah never became a province of thought in which they felt themselves strangers. Right from the beginning and with growing determination, they sought to master the world of the Halakhah as a whole and in every detail. From the outset, an ideology of the Halakhah is one of their aims. But in their interpretation of the religious commandments these are not represented as allegories of more or less profound ideas, or as pedagogical measures, but rather as the performance of a secret rite (or *mystery* in the sense in which the term was used by the Ancients).[28]

Whether one is appalled or not by this transformation of the Halakhah into a sacrament, a mystery rite, by this revival of myth in the very heart of Judaism, the fact remains that it was this transformation which raised the Halakhah to a position of incomparable importance for the mystic, and strengthened its hold over the people. Every *mitswah* became an event of cosmic importance, an act which had a bearing upon the dynamics of the universe. The religious Jew became a protagonist in the drama of the world; he manipulated the strings behind the scene. Or, to use a less extravagant simile, if the whole universe is an enormous complicated machine, then man is the machinist who keeps the wheels going by applying a few drops of oil here and there, and at the right time. The moral substance of man's action supplies this "oil," and his existence therefore becomes of extreme significance, since it unfolds on a background of cosmic infinitude.

The danger of theosophical schematism or, as S. R. Hirsch put it,[29] of "magical mechanism" is, of course, inherent in such an interpretation of the Torah, and it has more than once raised its head in the development of Kabbalism. There is danger of imagining a magical mechanism to be operative in every sacramental action, and this imagination is attended by a decline in the essential spontaneity of religious action. But then this conflict is inseparable from any and every fulfilment of a religious command, since every prescribed duty is also conceived as assumed willingly and spontaneously. The antinomy is, in fact, inescapable, and can only be overcome by religious feeling so long as it is strong and unbroken. When it begins to flag, the contradiction between command and free-will increases in proportion and eventually gathers sufficient force to become destructive.

By interpreting every religious act as a mystery, even where its meaning was clear for all to see or was expressly mentioned in the written or oral Law, a strong link was forged between Kabbalah and Halakkah, which appears to me to have been, in large part, responsible for the influence of Kabbalistic thought over the minds and hearts of successive generations.

A good deal of similarity to what I have said about the Halakhah is apparent in the attitude of philosophers and mystics, respectively, to the Aggadah. Here too, their ways part right from the beginning. The Aggadah is a wonderful mirror of spontaneous religious life and feeling during the rabbinical period of Judaism. In particular, it represents a method of giving original and concrete expression to the deepest motive-powers of the religious Jew, a quality which helps to make it an excellent and genuine approach to the essentials of our religion. However, it was just this quality which never ceased to baffle the philosophers of Judaism. Their treatment of the Aggadah, except where it pointed an ethical moral, is embarrassed and fumbling. They almost certainly regarded it as a stumbling-block rather than as a precious heritage, let alone a key to a mystery. And thus it is not surprising that their allegorical interpretation of its meaning reflects an attitude which is not that of the Aggadah. Only too frequently their allegorizations are simply, as I have said, veiled criticism.

Here again the Kabbalists conceive their task differently, although it also involves a transformation of the subject's meaning. It would be too much to say that they leave the meaning of the Aggadah intact. What makes them differ from the philosophers is the fact that for them the Aggadah is not just a dead letter. They live in a world historically continuous with it, and they are able, therefore, to enhance it, though in the spirit of mysticism. Aggadic productivity has been a constant element of Kabbalistic literature, and only when the former disappears will the latter, too, be doomed to extinction. The whole of Aggadah can in a way be regarded as a popular mythology of the Jewish universe. Now, this mythical element which is deeply rooted in the creative forms of Aggadic production, operates on different planes in the old Aggadah and in Kabbalism. The difference between the Aggadic production of the Kabbalah and that of the early Midrash can be easily gauged: in the Aggadah of the Kabbalists the events take place on a considerably wider stage, a stage with a cosmic horizon. Earth and heaven meet already in the ancient Aggadah, but now an even greater stress is laid on the heavenly element which comes more and more to the fore. All events assume gigantic dimensions and a wider significance; the steps of the heroes of the Kabbalistic Aggadah are directed by hidden forces from mysterious regions, while their doings react, at the same time, upon the upper world. Seen that way, there is nothing more instructive than a comparison between the two great and truly comprehensive collections, or *Yalkutim*, each one representing, respectively, one of the two types of Aggadic creation. The compiler of the *Yalkut Shim'oni* collected in the thirteenth century the old Aggadahs which, as preserved by the Midrashic literature, accompanied the biblical text. In the *Yalkut Reubeni*, on the other hand, we have a collection of the Aggadic output of the Kabbalists during five centuries. The latter highly interesting work which was compiled during the second half of the seventeenth century bears full witness to the growing strength and preponderance of the mythical element and to the great difference between Aggadah and Kabbalah in their interpretation of the stories of Biblical heroes. At the same time it is obvious that in comparison with the older Aggadah the realistic element in the later Aggadah has decreased because the realistic foundations, in which Jewish life was rooted, have grown more and more narrow. In fact, this explanation falls in well with the historical experience of the different generations. The old Aggadah is fed by deep and comprehensive experience; the life which it reflects has not yet become colourless, nor did it lose its impetus. The Kabbalistic Aggadah, in contrast, reflects a narrow and circumscribed life which sought, nay, was compelled to seek, inspiration from hidden worlds, as the real world turned for them into the world of the Ghetto. The Aggadic myth of the *Yalkut Reubeni* expresses the historical experience of the Jewish people after the Crusades, and we may say that it is expressed with rather greater force because it is not directly mentioned at all. The depth of the penetration into the hidden worlds which can be encountered here at every step stands in direct proportion to the shrinking perimeter of their historical experience. There is thus a mighty difference of function between the two types of Aggadic creation but no difference of essence.

There is another point worth mentioning. No Kabbalist was ever embarrassed by or ashamed of an old Aggadah; in particular those Aggadahs, which were anathema to 'enlightened' Jews, were enthusiastically hailed by the Kabbalists as symbols of their own interpretation of the Universe. The anthropomorphical and paradoxical Aggadahs belong to this class, as well as certain epigrams, such as R. Abbahu's saying, that before making this world God made many others and destroyed them because he did not like them.[20] The philosophers, who had passed through the school of Aristotle, never felt at home in the world of Midrash. But the more extravagant and paradoxical these Aggadahs appeared to them, the more were the Kabbalists convinced that they were one of the keys to the mystical realm. Their vocabulary and favorite similes show traces of Aggadic influence in proportions equal to those of philosophy and Gnosticism; Scripture being, of course, the strongest element of all.

10

What has been said of the Halakhah and the Aggadah is also true of the liturgy, the world of prayer; the last of the three domains in which the religious spirit of post-Biblical Judaism has found its classical expression. Here too the conclusion is inescapable that the philosophers had little of value to contribute. Of entire prayers written by philosophers only a few have been preserved, and these are often somewhat anaemic and half-hearted in their approach, especially where the authors were not, like Solomon ibn Gabirol and Jehudah Halevi, motivated in the last resort by mystical leanings. There is in many of them a curious lack of true religious feeling. The case is entirely different when we turn to the Kabbalistic attitude towards prayer; there is perhaps no clearer sign that Kabbalism is essentially a religious and not a speculative phenomenon. The novelty of its attitude to prayer can be viewed under two aspects: the vast number of prayers whose authors were mystics themselves, and the mystical interpretation of the old traditional community prayers—the backbone of Jewish liturgy.

To begin with the former, it is hardly surprising that the new religious revelation, peculiar to the visionaries of the Kabbalah, for which there existed no liturgical equivalent in the older prayers, strove after some form of expression and had already inspired the earliest mystics to write their own prayers. The first prayers of a mystical character, which can be traced back to the Kabbalists of Provence and Catalonia,[31] are carried forward by a long and varied tradition to the prayers in which, about 1820, Nathan of Nemirov, the disciple of Rabbi Nahman of Brazlav, gave valid expression to the world of Hasidic Zaddikism.[32] This mystical prayer, which bears little outward resemblance to the older liturgy, and in particular of course to the classical forms of communal prayer, flows from the new religious experience to which the Kabbalists were entitled to lay claim. Often these prayers bear the mark of directness and simplicity, and give plain expression to the common concern of every form of mysticism. But not infrequently their language is that of the symbol and their style reveals the secret pathos of magical conjuration. This has found a profound expression in the mystical interpretation of the phrase of Psalm cxxx, 1 "Out of the depths I have called unto Thee"; which, according to the Zohar, means not

"I have called unto Thee from the depths [where I am]" but "from the depths [in which Thou art] I call Thee up."[33]

But side by side with these original productions of the Kabbalistic spirit we find from the earliest beginnings down to our time another tendency, that of mystical reinterpretation of the traditional community liturgy which transforms it into a symbol of the mystical way and the way of the world itself. This transformation, which has meant a great deal for the true life of the Kabbalist, has become crystallized in the conception of *Kawwanah,* i.e. mystical intention or concentration, which is its instrument.[34] In the words of the liturgy as in the old Aggadahs, the Kabbalists found a way to hidden worlds and the first causes of all existence. They developed a technique of meditation which enabled them to extract, as it were, the mystical prayer from the exoteric prayer of the community the text of which followed a fixed pattern. The fact that this form of prayer was conceived not as a free effusion of the soul but as a mystical act in the strict sense of the term, as an act, that is to say, which is directly linked with the inner cosmic process, invests this conception of *Kawwanah* with a solemnity which not only approaches but also passes the border of the magical. It is significant that of all the various forms of Kabbalistic thought and practice this meditative mysticism of prayer has alone survived and has taken the place of all the others. At the end of a long process of development in which Kabbalism, paradoxical though it may sound, has influenced the course of Jewish history, it has become again what it was in the beginning: the esoteric wisdom of small groups of men out of touch with life and without any influence on it.

11

As I have already said, mysticism represents, to a certain extent, a revival of mythical lore. This brings us to another and very serious point which I should like at least to mention. The Jewish mystic lives and acts in perpetual rebellion against a world with which he strives with all his zeal to be at peace. Conversely, this fact is responsible for the profound ambiguity of his outlook, and it also explains the apparent self-contradiction inherent in a great many Kabbalist symbols and images. The great symbols of the Kabbalah certainly spring from the depths of a creative and genuinely Jewish religious feeling, but at the same time they are invariably tinged by the world of mythology. In the lectures on the Zohar and on Lurianic Kabbalism I shall give a number of particularly outstanding instances of this fact. Failing this mythical element, the ancient Jewish mystics would have been unable to compress into language the substance of their inner experience. It was Gnosticism, one of the last great manifestations of mythology in religious thought, and definitely conceived in the struggle against Judaism as the conqueror of mythology, which lent figures of speech to the Jewish mystic.

The importance of this paradox can hardly be exaggerated; it must be kept in mind that the whole meaning and purpose of those ancient myths and metaphors whose remainders the editors of the book *Bahir*, and therefore the whole Kabbalah, inherited from the Gnostics[30], was simply the subversion of a law which had, at one time, disturbed and broken the order of the mythical world. Thus through wide and scattered provinces of Kabbalism, the revenge of myth upon its conqueror is clear for all to see, and together with it we find an abundant display of contradictory symbols. It is characteristic of Kabbalistic theology in its systematical forms that it attempts to construct and to describe a world in which something of the mythical has again come to life, in terms of thought which exclude the mythical element. However, it is this contradiction which more than anything else explains the extraordinary success of Kabbalism in Jewish history.

Mystics and philosophers are, as it were, both aristocrats of thought; yet Kabbalism succeeded in establishing a connection between its own world and certain elemental impulses operative in every human mind. It did not turn its back upon the primitive side of life, that all-important region where mortals are afraid of life and in fear of death, and derive scant wisdom from rational philosophy. Philosophy ignored these fears, out of whose substance man wove myths, and in turning its back upon the primitive side of man's existence, it paid a high price in losing touch with him altogether. For it is cold comfort to those who are plagued by genuine fear and sorrow to be told that their troubles are but the workings of their own imagination.

The fact of the existence of evil in the world is the main touchstone of this difference between the philosophic and the Kabbalistic outlook. On the whole, the philosophers of Judaism treat the existence of evil as something meaningless in itself. Some of them have shown themselves only too proud of this negation of evil as one of the fundamentals of what they call rational Judaism. Hermann Cohen has said with great clarity and much conviction: "Evil is non-existent. It is nothing but a concept derived from the concept of freedom. *A power of evil exists only in myth.*"[36] One may doubt the philosophical truth of this statement, but assuming its truth it is obvious that something can be said for 'myth' in its struggle with 'philosophy'. To most Kabbalists, as true seal-bearers of the world of myth, the existence of evil is, at any rate, one of the most pressing problems, and one which keeps them continuously occupied with attempts to solve it. They have a strong sense of the reality of evil and the dark horror that is about everything living. They do not, like the philosophers, seek to evade its existence with the aid of a convenient formula; rather do they try to penetrate into its depth. And by doing so, they unwittingly establish a connection between their own strivings and the vital interests of popular belief—you may call it superstition—and all of those concrete manifestations of Jewish life in which these fears found their expression. It is a paradoxical fact that none other than the Kabbalists, through their interpretation of various religious acts and customs, have made it clear what they signified to the average believer, if not what they really meant from the beginning. Jewish folklore stands as a living proof of this contention, as has been shown by modern research in respect of some particularly well-known examples.[37]

It would be idle to deny that Kabbalistic thought lost much of its magnificence where it was forced to descend from the pinnacles of theoretical speculation to the plane of ordinary thinking and acting. The dangers which myth and magic present to the religious consciousness, including that of the mystic, are clearly shown in the development of Kabbalism. If one turns to the writings of great Kabbalists one seldom fails to be torn between alternate admiration and disgust. There is need for being quite clear about this in a time like ours, when the fashion of uncritical and superficial condemnation of even the most valuable elements of mysticism threatens to be replaced by an equally uncritical and obscurantist glorification of the Kabbalah. I have said before that Jewish philosophy had to pay a high price for its escape from the pressing questions of real life. But Kabbalism, too, has had to pay for its success.

Philosophy came dangerously near to losing the living God; Kabbalism, which set out to preserve Him, to blaze a new and glorious trail to Him, encountered mythology on its way and was tempted to lose itself in its labyrinth.

12

One final observation should be made on the general character of Kabbalism as distinct from other, non-Jewish, forms of mysticism. Both historically and metaphysically it is a masculine doctrine, made for men and by men. The long history of Jewish mysticism shows no trace of feminine influence. There have been no women Kabbalists; Rabia of early Islamic mysticism, Mechthild of Magdeburg, Juliana of Norwich, Theresa de Jesus, and the many other feminine representatives of Christian mysticism have no counterparts in the history of Kabbalism.[38] The latter, therefore, lacks the element of feminine emotion which has played so large a part in the development of non-Jewish mysticism, but it also remained comparatively free from the dangers entailed by the tendency towards hysterical extravagance which followed in the wake of this influence.

This exclusively masculine character of Kabbalism was by no means the result of the social position of Jewish women or their exclusion from Talmudic learning. Scholasticism was as much exclusively a domain of men as Talmudism, and yet the social position of women in Islam and in Mediaeval Christianity did not prevent their playing a highly important part among the representatives—though not the theoreticians—of Islamic and Christian mysticism. It is hardly possible to conceive Catholic mysticism without them. This exclusive masculinity for which Kabbalism has paid a high price, appears rather to be connected with an inherent tendency to lay stress on the demonic nature of woman and the feminine element of the cosmos.

It is of the essence of Kabbalistic symbolism that woman represents not, as one might be tempted to expect, the quality of tenderness but that of stern judgment. This symbolism was unknown to the old mystics of the Merkabah period, and even to the Hasidim in Germany, but it dominates Kabbalistic literature from the very beginning and undoubtedly represents a constituent element of Kabbalistic theology. The demonic, according to the Kabbalists, is an off-spring of the feminine sphere. This view does not entail a negation or repudiation of womanhood—after all the Kabbalistic conception of the Shekhinah has room for the, to orthodox Jewish thought, highly paradoxical idea of a feminine element in God Himself—but it does constitute a problem for the psychologist and the historian of religion alike. Mention has already been made of the dislike shown by the Kabbalists for any form of literary publicity in connection with mystical experience, and of their tendency towards the objectivization of mystical vision. These traits, too, would appear to be connected with the masculine character of the movement, for the history of mystical literature shows that women were among the outstanding representatives of the tendency towards mystical autobiography and subjectivism in expressing religious experience.

If, finally, you were to ask me what kind of value I attach to Jewish mysticism, I would say this: Authoritative Jewish theology, both mediaeval and modern, in representatives like Saadia, Maimonides and Hermann Cohen, has taken upon itself the task of formulating an antithesis to pantheism and mythical theology, i. e.: to prove them wrong. In this endeavour it has shown itself tireless. What is really required, however, is an understanding of these phenomena which yet does not lead away from monotheism; and once their significance is grasped, that elusive something in them which may be of value must be clearly defined. To have posed this problem is the historic achievement of Kabbalism. The varying answers it supplied to the question may be as inadequate as you like; I shall certainly be the last to deny that its representatives often lost their way and went over the edge of the precipice. But the fact remains that they faced a problem which others were more concerned to ignore and which is of the greatest importance for Jewish theology.

The particular forms of symbolical thought in which the fundamental attitude of the Kabbalah found its expression, may mean little or nothing to us (though even today we cannot escape, at times, from their powerful appeal). But the attempt to discover the hidden life beneath the external shapes of reality and to make visible that abyss in which the symbolic nature of all that exists reveals itself: this attempt is as important for us today as it was for those ancient mystics. For as long as nature and man are conceived as His creations, and that is the indispensable condition of highly developed religious life, the quest for the hidden life of the transcendent element in such creation will always form one of the most important preoccupations of the human mind.

SECOND LECTURE

MERKABAH MYSTICISM AND JEWISH GNOSTICISM

1

The first phase in the development of Jewish mysticism before its crystallization in the mediaeval Kabbalah is also the longest. Its literary remains are traceable over a period of almost a thousand years, from the first century B.C. to the tenth A.D., and some of its important records have survived. In spite of its length, and notwithstanding the fluctuations of the historical process, there is every justification for treating it as a single distinct phase. Between the physiognomy of early Jewish mysticism and that of mediaeval Kabbalism there is a difference which time has not effaced. It is not my intention here to follow the movement through its various stages, from its early beginnings in the period of the Second Temple to its gradual decline and disappearance. To do so would involve a lengthy excursion into historical and philological detail, much of which has not yet been sufficiently clarified. What I propose to do is to analyze the peculiar realm of religious experience which is reflected in the more important documents of the period. I do not, therefore, intend to give much space to hypotheses concerning the origins of Jewish mysticism and its relation to Graeco-Oriental syncretism, fascinating though the subject be. Nor am I going to deal with the many pseudepigraphic and apocalyptic works such as the Ethiopic Book of Enoch and the Fourth Book of Ezra, which undoubtedly contain elements of Jewish mystical religion. Their influence on the subsequent development of Jewish mysticism cannot be overlooked, but in the main I shall confine myself to the analysis of writings to which little attention has hitherto been given in the literature on Jewish religious history.

In turning our attention to this subject, we are at once made aware of the unfortunate fact that practically nothing is known about those who espoused the oldest organized movement of Jewish mysticism in late Talmudic and post-Talmudic times, i.e. the period from which the most illuminating documents have come down to us. Like the authors of the Biblical Apocrypha and Pseudepigrapha, they have generally followed the practice of concealing their identity behind the great names of the past. There is little hope that we shall ever learn the true identity of the men who were the first to make an attempt, still recognizable and describable, to invest Judaism with the glory of mystical splendor.

It is only by accident that certain names from among the mystics of the later period have been preserved. Thus we hear of Joseph ben Abba who was head of the rabbinical academy of Pumbeditha around 814, and who is said to have been versed in mystical lore.[1] Another name which occurs with some frequency is that of Aaron ben Samuel, of Baghdad, the "father of mysteries." Although his individuality disappears behind an iridescent haze of legends there is no doubt that he was instrumental in bringing a knowledge of the mystical tradition, such as it had by that time become in Mesopotamia, to Southern Italy, and thence to the Jews of Europe.[2] But these are men of the ninth century, that is to say of a time when this particular form of mysticism was already fully developed and, in certain respects, even on the decline. For its classical period, approximately from the fourth to the sixth century, we are left completely in the dark as to the leading figures. It is true that we know the names of some of the Talmudic authorities of the fourth century who made a study of the secret doctrine—men like Rava and his contemporary, Aha ben Jacob—but we have no means of knowing whether they were in any way connected with the groups of Jewish gnostics whose writings are in our hands.

Palestine was the cradle of the movement, that much is certain. We also know the names of the most important representatives of mystical and theosophical thought among the teachers of the Mishnah. They belonged to a group of the pupils of Johanan ben Zakkai, around the turn of the first century A.D. There is good reason to believe that important elements of this spiritual tradition were kept alive in small esoteric circles; the writers who, at the end of the Talmudic epoch, attempted a synthesis of their new religious faith and thereby laid the foundations of an entirely new literature, appear to have received important suggestions from this quarter.

As we have seen, these writers no longer appear under their own names, but under those of Johanan ben Zakkai, Eliezer ben Hyrkanus, Akiba ben Joseph, and Ishmael the "High Priest."[3] These authentic personages are at the same time introduced as the chief characters of their writings, the "heroes" of mystical action, the keepers and trustees of secret wisdom. Not all of this is mere romancing, but it is impossible to treat the bulk of it as authentic. A good deal undoubtedly pertains to later stages of development in which older motifs have acquired a new significance or revealed new aspects. If the roots in many cases go far back, they do not necessarily go back to these orthodox rabbinic teachers of the Mishnaic period. Subterranean but effective, and occasionally still traceable, connections exist between these later mystics and the groups which produced a large proportion of the pseudepigrapha and apocalypses of the first century before and after Christ. Subsequently a good deal of this unrecognized tradition made its way to later generations independent of, and often in isolation from, the schools and academies of the Talmudic teachers.

We know that in the period of the Second Temple an esoteric doctrine was already taught in Pharisaic circles. The first chapter of Genesis, the story of Creation (*Maaseh Bereshith*), and the first chapter of Ezekiel, the vision of God's throne-chariot (the "Merkabah"), were the favorite subjects of discussion and interpretation which it was apparently considered inadvisable to make public. Originally these discussions were restricted to the elucidation and exposition of the respective Biblical passages.[4] Thus St. Jerome in one of his letters mentions a Jewish tradition which forbids the study of the beginning and the end of the Book of Ezekiel before the completion of the thirtieth year.[5] It seems probable, however, that speculation did not remain restricted to commentaries on the Biblical text. The *hayoth*, the "living creatures", and other objects of Ezekiel's vision were conceived as angels who form an angelologic hierarchy at the Celestial Court. As long as our knowledge is confined to the meagre fragmentary material scattered across different parts of the Talmud and the Midrashim we shall probably be unable to say how much of this was mystical and theosophical speculation in the strict sense. It is a well-known fact that the editor of the Mishnah, the patriarch Jehudah "the Saint," a pronounced rationalist, did all he could to exclude references to the Merkabah, the angelology, etc. A good deal of this material has been preserved in a second Mishnah collection, the so-called Tosefta, and it is from this and from other fragments that we are able to draw some inferences concerning the character of these speculations.

Our task in this respect would undoubtedly be considerably facilitated if we could be sure that certain apocryphal works written around similar themes, such as the Book of Enoch or the Apocalypse of Abraham⁶—to mention only some of the most outstanding— reproduce the essentials of the esoteric doctrine taught by the teachers of the Mishnah; but it is precisely here that we are left in the dark. Although an immense literature has grown up on the subject of these apocrypha, the truth is that no one knows for certain to what extent they reflect views shared by Mishnaic authorities. Be that as it may—and even granted that it may be possible to trace the influence of the Essenes in some of these writings—one fact remains certain: the main subjects of the later Merkabah mysticism already occupy a central position in this oldest esoteric literature, best represented by the Book of Enoch. The combination of apocalyptic with theosophy and cosmogony is emphasized almost to excess: "Not only have the seers perceived the celestial hosts, heaven with its angels, but the whole of this apocalyptic and pseudepigraphic literature is shot through with a chain of new revelations concerning the hidden glory of the great Majesty, its throne, its palace . . . the celestial spheres towering up one over the other, paradise, hell, and the containers of the souls.'"⁷—This is entirely correct and by itself sufficient to prove the essential continuity of thought concerning the Merkabah in all its three stages: the anonymous conventicles of the old apocalyptics; the Merkabah speculation of the Mishnaic teachers who are known to us by name; and the Merkabah mysticism of late and post-Talmudic times, as reflected in the literature which has come down to us. We are dealing here with a religious movement of distinctive character whose existence conclusively disproves the old prejudice according to which all the productive religious energies of early apocalyptic were absorbed by and into Christianity after the latter's rise.

2

What was the central theme of these oldest of mystical doctrines within the framework of Judaism? No doubts are possible on this point: the earliest Jewish mysticism is throne-mysticism. Its essence is not absorbed contemplation of God's true nature, but perception of His appearance on the throne, as described by Ezekiel, and cognition of the mysteries of the celestial throne-world. The throne-world is to the Jewish mystic what the *pleroma,* the "fullness", the bright sphere of divinity with its potencies, aeons, archons and dominions is to the Hellenistic and early Christian mystics of the period who appear in the history of religion under the names of Gnostics and Hermetics. The Jewish mystic, though guided by motives similar to theirs, nevertheless expresses his vision in terms of his own religious background. God's pre-existing throne, which embodies and exemplifies all forms of creation,[8] is at once the goal and the theme of his mystical vision. From the fourteenth chapter of the Ethiopic Book of Enoch, which contains the oldest description of the throne in the whole of this literature, a long succession of mystical documents of the most varied character[9] leads to the ecstatic descriptions of the throne-world in the tracts of the Merkabah visionaries to which we must now turn our attention. From the interpretation of the throne-world as the true centre of all mystical contemplation it is possible to deduce most of the concepts and doctrines of these ancient mystics. The following is therefore an excursion through the manifold variations on the one theme which forms their common point of departure.

The outstanding documents of the movement appear to have been edited in the fifth and sixth centuries when its spirit was still alive and vigorous. It is difficult to establish exact dates for the various writings, but everything points to the period before the expansion of Islam.[10] The world reflected in this literature has evoked in the mind of more than one scholar comparisons with the pattern of Byzantine society. But there is no reason for assuming that the descriptions of the celestial throne and the heavenly court simply reflect the mundane reality of the Byzantine or Sassanid court, if only because the roots of their central theme go much too far back for such an hypothesis. At the same time there can be no reasonable doubt that the atmosphere of these writings is in harmony with contemporary political and social conditions.

All our material is in the form of brief tracts, or scattered fragments of varying length from what may have been voluminous works; in addition there is a good deal of almost shapeless literary raw material. Much of this literature has not yet been published,[11] and the history of many texts still await clarification. Most of the tracts are called "Hekhaloth Books," i. e., descriptions of the *hekhaloth,* the heavenly halls or palaces through which the visionary passes and in the seventh and last of which there rises the throne of divine glory. One of them, whose title, "Book of Enoch", appears to belong to a very late period, was edited in 1928 by the Swedish scholar Hugo Odeberg.[12] Of still greater importance than this book are the so-called "Greater Hekhaloth" and "Lesser Hekhaloth". The Hebrew text of both tracts is available unfortunately only in very corrupt editions[13] which still await a critical edition as much as a translation. If this task were undertaken, a good deal of light would be thrown on a startling and remarkable chapter in the history of ancient Gnosticism. In the present context, with our chief interest restricted to the ideas of the mystics who were the authors of these writings, there is no room for a discussion of the rather intricate questions connected with the probable origin and composition of these texts. My own views on this subject are rather different from the very scholarly interpretation put forward by Odeberg.

The so-called "Third Book of Enoch," which Odeberg attributes to the third century, appears to me to belong to a later period than the "Greater Hekhaloth."[14] The latter in their turn come after the "Lesser Hekhaloth," the oldest text available to us,[15] in which Rabbi Akiba appears as the principal speaker. The texts of the "Greater Hekhaloth", with Rabbi Ishmael as the speaker, are made up of several different strata. They even include a compilation of materials —particularly in chapters 17 to 23—which go back in part to the second century; but in their present form, including certain apocalyptic revelations, they can hardly have been edited before the sixth. Generally speaking, these documents reflect different stages of development, although some of them may have coexisted with others. A good deal of precious old material is whirled along in this stream; not a few allusions to ideas apparently common in these circles have no meaning for us. But what interests us chiefly, the spiritual physiognomy and the religious mentality of these groups, is clear and understandable enough.

In this connection one important point is to be noted: the most important of these old tracts and compilations, such as the "Greater" and "Lesser" Hekhaloth, are precisely those which are almost entirely free from the exegetical element. These texts are not Midrashim, i.e. expositions of Biblical passages, but a literature *sui generis* with a purpose of its own. They are essentially descriptions of a genuine religious experience for which no sanction is sought in the Bible. In short, they belong in one class with the apocrypha and the apocalyptic writings rather than with the traditional Midrash. It is true that the vision of the celestial realm which forms their main theme originally proceeded from an attempt to transform what is casually alluded to in the Bible into direct personal experience; similarly, the basic categories of thought which appear in the description of the Merkabah are derived from the same Biblical source. But for all that, one meets here with an entirely new and independent spiritual and religious mood; only in the later stages of the movement, probably corresponding with its gradual decline, do the writings show a return to exegesis for its own sake.

The descriptions given to the contemplation of God's "Glory" and the celestial throne employ a terminology which has varied in the course of the centuries. In the period of the Mishnah, reference is usually made to a theosophic "Study of the Glory" or an "Understanding of the Glory"[16]; we even find the curious term "Employment of the Glory," in connection with Rabbi Akiba, who was found worthy of it.[17] Later, the Hekhaloth tracts usually speak of the "Vision of the Merkabah."[18] The sphere of the throne, the "Merkabah," has its "chambers,"[19] and, later on, its "palaces" — a conception foreign to Ezekiel and the earlier writers generally. According to an Aggadic tradition from the fourth century, Isaac had a vision on Moriah, at the moment when Abraham was about to perform the sacrifice, in which his soul perceived the "Chambers of the Merkabah."[20] At different times the visionary experience was also interpreted differently. In the early literature, the writers always speak of an "ascent to the Merkabah," a pictorial analogy which has come to seem natural to us. The "Lesser Hekhaloth"[21] emphasize this "ascent", and the same term recurs in a few out-of-the-way passages of the "Greater Hekhaloth,"[22] and in the introduction to the "Book of Enoch". But for reasons which have become obscure, the whole terminology had in the meantime undergone a change—it is difficult to say exactly when, probably around 500. In the "Greater Hekhaloth," which are of such importance for our analysis, and from then on in almost all the later writings, the visionary journey of the soul to heaven is always referred to as the "descent to the Merkabah." The paradoxical character of this term is all the more remarkable because the detailed description of the mystical process nonetheless consistently employs the metaphor of ascent and not of descent. The mystics of this group call themselves *Yorde Merkabah*, i. e. "descenders to the Merkabah" (and not "Riders in the Chariot," as some translators would have it),[2] and this name is also given to them by others throughout the whole literature down to a late period. The authors of the "Greater Hekhaloth" refer to the existence of these *Yorde Merkabah* as a group with some sort of organization and identify them in the usual legendary fashion with the circle of Johanan ben Zakkai and his disciples. Since the "Greater Hekhaloth" contain Palestinian as well as Babylonian elements—the earliest chapters in particular bear unmistakable traces, in their subject-matter as well as their style, of Palestinian influence—it is not inconceivable that the organization of these groups did indeed take place in late Talmudic times (fourth or fifth century) on Palestinian soil. As a matter of ascertained fact, however, we only know of their existence in Babylonia, from where practically all mystical tracts of this particular variety made their way to Italy and Germany; it is these tracts that have come down to us in the form of manuscripts written in the late Middle Ages.

To repeat, we are dealing with organized groups which foster and hand down a certain tradition: with a *school* of mystics who are not prepared to reveal their secret knowledge, their 'Gnosis,' to the public. Too great was the danger, in this period of ubiquitous Jewish and Christian heresies, that mystical speculation based on private religious experience would come into conflict with that "rabbinical" Judaism which was rapidly crystallizing during the same epoch.[24] The "Greater Hekhaloth" show in many and often highly interesting details[25] that their anonymous authors were anxious to develop their 'Gnosis' within the frame-work of Halakhic Judaism, notwithstanding its partial incompatibility with the new religious spirit; the original religious impulses active in these circles came, after all, from sources quite different from those of orthodox Judaism.

One result of this peculiar situation was the establishment of

certain *conditions of admission* into the circle of the Merkabah
mystics. The Talmudic sources already mention certain stipulations,
albeit of a very general character, in accordance with which admission to the knowledge of theosophical doctrines and principles is
made conditional on the possession of certain moral qualities. Only
a "court president" or one belonging to the categories of men named
in Isaiah III, 3 is found worthy of obtaining insight into the tradition of Merkabah mysticism. Chapter 13 of the "Greater Hekhaloth" lists eight moral requisites of initiation. In addition, however,
we find physical criteria which have nothing to do with the moral
or social status of the acolyte; in particular the novice is judged in
accordance with physiognomic and chiromantic criteria—a novel
procedure which appears to have been stimulated by the renaissance
of Hellenistic physiognomics in the second century A.D.

Apart from being a criterion for the admission of novices,[26]
physiognomy and chiromancy also figure in Hekhaloth mysticism as
a subject of esoteric knowledge among the adepts. It is therefore
not surprising that several manuscripts have retained a sort of introduction in the form of a chiromantic fragment[27]—incidentally the
oldest chiromantic document known to us, since no Assyrian or
Graeco-Roman texts of this kind have been preserved.[28] This pre-
amble to the other Hekhaloth books interprets the significance of
the favorable or unfavorable lines of the human hand, without
reference to astrology but on the basis of a fixed terminology which
to us is frequently obscure. One is perhaps justified in regarding the
appearance of these new criteria as a parallel to the growth of neo-
Platonic mysticism in the Orient during the fourth century. (It is
characteristic of this period that Jamblichus, in his biography of
Pythagoras—a book which throws a good deal more light on the
period of its writing than on its subject-matter—asserts that entry
into the Pythagorean school was conditional upon the possession of
certain physiognomic characteristics.[29]) The above mentioned fragment, in which the angel Suriyah reveals to Ishmael—one of the
two principal figures of our Hekhaloth tracts—the secrets of chiromancy and physiognomy, has a title taken from Isaiah III, 9:
Hakkarath Panim, i. e. "perception of the face," and in fact this
passage from Isaiah first received a physiognomic interpretation in
the fourth century, as a Talmudic reference to the subject shows.[30]

3

Those who passed the test were considered worthy to make the "descent" to the Merkabah which led them, after many trials and dangers, through the seven heavenly palaces, and before that through the heavens, their preparation, their technique, and the description of what is perceived on the voyage, are the subject-matter of the writings with which we are concerned.

Originally, we have here a Jewish variation on one of the chief preoccupations of the second and third century gnostics and hermetics: the ascent of the soul from the earth, through the spheres of the hostile planet-angels and rulers of the cosmos, and its return to its divine home in the "fullness" of God's light, a return which, to the gnostic's mind, signified Redemption. Some scholars consider this to be the central idea of Gnosticism.[31] Certainly the description of this journey, of which a particularly impressive account is found in the second part of the "Greater Hekhaloth,"[32] is in all its details of a character which must be called gnostic.

This mystical ascent is always preceded by ascetic practices whose duration in some cases is twelve days, in others forty. An account of these practices was given about 1000 A.D. by Hai ben Sherira, the head of a Babylonian academy. According to him, "many scholars were of the belief that one who is distinguished by many qualities described in the books and who is desirous of beholding the Merkabah and the palaces of the angels on high, must follow a certain procedure. He must fast a number of days and lay his head between his knees and whisper many hymns and songs whose texts are known from tradition. Then he perceives the interior and the chambers, as if he saw the seven palaces with his own eyes, and it is as though he entered one palace after the other and saw what is there."[33] The typical bodily posture of these ascetics is also that of Elijah in his prayer on Mount Carmel. It is an attitude of deep self-oblivion which, to judge from certain ethnological parallels, is favorable to the induction of pre-hypnotic autosuggestion. Dennys[34] gives a very similar description of a Chinese somnambulist in the act of conjuring the spirits of the departed: "She sits down on a low chair and bends forward so that her head rests on her knees. Then, in a deep measured voice, she repeats three times an exorcism, whereupon a certain change appears to come over her." In the Talmud, too, we find this posture described as typical of the self-oblivion of a Hanina ben Dosa sunk in prayer, or of a penitent who gives himself over to God.[35]

Finally, after such preparations, and in a state of ecstasy, the adept begins his journey. The "Greater Hekhaloth" do not describe the details of his ascent through the seven heavens, but they do describe his voyage through the seven palaces situated in the highest heaven. The place of the gnostical rulers (archons) of the seven planetary spheres, who are opposed to the liberation of the soul from its earthly bondage and whose resistance the soul must overcome, is taken in this Judaïzed and monotheistic Gnosticism by the hosts of "gate-keepers" posted to the right and left of the entrance to the heavenly hall through which the soul must pass in its ascent. In both cases, the soul requires a pass in order to be able to continue its journey without danger: a magic seal made of a secret name which puts the demons and hostile angels to flight. Every new stage of the ascension requires a new seal with which the traveller "seals himself" in order that, to quote a fragment, "he shall not be dragged into the fire and the flame, the vortex and the storm which are around Thee, oh Thou terrible and sublime."[36] The "Greater He-khaloth" have preserved a quite pedantic description of this passport procedure;[37] all the seals and the secret names are derived from the Merkabah itself where they "stand like pillars of flame around the fiery throne" of the Creator.[38]

It is the soul's need for protection on its journey which has produced these seals with their twin function as a protective armour and as a magical weapon. At first the magical protection of a single seal may be sufficient, but as time goes on the difficulties experienced by the adept tend to become greater. A brief and simple formula is no longer enough. Sunk in his ecstatic trance, the mystic at the same time experiences a sense of frustration which he tries to overcome by using longer and more complicated magical for-mulae, symbols of a longer and harder struggle to pass the closed entrance gates which block his progress. As his psychical energy wanes the magical strain grows and the conjuring gesture becomes progressively more strained, until in the end whole pages are filled with an apparently meaningless recital of magical key-words with which he tries to unlock the closed door.

It is this fact which explains the abundance of magical elements in many of the Hekhaloth texts. Such *voces mysticae* are particularly prominent in the unedited texts. Already the oldest documents of all, the "Lesser Hekhaloth", are full of them; nor is this surprising, for shadowy elements of this kind, so far from being later additions or signs of spiritual decadence—a prejudice dear to the modern mind—belong to the very core of their particular religious system. This fact has been placed beyond doubt by modern research into the history of Hellenistic syncretism, where we find, in the Greek and Coptic magical papyri written in Egypt under the Roman Empire, the closest and most indissoluble union of religious fervor and mystical ecstasy with magical beliefs and practices. These magical interpolations have their proper and natural place in the texts only to the extent that magical rites were actually practised. Every secret name seemed to provide a further piece of protective armour against the demons—up to the point where the magical energy was no longer sufficient to overcome the obstacles which blocked the way to the Merkabah. This point is really the end of the movement as a living force; from then on it degenerates into mere literature. It is therefore not surprising that the tracts in our possession clearly reflect two different stages: an older one, in which the movement is still a living reality and in which, therefore, the seals and secret names occupy an important place; and a second phase, in which the process of degeneration has set in and for this very reason the study of the texts presents few difficulties. In this second stage the magical contents cease to represent a psychical reality and are gradually eliminated; in this way the old texts are gradually replaced by a new devotional literature, at once stilted and lyrical, which employs the elements of the original Merkabah mysticism. In our case, the first stage is represented by the "Greater" and "Lesser" Hekhaloth. The second includes the numerous texts of the "Midrash of the Ten Martyrs" and the "Alphabet of Rabbi Akiba,"[39] both of them writings which were particularly popular among the Jews of the Middle Ages.

The dangers of the ascent through the palaces of the Merkabah sphere are great, particularly for those who undertake the journey without the necessary preparation, let alone those who are unworthy of its object. As the journey progresses, the dangers become progressively greater. Angels and archons storm against the traveller "in order to drive him out";[40] a fire which proceeds from his own body

threatens to devour him."[41] In the Hebrew Book of Enoch there is
an account of the description given by the Patriarch to Rabbi
Ishmael of his own metamorphosis into the angel Metatron, when
his flesh was transformed into "fiery torches." According to the
"Greater Hekhaloth," every mystic must undergo this transformation, but with the difference that, being less worthy than Enoch, he
is in danger of being devoured by the "fiery torches." This transition through the opening stage of the process of mystical transfiguration is an ineluctable necessity. According to another fragment,
the mystic must be able to stand upright "without hands and feet,"
both having been burned.[42] This standing without feet in bottomless space is mentioned elsewhere as a characteristic experience of
many ecstatics; a mystical stage closely approximating to it is referred to in the Apocalypse of Abraham.[43]

But the most remarkable passage of all is the interpretation given
already in the "Lesser Hekhaloth" of a famous fragment which is
found in the Talmud and the Tosefta. This little story is included
in the few pages of the Treatise *Hagigah* which the Talmud devotes
to the subject of contemporary mysticism:[44] "Four entered 'Paradise':
Ben Azai, Ben Zoma, Aher and Rabbi Akiba. Rabbi Akiba spoke
to them: 'When you come to the place of the shining marble plates,
then do not say: Water, water! For it is written: He that telleth lies
shall not tarry in my sight'."

Modern interpretations of this famous passage, which clearly
enough refers to a *real* danger in the process of ascending to 'Paradise,'[45] are extremely far-fetched and not a little irrational in their
determination at all costs to preserve the characteristic essentials of
rationalism. We are told[46] that the passages refers to cosmological
speculations about the *materia prima,* an explanation which lacks
all plausibility and finds no support in the context or in the subject-
matter itself. The fact is that the later Merkabah mystics showed a
perfectly correct understanding of the meaning of this passage, and
their interpretation offers striking proof that the tradition of Tan-
naitic mysticism and theosophy was really alive among them, although certain details may have originated in a later period. The
following quotation is taken from the Munich manuscript of the
Hekhaloth texts:[47] "But if one was unworthy to see the King in his
beauty, the angels at the gates disturbed his senses and confused
him. And when they said to him: 'Come in,' he entered, and in-

stantly they pressed him and threw him into the fiery lava stream. And at the gate of the sixth palace it seemed as though hundreds of thousands and millions of waves of water stormed against him, and yet there was not a drop of water, only the ethereal glitter of the marble plates with which the palace was tessellated. But he was standing in front of the angels and when he asked: 'What is the meaning of these waters,' they began to stone him and said: 'Wretch, do you not see it with your own eyes? Are you perhaps a descendant of those who kissed the Golden Calf, and are you unworthy to see the King in his beauty?' . . . And he does not go until they strike his head with iron bars and wound him. And this shall be a sign for all times that no one shall err at the gate of the sixth palace and see the ethereal glitter of the plates and ask about them and take them for water, that he may not endanger himself."

Thus the text. The authenticity of the story's core, the ecstatic's vision of water, hardly requires proof. Nothing could be more far-fetched than to treat it as a *post festum* interpretation of the Talmudic passage; there is no reason whatsoever to doubt that the mystical experience of the dangers of the ascent is really the subject of the anecdote.[48] Similar dangers are described in the so-called "Liturgy of Mithras" contained in the great magical papyrus of Paris,[49] where the description of the mystical ascent shows many parallels of detail and atmosphere with the account given in the "Greater Hekhaloth."

Particularly vivid descriptions are given in the "Greater Hekhaloth" of the last stages of the ascent, the passage through the sixth and seventh gates. These descriptions, however, are not uniform but appear rather to be a compilation of various documents and traditions concerning the relevant experiences of the Merkabah mystic. The discussions between the traveller and the gate-keepers of the sixth palace, the archons Domiel and Katspiel, which take up a good deal of space, clearly date back to very early times. One of their more unexpected features is the recurrence of rudiments of certain Greek formulae and standing expressions, which the editors in Babylonia were not longer capable of understanding and apparently regarded as magical names of the divinity.[50] The fact that the original Merkabah mystics in Palestine prescribed the use of specific Greek formulae for certain occasions deserves special attention. It is difficult to say whether it indicates a concrete influence of Hellenistic religion, or whether the employment of Greek words by the Aramaic-speaking Jewish mystics is merely analogous to the predilection for Hebraic or pseudo-Hebraic formulae characteristic of the Greek-speaking circles for whom the Egyptian magical papyri were written.

The idea of the seven heavens through which the soul ascends to its original home, either after death or in a state of ecstasy while the body is still alive, is certainly very old. In an obscure and somewhat distorted form it is already to be found in old apocrypha such as the Fourth Book of Ezra or the Ascension of Isaiah, which is based on a Jewish text.[51] In the same way, the ancient Talmudic account of the seven heavens, their names and their contents, although apparently purely cosmological, surely presupposes an ascent of the soul to the throne in the seventh heaven.[52] Such descriptions of the seven heavens, plus a list of the names of their archons, have also come down to us from the school of the Merkabah mystics in the post-Mishnaic period. It is precisely here that we still find an entirely esoteric doctrine. Thus for example in the "Visions of Ezekiel", which have recently become known,[53] Ezekiel sees the seven heavens with their seven Merkabahs reflected in the waters of the Chebar river. This form of speculation about seven Merkabahs corresponding to the seven heavens is still innocent of any mention of Hekhaloth, or chambers, of the Merkabah. Possibly both conceptions were known to different groups or schools of the same period. In any event, the second variant gradually became the dominant one.

4

This idea of the seven Hekhaloth transforms the old cosmological conception of the world structure revealed during the ascent into a description of the divine hierachy: the traveller in search of God, like the visitor at Court, must pass through endless magnificent halls and chambers. This change of emphasis, like other important aspects of the mystical system to which it belongs, appears to me to be connected with the fundamental religious experience of these mystics, namely, the decisive importance which they assigned to the interpretation of God as King. We are dealing here with a Judaized form of cosmocratorial mysticism concerning the divine King (or Emperor). This form of adoration takes first place, and cosmological mysticism is relegated to the writings concerned with the creation of the world, the commentaries to *Maaseh Bereshith*. Not without good reason has Graetz called the religious belief of the Merkabah mystic "Basileomorphism."

This point needs to be stressed, for it makes clear the enormous gulf between the gnosticism of the Hekhaloth and that of the Hellenistic mystics. There are many parallels between the two, but there is a radical difference in the conception of God. In the Hekhaloth, God is above all King, to be precise, Holy King. This conception reflects a change in the religious consciousness of the Jews—not only the mystics—for which documentary evidence exists in the liturgy of the period. The aspects of God which are really relevant to the religious feeling of the epoch are His majesty and the aura of sublimity and solemnity which surrounds Him.

On the other hand, there is a complete absence of any sentiment of divine immanence. J. Abelson has made a valuable contribution to the understanding of the subject in his "Immanence of God in Rabbinical Literature," where he has devoted a particularly searching analysis to the theory of the Shekhinah, God's "immanence" or "indwelling" in the world, in the literature of the Aggadah. Quite rightly he has stressed the connection between these ideas and certain mystical conceptions which have played a part in the later development of Jewish mysticism.[54] But in the Merkabah mysticism with which we are dealing here, the idea of the Shekhinah and of God's immanence plays practically no part at all. The one passage in the "Greater Hekhaloth" which has been adduced as proof of the existence of such conceptions is based on an obviously corrupt text.[55] The fact is that the true and spontaneous feeling of the Merkabah mystic knows nothing of divine immanence; the infinite gulf between the soul and God the King on His throne is not even bridged at the climax of mystical ecstasy.

Not only is there for the mystic no divine immanence, there is also almost no love of God. What there is of love in the relationship between the Jewish mystic and his God belongs to a much later period and has nothing to do with our present subject. Ecstasy there was, and this fundamental experience must have been a source of religious inspiration, but we find no trace of a mystical union between the soul and God. Throughout there remained an almost exaggerated consciousness of God's *otherness*, nor does the identity and individuality of the mystic become blurred even at the height of ecstatic passion. The Creator and His creature remain apart, and nowhere is an attempt made to bridge the gulf between them or to blur the distinction. The mystic who in his ecstasy has passed through all the gates, braved all the dangers, now stands before the throne; he sees and hears—but that is all. All the emphasis is laid on the kingly aspect of God, not his creative one, although the two belong together and the second, as we shall see, even becomes, in a certain perspective of this mysticism, the dominant one. True, the mysteries of creation and the hidden connection between all things existing in the universe are among the riddles whose solution is of deep interest to the authors of the Hekhaloth tracts. There are some references to them in the description of the Merkabah vision; thus the "Greater Hekhaloth" give promise of the revelation of "the mysteries and wonderful secrets of the tissue on which the perfection of the world and its course depends, and the chain of heaven and earth along which all the wings of the universe and the wings of the heavenly heights are connected, sewn together, made fast and hung up."[56] But the promise is not carried out, the secret not revealed. The magnificence and majesty of God, on the other hand, this experience of the *Yorde Merkabah* which overwhelms and overshadows all the others, is not only heralded but also described with an abundance of detail and almost to excess.

Strange and sometimes obscure are the names given to God, the King who thrones in His glory. We find names such as Zoharariel, Adiriron, Akhtariel,[57] and Totrossiyah (or Tetrassiyah, i. e. the Tetras or fourfoldness of the letters of God's name YHWH?[58]), names which to the mystics may have signified various aspects of God's glory. In this context it is well to remember that the chief peculiarity of this form of mysticism, its emphasis on God's might and magnificence, opens the door to the transformation of mysticism into theurgy; there the master of the secret "names" himself takes on the exercise of power in the way described in the various magical and theurgical procedures of which this literature is full. The language of the theurgist conforms to that of the Merkabah mystic. Both are dominated by the attributes of power and sublimity, not love or tenderness. It is entirely characteristic of the outlook of these believers that the theurgist, in adjuring the "Prince of Divine Presence," summons the archons as "Princes of Majesty,

Fear and Trembling."⁵⁹ *Majesty, Fear* and *Trembling* are indeed
the key-words to this Open Sesame of religion.

5

The most important sources for our understanding of this atmosphere are undoubtedly the numerous prayers and hymns which
have been preserved in the Hekhaloth tracts.⁶⁰ Tradition ascribes
them to inspiration, for, according to the mystics, they are nothing
but the hymns sung by the angels, even by the throne itself, in
praise of God. In chapter IV of the "Greater Hekhaloth," in which
these hymns occupy an important place, we find an account of how
Rabbi Akiba, the prototype of the Merkabah visionary, was inspired to hear them sung at the very throne of glory before which
his soul was standing. Conversely, their recitation serves to induce
a state of ecstasy and accompanies the traveller on his journey
through the gates. Some of these hymns are simply adjurations of
God; others take the form of dialogues between God and the heavenly dwellers, and descriptions of the Merkabah sphere. It would
be vain to look for definite religious doctrines, to say nothing of
mystical symbols, in these hymns which belong to the oldest products of synagogal poetry, the so-called *piyut*. Often they are curiously
bare of meaning, and yet the impression they create is a profound
one.

Rudolf Otto in his celebrated book "The Idea of the Holy" has
stressed the difference between a purely rational glorification of
God, in which everything is clear, definite, familiar and comprehensible, and one which touches the springs of the irrational, or
the "numinous", as he calls it, one which tries to reproduce in words
the *mysterium tremendum,* the awful mystery that surrounds God's
majesty. Otto⁶¹ has called compositions of this latter sort "numinous
hymns." The Jewish liturgy, and not only that of the mystics, contains a great number of these; and from the Jewish liturgy Otto
himself has drawn some of the most important of his examples.
In the Hekhaloth books we have as it were a full treasure-house of
such numinous hymns.

The immense solemnity of their style, the bombast of their magnificent phrases, reflects the fundamental paradoxy of these hymns:
the climax of sublimity and solemnity to which the mystic can at-

tain in his attempt to express the magnificence of his vision is also the *non plus ultra* of vacuousness. Philipp Bloch, who was the first to be deeply impressed by the problem presented by these hymns, speaks of their "plethora of purely pleonastic and unisonous words which do not in the least assist the process of thought but merely reflect the emotional struggle."[62] But at the same time he shows himself aware of the almost magical effect of this vacuous and yet sublime pathos on those who are praying when, for example, hymns composed in this spirit are recited on the Day of Atonement.[63] Perhaps the most famous example of this kind is the litany *haadereth vehaemunah lehay olamim* which is to be found—with a wealth of variations—in the "Greater Hekhaloth" and has been included in the liturgy of the High Holidays. The mediaeval commentators still referred to it as the "Song of the Angels,"[64] and it is probable that it called for the deepest devotion and solemnity on the part of those who prayed. But a formal demand of this kind can hardly have been necessary, for the mighty effect of these incomparably solemn and at the same time infinitely vacuous hymns, i. e. their numinous character, can be witnessed to this day in every synagogue. No wonder that to this day this hymn is recited by many Hasidic Jews every Sabbath among the morning prayers. The following is an approximate translation of the text, which is entirely a medley of praises of God and citations of the attributes that "appertain to Him who lives eternally":[65]

> Excellence and faithfulness—are His who lives forever
> Understanding and blessing—are His who lives forever
> Grandeur and greatness—are His who lives forever
> Cognition and expression—are His who lives forever
> Magnificence and majesty—are His who lives forever
> Counsel and strength—are His who lives forever
> Lustre and brilliance—are His who lives forever
> Grace and benevolence—are His who lives forever
> Purity and goodness—are His who lives forever
> Unity and honor—are His who lives forever
> Crown and glory—are His who lives forever
> Precept and practice—are His who lives forever
> Sovereignty and rule—are His who lives forever
> Adornment and permanence—are His who lives forever

Mystery and wisdom—are His who lives forever
Might and meekness—are His who lives forever
Splendor and wonder—are His who lives forever
Righteousness and honor—are His who lives forever
Invocation and holiness—are His who lives forever
Exultation and nobility—are His who lives forever
Song and hymn—are His who lives forever
Praise and glory—are His who lives forever

This—in its original language—is a classic example of an alphabetical litany which fills the imagination of the devotee with splendid concepts clothed in magnificent expression; the particular words do not matter. To quote Bloch again: "The glorification of God is not that of the psalm, which either describes the marvels of creation as proof of the grandeur and the glory of the Creator, or stresses the element of divine grace and guidance in the history of Israel as throwing light on the wisdom and benevolence of Providence; it is simply praise of God, and this praise is heaped and multiplied as if there were a danger that some honorific might be forgotten."[66]

Another passage from a hymn to "Zoharariel, Adonai, God of Israel," in the "Greater Hekhaloth," runs as follows:[67]

His throne radiates before Him and His palace is full of
                                                splendor.
His Majesty is becoming and His Glory is an adornment for
                                                Him.
His servants sing before Him and proclaim the might of His
                                                wonders,
as King of all kings and Master of all masters,
encircled by rows of crowns, surrounded by the ranks of the
                                   princes of splendor.
With a gleam of His ray he encompasses the sky
and His splendor radiates from the heights.
Abysses flame from His mouth and firmaments sparkle from
                                        His body.

Almost all the hymns from the Hekhaloth tracts, particularly those whose text has been preserved intact, reveal a mechanism comparable to the motion of an enormous fly-wheel. In cyclical rhythm the hymns succeed each other, and within them the adjurations of God follow in a crescendo of glittering and majestic attributes, each stressing and reinforcing the sonorous power of the world. The monotony of their rhythm—almost all consist of verses of four words —and the progressively sonorous incantations induce in those who are praying a state of mind bordering on ecstasy. An important part of this technique is the recurrence of the key-word of the numinous, the *kedushah*, the trishagion from Isaiah VI, 3, in which the ecstasy of the mystic culminates: holy, holy, holy is the Lord of Hosts. One can hardly conceive of a more grandiose proof of the irresistible influence which the conception of God's kingdom exercised on the consciousness of these mystics. The "holiness" of God, which they are trying to paraphrase, is utterly transcendent of any moral meaning and represents nothing but glory of His Kingdom. Through various forms of the prayer known as the *kedushah*, this conception has also found its way into the general Jewish liturgy and left its imprint on it.[63]

In spite of the last mentioned fact, it cannot be denied that this "polylogy", or verbiage, of the mystics, these magniloquent attempts to catch a glimpse of God's majesty and to preserve it in hymnical form, stands in sharp contrast to the tendencies which already during the Talmudical period dominated the outlook of the great teachers of the Law. They could not but feel repelled by it, and in the Talmud one early encounters a strong dislike for extravagant enthusiasm in prayer, much as the Sermon on the Mount had attacked the polylogy of the pagans, their effusive and wordy style. Passages like the following read like an attack on the tendencies reflected in the Hekhaloth tracts: "He who multiplies the praise of God to excess shall be torn from the world." Or: "In the presence of Rabbi Hanina, one went to the praying-desk to say the prayer. He said, 'God, Thou great, strong, terrible, mighty, feared, powerful, real and adorable!' He waited until the other had finished, then he said to him: 'Have you ended with the praise of your God? What is the meaning of all this? It is as if one were to praise a king of the world, who has millions of pieces of gold, for the possession of a piece of silver.' "[60]

But this resistance to an enthusiasm and a verbiage so different from the classical simplicity and rationality of the fundamental prayers of Jewish liturgy was of no avail. That much is clear not only from the prayers and hymns of the Merkabah mystics, but also from certain important parts of the liturgy proper whose spirit reflects the influence of the *Yorde Merkabah*. Bloch was the first to point out that the community prayer in its final form, which it received in late Talmudic and post-Talmudic times, represents a compromise between these two opposing tendencies. Some of these prayers are indeed much older than was thought by Bloch, who has overlooked certain passages of the Palestinian Talmud and attributed every prayer which mentions the angels of the Merkabah to the post-Talmudic period.[70] But since the mystical school of the *Yorde Merkabah* is in general of much earlier origin than Zunz, Graetz and Bloch assumed and may have been in existence in Palestine during the fourth century, this fact presents no difficulty for our contention.

While the Merkabah hymns with which we are dealing hardly go back beyond the fifth century, they continue a tradition already visible in the throne mysticism and the apocalyptic of the Mishnaic period. In the Apocalypse of Abraham, whose connection with the Merkabah mysticism has also struck its English editor, G. H. Box, the patriarch who ascends to the throne hears a voice speaking from the celestial fire "like a voice of many waters, like the sound of the sea in its uproar." The same terms are used in the "Greater Hekhaloth" in describing the sound of the hymn of praise sung by the "throne of Glory" to its King—"like the voice of the waters in the rushing streams, like the waves of the ocean when the south wind sets them in uproar." The same apocalypse contains the song which Abraham is taught by the angel who guides him on his way to heaven—and this song is nothing but the hymn sung by the angels who mount guard before the Throne.[71] Although the attributes of God are in some cases identical with those used in Greek and early Christian prayers,[72] this hymn already has the numinous character described above. God is praised as the Holy Being and also as the supreme master; this is quite in harmony with the characteristic outlook of these hymns, whether sung by the angels or by Israel, in which the veneration of God the King blends imperceptibly with the conjuring magic of the adept. The presentation of the crown to God is almost the only act through which the devotee can still bear witness to the religious destiny of man.

It is characteristic of these hymns that the traditional vocabulary of the Hebrew language, although by no means restricted in this field, no longer sufficed for the spiritual needs of the ecstatic eager to express his vision of God's majesty in words. This is evident from the large number of original and frequently bizarre phrases and word combinations, sometimes entirely novel creations,[73] all bearing a decidedly numinous character, and which perhaps mark the beginning of the flood of new verbal creations to be found in the oldest classics of Palestinian synagogal poetry since the seventh century A.D. Thus, for example, the influence of the Merkabah literature on Eleazar Kalir, the outstanding master of this school, is obvious enough.

The extent to which in these circles the hymn was regarded as the original language of the creature addressing itself to its Creator, the extent, therefore, to which they had adopted the prophetic vision of a redeemed world, in which all beings speak in hymns, is clear from a brief tract called *Perek Shirah*, i. e. the chapter of the song of creation.[74] Here all beings are gifted with language for the sole purpose that they may sing—in Biblical words—the praise of their Creator. Originally known only among mystics, this poem gradually made its way—against violent opposition, whose motives are not clear[75]—into the liturgy of the daily prayers.

To sum up, it would appear that the Merkabah mystics were led by logical steps in the direction of mystical prayer, without, however, having developed anything like a mystical theory of prayer. One is perhaps justified in seeing a first step towards such a theory in the characteristic exaggeration of the significance of Israel's prayer in the celestial realm. Only when Israel has sung may the angels join in. One of them, Shemuiel, the "great archon," stands at the window of heaven as a mediator between the prayers of Israel, which rise from below, and the denizens of the seventh heaven to whom he transfers them.[76] The angel who bears the name of Israel stands in the centre of heaven and leads the heavenly choir with the call, "God is King, God was King, God will ever be King."[77] But great though the importance of prayer undoubtedly is for him, the Merkabah mystic who pours out his heart in ecstatic and spontaneous hymns seeks no mysteries behind the words of prayer. The ascent of the words has not yet substituted itself for the ascent of the soul and of the devotee himself. The pure word, the as yet unbroken summons stands for itself; it signifies nothing but what it expresses. But it is not surprising that when the fire out of which these prayers had streamed to heaven had burned low, a host of nostalgic souls stirred the ashes, looking in vain for the spirit which had departed.

6

We have seen that the God of the Merkabah mystics is the Holy King who emerges from unknown worlds and descends "through 955 heavens"[78] to the throne of Glory. The mystery of this God in His aspect of Creator of the universe is one of those exalted subjects of esoteric knowledge which are revealed to the soul of the mystic in its ecstatic ascent; it is of equal importance with the vision of the celestial realm, the songs of the angels, and the structure of the Merkabah. According to an account given in the "Greater Hekhaloth", which one is tempted to correlate with a similar passage at the end of the Fourth Book of Ezra, it was even the custom to place scribes or stenographers to the right and left of the visionary who wrote down his ecstatic description of the throne and its occupants.[79] That the mystic in his rapture even succeeded in penetrating beyond the sphere of the angels is suggested in a passage which speaks of "God who is beyond the sight of His creatures and hidden to the angels who serve Him, but who has revealed Himself to Rabbi Akiba in the vision of the Merkabah."[80]

It is this new revelation, at once strange and forbidding, which we encounter in the most paradoxical of all these tracts, the one which is known under the name of *Shiur Komah,* literally translated, "Measure of the Body" (i. e. the body of God.).[81] From the very beginning, the frank and almost provocative anthropomorphism of the *Shiur Komah* aroused the bitterest antagonism among all Jewish circles which held aloof from mysticism.[82] Conversely, all the later mystics and Kabbalists came to regard its dark and obscure language as a symbol of profound and penetrating spiritual vision. The antagonism was mutual, for it is in this attitude towards anthropomorphism that Jewish rational theology and Jewish mysticism have parted company.

The fragment in question, of which several different texts are extant,[83] describes the "body" of the Creator, in close analogy to the description of the body of the beloved one in the fifth chapter of the "Song of Solomon," giving enormous figures for the length of each organ. At the same time, it indicates the secret names of the various organs with the help of letters and configurations which to us are meaningless. "Whoever knows the measurements of our Creator and the glory of the Holy One, praise be to Him, which are hidden from the creatures, is certain of his share of the world to come." Rabbi Ishmael and Rabbi Akiba, the two heroes of Merkabah mysticism, appear as the guarantors of this sweeping promise— "provided that this Mishnah is daily repeated."[84]

What is really meant by these monstrous length measurements is not made clear; the enormous figures have no intelligible meaning or sense-content, and it is impossible really to visualize the "body of the Shekhinah" which they purport to describe; they are better calculated, on the contrary, to reduce every attempt at such a vision to absurdity.[85] The units of measurement are cosmic; the height of the Creator is 236,000 parasangs[86]—according to another tradition, the height of His soles alone is 30 million parasangs. But "the measure of a parasang of God is three miles, and a mile has 10,000 yards, and a yard three spans of His span, and a span fills the whole world, as it is written: Who hath meted out heaven with the span."[87] Plainly, therefore, it is not really intended to indicate by these numbers any concrete length measurements. Whether the proportion of the various figures, now hopelessly confused in the texts, once expressed some intrinsic relationships and harmonies is a question to which we are not likely to find an answer. But a feeling for the transmundane and the numinous still glimmers through these blasphemous-sounding figures and monstrous groupings of secret names. God's holy majesty takes on flesh and blood, as it were, in these enormous numerical relationships. At any rate the idea that "God is King" lends itself more easily to such symbolical expression than the conception of God as Spirit. Again we see that it was the exaltation of His kingship and His theophany which appealed to these mystics, not His spirituality. It is true that occasionally we find a paradoxical change into the spiritual. All of a sudden, in the midst of the *Shiur Komah,* we read a passage like the following: "The appearance of the face is like that of the cheek-bones, and both are like the figure of the spirit and the form of the soul, and no creature may recognize it. His body is like chrysolite. His light breaks tremendously from the darkness, clouds and fog are around Him, and all the princes of the angels and the seraphim are before

Him like an empty jar. Therefore no measure is given to us, but only secret names are revealed to us."[88] In the writings of the second and third century gnostics, and in certain Greek and Coptic texts, which frequently reflect a mystical spiritualism, we find a similar species of mystical anthropomorphism, with references to the "body of the father,"[89] or the "body of truth." Gaster has pointed out the significance of such instances of anthropomorphism in the writings of the second century gnostic Markos (described by some scholars as "kabbalistic") which are hardly less bizarre and obscure than the analogous examples in the *Shiur Komah*.[90]

The fact probably is that this form of speculation originated among heretical mystics who had all but broken with rabbinical Judaism. At some date this school or group must have blended with the "rabbinical" Gnosticism developed by the Merkabah visionaries, i. e. that form of Jewish Gnosticism which tried to remain true to the Halakhic tradition. Here we come inevitably to the question *whose* bodily dimensions are the subject of these fantastic descriptions? The prophet Ezekiel saw on the throne of the Merkabah "a figure similar to that of a man" (Ez. 1, 26). Does it not seem possible that among the mystics who wrote the *Shiur Komah,* this figure was identified with the "primordial man" of contemporary Iranian speculation, which thus made its entry into the world of Jewish mysticism?[91] Going a step further we may ask whether there did not exist —at any rate among the Merkabah mystics to whom we owe the preservation of the *Shiur Komah*—a belief in a fundamental distinction between the appearance of God the Creator, the Demiurge, i. e. one of His aspects, and His indefinable essence? There is no denying the fact that it is precisely the "primordial man" on the throne of the Merkabah whom the *Shiur Komah* calls *Yotser Bereshith*, i. e. Creator of the world—a significant and, doubtless, a deliberate designation. As is well known, the anti-Jewish gnostics of the second and third centuries drew a sharp distinction between the unknown, "strange," good God, and the Creator, whom they identified with the God of Israel. It may be that the *Shiur Komah* reflects an attempt to give a new turn to this trend of thought, which had become widespread throughout the Near East, by postulating something like a harmony between the Creator and the "true" God. A dualism of the Gnostic kind would of course have been unthinkable for Jews; instead, the Demiurge becomes, by an exercise of mystical anthropomorphism, the appearance of God on the "throne of Glory," at once visible and yet, by virtue of His transcendent nature, incapable of being really visualized.

If this interpretation is correct, we should be justified in saying that the *Shiur Komah* referred not to the "dimensions" of the divinity, but to those of its corporeal appearance. This is clearly the interpretation of the original texts. Already the "Lesser Hekhaloth" interpret the anthropomorphosis of the *Shiur Komah* as a representation of the "hidden glory". Thus, for example, Rabbi Akiba says: "He is like us, as it were, but greater than everything; and that is His glory which is hidden from us."[92] This conception of God's hidden glory, which forms the subject of much theosophical speculation, is almost identical, as we have seen, with the term employed for the object of their deepest veneration by the actual representatives of the Mishnaic Merkabah mysticism, among them the historical Rabbi Akiba. One has only to compare it with the relevant passage of the *Shiur Komah* (already quoted above) where it says, "whoever knows the measurements of our Creator, and the glory of the Holy One, praise be to him," etc. The term employed: *shivho shel hakadosh barukh hu,* signifies not only praise of God—in this context that would be without any meaning—but glory, δόξα, *shevah* being the equivalent of the Aramaic word for glory, *shuvha*.[93] The reference, in short, is not to God's praise but to the vision of His glory. Later when the "Glory of God" had become identified with the *Shekhinah,* the "Alphabet of Rabbi Akiba" expressly referred to the "body of the Shekhinah"[94] as the subject of the *Shiur Komah.* The employment of this term is proof that its authors had in mind not the substance of divinity but merely the measurements of its appearance.

Shiur Komah speculation is already to be found in the earliest Hekhaloth texts and must be counted among the older possessions of Jewish gnosticism. Graetz' theory that it came into being at a late date under the influence of Moslem anthropomorphic tendencies is entirely fallacious and has confused matters down to our own day.[95] If there can be any question of external influence, it was certainly the other way round. This is also borne out by the assertion of the Arab doxograph Shahrastani—not, it is true, an altogether reliable witness—that these ideas made their way from Jewish into Moslem circles.[96] Still less is it possible to agree with

Bloch's hypothesis that the *Shiur Komah* with "its exaggerations and its dull dryness" (!) was "intended for school children."[97] The curious tendency of some nineteenth century Jewish scholars to treat profoundly mythical and mystical references to God and the world as pedagogical *obiter dicta* for the benefit of small children is certainly one of the most remarkable examples of misplaced criticism and insensitiveness to the character of religious phenomena which this period has produced.

7

The *Shiur Komah* is not the only subject of mystical vision in this group. There are several others, some of which undoubtedly originated from entirely different sources but were more or less closely mixed up with the *Shiur Komah* during the period when all these various tendencies crystallized in the classical Hekhaloth literature. To the later mystics they presented what appeared to be on the whole a uniform picture. The most important of these deviations from the main current is the Metatron mysticism which revolves round the person of Enoch who, after a lifetime of piety, was raised, according to the legend, to the rank of first of the angels and *sar ha-panim*, (literally: prince of the divine face, or divine presence). "God took me from the midst of the race of the flood and carried me on the stormy wings of the Shekhinah to the highest heaven and brought me into the great palaces on the heights of the seventh heaven Araboth, where there are the throne of the Shekhinah and the Merkabah, the legions of anger and hosts of wrath, the *shinanim* of the fire, the *cherubim* of the flaming torches, the *ofannim* of the fiery coals, the servants of the flames, and the seraphim of the lightning, and He stood me there daily to serve the throne of glory."[98] This Enoch, whose flesh was turned to flame, his veins to fire, his eye-lashes to flashes of lightning, his eye-balls to flaming torches,[99] and whom God placed on a throne next to the throne of glory, received after this heavenly transformation the name Metatron.

The visions of the heavenly traveller Enoch, as set out in the Ethiopic and Slavonic Books of Enoch, have become, in the Enoch book of the Merkabah mystics, accounts given to Rabbi Ishmael by Metatron of his metamorphosis and of the hierarchy of the throne and the angels. It is impossible to overlook the steady line of development in this Enoch mysticism; moreover, the Hebrew "Book of Enoch" is not the only link between the earlier Enoch legend and the later Jewish mysticism. Some of the oldest mythical motifs are to be found not in that book but in an extremely interesting— from the mythographical point of view—magical text, the *"Havdalah of Rabbi Akiba,"* of which several as yet unpublished manuscripts are in existence.[100] In the "Greater Hekhaloth," on the other hand, we find Metatron mentioned only once in a chapter belonging to the later stratum; the earlier chapters do not mention him at all.[101]

It was after the beginning of the second century A. D., probably not earlier, that the patriarch Enoch was identified following his metamorphosis with the angel Yahoel, or Yoel, who occupies an important and sometimes dominant position in the earliest documents of throne mysticism and in the apocalypses.[102] The most important characteristics of this angel are now transferred to Metatron. We also find Yahoel as the first in the various lists of the "Seventy Names of Metatron" compiled in the Gaonic period (7th to 11th centuries).[103] The Babylonian Talmud contains only three references to Metatron, and the most important of these passages is meaningless if thought to refer to the name Metatron.[104] It refers to a tradition from the beginning of the fourth century, according to which Metatron is the angel of whom it is said in Exod. XXIII, 20 ff.: "Beware of him for my name is in him." The explanation is to be found in the tenth chapter of the Apocalypse of Abraham, already mentioned several times, where the angel Yahoel says to Abraham: "I am called Yahoel . . . a power in virtue of the ineffable name that is dwelling in me." That the name Yahoel contains the name of God is obvious, Yaho being an abbreviation of the Tetragrammaton YHWH, which was used especially often in texts bearing on Jewish-Hellenistic syncretism. The same Yahoel is referred to in Jewish gnostical literature as the "lesser Yaho," a term which at the end of the second century had already made its way into non-Jewish gnostical literature,[105] but which was also retained by the Merkabah mystics as the most exalted cognomen of Metatron, one which to outsiders seemed to border on blasphemy.[106] Also in the Talmudic passage cited above the assumption that the verse in Exodus XXIV, 1 "Ascend to YHWH" refers to Metatron seems to contain an implicit recognition of the latter as the "lesser Yaho," which he becomes explicitly in later texts.[107]

Mention may be made, moreover, of a further and very striking example of the extreme stubbornness with which ancient traditions are preserved in Jewish mystical literature, often in out-of-the-way places. In the Apocalypse of Abraham, Yahoel appears as the spiritual teacher of the patriarch to whom he explains the mysteries of the throne world and the last judgment, exactly as Metatron does in the Hekhaloth tracts. Abraham is here the prototype of the novice who is initiated into the mystery, just as he appears at the end of the *Sefer Yetsirah*, the "Book of Creation", a document the precise age of which is not known but the character of which I propose to discuss at the end of this lecture. In the Apocalypse we find him being initiated into the mysteries of the Merkabah, just as in the *Sefer Yetsirah* he is allowed to penetrate into the mysteries of its cosmogonical speculation. It is somewhat surprising to read in a manuscript originating among the twelfth century Jewish mystics in Germany that Yahoel was Abraham's teacher and taught him the whole of the Torah. The same document also expressly mentions Yahoel as the angel who—in the above-mentioned Talmudic passage —invites Moses to ascend to heaven.[108] Thus the tradition attached to his name must still have been preserved in mediaeval literature.

If the meaning of the name Yahoel is fairly clear, that of *Metatron* is completely obscure. There have been very many attempts to throw light on the etymology of the word,[109] the most widely accepted interpretation being that according to which Metatron is short for *Metathronios,* i. e. "he who stands besides the (God's) throne," or "who occupies the throne next to the divine throne." Mention of this throne is indeed made in the later (Hebrew) "Book of Enoch," but there is not the slightest suggestion that the author saw any connection between the name of the archon and his throne. The fact is that all these etymologies are so much guess-work and their studied rationality leads nowhere. There is no such word as *Metathronios* in Greek and it is extremely unlikely that Jews should have produced or invented such Greek phrase. In Talmudic literature the word θρόνος is never used in the place of its Hebrew equivalent. On the other hand, the reduplication of the *t* and the ending *ron* follow a pattern which runs through all these texts. Both the ending and the repetition of the consonant are observable, for instance, in names like Zoharariel and Adiriron. It must also be borne in mind that *on* and *ron* may have been fixed and typical constituents of secret names rather than meaningful syllables. It is quite possible that the word Metatron was chosen on strictly symbolical grounds and represents one of the innumerable secret names which abound in the Hekhaloth texts no less than in the gnostical writings or in the magical papyri. Originally formed apparently in order to replace the name Yahoel as a *vox mystica,* it gradually usurped its place. It is interesting, by the way, that the spelling in the oldest quotations and manuscripts is מיטטרון—a fact which is usually overlooked; this would seem to suggest that the word was pronounced Meetatron rather than Metatron. As a transcription of the Greek *epsilon* in the word *Meta,* the *yod* in the name would appear to be quite superfluous.

In the often highly imaginative description of the angelic sphere which one finds in the Hebrew Enoch book of the Merkabah period, Metatron's rank is always placed very high. Nevertheless the classical writings of the Merkabah school contain no suggestion that he is to be regarded as being one with the glory that appears on the throne. Throughout this literature Metatron, or whatever name is given to him, remains in the position of the highest of all created beings, while the occupant of the throne revealed in the *Shiur Komah* is, after all, the Creator Himself. No attempt is made to bridge the gulf; what has been said of the relationship of the mystic in his ecstasy towards his God is true also of the supreme exaltation of the prince of angels himself. The latter, incidentally, is also called Anafiel, according to an independent tradition which has found its reflection in the "Greater Hekhaloth," and the characteristics given of this angel make it clear that Anafiel is not simply one more name for Metatron, but is the name of another figure which for some mystics retained that supreme rank.[110]

8

Several texts have preserved codifications of the throne mysticism abounding among the Merkabah travellers, and elaborate lists of the problems and questions relevant in this context. These do not all belong to one particular period; subjects which appear to be of great importance in one text are not even mentioned in the other. One such codification of pure throne mysticism, for example, is to be found in the brief "Treatise of the Hekhaloth" which probably dates back to the eighth century.¹¹¹ Here the imaginative description of objects which were originally really visualized, but are now treated at great length purely for the purpose of edification, has already reached baroque proportions.

A more concise and restrained account of the principal subjects of Merkabah mysticism—apparently based on a Hekhaloth tract—is to be found in the Midrash to Solomon's proverbs.¹¹² Here, too, Rabbi Ishmael appears as the representative of the esoteric tradition. In this case he enumerates the questions which the doctors of the Torah will be asked by God on the Day of Judgment; the crowning part of this examination are the questions referring to esoteric doctrine:

"If there comes before Him one who is learned in the Talmud, the Holy One, praise be to Him, says to him: 'My son, since you have studied the Talmud, why have you not also studied the Merkabah and perceived my splendor? For none of the pleasures I have in My creation is equal to that which is given to me in the hour when the scholars sit and study the Torah and, looking beyond it, see and behold and meditate these questions: How the throne of My glory stands; what the first of its feet serves as; what the second foot serves as; what the third and what the fourth serve as; how the *hashmal* (seen by Ezekiel in his vision) stands; how many expressions he takes on in an hour, and which side he serves; how the heavenly lightning stands; how many radiant faces are visible between his shoulders, and which side he serves; and even greater than all this: the fiery stream under the throne of My glory, which is round like a stone made of brick; how many bridges are spanned across it, how great is the distance between one bridge and the next, and, if I cross it, over which bridge do I cross; which bridge do the *ofannim* (a class of angels) cross, and which do the *galgalim* (another class) cross; even greater than all this: how I stand from the nails of My feet to the parting of My hair; how great is the measure of My palm, and what is the measure of My toes. Even greater than all this: how the throne of My glory does stand, and which side it does serve on every day of the week. And is this not My greatness, is not this My glory and My beauty that My children know My splendor through these measurements?' And of this David hath said: O Lord, how manifold are Thy works!"

It is apparent from this passage that all these questions were systematically discussed, although some of them are not mentioned in the texts which have been preserved. Of the bridges in the Merkabah world, for instance, which find almost no mention in the "Greater Hekhaloth" and the Book of Enoch, we have several vivid descriptions.

Among the most important objects which Metatron describes to Rabbi Ishmael is the cosmic veil or curtain before the throne, which conceals the glory of God from the host of angels. The idea of such a veil appears to be very old; references to it are to be found already in Aggadic passages from the second century. The existence of veils in the resplendent sphere of the aeons is also mentioned in a Coptic writing belonging to the gnostic school, the *Pistis Sophia*.[113] Now this cosmic curtain, as it is described in the Book of Enoch, contains the images of all things which since the day of creation have their pre-existing reality, as it were, in the heavenly sphere.[114] All generations and all their lives and actions are woven into this curtain; he who sees it penetrates at the same time into the secret of Messianic redemption, for like the course of history, the final struggle and the deeds of the Messiah are already pre-existently real and visible. As we have seen, this combination of knowledge relating to the Merkabah and the Hekhaloth with a vision of the Messianic end—the inclusion, that is to say, of apocalyptic and eschatologic knowledge—is very old. It dominates the Apocalypse of Abraham and the Book of Enoch no less than the various Hekhaloth tracts four or eight centuries later. All of them contain varying descriptions of the end of the world, and calculations of the date set for the redemption.[115] Indeed, there is a passage in the "Greater Hekhaloth" where the meaning of the Merkabah vision is summed up in the question: "When will he see the heavenly majesty? When will he hear of the final time of redemption? When will he perceive what no eye has yet perceived?"[116]—Incidentally, according to these mystics, that which now belongs to the domain of secret lore shall become universal knowledge in the Messianic age. The throne and the glory which rests on it "shall be revealed anon to all inhabitants of the world."[117] At the same time the reasons, now obscure, of the commandments of the Torah will also be revealed and made plain.[118]

It is safe to say that what might be termed apocalyptic nostalgia was among the most powerful motive-forces of the whole Merkabah mysticism. The attitude of these mystics towards the reality of history is even more pointedly negative than that of the contemporary Jewish theologians, the Aggadists.[119] The depressing conditions of the period, the beginning of the era of persecution by the Church since the fourth century, directed the religious interests of the mystics towards the higher world of the Merkabah; from the world of history the mystic turns to the prehistoric period of creation, from whose vision he seeks consolation, or towards the post-history of redemption. Unfortunately the sources at our disposal shed no light on the social environment of the founders and leaders of the movement. As I said at the beginning of this lecture, they have been only too successful in preserving their anonymity.

9

In contrast to the connection between throne mysticism and apocalyptic which, as we have seen, is very close, that between eschatology and cosmogony—the end of things and the beginning of things—is rather loose, at any rate in the writings which have come down to us. In this respect, Merkabah mysticism differs not only from the non-Jewish forms of Gnosticism but also from the Kabbalism of the later period, where the connection between the two is exceedingly close. Moreover, the comparatively sparse account devoted to this subject under the heading of reflections on the *Maaseh Bereshith* is cosmology rather than cosmogony, that is to say, the emphasis is laid—so far as we are in a position to judge—on the order of the cosmos rather than on the drama of its creation, which plays so large a part in the mythology of the Gnostics. One has only to read the "Baraitha on the Work of Creation," which includes some fragments belonging to this period, albeit in a comparatively recent edition, and whose connection with Merkabah mysticism is evident, to become aware of this difference between Merkabah speculation and Gnosticism proper.[120] Its cause is obvious: the realm of divine "fullness," the *pleroma* of the Gnostics, which unfolds dramatically the succession of aeons, is directly related to the problem of creation and cosmogony, while for the Merkabah mystics, who substituted the throne world for the *pleroma* and the aeons, this problem has no significance at all. The constituents of the throne world: the *hashmal*, the *ofannim* and *hayoth*, the *seraphim*, etc., can no longer be interpreted in terms of a cosmogonic drama; the only link between this realm and the problem of creation was, as we have seen, the idea of the cosmic curtain. Here we have one of the most important points of difference between Merkabah mysticism and Kabbalism; the latter is distinguished by renewed interest in purely cosmogonic speculation, whose spirit often enough is entirely Gnostic. In the earlier literature—certainly during the phase represented by the Hekhaloth—theoretical questions have no place; its spirit is descriptive, not speculative, and this is particularly true of the best examples of this genre. Nevertheless it is possible that there was a speculative phase in the very beginning and that the famous passage in the Mishnah which forbids the questions: "What is above and what is below? What was before and what will be after?" refers to theoretical speculation in the manner of the Gnostics who strove after "the knowledge of who we were, and what we have become, where we were or where we are placed, whither we hasten, from what we are redeemed."[111]

As a matter of fact there exists indubitable proof that among certain groups of Jewish Gnostics who tried to stay within the religious community of rabbinical Judaism, Gnostical speculation and related semi-mythological thought was kept alive. Traces of such ideas in Aggadic literature are few but they exist. Thus for instance there is the well-known saying of the Babylonian teacher Rav in the third century A.D.: "Ten are the qualities with which the world has been created: wisdom, insight, knowledge, force, appeal, power, justice, right, love and compassion."[112] Or the following reference to seven hypostases of similar general ideas of the kind so often found in the names of Gnostical aeons: "Seven *middoth* serve before the throne of glory: wisdom, right and justice, love and mercy, truth and peace."[113] What the aeons and the archons are to the Gnostics, the *middoth* are to this form of speculation, i. e. the hypostatized attributes of God.

Much more important are the relics of speculation concerning aeons preserved in the oldest Kabbalistic text, the highly obscure and awkward book *Bahir,* which was edited in Provence during the twelfth century.[114] This brief document of Kabbalistic theology consists, at least in part, of compilations and editions of much older texts which, together with other writings of the Merkabah school, had made their way to Europe from the East. It was my good fortune to make a discovery a few years ago which renders it possible to identify one of these Eastern sources, namely, the book *Raza Rabba*, "The Great Mystery," which some Eastern authors of the tenth century named among the most important of esoteric writings and which was hitherto thought to have been lost.[125] Fortunately, several lengthy quotations from it have been preserved in the writings of thirteenth century Jewish mystics in Southern Germany, which leave no doubt that the Book *Bahir* was to a large extent directly based on it.[126] It thus becomes understandable how gnostical *termini technici*, symbols, and mythologems came to be used by the earliest Kabbalists who wrote their works in Provence during the twelfth century. The point obviously has an important bearing on the question of the origins of mediaeval Kabbalism in general. It can be taken as certain that in addition to the *Raza Rabba*, which appears to have been a cross between a mystical Midrash and a Hekhaloth text, with a strong magical element thrown in, other similar fragments of ancient writings, with Gnostic excerpts written in Hebrew, made their way from the East to Provence. It was thus that remainders of Gnostic ideas transmitted in this fashion entered the main stream of mystical thought via the Book *Bahir*, to become one of the chief influences which shaped the theosophy of the thirteenth century Kabbalists.

10

The existence of speculative Gnostic tendencies in the immediate neighborhood of Merkabah mysticism has its parallel in the writings grouped together under the name of *Maaseh Bereshith*. These include a document—the *Sefer Yetsirah* or Book of Creation—which represents a theoretical approach to the problems of cosmology and cosmogony.[127] The text probably includes interpolations made at a later period, but its connection with the Merkabah literature is fairly evident, at least as regards terminology and style. Written probably between the third and the sixth century, it is distinguished by its brevity; even the most comprehensive of the various editions does not exceed sixteen hundred words. Historically, it represents the earliest extant speculative text written in the Hebrew language. Mystical meditation appears to have been among the sources from which the author drew inspiration, so far as the vagueness and obscurity of the text permits any judgment on this point. The style is at once pompous and laconic, ambiguous and oracular—no wonder, therefore, that the book was quoted in evidence alike by mediaeval philosophers and by Kabbalists. Its chief subject-matters are the elements of the world, which are sought in the ten elementary and primordial numbers—*Sefiroth,* as the book calls them—and the 22 letters of the Hebrew alphabet. These together represent the mysterious forces whose convergence has produced the various combinations observable throughout the whole of creation; they are the "thirty-two secret paths of wisdom," through which God has created all that exists. These *Sefiroth* are not just ten stages, or representative of ten stages, in their unfolding; the matter is not as simple as that. But "their end is in their beginning and their beginning in their end, as the flame is bound to the coal—close your mouth lest it speak and your heart lest it think." After the author has analysed the function of the *Sefiroth* in his cosmogony, or rather hinted at the solution in some more or less oracular statements, he goes on to explain the function of the letters in creation: "[God] drew them, hewed them, combined them, weighed them, interchanged them, and through them produced the whole creation and everything that is destined to be created." He then proceeds to discuss, or rather to unveil, the secret meaning of each letter in the three realms of creation known to him: man, the world of the stars and planets, and the rhythmic flow of time through the course of the year. The combination of late Hellenistic, perhaps even late Neoplatonic numerological mysticism with exquisitely Jewish ways of thought concerning the mystery of letters and language is fairly evident throughout.[125] Nor is the element of Merkabah mysticism lacking; the author appears to have searched the Merkabah for a cosmological idea, and not without success, for it seems that the *hayoth* in the Merkabah described by Ezekiel, i. e. the "living beings" which carry the Merkabah, are for him connected with the *Sefiroth* as "living numerical beings." For, indeed, these are very peculiar "numbers" of which it is said that "their appearance is like a flash of lightning and their goal is without end; His word is in them when they come forth [from Him] and when they return; at His bidding do they speed swiftly as a whirlwind, and before His throne they prostrate themselves."

Various peculiarities of the terminology employed in the book, including some curious neologisms which find no natural explanation in Hebrew phraseology, suggest a paraphrase of Greek terms, but most of the details still await a full clarification.[129] The precise meaning of the phrase *Sefiroth belimah* which the author constantly uses and which may be the key to the understanding of what he actually had in mind when speaking of the *Sefiroth*, is a matter of speculation. The second word *belimah* which may be taken to denote or to qualify the specific nature of these "numbers" has been explained or translated in accordance with the theories of the several writers or translators: infinite *Sefiroth*, or closed, abstract, ineffable, absolute *Sefiroth*, or even *Sefiroth* out-of-nothing. If the author of the book wanted to be obscure, he certainly succeeded beyond his wishes. Even the substance of its cosmogony, as set forth in the chapter dealing with the *Sefiroth*, is still a subject of discussion. On the question whether the author believes in the emanation of his *Sefiroth* out of each other and of God it is possible to hear directly conflicting views. According to some writers, he identifies the *Sefiroth* directly with the elements of creation (the spirit of God; ether; water; fire; and the six dimensions of space). Others, with whom I am inclined to agree, see in his description a tendency towards parallelism or correlation between the *Sefiroth* and the elements. In any event, the *Sefiroth* which, like the host of angels in the Merkabah literature, are visualized in an attitude of adoration before God's throne, represent an entirely new element which is foreign to the conception of the classical Merkabah visionaries.

On the other hand, one cannot overlook the connection between the "Book of Creation" and the theory of magic and theurgy which, as we have seen, plays its part in Merkabah mysticism.[130] The ecstatic ascent to the throne is not the only element of that mysticism; it also embraces various other techniques which are much more closely connected with magical practices. One of these, for example, is the "putting on, or clothing, of the name," a highly ceremonious rite in which the magician impregnates himself, as it were, with the great name of God[131]—i. e. performs a symbolic act by clothing himself in a garment into whose texture the name has been woven.[132] The adjuration of the prince or archon of the Torah, *Sar Torah*, belongs to the same category.[133] The revelation sought through the performance of such rites is identical with that of the Merkabah vision. The "Prince of the Torah" reveals the same mysteries as the voice which speaks from the throne of fire: the secret of heaven and earth, the dimensions of the demiurge, and the secret names the knowledge of which gives power over all things. It is true that in addition these magical practices also hold out a promise of other things, e. g. a more comprehensive knowledge of the Torah, chiefly reflected in the fact that the adept can no longer forget anything he has learned, and similar accomplishments: Matters which to the Hekhaloth mystics were important but not vital, much as they tried to remain in conformity with rabbinical Judaism—a tendency which finds its expression in the emphasis laid in the "Greater Hekhaloth" on the link with Halakhic tradition. These theurgical doctrines form a kind of meeting-place for magic and ecstaticism. The theurgical element is brought to the fore in various writings which display manifold points of contact with the Hekhaloth tracts, as, to take some instances, *Harba de-Moshe,* "The Sword of Moses," the *"Havdalah* of Rabbi Akiba" and the recipes that are preserved in the book *Shimmushe Tehillim,* the title of which means "The magical use of the psalms." The latter have had a long, if not quite distinguished career in Jewish life and folklore.[134]

11

If Merkabah mysticism thus degenerates in some instances into magic pure and simple, it becomes subject to a moral reinterpretation in others. Originally, the ascent of the soul was by no means conceived as an act of penitence, but in later days the ancient Talmudic saying "great is repentance . . . for it leads to the throne of Glory" came to be regarded—e. g. by the Babylonian Gaon Jehudai (eighth century)—as a reference to it. In this conception, the act of penitence becomes one with the ecstatic progress through the seven heavens.[135] Already in one of the Hekhaloth tracts the first five of the seven palaces through which the soul must pass are placed parallel to certain degrees or stages of moral perfection. Thus Rabbi Akiba says to Rabbi Ishmael: "When I ascended to the first palace I was devout (*hasid*), in the second palace I was pure (*tahor*), in the third sincere (*yashar*), in the fourth I was wholly with God (*tamim*), in the fifth I displayed holiness before God; in the sixth I spoke the *kedushah* (the trishagion) before Him who spoke and created, in order that the guardian angels might not harm me; in the seventh palace I held myself erect with all my might, trembling in all limbs, and spoke the following prayer: . . . 'Praise be to Thee who art exalted, praise be to the Sublime in the chambers of grandeur'."[136]

This tendency to set the stages of ascent in parallel with the degrees of perfection obviously raises the question whether we are not faced here with a mystical reinterpretation of the Merkabah itself. Was there not a temptation to regard man himself as the representative of divinity, his soul as the throne of glory, etc.? A step in this direction had been taken by Macarius the Egyptian, one of the earliest representatives of fourth century Christian monastic mysticism. "The opening of his first homily reads like a programme of his mystical faith. It offers a new explanation of the obscure vision of Ezekiel (i. e. of the Merkabah) . . . according to him, the prophet beholds 'the secret of the soul which is on the point of admitting its master and becoming a throne of his Glory'."[137] We find an analogous reinterpretation of the Merkabah among the Jewish mystics in the thrice repeated saying of the third century Palestinian Talmudist Simeon ben Lakish: "The Patriarchs (i. e. Abraham, Isaac and Jacob)—they are the Merkabah."[138] The author tries to justify this bold assertion by an ingenious exegetical reasoning based on certain Scriptural phrases, but it is plain that the exegesis provided only the occasion for making it, not the motive; the latter is genuinely and unmistakably mystical.

It must be emphasized that these tendencies are alien to the spirit of Hekhaloth literature; we find in it none of that symbolic interpretation of the Merkabah which was later revived and perfected by the Kabbalists. Its subject is never man, be he even a saint. The form of mysticism which it represents takes no particular interest in man as such; its gaze is fixed on God and his aura, the radiant sphere of the Merkabah, to the exclusion of everything else. For the same reason it made no contribution to the development of a new moral ideal of the truly pious Jew. All its originality is on the ecstatical side, while the moral aspect is starved, so to speak, of life. The moral doctrines found in Hekhaloth literature are pale and bloodless; the ideal to which the Hekhaloth mystic is devoted is that of the visionary who holds the keys to the secrets of the divine realm and who reveals these visions in Israel. Vision and knowledge, in a word, Gnosis of this kind, represents for him the essence of the Torah and of all possible human and cosmic wisdom.

THIRD LECTURE

HASIDISM IN MEDIAEVAL GERMANY

1

Mediaeval German Jewry held aloof from the discussions of theological and philosophical problems which exercised so deep an influence on contemporary Jewish thought in the East, in Spain and in Italy, and which gave an impetus to new and important developments in the cultural life of these communities. The introduction of new values and ideas into the fields of metaphysics, ethics and anthropology by the Jewish theologians and philosophers of the period, the whole movement which can be described as the struggle between Plato and Aristotle for the Biblical and Talmudic heritage of Judaism, was all but ignored by the Jewish communities of Germany and Northern France. True, the study of the Talmud was pursued with an enthusiasm which was nowhere surpassed; nowhere else was so much importance assigned to learning, so much zeal developed in the pursuit of study. But this interest in the casuistry of the Holy Law was not paralleled by a similar genius for, or devotion to, speculative thought.

That, however, is not to say that German Jewry made no significant contribution to the history of Jewish religion in the Diaspora. Its spiritual leaders were indeed strangely devoid of originality in the domain of metaphysics. They showed themselves unable to turn to productive account even the few elements of philosophic speculation which were gradually absorbed. But a significant and lasting imprint was made on the spirit of this great Jewish community by the upheaval of the Crusades, by the savage persecutions of the period and the Jews' own constant readiness for martyrdom. Henceforth there was to be a novel element in the character of German Judaism, an element which owed its growth to purely religious motives but which never found adequate philosophic expression. Its mark is to be found in the movement to which the name of German Hasidism has been given, i. e. in the activities of certain groups of men whom their contemporaries already called with special emphasis *Haside Ashkenaz,* i. e. "the devout of Germany."

The rise of Hasidism was the decisive event in the religious development of German Jewry. Of all the factors determining the deeper religion of that community it was the greatest until the change which took place in the seventeenth century under the influence of the later Kabbalism, which originated at Safed in Palestine. Strictly speaking, it was the only considerable religious event in the history of German Judaism. Its importance lies in the fact that it succeeded already during the Middle Ages in bringing about the triumph of new religious ideals and values which were acknowledged by the mass of the people; in Germany and for the German Jewish community at any rate the victory was complete. Where the thirteenth century Kabbalism of Spain failed—for it became a real historical factor only much later, after the expulsion of the Jews from Spain and after Safed had become the new centre—German Hasidism succeeded. So far from being isolated, the Hasidim were intimately connected with the whole of Jewish life and the religious interests of the common folk; they were recognized as representatives of an ideally Jewish way of life even where their principles were never completely translated into practice. Side by side with the great documents of the Halakhah, and (in spite of their deep reverence for the divine commandment) by no means always in perfect conformity with them, the classical literature of Hasidism retained a truly canonical prestige—not indeed among the representatives of Talmudic learning, who can hardly have read documents like the "Book of the Devout" without experiencing some qualms, but with the average pious Jewish burgher or "householder," the *baal bayith.* Thus the Hasidim escaped the fate of the early Kabbalists who always remained a small aristocratic sect and whose ideas and values never entered into the general consciousness of their contemporaries. Although the creative period of the movement was relatively short— about one century, from 1150 to 1250—its influence on the Jews of Germany was lasting; the religious ideas to which it gave rise and which it filled with life retained their vitality for centuries. It is to them that German Jewry largely owes the inner strength and devotion which it displayed when new storms of persecution arose.

Like the Talmudic aristocracy before it, Hasidism found its leading representatives among that remarkable family which for centuries provided the Jewish communities in the Rhineland with their spiritual leaders: the Kalonymides, who had come to the Rhine from Italy and who, in Speyer, Worms and Mainz, formed a natural aristocracy among the communities. The three men who moulded German Hasidism all belonged to this family. Samuel the Hasid, the son of Kalonymus of Speyer, who lived in the middle of the twelfth century[1]; his son Jehudah the Hasid, of Worms, who died in Regensburg in 1217[2]; and the latter's disciple and relative, Eleazar ben Jehudah, of Worms, who died between 1223 and 1232.[3] All three exercized a deep and lasting influence on their contemporaries; Jehudah the Hasid in particular held an unrivalled position as a religious leader so long as Hasidism itself remained a living force. A contemporary said of him, "he would have been a prophet if he had lived in the times of the prophets."[4] Like Isaac Luria of Safed in a later age, he, too, soon became a legendary figure of mythical proportions, and in much the same way the personalities of the other two leaders of German Hasidism tend to disappear behind the tropical jungle of legends that has grown up around them. These legends have been preserved not only in Hebrew but also in a Yiddish version, the *Maase Buch*, which Gaster has translated into English.[5] They do not always give a true picture of what Hasidism actually was, but rather tell us what popular imagination would have liked it to be. And this distortion, too, is not without significance for an understanding of the motive-powers which were active in this movement.

Of Samuel the Hasid's writings little has been preserved, while the more numerous writings of his son Jehudah have come down for the most part only in the form given to them by his disciples. On the other hand, Eleazar of Worms, the most zealous of all the apostles of his master, has left a whole literature which is a veritable store-house of early Hasidic thought, including in particular the entire body of earlier mystical doctrine in so far as it was known to the members of this group. Indeed, his life work seems to have been devoted to the task of codification, whether of the Halakhah (in his great work *Rokeah* of which several editions have appeared in print), or of other materials and traditions. His voluminous writings, many of them extant only in manuscripts of which a distin-

guished Jewish scholar once remarked that he hoped they would
never emerge from their "well-deserved oblivion", are of considerable interest for the study of Jewish mysticism. But the most im
portant literary monument of the movement which gives the fullest
insight into its origins and its originality, is the *Sefer Hasidim* or
"Book of the Devout", an edition of the literary testaments of the
three founders, and in particular of the writings of Jehudah the
Hasid.[6] Undistinguished and even awkward in style, often resem
bling a mass of casual jottings rather than a coherent literary composition, it is yet undoubtedly one of the most important and remarkable products of Jewish literature. No other work of the period
provides us with so deep an insight into the real life of a Jewish
community in all its aspects. For once we are able to study religion
and theology not detached from reality and as it were suspended in
the vacuum of Revelation, but in the closest and most intimate connection with everyday life. Where other authors or editors have
drawn a dogmatic, Halakhic or idyllic veil before the living reality
of religious experience, the book records in plain words the actual
conflicting motives which determined the religious life of a Jew in
mediaeval Germany. Life, as it is presented here, although lived in
the shadow of a great idea, is painted with a realism which has an
almost dramatic quality. Thus the "Book of the Devout" inaugu-
rates the all too brief series of Jewish writings—not a few of them
and not the least valuable written at a later stage in the development of Jewish mysticism—which are also genuine historical documents revealing the whole truth about the circumstances of their
time.

In his brilliant analysis of the "Religious Social Tendency
of the *Sefer Hasidim*," F. I. Baer has shown that the "teachings
of the Sefer Hasidim form a definite and consistent whole'"[7] and
that they reflect the spirit of a central dominating figure—Rabbi
Jehudah the Hasid, whose historical position, according to Baer, is
akin to that of his Christian contemporary, St. Francis of Assisi.
Baer has also raised anew the problem of the relationship between
the social philosophy of Hasidism and its Monkish-Christian environment.[8] It is in fact undeniable that certain popular religious
and social ideas common to the Roman Catholic West after the
Cluniacensian reform also filtered into the religious philosophy of
some Jewish groups. According to Baer, this was possible only in

Germany, while in Italy and Spain the spread of philosophical enlightenment among the Jews either prevented this infiltration or at least limited its scope by conducting an incessant fight against it. Although Baer describes these tendencies as "stimulants which merely served to hasten a spontaneous development" he goes further than Guedemann who also believed in a connection between the popular Christian mysticism of the period and the Hasidic movement, but makes a reservation in respect of their interdependence by arguing that "there is no need to speak of derivations; similar causes produce similar effects. Mysticism was in the air and its seeds fell on fertile soil both among Jews and Christians."[9]

2

It would, however, be a mistake to assume that the impact upon the Jewish religious consciousness of the terrible sufferings during the Crusades was the source of an entirely novel mystical disposition. The truth is that long before this period, and long before the great body of lay Christianity had come under the influence of mystical thoughts which in turn could have penetrated into Jewish circles, the Jewish communities of the Rhineland, the cultural centre of German Jewry, had begun to absorb elements of the early Merkabah mysticism. It seems probable that this infiltration of an older tradition, in whose wake an entire literature was transplanted, coincided with the immigration during the ninth century of the already mentioned Kalonymide family from Italy, where through the tireless activity of Aaron of Baghdad an understanding of this literature had spread among wider circles.[10] The extent to which this renaissance of Merkabah mysticism on Italian soil had gone can be gauged from the legends in the "Chronicle of Ahimaaz of Oria"—a precious document of eleventh-century Jewish life which has been preserved as though by a miracle in the library of the Cathedral of Toledo.[11] And one has only to read the religious poetry of the Jews of Southern Italy in the tenth century—especially the hymns of Amitai ben Shefatiah—to become aware of the enormous influence of Merkabah mysticism both on its style and its contents. That the *Sefer Yetsirah* was already known in Italy in the tenth century is proved by the commentary of Sabbatai Donnolo.[12] Together with it there came a great deal of related literature, semi-mystical or entirely mystical

Midrashim and various documents of whose existence we only know through quotations scattered in the writings of the Hasidim.

The influence of this literature on the Jews of Germany was profound. One finds its reflection in the writings of the old synagogal poets of the German and Northern French school which carried on the tradition of Palestine and Italy. This poetry is frequently incomprehensible unless one is familiar with the Merkabah literature. The voluminous commentary on a large number of these poems compiled by Abraham ben Azriel of Bohemia, publication of which has lately been started[13], deals largely with mystical ideas. It is equally obvious, though less generally realized, that the writings of many Talmudists and Tosafists—the name generally given to the school of Talmudic casuists in Germany and Northern France in the twelfth and thirteenth centuries—in so far as they deal at all with religious subjects, are steeped in the same kind of mystical thought. The tradition which ascribes to some of the most famous Tosafists a preference for the study of old mystical tracts, if not the actual practice of mystical rites, is by no means simply a legend. The various testimonies to this effect are quite independent of each other, and for the rest a careful study of their occasional ventures into theology leaves no doubt that they draw their inspiration from mystical ideas on the subject of creation, the Merkabah, and even the *Shiur Komah*. One of the greatest masters of this school of casuists, Isaac of Dampierre, whom one would be the last to suspect of mystical leanings, was said to be a visionary[14]; we have a commentary to the "Book of Creation," written by Elhanan ben Yakar of London, which was based on his lectures[15], and one of his most famous pupils, Ezra of Montcontour, whose cognomen "The Prophet" was by no means intended to be merely an honorific appellation, is known to have practised Merkabah mysticism. His "ascents to heaven" are attested by several witnesses, and his possession of prophetic gifts was regarded as proved.[16] "He showed signs and miracles. One heard a voice speak to him from a cloud, as God spoke to Moses. Great scholars, among them Eleazar of Worms, after days of fasting and prayer, were granted the revelation that all his words were truth and not deception. He also produced Talmudic explanations the like of which had never been heard before, and he revealed the mysteries of the Torah and the Prophets." When he announced that the Messianic age would begin in 1226 and culminate in 1240, the year 5000 of Creation, the rumor of this prediction spread far and wide.

These traditions concerning the way of life and the vision of the old ecstatics, by which the imagination continued to be powerfully affected although only a few followed in their footsteps, combined—probably in the main during the period of the Crusades—with various other and often quite heterogenous elements of thought. Thus the ideas of Saadia, the soberest of philosophic rationalists, who flourished in the first half of the tenth century, gradually became known and, paradoxically enough, they gained influence owing to the poetical, enthusiastic and quasi-mystical style of the old Hebrew translation, or rather paraphrase, of his magnum opus, the "Book of Philosophic Doctrines and Religious Beliefs," the original of which was written in Arabic. Apart from partly misunderstood elements of Saadia, there was the growing influence of Abraham ibn Ezra and Abraham bar Hiya, through which Neoplatonic thought, including some of purely mystical character, came to Northern France and to the Hasidim of Germany. The stream also carried along with it an indefinable mixture of traditions concerning occultism of which the sources are difficult to trace; the most extraordinary combinations of Hellenistic occultism, early Jewish magic, and ancient German belief in demons and witches are frequently encountered in the Hasidic literature of the period.[17] It is characteristic that Eleazar of Worms uses the term "philosopher" in the same sense in which it is used in the medieval Latin writings on alchemy and occultism, i. e. as the designation of a scholar versed in these occult sciences. Wherever in his book on psychology a "philosopher" makes his appearance, he introduces hermetical ideas of this kind.[18]

All these elements are intermingled in the richly varied literature of Hasidism, but rather in the form of an amorphous whole than as elements of a system. Its authors, as we have already had occasion to remark, showed themselves unable to develop these elements of thought or to produce anything like a synthesis; possibly they were not even conscious of the manifold inconsistencies among the various traditions, all of which were treated by them with the same reverence. As regards the form of their writings it is worth noting that they displayed nothing of that passion for anonymity, let alone pseudepigraphy, which is so characteristic of the Merkabah mystics.

Only a very small number of pseudepigraphic texts are grouped round the figure of one Joseph ben Uziel[19] who first makes his appearance in the "Alphabet of ben Sira" (tenth century), where he is introduced as the grandson of ben Sira and the greatgrandson of the Prophet Jeremiah. And even there it is not certain whether some of these texts, and possibly the "Alphabet" as well, did not originate in Italy. Whatever else there is to be found of pseudepigraphic elements in this literature apparently owes its origin less to deliberate intention than to misunderstanding and confusion, such as for example the awkward commentary on the "Book of Creation" written by a disciple of Eleazar of Worms but published under the name of Saadia.[20] For Saadia was actually considered by the Hasidim as "learned in the mysteries."

3

Notwithstanding the failure to establish doctrinal unity or rather the lack of any serious attempt to bring it about, these writings, with all their manifold contradictions and inconsistencies, display a certain community of outlook. The new impulse which deeply affected the precarious life led by the German Jews in the twelfth century left a powerful imprint on the character of their literature; its spirit somehow permates even the semi-philosophic arguments, the ancient mythologems scattered among the fragments, and the rest of this stream of traditions and reminiscences, replete with obvious misunderstandings and not infrequently showing a reversion to mythology.

For like the external world, the world of the spirit, too, had undergone a deep transformation. The force of the religious impulse which at one time found expression and satisfaction in the visionary perception of God's glory and in the apocalyptic vision of the downfall of the fiendish powers of evil, had waned and for a time ceased to shape the outlook of actively religious groups. Nothing, indeed, disappeared completely; all the old traditions were preserved, often in abstruse metamorphoses, for in this Hasidic world age is its own justification.

But in spite of the innate conservatism of German Judaism, the novel circumstances in the end called forth a new response. It will always remain a remarkable fact that the great catastrophe of the Crusades, the incessant waves of persecution which now broke

over the Jews of Germany, failed to introduce an apocalyptic element into the religious tenets of German Jewry. Not a single apocalypse was written during that period, unless this name be given
to the no longer extant "Prophecy" of Rabbi Troestlin the Prophet,
the work of a Merkabah mystic who lived in Erfurt and of whose
book a brief passage has been preserved.[21] It is true that the chron-
iclers of the persecutions and the writers of the new school of religious poetry, perhaps the most characteristic representatives of this
period, sought consolation in eschatological hopes, but they laid far
more stress on the blessed state of the martyrs and the transcendent
splendor of the coming Redemption than on the terrors of the end
and the vision of the Last Judgment.

As far as concerns the views of the Hasidic leaders, Jehudah the
Hasid himself was radically opposed to all speculation concerning
the time of the Messiah's arrival. In chronicling the account of the
journey of Petahyah of Regensburg, who made a voyage to Baghdad
and Persia around 1175, he even went so far as to censor the manuscript by leaving out the Messianic prophecy of one Samuel, an
astrologer of Niniveh, "so that it might not seem as though he believed in it." And in the "Book of the Devout" he says: "If you
see one making prophecies about the Messiah, you should know that
he deals in witchcraft and has intercourse with demons; or he is one
of those who seek to conjure with the names of God. Now, since
they conjure the angels or spirits, these tell them about the Messiah,
so as to tempt him to reveal his speculations. And in the end he is
shamed because he has called up the angels and demons, and instead a misfortune occurs at that place. The demons come and teach
him their calculations and apocalyptic secrets in order to shame
him and those who believe in him, for no one knows anything
about the coming of the Messiah."[22]

But for all the lack of apocalyptic elements in the Messianic conception of Hasidism it would be a mistake to overlook its eschatological character. There have been tendencies in this direction.
Thus J. N. Simhoni, one of the few writers on the subject who have
tried to go below the surface, has drawn a picture of Hasidism as a
movement distinguished by a frankly anti-eschatologic form of devotion which holds out no expectations of reward in life for meritorious deeds, ignores the hope of salvation and remains resolutely
wedded to the present.[23] "If heavy misfortune befall a man let him

think of the knights who go to war and do not flee before the sword, for they are ashamed to flee, and so as not to expose themselves to shame they let themselves be killed or wounded, and they receive no reward from their masters for their death in battle. Thus let him speak with the Scripture: 'Though he slay me, yet will I trust in Him', and I will serve him without hope of reward.'"[24] According to Simhoni, the legend which ascribes to Jehudah the Hasid an unsuccessful attempt, before his death, to unravel the date of the 'end' is typical of the belated efforts to represent Hasidism as more Messianic than it really was.

But is it possible to accept this fundamentally anti-eschatological interpretation of Hasidism? It is not borne out even by the "Book of the Devout," far less by the other documents of this group, such as, for example, the writings of Eleazar of Worms. If it is true that their religious interest does not center on the Messianic promise in the strict sense, it is no less true that the imagination of these writers is powerfully affected by everything which concerns the eschatology of the soul. The whole subject was of less direct interest to the apocalyptically inclined Merkabah mystics than to the older visionaries like the author of the Ethiopic book of Enoch, but it was studied in other circles and inspired several of the shorter Midrashim. Eschatological ideas concerning the nature of the state of bliss in Paradise, the dawn of Redemption, the nature of Resurrection, the beatific vision of the just, their bodies and garments, the problem of reward and punishment, etc., were of real importance to a man like Jehudah the Hasid.[25] These notions were by no means mere literary ballast carried along with many traditions of a different kind; indeed, they belong to the very heart and core of the religious faith of these men which manifested itself in so many different ways. Many were no doubt the spontaneous creation of the age, but even those which came from the East in the wake of the eschatological Aggadah, such as the description of the terrors of the judgment held in the grave itself in the first days after burial (*Hibbut Ha-Kever*), were eagerly taken up and embellished.[26]

At all times the vagueness of eschatological hopes the contents of which have not been dogmatically defined, has evoked more interest among the common people than some great Jewish theologians have been willing to allow. For Jehudah the Hasid, mysticism represents something like an anticipation of a knowledge which,

strictly speaking, belongs to Messianic times. There are secrets which
are revealed in the upper world and which are preserved there for
"the time to come." Only the mystics and the allegorists of this
world "absorb something of the odor of these secrets and mysteries."²⁷—Notwithstanding which there can be no doubt that speculations concerning the "end" never ceased to play a part in Hasidic
mysticism.²⁸

The scope and variety of Hasidic speculation is far greater than
that of the old Merkabah mysticism. In addition to the latter's
favorite subjects of meditation it introduces a species of mystical
thought on a number of new subjects. Thus we find a new theosophy, the "mystery of God's unity," which, without entirely abandoning the old mysticism of the Throne, goes far beyond it and forms
a special branch of mystical doctrine; a new mystical psychology,
conceived as an instrument of this theosophy²⁹; and extensive speculation concerning the "reasons of the Torah," i. e. above all the true
motives of the commandments—a subject which the old Aggadah, no
less than many of the Merkabah mystics, expressly reserved for Messianic times.³⁰ Thus while the ecstatic Merkabah vision, as we have
seen, left little room for exegetical speculation, such speculation,
whatever its forms or methods—and some of them were strange indeed—occupies a highly important place in the religious thought of
the Hasidim.³¹

Nor is this all. The Hasidic doctrine includes—in addition to a
social philosophy based on the conception of natural right and
probably derived from Christian sources—something like a rudi-
mentary theology of history. According to Eleazar of Worms, there
have been since the days of Creation historical forces of opposition,
"weeds" as he calls them, which counteract the divine purpose. The
verse Gen. III, 18 "thorns and thistles shall the earth bring forth to
thee" is to be understood not only in a natural but also in a historical sense, the earth signifying in this context the stage on which
man's history is enacted. "Thorns and thistles" are interpreted, by
a process of reasoning based on numerological mysticism, as representations of the profane history which in every generation stands
in opposition to the inner sacred historical process. The origin of
profane history is sought in the Fall which is also defined as the
cause of force and social inequality in the relations of men. But for
Adam's fall, man would have continuous concourse with the angels

and maintain a permanent relationship with God based on direct revelation. And even after the Fall, men might have avoided the division into rich and poor, the evil of social inequality, if they all had remained tillers of the soil.**

The point to be stressed here is the fact that side by side with theosophical speculation concerning the mysteries of the Creator and the Creation, Hasidism gives prominence, far more than does Merkabah mysticism, to ideas which are of direct concern to the religious existence of man. It sets up a definite human ideal, a type of man and a way of life to be followed, and includes among the main articles of its mystical faith, in addition to a peculiar form of mystical prayer, the ideal of *Hasiduth*, of which a fuller account must now be given.

4

Neither learning nor tradition of any kind are among the prime motive forces of Hasidism. What gave to the movement its distinctive character was, more than any other idea, its novel conception of the devout, the Hasid, as a religious ideal which transcended all values derived from the intellectual sphere and the realization of which was considered more desirable than any intellectual accomplishment. To be a Hasid is to conform to purely religious standards entirely independent of intellectualism and learning. The surprise expressed by Guedemann that the term Hasid was often used of "devout but otherwise not remarkable men"³³ reveals a significant inability—doubly remarkable in the case of so eminent a scholar— to appreciate a scale of values completely independent of the traditional Jewish veneration for the learned student of the Torah. For while Hasidism continued to place a premium on knowledge, it was nevertheless possible to be a Hasid without an understanding of more than, say, the text of the Bible. It is significant that the psalm reader became a figure of Hasidic legend: it is owing to him that an entire community is able to resist the great persecutions in the years of the "Black Death" (1348—52).³⁴ It is more than unlikely that such legends could have arisen in Spain. They could flourish only because the ground had been prepared by a new conception of ideal humanity. The Hasid is "remarkable" not by any intellectual standard of values but only within the categorical frame-work of *Hasiduth* itself.

The word *Hasid* has a specific meaning which is sharply distinguished from the much more vague and general significance of the same term in Talmudic usage.[35] Three things above all others go to make the true Hasid as he appears before us in the "Book of the Devout": Ascetic renunciation of the things of this world; complete serenity of mind; and an altruism grounded in principle and driven to extremes. Let us consider these points a little closer.[36]

The ascetic turn of mind is the corollary of a darkly pessimistic attitude towards life, a characteristic expression of which may be found in the interpretation given to an old Midrash by Eleazar of Worms. The "Midrash on the Creation of the Child" relates that after its guardian angel has given it a fillip upon the nose, the newborn child forgets all the infinite knowledge acquired before its birth in the celestial houses of learning. But why, Eleazar asks, does the child forget? "Because, if it did not forget, the course of this world would drive it to madness if it thought about it in the light of what it knew."[37] Truly a remarkable variant of the Platonic conception of cognition as recollection, anamnesis, which lies also at the root of this Midrash! For this doctrine, hope is present only in the eschatological perspective. As Eleazar put it in a somewhat drastic metaphor, man is a rope whose two ends are pulled by God and Satan; and in the end God proves stronger.[38]

In practice, this asceticism enjoins the renunciation of profane speech, of playing with children and of other innocent pleasures— "he who keeps birds only for ornament would do better to give the money to the poor." In short, it amounts to turning one's back on ordinary life as lived by ordinary people, *azivath derekh erets*, to quote the pregnant term used in the "Book of the Devout."[39] The Hasid must resolutely reject and overcome every temptation of ordinary life. By a natural corollary, this asceticism finds its antithesis in a magnified eschatological hope and promise; by renouncing the temptations of this world, by averting his eyes from women, he becomes worthy of an afterlife in which he will see the glory of the Shekhinah with his own eyes and rank above the angels.[40]

Secondly, the Hasid must bear insults and shame without flinching; indeed the very term *Hasid* is interpreted, with the aid of an ingenious play of words, as "one who bears shame." For to bear shame and derision is an essential part of the way of life of the true devotee; in fact, the Hasid proves himself worthy of his name pre-

cisely in such situations. Though he be insulted and pale with
shame, yet he remains deaf and dumb. "For even though his face
is now pale, Isaiah has already said (xxix, 22): 'neither shall his
face now wax pale'; for indeed his face shall be radiant hereafter."[41]
"When the psalmist says: 'for Thy sake are we killed all the day
long' he means those who bear shame and dishonor and humilia-
tion in carrying out His commands."[42] This constantly stressed im-
perviousness to the scorn and the mockery which the Hasid's way
of life cannot fail to evoke by its extremism, is the true imitation
of God. He, the ideal of the Hasid, is meant by the prophet when
he says (Isaiah XLII, 14): "I have long time holden my peace; I
have been still and refrained myself."[43] Here again the hope of
eternal bliss is the predominant note, although, as we have seen, it
is occasionally emphasized that this hope should not be the motive
of one's actions. "One abused and insulted a Hasid; the latter did
not mind while the other called down curses on his body and his
possessions. But when he cursed him by saying he wished him many
sins so that he might lose his share of eternal bliss, that grieved him.
When his disciples questioned him about it, he replied: When he
called me names, he could not wound me. I need no honor, for
when a man dies, what becomes of his honor? But when he called
curses down on my blessedness, then I began to fear that he might
bring me to sin."[44]

No less stress is laid on the third point: "The essence of *Hasiduth*
is to act in all things not on but within the line of strict justice—
that is to say, not to insist in one's own interest on the letter of the
Torah; for it is said of God, whom the Hasid strives to follow,
(Psalm CXLV, 17): The Lord is *hasid* in all his ways."[45] This
altruism is stressed already in the "Sayings of the Fathers," an ethical Mishnah treatise: "What is mine is yours, and what is yours is
yours—that is the way of the Hasid." The famous commentator
Rashi, too, repeatedly lays emphasis on the fact that the Hasid
does not insist on the letter of the law even though it may be to
his advantage to do so.[46]

There can be little doubt that the formulation of this principle
in the *Sefer Hasidim* only partially bridges the divergence between
this way of life and the normative canon of rabbinical Judaism,
the Halakhah. On the side of the Hasidim there was the ancient
Talmudic tradition of a special "Mishnah of the Hasidim," whose

commandments place far heavier demands upon the Hasid than the ordinary standards of common law. Tendencies of this kind appear only sporadically in Talmudic literature and have never been systematized; nevertheless, they could be used as a legitimation of those ideals of mediaeval Hasidism which were indirectly derived from contemporary religious movements.⁴⁷ In the "Book of the Devout" we find what amounts almost to a crystallization of this hitherto amorphous "Mishnah of the Hasidim." The "heavenly law," *din shamayim*, as conceived by the Hasid, i. e. the call to self-abnegation and altruism, in many instances goes far beyond the common law of the Torah as interpreted by the Halakhah. It is not difficult to perceive the latent antagonism between the two conceptions.⁴⁸ There are things chiefly concerning social relations which are permitted under rabbinical law but for which heaven nevertheless inflicts punishment.⁴⁹ As Baer has pointed out, this divergence between the law of the Torah and the heavenly law—the latter frequently used as a synonym for natural and humane fairness and equity—is a fundamental principle of the conception of morality outlined in the *Sefer Hasidim;* it is even made the criterion of what shall be considered right and just in everyday life.

True, even this higher law, which is considered binding only for the Hasid and which is set up in somewhat veiled opposition to the Halakhah, is capable of exegetical deduction from Scripture, an undertaking in which the author of the book displays considerable ingenuity.⁵⁰ But it is plain that anyone who proceeds from such assumptions can hardly be productive in the domain of strict Halakhah, however much veneration he may show for Halakhic tradition and however little he may feel inclined to adopt a "revolutionary" attitude towards it. And in fact we possess hardly a single new Halakhah from Jehudah the Hasid, in striking contrast to his productive influence in so many other fields. In the great Halakhic work *Or Zarua* written by his disciple, Isaac ben Moses of Vienna, who was with him in Regensburg during the last years of his life, not one Halakhah is introduced in the name of his master.⁵¹ What he does attribute to him are "miracle stories, exegetical commentaries, and original deductions and opinions", such as there are by the hundred —most of them taken no doubt from Jehudah—in the "Book of the Devout."

The Hasid, who in his outward behavior submits to the established law in all its rigour, at bottom denies its absolute validity for himself. It is a little paradoxical when Eleazar of Worms, at the outset of his *Sefer Rokeah,* in which he gives an outline of the religious law, makes an attempt to codify the Hasidic ideal in Hala-khic terms.[52] It is a remarkable fact that both Maimonides and his younger contemporary, Eleazar, preface their codifications of the law by attempts to extend the Halakhah to matters which, strictly speaking, lie beyond its province: in the case of Maimonides, a philo-sophic and cosmologic preface in which the ideas of Aristotelian enlightenment are introduced as elements of the Halakhah; in the case of Eleazar, a chapter devoted to the entirely unintellectual principles of *Hasiduth.* The coincidence is hardly fortuitous and throws an interesting light on the significance of the various reli-gious trends in Judaism; nor is it fortuitous that in both cases the attempts failed: The Halakhah was never organically linked with the quasi-Halakhah which preceded it.

5

Such *Hasiduth* leads man to the pinnacles of true fear and love of God. In its sublimest manifestations, pure fear of God is identical with love and devotion for Him, not from a need for protection against the demons, or from fear of temptation, but because in this mystical state a flood of joy enters the soul and sweeps away every trace of mundane and egotistical feeling.[53] "The soul is full of love of God and bound with ropes of love, in joy and lightness of heart. He is not like one who serves his master unwillingly, but even when one tries to hinder him, the love of service burns in his heart, and he is glad to fulfill the will of his Creator . . . For when the soul thinks deeply about the fear of God, then the flame of heartfelt love bursts in it and the exultation of innermost joy fills the heart . . . And the lover thinks not of his advantage in the world, he does not care about the pleasures of his wife or of his sons and daughters, but all this is as nothing to him, everything except that he may do the will of his Creator, do good unto others, keep sanctified the name of God . . . And all the contemplation of his thoughts burns in the fire of love for Him."[54]

It is characteristic of this stage that the fulfillment of the divine will becomes purely an act of love. As in the contemporaneous

Christian mystical love-poetry, the relation of the mystic to God is described in terms of erotic passion, not infrequently in a way which shocks our modern sensibilities.⁵⁵ The use of such metaphors goes back to the exhaustive treatment of the subject in Saadia's theologic magnum opus.⁵⁶ The earthly love, which he describes in considerable detail, was for the early German Hasidim a complete allegory of the heavenly passion, just as it was in a later age for Israel Baal Shem, the founder of Polish Hasidism, who is quoted as saying: "What Saadia says of love makes it possible to draw an inference from the nature of the sensual to that of the spiritual passion; if the force of sensual love is so great, how great must be the passion with which man loves God."⁵⁷ The mystical principles of this *Hasi- duth* which culminate in pure love of God are necessary for the understanding of theosophy and of what is here called Merkabah mysticism, and it is as such prerequisites that they are introduced by Eleazar of Worms.⁵⁸

It is clear that this ideal of the Hasidic devotee, an ideal which bears none of the traces of scholarly gravity that might be expected in a centre of Talmudic learning like mediaeval Germany, is closely related to the ascetic ideal of the monk and particularly to its most archaic traits. Its practical message is indistinguishable from the *ataraxy*, the "absence of passion" of the Cynics and Stoics—an ideal which, although originally not conceived from religious motives, powerfully affected the nascent asceticism of Christianity and, at a later period, the way of life of the ancient Mohammedan mystics, the Sufis. What we have before us in these writings is a Judaized version of Cynicism, which makes use of cognate tendencies in Talmudic tradition but relegates to the background or eliminates altogether those elements which did not fall into line with these tendencies. The influence of Cynicism is obvious in the ideal of complete indifference to praise or blame, which very often in the history of mysticism figures as a *sine qua non* of mystical illumination, not least in the writings of the Kabbalists. The point is well brought out in the following anecdote told by the Spanish Kabbalist Isaac of Acre (around 1300): "He who is vouchsafed the entry into the mystery of adhesion to God, *devekuth*, attains to the mystery of equanimity, and he who possesses equanimity attains to loneliness, and from there he comes to the holy Spirit and to prophecy. But about the mystery of equanimity the following was told to me by

Rabbi Abner: Once upon a time a lover of secret lore came to an anchorite and asked to be admitted as a pupil. Then he said to him: My son, your purpose is admirable, but do you possess equanimity or not? He replied: Indeed, I feel satisfaction at praise and pain at insult, but I am not revengeful and I bear no grudge. Then the master said to him: My son, go back to your home, for as long as you have no equanimity and can still feel the sting of insult, you have not attained to the state where you can connect your thoughts with God."[59]—There is nothing in this Kabbalistic or Sufic anecdote which is not entirely in harmony with the spirit of Hasidism. Very similar ideas have been expressed at the same time by the German mystic Meister Eckhart who quotes "the old" i. e. the Stoics as his authority.

Another element of Cynicism is evident in the way in which the practice of certain actions is carried to extremes and the whole moral and religious fervor of the mind concentrated on a single aspect of religious life or on a single moral quality. Already the old paraphrasis of Saadia, through which, as we have seen, numerous religious ideas were transmitted to these circles, defines the Hasid as one "who all his life devotes himself to one particular religious commandment to which he stays obedient under any circumstances, even though he may be inconsistent in fulfilling other commandments . . . But one who wavers from one day to another between the various commandments is not called a Hasid."[60] Here the element of radicalism and extremism, which later on Maimonides too regarded as characteristic of the Hasid,[61] appears already in the definition of the term. On the other hand, the element of indifference to praise or blame, the ideal of *ataraxy* which stands in such striking contrast to this religious radicalism, is nowhere referred to in the theological sources of Hasidism and must have come from outside, that is to say, probably from the Christian environment. Both are equally essential, for it is the paradoxical combination of these two spiritual qualities which makes the Cynic, and it is the ideal of the monkish Cynic which appears before us in a Jewish guise under the name of Hasidism. Generally accepted as the moral ideal by contemporary Christian society, glorified by saints, popular preachers and tract writers, it struck roots among the German Jews in the atmosphere created by the Crusades. The innumerable little stories in which the Hasidic ideal is developed in the "Book of the

Devout" have a close counterpart in the collections of those "examples" which Christian preachers were in the habit of introducing in their homilies.[62] Alongside a mass of folklore these contain not a few stories of profound moral interest, thoughts common to the mystics of every religion and which might have grown out of any one of them. Such tales travel fast and know no boundaries; a story such as that of the devout man who bears the odium of apparent depravity and lives among whores and gamblers in order to try to save them from at least one sin,[63] is cosmopolitan in its appeal.

For the old Merkabah mystics, the devotee, as we have seen, was at best the keeper of the holy mysteries. This conception differs radically from that of the Hasidim for whom humility, restraint and self-abnegation rank higher than the pride of heart which fills the Merkabah visionary in the mystical presence of God. The place of the ecstatic seer, whose mystical élan carries him across all barriers and hindrances to the steps of the heavenly throne, is taken by the meditative devotee, sunk in humble contemplation of the Omnipresent Infinite. However, this ideal of the purely contemplative mystic must be understood in its true religious and social context. The Hasid whose face is, as it were, turned towards God and away from the community, nevertheless functions as the latter's true guide and master. The guiding function appears very clearly in the manner in which Hasidic literature is at pains to make allowances for human weakness and to show every consideration for the conditions of life of the community. The moral casuistry of the "Book of the Devout", which in this respect goes far beyond the older Halakhic literature in its earth-bound realism, is a precious document of true humanity. For all the moral and religious radicalism of its demands upon the devout, Hasidism does not hesitate to condemn the ostentatious display of these qualities and what the Talmud already called "heedless" or "absurd" devotion. Its monkish character is also apparent in the quiet assumption that not everybody is destined to be a Hasid. Both Jehudah the Hasid and his father are pictured by the legend as saints in whom both aspects of this form of religious life were harmoniously combined: radical, anti-social, introspective devotion to the ideal, and loving care for the maintenance of the community.

To this trait must be added another: The helpless, selfless, indifferent Hasid figures in the minds of a public influenced by Hasidism as an enormously powerful being who can command the forces of all the elements. Here the popular conception of the true Hasid supplements the picture which the Hasidim have drawn of themselves, though not without causing some discrepancies. To take one example, Jehudah the Hasid, though fully convinced of the effectiveness of magic and other occult disciplines, was sharply opposed to their practice. He appears to have sensed very clearly the contrast between the magician who prides himself on his control of the elements, and the humble Hasid who craves no form of power. But his perception of the danger did not prevent the magical elements in his heritage from gaining the upper hand over his moral ideal. In the legend, he appears as the bearer and dispenser of all those magical powers and attributes which he was at such pains to renounce, and this legend is by no means the product of later generations: it began to form already during his lifetime.[64] In this conception, the Hasid appears as the true master of magical forces who can obtain everything precisely because he wants nothing for himself. Nowhere else in Judaism has man the magical creator been surrounded with such an halo. It is to Hasidism that we owe the development of the legend of the Golem, or magical homunculus—this quintessential product of the spirit of German Jewry—and the theoretical foundations of this magical doctrine.[65] In the writings of Eleazar of Worms, the most faithful of Jehudah's disciples, discourses on the essence of *Hasiduth* are to be found side by side with tracts on magic and the effectiveness of God's secret names, in one case even in the same book.[66] There one also finds the oldest extant recipes for creating the Golem—a mixture of letter magic and practices obviously aimed at producing ecstatic states of consciousness.[67] It would appear as though in the original conception the Golem came to life only while the ecstasy of his creator lasted. The creation of the Golem was, as it were, a particularly sublime experience felt by the mystic who became absorbed in the mysteries of the alphabetic combinations described in the "Book of Creation." It was only later that the popular legend attributed to the Golem an existence outside the ecstatic consciousness, and in later centuries a whole group of legends sprang up around such Golem figures and their creators.[68]

6

Obscurity still surrounds the question how far a certain form of magic was also involved in the prayer mysticism of the Hasidim which contemporary authors already regarded as particularly characteristic of their faith. Jacob ben Asher, whose father came to Spain from Germany, says on this subject: "The German Hasidim were in the habit of counting or calculating every word in the prayers, benedictions and hymns, and they sought a reason in the Torah for the number of words in the prayers."[69] In other words, this mysticism of prayer originates not from the spontaneous prayer of the devotee but from a study of the classical liturgy whose text was largely fixed by tradition. It is essentially not a new form of devotion, but mystical speculation concerning the background of an already firmly established tradition. Here and elsewhere in the literature of the Hasidism, prominence is given for the first time to certain techniques of mystical speculation which are popularly supposed to represent the heart and core of Kabbalism, such as *Gematria*, i. e. the calculation of the numerical value of Hebrew words and the search for connections with other words or phrases of equal value; *Notarikon*, or interpretation of the letters of a word as abbreviations of whole sentences; and *Temurah*, or interchange of letters according to certain systematic rules.[70] As a matter of historical fact, none of these techniques of mystical exegesis can be called Kabbalistic in the strict sense of the word. In the literature of the classical Kabbalah, during the thirteenth and fourteenth centuries, they often played a very minor part; the few important Kabbalists who made more marked use of them, such as Jacob ben Jacob Hacohen, or Abraham Abulafia, were clearly influenced by the German Hasidim. What really deserves to be called Kabbalism has very little to do with these 'Kabbalistic' practices.

The Hasidic literature on the subject of prayer is comprehensive and to a large extent still in our hands.[71] It shows that the number of words which constituted a prayer and the numerical values of words, parts of sentences, and whole sentences, were linked not only with Biblical passages of equal numerical value, but also with certain designations of God and the angels, and other formulas. Prayer is likened to Jacob's ladder extended from the earth to the sky; it is therefore conceived as a species of mystical ascent and appears in many of these "explanations" as a "highly formalized process full of hidden aspects and purposes."[72] But while we know a great deal about the external technique of these "mysteries of prayer" as the Hasidim called them, we are in the dark as regards the real meaning, the functional purpose of these mystical numerologies. Were certain meditations meant to go with certain prayers, or does the emphasis lie on the magical influence of prayer? In the former case we should be dealing with what the Kabbalah since 1200 referred to as *Kawwanah,* literally "intention," i.e. mystical meditation on the words of prayer while they are being spoken. *Kawwanah,* in other words, is something to be realized in the act of prayer itself.

Now among the German Hasidim, this fundamental doctrine of Kabbalistic mysticism of prayer does not yet ocur. Eleazar of Worms, in his great commentary on the prayers, makes no mention of it, and where, in another context, he refers in passing to a conception of *Kawwanah* which comes close to the Kabbalistic one—a fact which I shall discuss later—it is clear that this concerns not particular words but the whole of the prayer. As to how the Hasidim themselves interpreted the use of the above-mentioned "mysteries" I have been unable to come to a final conclusion, but it is plain that this mysticism of prayer stands in opposition to the old Merkabah mysticism. The emphasis is no longer on the approach of the mystic himself to God's throne but on that of his prayer. It is the word, not the soul, which triumphs over fate and evil. The enormous concern shown for the use of the correct phrase in the traditional texts, and the excessive pedantry displayed in this regard reveals a totally new attitude towards the function of words. Where the Merkabah mystics sought spontaneous expression for their oceanic feeling in the prodigal use of words, the Hasidim discovered a multitude of esoteric meanings in a strictly limited number of fixed expressions. And this painstaking loyalty to the fixed term does indeed seem to go hand in hand with a renewed consciousness of the magic power inherent in words.

As to when and how this mysticism of prayer or, as one should perhaps say, magic of prayer, first originated, the texts tell us nothing. Certainly it did not originate solely among the Hasidim, although all our knowledge is derived from these sources. A consensus of traditions handed down by the disciples of Jehudah the Hasid determines the new mysticism as the final link in a chain which reaches back through the Kalonymides to Italy, and from there to Aaron of Baghdad, whose name has already been mentioned. Certain intermediate links in the chain may appear dubious, but in its essence the view that the "mysteries of prayer" were brought to Germany from Italy, perhaps in a more primitive form, seems incontrovertible.[73] Eleazar of Worms tells us that when the father of Samuel the Hasid, R. Kalonymus, died around 1126, his son was too young to be told the secret by his father, in accordance with the traditional family usage. For this reason another scholar, at the time leader of prayers in the Speyer community, was entrusted by him with the mission of initiating the boy when he had grown up. This shows quite clearly that the origins of the secret doctrine go back beyond the period of the Crusades. Whether they lay in Babylonia and spread from there to Italy—simultaneously perhaps with the already declining Merkabah mysticism—must remain a matter for conjecture. At any rate there can be little doubt that the Kabbalistic mysticism of prayer, though its own subsequent development was entirely different, was taken over from the Hasidim.

The combination of ecstaticism and magic, already noted as characteristics of Merkabah mysticism, reappears on a new plane in this mysticism of prayer. As to whether it determined the theory of prayer, it is only possible to guess. In other respects its influence is plain. Moses Taku (of Tachau?) a follower of Jehudah the Hasid, who set himself to defend the undiluted doctrine of Talmudic Judaism, if necessary even against the teachings of his own master, has given an account of such practices of which he strongly disapproved and which he did not hesitate to condemn as heretical: "They set themselves up as prophets by practicing the pronounciation of holy names, or sometimes they only direct their intention upon them without actually pronouncing the words. Then a man is seized by terror and his body sinks to the ground. The barrier in front of his soul falls, he himself steps into the centre and gazes into the faraway, and only after a while, when the power of the name recedes, does he awaken and return with a confused mind to his former state. This is exactly what the magicians do who practice the exorcism of the demons. They conjure one from their midst with unclean exorcisms, in order that he may tell them what has perhaps been happening in a far away country. The conjurer falls down on the ground where he was standing and his veins become cramped and stiff, and he is as one dead. But after a while he rises without consciousness and runs out of the house, and if one does not hold him at the door he would break his head and his limbs. Then when he again becomes a little conscious of himself, he tells them what he has seen.'"⁴

It is well known how widespread such manifestations of the abnormal "metapsychic" life were during this period among the Christians in whose midst the Hasidim passed their life. A book like Josef Goerres' voluminous "Christliche Mystik" is a veritable thesaurus of instances of this genre. But that the Jewish mystics also attached the very greatest importance to such direct contact with the psychic world is clearly proved by the example of Jacob Halevi of Marvège, (around 1200) who seems to have belonged to a Hasidic circle. He has left us a whole collection of "Responses from Heaven" i. e. judgments (on controversial questions of rabbinic law) which were revealed to him as answers to "dream questions," *sheeloth halom*.'⁵ The asking of such questions was an extremely widespread magical practice for which we have hundreds of recipes.'⁶ While there were scholars who disparaged the solution of Halakhic problems on the basis of direct revelation instead of Talmudic casuistry, there were also many others who admired and imitated the practice. Indeed, the thing is as characteristic of the attitude of many followers of Hasidism towards the Halakhah as it is dubious from the point of view of strict Talmudism.

7

Thus the new religious spirit which finds expression in the ideal of the Hasid permeates every domain of traditional Jewish mysticism and theosophy and tries, albeit awkwardly and unsystematically, to transform them. This effort includes attempts to give a new interpretation to the Merkabah. Jehudah the Hasid relates to his pupil Eleazar how, when he was once standing in the synagogue with his father and there was a bowl with water and oil before them, his father drew his attention to the incomparable radiance which the light of the sun produced on the surface of the liquid, and said to him: "Fix your attention on this radiance, for it is the same as the radiance of the Hashmal" (one of the personified objects of Ezekiel's Merkabah vision).'⁷

We have seen how the new temper transformed the old spirit of prayer. But it also opened new spheres of religious experience—important in spite of all the doubts that they may raise in the minds of later generations—such as the theory and practice of penitence which here first in the development of Jewish mysticism acquired vehement force. Hitherto penitence had not been of paramount importance to the mystics; now it became the central fact of their existence. In the place of the heavenly journey of the self-absorbed ecstatic, and parallel to the new emphasis laid on the now enormously important act of prayer, the technique of penitence was developed into a vast and elaborate system until it became one of the cornerstones of true *Hasiduth*. It is important to realize that previously an elaborate casuistry of penitential acts corresponding to every conceivable degree of transgression had been almost unknown among Jews.[78] The Hasidim were thus not restricted by traditional obstacles when they undertook the task of formulating a ritual of penitence that was entirely in accordance with the new spirit they represented.

Here we are again undoubtedly faced with the after-effects of Christian influence. The whole system of penitence, particularly in the codified form given to it by Eleazar of Worms in several of his writings, closely corresponds to the practices prescribed by the early mediaeval Church in its literature on the subject, the "penitentiary books."[79] Among the latter, the Celtic and later the Frankish tracts developed a peculiar system of which the understanding is pertinent to our subject. Penitence is conceived as reparation for an insult to God through a personal act of restitution, the sinner undertaking to perform certain well-defined acts of a penitentiary character—a conception which inevitably led to the establishment of what can only be described as a tariff of penitence. These "forcible cures and powerful remedies," of which the history of ecclesiastical penitence is full, were doubtless suited to the comprehension of the recently Christianized Celts and Germans and accorded well with their primitive notions of justice, especially in the case of the Franks. But the point to be noted here is that they were also taken over by the Hasidim and adapted to the Jewish *milieu*. Although after the Gregorian reform of the Church in the eleventh century, Rome opened a fight against the old "penitentiary books," their authority remained unshaken among wide circles during the whole period of the Crusades, at a time, that is to say, when the Jewish communities in Germany were themselves under the influence of a mood favorable to their adoption. Authority could easily be ascribed to them by pointing to some scattered analogies in the older Jewish literature. In this manner it became possible to justify the adoption of a whole system of penitence, beginning with all sorts of fastings and leading through various acts, frequently of a highly bizarre nature, to the supreme punishment of voluntary exile—an act of penance already known to the Talmud.[80]

Generally speaking, the system as developed in the *Sefer Hasidim* and conserved in the moral literature of later generations distinguishes between four categories of penitence.[81] In its mildest form, penitence simply meant that the opportunity for committing the same sin again was not utilized (*teshuvah habaah*); but penitence could also amount to a system of voluntary restraints and the preventive avoidance of all occasions calculated to tempt one into committing a certain sin (*teshuvath hagader*); thirdly, the amount of pleasure derived from committing a sin could be made the criterion of the self-imposed askesis (*teshuvath hamishkal*); lastly, in the case of transgressions forbidden under pain of death by the Torah, the sinner must undergo "tortures as bitter as death"—often amounting to extravagantly painful and humiliating punishments—in order to obtain divine forgiveness and avoid the "extermination of the soul" which the Torah threatens for certain sins (*teshuvath hakatuv*). In regard to these practices we have the evidence not only of the Hasidic writings, whose exhortations might be dismissed as belonging purely to the realm of theory, but also of a good many accounts of actual happenings through which the fame of the German Hasidim soon spread far and wide. These stories, of which there are many, leave no doubt about the spirit of fanatical earnestness which animated the zealots. To sit in the snow or in the ice for an hour daily in winter, or to expose one's body to ants and bees in summer, was judged a common practice among those who followed the new call. It is a far cry from the Talmudic conception of penitence to these novel ideas and practices.

A story like the following is characteristic of the new mood: "A Hasid was in the habit of sleeping on the floor in summer, among the fleas, and placing his feet into a bucket with water in winter, until they froze into one lump with the ice. A pupil asked him:

Why do you do that? Why, since man is responsible for his life, do you expose yourself to certain danger? The Hasid replied: It is true that I have not committed any deadly sin, and though I am surely guilty of lighter transgressions there is no need for me to expose myself to such tortures. But it is said in the Midrash that the Messiah is suffering for our sins, as it is said (Isaiah LIII, 5): 'he is wounded for our transgressions', and those who are truly just take sufferings upon themselves for their generation. But I do not want anyone but myself to suffer for my sins."[82] And in fact the pupil who, after the death of his teacher, is perturbed by the thought that his death might have been due to his ascetic sufferings, and that he may now be punished for it, has a dream revelation in which he learns that his master has attained to an infinitely high place in heaven.

In the same manner we are told by the Kabbalist Isaac of Acre, in the fourteenth century: "I have heard tell of a Hasid in Germany, who was not a scholar but a simple and honest man, that he once washed away the ink from a strip of parchment on which were written prayers which included the name of God. When he learned that he had sinned against the honor of God's name, he said: I have despised God's honor, therefore I shall not think higher of my own. What did he do? Every day during the hour of prayer, when the congregation entered and left the synagogue, he lay down on the doorstep and old and young passed over him; and if one trod on him, whether deliberately or by accident, he rejoiced and thanked God. Thus he did for a whole year, taking as his guide the saying of the Mishnah: 'the wicked will be judged in hell for twelve months'."[83]—Long afterwards, the responses of German Rabbis still bear testimony to the powerful influence of Hasidic morality, as when Jacob Weil prescribes detailed penances for an adulterous young woman, or Israel Bruna for a murderer.[84] There is, however, one important respect in which Hasidism differs sharply from its Christian contemporaries: it does not enjoin sexual asceticism. On the contrary, the greatest importance is assigned in the *Sefer Hasidim* to the establishment and maintenance of a normal and reasonable marital life. Nowhere is penitence extended to sexual abstinence in marital relations. The asceticism of the typical Hasid concerns solely his social relations towards women, not the sexual side of his married life.

8

Turning to the influence which Hasidism as a whole has exercised upon the Jews of Germany one finds that its prcatical side, i. e. the new morality, the system of penitence, and the mysticism of prayer, have held their own much longer than the theological and theosophical ideas and the conception of God expounded in the writings of Jehudah the Hasid and his disciples. With the gradual infiltration, since the fourteenth century, of a more highly developed system of thought, the Kabbalism of Spain, early Hasidic theosophy lost ground, and in time—albeit never completely[85]—relinquished its hold on those Jewish circles which were at all concerned with theological questions.

Nevertheless, an understanding of Hasidism also requires an analysis of these theosophical ideas of which the literature of the thirteenth and fourteenth century is full; and here one is immediately forced to recognize the existence of a new religious mood with a strong tendency towards pantheism, or at least a mysticism of divine immanence. In the literature with which we are concerned, this element is combined with Aggadic traditions, with remnants from the heritage of Merkabah mysticism[86]—sometimes in a new guise—and above all with the consistently influential theology of Saadia. In the case of some of these representations and transformations of theosophical ideas, some doubt remains both as regards their origin and their rabbinical orthodoxy. Now and then, when they became entangled in mystical brooding, it seems as though these pious and naive mediaeval Jewish devotees unconsciously drew upon the religious heritage of heretics and sectarians. One even finds tendencies towards a kind of *Logos* doctrine.

The God of the old pre-Hasidic mystics was the Holy King who, from his throne in the *empyraeum,* listens to the ecstatic hymns of his creatures. The living relationship of these mystics to God rested upon the glorification of certain aspects of the divinity, its solemnity, the absence of everything profane, even its immensity and overwhelmingness. In contradistinction to this picture, German Hasidism now develops a different conception of God which poignantly contrasts with the older one.

The Hasidim like to employ Saadia's terminology in order to describe the pure spirituality and the immeasurable infiniteness of

God, two aspects of His being on which they lay the greatest emphasis. To these attributes was added a third which, like the two others,
played no part in the mysticism of the Merkabah period, namely
God's omnipresence, which in turn imperceptibly acquired the character of an immanence not easily reconciled with the supramundane
transcendence of the Creator, another Hasidic article of faith. As
the idea is finally developed by the outstanding representatives of
the new school, God is not so much the master of the universe as
its first principle and prime mover. Side by side with this new
conception, the earlier belief seems to linger on as though by force
of tradition. The new conception is formulated by Eleazar of Worms
in a significant passage where he says: "God is omnipresent and
perceives the just and the evil-doers. Therefore when you pray,
collect your mind, for it is said: I always place God against myself;
and therefore the beginning of all benedictions runs 'Praise be to
Thee, oh God'—as though a man speaks to a friend."[87] No Merkabah
mystic would have given this interpretation of the "Thee" with
which God is addressed. More than that, the change between the
second and the third persons in the formulae of the benedictions
("Praise be to Thee . . . who has blessed us") is quoted as proof
that God is at once the nearest and the farthest, the most plainly
revealed and the most completely hidden of all.[88]

God is even closer to the universe and to man than the soul is
to the body. This doctrine, propounded by Eleazar of Worms[89] and
accepted by the Hasidim, closely parallels Augustine's thesis—so
often approvingly quoted by the Christian mystics of the thirteenth
and fourteenth centuries—that God is closer to any of His creatures
than the latter to itself. In its most uncompromising form this doctrine of God's immanence is expressed in the "Song of Unity", a
hymn composed by a member of the inner circle around Jehudah
the Hasid—who seems to have written a commentary to it—which
gives an impressive version of Saadia's conception of God.[90] Thus
we read: "Everything is in Thee, and Thou art in everything; Thou
fillest every thing and dost encompass it; when everything was created, Thou wast in everything; before everything was created, Thou
wast everything." Expressions of this sort recur in every kind of
Hasidic writing. As Bloch has shown, they are nothing but enthusiastic embellishments of the idea of divine omnipresence as set out
in the old Hebrew paraphrase of Saadia's magnum opus.[91]

But from where are they taken? Whose spirit do they reflect? One is tempted to think of John the Scot, called Scotus Erigena, the "great light" of Neoplatonic mysticism in the ninth century. His influence was immense and could very well have extended to Jewish circles in Provence where, according to some scholars, the above-mentioned paraphrase of Saadia seems to have originated. It is well known that writers from these circles drew heavily upon early sources of Latin scholasticism. And indeed, it is the spirit of John the Scot, which is reflected in such formulae as those that I have quoted. Nobody would be surprised if they closed with the words: "For Thou shalt be everything in everything, when there shall be nothing but Thee alone"—words which are actually a transposition into direct speech of a sentence taken from John the Scot's book "On the Division of Nature."[92]

Not infrequently the idea of immanence is given a naturalistic twist, as when Moses Azriel, a thirteenth-century Hasid, defines it thus: "He is One in the cosmic ether, for He fills the whole ether and everything in the world, and nowhere is there a barrier before Him. Everything is in Him, and He sees everything, for He is entirely perception though He has no eyes, for He has the power to see the universe within His own being."[93] Some of these passages have been taken literally from Saadia's commentary to the *Sefer Yetsirah*, where he refers in very naturalistic terms to God's life as a positive attribute of His being.[94]

Here it should be remarked in passing that this widespread doctrine of divine immanence, which clearly corresponded to the deepest religious feeling of the Hasidim, had already been criticized sharply by a disciple of Jehudah the Hasid: Moses Taku expressed the fear that this pantheistic element in the conception of the divinity might be used as a justification of paganism, since it made it possible for the heathen to argue that "they were serving the Creator with their cult and their idols, seeing that He was omnipresent."[95] And in fact there have always been pronounced opponents of this form of pantheism who refused to permit the "Song of Unity" to be included in the communal prayer although it was included already at an early period in the liturgy. Instances of such opposition are related of Rabbi Solomon Luria in the 16th century and the famous Rabbi Elijah of Vilna, the "Gaon of Vilna," in the 18th century.[96]

Among the Hasidim, the doctrine of divine immanence persisted after they had come in contact with Spanish Kabbalism—hardly surprising in view of the fact that Kabbalism was by no means free of similar tendencies, including radically pantheistic notions. One of these part Hasidic, part Kabbalistic treatises contains a very illuminating explanation of the description of God as the "soul of the soul," in which it is explained that God inhabits the soul. This, we are told, is the true meaning of the word (Deut. VII, 21) "for the Lord thy God is in your midst," the "in your midst" being a pregnant reference not to the people—although this is doubtless the meaning of the verse—but to the individual."[97] Thus with the aid of mystical exegesis the theory of divine immanence and the conception of God as the inmost ground of the soul is traced back to the Torah itself—an idea wholly foreign to the old Merkabah mystics.

This doctrine of a God who in a mysterious fashion is immanent in all things does not always differentiate between the unknown God, the *deus absconditus* and His revelation as King, Creator and sender of prophecy. Frequently the same designation is applied in both contexts. But side by side with these general theological characteristics of spirituality, infinity and immanence, there also appears a form of theosophic speculation which attempts to differentiate between the various aspects under which God is revealed. Owing to the lack of talent, peculiar to the Hasidim, for precisely-worded abstract thought, this attempt has been the source of a good deal of confusion. There is overlapping in the texts, and the various conflicting religious motives are not harmonized. As religious philosophers the Hasidim were distinguished by the quality which a modern scholar, referring to Philo, has defined as "that model lack of clarity which, in conjunction with an extraordinary susceptibility, makes it possible for a large variety of contradictory ideas to coexist in one mind, so that one is struck now by one and now by the other."[98] There are three main thoughts which characterize the peculiar theosophy of the Hasidim and which plainly originate from different sources: (1) the conception of *Kavod*, i. e. divine glory; (2) the idea of a "holy" or specially distinguished cherub on the throne; and (3) their conception of God's holiness and greatness.

9

Before turning to the analysis of these ideas, it is necessary to make a prefatory remark. The question how it is possible for the unknown God to reveal himself as the Creator, this central problem of Spanish Kabbalism, does not exist for the Hasidim. The conception of God the Creator presents no problem to their minds. It is to them not a special development, a modification of the unknown omnipresent God: since both are *identical*, there can be no question of a *relationship* between the two. It is not the riddle of Creation for which a solution is sought in the ideas of the *Kavod* and the cherub. Those formulae of Merkabah mysticism which come closest to postulating a discrepancy between the *deus absconditus* and the appearance of God the King-Creator on his celestial throne are precisely those to which the Hasidim pay least attention. Their interest belongs not to the mystery of Creation but to that of Revelation. How can God reveal Himself to His creatures? What is the meaning of the frequent anthropomorphisms in the Bible and in the Talmud? These are the questions which the theosophy of German Hasidism undertakes to answer.[99]

The glory of God, the *Kavod*, i.e. that aspect of God which He reveals to Man, is to the Hasidim not the Creator but the First Creation. The idea is derived from Saadia whose doctrine of divine glory was intended to serve as an explanation of the Biblical anthropomorphisms and the appearance of God in the vision of the prophets. According to him, God, who remains infinite and unknown also in the role of Creator, has produced the glory as "a created light, the first of all creations."[100] This *Kavod* is "the great radiance called Shekhinah" and it is also identical with the *ruah ha-kodesh*, the "holy spirit", out of whom there speaks the voice and word of God. This primeval light of divine glory is later revealed to the prophets and mystics in various forms and modifications, "thus to one, and differently to the other, in accordance with the demands of the hour."[101] It serves as a guarantee of the authentic character of the words heard by the prophet and excludes any doubts as to their divine origin.

The importance of this conception for the religious thought of Hasidism is considerable. Its variations are manifold and the contradictions between them frequently quite obvious. God does not reveal

Himself, nor does He speak. He "maintains His silence and carries the universe," as Eleazar of Worms puts it in a magnificent metaphor. The silent divinity immanent in all things as their deepest reality speaks and reveals itself through the appearance of its glory. The assertion that the light of glory was created is, of course, a novelty introduced by Saadia of which the ancient Merkabah conception of *Kavod* knows nothing. For Saadia there was a special emphasis on the word "created" which became blurred in the Hasidic conception, since for the Hasidim there is not, as for Saadia, a sharp distinction between created and emanated glory. The idea that the *Kavod* was created has for them little more significance than the notion of a created *logos,* which he sometimes uses, had for Philo. While in Saadia's theology this as yet amorphous light of glory was born on the first day of creation, the Hasidim apparently regarded it as in some way existent prior to the seven days' work.

Jehudah the Hasid has laid down his own dotrine of *Kavod* in a "Book of the Glory," of which only some scattered quotations have survived.[102] It appears to have included also a variety of speculative thoughts not concerned with the theory of *Kavod.* Like his pupil, Eleazar, Jehudah distinguished between two kinds of glory: One is an "inner glory" (*Kavod Penimi*) which is conceived as being identical with the Shekhinah and the holy spirit and as having no form, but a voice.[103] While man cannot directly communicate with God, he can "connect himself with the glory."[104] There is some overlapping between the definition of God and that of the *Kavod Penimi,* as when the qualities of omnipresence and immanence are in one place attributed to God and in another only to the Shekhinah. Occasionally this inner glory is identified with the divine will, thereby giving rise to a sort of Logos mysticism.[105] Thus in the "Book of Life," a document written about 1200 A.D., the *Kavod* is actually defined as the divine will, the "holy spirit," the word of God, and conceived as inherent in all creatures.[106] The author of this book goes even further. According to him, the potency of the *Kavod,* from which every act of creation originates, is never the same but undergoes a gradual, insensible change from one moment to another. In this way, the mundane process of constant change corresponds to a secret life of the divine glory active in it—a conception not far distant from Kabbalism.[107] For Eleazar of Worms the ten Sefiroth of the "Book of Creation" have already ceased to represent the ten original numbers and have become aspects of Creation, the first Sefirah being identified with the all-transcending will or glory of God, and therefore occupying a position midway between the created and the uncreated.[108]

This 'inner' glory now has its pendant in the 'visible' glory. While the first is formless, the second has various changing forms of which each change is subject to the will of God. It is this second glory which appears on the throne of the Merkabah or in the prophetic vision, and which forms the subject of the enormous spatial measurements in the *Shiur Komah* speculations regarding the "body of the Shekhinah."[109] Through perceiving the *Kavod*, says Jehudah the Hasid in conscious or unconscious development of one of Saadia's thoughts, the prophet knows that his vision comes from God and that he is not deceived by demons, who are also able to speak to man, for the demons are powerless to produce the phenomena of the glory.[110]

The vision of the *Kavod* is expressly defined as the aim and the reward of Hasidic askesis.[111] As to the emanation of the visible from the invisible *Kavod,* the notions vary. According to some writers, they emanate directly from each other, while another view[112] ascribes to the light of the invisible *Kavod* thousands and myriads of reflections before it becomes visible even to the angels and holy seraphim.

Side by side with this conception of the two-fold *Kavod,* one finds another remarkable element of Hasidic theosophy, the idea of the holy cherub as the appearance on the throne of the Merkabah. This cherub, who is never mentioned by Saadia, figures in certain Merkabah tracts which were known to the Hasidim.[113] Since in the visions of Ezekiel reference is generally to a host of cherubim, the idea of a particularly distinguished angel probably goes back to the one passage in Ezekiel x, 4 where the singular is used: "Then the glory of the Lord went up from the cherub." For the Hasidim, this cherub is identical with Saadia's "visible glory."[114] He is the emanation of God's Shekhinah or His invisible glory—according to others, the product of the "great fire" of the Shekhinah whose flame surrounds the Lord, while the throne of glory, on which the cherub appears, springs from a less exalted fire. According to the mythical account,[115] the reflection of the divine light in the cosmic waters produced a radiance which became a fire and out of which the throne and the angels arose. From the "great fire" of the Shekhinah not only the cherub emanates but also the human soul, which therefore ranks above the angels. The cherub can take every form of angel, man or beast; his human form was the model in whose likeness God created man.[116]

What this idea of the cherub originally signified can only be guessed, for it is clear that the Hasidim merely adapted to their own thoughts a conception of much earlier origin. A hint is perhaps supplied by an idea which one encounters among certain Jewish sectaries of the period of Saadia. Philo thought that the *logos,* the divine 'word' acted as an intermediary in the process of Creation. This Philonic doctrine of creation was developed by these sectarians, who for a long time moved on the fringe of rabbinic Judaism, in a somewhat crude form which, incidentally, had been ascribed already in earlier writings to isolated heretics.[117] According to them, God did not create the world directly, but through the intermediary of an angel, whether this latter emanated from Him or was himself a created being. This angel, who thus appears as creator or demiurge, is also defined as the subject of all Biblical anthropomorphisms and as the being which is perceived in the vision of the prophets.

This discovery of an echo of Philonic thought need not surprise us. Although not many traces of it are to be found in Talmudic and early rabbinic literature, there can be no doubt, since Poznanski's researches on the subject, that the ideas of the Alexandrian theosophist somehow spread even to the Jewish sectarians in Persia and Babylonia who as late as the tenth century were in a position to quote from some of his writings.[118] It is by no means impossible that the cherub on the throne was originally nothing but the transformed *logos,* especially if one takes into account the fact that for the pre-Hasidic mystics—as we have seen in the previous lecture—the appearance on the throne is precisely that of the Creator of the world. Among the Hasidim, who saw no particular problem in the idea of the infinite God as the Creator of the finite things, the angel lost this character; nevertheless, he is given attributes which almost make a second God out of him.[119] In reading these descriptions one is reminded time and again of the *logos.* Even the names under which God appears in the Hekhaloth tracts: Akhtariel, Zohorariel, Adiriron, are occasionally resuscitated and applied to the *Kavod* and the cherub through which the *Kavod* appears.[120] The transformation is similar to the one which we have encountered in the previous lecture, where the angel Metatron is described as the "lesser JHWH," except that the cherub corresponds more closely to the idea of the logos.

To the question how such ideas could have penetrated to the pious German Hasidim, several answers are possible. In the first place, such logos speculations may have become part and parcel of orthodox Jewish Gnosticism already in some Merkabah texts of whose existence the Hasidim had knowledge. Secondly, there is the possibility that the Hasidim came into direct contact with heretical thoughts. Moses Taku mentions such writings which came from the East and wandered in the twelfth century through Russia to Regensburg, at that time one of the chief centres of trade with the Slav countries.[121] Moreover, we know from newly discovered fragments of a book whose author was Samuel ben Kalonymus, the father of Jehudah the Hasid, that "among the heretical scholars there are a few who know of something like a reflection of the mysteries [of the *Kavod*], though not of their substance."[122] Samuel the Hasid himself is known on good authority to have travelled outside Germany for several years and may well have come into contact with Jewish sectarians or heretics and their writings.

The third theosophic symbol of importance in this connection seems to have originated among the Hasidim themselves. In their literature there appears early a sort of continuous reference to the "holiness" of God, and his "greatness" which they also call his "kingdom." The point is that these qualities are not conceived as attributes of the divinity but—at any rate in those writings of which we have any knowledge[123]—as a created hypostasis of its glory. The "holiness" is the formless glory, the hidden presence of God in all things. But in the same way as a passage of the Talmud says of the Shekhinah that its essential locality is in the "West",[124] the holiness of God is given a special "western" location. Again, the "holiness" is identified by the Hasidim with the "world of light", the highest of the five worlds of the spirit—a half gnostic, half Neoplatonic conception borrowed from Abraham bar Hiya, an early twelfth century writer in Northern Spain who belonged to the Neoplatonic school. While God's voice and His word issue from His "holiness," the latter radiates light from the "West" on His "greatness" which is localized in the "East." There is also this difference that while the "holiness" is infinite like God's essence itself, His "greatness" or appearance as "King" is finite, that is to say, identical with the visible *Kavod* or the cherub. In this system, therefore, the infinite Creator is conceived without any attributes which are a matter of the Glory in its various modifications.

The doctrine of prayer is again of special importance in this context. "God is infinite and everything; therefore if He did not take form in the vision of the prophets and appear to them as King on the throne, they would not know to whom they were praying", says Eleazar of Worms.[125] For this reason the devout in his prayer calls to God as King—in the visible theophany of the glory. But the true intention (*kawwanah*)—according to the same author—is not directed towards the appearance on the throne, and still less towards the Creator himself who, as we have seen, is identified in this system with the hidden God. The real object of mystical contemplation, its true goal, is the hidden holiness of God, His infinite and formless glory, wherefrom there emerges the voice and the word of God.[126] The finite word of man is aimed at the infinite word of God. By the same token the Shekhinah is defined, in Eleazar's terminology, as the real aim of prayer. In view of the above-mentioned conception of the Shekhinah as a created light, this idea is plainly paradoxical. And in fact we read in one of the fragments from Samuel ben Kalonymus' work, to which reference has already been made, "the creatures praise the Shekhinah, which is itself created; but in the world to come they will praise "God Himself.""[127] In other words, a direct prayer to the Creator, in spite of His infiniteness and omnipresence, is possible only in the eschatological perspective. At present, it is directed only towards "the Shekhinah of our Creator, the spirit of the living God," i. e. His "holiness", which in spite of everything is almost defined as the *Logos*.

10

Side by side with this theosophy and the mysticism of immanence ascribed to the authority of Saadia, one finds a third element of thought which for all its lack of color and true metaphysical breadth merits the description of Neoplatonism. Certain ideas derived from the writings of Spanish-Jewish Neoplatonists were taken up by the Hasidim and incorporated in their own system. In a number of cases, of course, these ideas underwent a process of retrogression from the metaphysical to the theological or Gnostical sphere, if not to pure mythology.

It has been argued that the mystical theology of the Spanish Kabbalists and that of the German Hasidim represent two different schools of thought which have nothing whatsoever in common. The Spaniards, according to this reading of the facts, followed in the footsteps of the Neoplatonists, while the typical Hasidic conceptions go back to oriental mythology.[128] This appears to me to be an oversimplification. The fact is that Neoplatonic thought came to be known among both groups, but with the difference that in Spain and Provence these ideas became a potent factor in transforming the character of the early Kabbalism, which was almost entirely a Gnostical system, whereas in Germany the elements of such speculations as they engendered failed to make a lasting impression on Hasidic thought. To the Hasidic mind they carried no real life. Instead of transforming the doctrine of Hasidism they were themselves transformed by being deprived of their original speculative content. In the final stage of decomposition they are no longer even recognizable for what they were. Thus to take an example, Abraham bar Hiya's doctrine of the hierarchy of the five worlds—that of light, of the divinity, of the intellect, of the soul, and of (spiritual) nature—was incorporated in a highly peculiar fashion in the Hasidic system in which cosmological ideas played a not unimportant part.[129]

Of special interest in this connection is the doctrine of the archetypes—wholly foreign to Saadia—which dominates Eleazar's work on "The Science of the Soul," but is of importance also for the "Book of the Devout." According to this doctrine, every "lower" form of existence, including lifeless things,—"even the wood block" to say nothing of even lower forms of life, has its archetype, *demuth*.[130] In this conception we recognize the traits not only of Plato's theory of ideas, but also of the astral theory of correspondence between higher and lower planes, and of the astrological doctrine that everything has its "star." The archetypes, as we have already seen in connection with the Hekhaloth tracts,[131] are conceived as being pictorially represented in the curtain spread before the Throne of Glory. According to the Hasidim, this curtain consists of blue flame and surrounds the throne from all sides except from the west.[132] The archetypes themselves represent a special sphere of non-corporeal, semi-divine existence. In another connection, mention is actually made of an occult "Book of Archetypes."[133] The archetype is the deepest source of the soul's hidden activity. The fate of every being is contained in its archetype, and there is even an archetypal representation of every change and passing made of its existence.[134] Not only the angels and the demons draw their foreknowledge of human fate from these archetypes;[135] the prophet, too, is able to perceive them and thus to read the future.[136] Of Moses it is expressly said that God showed him the archetypes.[137] There is a hint that even guilt and merit have their "signs" in the archetypes.[138]

These mysteries of the Godhead and its glory, then, the archetypes of all existence in a mythically conceived realm of ideas, and the secret of man's nature and his path to God, are the principal subjects of Hasidic theosophy. In a curiously pathetic manner those who studied them became absorbed in a mixture of profound and abstruse ideas and tried to combine a naive mythical realism with mystical insight and occult experience.

There is little to connect these old Hasidim of the thirteenth century with the Hasidic movement which developed in Poland and the Ukraine during the eighteenth century with which we shall deal in the final lecture. The identity of name is no proof of real continuity. After all, the two are separated by two or three great epochs in the development of Kabbalistic thought. The later Hasidism was the inheritor of a rich tradition from which its followers could draw new inspiration, new modes of thought and, last but not least, new modes of expression. And yet it cannot be denied that a certain similarity between the two movements exists. In both cases the problem was that of the education of large Jewish groups in a spirit of mystical moralism. The true Hasid and the Zaddik of later Hasidism are related figures; the one and the other are the prototypes of a mystical way of life which tends towards social activity even where its representatives are conceived as the guardians of all the mysteries of divinity.

ABRAHAM ABULAFIA AND THE DOCTRINE OF PROPHETIC KABBALISM

1

As from the year 1200, the Kabbalists begin to emerge as a distinct mystical group which, while still not numerically significant, had nonetheless attained considerable prominence in many parts of Southern France and Spain. The main tendencies of the new movement are clearly defined and the modern student may without difficulty trace its development from the early stages about 1200 to the Golden Age of Kabbalism in Spain at the close of the thirteenth and the early fourteenth centuries. An extensive literature has preserved for us the highlights of thought and personalities dominating the new mysticism which for five or six generations was to exercise an ever increasing influence on Jewish life. Some of the outstanding leaders, it is true, are but lightly sketched and we have not sufficient data to give us a clear picture of them all, but research of the past thirty years has brought an unexpected harvest of illuminating facts. Nor must it be forgotten that each of the leading figures had his own clearly defined physiognomy and there was no vagueness of outline to lead to confusion of identity. The same clear lines of demarcation apply also to tendencies each of which can be distinguished by terminology as well as by the nuance of its mystic thought.

This demarcation is intelligible enough when we review the growth of mystic tradition. Teaching by word of mouth and implication rather than assertion, was the rule. The numerous allusions found in this field of literature, such as "I cannot say more", "I have already explained to you by word of mouth", "this is only for those familiar with the 'secret wisdom'" are not mere flights of rhetoric. This vagueness, indeed, is the reason why many passages have remained obscure to the present day. In many cases, whispers, and that in esoteric hints, were the only medium of transmission. It is therefore not surprising that such methods should lead to innovations, sometimes startling, and that differentiations arose between the various schools. Even the devout pupil who leaned heavily on the tradition of his master, found before him a wide field for interpretation and amplification if he were so inclined. Nor should it be forgotten that the primary source was not always a mere mortal. Supernatural illumination also plays its part in the history of Kabbalism and innovations are made not only on the basis of new interpretations of ancient lore but as a result of fresh inspiration or revelation, or even of a dream. A sentence from Isaac Hacohen of Soria (about 1270) illustrates the twin sources recognized by the Kabbalists as authoritative. "In our generation there are but a few, here and there, who have received *tradition* from the ancients . . . or have been vouchsafed the grace of divine *inspiration*." Tradition and intuition are bound together and this would explain why Kabbalism could be deeply conservative and intensely revolutionary. Even "traditionalists" do not shrink from innovations, sometimes far-reaching, which are confidently set forth as interpretations of the ancients or as revelation of a mystery which Providence had seen fit to conceal from previous generations.

This duality colors Kabbalistic literature for the succeding hundred years. Some scholars are staunch conservatives who will say nothing that has not been handed down by their masters and that only in enigmatic brevity. Others frankly delight in innovations based on fresh interpretation and we have the admission of Jacob ben Sheshet of Gerona:

> Were they not the findings of my heart
> I had believed . . . this Moses from Sinai did impart.

A third class propound their views, either laconically or at length, without citing any authority, while yet a fourth, such as Jacob Hacohen and Abraham Abulafia, lean frankly on divine revelation. But it is not surprising that so many Kabbalists, illuminates as well as commentators, display a reticence which is among the factors that led directly to the revival of pseudepigraphic forms in Kabbalistic literature. This pseudepigraphy was, in my opinion, based on two impulses, psychological and historic. The psychological stimulus emanates from modesty and the feeling that a Kabbalist who had been vouchsafed the gift of inspiration should shun ostentation.

The historic impulse, on the other hand, was bound up with the desire to influence the writer's contemporaries. Hence the search for historic continuity and the sanctification of authority, and the tendency to lend to Kabbalistic literature the lustre of some great name from Biblical or Talmudic times. The Zohar, or the "Book of Splendor", is the most famous, but by no means the sole example, of such pseudepigraphy. But not all Kabbalists, fortunately for us, preferred anonymity and it is thanks to them that we are able to place the authors of the pseudepigraphic writings in their proper historic setting. I think it will be appropriate to sum up the contribution of Spanish Kabbalism to the treasury of Jewish mysticism by characterizing the most outspoken representatives of its main currents, the outspoken illuminates and ecstatics and, on the other hand, the masters of pseudepigraphy.

In the opening lecture I referred to the fact that Jewish mystics are inclined to be reticent about the hidden regions of the religious life, including the sphere of experiences generally described as ecstasy, mystical union with God, and the like. Experiences of this kind lie at the bottom of many Kabbalistic writings, though not, of course, of all. Sometimes, however, this fact is not even mentioned by the author. Of one bulky volume, Rabbi Mordecai Ashkenazi's book *Eshel Abraham*,[1] I have been able to prove for instance that it was written against a background of visionary dreams. But for the fact that one of the author's notebooks, a kind of mystical diary, has come down to us, it would be impossible to guess this, for it is in vain that one looks for a single allusion to the source of his ideas.[2] The treatment of the subject remains throughout strictly objective. Other Kabbalists deal at length with the question of the individual's approach to mystical knowledge, without any reference to their own experience. But even writings of this kind, if they are really manuals of the more advanced stages of mystical practice and technique, have seldom been published. To this class belongs, for instance, a penetrating analysis of various forms and stages of mystical rapture and ecstasy written by Rabbi Dov Baer (died 1827), son of the famous Rabbi Shneur Zalman of Ladi, the founder of *Habad*-Hasidism, in his *Kuntras Ha-Hithpaaluth*—roughly translated "An Enquiry into Ecstasy."[3] Or take the case of the famous Kabbalist, Rabbi Hayim Vital Calabrese (1543-1620), the leading disciple of Rabbi Isaac Luria, himself one of the central figures of later Kabbalism. This celebrated mystic is the author of an essay called *Shaare Kedushah,* i. e., "The Gates of Holiness", which includes a brief and easily comprehensible introduction into the mystical way of life, beginning with a description of certain indispensable moral qualities and leading up to a whole compendium of Kabbalistic ethics. The first three chapters of the little book have been printed many times, and on the whole they make interesting reading. So far so good. But Vital has added a fourth chapter, in which he sets out in detail various ways of imbuing the soul with the holy spirit and prophetic wisdom, and which, by virtue of its copious quotations from older authors, is really an anthology of the teachings of the older Kabbalists on the technique of ecstasy. You will not, however, find it in any of the printed editions of the book; in its place the following words have been inserted: "Thus speaks the printer: This fourth part will not be printed, for it is all holy names and secret mysteries which it would be unseemly to publish." And in fact, this highly interesting chapter has survived in only a few handwritten copies.[4] It is the same, or almost the same, with other writings which describe either ecstatical experiences or the technique of preparing oneself for them.

Still more remarkable is the fact that even when we turn to the unpublished writings of Jewish mystics, we find that ecstatic experience does not play the all-important part one might expect. It is true that the position is somewhat different in the writings of the early mystics who lived before the development of Kabbalism and whose ideas have been outlined in the second lecture. Instead of the usual theory of mysticism, we are treated in these documents of Jewish Gnosticism to enthusiastic descriptions of the soul's ascent to the Celestial Throne and of the objects it contemplates; in addition, the technique of producing this ecstatic frame of mind is described in detail. In later Kabbalistic literature these aspects tend more and more to be relegated to the background. The soul's ascension does not, of course, disappear altogether. The visionary element of mysticism which corresponds to a certain psychological disposition, breaks through again and again. But, on the whole, Kabbalistic meditation and contemplation takes on a more spiritualized aspect. Moreover, the fact remains that, even leaving aside the distinction between earlier and later documents of Jewish mysticism, it is only in extremely rare cases that ecstasy signifies actual union with God, in which the human individuality abandons itself to the rapture of complete submersion in the divine stream. Even in this ecstatic frame of mind, the Jewish mystic almost invariably retains a sense of the distance between the Creator and His creature. The latter is joined to the former, and the point where the two meet is of the greatest interest to the mystic, but he does not regard it as constituting anything so extravagant as identity of Creator and creature.

Nothing seems to me to express better this sense of the distance between God and man, than the Hebrew term which in our literature is generally used for what is otherwise called *unio mystica*. I mean the word *devekuth,* which signifies "adhesion," or "being joined," viz., to God. This is regarded as the ultimate goal of religious perfection. *Devekuth* can be ecstasy, but its meaning is far more comprehensive. It is a perpetual being-with-God, an intimate union and conformity of the human and the divine will.[5] Yet even the rapturous descriptions of this state of mind which abound in later Hasidic literature retain a proper sense of distance, or, if you like, of incommensurateness. Many writers deliberately place *devekuth* above any form of ecstasy which seeks the extinction of the world and the self in the union with God.[6] I am not going to deny that there have also been tendencies of the opposite kind[7]; an excellent description of the trend towards pure pantheism, or rather acosmism, can be found in a well-known Yiddish novel, F. Schneerson's *Hayim Grawitzer,*[8] and at least one of the famous leaders of Lithuanian Hasidism, Rabbi Aaron Halevi of Starosselje, can be classed among the acosmists. But I do maintain that such tendencies are not characteristic of Jewish mysticism. It is a significant fact that the most famous and influential book of our mystical literature, the Zohar, has little use for ecstasy; the part it plays both in the descriptive and in the dogmatical sections of this voluminous work is entirely subordinate. Allusions to it there are,[9] but it is obvious that other and different aspects of mysticism are much nearer to the author's heart. Part of the extraordinary success of the Zohar can probably be traced to this attitude of restraint which struck a familiar chord in the Jewish heart.

2

Considering all the aforementioned facts, it is hardly surprising that the outstanding representative of ecstatic Kabbalism has also been the least popular of all the great Kabbalists. I refer to Abraham Abulafia, whose theories and doctrines will form the main subject of this lecture. By a curious coincidence, which is perhaps rather more than a coincidence, Abulafia's principal works and the Zohar were written almost simultaneously. It is no exaggeration to say that each marks the culminating point in the development of two opposing schools of thought in Spanish Kabbalism, schools which I should like to call the ecstatic and the theosophical. Of the latter I shall have something to say in the following lectures. For all their differences, the two belong together and, only if both are understood, do we obtain something like a comprehensive picture of Spanish Kabbalism.

Unfortunately, not one of Abulafia's numerous and often voluminous treatises has been published by the Kabbalists, while the Zohar runs into seventy or eighty editions. Not until Jellinek, one of the small band of nineteenth century Jewish scholars who probed deeper into the problem of Jewish mysticism, published three of his minor writings and some extracts from others, did any of them appear in print.[10] This is all the more remarkable as Abulafia was a very prolific writer who, on one occasion, refers to himself as the author of twenty-six Kabbalistic and twenty-two prophetic works.[11] Of the former, many still exist; I know of more than twenty, and it is a fact that a few among them enjoy a great reputation among Kabbalists to this day.[12]

While some of the more orthodox Kabbalists, such as Rabbi Jehudah Hayat (about 1500 A. D.) attacked Abaluafia with vehemence and warned their readers against his books[13], their criticism appears to have aroused only a faint echo.[14] At any rate, Abulafia's influence as a guide to mysticism continued to remain very great. He owed this to the remarkable combination of logical power, pellucid style, deep insight and highly colored abstruseness which characterizes his writings. Since, as we shall have occasion to see, he was convinced of having found the way to prophetic inspiration, and from there to the true knowledge of the Divine, he took pains to use a simple and direct style which went straight to the heart of every attentive reader. He went so far as to include among his works a number of what one might call manuals, which not only set out his theory but also constitute a guide to action. In fact they can be practised so easily as to go far beyond his intentions; the

point is that although Abulafia himself never thought of going beyond the pale of rabbinic Jewry, his teachings can be put into effect
by practically everyone who tries. That probably is also one of the
reasons why the Kabbalists refrained from publishing them. Very
likely they feared that once this technique of meditation, which
had a very broad appeal, became publicly known, its use would no
longer be restricted to the elect. Certainly the success of Abulafia's
writing made the ever-present danger of a clash between the mystical revelation and that of Mount Sinai seem more real than ever.
Thus, the whole school of practical mysticism, which Abulafia himself called Prophetic Kabbalism, continued to lead an underground
life. By witholding his writings from the public, the Kabbalists undoubtedly sought to eliminate the danger that people might go in
for ecstatic adventures without due preparation and lay dangerous
claims to visionary powers.

Generally speaking, lay mystics—self-taught and untutored by
Rabbinism—have always been a potential source of heretical
thought. Jewish mysticism tried to meet this danger by stipulating
in principle that entry into the domain of mystical thought and
practice should be reserved to rabbinic scholars.[15] In actual fact,
however, there has been no lack of Kabbalists who either had no
learning whatsoever, or who lacked the proper rabbinic training.
Thus enabled to look at Judaism from a fresh angle, these men
frequently produced highly important and interesting ideas, and
so there grew up, side by side with the scholarly Kabbalah of the
Rabbis, another line of prophetic and visionary mystics. The pristine
enthusiasm of these early ecstatics frequently lifted the heavy lid of
rabbinic scholasticism, and for all their readiness to compromise
occasionally came into conflict with it. It is also worth pointing out
that during the classical period of Kabbalism, i. e. up to 1300 A. D.,
as distinct from later periods, its representatives were, as a rule,
not men whom their contemporaries regarded as outstanding Rabbis. Great Kabbalists, who also contributed to strictly rabbinical
literature, men like Moses Nahmanides or Solomon ben Adret, were
rare.[16] Yet the Kabbalists were, in the great majority, men of rabbinic education. Abulafia marks an exception, having had little
contact with higher rabbinic learning. All the more extensive, however, was his knowledge of contemporary philosophy; and his writ-

ings, especially those of a systematic character, show him to have been, by the standards of his age, a highly erudite man.

3

About Abulafia's life and his person we are informed almost exclusively by his own writings.[17] Abraham ben Samuel Abulafia was born in Saragossa in 1240, and spent his youth in Tudela, in the province of Navarre. His father taught him the Bible with its commentaries as well as grammar and some Mishnah and Talmud. When he was eighteen years old he lost his father. Two years later he left Spain and went to the Near East in order, as he writes, to discover the legendary stream Sambation beyond which the lost ten tribes were supposed to dwell. Warlike disturbances in Syria and Palestine soon drove him back from Acre to Europe, where he spent about ten years in Greece and Italy.

During these years of travel, he steeped himself in philosophy and conceived for Maimonides an admiration that proved lifelong. For him there was no antithesis between mysticism and the doctrines of Maimonides. He rather considered his own mystical theory as the final step forward from the "Guide of the Perplexed" to which he wrote a curious mystical commentary. This affinity of the mystic with the great rationalist has its astounding parallel—as the most recent research has shown—in the relationship of the great Christian mystic Meister Eckhart to Maimonides, by whom he seems to be much more influenced than was any scholastic before him. While the great scholastics, such as Thomas Aquinas and Albertus Magnus, although having learned and, indeed, accepted much from him, none the less frequently oppose him, the Rabbi is—as Josef Koch has ascertained[18]—for the great Christian mystic a literary authority to whom Augustine at best is superior. In the same way Abulafia tries to connect his theories with those of Maimonides.[19] According to him, only the "Guide" and the "Book of Creation" together represent the true theory of Kabbalism.[20]

Coincidentally with these studies he seems to have been deeply occupied with the Kabbalistic doctrines of his age, without, however, being overmuch impressed by them. About 1270 he returned to Spain for three or four years, during which he immersed himself completely in mystical research. In Barcelona he began to study the book *Yetsirah* and twelve commentaries to it showing both philosophic and Kabbalistic inclinations.²¹ Here, too, he seems to have come into contact with a conventicle the members of which believed they could gain access to the profoundest secrets of mystical cosmology and theology "by the three methods of Kabbalah, being *Gematria, Notarikon,* and *Temurah.*" Abulafia especially mentions one Baruch Togarmi, precentor, as his teacher, who initiated him into the true meaning of the *Sefer Yetsirah.* We still possess a treatise of this Kabbalist—"The Keys to Kabbalah"—about the mysteries of the book *Yetsirah.*²² Most of them, he says, he felt not entitled to publish, nor even to write down. "I want to write it down and I am not allowed to do it, I do not want to write it down and cannot entirely desist; so I write and I pause, and I allude to it again in later passages, and this is my procedure."²³

Abulafia himself at times wrote in this vein, so typical of mystical literature. By immersing himself in the mystical technique of his teacher, Abulafia found his own way. It was at the age of 31, in Barcelona, that he was overcome by the prophetic spirit. He obtained knowledge of the true name of God, and had visions of which he himself, however, says, in 1285, that they were partly sent by the demons to confuse him, so that he "groped about like a blind man at midday for fifteen years with Satan to his right." Yet on the other hand he was entirely convinced of the truth of his prophetic knowledge. He travelled for some time in Spain, expounding his new doctrine, but in 1274 he left his native country for the second and last time, and from then on led a vagrant life in Italy and Greece. It was still in Spain that he exerted a deep influence upon the young Joseph Gikatila who later became one of the most eminent Spanish Kabbalists. In Italy too, he found disciples in various places and taught them his new way, partly in pursuit of the philosophy of Maimonides. Quick enthusiasm about his disciples turned quickly into disappointment and he complained bitterly of the unworthiness of some of those whom he had taught in Capua.²⁴

He became the author of prophetical writings wherein he prefers to designate himself by names of the same numerical value as his original name of Abraham. He prefers to call himself Raziel or Zechariah. Only in the ninth year after the beginning of his prophetic visions he began, as he says himself,²⁵ to compose distinctly prophetic writings, although he had written before that time other tracts on different branches of science, among them "writings on the mysteries of Kabbalah."[26] In the year 1280, inspired with his mission, he undertook a most venturesome and unexplained task: He went to Rome to present himself before the Pope and to confer with him "in the name of Jewry." It seems that at that time he nursed Messianic ideas. Well may he have read of such a mission of the Messiah to the Pope in a then very widely known booklet.[27] This contained the disputation of the famous Kabbalist Moses ben Nahman with the apostate Pablo Christiani in the year 1263. Here Nahmanides said: "When the time of the end will have come, the Messiah will at God's command come to the Pope and ask of him the liberation of his people, and only then will the Messiah be considered really to have come, but not before that."

Abulafia himself relates[28] that the Pope had given orders "when Raziel would come to Rome to confer with him in the name of Jewry, to arrest him and not to admit him into his presence at all, but to lead him out of town and there to burn him." But Abulafia, although informed of this, paid no attention, but rather gave himself up to his meditations and mystical preparations and on the strength of his visions wrote a book which he later called: "Book of Testimony," in remembrance of his miraculous rescue. For as he prepared himself to come before the Pope, "two mouths," as he obscurely expresses himself, grew on him, and when he entered the city-gate, he learned that the Pope—it was Nicholas III.—had suddenly died during the night. Abulafia was held in the College of the Franciscans for twenty-eight days, but was then set free.

Abulafia then wandered about Italy for a number of years. Of these he seems to have spent several in Sicily, where he remained longer than in any other place. Almost all his extant works were written during his Italian period, particularly between the years 1279 and 1291. We are altogether ignorant of his fate after the year 1291. Of his prophetic, or inspired, writings only his apocalypse, *Sefer ha-Oth,* the "Book of the Sign," a strange and not altogether comprehensible book, has survived.[29] On the other hand, most of his theoretical and doctrinal treatises are still extant, some of them in a considerable number of manuscripts.

He seems to have made many enemies by claiming prophetical inspiration and antagonizing his contemporaries in various other ways, for he very often complains of hostility and persecution. He mentions denunciations by Jews to Christian authorities[30], which may perhaps be explained by the fact that he represented himself as a prophet to Christians as well. He writes that he found among them some who believed more in God than the Jews to whom God had sent him first.[31] In two places Abulafia tells of his connection with non-Jewish mystics.[32] Once, he relates, he talked with them about the three methods of the interpretation of the Torah (literal, allegoric, and mystic), and he noted their agreement with one another when conversing with them confidentially "and I saw that they belong to the category of the 'pious of the gentiles', and that the words of the fools of whatever religion need not be heeded, for the Torah has been handed over to the masters of true knowledge."[33] Another time he tells of a dispute with a Christian scholar with whom he had made friends and in whose mind he had implanted the desire for the knowledge of the Name of God. "And it is not necessary to reveal more about it."[34]

These connections of Abulafia's do not, however, testify to a special inclination to Christian ideas as some scholars have assumed.[35] On the contrary, his antagonism to Christianity is very outspoken and intense.[36] He sometimes, indeed, intentionally makes use—among many other associations—of formulae which sound quite trinitarian, immediately giving them a meaning which has nothing whatsoever to do with the trinitarian idea of God.[37] But his predilection for paradox as well as his prophetic pretensions alienated from him the Kabbalists of a more strictly orthodox orientation. And indeed he acutely criticizes the Kabbalists of his times and their symbolism insofar as it is not backed by individual mystical experience.[38] On the other hand, some of his writings are devoted to the refutation of attacks directed against him by 'orthodox' Kabbalists.[39] But "poverty, exile, and imprisonment" were powerless to make Abulafia, a proud and unbending spirit, abandon the standpoint to which his personal experience of things divine had led him.

In the preface to one of his works, the main part of which has been lost, he compares his mission and his place among his contemporaries with that of the prophet Isaiah. He tells how a voice called him twice: "Abraham, Abraham" and, he continues, "I said: Here am I! Thereupon he instructed me in the right way, woke me from my slumber and inspired me to write something new. There had been nothing like it in my day." He realized only too well that his gospel would make enemies for him among the Jewish leaders.

Nevertheless he submitted to this "and I constrained my will and dared to reach beyond my grasp. They called me heretic and unbeliever because I had resolved to worship God in truth and not as those who walk in darkness. Sunken in the abyss, they and their kind would have delighted to engulf me in their vanities and their dark deeds. But God forbid that I should forsake the way of truth for that of falsehood."[40]

Yet for all his pride in the achievement of prophetic inspiration and his knowledge of the great Name of God, there was combined in his character meekness and a love of peace. Jellinek rightly points out that his moral character must be estimated very highly. When accepting desciples to his Kabbalah he is extremely fastidious in his requirements as to a high morality and steadiness of character and it may be concluded from his writings even in their ecstatic parts that he himself possessed many of the qualities he asked for in others.[41] He who gains the deepest knowledge of the true essentials of reality—so he says in one place—at the same time acquires the deepest humility and modesty.[42]

It is one of the many oddities of the history of modern research into Kabbalism that Abulafia, of all men, has sometimes been made out to be the anonymous author of the Zohar. This hypothesis, which still finds its supporters, was first advanced by M. H. Landauer, who—a hundred years ago—was the first to point to Abulafia at all. He says: "I found a strange man with whose writings the contents of the Zohar coincide most accurately down to the minutest details. This fact struck me at once with the first writing of his which came into my hands. But now that I have read many of his works and have come to know his life, his principles, and his character, there cannot exist any longer even the slightest doubt that we now have the author of the Zohar."[43] This seems to me an extraordinary example of how a judgment proclaimed with conviction as certainly true may nevertheless be entirely wrong in every detail. The truth is that no two things could be more different than the outlook of the Zohar and that of Abulafia.

4

I shall now try to give a brief synthetic description, one after the other, of the main points of his mystical theory, his doctrine of the search for ecstasy and for prophetic inspiration.[44] Its basic principles have been upheld with varying modifications by all those among the Kabbalists who found in Abulafia a congenial spirit, and its characteristic mixture of emotionalism and rationalism sets its seal on one of the main trends of Kabbalism.

Abulafia's aim, as he himself has expressed it, is "to unseal the soul, to untie the knots which bind it."[45] "All the inner forces and the hidden souls in man are distributed and differentiated in the bodies. It is, however, in the nature of all of them that when their knots are untied they return to their origin, which is one without any duality and which comprises the multiplicity."[46] The "untying" is, as it were, the return from multiplicity and separation towards the original unity. As a symbol of the great mystic liberation of the soul from the fetters of sensuality the "untying of the knots" occurs also in the theosophy of northern Buddhism. Only recently a French scholar published a Tibetan didactic tract the title of which may be translated: "Book on Untying Knots".[47]

What does this symbol mean in Abulafia's terminology? It means that there are certain barriers which separate the personal existence of the soul from the stream of cosmic life—personified for him in the *intellectus agens* of the philosophers, which runs through the whole of creation. There is a dam which keeps the soul confined within the natural and normal borders of human existence and protects it against the flood of the divine stream, which flows beneath it or all around it; the same dam, however, also prevents the soul from taking cognizance of the Divine. The "seals," which are impressed on the soul, protect it against the flood and guarantee its normal functioning. Why is the soul, as it were, sealed up? Because, answers Abulafia, the ordinary day-to-day life of human beings, their perception of the sensible world, fills and impregnates the mind with a multitude of sensible forms or images (called, in the language of mediaeval philosophers, "natural forms"). As the mind perceives all kinds of gross natural objects and admits their images into its consciousness, it creates for itself, out of this natural function, a certain mode of existence which bears the stamp of finiteness. The normal life of the soul, in other words, is kept within the limits determined by our sensory perceptions and emotions, and as long as it is full of these, it finds it extremely difficult to perceive the existence of spiritual forms and things divine. The problem, therefore, is to find a way of helping the soul to perceive more than the forms of nature, without its becoming blinded and overwhelmed by the divine light, and the solution is suggested by the old adage "whoever is full of himself has no room for God." All that which occupies the natural self of man must either be made to disappear or must be transformed in such a way as to render it transparent for the inner spiritual reality, whose contours will then become perceptible through the customary shell of natural things.

Abulafia, therefore, casts his eyes round for higher forms of perception which, instead of blocking the way to the soul's own deeper regions, facilitate access to them and throw them into relief. He wants the soul to concentrate on highly abstract spiritual matters, which will not encumber it by pushing their own particular importance into the foreground and thus render illusory the whole purpose of mental purgation. If, for instance, I observe a flower, a bird, or some other concrete thing or event, and begin to think about it, the object of my reflection has an importance or attractiveness of its own. I am thinking of this particular flower, bird, etc. Then how can the soul learn to visualize God with the help of objects whose nature is of such a sort as to arrest the attention of the spectator and deflect it from its purpose? The early Jewish mystic knows of no object of contemplation in which the soul immerses itself until it reaches a state of ecstasy, such as the Passion in Christian mysticism.

Abraham Abulafia is, therefore, compelled to look for an, as it were, absolute object for meditating upon; that is to say, one capable of stimulating the soul's deeper life and freeing it from ordinary perceptions. In other words, he looks for something capable of acquiring the highest importance, without having much particular, or if possible any, importance of its own. An object which fulfills all these conditions he believes himself to have found in the Hebrew alphabet, in the letters which make up the written language. It is not enough, though an important step forward, that the soul should be occupied with the meditation of abstract truths, for even there it remains too closely bound to their specific meaning. Rather is it Abulafia's purpose to present it with something not merely abstract but also not determinable as an object in the strict sense, for everything so determined has an importance and an individuality of its own. Basing himself upon the abstract and non-corporeal nature of script, he develops a theory of the mystical contemplation of letters and their configurations, as the constituents of God's name. For this is the real and, if I may say so, the peculiarly Jewish object of mystical contemplation: The Name of God, which is something absolute, because it reflects the hidden meaning and totality of existence; the Name through which everything else acquires its meaning and which yet to the human mind has no concrete, particular meaning of its own. In short, Abulafia believes that whoever succeeds in making this great Name of God, the least concrete and perceptible thing in the world, the object of his meditation, is on the way to true mystical ecstasy.[48]

Starting from this concept, Abulafia expounds a peculiar discipline which he calls *Hokhmath ha-Tseruf,* i. e. "science of the combination of letters." This is described as a methodical guide to meditation with the aid of letters and their configurations. The individual letters of their combinations need have no 'meaning' in the ordinary sense; it is even an advantage if they are meaningless, as in that case they are less likely to distract us. True, they are not really meaningless to Abulafia, who accepts the Kabbalistic doctrine of divine language as the substance of reality. According to this doctrine, as I have mentioned in the first lecture, all things exist only by virtue of their degree of participation in the great Name of God, which manifests itself throughout the whole Creation. There is a language which expresses the pure thought of God and the letters of this spiritual language are the elements both of the most fundamental spiritual reality and of the profoundest understanding and knowledge. Abulafia's mysticism is a course in this divine language.

The purpose of this discipline then is to stimulate, with the aid of methodical meditation, a new state of consciousness; this state can best be defined as an harmonious movement of pure thought, which has severed all relation to the senses. Abulafia himself has already quite correctly compared it with music. Indeed, the systematic practice of meditation as taught by him, produces a sensation closely akin to that of listening to musical harmonies. The science of combination is a music of pure thought, in which the alphabet takes the place of the musical scale. The whole system shows a fairly close resemblance to musical principles, applied not to sounds but to thought in meditation. We find here compositions and modifications of motifs and their combination in every possible variety. This is what Abulafia himself says about it in one of his unpublished writings: "Know that the method of *Tseruf* can be compared to music; for the ear hears sounds from various combinations, in accordance with the character of the melody and the instrument. Also, two different instruments can form a combination, and if the sounds combine, the listener's ear registers a pleasant sensation in acknowledging their difference. The strings touched by the right or left hand move, and the sound is sweet to the ear. And from the ear the sensation travels to the heart, and from the heart to the spleen (the centre of emotion), and enjoyment of the different melodies produces ever new delight. It is impossible to produce it except through the combination of sounds, and the same is true of the combination of letters. It touches the first string, which is comparable to the first letter, and proceeds to the second, third, fourth and fifth, and the various sounds combine. And the secrets, which express themselves in these combinations, delight the heart which acknowledges its God and is filled with ever fresh joy."[49]

The directed activity of the adept engaged in combining and separating the letters in his meditation, composing whole motifs on separate groups, combining several of them with one another and enjoying their combinations in every direction, is therefore for Abulafia not more senseless or incomprehensible than that of a composer. Just as—to quote Schopenhauer—the musician expresses in wordless sounds "the world once again," and ascends to endless heights and descends to endless depths, so the mystic: To him the closed doors of the soul open in the music of pure thought which is no longer bound to "sense," and in the ecstasy of the deepest harmonies which originate in the movement of the letters of the great Name, they throw open the way to God.

This science of the combination of letters and the practice of controlled meditation is, according to Abulafia, nothing less than the "mystical logic" which corresponds to the inner harmony of thought in its movement towards God.[50] The world of letters, which reveals itself in this discipline, is the true world of bliss.[51] Every letter represents a whole world to the mystic who abandons himself to its contemplation.[52] Every language, not only Hebrew, is transformed into a transcendental medium of the one and only language of God. And as every language issues from a corruption of the aboriginal language—Hebrew—they all remain related to it. In all his books Abulafia likes to play on Latin, Greek, or Italian words

to support his ideas. For, in the last resort, every spoken word consists of sacred letters, and the combination, separation and reunion
of letters reveal profound mysteries to the Kabbalist, and unravel to
him the secret of the relation of all languages to the holy tongue.[53]

5

Abulafia's great manuals, such as "The Book of Eternal Life,"[54]
"The Light of Intellect,"[55] "The Words of Beauty" and 'The Book
of Combination"[56] are systematic guides to the theory and practice
of this system of mystical counterpoint. Through its methodical exercise the soul is accustomed to the perception of higher forms with
which it gradually saturates itself. Abulafia lays down a method
which leads from the actual articulation of the permutations and
combinations, to their writing and to the contemplation of the written, and finally from writing to thinking and to the pure meditation of all these objects of the "mystical logic."

Articulation, *mivta*, writing, *miktav*, and thought, *mahshav*, thus
form three superimposed layers of meditation. Letters are the elements of every one of them, elements which manifest themselves in
ever more spiritual forms. From the motion of the letters of
thought result the truths of reason. But the mystic will not stop
here. He differentiates further between matter and form of the letters in order to approach closer to their spiritual nucleus; he immerses himself in the combinations of the pure forms of the letters,
which now, being purely spiritual forms, impress themselves upon
his soul. He endeavours to comprehend the connections between
words and names formed by the Kabbalistic methods of exegesis.[57]
The numerical value of words, *gematria*, is here of particular
importance.

To this must be added another point: the modern reader of
these writings will be most astonished to find a detailed description
of a method which Abulafia and his followers call *dillug* and *kefi-
tsah*, "jumping" or "skipping" viz., from one conception to another.
In fact this is nothing else than a very remarkable method of using
associations as a way of meditation. It is not wholly the "free play
of association" as known to psychoanalysis; rather it is the way of
passing from one association to another determined by certain rules
which are, however, sufficiently lax. Every "jump" opens a new
sphere, defined by certain formal, *not* material, characteristics.

Within this sphere the mind may freely associate. The "jumping" unites, therefore, elements of free and guided association and is said to assure quite extraordinary results as far as the "widening of the consciousness" of the initiate is concerned. The "jumping" brings to light hidden processes of the mind, "it liberates us from the prison of the natural sphere and leads us to the boundaries of the divine sphere." All the other, more simple, methods of meditation serve only as a preparation for this highest grade which contains and supersedes all the others.[58]

Abulafia describes in several places the preparations for meditation and ecstasy, as well as what happens to the adept at the height of rapture. The report of one of his disciples which I quote below, confirms his statements. Abulafia himself says in one place[59]:

"Be prepared for thy God, oh Israelite! Make thyself ready to direct thy heart to God alone. Cleanse the body and choose a lonely house where none shall hear thy voice. Sit there in thy closet and do not reveal thy secret to any man. If thou canst, do it by day in the house, but it is best if thou completest it during the night. In the hour when thou preparest thyself to speak with the Creator and thou wishest Him to reveal His might to thee, then be careful to abstract all thy thought from the vanities of this world. Cover thyself with thy prayer shawl and put *Tefillin* on thy head and hands that thou mayest be filled with awe of the Shekhinah which is near thee. Cleanse thy clothes, and, if possible, let all thy garments be white, for all this is helpful in leading the heart towards the fear of God and the love of God. If it be night, kindle many lights, until all be bright. Then take ink, pen and a table to thy hand and remember that thou art about to serve God in joy of the gladness of heart. Now begin to combine a few or many letters, to permute and to combine them until thy heart be warm. Then be mindful of their movements and of what thou canst bring forth by moving them. And when thou feelest that thy heart is already warm and when thou seest that by combinations of letters thou canst grasp new things which by human tradition or by thyself thou wouldst not be able to know and when thou art thus prepared to receive the influx of divine power which flows into thee, then turn all thy true thought to imagine the Name and His exalted angels in thy heart as if they were human beings sitting or standing about thee. And feel thyself like an envoy whom the king and his ministers are to send on a mission, and he is waiting to hear something about his mission from their lips, be it from the king himself, be it from his servants. Having imagined this very vividly, turn thy whole mind to understand with thy thoughts the many things which will come into thy heart through the letters imagined. Ponder them as a whole and in all their detail, like one to whom a parable or a dream is being related, or who meditates on a deep problem in a scientific book, and try thus to interpret what thou shalt hear that it may as far as possible accord with thy reason . . . And all this will happen to thee after having flung away tablet and quill or after they will have dropped from thee because of the intensity of thy thought. And know, the stronger the intellectual influx within thee, the weaker will become thy outer and thy inner parts. Thy whole body will be seized by an extremely strong trembling, so that thou wilt think that surely thou art about to die, because thy soul, overjoyed with its knowledge, will leave thy body. And be thou ready at this moment consciously to choose death, and then thou shalt know that thou hast come far enough to receive the influx. And then wishing to honor the glorious Name by serving it with the life of body and soul, veil thy face and be afraid to look at God. Then return to the matters of the body, rise and eat and drink a little, or refresh thyself with a pleasant odor, and restore thy spirit to its sheath until another time, and rejoice at thy lot and know that God loveth thee!"

By training itself to turn its back upon all natural objects and to live in the pure contemplation of the divine Name, the mind is gradually prepared for the final transformation. The seals, which keep it locked up in its normal state and shut off the divine light, are relaxed, and the mystic finally dispenses with them altogether. The hidden spring of divine life is released. But now that the mind has been prepared for it, this irruption of the divine influx does not overwhelm it and throw it into a state of confusion and self-abandonment. On the contrary, having climbed the seventh and last step of the mystical ladder,[60] and reached the summit, the mystic consciously perceives and becomes part of the world of divine light, whose radiance illuminates his thoughts and heals his heart. This is the stage of prophetic vision, in which the ineffable mysteries of the divine Name and the whole glory of its realm reveal themselves to the illuminate. Of them the prophet speaks in words which extoll the greatness of God and bear the reflection of His image.

Ecstasy, which Abulafia regards as the highest reward of mystical contemplation, is not, therefore, to be confused with semi-conscious raving and complete self-annihilation. These uncontrolled forms of ecstasy he treats with a certain disdain and even regards them as dangerous. Rationally prepared ecstasy, too, comes suddenly[61] and cannot be enforced, but when the bolts are shot back and the seals taken off, the mind is already prepared for the 'light of the intellect' which pours in. Abulafia, therefore, frequently warns against the mental and even physical dangers of unsystematic meditation and similar practices. In combining the letters, every one of which —according to the book *Yetsirah*—is co-ordinated to a special member of the body "one has to be most careful not to move a consonant or vowel from its position, for if he errs in reading the letter commanding a certain member, that member may be torn away and may change its place or alter its nature immediately and be transformed into a different shape so that in consequence that person may become a cripple."[62] In the account I am going to quote at the end Abulafia's disciple also mentions spasmodic distortions of the face.

Abulafia lays great emphasis on the newness and singularity of his prophecy. "Know that most of the vision which Raziel saw are based on the Name of God and its gnosis, and also on his new revelation which took place on earth now in his days and the like there was not from the time of Adam until his."[63] The prophets who draw from the knowledge of the true name, are at the same time, to his mind, the true lovers. The identity of prophecy with the love of God also finds its proof in the mysticism of numbers, and he who serves God out of pure love, is on the right path towards prophecy.[64] That is why the Kabbalists with whom the pure fear of God turns into love, are for him the genuine disciples of the prophets.[65]

6

In the opinion of Abulafia, his own doctrine of prophetic ecstasy is in the last resort nothing but the doctrine of prophecy advanced by the Jewish philosophers, more especially by Maimonides, who also defines prophecy as a temporary union of the human and the divine intellect, deliberately brought about through systematic preparation. The prophetic faculty, according to this doctrine, represents the union of the human intellect at the highest stage of its development, with a cosmic influence normally domiciled in the intelligible world, the so-called active intellect (*intellectus agens*). The influx of this active intellect into the soul manifests itself as prophetic vision. Abulafia is concerned to prove the substantial identity of this theory of prophecy, which was widely recognized in the Middle Ages, with his own doctrine.[66] These rationalizations cannot, however, obscure the fact that his teachings represent but a Judaized version of that ancient spiritual technique which has found its classical expression in the practices of the Indian mystics who follow the system known as *Yoga*. To cite only one instance out of many, an important part in Abulafia's system is played by the technique of breathing;[67] now this technique has found its highest development in the Indian *Yoga,* where it is commonly regarded as the most important instrument of mental discipline. Again, Abulafia lays down certain rules of body posture, certain corresponding combinations of consonants and vowels, and certain forms of recitation,[68] and in particular some passages of his book "The Light of the Intellect" give the impression of a Judaized treatise on *Yoga*. The similarity even extends to some aspects of the doctrine of ecstatic vision, as preceded and brought about by these practices.

For what is the reward of reaching this supreme stage of vision? We are repeatedly told by Abulafia that the visionary perceives the image of his spiritual mentor, usually visualized either as a young or as an old man, whom he not only sees but also hears.[69] "The body," Abulafia says, "requires the physician of the body, the soul the physician of the soul, to wit the students of the Torah, but the intellect (the highest power of the soul) requires a mover from outside who has received Kabbalah concerning the mysteries of the Torah and a mover from inside, *me'orer penimi,* who opens the closed doors before him."[70] Elsewhere too he differentiates between the human and the divine teacher. If need be, one could manage without the former: Abulafia assumes that his own writings may possibly replace an immediate contact between disciple and teacher,[71] yet by no means could one forego the spiritual teacher who confronts man at the secret gates of his soul. This spiritual mentor—in Indian terminology the *Guru*—personifies the *intellectus agens* through the mythical figure of the angel Metatron, but he is also, according to certain passages, God Himself as *Shaddai*.[72] Of Metatron, the Talmud says "his name is like the name of his master,"[73] the Hebrew word for master also signifying "teacher." Abulafia applies this statement to the relation between the visionary and his *Guru*, his spiritual teacher. Its significance is seen to lie in the fact that in the state of ecstasy, man becomes aware of his intrinsic relationship with God. Although he is apparently confronted with his master, he is yet in some way identical with him. The state of ecstasy, in other words, represents something like a mystical transfiguration of the individual. This experience of self-identification with one's guide or master, and indirectly with God, is mentioned several times by Abulafia, but nowhere does he write about it with complete and utter frankness.[74] The following passage, for instance, is taken from an unpublished fragment called *The Knowledge of the Messiah and the Meaning of the Redeemer*:[75]

"This science [of mystical combination] is an instrument which leads nearer to prophecy than any other discipline of learning. A man who gains his understanding of the essentials of reality from books is called *Hakham*, a scholar. If he obtains it from the Kabbalah, that is to say from one who has himself obtained it from the contemplation of the divine names or from another Kabbalist, then he is called *Mevin*, that is, one who has insight, but if his understanding is derived from his own heart, from reflecting upon what he knows of reality, then he is called *Daatan*, that is, a gnostic. He whose understanding is such as to combine all three, to wit, scholarly erudition, insight obtained from a genuine Kabbalist, and wisdom from reflecting deeply upon things, of him I am not indeed going to say that he deserves to be called a prophet, especially if he has not yet been touched by the pure intellect, or if touched [that is to say, in ecstasy] does not yet know by whom. If, however, he has felt the divine touch and perceived its nature, it seems right and proper to me and to every perfected man that he should be called 'master', because his name is like the Name of his Master, be it only in one, or in many, or in all of His Names. For now he is no longer separated from his Master, and behold he is his Master and his Master is he; for he is so intimately adhering to Him [it is here that the term *Devekuth* is used], that he cannot by any means be separated from Him, for he is He ["he is He" being a famous formula of advanced Moslem pantheism]. And just as his Master, who is detached from all matter, is called *Sekhel, Maskil* and *Muskal,* that is the *knowledge,* the *knower* and the *known,* all at the same time, since all three are one in Him,[76] so also he, the exalted man, the master of the exalted name, is called *intellect,* while he is actually knowing; then he is also *the known,* like his Master; and then there is no difference between them, except that his Master has His supreme rank by His own right and not derived from other creatures, while he is elevated to his rank by the intermediary of creatures."

In this supreme state, man and Torah become one. This Abulafia expresses very deftly when he supplements the old word from the "Sayings of the Fathers" about the Torah: "Turn it round and round, for everything is in it" by the words: "for it is wholly in thee and thou art wholly in it."[77]

To a certain extent, as we have seen, the visionary identifies himself with his Master; complete identification is neither achieved nor intended. All the same, we have here one of the most thoroughgoing interpretations of the meaning of ecstatic experience to which rabbinical Jewry has given birth. Hence the fact that nearly all Kabbalists who in everything else follow the steps of Abulafia, have as far as I can see recoiled from this remarkable doctrine of ecstatic identification. Let us take as an instance a little tract called *Sullam Ha-Aliyah,* "the Ladder of Ascent"—i. e., ascent to God—written in Jerusalem by a pious Kabbalist, Rabbi Jehudah Albottini, or Albuttaini one of the exiles of Spain. It contains a brief statement of Abulafia's doctrine, and its tenth chapter, which I once had an occasion to publish, describes "the paths of loneliness and the preliminaries of adhesion *(devekuth)"*; in other words, the theory of ecstaticism.[78] But nowhere does it make the slightest mention of those radical consequences of Abulafia's methods and of the images employed by him, although for the rest its description is interesting and impressive enough.

The content of ecstasy is defined by the followers of prophetic Kabbalism by yet another and even stranger term which deserves, for the unexpected turn it takes, the special attention of the psychologist. According to this definition, in prophetic ecstasy man encounters his own self confronting and addressing him. This occult experience was estimated higher than the visions of light usually accompanying ecstasy.[79] The Midrash says of the anthropomorphic utterances of the prophets: Great is the strength of the prophets who assimilate the form to Him who formed it,[80] that is to say who compare man to God. Some Kabbalists of Abulafia's school, however, interpret this sentence differently. The form being compared to its creator, i. e., being of divine nature, is the pure spiritual self of man departing from him during prophecy. The following fine passage has been conserved by a collector of Kabbalistic traditions:[81] "Know that the complete secret of prophecy consists for the prophet in that he suddenly sees the shape of his self standing before him and he forgets his self and it is disengaged from him and he sees the shape of his self before him talking to him and predicting the future, and of this secret our teachers said: Great is the strength of the prophets who compare the form [appearing to them] to Him who formed it. Says Rabbi Abraham ibn Ezra: 'In prophecy the one who hears is a human being and the one who speaks is a human being.'[82] . . . And another scholar writes: 'I know and I understand with absolute certainty that I am neither a prophet nor the son of a prophet, that the holy spirit is not in me and that I have no power over the "divine voice"; for of all these things I have not been found worthy, for I did not take off my dress nor did I wash my feet—and yet I call heaven and earth to witness that one day I sat and wrote down a Kabbalistic secret; suddenly I saw the shape of my self standing before me and myself disengaged from me and I was forced to stop writing!" This explanation of the occult character of prophecy as self-confrontation sounds like a mystical interpretation of the old Platonic prescript: "Recognize thyself", as "Behold thy self."

The state of ecstasy as described by Abulafia, frequently, so it seems, on the basis of personal experience, also carries with it something like an anticipatory redemption. The illuminate feels himself not only aglow with a heavenly fire, but also as it were anointed with sacred and miraculous oil. He becomes, as Abulafia puts it, by playing upon the double meaning of the Hebrew word *Mashiah,* the Lord's anointed.[83] He is, so to speak, his own Messiah, at least for the brief period of his ecstatical experience.

7

Abulafia calls his method "The Path of the Names," in contrast to the Kabbalists of his time, whose doctrine concerning the realization of the divine attributes it referred to as "The Path of the Sefiroth."[84] Only together the two paths from the whole of the Kabbalah, the Path of the Sefiroth the 'rabbinical' and that of the Names the 'prophetic' Kabbalah. The student of Kabbalah is to begin with the contemplation of the ten Sefiroth.[85] These, indeed, during meditation are to become objects of quickened imagination rather than objects of an external knowledge acquired by merely learning their names as attributes or even symbols of God.[86] For in the Sefiroth, too, according to Abulafia, there are revealed the 'profundities of the *intellectus agens*', that cosmic power which for the mystic coincides with the splendor of the Shekhinah.[87] Only from there is he to proceed to the twenty-two letters which represent a deeper stage of penetration.

For what he calls the Path of the Names, the ancient Jewish Gnostics, as we have seen, employed another term, namely *Maaseh Merkabah,* literally translated "The Work of the Chariot," because of the Celestial chariot which was supposed to carry the throne of God the Creator. Abulafia, with his penchant for playing upon words, introduces his new doctrine as the true *Maaseh Merkabah*— a term which can also be taken to mean "combination". The theory of combining the letters and names of God—that is the true vision of the Merkabah.[88] It is true that where he describes the seven stages of knowledge of the Torah, from the inquiry into the literal meaning of the word to the stage of prophecy, he draws a distinction between prophetic Kabbalism, which is the sixth stage, and the holy of holies to which it is merely the preliminary. The substance of this final stage, in which "the language which comes from the active intellect" is understood, may not be divulged even if it were possible to clothe it in words.[89] But as we have seen, Abulafia himself, despite this solemn vow, has lifted a corner of the veil.

It remains to be said that Abulafia is far from despising philosophical knowledge. Indeed, he even says in one place that philosophy and Kabbalah both owe their existence to the active intellect, with the difference that Kabbalism represents a more profound manifestation of the spirit and probes into a deeper and more spiritual region.[90] At the same time, however, he is definitely of the opinion that certain philosophical problems are meaningless, except insofar as they serve to lead the mind astray. It is interesting to hear his comment on the dispute concerning the supposed eternity or non-eternity of the universe, by and large one of the main issues of Jewish philosophy in its struggle against pure Aristotelianism. The fact that the Torah advances no proof for either contention is explained by Abulafia by remarking that from the point of view of prophetic Kabbalism, itself the crowning achievement of the Torah, the whole question is meaningless. "The prophet, after all, demands nothing from the Torah except that which helps him to reach the stage of prophecy. What then does it mean to him whether the world is eternal or created, since its eternity can neither advance his development nor take anything away from him. And the same is true of the hypothesis that the world came into existence at a given moment."[91] Religious importance attaches solely to that which contributes to man's perfection, and that is above all else the Path of the Names. Although Abulafia himself denies the eternity of the world,[92] he is inclined to adopt a strictly pragmatic attitude and to dismiss the whole argument as sterile.

In short, Abulafia is before all else what one might call an eminently practical Kabbalist. It is true that in Kabbalistic parlance 'Practical Kabbalism' means something entirely different. It simply means magic, though practised by means which do not come under a religious ban, as distinct from black magic, which uses demonic powers and probes into sinister regions. The fact is, however, that this consecrated form of magic, which calls out the tremendous powers of the names, is not very far removed from Abulafia's method; if the sources from which he drew the elements of his doctrine are investigated more closely—a task which is outside the scope of this lecture—it becomes plain that all of them, both the Jewish and the non-Jewish, are in fact closely connected with magical traditions and disciplines. This is true both of the ideas of the mediaeval German Hasidim, which seem to have made a deep impression upon him,[93] and of the tradition of *Yoga* which in devious ways had also influenced certain Moslem mystics, and with which he may have become acquainted during his Oriental travels. But it is no less true that Abulafia himself has decisively rejected magic and condemned in advance all attempts to use the doctrine of the holy names for magical purposes. In countless polemics he condemns magic as a falsification of true mysticism;[94] he does admit a magic directed towards one's own self, a magic of inwardness—I think that is the general name one could give to his doctrine—but none which aims at bringing about external sensory results, even though the means may be inward, permissible and even sacred. Such magic is possible, according to Abulafia, but he who practices it is accursed.[95] Already in his first known work Abulafia maintains that conjuration of demons, although as a matter of fact based on a delusive fantasy, was just good enough to strike the rabble with a healthy terror of religion.[96] Elsewhere he warns against the use of the "Book of Creation" for the purpose of creating to oneself—in the words of the Talmud—a fat calf. They who want this, he says bluntly, are themselves calves.[97]

Abulafia has resolutely taken the path that leads inwards, and I think one can say he has pursued it as far as anybody in latter-day Jewry. But this path runs along the border between mysticism and magic, and for all the irreconcilable difference that appears to exist between the two, their interrelation is more profound than is usually taken for granted. There are certain points at which the belief of the mystic easily becomes that of the magician, and Abulafia's magic of inwardness, which I have just outlined, is one of them. Although he himself escaped the danger of sliding insensibly from the meditative contemplation of the holy names into magical practices aimed at external objects, many of his successors fell into confusion and tended to expect from the inward path the power to change the outer world. The magician's dream of power and lordship over nature by mere words and strained intention, found its dreamers in the Ghetto also and formed manifold combinations with the theoretical and practical interests of mysticism proper. Historically, Kabbalism presents itself almost invariably as a combination of the two. Abulafia's doctrine of combination (*Hokhmath ha-Tseruf*) came to be regarded by later generations as the key not only to the mysteries of Divinity but also to the exercise of magical powers.

In the literature of the 14th to 16th centuries on the *Hokhmath ha-Tseruf* we find a blend of ecstatic and theosophic Kabbalism. Thus for instance a writing of this character could even be ascribed to Maimonides who appears here as a practical magician and thaumaturge.⁹⁸ And thus instructions concerning meditation on the different possibilities of vocalizing the Tetragrammaton are given in the very awkward book *Berith Menuhah*, "Order of Calmness", which was almost the only one of these books to be printed.⁹⁹ These instructions concerning meditation describe the lights flashing up in the soul of the devotee, but at the same time dwell rather extensively on the magical application of the names of God. Yet in the two great works of the Kabbalist Josef ibn Sayah of Jerusalem, which were composed about 1540 and which we possess in manuscript, both sides of this Jewish Yoga are brought into a system and pushed to excess: meditation endeavoring to reveal ever deeper layers of the soul and more of its secret lights, and magical application of the forces of the soul thus revealed by inward meditation.¹⁰⁰

Finally, it may be interesting to note, that in the writings of some Kabbalists the Great Name of God appears as the supreme object of meditation in the last hour of the martyrs. In a powerful speech of the great mystic Abraham ben Eliezer Halevi of Jerusalem (died about 1530) we find a recommendation to those who face martyrdom. He advises them to concentrate, in the hour of their last ordeal, on the Great Name of God; to imagine its radiant letters between their eyes and to fix all their attention on it. Whoever does this, will not feel the burning flames or the tortures to which he is subjected. "And although this may seem improbable to human reason, it has been experienced and transmitted by the holy martyrs."¹⁰¹

8

Of the attractive power of these ideas and practices we possess a very precious testimonial. An anonymous disciple of Abulafia's wrote a book in 1295, apparently in Palestine, in which he set forth the basic ideas of prophetic Kabbalism.¹⁰² Discussing three paths of "expansion", i. e. of the progress of the spirit from corporeality to an ever purer spiritual apprehension of objects, he has interpolated an autobiographical account. In it he describes very accurately and without doubt reliably his own development, as well as his experiences with Abulafia and the latter's Kabbalah. He does not name Abulafia, but from the description he gives and the kindred ideas he employs, there can be no doubt to whom he alludes. This book is called *Shaare Tsedek*, "Gates of Justice." Four manuscripts of it are extant. But only two of them[103] contain this autobiographical account which obviously in the other two has fallen a prey to that previously mentioned self-censorship of the Kabbalists who are adverse to confessions of an all too intimate character concerning mystical experiences, and before whom the author deems it necessary to apologize for his candor.

I believe it will be a good illustration for what I have been saying if I give the main parts of this account, which in my opinion, is of extraordinary psychological interest.[104]

"I, so and so, one of the lowliest, have probed my heart for ways of grace to bring about spiritual expansion and I have found three ways of progress to spiritualization: the vulgar, the philosophic, and the Kabbalistic way. The vulgar way is that which, so I learned, is practiced by Moslem ascetics. They employ all manner of devices to shut out from their souls all 'natural forms', every image of the familiar, natural world. Then, they say, when a spiritual form, an image from the spiritual world, enters their soul, it is isolated in their imagination and intensifies the imagination to such a degree that they can determine beforehand that which is to happen to us. Upon inquiry, I learned that they summon the Name, ALLAH, as it is in the language of Ishmael. I investigated further and I found that, when they pronounce these letters, they direct their thought completely away from every possible 'natural form', and the very letters ALLAH and their diverse powers work upon them. They are carried off into a trance without realizing how, since no Kabbalah has been transmitted to them. This removal of all natural forms and images from the soul is called with them *Effacement*.[105]

"The second way is the philosophic, and the student will experience extreme difficulty in attempting to drive it from his soul because of the great sweetness it holds for the human reason and the completeness with which that reason knows to embrace it. It consists in this: That the student forms a notion of some science, mathematics for instance, and then proceeds by analogy to some natural science and then goes on to theology. He then continues further to circle round this centre of his, because of the sweetness of that which arises in him as he progresses in these studies. The sweetness of this so delights him that he finds neither gate nor door to enable him to pass beyond the notions which have already been established in him. At best, he can perhaps enjoy a [contemplative] spinning out of his thoughts and to this he will abandon himself, retiring into seclusion in order that no one may disturb his thought until it proceed a little beyond the purely philosophic and turn as the flaming sword which turned every way. The true cause of all this is also to be found in his contemplation of the letters through which, as intermediaries, he ascertains things. The subject which impressed itself on his human reason dominates him and his power seems to him great in all the sciences, seeing that this is natural to him [i. e. thus to ascertain them]. He contends that given things are revealed to him by way of prophecy, although he does not realize the true cause, but rather thinks that this occured to him merely because of the extension and enlargement of his human reason . . . But in reality it is the letters ascertained through thought and imagination, which influence him through their motion and which concentrate his thought on difficult themes, although he is not aware of this.

"But if you put the difficult question to me: 'Why do we nowadays pronounce letters and move them and try to produce effects with them without however noticing any effect being produced by them?'—the answer lies, as I am going to demonstrate with the help of *Shaddai,* in the third way of inducing spiritualization. And I, the humble so and so, am going to tell you what I experienced in this matter.

"Know, friends, that from the beginning I felt a desire to study Torah and learned a little of it and of the rest of Scripture. But I found no one to guide me in the study of the Talmud, not so much because of the lack of teachers, but rather because of my longing for my home, and my love for father and mother. At last, however, God gave me strength to search for the Torah, I went out and sought and found, and for several years I stayed abroad studying Talmud. But the flame of the Torah kept glowing within me, though without my realizing it.

"I returned to my native land and God brought me together with a Jewish philosopher with whom I studied some of Maimonides' "Guide of the Perplexed" and this only added to my desire. I acquired a little of the science of logic and a little of natural science, and this was very sweet to me for, as you know, 'nature attracts nature.' And God is my witness: If I had not previously acquired strength of faith by what little I had learned of the Torah and the Talmud, the impulse to keep many of the religious commands would have left me although the fire of pure intention was ablaze in my heart. But what this teacher communicated to me in the way of philosophy [on the meaning of the commandments], did not suffice me, until the Lord had me meet a godly man, a Kabbalist who taught me the general outlines of the Kabbalah. Nevertheless, in consequence of my smattering of natural science, the way of Kabbalah seemed all but impossible to me. It was then that my teacher said to me: 'My son, why do you deny something you have not tried? Much rather would it befit you to make a trial of it. If you then should find that it is nothing to you—and if you are not perfect enough to find the fault with yourself—then you may say that there is nothing to it.' But, in order to make things sweet to me until my reason might accept them and I might penetrate into them with eagerness, he used always to make me grasp in a natural way everything in which he instructed me. I reasoned thus within myself: There can only be gain here and no loss. I shall see; if I find something in all of this, that is sheer gain; and if not, that which I have already had will still be mine. So I gave in and he taught me the method of the permutations and combinations of letters and the mysticism of numbers and the other 'Paths of the book *Yetsirah*.' In each path he had me wander for two weeks until each form had been engraven in my heart, and so he led me on for four months or so and then ordered me to 'efface' everything.

"He used to tell me: 'My son, it is not the intention that you come to a stop with some finite or given form, even though it be of the highest order. Much rather is this the "Path of the Names": The less understandable they are, the higher their order, until you arrive at the activity of a force which is no longer in your control, but rather your reason and your thought is in its control. I replied: 'If that be so [that all mental and sense images must be effaced], why then do you, Sir, compose books in which the methods of the natural scientists are coupled with instruction in the holy Names?'[106] He answered: 'For you and the likes of you among the followers of philosophy, to allure your human intellect through natural means, so that perhaps this attraction may cause you to arrive at the knowledge of the Holy Name.' And he produced books for me made up of [combinations of] letters and names and mystic num-

bers [*Gematrioth*], of which nobody will ever be able to understand anything for they are not composed in a way meant to be
understood. He said to me: 'This is the [undefiled] Path of the
Names.' And indeed, I would see none of it as my reason did not
accept it. He said: 'It was very stupid of me to have shown them
to you.'

"In short, after two months had elapsed and my thought had
disengaged itself [from everything material] and I had become
aware of strange phenomena occurring within me, I set myself the
task at night of combining letters with one another and of ponder-
ing over them in philosophical meditation, a little different from
the way I do now, and so I continued for three nights without telling him. The third night, after midnight, I nodded off a little, quill
in hand and paper on my knees. Then I noticed that the candle
was about to go out. I rose to put it right, as oftentimes happens to
a person awake. Then I saw that the light continued. I was greatly
astonished, as though, after close examination, I saw that it issued
from myself. I said: 'I do not believe it.' I walked to and fro all
through the house and, behold, the light is with me; I lay on a
couch and covered myself up, and behold, the light is with me all
the while. I said: 'This is truly a great sign and a new phenomenon
which I have perceived.'

"The next morning I communicated it to my teacher and I
brought him the sheets which I had covered with combinations of
letters. He congratulated me and said: 'My son, if you would devote
yourself to combining holy Names, still greater things would happen to you. And now, my son, admit that you are unable to bear
not combining. Give half to this and half to that, that is, do combinations half of the night, and permutations half of the night.' I practiced this method for about a week. During the second week the
power of meditation became so strong in me that I could not manage to write down the combinations of letters [which automatically
spurted out of my pen], and if there had been ten people present
they would not have been able to write down so many combinations
as came to me during the influx. When I came to the night in which
this power was conferred on me, and midnight—when this power
especially expands and gains strength whereas the body weakens—
had passed, I set out to take up the Great Name of God, consisting
of seventy-two names, permuting and combining it.[107] But when I

had done this for a little while, behold, the letters took on in my eyes the shape of great mountains, strong trembling seized me and I could summon no strength, my hair stood on end, and it was as if I were not in this world. At once 1 fell down, for I no longer felt the least strength in any of my limbs. And behold, something resembling speech emerged from my heart and came to my lips and forced them to move. I thought—perhaps this is, God forbid, a spirit of madness that has entered into me? But behold, I saw it uttering wisdom. I said: 'This is indeed the spirit of wisdom.' After a little while my natural strength returned to me, I rose very much impaired and I still did not believe myself. Once more I took up the Name to do with it as before and, behold, it had exactly the same effect on me. Nevertheless I did not believe until I had tried it four or five times.

"When I got up in the morning I told my teacher about it. He said to me: 'And who was it that allowed you to touch the Name? Did I not tell you to permute only letters?' He spoke on: 'What happened to you, represents indeed a high stage among the prophetic degrees.' He wanted to free me of it for he saw that my face had changed. But 1 said to him: 'In heaven's name, can you perhaps impart to me some power to enable me to bear this force emerging from my heart and to receive influx from it?' For I wanted to draw this force towards me and receive influx from it, for it much resembles a spring filling a great basin with water. If a man [not being properly prepared for it] should open the dam, he would be drowned in its waters and his soul would desert him. He said to me: 'My son, it is the Lord who must bestow such power upon you for such power is not within man's control."

"That Sabbath night also the power was active in me in the same way. When, after two sleepless nights, I had passed day and night in meditating on the permutations or on the principles essential to a recognition of this true reality and to the annihilation of all extraneous thought—then I had two signs by which I knew that I was in the right receptive mood. The one sign was the intensification of natural thought on very profound objects of knowledge, a debility of the body and strengthening of the soul until 1 sat there, my self all soul. The second sign was that imagination grew strong within me and it seemed as though my forehead were going to burst. Then I knew that I was ready to receive the Name. I also that

Sabbath night ventured at the great ineffable Name of God [the name JHWH]. But immediately that I touched it, it weakened me and a voice issued from me saying: 'Thou shalt surely die and not live! Who brought thee to touch the Great Name?' And behold, immediately I fell prone and implored the Lord God saying: 'Lord of the universe! I entered into this place only for the sake of Heaven, as Thy glory knoweth. What is my sin and what my transgression? I entered only to know Thee, for has not David already commanded Solomon: Know the God of thy father and serve Him; and has not our master Moses, peace be upon him, revealed this to us in the Torah saying: Show me now Thy way, that I may know Thee, that I may there find grace in Thy sight?' And behold, I was still speaking and oil like the oil of the anointment anointed me from head to foot and very great joy seized me which for its spirituality and the sweetness of its rapture I cannot describe.

"All this happened to your servant in his beginnings. And I do not, God forbid, relate this account from boastfulness in order to be thought great in the eyes of the mob, for I know full well that greatness with the mob is deficiency and inferiority with those searching for the true rank which differs from it in genus and in species as light from darkness.

"Now, if some of our own philosophizers, sons of our people who feel themselves attracted towards the naturalistic way of knowledge and whose intellectual power in regard to the mysteries of the Torah is very weak, read this, they will laugh at me and say: See how he tries to attract our reason with windy talk and tales, with fanciful imaginations which have muddled his mind and which he takes at their face value because of his weak mental hold on natural science. Should however Kabbalists see this, such as have some grasp of this subject or even better such as have had things divulged to them in experiences of their own, they will rejoice and my words will win their favor. But their difficulty will be that I have disclosed all of this in detail. Nevertheless, God is my witness that my intention is *in majorem dei gloriam* and I would wish that every single one of our holy nation were even more excellent herein and purer than I. Perhaps it would then be possible to reveal things of which I do not as yet know . . . As for me, I cannot bear not to give generously to others what God has bestowed upon me. But since for this science there is no naturalistic evidence, its premises being as spiritual as are its inferences, I was forced to tell this story of the experience that befell me. Indeed, there is no proof in this science except experience itself . . . That is why I say, to the man who contests this path, that I can give him an experimental proof, namely, my own evidence of the spiritual results of my own experiences in the science of letters according to the book *Yetsirah*. I did not, to be sure, experience the corporeal [magic] effects [of such practices]; and even granting the possibility of such a form of experience, I for my part want none of it, for it is an inferior form, especially when measured by the perfection which the soul can attain spiritually. Indeed, it seems to me that he who attempts to secure these [magic] effects desecrates God's name, and it is this that our teachers hint at when they say: Since licence prevailed, the name of God has been taught only to the most reticent priests.[108]

"The third is the Kabbalistic way. It consists of an amalgamation in the soul of man of the principles of mathematical and of natural science, after he has first studied the literal meanings of the Torah and of the faith, in order thus through keen dialectics to train his mind and not in the manner of a simpleton to believe in everything. Of all this he stands in need only because he is held captive by the world of nature. For it is not seemly that a rational being held captive in prison should not search out every means, a hole or a small fissure, of escape. If today we had a prophet who showed us a mechanism for sharpening the natural reason and for discovering there subtle forms by which to divest ourselves of corporeality, we should not need all these natural sciences in addition to our Kabbalah which is derived from the basic principles or heads of chapters of the book *Yetsirah* concerning the letters [and their combinations] . . . For the prophet would impart to us the secrets of the combination of consonants and of the combination of vowels between them, the paths by which the secret and active powers emanate, and the reason that this emanation is sometimes hindered from above . . . All this he would convey to us directly whereas now we are forced to take circuitous routes and to move about restrainedly and go out and come in on the change that God may confront us. For as a matter of fact every attainment in this science of Kabbalah looked at from its point of view is only a chance, even though, for us, it be the very essence of our being.[109]

"This Kabbalistic way, or method, consists, first of all, in the cleansing of the body itself, for the bodily is symbolic of the spiritual. Next in the order of ascent is the cleansing of your bodily disposition and your spiritual propensities, especially that of anger, or your concern for anything whatsoever except the Name itself, be it even the care for your only beloved son; and this is the secret of the Scripture that 'God tried Abraham.' A further step in the order of ascent is the cleansing of one's soul from all other sciences which one has studied. The reason for this is that being naturalistic and limited, they contaminate the soul, and obstruct the passage through it of the divine forms. These forms are extremely subtle; and though even a minor form is something innately great in comparison with the naturalistic and the rational, it is nevertheless an unclean, thick veil in comparison with the subtlety of the spirit. On this account seclusion in a separate house is prescribed, and if this be a house in which no [outside] noise can be heard, the better. At the beginning it is advisable to decorate the house with fresh greens in order to cheer the vegetable soul which a man possesses side by side with his animal soul. Next, one should pray and sing psalms in a pleasant melodious voice, and [read] the Torah with fervor, in order to cheer the animal soul which a man possesses side by side with his rational soul. Next, one directs his imagination to intelligible things and to understanding how one thing proceeds from another. Next, one proceeds to the moving of letters which [in their combinations] are unintelligible, thus to detach the soul [from the senses] and to cleanse it of all the forms formerly within it. In the same way one proceeds with the improvement of his [bodily] matter by meat and drink, and improves it [the body] by degrees. As to the moving of letters we shall deal with some methods in the chapter 'Letters.' Next, one reaches the stage of 'skipping' as Scripture says, 'and his banner over me was love.'¹¹⁰ It consists of one's meditating, after all operations with the letters are over, on the essence of one's thought, and of abstracting from it every word, be it connected with a notion or not. In the performance of this 'skipping' one must put the consonants which one is combining into a swift motion. This motion heats the thinking and so increases joy and desire, that craving for food and sleep or anything else is annihilated. In abstracting words from thought during contemplation, you force yourself so that you pass beyond the control of your natural mind and if you desire *not* to think, you cannot carry out your desire. You then guide your thinking step by step, first by means of script and language and then by means of imagination. When, however, you pass beyond the control of your thinking, another exercise becomes necessary which consists in drawing thought gradually forth—during contemplation—from its source until through sheer force that stage is reached where you do not speak nor can you speak. And if sufficient strength remains to force oneself even further and draw it out still farther, then that which is within will manifest itself without, and through the power of sheer imagination will take on the form of a polished mirror. And this is 'the flame of the circling sword', the rear revolving and becoming the fore. Whereupon one sees that his inmost being is something outside of himself.[111] Such was the way of the *Urim* and *Tummim,* the priest's oracle of the Torah, in which, too, at first the letters shine from inside and the message they convey is not an immediate one nor arranged in order, but results only from the right combination of the letters. For a form, detached from its essence, is defective until it clothe itself in a form which can be conceived by imagination, and in this imaginable form the letters enter into a complete, orderly and understandable combination. And it seems to me that it is this form which the Kabbalists call 'clothing', *malbush.*"[112]

THE ZOHAR
I. THE BOOK AND ITS AUTHOR

I

In the years immediately following 1275, while Abraham Abulafia was expounding his doctrine of prophetic Kabbalism in Italy, a book was written somewhere in the heart of Castile which was destined to overshadow all other documents of Kabbalist literature by the success and the fame it achieved and the influence it gradually exerted; this was the *Sefer Ha-Zohar,* or "Book of Splendor." Its place in the history of Kabbalism can be gauged from the fact that alone among the whole of post-Talmudic rabbinical literature it became a canonical text, which for a period of several centuries actually ranked with the Bible and the Talmud. This unique position, however, was only achieved gradually. It took the better part of two centuries to raise the Zohar from the comparative obscurity of its early beginnings to the foremost eminence in Kabbalistic literature. Moreover, there is little doubt that its author, whoever he may have been, had nothing so far-reaching in mind. Everything goes to suggest that when writing the Zohar his primary object was simply to find a congenial expression for his thought. His mind was completely immersed in the world of Kabbalistic thought, but the manner in which he deals with the subject bears the imprint of his own personality, much as he tried to obscure the personal aspect. As a writer, he can claim to have achieved his object, for whatever one may think of the book's merits, it was undeniably a success, first among the Kabbalists and later, particularly after the exodus from Spain, among the whole Jewish people. For centuries it stood out as the expression of all that was profoundest and most deeply hidden in the innermost recesses of the Jewish soul. The story is told of Rabbi Phineas of Koretz, a famous Hasidic saint (died about 1791), who was wont to praise and thank God because he had not been born while the Zohar was still unknown to the world; *"denn der Zohar hot mich derhalten bei Yiddishkeit* (for the Zohar has helped me to remain a Jew.) "¹ Such a remark, coming from such a man, sets one thinking, for the Zohar is perhaps the classical example of that mythical reaction in the heart of Judaism which I have mentioned in the first lecture. If notwithstanding this fact a great many Jewish mystics have felt it to be the expression of their deepest emotions and volitions, we shall have to ask ourselves in what the secret of its influence consisted and why the same success was denied to other documents of mystical literature.

The Zohar is written in pseudepigraphic form, almost, one might say, in the form of a mystical novel. In itself, this is not a new departure in style, for the pseudepigraphic form had been employed by many previous writers, including Kabbalists. Already the authors of the Book *Bahir* made use of the device and spoke through the mouths of older authorities—some of them mere names of fiction, such as Rabbi Amora or Rabbi Rehumai. But neither before nor since has any Kabbalist shown anything like the same delight in letting his fancy elaborate upon the details of his mystification. Against the background of an imaginative Palestinian setting, the famous Mishnah teacher, Rabbi Simeon ben Yohai, is seen wandering about with his son Eleazar, his friends and his disciples, and discoursing with them on all manner of things human and divine. The literary method employed is modelled on that of the Midrash, that is to say, where possible it avoids theoretical, let alone systematic, disquisition; preference is given to homiletics. Its favorite way of putting forward an idea is to work at the mystical interpretation of a Scriptural saying. As a stylist the author is inclined to be verbose and long-winded in contrast to the terse and pregnant style of true Midrash. Where he employs the pointed language of the ancient sages he is usually less successful than they in making himself understood. Often several discourses are skilfully worked into the pattern of a longer story. The whole of these shorter or longer discourses, stories and monologues is assembled in the form of a Midrash to the Torah, the Song of Songs and the Book of Ruth. But because its parts are strung on a selection of Scriptural sayings chosen at random and as best suited to serve as vehicles for the writer's own train of thought, it is very far from constituting anything like a real commentary. It remains to be added that from the point of view of style, a highly effective ingredient is supplied by the solemn Aramaic language of the book.

I have already said that the author is a homiletical rather than a systematic thinker. In this, however, he is at one with a deeply rooted tendency in Jewish thought. The more genuinely and characteristically Jewish an idea or doctrine is, the more deliberately unsystematic is it. Its principle of construction is not that of a logical system. Even the Mishnah, which comes nearest to presenting an orderly array of thought, reflects this lack of systematization. True, there have been attempts to express Kabbalistic thought in systematic form; indeed, most of the fundamental ideas found in the Zohar were expressed only a little later in a systematically constructed treatise, *Maarekheth Ha-Elohuth*, "The Order of God."³ But how dry and lifeless are these bare skeletons of thought compared with the flesh and blood of the Zohar! To repeat, the Zohar does not so much develop an idea as it applies it in a homily, and it must be said that the author is distinctly a genius of homiletical thought. Under his touch the most unpretentious verses of Scripture acquire an entirely unexpected meaning. As David Neumark, that searching historian of Jewish philosophy, once said, even the critical reader is occasionally plagued by doubts whether the true interpretation of certain passages of the Torah may not after all be found here and nowhere else! Frequently the author loses himself in mystical allegorizations, and not infrequently he becomes abstruse, but again and again a hidden and sometimes awful depth opens before our eyes, and we find ourselves confronted with real and profound insight. His style, tortuous on other occasions, is then lightened up by a magnificent clarity of expression, by a profound symbol of that world into whose hidden regions his mind has so deeply penetrated.

I have spoken of an "author" of the Zohar and therefore assumed his existence, but we must now turn to the question whether there ever was a single author. On this subject it is still possible to hear widely divergent views. Was there one author or were there several? Was the Zohar the work of many generations, or at any rate a compilation from more than one author, rather than the work of one man? Do its several parts, of which we shall presently hear more, correspond to different strata or periods? In short, we have to face the crucial questions of "higher criticism": What can be said to be known about the compilation of the Zohar, the time of its writing and its author or authors? I have spent many years trying to lay a stable foundation for critical work of this kind, and it seems to me that in so doing I have arrived at a number of incontrovertible conclusions.[3] Research work of this kind has something of the character of a detective story, but fascinating though it is, at least to me, this is not the place to describe it in detail. What I propose to do in this lecture is to give as precise an account as possible of my views on the subject and the manner in which I have arrived at my final conclusions.

To begin briefly with the latter, I have come to accept in substance the contention of Graetz—itself only the most articulate expression of a whispered tradition of centuries—that the Spanish Kabbalist Moses de Leon must be regarded as the author of the Zohar. The fact that Graetz was in a surprisingly large number of respects unable to supply satisfactory proof of his theory[4] has facilitated the more general acceptance of the contrary view, very common now, viz., that the Zohar represents only a final edition of writings composed over a long period—so long as to make it seem possible that they still contain rudiments of the original mystical thought of Simeon ben Yohai.[5] I may say that when I began to study the Zohar twenty years ago, I also inclined to this view,[6] as is probably the case with everyone who reads the Zohar for the first time (not to mention those who read it only once in their lives). But in the attempt to base my preference for this explanation on solid philological grounds, I gradually became convinced that I had been on the wrong track.[7]

2

At first sight, the existence of a multitude of writings of apparently very different character, loosely assembled under the title of "Zohar," seems to leave no argument against the view that they do in fact belong to different writers and different periods. Our first task, therefore, must be to examine more closely the major components which make up the five full volumes of the "Zoharic literature."[8] These may be summarized under the following heads:

a) A bulky part which has no specific title and is wholly composed of discursive commentaries on various passages from the Torah.

Everything that I have said of the literary character of the Zohar applies fully to this part, in which discourses, discussions and longer or shorter stories are mingled throughout in about the same proportion.

b) *Sifra di-Tseniutha,* or "Book of Concealment",[9] a document of only six pages[10] containing a sort of commentary on passages from the first six chapters of Genesis which form a single section in the synagogical division of the Torah. Its style is highly oracular and obscure, not a single name being mentioned, and only the briefest allusions are made to the various doctrines, while no explanations of any sort are vouchsafed.

c) *Idra Rabba,* or "Greater Assembly."[11] Under this head, the oracular hints and allusions of the preceding chapter are now fully developed and explained.[12] Simeon ben Yohai assembles his faithful followers in order to reveal to them the mysteries hitherto hidden from their eyes. Each in turn rises to speak and is praised by the Master. The composition of this part is architecturally perfect; the totality of the speeches constitutes a systematic whole, in so far as this expression can be at all applied to anything in the Zohar. As the unravelling of the mystery progresses, the participants are increasingly overcome by ecstasy, and in the final dramatic apotheosis, three of them die in a state of ecstatic trance.

d) *Idra Zutta,* or "Lesser Assembly."[13] Here the death of Simeon ben Yohai is described in the same dramatic fashion, and the lengthy speech is quoted in which he sums up the mysteries of the great *Idra,* at the same time introducing certain novel specifications.

e) *Idra di-be-Mashkana,* i. e. "Assembly on the occasion of a lecture in connection with the Torah section concerning the Tabernacle."[14] This chapter follows in its composition the example of the *Idra Rabba,* but deals with different questions, particularly those relating to the mysticism of prayer.

f) *Hekhaloth,* a description of the seven "palaces" of light perceived by the soul of the devout after his death, or by the inner vision of the mystic during prayer. The same description recurs in another passage, but at five times its length and with many new and picturesque embellishments, particularly of the angelology.[15]

g) *Raza de-Razin,* i. e. "Secretum Secretorum."[16] Here we find separate pieces on physiognomy and chiromancy:[17] evidently two parallel attempts to deal with the subject in different ways. One chapter is

THE ZOHAR I: THE BOOK AND ITS AUTHOR

completely anonymous, the other employs the customary stage setting, with Simeon ben Yohai and his pupils in the foreground.

h) *Sava,* "The Old Man."[18] A romantic story centering on the speech made by a mysterious old man who, under the beggarly appearance of a donkey driver, reveals himself before Simeon ben Yohai's pupils as one of the greatest Kabbalists—a literary fiction which is also employed in many of the tales of which part a is compounded. The speaker's elaborately styled discourse deals mainly with the mysteries of the soul, the roots of which he traces in the legal code of the Torah concerning the treatment of the Hebrew slave.

i) *Yenuka,* "The Child." The story of an infant prodigy and its own discourse on the mysteries of the Torah and the saying of grace after meals.[19] Like other child prodigies mentioned in part a,[20] this child is discovered by the pupils of Simeon ben Yohai after its own parents and relatives have come to regard it as incapable of learning.

k) *Rav Methivtha,* "The Head of the Academy."[21] A description of a visionary journey through Paradise undertaken by members of the circle, and a discourse by one of the heads of the celestial academy on the destinies of the soul, particularly in the other world.

l) *Sithre Torah,* "Secrets of the Torah."[22] Allegorical and mystical interpretations of some passages of the Torah, with a tendency towards theosophy and mystical psychology; part anonymous, part in accordance with the usual style of legend.

m) *Mathnithin,* i. e. "Mishnas," and "Tosefta."[23] These chapters show a deliberate attempt to follow the characteristically laconic style of the second century Halakhic *compendia* known as Mishnah and Tosefta, though of course on a purely Kabbalistic basis. They are apparently meant to serve as brief introductions to the lengthy speeches and discussions on part a based upon the sections of the Torah, just as the Mishnah, with its brief passages, serves as an introduction to the discussions of the Talmud. The mystical Mishnas are anonymous and written in a high-flown style. They seem to express some sort of revelation of heavenly voices.

n) *Zohar* to the *Song of Songs,* a purely Kabbalistic commentary to the first verses of the *Song of Solomon,* with numerous digressions from the central train of thought.[24]

o) *Kav Ha-Middah,* "The Mystical Standard of Measure."[25] A very profound and searching interpretation of the meaning of Deut. VI, 4, the *Shema Israel*.

p) *Sithre Othioth*, "Secrets of the Letters."[26] A Kabbalistic monologue by Rabbi Simeon on the letters which occur in the names of God, and on the origins of Creation.

q) A commentary, for which no title is supplied, on Ezekiel's vision of the Merkabah.[27]

r) *Midrash Ha-Neelam*, i. e. "Mystical Midrash," on the Torah.[28] Here we encounter not only Simeon ben Yohai and his pupils but also a host of other authorities, who, like the others, are either legendary figures or Talmudic teachers of the second, third and fourth centuries. (For further details see below.)

s) *Midrash Ha-Neelam* on the *Book of Ruth*. A close parallel to the one just mentioned. Both are partly written in Hebrew.

t) *Raya Mehemna*, "The Faithful Shepherd."[30] A Kabbalistic interpretation of the commandments and prohibitions of the Torah.

u) *Tikkune Zohar*. A new commentary on the first section of the Torah, divided into seventy chapters each of which begins with a new interpretation of the first word of the Torah, *Bereshith*. In print this part constitutes a separate bibliographical unit.[31]

v) Further additions to the last mentioned, or texts written in the same style, e. g., a new commentary to Ezekiel's Merkabah, etc.[32]

These are the main components of the Zohar, i. e. all except a few brief texts of little importance and some "forged" parts, imitations of the main work, written at a much later time and only partly incorporated into the printed editions.[33] In the published volumes of the Zohar, these writings cover about two thousand four hundred closely printed pages, of which only about half—chiefly the material headed under a and h to k—are contained in the English translation of the Zohar by Harry Sperling and Maurice Simon published in five volumes a few years ago.[34]

Upon closer examination of these writings themselves and their relation to each other, it becomes plain that they must be divided into two groups. One includes the first eighteen items of our list, among which, however, the two sections of the *Midrash Ha-Neelam* occupy a special position; the last three items form a second group which differs radically from the first.

Of the eighteen items which make up the first group and may be said to constitute what is to all intents and purposes the real

Zohar, it can be definitely asserted that they are the work of one author. It is neither true that they were written at different periods or by different authors, nor is it possible to detect different historical layers within the various parts themselves. Here and there a sentence or a few words may have been added at some later date, but in the main the distinction—still popular with some writers—between so-called authentic parts and subsequent interpolations does not bear serious investigation." The truth is that the general impression left by these writings is one of surprising uniformity despite their wealth of color; the physiognomy of their author is more or less clearly reflected in all of them, and the picture which emerges is that of a distinctive personality with all its strength and weaknesses, both as a thinker and as a writer. Evidence of this identity is to be found in the language of the book, in its literary style, and, last but not least, in the doctrine which it sets forth.

3

The Aramaic language of all these eighteen sections is throughout the same, and throughout it displays the same individual peculiarities. This is all the more important because it is not in any sense a living language which Simeon ben Yohai and his friends in the first half of the second century A. D. in Palestine might conceivably have spoken. The Aramaic of the Zohar is a purely artificial affair, a literary language employed by a writer who obviously knew no other Aramaic than that of certain Jewish literary documents, and who fashioned his own style in accordance with definite subjective criteria. The expectation expressed by some scholars that philological investigation would reveal the older strata of the Zohar has not been borne out by actual research. Throughout these writings, the spirit of mediaeval Hebrew, specifically the Hebrew of the thirteenth century, is transparent behind the Aramaic facade. It is a further important point that all the resultant peculiarities of the language in which the Zohar is written, and which set it off from spoken Aramaic dialects, are to be found equally in all its various parts. It is true that the style shows a great many variations; it runs all the way from serene beauty to labored tortuousness, from inflated rhetoric to the most paltry simplicity, and from excessive verbosity to laconic and enigmatic brevity,—all depending on the subject and the mood of the author. But these stylistic variations all play upon a single theme and never obscure the essential identity of the mind behind them. It remains to be added that the author's vocabulary is extremely limited, so that one never escapes a feeling of surprise at his ability to express so much with the aid of so little.

In general, the language of the Zohar may be described as a mixture of the Aramaic dialects found in the two books with which the author was above all familiar: The Babylonian Talmud and the Targum Onkelos, the old Aramaic translation of the Torah; in particular, the grammatical forms of the latter are given preference over all others. The author apparently regarded the language of the Targum Onkelos as the dialect which was spoken in Palestine around 100 A. D. Nevertheless, linguistic elements from the Babylonian Talmud occur in almost every line. It is noteworthy that the Palestinian Talmud has exercised virtually no influence on the language of the Zohar, although elements of it are traceable in some of its contents. Evidently it was not one of the author's standard books of reference. To take an example, the terminology of the discussion on questions of exegesis and Halakhah is wholly derived from the Babylonian Talmud, albeit not copied literally but enriched by certain stylistic novelties.

This motley display of different styles is equally evident in the use of pronouns and particles and in the employment of verbal forms and endings of nouns. In some cases, the forms used are those of the Targum Jerushalmi. Frequently, the various forms appear quite indiscriminately in the same sentence. As a result, every page of the Zohar displays a rainbow picture of linguistic eclecticism, the constituent elements of which, however, remain constant throughout. The syntax is extremely simple, almost monotonous, and wherever there are differences between Hebrew and Aramaic, the construction is distinctly Hebrew. Syntactical peculiarities of mediaeval Hebrew recur in Aramaic disguise.[36]

As in the case of every artificial language, a characteristic note is introduced by misunderstandings and grammatical misconstructions. Thus the author in many cases confuses the verb-stems of *Kal* with those of *Pael* and *Aphel,* and vice versa.[37] He employs entirely wrong forms of *Ethpael,*[38] and gives a transitive meaning to verbs in *Ethpael.*[39] He mixes up finite verb-forms, chiefly in the many cases where the endings of the participle are tacked on the perfect;

and his use of prepositions and conjunctions is often quite preposterous.[40]

The same is also true of his vocabulary. One frequently encounters mediaeval Hebrew expressions, particularly from the language of the philosophers, in Aramaic disguise.[41] Thus in a hundred places one finds for "nevertheless" or "despite", the word *im kol da,* which is nothing but a metaphrase of the Hebrew word, introduced by the Tibbonide family of translators in conscious imitation of the Arabic adverb and gradually naturalized in the thirteenth century. Some recurrent expressions are simply Arabic, like the word *taan,* in the sense of goading an animal,[42] or Spanish, like *gardina* = guardian.[43] The Zohar's standing expression for "mitigating or allaying the stern judgment" is coined from a Spanish phrase.[44] In a number of cases, the author choses the wrong metaphrases, i. e. he attributes to the Aramaic roots all the meanings that the derivatives of the corresponding Hebrew roots may carry, irrespective of the actual Aramaic usage.[45] Simple misunderstandings of expressions which he found in his literary sources also play a part.

Many words have a meaning of their own in the Zohar that they could not have had in any spoken Aramaic dialect. A study of the manner in which the author has extracted from them these new and often quite fantastic meanings not infrequently throws new light on his sources. To take a few instances, the Talmudic word for an Arab becomes a term for a Jewish donkey driver;[46] what is there a word for ship, is here a word for a treasure-house;[47] the same word which in the Talmud signifies strength, comes to mean also the mother's breast or lap;[48] the word for thirst now signifies clarity.[49] The verb: to lend someone something, now means: to accompany someone.[50] And so on through a long list of cases in all of which the author's method in his misunderstandings is on the whole one and the same: He stretches the meaning of ancient words in an entirely arbitrary fashion and frequently employs them for the purpose of paraphrasing mystical *termini technici.*[51] He also likes to play on double meanings by using ambiguous expressions in which the original and the secondary meaning give an opaque character to the word.[52] He is careful to avoid expressions which appear to have too much of a modernistic sound, such as *Kabbalah* and *Sefiroth.* In their place he employs paraphrases, often with a fine absence of awareness that modern forms of thought are perceptible even in archaic disguise. He does not seem to have realized that the Hebrew of his day, which he tried to translate into Aramaic, totally differed as a language from that of the ancient books. With all his vast erudition he was anything but a philologist, and modern criticism can benefit a good deal from an analysis of his not infrequent "howlers". In some instances it is possible to show that he made use of the standard Hebrew and Aramaic dictionaries of the period. In other cases he evidently employed expressions newly coined by himself, either by inventing completely new words[3] or by altering old ones,[54] and it is of some interest that the same three or four consonants recur in most of these neologisms (*Teth, Samekh* and in particular *Koph*).[55]

These peculiarities of language and style are uniformly present in every one of the eighteen writings on our list, from the *Midrash Ha-Neelam* and the *Idroth* to the *Mishnas* and the tracts on physiognomy. The *Sifra di-Tseniutha,* which some writers have assigned to remote antiquity, without offering the least proof of so far-reaching a thesis, is distinguished in nothing from the Aramaic sections of the *Midrash Ha-Neelam* which, according to the same authorities, were written a long time after the main part of the Zohar.[56]

Everything that has been said of the vocabulary of the Zohar also applies to its phraseology. Whether the style is elliptic and oracular or verbose and circumstantial, there is the same tendency to employ words such as all-profundity, all-completion, all-connection, all-configuration, all-mystery, etc.,—expressions in which the word *de-kola* ("of the whole") is tacked on to the substantive.[57] Such expressions, although used a good deal by the Gnostics, are not to be found in the language of the ancient Jewish literature; in the literature of Kabbalism, their appearance in the wake of the Neoplatonic revival constitutes one of the most striking examples of the gradual penetration of Neoplatonic terminology into Kabbalism. Also due to the same influence is the increasing vogue enjoyed by superlatives on the pattern of "mystery of mysteries," "bliss of blisses," "depth of depths," etc., of which a large number are to be found in all parts of the Zohar.

Another characteristic peculiarity of style which must be mentioned in this context is the author's predilection for oxymora and paradoxes. Rhetorical figures of speech such as "cooked and uncooked" also occur in the Talmud, but there they signify—in our instance—"half-baked". The long list of similiar expressions in the Zohar is usually employed to indicate that a certain act is of a spiritual and impenetrable nature. "It is and is not" signifies, not that something exists, as it were, only partially, but that its existence is of an exquisitely spiritual nature and cannot therefore be properly described. Whole sentences couched in grand and magniloquent style, which at first sight seem to be pure nonsense, are employed for the sole purpose of drawing the attention of the reader to what is to follow.

"Which is the serpent that flies in the air and walks alone, and meanwhile an ant resting between its teeth has the enjoyment, beginning in community and ending in isolation? Which is the eagle whose nest is in the tree that does not exist? Which are his young which grow up, but not among the creatures, which were created in the place where they were not created? What are those which, when they ascend, descend, and when they descend, ascend, two which are one, and one which is three?[58] Who is the beautiful girl on whom nobody has set his eyes, whose body is concealed and revealed, who goes out in the morning and hides in the day, who puts on the ornaments which are not there?"—Thus the "Old Man" (see item h of our list) begins his great discourse. The mystifying purpose is plain. It is also apparent in the not infrequent sentences containing some brief impressive-sounding *obiter dictum* which is not only in most cases entirely obscure but which in many instances cannot even be properly construed grammatically.[59] It is sometimes difficult to avoid the impression that the author was acting on the good old principle of *épater le bourgeois*. However that may be, his capacity for declamatory, pathetical and sonorous prose was without doubt highly developed, and it is undeniable that he was a sovereign master on the instrument which he himself had fashioned.

These artifices of style also include a peculiar form of hendiadys by which special emphasis is placed on a notion through the negation of its opposite: "Hidden and not evident", "sealed and not comprehensible", "short and not long", etc. The formulae with which distinctions between different categories of the same general application are introduced are everywhere the same.[60] Nor must the stereotyped homiletical phrases be forgotten which are entirely foreign to the old Midrash and which the author has borrowed in part from the later Midrash, but chiefly from the stock of standing expressions habitually employed by the preachers of his age: "This verse must be more closely examined." "Now the time has come to reveal the meaning." "Let us return to the earlier words." "This the friends have already dealt with,"—typical cliches of this genre are to be found on almost every page.

Compared with this style, that of the *Raya Mehemna* and the *Tikkunim* at once reveals an important difference. Here we evidently have before us a deliberate imitation of the uniform language of the other parts, but executed in a rather lame fashion and without any originality. The author of this group of writings knows vastly less Aramaic even than his predecessor. His use of words is quite preposterous and the transcription largely limited to pure Hebrew with an *aleph* tacked on at the end, in order to give a quasi-Aramaic appearance to the substantive. In place of many of the Aramaic expressions used in the magnum opus, there is an indiscriminate use of Hebraisms not to be found in the writings which he is trying to imitate. With two or three exceptions, he makes no use of the new words peculiar to the vocabulary of the Zohar, and the same applies to the peculiarities of style just mentioned. The syntax is entirely different, and so are the formulae with which Biblical verses or Talmudic quotations are introduced. Of the glamour which distinguishes the best passages of the Zohar in spite of the artificiality of their language there is not a trace; everything is pale and lifeless. On the other hand, there are no marked differences in style between the *Raya Mehemna* and the *Tikkunim*, except perhaps that the style of the *Tikkunim* is even less distinguished than that of the *Raya Mehemna*.

4

If one turns from purely philological to literary criteria, the results are no different. Whether it be the form or the content of the Zohar that is subjected to critical analysis, the conclusion to which one is led is invariably the same, namely, that all those parts which I propose to call the real Zohar are to be defined as the work of one author, and that the *Raya Mehemna* and *Tikkunim* must be regarded as an imitation of it.

The first point that strikes one in analyzing the literary form of the "real" Zohar is its peculiar stage-setting: The Palestine which is described in all its parts is not the real country such as it exists or existed, but an imaginary one. So far from proving that the Zohar originated in Palestine,[61] the various topographical and sundry descriptions of the natural background of the miraculous actions and happenings attributed to Rabbi Simeon and his friends provide the most convincing proof possible that the author had never so much as set foot in Palestine and that his knowledge of the country was derived entirely from literary sources.[62] Localities which owe their existence in literature to the misreading of mediaeval Talmudic manuscripts are selected as the stage of mystical revelations.[63] Whole villages are set up on the authority of some Talmudic passage the meaning of which has eluded the author. The most characteristic example of this kind is the frequent mention of a place called Kapotkia, which for the author is not the province of Kappadocia in Asia Minor, but a village, apparently in Lower Galilee, frequently visited by the adepts on their journeys. What the Zohar has to say about the character of its inhabitants leaves no doubt that—as Samuel Klein has shown[64]—a passage from the Palestinian Talmud containing some rather unfriendly remarks on "the Kappadocians in Sepphoris," i. e. the settlement of Kappadocian Jews in the town of Sepphoris, has prompted the author to found his mythical village of "Kapotkia." This is on a par with his treatment of Palestinian topography, of which he had evidently read a good deal in his Talmudic and Midrashic sources, but remembered only what suited his imagination. His descriptions of the mountains of Palestine, for example, are of the most romantic kind and accord far better with the reality of Castile than with that of Galilee.

Much the same applies to the fanciful treatment of the personalities of the narrative. Here again, the author's misconceptions are inexplicable on the assumption that he was drawing on ancient and authentic sources. The legend which he builds up, in the *Midrash Ha-Neelam* and in the "real" Zohar, around the figure of Simeon ben Yohai is fanciful in the last degree. He has even misunderstood the family relations of his hero: the famous saint Phineas ben Yair is mentioned in the Talmud as the son-in-law of Simeon ben Yohai;[65] the author, having evidently misread a word, described him as his father-in-law![66] The name of the father-in-law of Eleazar, Rabbi Simeon's son, he seems to have changed deliberately.⁶⁷ Nor is he worried by chronology: where it is a question of giving the names of the initiates who gathered round Simeon ben Yohai he lets his imagination roam freely and introduces the names of Talmudic teachers who lived generations later.⁶⁸ He even goes so far as to introduce the legendary figure of Rabbi Rehumai, who first appears as a Kabbalistic authority in the book *Bahir,* as a sort of older mystical colleague of Simeon ben Yohai—thereby involuntarily betraying the true historical position of the Zohar in relation to the book *Bahir.*⁶⁹ The names of the most important members of the group around Simeon ben Yohai are largely taken from a pseudepigraphical Midrash and given a spurious appearance of authenticity by the addition of the name of the father or other cognomens. This particular Midrash, the *Pirke Rabbi Eliezer,* dating from the eighth century, is one of the most important sources for the Aggadah of the Zohar in general. As for the descriptions of the contemplative life led by anchorites and mystics in the desert, it is possible to show that so far from describing—as Gaster assumed⁷⁰ —the real conditions of Trans-Jordan in the first centuries of the Christian era, the author simply made use of the description of hermits given by the Spanish-Jewish moral philosopher Bahya ibn Pakuda on the basis of Arab mystical sources.⁷¹

In sharp contradistinction to this pseudo-realism, the scenery and the personalities of the *Raya Mehemna* and the *Tikkunim* show no attempt to describe concrete situations. In these later writings, the tendency to obscure all earthly happenings and to transfer the stage from earth to heaven has completely triumphed. Not Palestine, however romantically draped and disfigured, but the celestial house of learning provides the stage of the *Raya Mehemna.* Simeon ben Yohai is shown in conversation not with his pupils, Rabbi Abba, Rabbi Jehudah, Rabbi Hizkiah, etc., but with Moses, "the faithful shepherd", whose cognomen has suggested the title of the book, with an "ancient of the ancients," with the Prophet Elijah, with the "Tannaites and Amoraites" collectively, and, finally, even with God Himself. It is plain that the author intended to write a sort of continuation of the Zohar, which he had of course read; the justification being that, following the death of Simeon ben Yohai, his further revelations in Heaven and among its residents, from God to the spirits of the blessed, remained to be dealt with. The author significantly refers to the real Zohar, whose stage is the sublunary

world, as the "earlier work."[2] His own contribution is independent
of it in character, and in a number of places, particularly in the
Tikkunim, he actually introduces a sort of systematic commentary
to Zoharic passages.

A close analysis of the Zohar's literary composition supplies further proof of the view set out in the preceding paragraphs. Its construction is on the whole regular and systematic and exhibits certain recurrent characteristics. There is no difference between the
structure of the various quasi-independent writings on our list and
that of the numerous briefer compositions scattered throughout
part a, which outwardly imitates the form of the Midrash. It is
evident that the author had no clear perception of the difference
between the old Midrash, whose tradition he tried to carry on, and
the mediaeval homily which issued from his pen without his being
aware of it. Like the old Midrashim, the Zohar follows the division
of the Torah into sections for synagogal use. Within each section
—*Sidra*—one finds introductions, systematic mystical Midrash to
certain verses, and, scattered among these homiletic explanations,
various literary compositions in the form of anecdotes, etc., referring to some subject mentioned in the *Sidra.* The personalities
who figure in these proto-anecdotes or tales are frequently made to
hold lengthy discourses whose construction is always the same. As
regards the introductions which precede the interpretation proper
of the Torah verse there is the same superficial imitation of the
Midrash, usually in the form of taking a verse from the Prophets
or the Hagiographa as the starting-point and linking its interpretation with that of the Torah verse in question. But whereas in
the old Midrash these introductions display a loose mosaic of authentic remarks and sayings, their imitations in the Zohar are really
like homilies carefully built up with an eye to formal unity and
coherence of thought. Even in those parts which purport to be independent writings, the development of the argument is always
preceded by such homiletical introductions.

Uniformity is also the mark of the illustrative or explanatory
proto-excursions into story-telling. The same small number of literary motifs is juggled in all of them. The figurants change, but the
story remains the same. Of differences in the historical strata going
beyond a period of a few years there can be no question. These
stories are not only as a rule built up in strict accordance with

certain archetypes, but they are also closely linked with each other—
and with the more loosely constructed homilies to the various verses
of the Torah—both directly, by cross-reference, and by implication.
Thus it may happen that an idea developed in a story or an introductory homily is simply continued in the subsequent "Midrash,"
and vice versa. The further one carries the analysis of these cross-
references and implications, the general form of the arguments and
their architectural structure, the more clearly does one perceive
that long passages have been written on the spur of the moment,
and occasionally under the spell of inspiration. Subsequently, on
reading through what he had written, the author made certain
emendations and corrections, including cross-references where he
found them advisable. When all the facts are fairly considered,
there is never any proof that these subsidiary notes amount to more,
i. e. that they are traceable to independent sources. The lengthy
chapters on the history of the patriarchs and the first two hundred
pages of the Zohar on Leviticus are instances of such parts composed at a single stretch. Here and there one encounters a brief
passage whose genuine connection with the rest might conceivably
seem doubtful, but such passages are never of particular importance
for the subject-matter. It is part of the same general picture that the
author tends to repeat himself. Occasionally he goes so far as to
introduce the same passage in different contexts,[13] but as a rule he
prefers to vary the same idea. But whenever that happens we are
plainly dealing with homiletical variations on one subject, and not
with a plurality of writers.

5

Finally we come to the important question of the literary sources
of which the author has made use. Again one is struck by the uniformity of the picture; although the same sources are not constantly
used throughout, one obtains a fairly clear impression of his "library." I do not mean to imply that in the actual process of writing
he surrounded himself with books to which he constantly went for
reference. It is more probable that, being an omnivorous reader
gifted with an excellent memory, and having, moreover, made an
intensive study of certain writings, he was able to quote more or
less textually from memory, in the manner generally accepted in
the Middle Ages. Now and then, of course, memory failed him,

and the resultant inaccuracies and errors are sometimes very illuminating.

Among the writings which must be regarded as his principal sources are the Babylonian Talmud, the *Midrash Rabba* in its various parts, the Midrash to the Psalms, the *Pesiktoth* and the *Pirke Rabbi Eliezer,* and also the *Targumim,* and Rashi's commentary to the Bible and the Talmud. Over and above these there emerges a long list of other writings of which use is made more occasionally.[74] As Bacher has shown in a brilliant essay on the subject,[75] he drew heavily upon the mediaeval Scriptural commentators. More than that, it is possible to show that he also made use of the main writings of Jehudah Halevi[76] and Moses Maimonides, and that some of his ideas on questions of the first order which were among his favorite subjects are directly based on the views of Maimonides, such as for instance his frequent references to paganism as a form of astral worship closely linked with magic and idolatry.[77]

To this can be added that he has clearly made much use of thirteenth century literature, both Hasidic and Kabbalistic; and in particular he has drawn freely upon the writings published by the school of Kabbalists whose center was the little Catalan town of Gerona and who between the years 1230 and 1260 did more than any other contemporary group to unify and consolidate what was pregnant and living in the Kabbalism of Spain. There can be no doubt that the writings of Ezra ben Solomon, Azriel[78] and of Moses ben Nahman,[79] the leading figure of this group, influenced him not only generally but also down to certain peculiar details of his own doctrine. The latest ascertainable source of a highly important *terminus technicus* adopted by the Zohar is Joseph Gikatila's *Ginnath Egoz,* the "Nut Garden," which was written in 1274. This book is the source both of the term used to describe the "primordial point," or mystical centre, which one encounters in widely separated parts of the Zohar,[80] and of the highly original manner in which the conception of the primordial point is linked with that of the primordial Torah conceived as the wisdom of God.[81]

Naturally these sources are not mentioned. Instead, the author contents himself—and discontents the reader—with vague references to ancient writings or mystical tracts dealing with the same topics. Thus the discovery of the real sources, which he is so careful to obscure, is one of the main prerequisites for a correct appreciation

of the historical and doctrinal significance of the Zohar.[82] The task
is made all the more intricate and amusing because the author not
only fails to indicate his real sources but supplies fantastic references to non-existent ones. The whole book is full of fictitious quotations and other bogus references to imaginary writings which
have caused even serious students to postulate the existence of lost
sources for the mystical parts of the Zohar. But these "quotations"
from the Book of Adam, the Book of Enoch, the Book of King
Solomon, the Book of Rav Hamnuna Sava, etc.—we owe to a writer
with a sense of humor the publication of a catalogue of this
"library from the upper world"[83]—are entirely of a piece with the
context in which they stand, both in style and terminology, and
as a rule they are part of the argument as well. It is only in very
rare cases that these references do actually refer to an existing book,
and whenever that happens the document in question is the very
reverse of a text of hoary antiquity. The "Alphabet of ben Sira",
a very late text (tenth century) from which the author has obviously taken the myth of Lilith as Adam's first wife, is a case in
point.[84] Not in a single instance are we confronted with genuine
quotations from earlier writings which have since disappeared.

The same independence of mind characterizes the author's treatment of his sources. As often as not he displays a sovereign contempt
for the literal text, using it freely as plastic material for his own
constructive purposes and giving free rein to his imagination in
making vital changes, emendations and reinterpretations of the
original. His favorite method is to take the motifs of the old
Aggadah and weave them into his own fabric of thought, even
where he does not convert their meaning into outright mysticism.
Such excursions into Aggadic legends nowhere else found in this
form are, therefore, not necessarily based on lost writings. Their
source is simply the author's own imagination. His treatment of
such subjects is characterized by a tendency towards dramatization,
equally apparent in the architecture of whole compositions and in
the manner in which brief Talmudic stories or legends are converted into lively Aggadoth on the same subject.[85] Where an Aggadah already contains mystical elements, these are of course duly
emphasized and occasionally woven into an entirely new myth.[86]

In all this busy reinterpretation of old material the author displays a passion for his subject and a naïveté which are not among

the least peculiar of his characteristics as a writer. One may explain
them by recalling that, for all his familiarity with the elements of
mediaeval Jewish culture, and his own frequent development of
profoundly mystical and dialectical ideas, the author's spiritual life
is centered as it were in a more archaic layer of the mind. Again
and again one is struck by the simultaneous presence of crudely
primitive modes of thought and feeling, and of ideas whose profound contemplative mysticism is transparent. And it is perhaps
noteworthy that the two harmonize better than might be imagined.
There cannot even be a question of relating them to different literary sources[87]; what we have before us is the reflection of their living conflict in the mind of a very remarkable personality in whom,
as in so many mystics, profound and naive modes of thought existed
side by side.

It may be observed here that the author of the Zohar is not
the only thirteenth century Kabbalist who displays this peculiar
and fruitful combination of seemingly divergent traits, though there
is hardly another writer of the period whose personality is of such
arresting interest to us. It must be borne in mind that by his outlook, and probably also through personal relations, he belonged
to a group of writers in Spain, and more particularly in Castile, who
might be described as the representatives of the Gnostical reaction
in the history of Spanish Kabbalism. The Kabbalah of the early
thirteenth century was the offspring of a union between an older
and essentialy Gnostical tradition represented by the book *Bahir,*
and the comparatively modern element of Jewish Neoplatonism.
The growing influence of the latter in turn provoked a reaction
which naturally stressed the Gnostical elements of the Kabbalistic
outlook. In the second half of the thirteenth century, this tendency
was represented by such writers as the brothers Isaac and Jacob
Hacohen of Soria, Todros ben Joseph Abulafia of Toledo, and
Moses ben Simon of Burgos. We still have a number of their writings,[88] and it is not difficult to detect in them (particularly in those
of the two last mentioned), a mood which is closely related to that
of the Zohar, though they possess hardly any of the glamor and
originality which distinguishes that great work.

To return to our critical examination of the Zohar's sources,
the statement that the use which the author makes of older literary
material is consistent and uniform throughout is also true if we con-

sider as that material ideas which belong to the general consciousness of the epoch rather than to specific writers. This category includes, for example, the liturgy which the Zohar takes for granted
in dealing with the mysticism of prayer and which is without any
doubt that current in Spain during the twelfth and thirteenth centuries. The same is true of the frequent references to popular Jewish usages, the customary forms of polite intercourse which are here
treated as natural,[89] the author's ideas on the subject of medicine,[90]
and above all his views on sorcery, magic and demonology which
play an important part in his doctrine. The constituent elements of
his theory of magic are clearly traceable to the popular mediaeval
views on the subject, though leavened with a strong dose of personal
fancy. A detailed analysis of the resultant conception of magic could
hardly fail to be of considerable interest, for the power of evil is a
problem which exercised a special fascination upon his mind, and
as I shall try to show in the following lecture, it forms one of the
main subjects of his writings, both in their theoretical and in their
homiletical aspects. In the same manner, some of the basic ideas of
his eschatology, such as the distinction between an earthly and a
heavenly paradise, are in conformity with Jewish and Christian
beliefs of the time.

6

And what has been said of his style and his attitude towards the
heritage of Jewish thought is true also of his own doctrines. Here
again the various parts of the real Zohar form a whole, distinct from
the *Raya Mehemna* and the *Tikkunim*. Of the substance of these
ideas, or at any rate of some of the most important of them, I shall
have something to say in the following lecture. Here we are concerned with their bearing upon the question of the authorship of
the Zohar, and the point which must be stressed before all others
is the fact that the line of thought which runs through all these
writings is consistent in spite of occasional minor contradictions.[91]
The mystical terminology is virtually the same throughout, representing as it does a development of the terminology employed by
the Kabbalists of the Geronese school. The mass of symbols follow
a more or less uniform rule, so much so that it would be possible
to interpret them in detail even if we had no other document of
early Kabbalism than the Zohar. The same fundamental symbolic

configurations are repeated innumerable times in various forms, and what is chiefly alluded to in one place is lengthily explained in another. It is clear that when an author writes a number of homilies on one and the same verse he is able to express entirely different thoughts without abandoning the unity of his fundamental conception, a fact which explains such minor contradictions as are to be found in the more doctrinal and theoretical passages. To some questions he has propounded different solutions, but these do not belong to different "layers" but are deliberately introduced into the same complex of discursive tales, and sometimes even into the same discourse.

What then is the special peculiarity of the Zohar on its theoretical side? It must be admitted that as a matter of fact the existence of a personal note is more apparent in the author's style than in the substance of his thought. The chief doctrines he puts forward are essentially the consummation of the development of Kabbalistic thought during the first three-quarters of the thirteenth century. The point to be noted, however, is that he does not indiscriminately adopt the whole of this spiritual legacy. His point of view is that of a clearly defined school of thought in Spanish Kabbalism, the "Gnostical" school already mentioned. Spanish Kabbalism as a whole included a considerable variety of more or less clearly grouped tendencies and schools. The manifold views on such subjects as the depths of the Godhead, the destiny of man, and the significance of the Torah which one finds in the Zohar, were the product of the hundred years of intensive development of thought which separate the Zohar from the book *Bahir*. From this welter of frequently conflicting views the author makes his own selection and gives prominence to that which appeals most strongly to his mind, often in a highly personal manner characteristic of his intensive preoccupation with the subject.

Thus he displays the greatest interest in a group of ideas which owes its very development to the already mentioned Gnostical school: the idea of a "left emanation," i. e. of an ordered hierarchy of the potencies of evil, the realm of Satan, which, like the realm of light, is organized in ten spheres or stages. The ten "holy" Sefiroth have their counterparts in ten "unholy" or "impure" ones; the latter, however, are distinguished from the former in that each one has a highly personal character. Each therefore has a personal name proper to itself, while the names of the divine Sefiroth merely represent abstract qualities such as wisdom, intelligence, grace, beauty, etc. Complete mythologies of this realm of darkness are to be found above all in the writings of Isaac ben Jacob Hacohen and Moses of Burgos.[92] The author of the Zohar adopts these ideas but plays new variations on the original theme. Starting out from the same assumptions as the writers we have just mentioned, he yet arrives at a doctrine of the "other side," *sitra ahra,* which closely parallels but does not converge with that of his contemporaries.

But, and this carries us a step further, the individuality of the author is no less clearly expressed in what he omits than in what he emphasizes. To take a particularly striking example, he completely ignores a form of speculation very popular among thirteenth century Kabbalists, namely, the idea of successive periods of cosmic development, each lasting seven thousand years, in which the universal process follows certain theosophic laws, until in the fifty thousandth year, the Great Jubilee, it returns to its source.

This theory was first expounded in the book *Temunah* (around 1250)[93] in the form of a mystical interpretation of the twenty-two letters of the Hebrew alphabet, and was based on a new interpretation of the Biblical prescriptions for the Sabbath year, the *Shemitah,* and the Jubilee, when all things shall return to their possessor. To the Kabbalists of Catalonia, these rules were but symbolical representations of the stages of the process in which all things emanate from God and return to Him. The literature of the thirteenth and fourteenth centuries is full of speculations on this subject. The question how many world-periods or Jubilees there are was of as much importance to some Kabbalists as that of the state of the world in the various *Shemitahs.* Indeed, the assumption was even made that the Torah was read in different ways during the various successive periods, without however being changed in its literal content as the secret name of God, i. e. that it is capable of revealing more than one meaning. The current period, according to the book *Temunah,* is that of stern judgment, i. e. that which is dominated by the Sefirah, the divine quality, of rigor, and in which there are accordingly commandments and prohibitions, pure and impure things, holy and profane matters—in accordance with the present reading of the Torah. But in the coming aeon, the next

Shemitah, the Torah will no longer contain prohibitions, the power of evil will be curbed, etc., in brief, Utopia will at last be realized.

It is difficult to avoid the impression that we are dealing here with an independent Jewish parallel to the doctrine of Joaquin of Fiore concerning the three cosmic stages which accord with the three figures of the Christian Trinity. This doctrine, which was first developed in far-off Calabria towards the end of the twelfth century, became of importance in the forties of the thirteenth century when it was taken up and developed further by the Franciscans of Italy.⁹⁴ By a curious coincidence, the doctrine of the *Shemitahs* was codified in Gerona at about the same time. Of a direct historical connection between the two there is no proof and the idea carries little probability. Moreover, the *Shemitahs* concern not only the process of our present cosmos, like the three world-periods of the Father, the Son and the Holy Spirit in the writings of Joaquin, but its past and future as well. Nevertheless, it remains a remarkable fact that in both doctrines the various manifestations of the Divine—the Trinity and the Sefiroth—appear as successive principles each of a particular cosmic unit, an aeon. It is clear that in the eschatological perspective this doctrine opened up a vast number of new vistas: the probable meaning of the Messianic time, the transformation of all things before the rebirth of the world in the new *Shemitah,* the continuity of the soul in this process of change, and other questions which to the followers of this doctrine inevitably appeared in a new light.

Now the remarkable fact is that our author, for all his lively interest in the eschatological fate of the soul, appears to have strongly disapproved of this doctrine which I have just outlined. In the whole of his great work there is not a single mention to be found of the *Shemitahs* in this pregnant sense of the term, although he too refers to the passage of fifty thousand years before the "Great Jubilee."⁹⁵ It is as though he was repelled by something in this doctrine, perhaps its latent antinomianism which is perceptible behind the utopian expectation of a change in the commandments and prohibitions of the Torah during the coming *Shemitahs.* A good example of this antinomian tendency is to be found in the doctrine expounded by a writer of this school which postulates the existence of a twenty-third letter of the Hebrew alphabet, invisible in our present aeon but to be resuscitated in the next—a theory which of course implies a complete change in the

traditional attitude towards the Torah.[95] Notions of this kind are
as foreign to the author of the genuine Zohar as they are dear to
the heart of the writer who has produced the *Raya Mehemna*. The
latter is full of references to the "two trees": the "tree of knowledge
of good and evil" which dominates our world age, and the "tree
of life" which is to preside over the coming Messianic aeon. The
difference between these two cosmic forces is vividly described,
and it is obvious that the writer is greatly fascinated by the idea
of the coming liberation from the yoke of commandments and prohibitions. Nothing of the sort is to be found in the genuine Zohar.
Nor is a very pointed social criticism in an apocalyptical vein typical of the Zohar, whereas it is an outstanding feature of the *Raya
Mehemna* whose burning hate of the oppressive groups in contemporary Jewish society is unmistakable. He speaks not so much
as a reformer as does the author of the Zohar, but rather as an
apocalyptical revolutionary who is confined by circumstances to
solitary dreams of the great upheaval that is to precede the mystical
utopia.[97] In the same way we find in the Zohar little or no mention of various Kabbalistic doctrines with which the author must
certainly have been familiar. He selects from the wealth of material
what is proper and adequate for his own purpose and ignores what
he cannot use. It seems, for example, that the author of the Zohar
disliked, for some reason or other, the catalogues or inventories of
demonic and angelic beings which abound in the writings of the
Spanish Kabbalists in whose circle he moved. He replaced them
by fanciful beings of his own creation.

Having now asserted proof of the essential unity of the bulk of
the Zohar and the somewhat later date of writing of the subsidiary
part, a few words must be said about the literary and ideological
character of the *Raya Mehemna* and the *Tikkunim*. Their literary
merit requires little comment; it is poor indeed and far inferior to
that of the Zohar. Compared with the latter, these writings are as
much distinguished by the poverty of their style as by their excessive fondness for verbal association. It frequently happens that instead of the systematic development of a train of thought characteristic of the Zohar, we find nothing but a confused meandering from
one association to the next. Secondly, as regards the doctrines put
forward in the *Raya Mehemna* and the *Tikkunim*, it suffices to say
that they are as closely alike as they are sharply different in im-

portant respects from those of the Zohar, although their author was evidently intent on making his writings a continuation of the latter. The author of the Zohar proper, as we shall have occasion to see, inclines towards pantheism, while the Kabbalah outlined in the *Raya Mehemna* is strictly theistic.[98] Its treatment of the Sefiroth is much less lively and colorful, and in many details different from that of the major part. Lastly, it might be remarked that as a Talmudist (in the casuistical sense), the author of the *Raya Mehemna* is markedly superior to that of the Zohar, whose frequent attempts to introduce mystical interpretations of the Halakhah are distinguished by a good deal of uncertainty and some rather elementary misunderstandings of Talmudic law.

7

Assuming the bulk of the Zohar to be the work of one author we come to the question whether it is still possible to trace the stages in the composition of so vast a literary opus. Where did the author begin and how ought one to picture his method of working? The first question can be answered in my opinion quite simply and somewhat surprisingly. Even those scholars who realized that the Zohar was written at a comparatively late date usually proceeded upon the assumption that certain chapters of the major part, such as the two *Idras,* made the beginning, followed by the Midrashic parts, after which the *Midrash Ha-Neelam* was added, perhaps even by another author.[99] In the same way, many Kabbalists regarded the *Midrash Ha-Neelam,* in which the mediaeval element is not cloaked by the Aramaic language, as a later addition to the Zohar properly speaking.[100]

This view I consider to be mistaken. One of the most striking results to which I have been led by a closer analysis of the Zohar is the recognition that the *Midrash Ha-Neelam* to the first sections *(Sidras)* of the Torah, and the *Midrash Ha-Neelam* to the Book of Ruth are the two oldest constituents of the whole work. The following are some of the main considerations by which I have been guided.

(a) A careful analysis of all the cross-references in the Zohar, and of those passages which necessarily imply certain other passages leads to the conclusion that in many cases the first reference is to

be found in the two sections of the *Midrash Ha-Neelam,* but never
vice versa. This is true not only of doctrinal material but also of
the legendary form of certain essential pieces of the major part,
which either assume or directly refer to points mentioned in the
Midrash Ha-Neelam, while the reverse is never the case.[101]

(b) In a number of cases, the same homily or identical tale—
the identity being that of motif—appears both in the *Midrash Ha-
Neelam* and in the other parts of the genuine Zohar. Analysis always
shows that the literary form employed in the former is more primitive, more clearly dependent on the original sources, and more awkward in style than in the corresponding passages of the other parts.
Frequently the difference is most striking; one clearly sees how the
author treats the passage in the *Midrash Ha-Neelam* as raw material for a second edition more in accordance with the subsequent
improvement of his literary taste.[102] I was very surprised myself when
after making a number of such comparisons, without any reference
to the literary problem of the *Midrash Ha-Neelam,* I suddenly became aware that priority belonged throughout to this part.

(c) Only in the *Midrash Ha-Neelam* is it still possible to find
some uncertainty regarding the group of personalities whom the
author meant to place into the center of his imaginative construction. While in the other parts the stage is dominated by Simeon
ben Yohai and his disciples, the *Midrash Ha-Neelam* shows the author wavering between three different solutions: (1) to do without a
hero and follow the tradition of the genuine Midrash in ranging
together the largest possible number of dicta purporting to represent the true views of a large number of authorities throughout the
Talmudic period; (2) to build up the legendary scenery around the
Mishnaic teacher Eliezer ben Hyrkanus; in this the author was undoubtedly influenced by a favorite piece of mystical literature, the
Midrash *Pirke Rabbi Eliezer,* which had already done the same,
as well as by the fact that this teacher was already mentioned as a
mystical authority by the Merkabah mystics; (3) to center the tale
on Simeon ben Yohai, whose historical personality was not ill-fitted
for the purpose but who is nowhere mentioned as a mystical authority, if one excepts two early mediaeval apocalypses in which he
figures as the hero. Throughout large parts of the *Midrash Ha-
Neelam,* Simeon ben Yohai and his circle play no part at all. Apparently the author finally decided in his favor only while he was

already busy writing the book. He did not, however, sacrifice Eliezer
ben Hyrkanus altogether. In a minor writing apparently thrown off
during a pause in working on the Zohar, he develops the legend of
Eliezer and makes him voice certain ideas which he puts forward
simultaneously in the Zohar. The fact that the "Testament of
Rabbi Eliezer"—the title of this little Hebrew book which went into
many editions—really belongs to the Zohar literature has never so
far been recognized,[103] and various mistaken theories have been
advanced concerning its origin.

(d) In the *Midrash Ha-Neelam*, the author is still endeavoring to find for his thought a place within the frame-work of the old
Merkabah mysticism; the other parts no longer show any trace of
this tendency. In the *Midrash Ha-Neelam*, too, his literary method
is more dependent on the genuine older Midrashic literature than
in the later parts. The title also shows that the writer's purpose was
to create a "mystical Midrash" as distinct from the purely Aggadic
one; for that, and not "a hitherto unknown Midrash", is the distinctive meaning of the title *Midrash Ha-Neelam*, as the occurence
of the same term in the writings of other Kabbalists of the same
period conclusively shows.[104]

(e) In the *Midrash Ha-Neelam*, the use of direct quotations
from Talmudic sources is much more open than in the later writings. The author also shows no hesitation to quote genuine documents with their real title, although he already begins with the in-
vention of titles from his "celestial library."

(f) The doctrinal differences which exist in several important
points between the *Midrash Ha-Neelam* and the other parts are
psychologically explicable only on the assumption that the simpler
conception of the *Midrash* preceded the more complicated one of
the texts which I have come to regard as having been written later.
On this assumption the author, like all the followers of Maimonides,
began with philosophical allegorization, and gradually came to
mysticism—a process of development which in the circumstances of
the period is far more plausible than the reverse. In the beginning
he was closer to philosophy and further away from Kabbalism. In
the course of time he was progressively drawn more deeply into the
realm of mystical thought, and the philosophic elements of his doctrine were either relegated to the background or given a mystical
twist. The philosophizer becomes a theosophist. In the *Midrash*

Ha-Neelam, the doctrine of the Sefiroth is very far from being his main subject, a position occupied by all kinds of allegorical homilies on cosmological, psychological and eschatological subjects. His psychological ideas here and in the later parts show a definite development, without, however, necessitating the assumption that they reflect the influence of more than one mind. In the *Midrash Ha-Neelam,* the psychological theories current in the Middle Ages, and more particularly a blend of those of Maimonides and the Neoplatonists, are put forward as the author's own opinion, but their mystical coloring is already apparent. In the main part, this progress towards a purely mystical psychology, which can be traced in close detail, is already in a much more advanced stage.

(g) The author's Hebrew, which in the *Midrash Ha-Neelam* still alternates with Aramaic, is unquestionably that of the late Middle Ages. At the same time, it is still possible to distinguish quite clearly in a number of cases which Hebrew phrases were formerly employed in the place of the later and artificial Aramaic ones.

As against these considerations, there is not a single one which argues conclusively in favor of placing the main part before the *Midrash Ha-Neelam.* In some of its chapters, e. g. in the *Sithre Torah,* one still notices something like a wavering in the direction of the *Midrash Ha-Neelam.* In some tales we make the acquaintance of figures which are to be found only there. Generally speaking, however, the character of the picture has changed. Above all, the author's literary ability and his power of expression have considerably improved. It is evident that he has in the meantime had moments of inspiration, but also that he has made much progress in the technique of writing. Instead of brief tales and discursions one finds elaborate and often well-constructed compositions. One has the impression that he wrote the later parts of the *Midrash Ha-Neelam* simultaneously with the main part —a) -q) of our list—as though he was occasionally tempted to continue for a while in the old direction; but here again one finds references to the later work only in two or three places, and it may well be that these passages, too, were on the whole written before he turned to the main part. In any case he broke off his work on the *Midrash Ha-Neelam* when he had come to the middle of Genesis. To the other books of the Torah he wrote only a few commentaries, particularly a beginning to Exodus. Instead of continuing with this work he appears to have concentrated on the various parts of the real Zohar which were probably completed in five or six years of intensive productivity. In later years, he may have made a few additions, including probably the beginnings of an anonymous explanation of the commandments, called *Pikkuda,* a piece which is still written in the true style and language of the real Zohar and which seems to have furnished the author of the *Raya Mehemna* with a stimulus for his own book. At any rate he uses these rather fragmentary beginnings as a starting-point and then develops the argument in his own manner: the transition from one style to the other can be quite distinctly observed.[104]

The fact that the whole work is a torso—to Deuteronomy there are only a few Zohar passages—can be explained in several ways. The least plausible explanation is that a great deal has been lost. The manuscripts we have correspond on the whole very well to the printed text, although their closer analysis occasionally still yields interesting results. Thus for example one finds that the author has made two versions of a very important part of the *Midrash Ha-Neelam,* of which the older is extant only in a fourteenth century manuscript now in Cambridge,[105] while most of the manuscripts and all the printed editions have made use only of the other. Similarly, the quotations found in writers before 1350 show that they had knowledge of only very few texts of the genuine Zohar which are no longer traceable.[107] Thus while it is certain that some minor passages have been lost in the course of time, there is nothing to show that the work was ever completed in a formal sense. Rather does it seem probable that the author at some point felt that he had done enough and turned his attention to a new subject. At any rate that seems to me a more plausible explanation, particularly in view of the character of his later work. It may also be that he had in those years more or less exhausted his productive power.

The precise order in which the different parts of the Torah commentary and the various subsidiary texts outside its framework were written can no longer be ascertained with anything like certainty, but since the whole task probably occupied no more than a few years, the question is not one of great importance. On the whole one has the impression that the *Idra Rabba* and the *Sifra di-Tseniutha* were among the first major writings to be completed.

In this connection it is of interest that the pages following directly upon the conclusion of the *Idra* represent a conscious return to the *Midrash Ha-Neelam*. To the first section of the Torah, which was of course of the greatest importance for him, he has written no less than three commentaries, apart from the *Midrash Ha-Neelam*. Such instances of recurrent attempts to solve the same problem in different ways are as characteristic of his method as they are eloquent of the fundamental unity and coherence of his thought.

8

What after all this is our answer to the question when the book was written? It appears to me that what has been said above of the result to which one is led by an analysis of the sources is also confirmed by other considerations. We have seen that the author was familiar with a group of writings of which the latest was written in 1274. This gives us a definite *terminus post quem,* the significance of which is enhanced by the general character of the allusions made both in the *Midrash Ha-Neelam* and in other chapters to contemporary events and institutions. From these allusions it is not difficult to draw the inference that the author was writing at a time when Palestine, after the vicissitudes of the Crusades, was again in the hands of the Arabs.[108] There is no lack of polemical references to Christianity and Islam,[109] nor of remarks alluding to the moral atmosphere of Jewry which harmonize with what we know of the conditions around 1280. The data can be narrowed down a little further. In several places the author introduces apocalyptical calculations all of which set the end of exile around the year 1300 and the following years.[110] In one passage, however, the assumption is made that since the destruction of the Second Temple—in the year 68, according to the Jewish calendar—twelve hundred years of exile have already passed, and that Israel is now living in the darkness which precedes the dawn.[111] In other words, he is writing some years after 1268.

Now this date accords perfectly with everything we know of the circumstances of the book's publication. All sources are agreed that the Zohar was first circulated in the eighties or nineties of the thirteenth century by the Kabbalist Moses ben Shemtob de Leon who lived until 1290 in the little town of Guadalajara in the heart of

Castile,[112] then led a wandering life and finally spent his last years in Avila to which town he may have been attracted by the brief sensation caused by the appearance of a Jewish "prophet" in 1295. He died in 1305 in the little town of Arevalo on a return journey to Avila from the Royal Court at Valladolid.[113]

Apart from these brief data on his life we know that Moses de Leon published under his own name a considerable number of Hebrew writings, most of which have been preserved, although only two have been printed.[114] We also know that he was in close touch with the family of Todros Abulafia whom we have met as a member of the Gnostical school of Kabbalism; in other words, he belonged to the circle of a man who occupied a very high position in the Jewish community of Castile between 1270 and 1280. We are told by himself that his first book, i. e. the first book whose authorship he admitted, was the *Shushan Eduth* or "Rose of Testimony." This book, of which about half has been preserved, was written in 1286.[115] In the following year he published a fairly voluminous treatise on the meaning of the Commandments, *Sefer Ha-Rimmon,* the "Book of the Pomegranate."[116] Both, but in particular the latter, are replete with allusions to mystical sources. Although the Zohar is never directly mentioned, a detailed analysis shows that he is already making systematic use of all its parts, from the *Midrash Ha-Neelam* to the commentaries of the main part on Leviticus and Numbers.

But even before Moses de Leon made his appearance as a Hebrew author, quotations from the Zohar—to be exact, from the *Midrash Ha-Neelam*—began to appear in the writings of two other Kabbalists, thus confirming our view of the order in which the various parts of the Zohar were written and began to circulate. The oldest quotation from the Zohar dates from the year 1281 and is to be found at the end of the *Mashal Ha-Kadmoni,* by Isaac ibn Abu Sahulah. It is a passage taken from the *Midrash Ha-Neelam,* or rather from the above-mentioned version, hitherto unknown, of a paragraph on Genesis which I had the good fortune to discover in a Cambridge manuscript of the Zohar.[117] The author, who like Moses de Leon lived in Guadalajara, two years later wrote a mystical commentary to the Song of Songs. He does not there quote the full text of the passages from the genuine Midrashim to which he alludes, but he does make use of a good number of quotations from an obviously unknown and unpublished Midrash—none other than the *Midrash Ha-Neelam* to the first three *Sidras* of the Torah.[118] At about the same time, Todros Abulafia appears to have written his *Otsar Ha-Kavod,* "Treasure of Glory," where one finds two quotations from the *Midrash Ha-Neelam,* the title of which is again not mentioned. Both writers, who for various reasons may safely be excluded from the list of possible authors of the Zohar, maintained close relations with Moses de Leon, the former being a resident of the same locality and the latter a wealthy friend to whose son several of Moses de Leon's works are dedicated.[119]

Taken all together, these facts permit us to draw the following conclusion: The *Midrash Ha-Neelam,* the forerunner of the Zohar proper, was written between 1275 and 1280, probably not long before the latter year, while the bulk of the work was completed in the years 1280—86. After the latter date, Moses de Leon in his various writings mingles a constant proportion of quotations from the Zohar among his other quotations from Midrashim and commentaries. Till about 1293 in particular he appears to have worked fairly intensively on the publication of writings designed to propagate the doctrines of the Zohar. Probably in conjunction with this work, certainly after 1290, he also began to circulate copies of the main Zohar among other Kabbalists. Bahya ben Asher of Saragossa, who started work on his great Torah commentary in 1291, appears to have read certain chapters of these copies of the new Kabbalistic Midrash, which was at first circulated not only under the title "Zohar," but also as the "Midrash of Rabbi Simeon ben Yohai."[120] Probably on the basis of these texts, another Kabbalist, either in the nineties of the thirteenth or at the beginning of the fourteenth century, wrote the *Raya Mehemna* and the *Tikkunim.* In general, there seems to have been no lack of imitations; David ben Jehudah, the grandson of Nahmanides, in his *Maroth Ha-Tsoveoth,* written at the beginning of the fourteenth century, quotes, apart from various authentic Zoharic passages, some lengthy pieces written in the manner of the *Midrash Ha-Neelam* and the Zohar, whose contents show them to be imitations of these two books.[121]

That such imitations were produced is in itself proof that some Kabbalists did not take the literary form of the Zohar too seriously, but regarded it as pure fiction which they had no hesitation to copy. No doubt there were also unsophisticated souls who accepted the book as a genuine Midrash, even as an authentic work of the disciples of Simeon ben Yohai. Its masterly presentation of the secret thoughts and feelings of the contemporary Kabbalists was far too true to reality not to have excited the wish that this romantic projection of their own spiriual world might really prove to have been the secret doctrine of the Midrash teachers,[122] at once hoary with antiquity and sanctified by authority. The proportion of critical minds at that time was no greater than it is in our own day. Nevertheless, criticism was not completely lacking. As late as 1340, Joseph ibn Wakkar of Toledo—almost the only Kabbalist known to us who wrote in Arabic[123]—warned his readers to exercise caution in using the Zohar as it contained "a great many errors."[124]

This solution of the Zoharic problem accords, so far as I can see, completely with all the circumstances which the critic must bear in mind. As to the motive which prompted the writing of the Zohar immediately prior to its publication, the general remarks of Eduard Zeller, the historian of Greek philosophy, are still true. "An author who writes under an assumed name wants to produce a certain effect *in his own time;* he will therefore circulate his work immediately, and if the first who read it regard it as genuine, the growth of its circulation will perhaps be more rapid than if it had appeared under the real name of its author. Only where a book is inadvertently attributed to the wrong author because the real one is unknown, and without its author having any part in the mistake, will a length of time be required as a rule before it begins to circulate."[125] Having disposed of all the fantasies about the various parts of the Zohar belonging to different periods, about its sources and its supposed derivation from the East, as well as of all doubts that it was not only published but also written in Castile, the inner dynamic of the process which led to its inception and circulation is now clearly revealed before our eyes.

There is another consideration which may be mentioned at least in passing. Some defenders of the Zohar as a book composed of many different elements and in different periods have argued that it is impossible to assume that a vast production like the "Zoharic literature" could have been the result of a few years' work (in our case of six years). This is a serious error in judgment. Precisely the contrary is true: if a man writes under the spell of inspiration, if he has found an "Archimedean point" around which his spiritual world is focussed, it is indeed easy for him to produce thousands of pages within a very limited period. We have the example of the famous German mystic Jacob Boehme who produced during the six years 1618-1624 an even vaster theosophic literature than the Zohar.

9

There remains only one last question: Who was the author? Was it Moses de Leon himself or an unknown writer who moved in Moses de Leon's circle and managed to shield his identity from the glaring light of posterity? Can the possibility be wholly discarded that another Kabbalist, whose identity has been lost in the dark remoteness of the past, had the main share in the work? It can at least be said that by some of his contemporaries, Moses de Leon was already described as the author of the Zohar. That much at any rate we know from the much-discussed testimony of the Kabbalist Isaac ben Samuel of Acre, one of the two documents of the period, apart from Moses de Leon's own writings, in which we find him mentioned.[126] Isaac left his home when he was still a young student after the conquest of Acre by the Moslems (1291), apparently for Italy where he also seems to have heard of the Zohar, and finally went to Spain in 1305, where he began to take an interest in the circumstances under which the book was published. His diary, of which a few other parts have also been preserved in manuscript, gives a rather naive account of the information he gathered on the subject. We are told that he met Moses in Valladolid and was informed under oath that he (Moses de Leon) was in possession of "the ancient book written by Simeon ben Yohai" and would show it to him in his house at Avila. Subsequently, when after Moses de Leon's death he came to Avila, he was told that a rich citizen of the town, Joseph de Avila, had offered to marry his son to the daughter of the deceased in exchange for the original manuscript of the Zohar, said to be ancient as well as authentic, from which Moses de Leon was supposed to have copied, but that both the widow of the deceased and his daughter had denied the existence of such an original. According to them, Moses de Leon had written the Zohar all by himself, and, to his wife's question why he did not claim the authorship of the work, had replied: "If I told people that I am the author, they would pay no attention nor spend a farthing on the book, for they would say that these are but the workings of my own imagination. But now that they hear that I am copying from the book Zohar which Simeon ben Yohai wrote under the inspiration of the holy spirit, they are paying a high price for it as you know." Isaac of Acre, who did not himself speak to Moses de Leon's widow but relates all this as second, or rather third hand information, also speaks of further researches, but unfortunately his account, as quoted by a later chronicler of the fifteenth century, breaks off at the very point where he proposes to disclose what he was told under solemn oath by a pupil of Moses de Leon about "the book Zohar which was written by Rabbi Simeon ben Yohai." Whether Isaac of Acre, who later became one of the leading Kabbalists of the first half of the fourteenth century, believed in the authenticity of the Zohar remains obscure. That he quotes it several times in his own writings does not imply belief in its antiquity. On the other hand, it is of some interest that he repeatedly contrasts the Catalan and the Castilian tradition of Kabbalism. According to him, the former school based its teachings on the doctrine expounded in the book *Bahir,* the latter on the Zohar.[127] In other words, he postulates a close connection between the Zohar and the Kabbalism of Castile!

On the account given by Isaac of Acre, and in particular on the alleged evidence of Moses de Leon's widow, Graetz has based his impression of Moses de Leon, on whom he pours the full measure of the wrath kindled in him by the "book of lies."[128] According to him, Moses de Leon was an idle and impecunious charlatan who "made use of the increasingly fashionable Kabbalah in order to pose as a writer on the subject and thus opened up a rich source of income for himself."[129] The foundation of this startling assertion is the mistaken assumption that Moses de Leon began by writing under his own name and descended to pseudepigraphy from thoroughly mean and worthless motives, i. e. because his original writings had failed to win him sufficient laurels and profits. Hence he is supposed to have written the whole Zohar after 1293, including the *Midrash Ha-Neelam,* the *Raya Mehemna* and the *Tikkunim.* That this view of the author's personality and the date and form of his work is thoroughly mistaken should be clear after our conclusions on the subject which are the result of a somewhat more detailed analysis. Having established this point I have no hesitation in saying that

Graetz' fanciful picture of Moses de Leon as a base and despicable swindler who tried to parade a fake profundity of thought, and his other moral strictures on his character, can be dismissed as pure fantasy.[130] There is nothing in the character of the Zohar and of Moses de Leon's Hebrew writings which justifies this view of the book and its author. Nor is there anything in them which might predispose one to regard the alleged cynical remark to his wife as authentic; on the contrary, the manner in which this remark is related rather suggests that it owes its origin to the spite of persons ill disposed towards the author.

That his widow described him as the author of the book is indeed well possible and, as we shall see, in entire accordance with the facts. But the supposed authenticity of her particular words is a question on which it is well to exercise some restraint. One thing is certain: the actual relationship between the Zohar and Moses de Leon's other writings is the reverse of that assumed by Graetz. A detailed analysis of all the books written under his own name proves that they presuppose the existence of the Zohar as a completed work, and their obvious purpose is to prepare the readers for its publication, unobtrusively at first and gradually with growing emphasis. It appears indeed that they were intended to prepare the ground for the publication of those copies of the Zohar to which he seems to have devoted the better part of the remaining twelve years of his life, for it is difficult to believe that he can have done much copying work in the seven years between 1286 and 1293 during which he was engaged in producing Hebrew writings, of which the part that is still preserved alone runs into close on a thousand pages.

It is interesting to note the gradual process by which quotations from the Zohar are introduced with ever growing frequency and forthrightness in the course of these seven years. In the beginning, we find the author referring in suitably vague terms to "sayings of the wise" or "commentaries" by "mystics", but as time goes on, his introductions become more and more enthusiastic, and in the *Mishkan Ha-Eduth,* written in 1293, there are whole long passages in which he refers in a very remarkable manner to the character of these antique pearls of wisdom newly 'discovered' by him and finally revealed. A closer analysis of this book removes the last doubt that it was intended to serve as a propagandist introduction to the Zohar which had just been, or was on the point of being, published. Although it is to some extent devoted to the further development of those ideas relevant to its central theme (the eschatology of the soul), which are expounded in the Zohar, its main purpose is clearly propagandist.

But notwithstanding all that has been said of the author's motives and the chronological sequence in which the Zohar was written, the question of its authorship cannot yet be said to have been answered. After all, it is still possible that Moses de Leon made use of writings which were in his possession but not written by himself. The question, therefore, is whether it is possible to find proof positive that he was really the author of the Zohar.

In regard to this question all I can say is that after making a close study of Moses de Leon's Hebrew writings and their relation to the *Midrash Ha-Neelam* and the components of the Zohar, I have come to the conclusion that they were all written by the same man. I am bound to admit that for many years, even after I had become convinced that the Zohar is the work of one writer, I was in doubt on this point. For a long time I searched for criteria which would positively exclude the possibility of Moses de Leon being the author, such as for example repeated flagrant misunderstandings of the text of the Zohar by Moses de Leon himself. But although hundreds of quotations from the Zohar occur in the writings published under his own name, be it textually or paraphrased, I have been unable to discover a single case in which it is possible to speak of a significant misunderstanding. I have thus come to abandon the idea that the theory of another authorship is capable of being proved. On the other hand, the assumption that the author of the Zohar was also the author of the Hebrew writings supplies an adequate explanation of all doubtful points, if it be fairly borne in mind that the writer was not willing to disclose the pseudepigraphic character of his work on the Zohar.

What I have said does not mean that the personality of Moses de Leon and his authorship of the Zohar no longer offer any problem. To say that would be to overlook that we possess too little documentary material which goes beyond the bare rehearsal of his theosophic doctrines. Even if the proof of Moses de Leon's authorship which I shall advance is conclusive, the acceptance of this theory still leaves a number of questions unanswered. These questions in particular concern the various stages of Moses de Leon's religious development and the events which brought about his pseudepigraphic activity. This applies for instance to the still unsolved problem of his relationship to Joseph Gikatila.

There can be no doubt that Moses de Leon, too, began as a follower of Maimonides and was only gradually attracted by the study of Kabbalism. This is plain enough from the philosophical elements of his Hebrew writings, and in addition we have the clearest documentary proof in the form of a manuscript—described in the autographed catalogue of the Guenzburg collection of Hebrew manuscripts, now in Moscow—of the Hebrew translation of Maimonides' "Guide of the Perplexed", which was written in 1264 "for the erudite (ha-maskil) Rabbi Moses de Leon."[131] The absence of further honorifics suggests that he was at that date still a young man, although of sufficient means to be able to pay for a private copy of so voluminous a book. We shall probably not go wrong in assuming that he was born around 1240. The period of more than twenty years between 1264 and 1286 we may picture as being filled with intensive study and gradual development towards mysticism, with its latter half devoted to the writing of the Zohar in the manner outlined in the foregoing pages.

From all we know it would appear that in the seventies he made the acquaintance of Joseph Gikatila who at that time was a zealous follower of the school of Prophetic Kabbalism founded by Abraham Abulafia. Although the two Kabbalists never mention each other by name, a study of their writings leads one to the conclusion that each had a considerable share in influencing the other. To begin with Moses de Leon, it is plain enough that, although he nowhere approaches the main points of Abulafia's doctrine itself, which does not seem to have aroused his enthusiasm, his writings, and particularly those in Hebrew, reflect the influence of Gikatila's *Ginnath Egoz* in their treatment of the mysticism of letters and similar subjects.[132] In some passages, the influence of the *Ginnath Egoz* is so striking that on the face of it one might be inclined to ascribe the authorship to Gikatila.[133] On the other hand, it is certain that it was not Gikatila through whom Moses de Leon was led to the Sefirothic Kabbalah, for Gikatila during the first period of his literary activity, i. e. the period during which the Zohar was written, showed hardly any understanding for the theosophic conception of mysticism. The spiritual development of Gikatila, too, shows evidence of a definite change of outlook. In his later writings there is hardly a trace of the influence of Abulafia and the characteristic ideas of the *Ginnath Egoz*. Instead, he displays all signs of having gone over body and soul to the doctrine of theosophic Kabbalism. The influence of the Zohar is plain in all his later writings, though the form in which it is expressed differs widely from that which we find in the case of Moses de Leon. It would appear that Moses de Leon's theosophical trend of mind very deeply influenced his own development.

Unfortunately we have no knowledge of the actual personal relations between these two Kabbalists. Did Gikatila know of the pseudepigraphic character of the Zohar? He too propagates its ideas, particularly in his *Shaare Orah*, but his references to the source of these doctrines are limited to vague allusions to "the words of the wise."[134] This systematic failure to mention the name of the Zohar must have been in accordance with some definite purpose. The title of Gikatila's book originally was *Sefer Ha-Orah*, i.e., "Book of Light",[135] which sounds almost like a paraphrase of *Sefer Ha-Zohar* or "Book of Splendor." By all accounts it was written during the years when Moses de Leon had begun to circulate the first copies of the Zohar. Already in 1293, Moses de Leon in three different passages of his book *Mishkan Ha-Eduth* quotes the "words of the wise in the *Shaare Orah*." It is not clear whether "Gates of Light" is one of the several assumed names under which the Zohar appears in Moses de Leon's other writings, or whether the reference is to Gikatila's book. On the one hand, there is the fact that one of the passages quoted is in fact to be found in the first chapter of Gikatila's book, and is written in a terminology particularly characteristic of this writer.[136] On the other hand, the two other passages mentioned are not to be found in Gikatila's work, and there is the further point that since Gikatila wrote under his own name, his book does not purport to be the work of the ancient Rabbis. Is it therefore permissible to conclude that Moses de Leon had read only the first chapter of Gikatila's still incomplete work and that in his veiled hints as to the existence of the Zohar he made playful use of the title of his friend's book? That would at least not be out of harmony with his general habits as a writer. In any event it appears likely that Gikatila had read the Zohar already before 1293 and that he had conceived the idea of making its mystical smybolism the subject of one of his own works. It may be that in propagating the new ideas he acted in accordance with Moses de Leon's own wishes. He himself cannot possibly have been the author of the Zohar. Not one of the criteria of authorship to which we must now turn our attention applies to his own original writings as compared with the Zohar. But it is likely enough that as a member of Moses de Leon's closest circle, as his friend who was at one and at the same time his teacher and his disciple, he played a part in the preliminaries of the writing and publication of the Zohar, a part which, at the present time, we are still unable to determine.

10

It goes without saying that it is no more possible to solve the riddle of Moses de Leon's authorship without a detailed analysis of all the factors involved, than it is possible to answer the question when and how the Zohar as a work of literature was composed without thorough research. Nevertheless, the conclusions at which I have arrived can be summarized comparatively briefly.

Moses de Leon's Hebrew writings are distinguished by a style which is peculiarly their own and, in some respects, differs sharply from that of Gikatila. Its special mark is an admixture of rhymed prose and an abundance of Scriptural "tags" in the precious and flowery manner of erudite Hebrew literature in mediaeval Spain and a very awkward prose-fabric of his own. Clearly it would be idle to look for anything like that in the Zohar where the author had to put up with a language—Aramaic—which did not offer him the advantage of a stock of ready-made phrases and semi-poetical quotations. On the other hand, this flowery style—which he drops not infrequently—does not prevent one from discerning the texture of what might be called with some justification his real language.

Now the point is that while the many peculiarities of his authentic speech are not found in the writings of any other contemporary author, not even Gikatila to whom he is very close in other respects, they do correspond in the most striking manner to certain peculiarities of the language of the Zohar. One finds in both the same deviations from common usage, in some cases even the same mistakes. And these mistakes occur not only in Hebrew passages which might be thought to be translations of the corresponding Aramaic passages of the Zohar, but also where this possibility is excluded. The same wrong constructions, the same words with peculiar new meanings, the same wrong verb inflections, the same manner of confusing the verb-stems of *Kal* and *Hif'il*—all these and many other characteristics of Moses de Leon's Hebrew language are also to be found in the Zohar.[187] Any translator of the Zohar would have corrected these mistakes, especially in the many cases where they are in flagrant contradiction with the usage common in Hebrew. Moses de Leon does nothing of the sort. He displays precisely the same preference for endless repetition, verbal bombast and the indiscriminate use of certain terms which are thereby almost robbed of their meaning. No other writer, for example, uses the word "mystery" half as often as he and the author of the Zohar—in most cases to very little purpose.

Again, both Moses de Leon and the author of the Zohar display the same aversion to the terms *Kabbalah* and *Sefiroth,* the infrequent use of which in his Hebrew writings is doubly striking in view of the plethora of Kabbalistic terms which crowd every page of his books. And if one turns from the use of words to the construction of sentences, one is struck by the many instances where one of his Hebrew passages—freely written and not taken from the Zohar—in its construction and its use of words reads for all the world like a translation from the Zohar. This is particularly true of the parallelism with the Hebrew part of the *Midrash Ha-Neelam.* Often one scarcely realizes that a passage one has just read in its own proper context is to all intents and purpose nothing but an almost literal repetition of a passage from the *Midrash Ha-Neelam.* The chief difference between the two is that in Moses de Leon's other Hebrew writings, the style has usually been touched up and embellished by flowery Scriptural phrases for which there was of course no room in a pseudo-Midrash.

Again, in analyzing those passages of which it is expressly said that their sources are antique, and which are in fact to be found only in the Zohar, one comes upon a highly significant uncertainty of phrasing in the introductory formulae. No mediaeval author would ever have thought of referring to the Talmud or the Midrash as the work of "commentators," a term reserved exclusively for mediaeval writers. Moses de Leon, nevertheless, thinks nothing of introducing quotations from the Zohar alternatively as "words of the wise", and as the opinion of the "commentators".

To this must be added the further significant fact that these quotations frequently differ in no way from their context where the author advances as his own literary product what is simply taken from the Zohar, without troubling to quote his references. Nothing could be more mistaken than to imagine that Moses de Leon, in quoting the Zohar (or whatever name he gave it), is careful to distinguish what he quotes from what he puts forward as his own brain-child. His way of quoting the Zohar is to some extent conditioned by the need of masking the true position. The *Sefer Ha-Rimmon* in particular abounds with such quotations where the quotation marks are actually applied to only a very small portion of long passages lifted textually from the Zohar, sometimes even from a single paragraph. He is simply quoting himself under another name; even where he paraphrases a Zoharic passage with his "own" words, these turn out upon analysis to be nothing but a repetition of the words used in some other part of the Zohar!

The manner in which Moses de Leon makes use of the Zohar contrasts sharply with the attitude he displays where his source is a genuine Midrash. With the latter, he does not vary quotations or combine them into a new context. With the Zohar, however, he shows no hesitation in employing his material in a new form. Sometimes he quotes an idea almost without changing an expression, but as often as not he strings together scattered thoughts from the original, and vice versa. His method is that of the artist who shapes the material into any form he desires. One never has the feeling that the author is laboriously groping through the text for suitable quotations which can be incorporated in his own work. On the contrary, every word breathes the same spirit, and it is left to the critic to discover, with no small amount of labor, that the constituent thoughts of a firmly constructed homily are to be found scattered among various Zoharic passages. When one has analyzed a number of such examples one begins to realize that in many cases the author is strictly speaking not dealing in literary quotations at all, but merely adapting the method already worked out in the Zohar, whose subject-matter is constantly present in his mind. The *motifs* of his homiletics being always before his eye so to speak, his technique consists in presenting them now in this way, now in that, often without adhering strictly to the particular construction of thought which was dominant in his mind when he wrote the Zohar. In this sense, his Hebrew writings are a genuine continuation, and in some cases a further development, of the Zohar. The same fact also explains why Jellinek, who was the first to undertake a comparative study of the Zohar and one of Moses de Leon's Hebrew texts,[138] was led to the wrong conclusion that the latter were written before the Zohar. This idea may have suggested itself to him because he found that a single train of thought in Moses de Leon's Hebrew book recurred in the form of three scattered fragments in the Zohar. Had he considered the possibility that the author might have continued his work on the same *motifs* after completing the Zohar, he would have been led to more fruitful conclusions.

The same technique of variation on themes begun in the Zohar is evident in the way in which he employs parables and similes capable of illustrating more than one idea, modifying them as the context demands.[139] Or he translates a piece of cosmic symbolism, which he has introduced in the Zohar, into the equivalent psychological symbol. A conversation in the Zohar between the sun and the moon concerning her waning—a variation of a Talmudic Aggadah —is converted, in Moses de Leon's *Mishkan Ha-Eduth,* into a dialogue between God and the Soul.[140] In every instance it is evident that the author is completely familiar with the subject and is making use of it as one would with one's own work, although he is careful to conceal this fact as far as this is possible.

Again, Moses de Leon's "library" is exactly the same as that of the Zohar. How often has it happened that some more or less unfamiliar source of a Zoharic passage which I noted down as such, next turned up in Moses de Leon's treatment of the same subject.[141] The very mistakes he makes in quoting his sources throw light on his authorship of the Zohar. Let us take an example. In the Midrash known under the name *Pesikta,* the inauguration of the Tabernacle is compared to a wedding,[142] the comparison resting on a play of words which in turn suggested a further idea to the Kabbalists. For the 'marriage' of God and the Community of Israel they substituted that of Moses and the Shekhinah, the description of Moses as the 'Man of God' thus being made to signify, according to them, that he was indeed the 'husband of the Shekhinah.' This interpretation, which is of course entirely foreign to the *Pesikta*, is advanced by more than one Kabbalist of the period with which we are concerned and also plays an important part in the Zohar where it appears in several variations: Moses, according to the Zohar, was the only mortal who was vouchsafed the mystical union with the Shekhinah during his earthly life, and who from then on constantly remained in this state of 'mystical marriage'. Moses de Leon, whose mind dwells entirely in these constructions, quotes one of the most remarkable Zoharic passages on this subject, but from the *Pesikta!*[143] The mystical interpretation which he has himself read into this *Pesikta* passage is so dominant in his mind that he inadvertently quotes the Midrash in support of an idea which he has actually developed in the Zohar.

In addition to the genuine sources of his ideas which he is in the habit of referring to with more or less circumstantial accuracy, there is also in his Hebrew writings more than a trace of pseudepigraphy. Thus he quotes long passages from the Book of Enoch which are not to be found in the Zohar but which have the advantage of fitting in admirably, both in content and in style, with his own train of thought. There can be no question of his having used an Arabic Book of Enoch unknown to us, or anything else of the sort[144]; nor is it necessary to assume that he had himself written such a book before he quoted it, although he may have intended to do so or even have begun writing it. He is the first to quote from the above mentioned "Testament of Eliezer ben Hyrkanus,"[145] of which I have said that it must have been written by the author of the Zohar himself. The same applies to non-authentic pieces from alleged *responsa* of the Babylonian savant Hai Gaon, which contain several passages in the vein of the *Midrash Ha-Neelam* and concerning the origin of which there has hitherto been some obscurity. Here again, Moses de Leon, the author of the *Midrash Ha-Neelam*, is the first to quote one of these bogus *responsa*[146] which even a scholar of the rank of David Luria eighty years ago adduced as proof of the hoary antiquity of the Zohar.[147] It follows that he must have had a share in the writing of these pseudepigraphic *responsa*, even if he did not write all of them. And generally speaking, there is no lack in his Hebrew writings of curious parables, legends, etc., which, while they are not to be found in the Zohar, are entirely in harmony with its spirit, and in some of which we encounter legendary persons whom we met in the Zohar as the alleged authors of mystical texts.[148]

It is worth mentioning that in his Hebrew writings, Moses de Leon not infrequently deals very fully with matters which the Zohar mentions only in passing, thereby incidentally confirming the authenticity of Zoharic passages which critics, as well as later Kabbalists, have treated as interpolations.[149] A study of his Hebrew writings in fact supplies the best commentary to large parts of the Zohar. On the literary side, it helps one to realize that Moses de Leon as a writer was fully equal to the task of writing the Zohar, but it is also plain how important the artificial patina of his Aramaic, with its strangeness and its solemnity, was for the literary success of the Zohar. Had it been written in Hebrew and without that picturesque background, I rather doubt whether it would have produced anything like the same impression.

11

If proper account is taken of all these facts, certain allusions in Moses de Leon's writings to his mystical 'sources' appear no longer as anything but veiled references to his own authorship. Thus in 1290 he remarks in his "Book of the Rational Soul," that "only recently the spring of mystery has begun to flow in the land"[150]— a plain allusion to the recent publication of some of the Zoharic writings. But the most remarkable hints of this genre are to be found in the *Mishkan Ha-Eduth*, written in 1293, from which I shall quote, as literally as possible, the most important passage, one which, like so much else, has escaped the notice of writers on the subject. In a passage where he discusses the theory of a two-fold *Gehenna*—a close parallel to the above-mentioned idea of a double Paradise—he prefaces his Zoharic variations on the subject by the following remarks:

"Concerning this matter there are hidden mysteries and secret things which are unknown to men. You will now see that I am revealing deep and secret mysteries which the holy sages regarded as sacred and hidden, profound matters which properly speaking are not fit for revelation so that they may not become a target for the wit of every idle person. These holy men of old have pondered all their lives over these things and have hidden them, and did not reveal them to every one, and now I have come to reveal them. Therefore keep them to yourself, unless it be that you encounter one who fears God and keeps His Commandments and the Torah . . . I looked at the ways of the children of the world and saw how in all that concerns these [theological] matters, they are enmeshed in foreign ideas and false, extraneous [or heretical] notions. One generation passes away and another generation comes, but the errors and falsehoods abide for ever. And no one sees and no one hears and no one awakens, for they are all asleep, for a deep sleep from God has fallen upon them, so that they do not question and do not read and do not search out. And when I saw all this *I found myself constrained to write and to conceal and to ponder, in order to reveal it* to all thinking men, and to make known all these things with which the holy sages of old concerned themselves all their lives. For they are scattered in the Talmud and in their [other] words and secret sayings, precious and hidden better even than pearls. And they [the sages] have closed and locked the door behind their words and hidden all their mystical books, because they saw that the time had not come to reveal and publish them. Even as the wise king has said to us: 'Speak not in the ears of a fool.' Yet I have come to recognize that it would be a meritorious deed to bring out to light what was in the dark and to make known the secret matters which they have hidden.''[161] And a few pages later he says: "And though I now reveal their mysteries, the Almighty God knows that my purpose in doing so is good, in order that many may become wise and retain their faith in God, and hear and learn and fear in their soul and rejoice because they know the truth.''[162]

Now this appears to me a highly significant statement. To refer in such a manner and in so many ambiguous terms to a work which, as we have seen, was without any doubt written shortly before, is to reveal one's authorship. Short of abandoning the pseudepigraphical fiction—a thing not to be expected of him—Moses de Leon could hardly go farther in proclaiming himself to be the author of these "words of the wise" which he feels compelled *to write and to conceal,* as his own excellent phrase puts it. He does not explicitly claim to have discovered the old books themselves; his purpose is merely to reveal what must be contained in them if they were in accordance with that meaning of the Kabbalah which was to him natural and supremely important.

At the same time, the evidence he provides in these passages also supplies a clear picture of the motives which led him to write the Zohar and which are expressed with special emphasis in his long preface to the *Sefer Ha-Rimmon*. Jellinek, who was the first to discern these motives from the much briefer allusions in the "Book of the Rational Soul,"[153] and Graetz who followed him on this point, were right in their assertion: Moses de Leon wrote the Zohar in order to stem the growth of the radical rationalistic mood which was widespread among his educated contemporaries and with regard to which we have quite a number of interesting testimonials. He refers in one of his books to the opinions and habits of these circles who had already broken in theory as well as in practice with large parts of Jewish tradition and religious law.[154] In opposition to them he strives to maintain the undefiled Judaism of the Torah, as he interpreted it in his mystical way. A mystical Midrash which presented an impressive picture of the profundity of the divine word appeared to him as the best instrument for awakening an understanding of the grandeur of true Judaism, when it is properly, i. e. mystically, understood. And since he was a man of genius he succeeded, over and above the immediate purpose which he set himself and which is now clear to us, in giving magnificent expression to the spirit of that contemporary world of Spanish Kabbalism which was the abode of his own restless mind.

The figure of the man now stands clearly before us. He came from the world of philosophic enlightenment against which he subsequently conducted so unremitting a fight. In his youth we see him brooding over Moses Maimonides' great work and going to some expense to procure a private copy. Somewhat later his mystical inclinations turn him in the direction of Neoplatonism. There can be no doubt that he read those extracts from Plotinus' Enneads which were current in the Middle Ages under the title of "The Theology of Aristotle." He quotes in one of his writings Plotinus' description of the philosopher's ecstatic ascent into the world of pure intelligence and his vision of the One.[155] But at the same time he is more and more attracted by the mystical side of Judaism, which appears to him as its true core, and gradually he comes to ponder the mystery of the Godhead as it was presented by the Kabbalistic theosophy of his age. He studies, alters, selects and develops these ideas and links them with his own thoughts on a mystical theory of morals—

thoughts which play so large a part in the Zohar, as well as in all his Hebrew writings.[156] But the theosophist and moralist in whom the genius comes to life has also developed the adventurous side of his being, for it is plain that he embarked on a great adventure in writing and propagating the *Midrash Ha-Neelam* and the Zohar, even if one concedes him his great hours of inspiration, as I for one am prepared to do. For him, however, there was no paradox in what he did, and I am almost inclined to say that he was right. Pseudepigraphy is far removed from forgery. The mark of immorality, which is inseparable from falsehood, does not stain it, and for this reason it has always been admitted as a legitimate category of religious literature of the highest moral order. The historian of religion in particular has no cause to express moral condemnation of the pseudepigraphist. The Quest for Truth knows of adventures that are all its own, and in a vast number of cases has arrayed itself in pseudepigraphic garb. The further a man progresses along his own road in this Quest for Truth, the more he might become convinced that his own road must have already been trodden by others, ages before him. To the streak of adventurousness which was in Moses de Leon, no less than to his genius, we owe one of the most remarkable works of Jewish literature and of the literature of mysticism in general.

THE ZOHAR
II. THE THEOSOPHIC DOCTRINE OF THE ZOHAR

1

Taken as a whole, the Zohar must be regarded as the complete antithesis to the now familiar system of Abulafia. That esoteric doctrine centered round a pragmatic philosophy of ecstasy for the elect, which laid exclusive emphasis on meditation as the way to the cognition of God. By contrast, the Zohar is chiefly concerned with the object of meditation, i.e. the mysteries of *mundus intelligibilis*. Again, the doctrine of prophetic Kabbalism presents itself as the most aristocratic form of mysticism, whereas the language of the Zohar is that of a writer who has experienced the common fears of mankind as profoundly as anyone. For this reason if for no other it struck a chord which resounded deeply in human hearts and assured it a success denied to other forms of early Kabbalism. Last but not least, Abulafia presents the reader with something very much like a system, and his ideas are set out on the whole without reference to Scripture. (Of course, Abulafia, too, has written mystical commentaries to the Torah,[1] but his particular contribution to mysticism did not grow out of these writings.) Here again the Zohar strikes a different note: throughout it reflects the homiletic viewpoint and remains closely bound to the Scriptural text. Often an idea is not so much extrapolated and projected into the Biblical word but rather conceived in the process of mystical reflection upon the latter. In making this approach the Zohar remains true to the tradition of Jewish speculative thought which, to repeat, is alien to the spirit of systematization.

If I were asked to characterize in one word the essential traits of this world of Kabbalistic thought, those which set it apart from other forms of Jewish mysticism, I would say that the Zohar represents Jewish theosophy, i. e., a Jewish form of theosophy. Thirteenth century Kabbalism with its theosophic conception of God is essentially an attempt to preserve the substance of naive popular faith, now challenged by the rational theology of the philosophers. The new God of Kabbalism who, according to the Kabbalists, is simply the old God of creation and revelation and man in his relation to Him—these are the two poles of Kabbalistic doctrine round which the system of Zoharic thought revolves.

Before proceeding further, I should like to indicate in a few words what I am trying to express by using this much abused term *theosophy*. By theosophy I mean that which was generally meant before the term became a label for a modern pseudo-religion,[2] i. e. *theosophy* signifies a mystical doctrine, or school of thought, which purports to perceive and to describe the mysterious workings of the Divinity, perhaps also believing it possible to become absorbed in its contemplation. Theosophy postulates a kind of divine emanation whereby God, abandoning his self-contained repose, awakens to mysterious life; further, it maintains that the mysteries of creation reflect the pulsation of this divine life. Theosophists in this sense were Jacob Boehme and William Blake, to mention two famous Christian mystics.

I shall now try to go a little deeper into the meaning of this theosophical conception of God, which, it can hardly be doubted, has exercised a decisive influence on the majority of Kabbalistic writers. It rests upon a basic assumption to which I have referred in the course of the first lecture, where I tried to trace its origin in the problem of the divine attributes. There I also mentioned the Kabbalistic term *Sefiroth*—a term for which the approximate translation would be 'spheres' or 'regions' (although the Hebrew word *sefirah* has nothing to do with the Greek *sphaira,* various hypotheses to the contrary notwithstanding). In the "Book of Creation" from which it was originally taken, Sefiroth simply meant numbers,[3] but with the gradual development of mystical terminology, with which I cannot deal here, it changed its meaning until it came to signify the emergence of divine powers and emanations.

It may be useful at this point to consider the difference between the old Merkabah mysticism and the Kabbalistic system. The world of the Merkabah, with its celestial throne, its heavenly household, and its palaces through which the wanderer passes, is for the Kabbalist no longer of supreme importance, though its core, frequently clothed in new disguise, never ceases to attract his interest. All knowledge concerning it is, for him, merely provisional. Indeed, some Kabbalists go so far as to refer to Ezekiel's Merkabah as the *second Merkabah*.[4] In other words, the new Kabbalistic Gnosis or cognition of God, which in the Hekhaloth tracts is not even mentioned, is related to a deeper layer of mystical reality, an "inner Merkabah",[5] as it were, which can be visualized only in a symbolical way, if at all. Briefly, this gnosis concerns God Himself. Where previously the vision could go no farther than to the perception of the glory of his appearance on the throne, it is now a question, if the expression be permitted, of the inside of this glory. In the early period of Kabbalistic thought, represented by the book *Bahir* and various smaller writings down to the middle of the thirteenth century,[6] these two domains, the world of the throne and that of the divinity—the original *pleroma* of the Gnostics—are not yet completely differentiated. Nevertheless the tendency to separate them, and to penetrate into a new field of contemplation beyond the sphere of the throne, is at the roots of the original impulse of the Kabbalah.

Historically, Jewish mysticism has tended to carry this process ever further, striving to detect successively new layers in the mystery of the Godhead. These worlds of the Sefiroth, too, became, in their turn, a starting-point of fresh attempts to push on into yet more remotely hidden worlds where the radiance of the divine light is mysteriously refracted in itself.[7] The more the original perception, born from deep meditation, of a given mode of divine reality, was externalized and transformed into mere book-learning, in which the symbols lost their tremendous meaning and unfettered allegory filled their empty husks, the more did original thinkers among the Kabbalists strive to penetrate into new and yet deeper layers of mystical consciousness; hence the adoption of new symbols. For the Zohar, however, the Sefiroth still had the unbroken reality of mystical experience. To the analysis of this experience, or at least of some of its essential traits, we must now turn our attention.

2

The hidden God, the innermost Being of Divinity so to speak, has neither qualities nor attributes. This innermost Being the Zohar

and the Kabbalists like to call *En-Sof,* i. e., the Infinite.⁸ Insofar,
however, as this hidden Being is active throughout the universe,
it has also certain attributes which in turn represent certain aspects
of the divine nature; they are so many stages of the divine Being,
and divine manifestation of His hidden life. That is to say, they
are not meant to be mere metaphors. To the mediaeval philosopher,
a Scriptural allusion to the "arm of God" was simply an analogy to
the human arm, which is the only one that exists, i. e. the "arm of
God" is merely a figure of speech. To the mystic, on the contrary,
the arm of God represents a higher reality than the human arm.⁹
The latter exists only by virtue of the former's existence. Isaac ibn
Latif, a 13th century mystic, puts it in the shortest terms: "All names
and attributes are metaphoric with us but not with Him" which,
according to him, is the true key to a mystical understanding of
the Torah. In other words, the mystic believes in the existence of
a sphere of divine reality to which this term, among others, is really
applicable. Each sphere of this sort constitutes one of the Sefiroth.
The Zohar¹⁰ expressly distinguishes between two worlds, which both
represent God. First a primary world, the most deeply hidden of
all, which remains insensible and unintelligible to all but God, the
world of *En-Sof;* and secondly one, joined unto the first, which
makes it possible to know God, and of which the Bible says: "Open
ye the gates that I may enter", the world of attributes. The two in
reality form one, in the same way—to use the Zohar's simile"—as
the coal and the flame; that is to say, the coal exists also without a
flame, but its latent power manifests itself only in its light. God's
mystical attributes are such worlds of light in which the dark nature
of *En-Sof* manifests itself.

According to the Kabbalists, there are ten such fundamental attributes to God, which are at the same time ten stages through which
the divine life pulsates back and forth. The point to keep in mind
is that the Sefiroth are not secondary or intermediary spheres which
interpose between God and the universe. The author does not regard them as something comparable to, for example, the 'middle
stages' of the Neoplatonists which have their place between the Absolute One and the world of the senses. In the Neoplatonic system,
these emanations are "outside" the One, if it is possible to use that
expression. There have been attempts to justify an analogous in-

terpretation of the theology of the Zohar and to treat the Sefiroth as secondary stages or spheres outside of, or apart from the divine personality. These interpretations, which have been advanced above all by D. H. Joel,[12] have the distinct advantage of avoiding the problem of God's unity in the Sefiroth, but it may be said not unfairly that they ignore the crucial point and misrepresent the intention of the author. True, the Zohar frequently refers to the Sefiroth as stages, but they are plainly regarded not as the steps of a ladder between God and the world, but as various phases in the manifestation of the Divinity which proceed from and succeed each other.

The difficulty lies precisely in the fact that the emanation of the Sefiroth is conceived as a process which takes place *in* God and which at the same time enables man to perceive God. In their emanation something which belongs to the Divine is quickened and breaks through the closed shell of His hidden Self. This something is God's creative power, which does not reside only in the finite universe of creation, although of course there, too, it is immanent and even perceptible. Rather do the Kabbalists conceive their creative power to be an independent theosophical world of its own, which antedates the natural world and represents a higher stage of reality. The hidden God, *En-Sof*, manifests himself to the Kabbalist under ten different aspects, which in turn comprise an endless variety of shades and gradations. Every grade has its own symbolical name, in strict accordance with its peculiar manifestations. Their sum total constitutes a highly complex symbolical structure, in which almost every Biblical word corresponds to one of the Sefiroth. This correspondence, which in turn could be subjected to the most searching investigation regarding its motives,[13] enables the Kabbalists to base their interpretation of Scripture on the assumption that every verse not only describes an event in nature or history but in addition is a symbol of a certain stage in the divine process, an impulse of the divine life.

The mystical conception of the Torah, of which mention has been made in the first lecture, is fundamental for the understanding of the peculiar symbolism of the Zohar. The Torah is conceived as a vast *corpus symbolicum* representative of that hidden life in God which the theory of the Sefiroth attempts to describe. For the mystic who starts out with this assumption, every word is capable of becoming a symbol, and the most inconspicuous phrases or verses are precisely the ones into which at times the greatest importance is read.[14] For the peculiar speculative genius which discovers in the Torah layer upon layer of hidden meaning, there is in principle no limit. In the last resort, the whole of the Torah, as is often stressed by the author, is nothing but the one great and holy Name of God. Seen that way it cannot be "understood"; it can only by "interpreted" in an approximate manner. The Torah has "seventy faces" shining forth to the initiate. Later Kabbalism has tended to give a more individualistic turn to this idea. Isaac Luria taught that there are 600,000 "faces" of the Torah, as many as there were souls in Israel at the time of the Revelation. This meant that, in principle, everybody in Israel has his own way of reading and interpreting the Torah, according to the "root of his soul", or to his own lights. The hackneyed phrase acquires here a very precise meaning: the divine word sends out to every man another ray of light which indeed is all his own.

The Zohar is the first book in which the theory of the four methods of interpreting Scripture, originally developed by Christian exegetes, is taken up by a Jewish author.[15] But of the four layers of meaning: the literal, the Aggadic or homiletic, the allegorical, and the mystical, in the last resort only the fourth—*Raza,* i. e. "The Mystery", in the terminology of the Zohar—matters to the author. It is true that he also advances numerous examples of Scriptural interpretation based on the other three methods, but these are either taken from other writings or, at the most, developed from ideas not peculiar to Kabbalism.[16] Only when it is a question of revealing the mystery of a verse—or rather one of its many mysteries —does the author show real enthusiasm. And, as we have seen, the "mystery" in every case concerns the interpretation of the Biblical word as a symbol pointing to the hidden world of God and its inner processes.

Incidentally, the author frequently takes issue with those among his contemporaries who reject the view that the Torah has more than one meaning. He does not, it is true, in any sense question or deny its literal meaning, but he makes the assumption that it merely hides and envelopes the inner mystical light.[17] Indeed, he goes so far as to assert that if the Torah really contained merely those tales,

genealogies and political precepts which are capable of being literally understood, we should be able even today to write a much
better one.[18]

Still more radical are the ideas developed by the author of the
Raya Mehemna; here we already find sharp invective against the
representatives of purely literal exegesis and the dogmatic advocates
of an exclusively Halakhic study of the Talmud who, in his view,
show no understanding of the religious problems with which the
mystics are wrestling.[19] This sharply critical attitude towards non-
mystical Judaism reached its climax in the second half of the fourteenth century, when an anonymous Kabbalistic theosophist in
Spain summed up the doctrine of his school in two important
works, the book *Peliah* and the book *Kanah*—the first a commentary to the first six chapters of Genesis, the second an explanation
of the meaning of the religious commandments.[20] This writer goes
so far as to proclaim the literal meaning even of the rabbinical
sources, and above all the Talmud, to be identical with the Kabbalistic interpretation. By applying the method of immanent criticism he tries to prove that the Talmudic discourses on the law become meaningless unless they are so interpreted.[21] Here then we have
nothing less than a *reductio ad absurdum* of traditional Judaism
and an attempt to replace it by an entirely mystical system within
the framework of tradition. In this system, nothing exists except
symbols, and signs mean nothing independently of the symbols
manifest in them. It is not surprising that a latent anti-Talmudism
has been diagnosed in these writings,[22] nor does it surprise us to
learn that the Messiah of Kabbalism, Sabbatai Zevi, studied no other
Kabbalistic books in his youth than the Zohar and the book *Kanah,*
the latent antinomianism of which became manifest in the movement inaugurated by him.

3

The nature of this mystical symbolism is one of the main obstacles to a true understanding of a work of mystical exegesis like
the Zohar, and yet this elaborate and often bizarre symbolism is the
key to its particular religious world. Even a writer of the distinction
of R. T. Herford who has given proof of his understanding of Judaism, speaks of a "symbolism which often appears to be wildly extra-

vagant and sometimes gross and repulsive."[23] The fact is that it is hardly possible at first contact with the world of Kabbalistic symbolism to escape a sense of bewilderment.

There is, of course, no question of the symbolism of the Zohar having fallen from heaven—it is the result of the development of the four generations since the book *Bahir,* and especially that of the school of Gerona. Already in the earlier writings we find the same principle and often even the same details. It is true, however, that they made free use with the details and every Kabbalist of importance grouped the symbols in his own way. For our purpose there is no need to dwell on these differences, however great their importance for the internal history of many Kabbalistic ideas might be.

In the course of a brief lecture it is not possible to give more than a few examples of the manner in which the Zohar seeks to describe in symbolical terms the theosophic universe of God's hidden life. Joseph Gikatila's *Shaare Orah,* "The Gates of Light," is still much the best work on the subject.[24] It gives an excellent description of Kabbalistic symbolism and also analyzes the motives which determine the correlation between the Sefiroth and their Scriptural symbols. Gikatila wrote only a few years after the appearance of the Zohar, and although he leans heavily on it, his book is also marked by quite a few original departures in thought. In English literature on the subject A. E. Waite's "The Secret Doctrine in Israel" represents a serious attempt to analyze the symbolism of the Zohar. His work, as I have had occasion to remark at the outset of these lectures, is distinguished by real insight into the world of Kabbalism; it is all the more regrettable that it is marred by an uncritical attitude towards facts of history and philology, to which it must be added that he has frequently been led astray by Jean de Pauly's faulty and inadequate French translation of the Zohar, which, owing to his own ignorance of Hebrew and Aramaic, he was compelled to accept as authoritative.[25]

For the succession of the ten Sefiroth, the Kabbalists have a number of more or less fixed terms; this terminology is also quite often employed by the Zohar, although even more frequently its author operates with the innumerable symbolical names correlated to each Sefirah and its various aspects. These fixed or common names of the Sefiroth are:

1. *Kether Elyon,*   the "supreme crown" of God;

2. *Hokhmah,*   the "wisdom" or primordial idea of God;

3. *Binah,*   the "intelligence" of God;

4. *Hesed,*   the "love" or mercy of God;

5. *Gevurah* or *Din,*   the "power" of God, chiefly manifested as the power of stern judgment and punishment;

6. *Rahamim,*   the "compassion" of God, to which falls the task of mediating between the two preceding Sefiroth; the name *Tifereth* "beauty", is used only rarely.

7. *Netsah,*   the "lasting endurance" of God;

8. *Hod,*   the "majesty" of God;

9. *Yesod,*   the "basis" or "foundation" of all active forces in God;

10 *Malkhuth,*   the "kingdom" of God, usually described in the Zohar as the *Keneseth Israel,* the mystical archetype of Israel's community, or as the Shekhinah.

These are the ten spheres of divine manifestation in which God emerges from His hidden abode. Together they form the "unified universe" of God's life, the "world of union," *alma de-yihuda,* both the ensemble and the particulars of which the Zohar attempts to interpret in an unending variety of speculation. Of this multitude of symbols I can only quote and try to interpret a few.

The manner in which the Sefiroth are described in the Zohar which, it should be pointed out, avoids this classical term and uses others instead, throws some light on the extent to which the idea of God's mystical qualities have moved away from the conception of divine attributes. They are called "mystical crowns of the Holy King"[26] notwithstanding the fact that "He is they, and they are He."[27] They are the ten names most common to God, and in their entirety they also form his one great Name. They are "the King's faces,"[28] in other words, his varying aspects, and they are also called

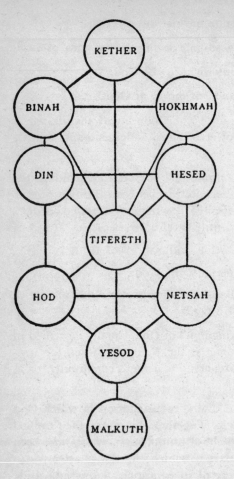

the inner, intrinsic or mystical Face of God. They are the ten stages of the inner world, through which God descends from the inmost recesses down to His revelation in the Shekhinah. They are the garments of the Divinity, but also the beams of light which it sends out.[29]

The world of Sefiroth is described, for instance, as a mystical organism, a symbol which has the additional advantage of supplying the Kabbalist with a ready justification for the anthropomorphic mode of Scriptural expression. The two most important images used in this connection are that of the tree—see the drawing —and that of the man.

"All the divine powers form a succession of layers and are like a tree"—we read already in the book Bahir,[30] through which, as we have seen, the thirteenth century Kabbalists became the heirs of Gnostical symbolism. The ten Sefiroth constitute the mystical Tree of God or tree of divine power each representing a branch whose common root is unknown and unknowable. But En-Sof is not only the hidden Root of all Roots, it is also the sap of the tree; every branch representing an attribute, exists not by itself but by virtue of En-Sof, the hidden God. And this tree of God is also, as it were, the skeleton of the universe; it grows throughout the whole of creation and spreads its branches through all its ramifications. All mundane and created things exist only because something of the power of the Sefiroth lives and acts in them.

The simile of the man is as often used as that of the Tree. The Biblical word that man was created in the image of God means two things to the Kabbalist: first, that the power of the Sefiroth, the paradigm of divine life, exists and is active also in man. Secondly, that the world of the Sefiroth, that is to say the world of God the Creator, is capable of being visualized under the image of man the created. From this it follows that the limbs of the human body, to repeat the instance I have already given, are nothing but images of a certain spiritual mode of existence which manifests itself in the symbolic figure of *Adam Kadmon,* the primordial man.[31] For, to repeat, the Divine Being Himself cannot be expressed. All that can be expressed are His symbols. The relation between *En-Sof* and its mystical qualities, the Sefiroth, is comparable to that between the soul and the body, but with the difference that the human body and soul differ in nature, one being material and the other spiritual, while in the organic whole of God all spheres are substantially the same.[32] Nevertheless the question of the essence and substance of the Sefiroth, with which the Zohar itself is not concerned, subsequently became to theosophical Kabbalism a special problem whose consideration we must forego here.[33] The conception of God as an organism had the advantage of answering the question why there are different manifestations of the divine power, although the divine Being is an Absolute Whole. For is not the organic life of the soul one and the same, although the function of the hands differs from that of the eyes, etc.[34]

Incidentally, the conception of the Sefiroth as parts or limbs of the mystical anthropos leads to an anatomical symbolism which does not shrink from the most extravagant conclusions. Thus, for instance, the concept of the various aspects of the beard worn by the "most ancient one" is stated to be symbolical of varying shades of God's compassion. The *Idra Rabba* is almost entirely devoted to a most radical symbolism of this kind.

Side by side with this organic symbolism, other ways of symbolical expression present themselves to the theosophist who is concerned to describe the realm of Divinity. The world of the Sefiroth is the hidden world of language, the world of the divine names. The Sefiroth are the creative names which God called into the world, the

names which He gave to Himself.[35] The action and development of
that mysterious force which is the seed of all creation is, according
to the Zohar's interpretation of the Scriptural testimony, none other
than speech. "God spoke—this speech is a force which at the beginning of creative thought was separated from the secret of *En-
Sof*."[36] The process of life in God can be construed as the unfolding
of the elements of speech. This is indeed one of the Zohar's favorite
symbols. The world of divine emanation is one in which the faculty
of speech is anticipated in God. Varying stages of the Sefiroth-Uni-
verse represent, according to the Zohar, the abysmal will, thought,
inner and inaudible word, audible voice, and speech, i. e. articulated
and differentiated expression.[37]

The same conception of progressive differentiation is inherent in
other symbolisms of which I should like to mention only one, that
of the I, You and He. God in the most deeply hidden of His manifestations, when he has as it were just decided to launch upon His
work of creation, is called He. God in the complete unfolding of
his Being, Grace and Love, in which He becomes capable of being
perceived by the "reason of heart," and therefore of being expressed,
is called "You." But God, in His supreme manifestation, where the
fullness of His Being finds its final expression in the last and all-
embracing of His attributes, is called "I."[38] This is the stage of true
individuation in which God as a person says "I" to Himself. This
divine Self, this "I", according to the theosophical Kabbalists—and
this is one of their most profound and important doctrines—is the
Shekhinah, the presence and immanence of God in the whole of
creation. It is the point where man, in attaining the deepest understanding of his own self, becomes aware of the presence of God.
And only from there, standing as it were at the gate of the Divine
Realm,[39] does he progress into the deeper regions of the Divine,
into His "You" and "He" and into the depths of Nothing. To gauge
the degree of paradox implied by these remarkable and very influential thoughts one must remember that in general the mystics, in
speaking of God's immanence in His creation, are inclined to
depersonalize Him: the immanent God only too easily becomes an
impersonal God-head. In fact, this tendency has always been one
of the main pitfalls of pantheism. All the more remarkable is the
fact that the Kabbalists and even those among them who are inclined to pantheism managed to avoid it, for as we have seen the

Zohar identifies the highest development of God's personality with precisely that stage of His unfolding which is nearest to human experience, indeed which is immanent and mysteriously present in every one of us.

4

Among the symbolical descriptions of the unfolding of God in His revelation, special attention must be given to that which is based on the concept of the mystical Nothing. To the Kabbalist the fundamental fact of creation takes place *in* God; apart from that he admits of no act of creation worth that name which might be conceived as fundamentally different from the first inmost act and which takes place outside the world of the Sefiroth. The creation of the world, that is to say, the creation of something out of nothing, is itself but the external aspect of something which takes place in God Himself. This is also a crisis of the hidden *En-Sof* who turns from repose to creation, and it is this crisis, creation and Self-Revelation in one, which constitutes the great mystery of theosophy and the crucial point for the understanding of the purpose of theosophical speculation. The crisis can be pictured as the break-through of the primordial will, but theosophic Kabbalism frequently employs the bolder metaphor of Nothing. The primary start or wrench in which the introspective God is externalized and the light that shines inwardly made visible, this revolution of perspective, transforms *En-Sof*, the inexpressible fullness, into nothingness. It is this mystical 'nothingness' from which all the other stages of God's gradual unfolding in the Sefiroth emanate and which the Kabbalists call the highest Sefirah, or the "supreme crown" of Divinity. To use another metaphor, it is the abyss which becomes visible in the gaps of existence. Some Kabbalists who have developed this idea, for instance Rabbi Joseph ben Shalom of Barcelona (1300), maintain that in every transformation of reality, in every change of form, or every time the status of a thing is altered, the abyss of nothingness is crossed and for a fleeting mystical moment becomes visible.[40] Nothing can change without coming into contact with this region of pure absolute Being which the mystics call Nothing. The difficult task of describing the emergence of the other Sefiroth from the womb of the first—the Nothing—is somehow managed with the aid of copious metaphors.

In this connection it may be of interest to examine a mystical *jeu de mots* which comes very close to the ideas of the Zohar and was already used by Joseph Gikatila.[41] The Hebrew word for nothing, *ain* has the same consonants as the word for I, *ani*—and as we have seen, God's "I" is conceived as the final stage in the emanation of the Sefiroth, that stage in which God's personality, in a simultaneous gathering together of all its previous stages, reveals itself to its own creation. In other words, the passage from *ain* to *ani* is symbolical of the transformation by which the Nothing passes through the progressive manifestation of its essence in the Sefiroth, into the I—a dialectical process whose thesis and antithesis begin and end in God: surely a remarkable instance of dialectical thought. Here as elsewhere, mysticism, intent on formulating the paradoxes of religious experience, uses the instrument of dialectics to express its meaning. The Kabbalists are by no means the only witnesses to this affinity between mystical and dialectical thinking.

In the Zohar, as well as in the Hebrew writings of Moses de Leon, the transformation of Nothing into Being is frequently explained by the use of one particular symbol, that of the primordial point.[42] Already the Kabbalists of the Geronese school employed the comparison with the mathematical point, whose motion creates the line and the surface, to illustrate the process of emanation from the "hidden cause."[43] To this comparison, Moses de Leon adds the symbolism of the point as the centre of the circle.[44] The primordial point from Nothing is the mystical center around which the theogonical processes crystallize. Itself without dimensions and as it were placed between Nothing and Being, the point serves to illustrate what the Kabbalists of the thirteenth century call "the Origin of Being",[45] that "Beginning" of which the first word of the Bible speaks. The somewhat pompous phrases in which the opening lines of the Zohar's interpretation of the story of creation describe this emergence of the primordial point—not indeed from the Nothing as remarked in another context, but from the ethereal aura of God —can serve as an example of the mystical imagery of the whole book[46]:

"In the beginning, when the will of the King began to take effect, he engraved signs into the divine aura. A dark flame sprang forth from the innermost recess of the mystery of the Infinite, *En-Sof*, like a fog which forms out of the formless, enclosed in the ring of this aura, neither white nor black, neither red nor green, and of no color whatever. But when this flame began to assume size and extension it produced radiant colors. For in the innermost center of the flame a well sprang forth from which flames poured upon everything below, hidden in the mysterious secrets of *En-Sof.* The well broke through, and yet did not entirely break through, the ethereal aura which surrounded it. It was entirely unrecognizable until under the impact of its break-through a hidden supernal point shone forth. Beyond this point nothing may be known or understood, and therefore it is called *Reshith,* that is 'Beginning', the first word of creation".[47]

By the Zohar, as by the majority of the other Kabbalistic writers, this primordial point is identified with the wisdom of God, *Hokhmah.* God's wisdom represents the ideal thought of Creation, conceived as the ideal point which itself springs from the impulse of the abysmal will. The author extends the comparison by likening it to the mystical seed which is sown into Creation,[48] the point of comparison apparently being not only the subtlety of both but also the fact that in either the possibilities of further being are potentially, though as yet invisibly, existent.

Insofar as God appears through the manifestation of *Hokhmah,* He is perceived as wise, and in His wisdom the ideal existence of all things is as it were enshrined; if still undeveloped and undifferentiated, the essence of all that exists is nevertheless derived from God's *Hokhmah.*[49] Between this primordial mode of existence in God's thoughts, and the concretest of reality, there is no second transition or crisis, no second creation from the uncreated in the theological sense.

In the following Sefirah, the point develops into a "palace" or "building"—an allusion to the idea that from this Sefirah, if it is externalized, the "building" of the cosmos proceeds.[50] What was hidden and was as it were folded up in the point is now unfolded. The name of this Sefirah, *Bina,* can be taken to signify not only "intelligence", but also "that which divided between the things", i.e. differentiation. What was previously undifferentiated in the divine wisdom exists in the womb of the *Binah,* the "supernal mother", as the "pure totality of all individuation."[51] In it all forms are already preformed, but still preserved in the unity of the divine intellect which contemplates them in itself.

In the passage from the Zohar which has been quoted above, the image of the point is already combined with the more dynamic one of the fountain which springs from the heart of the mystical Nothing. In many places, the primordial point is directly identified with this fountain from which all bliss and all blessings flow. This is the mystical Eden—Eden meaning literally bliss or joy—and from here the stream of divine life takes its course and flows through all the Sefiroth and through all hidden reality, until at last it falls into the "great sea" of Shekhinah, in which God unfolds His totality. The seven Sefiroth which flow from the maternal womb of the *Binah* are the seven primeval days of creation.[52] What appears in time as the epoch of actual and external creation is nothing but the projection of the archetypes of the seven lower Sefiroth which, in timeless existence, are enshrined in God's inwardness. One is tempted to apply to this hidden life of the Sefiroth in their relation to *En-Sof* Shelley's lines:[53]

> *Life, like a dome of many-coloured glass,*
> *Stains the white radiance of Eternity.*

It is true that this supreme entity which springs out of Nothing, this entity in God, this substance of divine wisdom, lies beyond the horizon of human experience. It cannot be questioned or even visualized; it precedes the division between the subject and the object of consciousness without which there is no intellectual cognition, that is to say, no knowledge. In describing this division of the divine consciousness, the Zohar in one of its profoundest symbolisms,[54] speaks of it as a manifestation of God's progressive unfolding. Among the manifestations of God, there is one—for several reasons the Kabbalists identify it with *Binah,* the divine Intelligence—in which He appears as the eternal subject, using the term in its grammatical sense, as the great Who, *Mi,* who stands at the end of every question and every answer; a thought which suggests the idea of an apotheosis of the well-known Jewish penchant for putting questions. There are certain spheres of Divinity where questions can be asked and answers obtained, namely the spheres of "this and that", of all those attributes of God which the Zohar symbolically calls *Eleh,* i. e., the determinable world. In the end, however, meditation reaches a point where it is still possible to question "who", but no longer possible to get an answer; rather does the question itself constitute an answer; and if the domain of *Mi,* of the great Who, in which God appears as the subject of the mundane process, can at least be questioned, the higher sphere of divine wisdom represents something positive beyond the reach of questioning, something which cannot even be visualized in abstract thought.

This idea is expressed in a profound symbol: the Zohar, and indeed the majority of the older Kabbalists, questioned the meaning of the first verse of the Torah: *Bereshith bara Elohim,* "In the beginning created God"; what actually does this mean? The answer is fairly surprising. We are told[55] that it means *Bereshith*—through the medium of the "beginning," i. e., of that primordial existence which has been defined as the wisdom of God,—*bara,* created, that is to say, the hidden Nothing which constitutes the grammatical subject of the word *bara,* emanated or unfolded,—*Elohim,* that is to say, its emanation is *Elohim.* It is the object, and not the subject of the sentence. And what is *Elohim? Elohim* is the name of God, which guarantees the continued existence of creation insofar as it represents the union of the hidden subject *Mi* and the hidden object *Eleh.* (The Hebrew words *Mi* and *Eleh* have the same consonants as the complete word *Elohim*).—In other words, Elohim is the name given to God after the disjunction of subject and object has taken place, but in which this gap is continuously bridged or closed. The mystical Nothing which lies before the division of the primary idea into the Knower and the Known, is not regarded by the Kabbalist as a true subject. The lower ranges of God's manifestation form the object of steady human contemplation, but the highest plane which meditation can reach at all, namely the knowledge of God as the mystical *Mi* (Who), as the subject of the mundane process, this knowledge can be no more than an occasional and intuitive flash which illuminates the human heart, as sunbeams play on the surface of water—to use Moses de Leon's metaphor.[56]

5

These are only a few instances of the method by which the author of the Zohar seeks to describe in symbolical terms the theosophical universe of God's hidden life. At this point we are faced with the problem of the world outside the Sefiroth, or in other words, that of creation in the narrower sense and its relations to God—a prob-

lem involving that of pantheism. In the history of Kabbalism,
theistic and pantheistic trends have frequently contended for mas-
tery. This fact is sometimes obscured because the representatives of
pantheism have generally endeavoured to speak the language of
theism; cases of writers who openly put forward pantheistic views
are rare.[57] Most of the texts, and in particular the classical writings
of the theosophic school, contain elements of both tendencies. The
author of the Zohar inclines towards pantheism, a fact made even
clearer by the Hebrew writings of Moses de Leon, but one would
look in vain for confession of his faith beyond some vague formulae
and hints at a fundamental unity of all things, stages and worlds.
On the whole, his language is that of the theist, and some penetration is needed to lift its hidden and lambent pantheistic core to
the light.

We read in one passage:[58] "The process of creation, too, has taken
place on two planes, one above and one below, and for this reason
the Torah begins with the letter "Beth", the numerical value of
which is two. The lower occurrence corresponds to the higher; one
produced the upper world (of the Sefiroth), the other the
nether world (of the visible creation)."—In other words, the work
of creation as described in the first chapter of Genesis has a twofold
character: Insofar as it represents, in a mystical sense, the history
of God's self-revelation and His unfolding in the life of the Sefiroth,
the description is theogony—it is difficult to find a more suitable
term, for all its mythological connotations—and only in so far as
it brings the "nether" world into being, i.e. creation in the strict
sense of a *processio Dei ad extra,* as the scholastic definition goes,
can it be described as cosmogony. Both differ, as we are told in the
continuation of the above quoted passage,[59] only in that the higher
order represents the dynamic unity of God, while the lower leaves
room for differentiation and separation. For the description of this
lower realm the Zohar favors the term *alma de-peruda,* the "world
of separation".[60] Here there exist things which are isolated from
each other and from God. But, and at this point the pantheistic
tendency comes to the surface, to the eye which penetrates more
deeply this isolation, too, is only apparent. "If one contemplates the
things in mystical meditation, everything is revealed as one."[61] Already Gikatila has the formula, "He fills everything and He *is*
everything."

Theogony and Cosmogony represent not two different acts of creation, but two aspects of the same. On every plane—in the world of the Merkabah and the angels, which is below the Sefiroth, in the various heavens, and in the world of the four elements—creation mirrors the inner movement of the divine life. The "vestiges" of the innermost reality are present even in the most external of things.[62] Everywhere there is the same rhythm, the same motion of the waves. The act which results beyond and above time in the transformation of the hidden into the manifest God, is paralleled in the time-bound reality of every other world. Creation is nothing but an external development of those forces which are active and alive in God Himself. Nowhere is there a break, a discontinuity. Though the "palaces" (Hekhaloth) of the Merkabah world emanate from the light of the Shekhinah,[63] this is not a creatio ex nihilo, which at this stage would no longer be a mystical metaphor.

The most frequent illustration of this doctrine to be found in Moses de Leon's Hebrew writings is that of the chain and the links of which it consists. There are in this chain, the links of which are represented by the totality of the different worlds, different grades of links, some deeply hidden and others visible from outside, but there is no such thing as isolated existence: "Everything is linked with everything else down to the lowest ring on the chain, and the true essence of God is above as well as below, in the heavens and on the earth, and nothing exists outside Him. And this is what the sages mean when they say: When God gave the Torah to Israel, He opened the seven heavens to them, and they saw that nothing was there in reality but His Glory; He opened the seven worlds to them and they saw that nothing was there but His Glory; he opened the seven abysses before their eyes, and they saw that nothing was there but His Glory. Meditate on these things and you will understand that God's essence is linked and connected with all worlds, and that all forms of existence are linked and connected with each other, but derived from His existence and essence."[64]

The pantheistic side of this conception has its limits and can be shelved altogether if necessary. All created existence has a certain kind of reality to itself in which it appears independent of these mystical worlds of unity. But in the sight of the mystic the separate outlines of things become blurred until they, too, represent nothing but the Glory of God and His Hidden Life which pulsates in everything.

It is true that this is not all. As we shall see further on, this limited and isolated existence of separate things is not really a primary and essential component of the divine scheme of creation. Originally, everything was conceived as one great whole, and the life of the Creator pulsated without hindrance or disguise in that of his creatures. Everything stood in direct mystical rapport with everything else, and its unity could have been apprehended directly and without the help of symbols. Only the Fall has caused God to become "transcendent". Its cosmic results have led to loss of the original harmonious union and to the appearance of an isolated existence of things. All creation was originally of a spiritual nature and but for the intervention of evil would not have assumed material form. No wonder that where the Kabbalists of this school describe the state of the Messianic world and the blissful knowledge of the devotee in a world purged of its blemish, the emphasis is on the restoration of the original coexistence and correlation of all things.[65] What is at present reserved to the mystic whose gaze penetrates through the outer shell to the core of the matter, will anon be the common property of mankind in the state of redemption.

It is true that despite this multiformity of stages and manifestations, the theosophist tries to maintain the unity of God and to avoid the danger of postulating a plurality. Theoretically he manages this frequently with the aid of the philosophical formula that the semblance of difference between God's compassion, wrath, etc., exists only in the mind, but not in the objective reality of God's existence. In other words, the appearance of a multitude of manifestations is due to the existence of a medium, the finite creature, which perceives the divine light in its own way.[66] However, it is impossible to escape from the fact that such formulae, ingenious as they are, do not entirely correspond to the essence of the particular religious feeling which has found its expression in the doctrine of the Sefiroth.

As I have said previously, these symbolically conceived spheres of God are more than the attributes of theology, or the meditations and hypostases which Plotinus, in his doctrine of emanation, interposed between the Absolute and the phenomenal world. The Sefiroth of Jewish theosophy have an existence of their own; they form combinations, they illuminate each other, they ascend and descend. They are far from being static. Although each has its ideal place in the hierarchy, the lowest can under a certain aspect appear as the highest.⁵⁷ In other words, what we have here is something like a real process of life in God, the fluctuations of which the theosophist perceives, if his experience can be called perception, the organ of perception being, so to speak, the heart. To reconcile this process with the monotheistic doctrine, which was as dear to the Kabbalists as it was to every Jew, became the task of the theorists of Kabbalistic theosophy. Although they applied themselves bravely to it, it cannot be said that they were completely successful. Even the most grandiose efforts to establish a complete synthesis, like the one made by Moses Cordovero of Safed,⁵⁸ left an indissoluble remainder which defied rationalization. It is impossible to avoid the conclusion that the problem was from the beginning insoluble, that mysticism originally perceived an aspect of God which is beyond rationality and which becomes paradoxical the moment it is put into words. The author of the Zohar seldom makes a direct approach to the problem; the theosophic world of Sefiroth is so real to him as to be, according to him, perceptible in almost every word of the Bible. The symbols and images which serve to describe it are, after all, more than mere metaphors to him. He is not simply a mystic who hunts for expressions to describe his irrational experience; he is that, too, and the origin of the mystical symbol, described by E. Récéjac in his "Essay on the Bases of the Mystical Knowledge" (1899), can be traced in many a striking passage. But at the same time the Zohar, indeed the whole of theosophical Kabbalism, reflects a very ancient heritage of the soul, and it would be too much to say that this mythical heritage has everywhere been successfully integrated into the doctrine of monotheism.

6

Some of these mythical symbols afford a particularly striking instance of the way in which genuine Jewish thought became indissolubly mixed up with primitive mythical elements. This is true above all of sexual symbolism. It is well known that those deepest regions of human existence which are bound up with the sexual life play an important part in the history of mysticism. With few exceptions mystical literature abounds in erotic images. Even the mystical relation to God is frequently described as love between the soul and God, and Christian mysticism in particular has become notorious for the way in which it pushed this metaphor to extremes. The first fact to be noted is that this particular interpretation of man's relation to God plays hardly any part in the documents of the older, and particularly the Spanish, Kabbalah. It may be remarked in passing that the older Kabbalists never interpreted the "Song of Songs" as a dialogue between God and the soul, i. e., an allegorical description of the path to the *unio mystica*—an interpretation common to Christian mystics since the days of Bernard of Clairvaux. The mystical school of Safed in the sixteenth century was the first to have its attention drawn to it.[69]

It is true that for the Kabbalists, as well as for the Hasidim of Germany, love towards God is a matter of the greatest importance. Again and again the Zohar recurs to the problem of the two-fold attitude towards God, that of love and that of fear.[70] Like Eleazar of Worms, whose writings, as well as similar mystical tracts on morality, were doubtless known to him, Moses de Leon, too, postulates the identity of the deepest fear with the purest love. But even in the most extravagant descriptions of this love its character remains that of the love of the child for its father; it is never the passion of the lover for his beloved. Here the Kabbalists of Spain differ radically from the Hasidim of Germany who, as we have seen, did not shrink from taking this final step. The Zohar, in its description of the soul's fate after death, speaks of an ascent of the soul into higher regions until in the end it enters the "chamber of love". There the last veil falls and the soul stands pure and undisguised before its Maker. But this is not the bridal chamber of contemporary Christian mysticism: "Like a daughter" to quote the Zohar, the soul receives the kiss of its father as the mark and seal of the highest state of bliss.[71]

There is only one instance in which the Zohar refers to the relation of a mortal to the Divinity, to be exact, the Shekhinah, in terms of sexual symbolism. The exception is provided by Moses, the man of God; of him and of him alone it is said in a striking phrase that he had intercourse with the Shekhinah.[72] Here for once, the continuous relation with the Divinity is pictured in terms of a mystical marriage between Moses and the Shekhinah. From certain passages in the Midrash where mention is made of the termination of Moses' sexual relationship with his wife after he had been vouch-safed personal intercourse with God "from face to face", Moses de Leon has drawn the conclusion that for him, the marriage with the Shekhinah had taken the place of earthly marriage.

But while in all other instances the Kabbalists refrain from em-ploying sexual imagery in describing the relation between man and God, they show no such hesitation when it comes to describing the relation of God to Himself, in the world of the Sefiroth. The mys-tery of sex, as it appears to the Kabbalist, has a terribly deep significance.[73] This mystery of human existence is for him nothing but a symbol of the love between the divine "I" and the divine "You," the Holy one, blessed be He and His Shekhinah. The ἱερὸς γάμος,, the "sacred union" of the King and the Queen,[74] the Celestial Bridegroom and the Celestial Bride, to name a few of the symbols, is the central fact in the whole chain of divine mani-festations in the hidden world. In God there is a union of the active and the passive, procreation and conception, from which all mundane life and bliss are derived.

This sexual imagery is employed again and again, and in every possible variation. One of the images employed to describe the un-folding of the Sefiroth pictures them, as I have said above, as the offspring of mystical procreation, in which the first ray of divine light is also the primeval germ of creation; for the ray which em-erges from Nothing is, as it were, sown into the "celestial mother", i.e. into the divine Intellect, out of whose womb the Sefiroth spring forth, as King and Queen, son and daughter. Dimly we perceive behind this mystical images the male and female gods of antiquity, anathema as they were to the pious Kabbalist.[75]

The ninth Sefirath, *Yesod,* out of which all the higher Sefiroth —welded together in the image of the King—flow into the Shekhi-nah, is interpreted as the procreative life force dynamically active in the universe. Out of the hidden depth of this Sefirah the divine life overflows in the act of mystical procreation. The holy sign of circumcision is proof to the Kabbalist that within the limits of the holy law, these forces have their rightful place. It cannot be denied that this whole sphere exercises a strong fascination upon the mind of the author of the Zohar. The mythical character of his thought is more strongly pronounced in these passages than in any others, and that is saying a good deal. It is to be noted that the Zohar makes prominent use of phallic symbolism in connection with speculations concerning the Sefirah *Yesod*—not a minor psychological problem considering the author's strict devotion to the most pious conceptions of Jewish life and belief.[16] There is, of course, ample room here for psychoanalytical interpretation; indeed, the ease with which this method can be applied to the subject is only too apparent, but there is little hope, in my opinion, that real light can be shed on the matter in this way. An attempt to interpret the "Eroticism of the Kabbalah" in psychoanalytical terms has actually been made,[17] but the author has not advanced beyond the common catch-phrases which not a few adherents of the school unfortunately seem to regard as a sufficient answer to problems of this nature.

Certain it is that in the Zohar this form of symbolism confronts us in a far more uncompromising form than it wears in any other literary document of Spanish Kabbalism, though to some extent it is common to the whole of this literature. We are obviously dealing here with a special individual characteristic of our author and it is not surprising that it has aroused the criticism of the opponents of Kabbalism. An example of his radicalism is to be found in one of the sublimest passages of the whole book, where he describes the end of his hero, Simeon ben Yohai: Death comes to him at the moment when, after a long monologue on the deepest mysteries, he concludes with a symbolical description of the "holy union" in God, a description, whose drastic and paradoxical character can scarcely be excelled.[18] Here as elsewhere, an unprejudiced analysis of this phenomenon would be of greater assistance for the understanding of the Zohar than the eloquent denunciation of so-called obscenities which Graetz and other detractors of this "book of lies" have permitted themselves. Charges of this kind simply misconstrue both the morality and the tendency of the Zohar, and are hardly relevant even to the literary form of presentation; but above all they completely ignore the problem presented by the resurrection of mythology in the heart of mystical Judaism, of which the Zohar is the classical representative. Undoubtedly the author has gone farther in the Aramaic disguise, and under cover of pseudepigraphy, than in his Hebrew writings in which these tendencies have found a far more moderate expression. But it is precisely the comparatively uninhibited language of the Zohar which provides us with that deeper insight into his mind denied us by the majority of the writings of this school.

7

In this connection, attention must be directed above all to the new meaning infused into the idea of the Shekhinah. This restatement of an ancient conception actually represents one of the most important constituent elements of Kabbalism. In all the numerous references to the Shekhinah in the Talmud and the Midrashim—I have already referred in the second lecture to Abelson's work on the subject—there is no hint that it represents a feminine element in God. Not a single metaphor employs such terms as Princess, Matron, Queen, or Bride to describe the Shekhinah. It is true that these terms frequently occur where reference is made to the Community of Israel in its relation to God, but for these writers the Community has not yet become a mystical hypostasis of some divine force; it is simply the personification of the real Israel. Nowhere is there a dualism, with the Shekhinah, as the feminine, opposed to the "Holy one, praise be to Him," as the masculine element in God. The introduction of this idea was one of the most important and lasting innovations of Kabbalism. The fact that it obtained recognition in spite of the obvious difficulty of reconciling it with the conception of the absolute unity of God, and that no other element of Kabbalism won such a degree of popular approval, is proof that it responded to a deep-seated religious need. I have already suggested in the first lecture that the mystics, for all their aristocratic tendencies, were the true representatives of the living, popular religion of the masses, and that the secret of their success is to be found in this fact. Not only for the philosophers, but for the strict Talmudists as well, insofar as they were not themselves mystics, the conception of the Shekhinah as the feminine element in God was one of the main stumbling-blocks in approaching the Kabbalistic system. It says something for its vitality that, despite the opposition of such powerful forces, this idea became part and parcel of the creed of wide circles among the Jewish communities of Europe and the East.

Traces of this conception are to be found already in the book *Bahir,* the oldest document of Kabbalist thought, upon whose relation to earlier Gnostic sources I have already commented in a few places." This fact is further proof, if proof were needed, that, so far from being Christian, the idea originally belonged to the sphere of pagan mythology. In the Gnostic speculations on the male and female aeons, i. e. divine potencies, which constitute the world of the *pleroma*, the 'fullness' of God, this thought assumed a new form in which it became known to the earliest Kabbalists through the medium of scattered fragments. The similes employed in the book *Bahir* to describe the Shekhinah are extremely revelatory in this respect. For some Gnostics, the "lower Sophia," the last aeon on the rim of the *pleroma*, represents the "daughter of light" who falls into the abyss of matter. In close parallel with this idea, the Shekhinah, as the last of the Sefiroth, becomes the "daughter" who, although her home is the "form of light," must wander into far lands.[80] Various other motives helped to complete the picture of the Shekhinah as drawn in the Zohar; above all, she was now identified with the "Community of Israel," a sort of Invisible Church, representing the mystical idea of Israel in its bond with God and in its bliss, but also in its suffering and its exile. She is not only Queen, daughter and bride[81] of God, but also the mother of every individual in Israel. She is the true "Rachel weeping for her children," and in a magnificent misinterpretation of a Zoharic passage, the Shekhinah weeping in her exile becomes for later Kabbalism "the beauty who no longer has eyes."[82] It is as a woman that she now appears to the visionaries among the Kabbalists, like the Abraham Halevi, a disciple of Luria, who in 1571 saw her at the Wailing Wall in Jerusalem as a woman dressed in black and weeping for the husband of her youth.[83] In the symbolic world of the Zohar, this new conception of the Shekhinah as the symbol of "eternal womanhood"[84] occupies a place of immense importance and appears under an endless variety of names and images. It marks the sphere which is the first to open itself to the meditation of the mystic, the entrance to that inwardness of God which the Zohar very frequently paraphrases by the term *raza de-mehemanutha*, "the mystery of faith," i. e. a domain which discloses its secret only to those who approach it in a spirit of complete devotion.[85]

8

The union of God and the Shekhinah constitutes the true unity of God, which lies beyond the diversity of His various aspects, *Yihud* as the Kabbalists call it. Originally, according to the Zohar, this unity was a steady and continuous one. Nothing disturbed the blissful union of the rhythms of divine existence in the one great melody of God. Equally, nothing disturbed at first the steady contact of God with the worlds of creation, in which His life pulsates, and particularly with the human world.

In his original paradisical state, man had a direct relation to God. As Moses de Leon, using an older formula, frequently expresses it: Man is a synthesis of all the spiritual forces which have gone into the work of creation.[86] He reflects, as we have seen, in his organism the hidden organism of God's own life. However, an important modification is to be noted: Man was originally a purely spiritual being.[87] The ethereal shape which enclosed him and which was later transformed into the organs of his body stood in an entirely different relation to its nature than his body does now. It is to sin that he owes his corporeal existence, born from the pollution of all matter by the poison of sin. Sin, a subject on which the Jewish mystics have lavished an immense amount of speculation, has destroyed the immediate relation between man and God and thereby also in some way affected the life of God in His creation. It is only now that the distinction between the Creator and creation assumes the nature of a problem. To quote Joseph Gikatila: "In the beginning of creation, the core of the Shekhinah was in the lower regions. And because the Shekhinah was below, heaven and earth were one and in perfect harmony. The well springs and the channels through which everything in the higher regions flows into the lower were still active, complete and unhindered, and thus God filled everything from above to below. But when Adam came and sinned, the order of things was turned into disorder, and the heavenly channels were broken."[88]

I have said that the mystics were deeply concerned with the problem of sin and, especially, with the nature and meaning of Adam's fall, and that this problem was amply discussed in Kabbalistic literature. This is true with but one exception, that of the Zohar. Whilst the Kabbalists of Gerona deal at length with this subject, and also some of Moses de Leon's circle seem to display a predilection for it, passages referring to the question of original sin are scanty in the Zohar, and especially in its main parts. Moreover, these passages are written with a restraint which cannot be said to have been exercised by the author in regard to the other fundamental doctrines of the Kabbalah. The meager treatment of the subject in the Zohar is also in sharp contrast with the profusion with which the problem was discussed in the contemporary Kabbalistical work *Ma'arekhet Ha-Elohut*, "The Order of the Godhead." This reticence is not accidental; it is evident that the author of the Zohar considered the subject as extremely dangerous, as it touched the great question, where and how the unity of God's life has been disturbed and whence comes the breach which is now manifest in the whole universe. As a matter of fact, in the *Midrash Ha-Neelam* the author reveals the reason for his silence or reserve, by putting into the mouth of Adam bitter complaints against those Kabbalists who indulge in too much talk on the mystery of his fall. Why reveal a secret which has been left undisclosed by the Torah, why not content themselves with allusions only, especially when speaking to the rabble? The secret must be kept inside the circle of the initiates. On the other hand, in the *Midrash Ha-Neelam* as well as in the other parts of the Zohar Simeon ben Yohai alludes to different explanations of this mystery and leaves little doubt indeed that his opinion is essentially the same as that of the aforementioned Kabbalists. And as though to conceal his esoteric views, the author accompanies them by entirely rationalistic explanations which are most astonishing in the Zohar and contain nothing of the main Gnostic interpretation. This interpretation says that the Sefiroth were revealed to Adam in the shape of the Tree of Life and the Tree of Knowledge, i.e. the middle and the last Sefirah; instead of preserving their original unity and thereby unifying the spheres of 'life' and 'knowledge' and bringing salvation to the world, he separated one from the other and set his mind to worship the Shekhinah only without recognizing its union with the other Sefiroth. Thus he interrupted the stream of life which flows from sphere to sphere and brought separation and isolation into the world.

From this time on there has been a mysterious fissure, not indeed in the substance of Divinity but in its life and action. This doctrine has been completely hedged round with reservations, but its basic meaning for all that is clear enough. Its pursuit led to the conception of what the Kabbalists call "the exile of the Shekhinah."[89] Only after the restoration of the original harmony in the act of redemption, when everything shall again occupy the place it originally had in the divine scheme of things, will "God be one and His name one," in Biblical terms, truly and for all time.[90]

In the present unredeemed and broken state of the world this fissure which prevents the continuous union of God and the Shekhinah[91] is somehow healed or mended by the religious act of Israel: Torah, *mitswoth* and prayer. Extinction of the stain, restoration of harmony—that is the meaning of the Hebrew word *Tikkun*, which is the term employed by the Kabbalists after the period of the Zohar, for man's task in this world. In the state of redemption, however, "there shall be perfection above and below, and all worlds shall be united in one bond."

In the Community of Israel, whose mundane life reflects the hidden rhythm of the universal law revealed in the Torah, the Shekhinah is immediately present, for the earthly Community of Israel is formed after the archetype of the mystical Community of Israel which is the Shekhinah. Everything that is done by the individual or the community in the mundane sphere is magically reflected in the upper region, i.e. the higher reality which shines through the acts of man. To quote a favorite expression of the Zohar: "The impulse from below (*itharuta dil-tata*) calls forth that from above."[92] The earthly reality mysteriously reacts upon the heavenly, for everything, including human activity, has its "upper roots"[93] in the realm of the Sefiroth. The impulse which originates from a good deed guides the flow of blessing which springs from the superabundance of life in the Sefiroth into the secret channels leading into the lower and the outer world. The devotee, it is even said, through his acts links the visible and practicable Torah with the invisible and mysterious one.

The supreme religious value which the Zohar, in common with the whole of Spanish Kabbalism, places in the center of its ethical system is *devekuth*, the continuous attachment or adhesion to God, that direct relationship which—as I have already mentioned in a previous lecture—almost takes the whole place of the previous ecstatic experience.[94] Although *devekuth* is definitely a contemplative value, it is not predicated upon special or abnormal modes of consciousness. Indeed, according to Moses ben Nahman—a generation before the Zohar—true *devekuth* can be realized in the normal life of the individual within the community.[95] It is therefore capable of being transformed into a social value, a point of great importance in the subsequent influence of Kabbalism on popular ethics. All the other values of Kabbalist ethics—fear of God, love of

God, purity of thought, chastity, charity, study of the Torah, penitence and prayer—are set in relation to this highest ideal and take
their ultimate significance from it. Those that I have mentioned
may be said to represent the meritorious acts to which the Zohar
attaches special importance. Together they constitute an ideal
which unites, through a mystical revaluation, the virtues of the
poor and the devotee in a manner interesting also from the point of
view of social ethics.

In harmony with this tendency, the Zohar, for the first time in the
history of rabbinical Judaism, lays special stress on the glorification
of poverty as a religious value. It has been suggested by F. I. Baer
that this mood reflects the influence of the popular movement led by
the radical wing of the Franciscans, known as the "Spirituals," which
spread through southern Europe in the thirteenth century and
found its most impressive representative in Petrus Olivi in Spain
during the very years in which the Zohar was written. Whatever the
facts, it is undeniable that the glorification of poverty found in the
Psalms was considerably dimmed in the later development of
rabbinical Judaism[90] until its revival in the *Sefer Hasidim* on the
one hand, and in the Zohar on the other. To the mystic, the poor
are "God's broken vessels," to quote the frequent metaphor which
one would look for in vain in the old Midrash.[97] This spiritualistic
identification of the poor and the devotee finds further expression
in the fact that Moses de Leon, in his Hebrew writings, uses the
same term for the poor which in the Zohar he very often employs
for the mystics, the true devotees: they are *bne hekhla de-malka,*
the true "Court" of God.[98]

In the *Raya Mehemna,* written shortly after the Zohar, these
tendencies are systematized into a radical spiritualistic criticism of
contemporary Jewish society. The Zohar itself as yet draws no such
consequences,[99] but it already contains an interpretation of theosophic thoughts in which the quality of poverty is attributed to the
Shekhinah, in other words to God Himself in the last of his manifestations: the Shekhinah is poor for "she has nothing from herself," but only what she receives from the stream of the Sefiroth.[100]
The alms from which the poor live symbolically reflect this mystical
state of the Shekhinah. The "just," or righteous man, the *Zaddik*
of the Zohar, therefore, is he who attains to the state of *devekuth*
with God. It is hardly an accident that among the ethical values

glorified by the Kabbalists, those of a purely intellectual nature—apart from the study of the Torah—are all but entirely absent. In this conception of ethics, which lays so much more stress on the voluntaristic than on the intellectualist element, the Kabbalists again prove themselves close to the religious faith of the common people.

To repeat what I said before, the Zohar's sexual symbolism reflects the influence of two different tendencies. Insofar as it shows a positive attitude towards the function of sexual life, within the limits ordained by divine law, it may be said to represent a genuinely Jewish outlook. Chastity is indeed one of the highest moral values of Judaism: Joseph, who by his chastity has "upheld the covenant" is regarded by the Midrash and the Kabbalah as the prototype of the righteous man, the true Zaddik.[101] But at no time was sexual asceticism accorded the dignity of a religious value, and the mystics make no exception. Too deeply was the first command of the Torah, Be fruitful and multiply, impressed upon their minds. The contrast to other forms of mysticism is striking enough to be worth mentioning: non-Jewish mysticism, which glorified and propagated asceticism, ended sometimes by transplanting eroticism into the relation of man to God. Kabbalism, on the other hand, was tempted to discover the mystery of sex within God himself. For the rest it rejected asceticism and continued to regard marriage not as a concession to the frailty of the flesh but as one of the most sacred mysteries. Every true marriage is a symbolical realization of the union of God and the Shekhinah. In a tract on the "union of a man with his wife" which was later ascribed to Nahmanides, Joseph Gikatila gave a similar interpretation of the mystical significance of marriage.[102] The Kabbalists deduced from Gen. IV, 1: "And Adam knew Eve his wife" that "knowledge" always means the realization of a union, be it that of wisdom (or reason) and intelligence, or that of the King and the Shekhinah. Thus knowledge itself received a sublime erotic quality in this new Gnostical system, and this point is often stressed in Kabbalistic writings.[103]

9

We find the same curious mixture of mystical and mythical strains in the Zohar's interpretation of the nature of evil. The ancient Christian, and the mediaeval Jewish Gnostic, have both asked the question, *unde malum?* What is the source of evil? For the theosophical school of Kabbalism, which in addition to a definite similarity in outlook was, through certain channels, historically connected with Gnosticism, this was indeed a fundamental question. In dealing with it, as I propose to do now, one becomes more than ever aware of the difference between religious and intellectual motives of thought. To the intellect the problem is no real problem at all. All that is needed is to understand that evil is relative, more, that it does not really exist. This done, it really *has* ceased to exist, or so the intellect imagines, whereas the religious consciousness demands that evil should be really vanquished. This demand is based on the profound conviction that the power of evil is real, and the mind which is conscious of this fact refuses to content itself with intellectual tours de force, however brilliant, which try to explain away the existence of something which it knows to be there.

That is also the position of the theorists of evil in the old Kabbalah, mystics like Isaac ben Jacob Hacohen of Soria, Moses ben Simon of Burgos,[104] Joseph Gikatila and Moses de Leon. The Zohar itself puts forward several different attempts at a solution which have this in common—that they all assume the reality of evil. For the rest, the author of the Zohar often treats as one various aspects of evil—such as the metaphysical evil, the imperfect state of all beings, the physical evil, the existence of suffering in the world, and the moral evil in human nature—while sometimes he is specially concerned with the latter. The task of reducing the conception of evil in the theosophic school of Kabbalism to a brief formula is made difficult by the fact that its adherents advance not one theory but several. Sometimes the existence of evil is identified with that of a metaphysical domain of darkness and temptation which exists independently of human sinfulness; on other occasions we are told that man's sinfulness actualized the potentially evil, i.e. made it tear itself away from the Divine. In fact, moral evil, according to the Zohar, is always either something which becomes separated and isolated, or something which enters into a relation for which it is not made. Sin always destroys a union, and a destructive separation of this kind was also immanent in the Original Sin through which the fruit was separated from the tree, or as another Kabbalist puts it, the Tree of Life from the Tree of Knowledge.[105] If man falls into such isolation—if he seeks to maintain his own self, instead of remaining in the original context of all things created, in which he, too, has his place—then this act of apostasy bears fruit in the demiurgical presumption of magic in which man seeks to take God's place and to join what God has separated.[106] Evil thus creates an unreal world of false contexts[107] after having destroyed or deserted the real.

However, the fundamental causes of evil lie deeper than that; in fact they are bound up, according to an important Zoharic doctrine, with one of the manifestations or Sefiroth of God. This must be explained. The totality of divine potencies forms a harmonious whole, and as long as each stays in relation to all others, it is sacred and good. This is true also of the quality of strict justice, rigor and judgment in and by God, which is the fundamental cause of evil. The wrath of God is symbolized by His left hand, while the quality of mercy and love, with which it is intimately bound up, is called His right hand. The one cannot manifest itself without involving the other. Thus the quality of stern judgment represents the great fire of wrath which burns in God but is always tempered by His mercy. When it ceases to be tempered, when in its measureless hypertrophical outbreak it tears itself loose from the quality of mercy, then it breaks away from God altogether and is transformed into the radically evil, into Gehenna and the dark world of Satan.[108]

It is impossible to overlook the fact that this doctrine, whose fascinating profundity is undeniable, found a highly remarkable parallel in the ideas of the great theosophist Jacob Boehme (1575-1624), the shoemaker of Goerlitz whose thoughts exercised so great an influence on many Christian mystics of the seventeenth and eighteenth centuries, especially in Germany, Holland and England. Boehme's doctrine of the origins of evil, which created such a stir, indeed bears all the traits of Kabbalistic thought. He, too, defines evil as a dark and negative principle of wrath in God, albeit eternally transfigured into light in the theosophical organism of divine life. In general if one abstracts from the Christian metaphors in which he tried, in part at least, to express his intuitions, Boehme, more than any other Christian mystic, shows the closest affinity to Kabbalism precisely where he is most original. He has, as it were, discovered the world of Sefiroth all over again. It is possible, of course, that he deliberately assimilated elements of Kabbalistic thought after he had made, in the period following upon his illumination, their acquaintance through friends who, unlike himself, were scholars. At any rate, the connection between his ideas and those of the theosophic Kabbalah was quite evident to his followers, from Abraham von Franckenberg (died 1652) to Franz von Baader (died 1841),[109] and it was left to the modern literature on the subject to obscure it. F. C. Oetinger, one of the later followers of Boehme, relates in his autobiography[110] that in his youth he asked the Kabbalist Koppel Hecht in Frankfort-on-Main (died 1729) how he might best gain an understanding of Kabbalism, and that Hecht referred him to a Christian author who, he said, spoke of Kabbalism more openly than the Zohar. "I asked him which he meant, and he replied: Jacob Boehme, and also told me of the parallels between his metaphors and those of the Kabbalah."—There is no reason to doubt the authenticity of this story. It should also be recalled that at the end of the seventeenth century, a follower of Boehme, Johann Jacob Spaeth, was so impressed by this astonishing affinity with Kabbalism that he even became a convert to Judaism.

To return to the subject matter, the metaphysical cause of evil is seen in an act which transforms the category of judgment into an absolute. As I have said before, the Zohar supplies no completely unequivocal answer to the questions why this transformation takes place, whether it is rooted in the essence of the theosophic process, or whether its origin is to be found in human sin. The two ideas intermingle; on the whole the author appears to incline to the first: Evil fell upon the world not because Adam's fall actualized its potential presence, but because it was so ordained, because evil has a reality of its own. This was also the doctrine of Gnosticism: Evil is by its very nature independent of man; it is woven into the texture of the world, or rather into the existence of God. It is this thought which leads the Zohar to interpret evil as a sort of residue or refuse of the hidden life's organic process. This peculiar idea, in itself an audacious consequence of interpreting God as a living organism, has found frequent expression in a variety of similes. Even as the tree cannot exist without its bark, or the human body without shedding "unclean blood," so, too, all that is demonic has its root somewhere in the mystery of God.[111] The incompatibility of these varying explanations does not appear to have struck the author of the Zohar, who sees no contradiction in alternatively using metaphysical and physical or biological metaphors. One of these metaphors has become predominant in later Kabbalism. It is that which considers evil as the *Kelipah,* or the "bark" of the cosmic tree[112] or "the shell" of the nut. (The nut as a symbol of the Merkabah was taken over by the Zohar from the writings of Eleazar of Worms.)

It is true that some Kabbalists of this school have advanced another theory according to which evil represents an illegitimate inroad upon the divine realm of light, and that it becomes evil only because something which is good in its right place tries to usurp a place for which it is not fitted. Thus Joseph Gikatila, who laid great emphasis upon this point.[113] The Zohar, on the other hand, takes an entirely different view; according to its author, evil is indeed something which has its ordained place, but in itself it is dead, it comes to life only because a ray of light, however faint, from the holiness of God falls upon it[114] or because it is nourished and quickened by the sin of man[115]; by itself it is simply the dead residue of the process of life. A spark of God's life burns even in Sammael,[116] the personification of evil, the "other" or "left side."[117] This sinister demonic world of evil which forms the dark side of everything living and threatens it from within, exercises a peculiar fascination upon the author of the Zohar. A comparison of the very scanty attention paid to these ideas in the *Midrash Ha-Neelam* and the *embarras de richesse* which confronts us in the parts written later clearly reveals their progressive influence upon his thought. It is true that these philosophical and Gnostical speculations, including the conception of evil as the remains of the primeval world which existed before God destroyed it,[118] are intermingled with less sophisticated ideas. Thus we read for instance that, far from being rooted in a theogonic or cosmogonic process, evil is there simply in order to increase man's chances; because God wanted man to be free, he ordained the real existence of evil, that he might prove his moral strength in overcoming it.[119]

10

The Kabbalistic view of the nature of man and the essence of sin is of course closely connected with the theory of the soul set out in the Zohar. The intimate connection between cosmogony and psychology in all Gnostical systems is so well known that its appearance in the Zohar is hardly a cause for surprise. In a mystical hymn, Moses ben Nahman has described the birth of the soul in the depth of the divine spheres from where its life streams forth. For the soul,

too, is a spark of the divine life and bears in it the life of the
divine stages through which it has wandered. These are the words
of Nahmanides[120]:

> From the beginning of time, through eternities
> I was among his hidden treasures.
> From Nothing he called me forth, but at the end of time
> I shall be reclaimed by the King.
>
> My life flows from the depth of the spheres
> Which give order and form to the soul;
> Divine forces build it and nourish it;
> Then it is preserved in the chambers of the King.
>
> He radiated light to bring her forth,
> In hidden well-springs, right and left.
> The soul descended the ladder of heaven,
> From the primeval pool of Siloam to the garden of the
>
> King.[121]

The psychology of the Zohar shows a peculiar mixture of two
doctrines held by certain schools of mediaeval philosophy. The first
distinguished between the vegetative, the animal, and the rational
soul—three stages which Aristotelian doctrine regarded as different
faculties of the one soul, while the mediaeval followers of Plato
were inclined to think of them as three different entities. The second,
which was generally held by the Arab philosophers and popularized
among the Jews by Maimonides, is based on the conception of the
"acquired intellect." According to this view, the rational faculty
latent in the mind is actualized in the process of cognition, and this
realization of the intellect is the sole guide to immortality.[122] To this
doctrine, the Zohar now gives a Kabbalistic turn. It retains the
distinction between three spiritual agencies: *Nefesh* or life; *Ruah*
or spirit; and *Neshamah* or soul proper, but abandons the idea that
they represent three different faculties of the soul. Rather all three
are already latently present in the first, *Nefesh,* and the higher grades
correspond to the new and deeper powers which the soul of the
devotee acquires through the study of the Torah and through meritorious actions.

In particular, *Neshamah,* the "holy soul," can be realized only by the perfect devotee, who, for the author of the Zohar, is identical with the Kabbalist, and it is only by penetrating into the mysteries of the Torah, that is to say, through the mystical realization of his cognitive powers, that he acquires it.[123] *Neshamah* is the deepest intuitive power which leads to the secrets of God and the universe. It is therefore natural that *Neshamah* is also conceived as a spark of *Binah,* the divine intellect itself.[124] By acquiring it, the Kabbalist thus realizes something of the divine in his own nature. The various detailed theories concerning the functions, origins and destinies of the three souls of man are obscure and sometimes contradictory, as well as involved, and it is not my intention here to analyze them, but it is perhaps worth noting that, on the whole, our author holds to the view that only *Nefesh,* the natural soul given to every man, is capable of sin: *Neshamah,* the divine, innermost spark of the soul, is beyond sin. In his Hebrew writings, Moses de Leon actually propounds the question: How is it possible for the soul to suffer in Hell, since *Neshamah* is substantially the same as God, and God therefore appears to inflict punishment upon Himself?[125] His solution of the problem—which incidentally throws a flood of light on the pantheism at the bottom of his system—is that in the act of sin, *Neshamah,* the divine element, abandons man, and its place is taken by an impure spirit from the "left side" who takes up his abode in the soul and who alone suffers the torments of retribution. *Neshamah* itself is not affected, and if it descends to Hell, it is only to guide some of the suffering souls up to the light. In the Zohar, too, the punishment of the soul after death is similarly restricted to *Nefesh,* and in some passages extended to *Ruah,* but never to *Neshamah.*[126]

The story of the soul's fate after death, of reward and punishment, of the bliss of the devout and the torments of the sinner, in short the eschatology of the soul, is the last of the major problems with which the author is concerned.[127] Its connection with the fundamental thoughts of his theosophy is but loose, but his vivid imagination constantly produces new variations on the theme whose detailed exemplification fills a considerable part of the Zohar. Taken by and large, the doctrine expounded by the author is fairly consistent. Like all Kabbalists he teaches the pre-existence of all souls since the beginning of creation. Indeed, he goes so far as to assert that the pre-existent souls were already pre-formed in their full individuality while they were still hidden in the womb of eternity. "Since the day when it occurred to God to create the world, and even before it was really created, all the souls of the righteous were hidden in the divine idea, every one in its peculiar form. When He shaped the world, they were actualized and they stood before Him in their various forms in the supreme heights [still in the Sefirotic world], and only then did He place them in a treasure-house in the upper Paradise."[128] There the souls live in pure celestial garments and enjoy the bliss of the beatific vision. Their progress from the Sefirotic sphere to the paradisical realm, which latter is already outside God, is interpreted as a consequence of the mystical "union of the King and the Shekhinah."[129] But already in this pre-existent state, there are differences and gradations in the position of the souls.

On more than one occasion we read of the 'audience' given to the soul by God[130] before its descent into a mundane body and the vow taken by the soul to complete its mission on earth by pious acts and mystical cognition of God. From its good deeds, *mitswoth,* nay from the days on which it has accomplished good, as the poetic description has it, the soul during its earthly stay weaves the mystical garment which it is destined to wear after death in the lower Paradise.[131] This notion of heavenly garments of the souls has a special attraction for the author. Only the souls of the sinners are "naked," or at any rate the garment of eternity which they weave in time and out of time has "holes." After death, the various parts of the soul, having accomplished their mission, return to their original location, but those which have sinned are brought to court and are purified in the 'fiery stream" of Gehenna, or, in the case of the most shameful sinners, burned.[132]

Here the doctrine of transmigration, *Gilgul,* also plays a part. One encounters it first in the book *Bahir.*[133] Unless it goes back to the literary sources of this work, it is reasonable to assume that the Kabbalists of Provence who wrote or edited the book *Bahir* owe it to the influence of the Catharists, the chief religious force in Provence until 1220, i. e. during the years which saw the rise of Kabbalism. The Catharist heresy, which was only stamped out after a bloody Crusade, represented a late and attenuated form of Manichaeism, and as such clung to the doctrine of metempsychosis which the Church condemned as heretical.[134] It must be kept in mind, however, that to the early Kabbalists metempsychosis was not the general destiny of the soul but, according to the Zohar, an exception brought about, above all, by offences against procreation.[135] He who has not obeyed the first commandment of the Torah assumes a new existence in a new bodily abode, be it as a form of punishment or as a chance or restitution. Thus the institution of the levirate is explained by the theory of transmigration. If the dead man's brother marries his widow, he "draws back" the soul of the deceased husband. He builds it up again and it becomes a new spirit in a new body.[136] On the other hand, Moses de Leon, unlike other early Kabbalists, seems to have disapproved of the theory of transmigration into non-human forms of existence. Such transmigration is mentioned as a punishment in the case of certain sins by Menahem of Recanati (1300) who quotes several details about it from the "modern Kabbalists." However, the conception of metempsychosis as a general form of divine retribution is not unknown to the early Kabbalist tradition.[137] The fundamental contradiction between the ideas of punishment in Hell and of metempsychosis—two forms of retribution which in the strict sense are mutually exclusive—is blurred in the Zohar by the limitation of the idea of punishment proper to the process of torment in Hell.

Taken altogether, the spiritual outlook of the Zohar might well be defined as a mixture of theosophic theology, mythical cosmogony and mystical psychology and anthropology. God, the universe and the soul do not lead separate lives, each on its own plane. The original act of creation in fact knows nothing of such clear-cut division which, as we have seen, was the cosmic fruit of human sin. The close interrelation of all three which we find in the Zohar is also characteristic of all later Kabbalism. Reference to one often shades off imperceptibly into talk of the other. Later Kabbalists have sometimes tried to deal separately with them, but as far as the Zohar is concerned its fascinating appeal to the mind is to a large extent bound up with its unique combination of the three elements into a colorful though not unproblematic whole.

SEVENTH LECTURE

ISAAC LURIA AND HIS SCHOOL

1

After the Exodus from Spain, Kabbalism underwent a complete transformation. A catastrophe of this dimension, which uprooted one of the main branches of the Jewish people, could hardly take place without affecting every sphere of Jewish life and feeling. In the great material and spiritual upheaval of that crisis, Kabbalism established its claim to spiritual domination in Judaism. This fact became immediately obvious in its transformation from an esoteric into a popular doctrine.

When the Jews were expelled from Spain in 1492, the Kabbalistic form of Jewish mysticism had reached the end a certain stage of development. The main currents of twelfth and thirteenth century Kabbalism had run their course by the close of the fourteenth century and the beginning of the fifteenth. This coincided with the beginning of the persecution of the Jews in Spain and the appearance of Marrano Judaism after 1391, and the literature of the fifteenth century reflects an unmistakable flaccidity of religious thought and expression.

The Kabbalists of the time were a small group of esoterics who had little desire to spread their ideas,[1] and who would have been the last to promote any movement for introducing radical changes into Jewish life, or for altering its rhythms. Only two isolated mystics, the authors of the *Raya Mehemna* and of the book *Peliah*, had been dreaming about a mystical revolution in Jewish life, and nothing had responded to their call.[2] Kabbalism was essentially the privilege of the elect who pursued the path of ever deeper penetration into the mysteries of God. This attitude was clearly manifest in the older Kabbalah, with its 'neutralization' of all Messianic tendencies which, though not complete, was very marked. This comparative indifference to the suggestion that the course of history might be somewhat shortened by mystical means was due to the fact that originally the mystics and apocalyptics had turned their thoughts in the reverse direction: the Kabbalists concentrated all their mental and emotional powers not upon the Messianic end of the world, upon the closing stage of the unfolding universe, but rather upon its beginning. Or to put it in other words, in their speculation they were on the whole more concerned with creation than with redemption. Redemption was to be achieved not by storming onward in an attempt to hasten historic crises and catastrophes, but rather by retracing the path that leads to the primordial beginnings of creation and revelation, at the point where the world-process (the history of the universe and of God) began to evolve within a system of laws. He who knew the way by which he had come might hope eventually to retrace his steps.

The mystical meditations of the Kabbalists on theogony and cosmogony thus produced a non-Messianic and individualistic mode of redemption or salvation. In union—says a fourteenth century Kabbalist[3]—there is redemption. In these meditations history was purged of its taint, since the Kabbalists sought to find their way back to the original unity, to the world-structure prior to Satan's First Deception, with the consequences of which they were bound to identify the course of history. Given a new emotional approach at this point, the Kabbalah might have absorbed the intensity of Messianism and become a powerful apocalyptic factor, because retracing the spiritual process to the ultimate foundations of existence might in itself have been regarded as the redemption, in the sense that the world would thus return to the unity and purity of its beginnings. This return to the cosmogonic starting-point, as the central aim of the Kabbalah, need not always have proceeded in the silent and aloof meditations of the individual, which have and can have no relation to outward events.

After the catastrophe of the Spanish Expulsion, which so radically altered the outer aspect of the Kabbalah if not its innermost content, it also became possible to consider the return to the starting-point of creation as the means of precipitating the final world-catastrophe, which would come to pass when that return had been achieved by many individuals united in a desire for 'the End' of the world. A great emotional upheaval having taken place, the individual mystic's absorption could have been transformed, by a kind of mystical dialectics, into the religious aspiration of the whole community. In that event, what had been hidden under the mild aspect of *Tikkun* (striving for the perfection of the world) would be revealed as a potent weapon, one capable of destroying all the forces of evil; and such destruction would in itself have been tantamount to redemption.

Though Messianic calculations, ideas, and visions were not an essential part of the older Kabbalah, it was by no means lacking in these matters, and it should not be inferred that Kabbalism altogether disregarded the problem of redemption "in our time." The point is that if and when it did concern itself with it, it did so in a spirit of supererogation. Typical of the catastrophic aspects of redemption—of which the Kabbalists were fully aware—is the gruesome fact that, long before 1492, some Kabbalistic writers had proclaimed that catastrophic year as the year of the redemption. However, 1492 brought no liberation from above, but a most cruel exile here below. The consciousness that redemption signified both liberation and catastrophe permeated the new religious movement to such an extent that it can only be called the obverse side of the apocalyptic temper predominating in Jewish life.

The concrete effects and consequences of the catastrophe of 1492 were by no means confined to the Jews then living. As a matter of fact, the historic process set going by the expulsion from Spain required several generations—almost an entire century—to work itself out completely. Only by degrees did its tremendous implications permeate ever more profound regions of being. This process helped to merge the apocalyptic and Messianic elements of Judaism with the traditional aspects of Kabbalism. The last age became as important as the first; instead of reverting to the dawn of history, or rather to its metaphysical antecedents, the new doctrines laid the emphasis on the final stages of the cosmological process. The pathos of Messianism pervaded the new Kabbalah and its classical forms of expression as it never did the Zohar; the 'beginning' and the 'end' were linked together.

The contemporaries of the Expulsion were aware chiefly of the concrete problems it had created, but not of its deep-lying implications for religious thought and its theological expression. For the exiles from Spain the catastrophical character of the "End" was again made clear. To summon up and to release all the forces capable of hastening the "End," became once more the chief aim of the mystics. The messianic doctrine, previously the concern of those interested in apologetics, was made for a time the subject of an aggressive propaganda. The classic compendia in which Isaac Abarbanel codified the Messianic doctrines of Judaism a few years after the Expulsion were soon followed by numerous epistles, tracts, homilies, and apocalyptic writings in which the repercussions of the catastrophe reached their most vigorous expression. In these writings, whose authors were at great pains to link up the Expulsion with the ancient prophecies, the redemptive character of the 1492 catastrophe was strongly emphasized. The birthpangs of the Messianic era, with which history is to "end" or (as the apocalyptics would have it) to "collapse," were therefore assumed to have set in with the Expulsion.[5]

The sharply etched and impressive figure of Abraham ben Eliezer Ha-Levi in Jerusalem, an untiring agitator and interpreter of events "pregnant" with redemption, is typical of a generation of Kabbalists in which the apocalyptic abyss yawned, but without swallowing up the traditional categories of the mystical theology or, as happened later, transforming it.[6] The emotional force and eloquence of a preacher of repentance were here combined with a passion for the apocalyptic interpretation of history and of historical theology; but the very belief that redemption was near prevented the drastic experiences of the Expulsion, vividly as they were still remembered, from being transmuted into ultimate religious concepts. Only gradually, as the Expulsion ceased to be regarded in a redemptive light and loomed up all the more distinctly in its catastrophic character, did the flames which had flared up from the apocalyptical abyss sweep over wide areas of the Jewish world until they finally seized upon and recast the mystical theology of Kabbalism. The new Kabbalah, which was fashioned by this transforming and fusing process in "the Community of the Devout" at Safed, bore enduring marks of the event to which it owed its origin. For, once the catastrophic had been sown as a fertile seed in the heart of this new Kabbalah, its teachings were bound to lead to that further catastrophe which became acute with the Sabbatian movement.

The mood which prevailed in Kabbalistic circles enkindled by the apocalyptic propaganda and in the groups influenced by them, is reflected most revealingly in two anonymous works—*Sefer Ha-Meshiv* "The Book of Revelations," and *Kaf Ha-Ketoreth* "The Censer"—written about 1500 and preserved in manuscript.[7] The first is a commentary on the Torah and the second a commentary on the Psalms. Both authors tried to force apocalyptic meanings into every word of the Scriptures. The Scriptures were alleged to have seventy "faces," and to manifest a different face to each generation, with a different mode of address. In their own generation every word of the Bible was assumed to refer to Exile and Redemption. The entire Scriptures were interpreted as a series of symbols of the preliminary events, sorrows, and travail of the redemption, which these authors most vividly envisaged as a catastrophe.

The author of *Kaf Ha-Ketoreth*, in particular, took up a very radical position. Employing every device of that mystical precision with which the Kabbalists read the Bible, he infused extraordinary apocalyptical meanings into the words of the Psalms, and held up the Psalter as a textbook of the millenium and the Messianic catastrophe. He furthermore developed an exceedingly bold theory of the Psalms as apocalyptic hymns and of the comfort which these hymns yield to worshippers.[8] The secret function of true hymns was to serve as magical weapons to be wielded in the final struggle, weapons which were endowed with unlimited powers of purification and destruction so that they might annihilate all the forces of evil. Seen in this light, the words of the Psalms stood forth as "sharp swords in Israel's hand and deadly weapons,"[9] and the Psalter itself was envisaged in the double capacity of a book of war songs and an arsenal of weapons for the "last war." Before the final apocalyptic struggle in which these weapons were to be used, the tremendous apocalyptic power latent in the words of the Psalms is to manifest itself in the form of comfort, which is really the glow and secret crackling of the apocalyptic fires in their depths. Comfort is the classical symbol of delay. Even the delay of the final consummation, undesirable as it is, has a healing force. Comfort paves the way for the apocalyptic struggle. But when once the absolute power of the divine words erupts from beneath the comforting guise of meditation and promise, "all the forces will be transformed," as the author puts it in the language of apocalyptic dialectics.

Such deep-seated feeling as to the religious significance of catastrophes was bound, after the acute apocalyptic phase had sub-sided, to be transferred to more solid and substantial regions and there to struggle for expression. This expression was achieved in the far-reaching changes in the outlook on life, and in the new reli-gious conceptions with which the Kabbalah of Safed laid claim to dominate the Jewish world, and did in fact so dominate it for a long time.

The exiles from Spain must have held an intense belief in the fiendish realities of Exile, a belief that was bound to destroy the illusion that it was possible to live peacefully under the Holy Law in Exile. It expressed itself in a vigorous insistence upon the fragmen-tary character of Jewish existence, and in mystical views and dog-mas to explain this fragmentariness with its paradoxes and tensions. These views won widespread acceptance as the social and spiritual effects of the movement which originated either in the catastrophe of 1492 itself or in the Kabbalistic-apocalyptic propaganda attached to that event, made themselves increasingly felt. Life was conceived as Existence in Exile and in self-contradiction, and the sufferings of Exile were linked up with the central Kabbalistic doctrines about God and man. The emotions aroused by these sufferings were not soothed and tranquilized, but stimulated and whipped up. The ambiguities and inconsistencies of "unredeemed" existence, which were reflected in the meditations on the Torah and the nature of prayer, led that generation to set up ultimate values which differed widely from those of the rationalist theology of the Middle Ages, if only because the religious ideals it affirmed had no connection with a scale of values based on an intellectual point of view. Aristotle had represented the essence of rationalism to Jewish minds; yet his voice, which had not lost its resonance even in mediaeval Kabbalism despite its passage through a variety of media, now began to sound hollow and spectral to ears attuned to the new Kabbalah. The books of the Jewish philosophers became "devilish books."[10]

Death, repentance, and rebirth were the three great events in human life by which the new Kabbalah sought to bring man into blissful union with God. Humanity was threatened not only by its own corruption, but by that of the world, which originated in the first breach in creation, when subject and object first parted com-pany. By its emphasis upon death and rebirth (rebirth either in the sense of reincarnation or by the spiritual process of repentance), the

Kabbalistic propaganda, through which the new Messianism sought to win its way, gained in directness and popularity. This propaganda shaped the new attitudes and social customs which originated in Safed no less than the new systems and theologumena on which they were based. There was a passionate desire to break down the Exile by enhancing its torments, savouring its bitterness to the utmost (even to the night of the Exile of the Shekhinah itself), and summoning up the compelling force of the repentance of a whole community. (The Zohar promised redemption if only a single Jewish community would repent whole-heartedly.[11] The strength of the belief in this promise was demonstrated in Safed even while the attempt itself failed.[12]) Attempts to curtail or end the Exile by organized mystical action not rarely took on a social or even quasi-political character. All these tendencies, which were manifested in the very theatre of the redemption—Eretz Israel—clearly reflect the circumstances in which the Kabbalah became the authentic voice of the people in the crisis produced by the banishment from Spain.

The horrors of Exile were mirrored in the Kabbalistic doctrine of metempsychosis, which now won immense popularity by stressing the various stages of the soul's exile. The most terrible fate that could befall any soul—far more ghastly than the torments of hell—was to be "outcast" or "naked," a state precluding either rebirth or even admission to hell. Such absolute exile was the worst nightmare of the soul which envisaged its personal drama in terms of the tragic destiny of the whole people. Absolute homelessness was the sinister symbol of absolute Godlessness, of utter moral and spiritual degradation. Union with God or utter banishment were the two poles between which a system had to be devised in which the Jews could live under the domination of Law, which seeks to destroy the forces of Exile.

This new Kabbalism stands and falls with its programme of bringing its doctrines home to the community, and preparing it for the coming of the Messiah.[13] On the lofty pinnacles of speculative thought, sustained by the deep founts of mystical contemplation, it never proclaimed a philosophy of escape from the madding crowd; it did not content itself with the aristocratic seclusion of a few elect, but made popular education its business. In this it was for a long time surprisingly successful. A comparison of typical popular moralizing and edifying treatises and writings, before and after 1550, reveals the fact that until and during the first half of the sixteenth century this type of popular literature showed no trace of Kabbalistic influence. After 1550, the majority of these writers propagated Kabbalistic doctrines. In the centuries that followed, almost all the outstanding treatises on morals were written by mystics, and, with the exception of Moses Hayim Luzzatto in his "Path of the Upright" *Mesilath Yesharim,* their authors made no attempt to conceal this fact. Moses Cordovero's *Tomer Deborah,* Elijah de Vidas' *Reshith Hokhmah,* Eliezer Azikri's[14] *Sefer Haredim,* Hayim Vital's *Shaare Kedushah,* Isaiah Horovitz' *Shne Luhoth Ha-Berith,* Zevi Koidanover's *Kav Ha-Yashar,* to mention only a few of a long list of similar writings between 1550 and 1750—all played their part in carrying the religious message of the Kabbalah into every Jewish home.

2

The most important period in the history of the older Kabbalah is linked up with the little Spanish town of Gerona in Catalonia, where a whole group of mystics were active in the first half of the thirteenth century; this group was also the first which succeeded in familiarizing influential circles of Spanish Jewry with Kabbalist thought. It was mainly their spiritual heritage that was brought to the fore in the Zohar. Similarly the small town of Safed, in Upper Galilee, became about forty years after the exodus from Spain the center of the new Kabbalistic movement. There its peculiar doctrines were first formulated, and from there they began their victorious march through the Jewish world.

Strange as it may seem, the religious ideas of the mystics of Safed, which had such an immense influence, have to this day not been properly explored.[15] The fact is that all the scholars who followed Graetz and Geiger were inclined to single out the Lurianic school of Kabbalism for attack and to pillory it. Hence anyone can read in our historical literature how deeply Isaac Luria injured Judaism, but it is not so easy to discover what Luria actually thought. The mystical system, the influence of which on Jewish history has certainly been no less considerable than that of Maimonides' "Guide of the Perplexed," was considered by nineteenth century rationalism a slightly unsavory subject. This view no longer holds good. There is a valuable introduction to the subject in

Schechter's beautiful essay "Safed in the Sixteenth Century," where he describes the general characteristics of the movement and more particularly some of the leading figures.[16] But Schechter who says "I lay no claim to be initiated in the science of the invisible,"[17] studiously refrains from giving what would amount to an analysis of their mystical ideas. It is here that our task really begins.

The Kabbalists of Safed have left numerous and sometimes voluminous writings, some of them complete systems of mystical thought, of which the two most famous are those of Moses ben Jacob Cordovero and of Isaac Luria. It would be a fascinating task to compare and contrast the personalities and ideas of the two men, in the manner which Plutarch developed in his famous biographies, for they differ as much from one another as they are intimately related to each other. I must leave such an analysis for another occasion. Let me, however, say this much: Cordovero is essentially a systematic thinker; his purpose is to give both a new interpretation and a systematic description of the mystical heritage of the older Kabbalah, particularly the Zohar. One may say that this thinking, rather than a new stage of mystical insight, leads him to new ideas and formulas. To describe him in the terms of Evelyn Underhill, he is a mystical philosopher rather than a mystic, although he was by no means lacking mystical experience altogether.[18]

Of the theoreticians of Jewish mysticism Cordovero is undoubtedly the greatest. He was the first to make an attempt to describe the dialectical process through which the Sefiroth pass in the course of their development, with particular emphasis on that side of the process which may be said to take place inside each. Again, it was he who tried to interpret the various stages of emanation as stages of the divine mind. The problem of the relation of the substance of En-Sof to the "organism," the "instruments" (kelim: i. e. vessels or bowls), through which it works and acts was one to which he returned again and again. The intrinsic conflict between the theistic and the pantheistic tendencies in the mystical theology of Kabbalism is nowhere brought out more clearly than in his thought, and his attempts to synthetize the contradiction not only dominated the speculative side of his thinking but also produced tentative solutions which are frequently as profound and audacious as they are problematical. His ideas on the subject are summed up in the formula —a century before Spinoza and Malebranche,—that "God is all reality, but not all reality is God."[19] *En-Sof*, according to him, can also be called thought (i. e. thought of the world) "insofar as everything that exists is contained in His substance. He encompasses all existence, but not in the mode of its isolated existence below, but rather in the existence of the substance, for He and existing things are [in this mode] one, and neither separate nor multifarious, nor externally visible, but rather His substance is present in His Sefiroth, and He Himself is everything, and nothing exists outside Him."[20]

Cordovero's fecundity as a writer is comparable to that of Bonaventura or Thomas Aquinas, and like the latter he died comparatively young. When death carried him away in 1570, he was only 48 years old. The bulk of his writings is still extant, including an immense commentary on the Zohar, which has come down to us in a complete copy from the original.[21] He had the gift of transforming everything into literature, and in this as in many other things he was the complete antithesis of Isaac Luria, in whom we meet the outstanding representative of later Kabbalism. Luria was not only a true "Zaddik" or saintly man—that Cordovero was no less, from all we know about him[22]—but in addition there was also in him that creative power which has led every successive generation to regard him as the leader of the Safed movement. He was also the first Kabbalist whose personality impressed his disciples so deeply that some thirty-odd years after his death a kind of "saint's biography" began to circulate which relates not only a multitude of legends, but a faithful description of many of his personal traits. It is contained in three letters written by one Solomon, better known as Shlomel Dresnitz, who came from Strassnitz in Moravia to Safed in the year 1602 and from there spread Luria's fame in his letters to his Kabbalistic friends in Europe.[23]

Luria was no less a scholar than many other Kabbalists; during his formative years in Egypt he had his fill of rabbinical learning. But although he speaks the symbolical language of the old Kabbalists, particularly that of the anthropomorphists among them, it is evident that he is looking for ways of expressing new and original thoughts. Unlike Cordovero he left no written legacy when he passed away in 1572 at the age of 38; indeed he seems to have lacked the literary faculty altogether. When one of his disciples, who seem to have worshipped him like a superior being, asked him once why he did not set out his ideas and teaching in book form, he is said to have replied: "It is impossible, because all things are interrelated. I can hardly open my mouth to speak without feeling as though the sea burst its dams and overflowed. How then shall I express what my soul has received, and how can I put it down in a book?"²⁴ Actually, a critical analysis of the very numerous written tracts which circulate under his name and to which the Kabbalists always reverently referred as *Kithve Ha-Ari,* "The writings of the Sacred Lion," shows that either before or during his stay in Safed, which lasted only about three years, Luria did make an attempt to put his thoughts down in a book, which is undoubtedly authentic and in our possession. This is his commentary to the *Sifra di-Tseniuta,* "The Book of Concealment," one of the most difficult parts of the Zohar.²⁵ But here we find but little that is peculiar to him. In addition, a number of his commentaries on certain passages of the Zohar have survived. Finally there are his three mystical hymns for the Sabbath meals, which are among the most remarkable products of Kabbalistic poetry and may be found in almost every prayer-book of Eastern Jewry.

On the other hand, all we happen to know of his system is based on his conversations with his disciples; conversations which were as diffuse and unsystematic as possible. Luckily for us his pupils have left us several compilations of his ideas and sayings, including some which were written independently of each other, so that we are not, as has sometimes been said, dependent upon a single source. His most important follower, Hayim Vital (1543–1620), is the author of several versions of Luria's system, the most elaborate of which runs into five folio volumes, the so-called "Eight Gates" *(Shemonah Shearim)* into which he has divided his life work, *Ets Hayim,* "The Tree of Life."²⁶ In addition we have several anonymous writings, also by his followers, as well as a more compact presentation of the theosophical side of his system by Rabbi Joseph ibn Tabul, the most authoritative of his disciples after Vital.²⁷ Tabul's book in manuscript was for a long time buried in various libraries, with nobody paying any attention to it, and even when it was finally published by pure accident in 1921,²⁸ it was attributed to the more famous Vital—ironically enough, since Vital seems to have had little sympathy for his rival. What is common to both versions may safely be regarded as the authentic Lurianic doctrine.

As regards Luria's personality it is fortunate that Vital has carefully jotted down hundreds of little personal traits which bear the unmistakable imprint of authenticity.[29] Altogether Luria's personality comes out much clearer than that of Cordovero. Although not long after his death he had already become a legendary figure, there remains enough genuine biographical material to show us the man. First and foremost he was a visionary. As a matter of fact, we owe to him a good deal of insight into the strength and the limits of visionary thinking. The labyrinth of the hidden world of mysticism —for that is the way it appears in the writings of his disciples— was as familiar to him as the streets of Safed. He himself dwelt perpetually in this mysterious world, and his visionary gaze caught glimpses of psychical life in all that surrounded him; he did not differentiate between organic and inorganic life, but insisted that souls were present everywhere and that intercourse with them was possible. He had many uncanny visions, as for example when he frequently pointed out to his disciples, while walking with them in the vicinity of Safed, the graves of pious men of old with whose souls he held intercourse. Since the world of the Zohar was to him completely real, he not infrequently "discovered" the tombs of men, who were nothing but literary phantoms, derived from the romantic trappings of that remarkable book.[30]

Vital's account of his master's critical remarks on earlier Kabbalistic literature is also interesting; he warns against all the Kabbalists between Nahmanides and himself, because the prophet Elijah had not appeared to them and their writings were based purely on human perceptions and intelligence, and not on true Kabbalah. But the books he recommends, such as the Zohar, the commentary of the so-called pseudo-Abraham ben David to the "Book of Creation," the book *Berith Menuhah* and the book *Kanah*, were without exception written during the period which he condemns. Moreover, Luria, who rejected the lyrical poetry of the mediaeval poets, had a very high regard for the hymns of Eleazar Kalir and spoke of them as being representative of the true spirit of mysticism, doubtless because in accordance with an ancient tradition he believed this poet to be one of the great teachers of the period of the Mishnah,[31] the period which he also unsophisticatedly believed to be the background of the heroic figures which make their appearance in the great Kabbalistic pseudepigrapha.

By inclination and habit of mind, Luria was decidedly conservative. This tendency is well expressed in his persistent attempts to relate what he had to say to older authorities, especially to the Zohar, and in his attitude towards minor matters. He was always in favor of retaining what had a clearly defined character of its own and ever ready to grant the mystical truth of contradictory assertions. Even the various types of the Hebrew script have, according to him, each its own mystical significance.[32] In the same way he accorded equal rights so to speak to the different orders of prayer established by the various Jewish communities, on the ground that each of the twelve tribes of Israel had its own entrance to heaven which correspond to a certain form of prayer; and since no one knew to which tribe he belonged, there was no harm in being faithful to the traditions and usages of one's particular geographical group, the Spanish Jews remaining loyal to their customs, the Jews of Poland to theirs, and so on.[33]

The story of the gradual spread of Lurianic Kabbalism is remarkable and, like the creation of the Zohar, not without its dramatic side. Luria's original disciples did comparatively little to spread his ideas. Although Hayim Vital began to systematize Luria's thought immediately after his master's death he was jealously on guard against any attempt by others to claim possession of the key to the mystery. For a time he gave lectures before his former co-disciples on the new doctrines whose theosophic principles he surrounded with a great deal of scholastic detail. We still have the text of a document from the year 1575 in which almost all the more important pupils of Luria, insofar as they were still living in Safed, undertook in writing to recognize Vital's authority as supreme: "We shall study the Kabbalah with him and truly remember all he tells us and relate to no one else anything of the mysteries which we shall learn from him or which he has taught us in the past, even of what he has taught us in the life-time of our teacher, the great Rabbi Isaac Luria Ashkenazi, except it be that we receive his permission.[34] Subsequently Vital withdrew completely from this activity and only very reluctantly admitted others to the knowledge of his Kabbalistic writings. Until his death in Damascus in 1620, not a single one of his books was reproduced and circulated with his permission. A large number of them were, however, secretly copied in Safed in 1587 while he was dangerously ill—his brother having received a bribe of fifty pieces of gold for handing them over—and thereafter circulated among the adepts in Palestine. Nor can it be said of Joseph ibn Tabul, Luria's second most important follower, that he was a zealous propagandist, although he seems to have been somewhat more active in teaching his master's doctrine in Safed itself. He was not among those who signed the above mentioned declaration, and it is known that he also taught pupils who had not studied under Luria.[35]

On the whole, the spread of Lurianic Kabbalism was almost entirely due to the activity of another Kabbalist, Israel Sarug, who between 1592 and 1598 carried on a lively propaganda in the interests of the new school among the Kabbalists of Italy.[36] He posed as one of Luria's principal disciples, although it seems certain that he had no claim to this title and that all his knowledge of Lurianic doctrine was derived from those stolen copies of Vital's writings which had come into his hands in Safed. A man of considerable intellectual originality, he concieved himself to have penetrated more deeply than Luria's genuine pupils into the mysteries of the new doctrine. This fact probably explains why his missionary zeal led him to claim an authority which strictly speaking he did not possess. The deception passed unnoticed, and down to our own days Sarug has been treated both by adherents and opponents of Kabbalism as an authentic interpreter of Luria. The truth is that in certain essential points he gave an entirely new turn to Luria's thought and enriched it by speculative ideas of his own with which I cannot deal in this context. They are to be found chiefly in his book *Limmude Atsiluth*, "Doctrines on Emanation." The essence of Sarug's interpretation of Luria may be described as an attempt to provide a quasi-philosophical basis for Luria's distinctly unphilosophical doctrine by injecting a species of Platonism into it, and the singular success his interpretation achieved was due in part to those elements of his teaching which were not genuinely Lurianic.

One of Sarug's own followers subsequently carried these tendencies to a particularly radical conclusion and produced a system of Kabbalism which represents a curious eclectical mixture of the Neoplatonism fashionable in the Italy of the Renaissance and Luria's doctrine according to the interpretation of Sarug. He was Abraham Cohen Herrera of Florence (died in Amsterdam 1635 or 1639), the descendant of a Marranic family and the only Kabbalist who wrote in Spanish. His books were translated from the Spanish, in which they have been preserved only in manuscript form,[37] into Hebrew, and a Latin compendium which appeared in 1677 played a very considerable role—not least because it was written in a more or less comprehensible style[38]—in moulding the prevailing Christian view of the character of Kabbalism, and its alleged pantheism or Spinozism,[39] down to the beginning of the nineteenth century.

While the authentic writings of Luria's eastern followers achieved a wide circulation already in the seventeenth century, but almost without exception only in the form of manuscripts, the type of Lurianic Kabbalism represented by the followers of Sarug—specifically in Italy, Holland, Germany and Poland—predominates in the small number of printed books devoted to the propagation of Luria's ideas before the outbreak of the Sabbatian movement (1665). Of special importance in this connection was the great folio volume of Naphtali ben Jacob Bacharach, of Frankfort-on-Main, which appeared in 1648 under the title *Emek Ha-Melekh*. (A correct translation of this title might be "The Mystical Depths of the King," rather than "The Valley of the King.") The book relies wholly on Sarug's interpretation of Luria. It was sharply criticized in parts, by Kabbalists among others, but it was not before the end of the eighteenth century, and in some respects only in the nineteenth, that the Kabbalists consented to the publication of Vital's own books in print. However, the innovation did not add much to their popularity, for during the eighteenth century the business of copying his writings from manuscripts had become in some places, e. g. Jerusalem, Italy and Southern Germany, almost an industry.

3

In the years following his death, Luria's mystical inspiration was generally recognized in Safed, and precisely those ideas which were peculiar to him became the common property of later Kabbalism—not at once but through a process of expansion and development which began shortly before 1600.

I have spoken of Luria's mystical inspiration. But it must not be assumed that his doctrine came entirely out of the blue. It is true that at first it strikes one as being entirely different, in its outlook and its basic conceptions, from the earlier doctrine of the Safed school, and especially from Cordovero's system. However, closer comparison makes it apparent that a good many points in Luria's system are based on Cordovero's ideas, although they are developed in such an original way as to lead Luria to quite different and novel conclusions.

There is hardly any difference between Cordovero and Luria as far as the practical application of Kabbalistic thought is concerned, although some modern writers have been at pains to prove that this is the real point at issue. Nothing could be further from the truth; it is entirely wrong to say that Cordovero stands for the theory and Luria for the practice of Kabbalism, or alternatively, that Cordovero is the heir of Spanish Kabbalism, while Luria, an Ashkenazic Jew, whose parents appear to have come to Jerusalem only a short time before he was born, represents the consummation of the tradition of Jewish asceticism in mediaeval Germany.[40] Luria's Kabbalah is just as much or as little "practical" as that of the other Safed mystics. They all have something to do with "practical Kabbalism" and the things it connotes to the Kabbalist mind, to which I have drawn attention in the fourth lecture, but all of them were equally anxious to draw a distinction between their practical mysticism and its possible degeneration into magic. As for the ascetic ways of life which Lurianic Kabbalism propagated, it is difficult to find here anything that owes its influence to Luria. On the whole they are no more than a reflex of religious life in Safed as it existed before Luria's time as well as after him. It is to be hoped that the unfortunate term *practical Kabbalism* as a description of Luria's system, which is already finding its way into our historical text-books, will be given its quietus. The hegemony of the Safed school and more especially of its most important offshoot, the Lurianic Kabbalah, may justly be described as a period in which practical mysticism dominated, but for the specific difference between the Lurianic doctrine and its immediate predecessors we must look elsewhere.

To repeat, Luria's ideas are developed by him out of those of his predecessors, including not only Cordovero but far older authors. In the case of certain important details, for which he went back to the old Kabbalists, it can be said that these played no conspicuous part in their writings, while to Luria they were all-important. These connections between Luria and a few half-forgotten Spanish Kabbalists still await an adequate historical analysis.[41]

4

As we shall see later on, the form in which Luria presented his ideas is strongly reminiscent of the Gnostic myths of antiquity. The similarity is, of course, unintentional; the fact is simply that the structure of his thoughts closely resembles that of the Gnostics. His cosmogony is intensely dramatic, and I am inclined to believe that this quality, which was lacking in Cordovero's system, partly explains its success. Compared to that of the Zohar, whose authentic interpretation—on the basis of Elijah's revelations—it purports to be, his cosmogony is both more original and more elaborate. The older Kabbalists had a much simpler conception of the cosmological process. According to them, it begins with an act in which God projects His creative power out of His own Self into space. Every new act is a further stage in the process of externalization, which unfolds, in accordance with the emanationist doctrine of Neoplatonism, in a straight line from above downwards. The whole process is strictly one-way and correspondingly simple.

Luria's theory has nothing of this inoffensive simplicity. It is based upon the doctrine of *Tsimtsum,* one of the most amazing and far-reaching conceptions ever put forward in the whole history of Kabbalism. *Tsimtsum* originally means "concentration" or "contraction," but if used in the Kabbalistic parlance it is best translated by "withdrawal" or "retreat." The idea first occurs in a brief and entirely forgotten treatise which was written in the middle of the thirteenth century and of which Luria seems to have made use,[42] while its literary original is a Talmudic saying which Luria inverted. He stood it on its head, no doubt believing that he had put it on its feet. The Midrash—in sayings originating from third century teachers—occasionally refers to God as having concentrated His Shekhinah, His divine presence, in the holiest of holies, at the place of the *Cherubim,* as though His whole power were concentrated and contracted in a single point.[43] Here we have the origin of the term *Tsimtsum,* while the thing itself is the precise opposite of this idea: to the Kabbalist of Luria's school *Tsimtsum* does not mean the concentration of God *at* a point, but his retreat *away* from a point.

What does this mean? It means briefly that the existence of the universe is made possible by a process of shrinkage in God. Luria begins by putting a question which gives the appearance of being naturalistic and, if you like, somewhat crude. How can there be a world if God is everywhere? If God is 'all in all,' how can there be things which are not God? How can God create the world out of nothing if there is no nothing? This is the question. The solution became, in spite of the crude form which he gave it, of the highest importance in the history of later Kabbalistic thought. According to Luria, God was compelled to make room for the world by, as it were, abandoning a region within Himself, a kind of mystical primordial space from which He withdrew in order to return to it in the act of creation and revelation.⁴⁴ The first act of *En-Sof*, the Infinite Being, is therefore not a step outside but a step inside, a movement of recoil, of falling back upon oneself, of withdrawing into oneself. Instead of emanation we have the opposite, contraction. The God who revealed himself in firm contours was superseded by one who descended deeper into the recesses of His own Being, who concentrated Himself into Himself,⁴⁵ and had done so from the very beginning of creation. To be sure, this view was often felt, even by those who gave it a theoretical formulation, to verge on the blasphemous. Yet it cropped up again and again, modified only ostensibly by a feeble 'as it were' or 'so to speak.'

One is tempted to interpret this withdrawal of God into his own Being in terms of Exile, of banishing Himself from His totality into profound seclusion. Regarded this way, the idea of *Tsimtsum* is the deepest symbol of Exile that could be thought of, even deeper than the 'Breaking of the Vessels.'⁴⁶ In the 'Breaking of the Vessels,' with which I propose to deal later, something of the Divine Being is exiled out of Himself, whereas the *Tsimtsum* could come to be considered as an exile into Himself. The first act of all is not an act of revelation but one of limitation. Only in the second act does God send out a ray of His light and begin his revelation, or rather his unfolding as God the Creator, in the primordial space of His own creation. More than that, every new act of emanation and manifestation is preceded by one of concentration and retraction.⁴⁷ In other words, the cosmic process becomes two-fold. Every stage involves a double strain, i. e. the light which streams back into God and that which flows out from Him, and but for this perpetual tension, this ever repeated effort with which God holds Himself back, nothing in the world would exist. There is fascinating power and profundity in this doctrine. This paradox of *Tsimtsum*—as Jacob Emden said⁴⁸—is the only serious attempt ever made to give substance to the idea of Creation out of Nothing. Incidentally, the fact that an idea which at first sight appears so reasonable as "Creation out of Nothing" should turn out upon inspection to lead to a theosophical mystery shows us how illusory the apparent simplicity of religious fundamentals really is.

Apart from its intrinsic importance, the theory of *Tsimtsum* also acted as a counterpoise to the pantheism which some scholars think is implied by the theory of emanation.⁴⁹ Not only is there a residue of divine manifestation in every being, but under the aspect of *Tsimtsum* it also acquires a reality of its own which guards it against the danger of dissolution into the non-individual being of the divine "all in all." Luria himself was the living example of an outspoken theistic mystic. He gave the Zohar, for all its intrinsic pantheism, a strictly theistic interpretation. Nothing is more natural, therefore, than that the pantheistic tendencies which began to gain momentum in Kabbalism, especially from the period of the European Renaissance onwards, clashed with the Lurianic doctrine of *Tsimtsum,* and that attempts were made to re-interpret it in such a way as to strip it of its meaning. The question whether it should be interpreted literally or metaphorically came sometimes to be symbolical of the struggle between theistic and pantheistic trends, so much so that in later Kabbalism the position which a writer occupied in this struggle is to a certain extent implied by his stand on the question of *Tsimtsum.*⁵⁰ For if *Tsimtsum* is merely a metaphor to which no real act or occurence, however shrouded and mysterious, corresponds, then the question how something that is not God can really exist remains unsolved. If the *Tsimtsum*—as some later Kabbalists have tried to prove—is only a veil which separates the individual consciousness from God in such a way as to give it the illusion of self-consciousness, in which it knows itself to be different from God, then only an imperceptible change is needed so that the heart may perceive the unity of divine subsistence in all that exists. Such a change would necessarily destroy the conception of *Tsimtsum* as one intended to provide an explanation for the existence of something other than God.

As I have already said, the doctrine of *Tsimtsum* played an extremely important part in the development of Lurianic thought, and new attempts to formulate it were made continuously. The history of this idea from Luria down to our own days would give a fascinating picture of the development of original Jewish mystical thought.[51] Here I must content myself with stressing one more aspect which Luria himself undoubtedly regarded as highly important and for which our source is an authentic remark by himself.[52] According to this, the essence of the Divine Being, before the *Tsimtsum* took place, contained not only the qualities of love and mercy, but also that of Divine Sternness which the Kabbalists call *Din* or Judgment. But *Din* was not recognizable as such; it was as it were dissolved in the great ocean of God's compassion, like a grain of salt in the sea, to use Joseph ibn Tabul's simile. In the act of *Tsimtsum*, however, it crystallized and became clearly defined, for inasmuch as *Tsimtsum* signifies an act of negation and limitation it is also an act of judgment.[53] It must be remembered that to the Kabbalist, judgment means the imposition of limits and the correct determination of things. According to Cordovero the quality of judgment is inherent in everything insofar as everything wishes to remain what it is, to stay within its boundaries.[54] Hence it is precisely in the existence of individual things that the mystical category of judgment plays an important part. If, therefore, the Midrash says that originally the world was to have been based on the quality of strict judgment, *Din*, but God seeing that this was insufficient to guarantee its existence, added the quality of mercy, the Kabbalist who follows Luria interprets this saying as follows: The first act, the act of *Tsimtsum*, in which God determines, and therefore limits, Himself, is an act of *Din* which reveals the roots of this quality in all that exists; these "roots of divine judgment" subsist in chaotic mixture with the residue of divine light which remained after the original retreat or withdrawal within the primary space of God's creation. Then a second ray of light out of the essence of *En-Sof* brings order into chaos and sets the cosmic process in motion, by separating the hidden elements and moulding them into a new form.[55] Throughout this process the two tendencies of perpetual ebb and flow—the Kabbalists speak of *hithpashtuth*, egression, and *histalkuth*, regression[56]—continue to act and react upon each other. Just as the human organism exists through the double process of inhaling and exhaling and the one cannot be conceived without the other, so also the whole of Creation constitutes a gigantic process of divine inhalation and exhalation. In the final resort, therefore, the root of all evil is already latent in the act of *Tsimtsum*.

True to the tradition of the Zohar, Luria regards the cosmic process, up to a certain point, after the *Tsimtsum,* as a process *within* God—a doctrine, incidentally, which has never failed to involve its adherents in difficulties of the most complex sort. This assumption was made easier for him by his belief, already mentioned in passing, that a vestige or residue of the divine light—*Reshimu* in Luria's terminology—remains in the primeval space created by the *Tsimtsum* even after the withdrawal of the substance of *En-Sof.*[57] He compares this with the residue of oil or wine in a bottle the contents of which have been poured out.[58] This conception makes it possible to lay stress alternatively on the divine character of the *Reshimu,* or on the fact that the essence of *En-Sof* has been withdrawn so that what comes into being as the result of this process must stand outside God. It remains to be added that some of the more decided theists among the Kabbalists have solved the dilemma by disregarding the *Reshimu* altogether.

Before going further it may be of interest to point out that this conception of the *Reshimu* has a close parallel in the system of the Gnostic Basilides who flourished about 125 A.D. Here, too, we find the idea of a primordial "blessed space, which can neither be conceived of, nor characterized by any word, yet is not entirely deserted from the Sonship"; the latter is Basilides' term for the most sublime consummation of the universal potentialities. Of the relation of the Sonship to the Holy Spirit, or Pneuma, Basilides says that even when the Pneuma remained empty and divorced from the Sonship, yet at the same time it retained the latter's flavor which permeates everything above and below, even as far as formless matter and our own state of existence. And Basilides, too, employs the simile of a bowl in which the delicate fragrance of a "sweetest smelling unguent" remains though the bowl be emptied with the greatest possible care. Moreover, we have an early prototype of the *Tsimtsum* in the Gnostic "Book of the Great Logos," one of those astounding remains of Gnostic literature that have been preserved through Coptic translations. Here we are taught that all primordial spaces and their "fatherhoods" have come into being because of the "little idea," the space of which God has left behind as the shining world of light when He "withdrew Himself into Himself." This withdrawal that precedes all emanation is repeatedly stressed.[59]

5

Side by side with this conception of the cosmic process, we find two other important theosophical ideas. Luria has expressed them in bold mythical language, at times perhaps rather too bold. These two ideas are the doctrine of *Shevirath Ha-Kelim*, or "Breaking of the Vessels," and that of *Tikkun*, which means mending or restitution of a defect. The influence of these two ideas on the development of later Kabbalistic thought has been as great as that of the doctrine of *Tsimtsum*.

Let us begin by considering the former. We have to assume that the divine light which flowed into primordial space—of which three-dimensional space is a late development—unfolded in various stages and appeared under a variety of aspects. There is no point in going here into the details of this process. Luria and his followers are inclined to lose themselves partly in visionary, partly in scholastic, descriptions of it.[60] It came to pass within a realm of existence which, to use a Gnostic term, might well be called the sphere of *Pleroma*, or the "fullness" of divine light. The decisive point is that, according to this doctrine, the first being which emanated from the light was *Adam Kadmon*, the "primordial man."

Adam Kadmon is nothing but a first configuration of the divine light which flows from the essence of *En-Sof* into the primeval space of the *Tsimtsum*—not indeed from all sides but, like a beam, in one direction only. He therefore is the first and highest form in which the divinity begins to manifest itself after the *Tsimtsum*. From his eyes, mouth, ears and nose, the lights of the Sefiroth burst forth. At first these lights were coalesced in a totality without any differentiation between the various Sefiroth; in this state they did not require bowls or vessels to hold them. The lights coming from the eyes, however, emanated in an 'atomized' form in which every Sefirah was an isolated point. This "world of punctiform lights," *Olam Ha-Nekudoth*, Luria also calls *Olam Ha-Tohu*, i. e., "world of confusion or disorder."[61] In reply to a question regarding the difference between his doctrine and that of Cordovero, Luria expressed himself in the sense that the Kabbalah of his predecessor dealt on the whole only with events in this realm and a state of the world corresponding to them.[62] Since, however, the divine scheme of things involved the creation of finite beings and forms, each with its own allotted place in the ideal hierarchy, it was necessary that these isolated lights should be caught and preserved in special "bowls" created—or rather emanated—for this particular purpose. The vessels which corresponded to the three highest Sefiroth accordingly gave shelter to their light, but when the turn of the lower six came, the light broke forth all at once and its impact proved too much for the vessels which were broken and shattered. The same, though not to quite the same extent, also occurred with the vessel of the last Sefirah.[63]

This idea of the "breaking of the vessels" was developed by Luria in a highly original manner from a suggestion made in the Zohar. In a Midrash to which I have referred already in the first Lecture, mention is made of the destruction of worlds before the creation of the now existing cosmos.[64] The Zohar's interpretation of this Aggadah is that it refers to the creation of worlds in which only the forces of *Gevurah*, the Sefirah of stern judgment, were active, and which were therefore destroyed by this excess of sternness. This event in turn is placed in relation to the list of the Kings of Edom in chapter 36 of Genesis, of whom nothing is said but that they built a town and died. "And these are the Kings that reigned in the land of Edom,"—Edom signifying the realm of stern judgment untempered by compassion.[65] But the world is maintained only through the harmony of grace and strict judgment, of the masculine and the feminine, a harmony which the Zohar calls the "balance."[66] The death of the "primordial kings," of which more is said in the *Idra Rabba* and the *Idra Zutta* in the Zohar, now re-appears in Luria's system as the "breaking of the vessels."

In the description given of this event by Luria's original disciples, it has none of the characteristics of chaos or anarchy. On the contrary, it is a process which follows certain very definite laws or rules which are described in considerable detail. Subsequently, however, popular imagination took hold of the picturesque side of the idea and gave a literal interpretation, so to speak, to metaphors like "breaking of the vessels" or "world of the *tohu*"; in this manner, the emphasis was gradually shifted from the lawful to the catastrophic nature of the process.

The cause of this "breaking of the vessels," which releases the whole complexity of the cosmological drama and determines man's place in it, appears in Luria's and Vital's doctrine under varying aspects. In the immediate sense, the event is traced back to certain technical flaws in the structure of the Sefirotic atom-cosmos from which the 'accident' follows with necessity.[67] In a profounder sense, however, the event is due to what I propose to term, with Tishby,[68] the cathartic cause. For Luria, the deepest roots of the *Kelipot*, or "shells," i. e. the forces of evil, existed already before the breaking of the vessels and were mixed up, so to speak, with the lights of the Sefiroth and the above-mentioned *Reshimu*, or residue of *En-Sof* in the primordial space. What really brought about the fracture of the vessels was the necessity of cleansing the elements of the Sefiroth by eliminating the *Kelipot*, in order to give a real existence and separate identity to the power of evil.[69] The Zohar, as we have seen, already defines evil as a by-product of the life process of the Sefiroth, and more particularly, of the Sefirah of strict judgment. According to Luria, these waste products were originally mixed with the pure substance of *Din* (sternness), and it was only after the breaking of the vessels and the subsequent process of selection that the evil and demonic forces assumed real and separate existence in a realm of their own. Not from the fragments of the broken vessels but from the "dross of the primordial kings" did the domain of the *Kelipah* arise. More than that, the Zohar's organological imagery is developed to its logical conclusion: the *Shevirah* is compared to the "breakthrough" of birth, the deepest convulsion of the organism which, incidentally, is also accompanied by the externalization of what might be described as waste products.[70] In this manner, the mystical "death of the primordial kings" is transformed into the far more plausible symbol of a mystical 'birth' of the pure new vessels.

This cathartic interpretation of the meaning of the *Shevirah* was accepted by all the Kabbalists of the Lurianic school. For some of them, however, the idea that the roots of evil lie in the 'world of points' remained a stumbling-block, since it seemed to suggest a dualistic conception of God, i. e. one of the most serious heresies.[71] They therefore held to the view that the powers of evil developed out of the scattered fragments of the vessels which have sunk into the lower depths of the primordial space and there constitute the "depth of the great abyss" in which the spirit of evil dwells. Like all attempts to answer the question, *Unde malum?*, this effort to find a rational explanation of the existence of evil, or rather of its myth, fails to give complete satisfaction. Again the Gnostical character of the doctrine is clearly evident. The mythology of the Gnostical systems, too, recognizes in the *pleroma* dramatic processes in which particles of the light of the aeons are driven out and fall into the void. In the same manner, Luria accounts for the fall of divine "sparks of light" from the divine realm into the lower depths.

Later Kabbalists have lavished a great deal of further speculative thought on this point. According to some of them, the Breaking of the Vessels is connected, like so many other things, with the law of organic life in the theosophical universe. Just as the seed must burst in order to sprout and blossom, so too the first bowls had to be shattered in order that the divine light, the cosmic seed so to speak, might fulfill its function.[12] At any rate the Breaking of the Bowls, of which we find exhaustive descriptions in the literature of Lurianic Kabbalism, is the decisive turning point in the cosmological process. Taken as a whole, it is the cause of that inner deficiency which is inherent in everything that exists and which persists as long as the damage is not mended. For when the bowls were broken the light either diffused or flowed back to its source, or flowed downwards. The fiendish nether-worlds of evil, the influence of which crept into all stages of the cosmological process, emerged from the fragments which still retained a few sparks of the holy light—Luria speaks of just 288.[13] In this way the good elements of the divine order came to be mixed with the vicious ones.[14] Conversely the restoration of the ideal order, which forms the original aim of creation, is also the secret purpose of existence. Salvation means actually nothing but restitution, re-integration of the original whole, or *Tikkun,* to use the Hebrew term. Naturally enough the mysteries of *Tikkun* are the chief concern of Luria's theosophical system, theoretical and practical. Its details, particularly on the theoretical side, are of a highly technical nature and I shall not go to the length of describing them here.[15] What we have to consider are the few basic ideas which find their expression in the theory of *Tikkun.*

6

These parts of the Lurianic Kabbalah undoubtedly represent the greatest victory which anthropomorphic thought has ever won in the history of Jewish mysticism. It is as certain that many of these symbols reflect highly developed mystical meditations, which are almost impenetrable to rational thought, as it is undeniable that, taken as a whole, this symbolism is of a somewhat crude texture. The tendency to interpret human life and behavior as symbols of a deeper life, the conception of man as a *micro-cosmos* and of the living God as a *macro-anthropos,* has never been more clearly expressed and driven to its farthest consequences.

In the stage which corresponds to the manifestation of God under the aspect of *Adam Kadmon,* before the Breaking of the Vessels, the forces in action are not yet altogether parts of an organic whole and likewise have not yet assumed a distinctive, personal and characteristic configuration. Now that the vessels are broken a new stream of light wells from the original source of *En-Sof* and, bursting forth from the forehead of *Adam Kadmon,* gives a new direction to the disordered elements. The lights of the Sefiroth streaming from *Adam Kadmon* are organized in new configurations in each of which *Adam Kadmon* is reflected in certain definite forms. Every Sefirah is transformed from a general attribute of God into what the Kabbalists call a *Partsuf,* a "countenance" of God, which means that all the potentialities implied in every Sefirah are now brought under the influence of a formative principle,[76] and that in each the entire personality of God becomes apparent, if always under the aspect of a distinctive feature. The God who manifests Himself at the end of the process, represents a great deal more than the hidden *En-Sof;* He is now the living God of religion, whom Kabbalism attempted to portray. The whole attempt of Lurianic Kabbalism to describe the theogonic process in God in terms of human existence represents an effort to arrive at a new conception of the personal God,[77] but all it does is to culminate in a new form of Gnostical mythology. There is no use trying to get away from this fact; Luria tries to describe how in the process of *Tikkun,* of restoring the scattered lights of God to their right place, the various aspects, under which God manifests Himself, emerge one from the other as so many *Partsufim;* the conception of these is already quite personalistic.

In reading these descriptions one is easily tempted to forget that for Luria they refer to purely spiritual processes. Superficially at least, they resemble the myths through which Basilides, Valentinus or Mani tried to describe the cosmic drama, with the difference that they are vastly more complicated than these Gnostical systems.

The chief *Partsufim* or configurations are five in number.[78] Their names were suggested to Luria by the symbolism of the Zohar, par-

ticularly in the Idras; but the function and significance which he
assigns to them is to a large extent novel.

Where the flowing potencies of pure mercy and divine love which
are contained in the supreme Sefirah are gathered together in a
personal figure, there, according to the Zohar, arises the configuration of *Arikh Anpin,* occasionally translated "The Long Face," but
actually signifying "the Long-Suffering," i. e. God the long-suffering
and merciful.[79] In the Zohar, *Arikh* is also called *Attika Kaddisha,*
i. e. "the Holy Ancient One." For Luria, the former is to some extent a modification of the latter. The potencies of the Sefiroth of
divine wisdom and intelligence, *Hokhmah* and *Binah,* have become
the *Partsufim* of "father and mother," *Abba* and *Imma.*[80] The potencies of the six lower Sefiroth (with the exception of the Shekhinah), in which therefore mercy, justice and compassion are in
harmonious balance, are organized into a single configuration which
Luria, in accordance with the Zohar, calls *Zeir Anpin.* Again, the
correct translation is not "The Short Face," but "The Impatient,"[81]
as opposed to "The Long-Suffering." In this configuration, the quality of stern judgment, which has no place in the figure of the "Holy
Ancient One," plays an important part.

In the same manner in which, according to the Zohar, the six
Sefiroth, corresponding to the six days of creation, play the chief
part in the cosmic process and through the unity of their motion
represent God as the living Lord of the universe, so the figure of
Zeir Anpin stands in the centre of Lurianic theosophy insofar as the
latter refers to the process of *Tikkun. Zeir Anpin* is "The Holy One,
praise be to Him." What the "Holy One, praised be He," and the
Shekhinah were for the Zohar, *Zeir Anpin* and *Rachel,* the mystical
configuration, or *Partsuf,* of the Shekhinah, are to Luria. As long as
the *Tikkun* is not complete they form two *Partsufim,* although the
doctrine essentially concerns the one fully developed personality of
the living God which is carved out of the substance of *En-Sof* by
the immeasurably complicated process of *Tikkun.* The doctrine of
Zeir and *Rachel,* therefore, is the real focal point of the theoretical
side of the *Tikkun.* The origin of *Zeir Anpin* in the womb of the
'celestial mother,' his birth and development, as well as the laws in
accordance with which all the 'upper' potencies are organized in
him, form the subject of detailed exposition in the system developed
by Luria's followers.[82] There is something bewildering in the eccen-

tricity of these over-detailed expositions—the architecture of this mystical structure might be styled baroque.

Luria is driven to something very much like a mythos of God giving birth to Himself; indeed, this seems to me to be the focal point of this whole involved and frequently rather obscure and inconsistent description. The development of man through the stages of conception, pregnancy, birth and childhood, to the point where the developed personality makes full use of its intellectual and moral powers,[83] this whole process appears as a bold symbol of the *Tikkun* in which God evolves His own personality.

The conflict here is latent but inescapable: Is *En-Sof* the personal God, the God of Israel, and are all the *Partsufim* only His manifestations under various aspects, or is *En-Sof* the impersonal substance, the *deus absconditus,* who becomes a person only in the *Partsufim?* What could easily be managed so long as it concerned only the theological interpretation of the doctrine of the Zohar, with its immediate relationship between *En-Sof* and the Sefiroth, becomes a pressing problem in this very complicated process of *Tsimtsum* and *Shevirah* and the long chain of events leading up to the development of *Zeir Anpin.* The more dramatic the process in God becomes, the more inevitable is the question: Where in all this drama is God?

For Cordovero, only *En-Sof* was the real God of whom religion speaks, and the world of divinity with all its Sefiroth nothing but the organism in which He constitutes Himself in order to bring forth the universe of creation, and to act in it. In reading the authentic literature of Lurianic Kabbalism, one is frequently struck by the opposite impression: *En-Sof* has little religious interest for Luria. His three hymns for the three Sabbath meals are directed to the mystical configurations of God: the "Holy Ancient One," the *Zeir Anpin,* and the *Shekhinah* for whom he employs a Zoharic symbol, the "holy apple garden."[84] These hymns have the magnificent sweep of mind which visualizes a mystical process, half describing it, half conjuring and producing it through these very words. Their solemnity is highly suggestive, and the third hymn in particular deserves its immense popularity, so well does it express the mood which envelopes the mind when the growing dusk proclaims the end of the Sabbath. In these hymns, then, Luria appears to address the *Partsufim* as separate personalities. This is an extreme attitude.

There have always been Kabbalists who declined to go so far and, like Moses Hayim Luzzatto, insisted on the personal character of *En-Sof*. These outspoken theists among the theosophists never ceased to reinterpret the doctrine of the *Partsufim* in a sense designed to strip it of its obvious mythical elements, a tendency particularly interesting in the case of Luzzatto whose doctrine on the world of divinity was the offspring not of pure theory but of mystical vision. For the rest, the manifold contradictions and *non sequiturs* in Vital's writings supplied these Kabbalists with a sufficiency of arguments in favor of their own theistic exegesis.

According to Luria, this evolution of personality is repeated and as it were reflected at every stage and in every sphere of divine and mundane existence. From earlier sources, the Kabbalists of Safed, and in particular Cordovero, had adopted the doctrine of four worlds placed between the *En-Sof* and our earthly cosmos—a doctrine of which no trace is to be found in the major part of the Zohar.[85] In Safed, this theory was for the first time more fully elaborated and Luria, too, accepted it, though in his own way. The four worlds are: (1) *Atsiluth*, the world of emanation and of the divinity which has so far been our subject; (2) *Beriah*, the world of creation, i. e. of the Throne, the *Merkabah* and the highest angels; (3) *Yetsirah*, the world of formation, the chief domain of the angels; and (4) *Asiyah*, the world of making (and not, as some translators would have it, action). This fourth world, similar to Plotinus' hypostasis of "Nature," is conceived as the spiritual archetype of the material world of the senses. In every one of these four worlds, the mystical vision which unravels their innermost structure perceives the above mentioned configurations of the Godhead, the *Partsufim*, albeit shrouded in progressively deeper disguise, as is shown in the last part of Vital's "Tree of Life."[86]

For Luria and his followers, there is no break in this continuous process of evolution. This fact makes the problem of Luria's theism doubly acute, for the pantheistic implications of this doctrine are too manifest to require emphasis. Luria's reply to the question takes the form of a subtle distinction between the world of *Atsiluth* and the three other spheres: the former, or at any rate an important part of it, is conceived as being substantially identical with the divinity and the *En-Sof*, but from then on Luria tries to draw a firm dividing line. Between the world of *Atsiluth* and that of *Beriah*, and similarly between each of the following ones, he postulates a curtain or partition wall which has a double effect. In the first place it causes the divine substance itself to flow upwards; the Light of *En-Sof* is refracted. Secondly, the power which emanates from the substance, if not the latter itself, passes through the filter of the 'curtain.' This power then becomes the substance of the next world, of which again only the power passes into the third, and so through all four spheres. "Not *En-Sof* itself is dispersed in the nether worlds, but only a radiance [differing from his substance], *haarah*, which emanates from him."[87] In this fashion, that element of the nether worlds which, as it were, envelopes and hides the *Partsufim* in them assumes the character of a creature in a stricter sense. These "garments of the divinity" are no longer substantially one with God. It is true that there is no lack of speculative discursions in entirely different connections which are calculated to throw doubt on the definiteness of this solution[88] and which have in fact encouraged various pantheistic reinterpretations of the Lurianic system. More radical theists like Moses Hayim Luzzatto have tried to guard against this danger by denying altogether the continuity of the process in the four worlds and assuming that the Godhead, after manifesting itself in all its glory in the world of *Atsiluth,* proceeded to bring forth the three other worlds by an act of "creation out of nothing" no longer conceived as a mere metaphor.[89] Others have gone further and assumed that even the ray from *En-Sof,* whose incursion into primordial space forms the starting-point of all the processes after the *Tsimtsum,* was not of the same substance as *En-Sof* but was created *ex nihilo.*[90] All these interpretations must, however, be regarded as deviations from Luria's authentic teachings.

7

This brings us to a further aspect of the doctrine of *Tikkun,* which is also the more important for the system of practical theosophy. The process in which God conceives, brings forth and develops Himself does not reach its final conclusion in God. Certain parts of the process of restitution are allotted to man. Not all the lights which are held in captivity by the powers of darkness are set free by their own efforts; it is man who adds the final touch to the divine countenance; it is he who completes the enthronement of

God, the King and the mystical Creator of all things, in His own Kingdom of Heaven; it is he who perfects the Maker of all things! In certain spheres of being, divine and human existence are intertwined. The intrinsic, extramundane process of *Tikkun,* symbolically described as the birth of God's personality, corresponds to the process of mundane history. The historical process and its innermost soul, the religious act of the Jew, prepare the way for the final restitution of all the scattered and exiled lights and sparks. The Jew who is in close contact with the divine life through the Torah, the fulfilment of the commandments, and through prayer, has it in his power to accelerate or to hinder this process. Every act of man is related to this final task which God has set for His creatures.

It follows from this that for Luria the appearance of the Messiah is nothing but the consummation of the continuous process of Restoration, of *Tikkun.*[71] The true nature of redemption is therefore mystical, and its historical and national aspects are merely ancillary symptoms which constitute a visible symbol of its consummation. The redemption of Israel concludes the redemption of all things, for does not redemption mean that everything is put in its proper place, that the original blemish is removed? The 'world of *Tikkun*' is therefore the world of Messianic action. The coming of the Messiah means that this world of *Tikkun* has received its final shape.

It is here that we have the point where the mystical and the Messianic element in Luria's doctrine are welded together. The *Tikkun,* the path to the end of all things, is also the path to the beginning. Theosophic cosmology, the doctrine of the emergence of all things from God, becomes its opposite, the doctrine of Salvation as the return of all things to their original contact with God. Everything that man does, reacts somewhere and somehow on this complicated process of *Tikkun.* Every event and every domain of existence faces at once inwardly and outwardly, which is why Luria declares that worlds in all their externals are dependent on acts of religion, on the fulfilment of the commandments and meritorious deeds. But, according to him, everything internal in these worlds depends on spiritual actions, of which the most important is prayer.[72] In a sense, therefore, we are not only masters of our own destiny, and in the last resort are ourselves responsible for the continuation of the *Galuth,* but we also fulfil a mission which reaches far beyond that.

In a previous lecture I mentioned the magic of inwardness connected with certain Kabbalistic doctrines. In Lurianic thought these elements, under the name of *Kawwanah,* or mystical intention, occupy a highly important position. The task of man is seen to consist in the direction of his whole inner purpose towards the restoration of the original harmony which was disturbed by the original defect —the Breaking of the Vessels—and those powers of evil and sin which date from that time. To *unify* the name of God, as the term goes, is not merely to perform an act of confession and acknowledgment of God's Kingdom, it is more than that; it is an action rather than an act. The *Tikkun* restores the unity of God's name which was destroyed by the original defect—Luria speaks of the letters JH as being torn away from WH in the name JHWH—and every true religious act is directed towards the same aim.

In an age in which the historical exile of the people was a terrible and fundamental reality of life, the old idea of an exile of the Shekhinah gained a far greater importance than ever before. For all their persistent claim that this idea represents a mere metaphor, it is clear from their own writings that the Kabbalists at bottom saw something else in it. The exile of the Shekhinah is not a metaphor, it is a genuine symbol of the 'broken' state of things in the realm of divine potentialities. The Shekhinah fell, as the last Sefirah, when the vessels were broken. When the *Tikkun* began and the last Sefirah was reorganized as 'Rachel,' the celestial bride, she gathered fresh force and had all but achieved complete unification with the *Zeir Anpin* when, through an act described as the 'lessening of the Moon,' she was for the second time deprived of some of her substance.[93] Again, with the creation of the earthly Adam the *Tikkun* was strictly speaking at an end; the worlds were almost in the state for which they had been prepared, and if Adam had not fallen into sin on the sixth day, the final redemption would have been brought about on the Sabbath by his prayers and spiritual actions.[94] The eternal Sabbath would have come and "everything would have returned to its original root."[95] Instead, Adam's fall again destroyed the harmony, hurled all the worlds from their pedestals,[96] and again sent the Shekhinah into exile. To lead the Shekhinah back to her Master, to unite her with Him, is in one way or other the true purpose of the Torah. It is this mystical function of human action which lends it a special dignity. The fulfilment of each and every commandment was to be accompanied by a formula declaring that this was done "for the sake of uniting the Holy One, praised be He, and his Shekhinah, out of fear and love."[97]

But the doctrine of *Kawwanah,* particularly of the *Kawwanah* of prayer, does not stop there. To Luria, the heir of a whole school of thought in classical Kabbalism which he merely developed further, prayer means more than a free outpouring of religious feeling. Nor is it merely the institutionalized acknowledgment and praise of God as Creator and King by the religious community, in the standard prayers of Jewish liturgy. The individual's prayers, as well as those of the community, but particularly the latter, are under certain conditions the vehicle of the soul's mystical ascent to God.[98] The words of prayer, more particularly of the traditional liturgical prayer with its fixed text, become a silken cord with the aid of which the mystical intention of the mind gropes its dangerous way through the darkness towards God. The purpose of mystical meditation in the act of prayer, and in reflecting upon this act, is to discover the various stages of this ascent, which of course can also be called a descent into the deepest recesses of the soul. Prayer, according to Luria, is a symbolical image of the theogonic and cosmic process. The devout worshipper who prays in a spirit of mystical meditation moves through all the stages of this process, from the outermost to the innermost.[99] More than that: prayer is a mystical action which has an influence on the spheres through which the mystic moves in his *Kawwanah*. It is part of the great mystical process of *Tikkun*. Since *Kawwanah* is of a spiritual nature, it can achieve something in the spiritual world. It can become a most powerful factor, if used by the right man in the right place. As we have seen, the process of restoring all things to their proper place demands not only an impulse from God, but also one from His creature, in its religious action. True life and true amends for original sin are made possible by the confluence and concurrence of both impulses, the divine and the human.

The true worshipper, in short, exercises a tremendous power over the inner worlds, just as he bears a correspondingly great responsibility for the fulfilment of his Messianic task. The life of every world and every sphere is in continuous movement; every moment is a new stage in its development.[100] At every moment it strives to find the natural form which will lift it out of the confusion. And therefore there is in the last resort a new *Kawwanah* for every new moment. No mystical prayer is completely like any other. True prayer is modelled on the rhythm of the hour for which and in which it speaks.[101] Since everyone makes his individual contribution to the task of *Tikkun,* in accordance with the particular rank of his soul in the hierarchy, all mystical meditation is of an individual nature. As for the general principles concerning the direction of such meditation, the principles which everyone may apply in his own way and in his own time to the standard prayers of the liturgy, Luria believed he had found them, and his followers developed them in great detail. They represent an application of Abulafia's theory of meditation to the new Kabbalah. The emphasis on the strictly individual character of prayer, which occupies an important place in Hayim Vital's theory of *Kawwanah,* is all the more important because we are here in a region of mysticism where the danger of degeneration into mechanical magic and theurgy is greatest.

Luria's doctrine of mystical prayer stands directly on the borderline between mysticism and magic, where the one only too easily passes into the other. Every prayer which is more than mere acknowledgment of God's Kingdom, indeed every prayer which in a more or less clearly defined sense is bound up with the hope of its being granted, involves the eternal paradox of man's hope to influence the inscrutable ways and eternal decisions of Providence. This paradox, in the unfathomable depths of which religious feeling has its abode, leads inevitably to the question of the magical nature of prayer. The facile distinction between magic and so-called true mysticism, which we find in the writings of some modern scholars, (and which we have also met in Abulafia's account of his own system), with their abstract definition of the term *mysticism,* is quite irrelevant to the history and to the lives of many mystical thinkers. Granted that magic and mysticism represent fundamentally different categories, that does not disprove the fact that they are capable of meeting, developing and interacting in the same mind. History shows that particularly those schools of mysticism which are not purely pantheistic and show no tendency to blur the distinction between God and Nature, represent a blend of the mystical and the magical consciousness. That is true of many forms of Indian, Greek, Catholic and also of Jewish mysticism.

That the doctrine of *Kawwanah* in prayer was capable of being interpreted as a certain kind of magic seems clear to me; that it invólves the problem of magical practices is beyond any doubt. Yet the number of Kabbalists who weakened under the temptation is surprisingly small. I have had occasion in Jerusalem to meet men who to this day adhere to the practice of mystical meditation in prayer, as Luria taught it, for among the 80,000 Jews of Jerusalem there are still thirty or forty masters of mystical prayer who practise it after years of spiritual training.[102] I am bound to say that in the majority of cases a glance is sufficient to recognize the mystical character of their devotion. None of these men would deny that the inner *Kawwanah* of prayer is easily capable of being externalized as magic, but they have evolved, or perhaps one should say inherited, a system of spiritual education in which the center of gravity lies on mystical introspection. The *Kawwanah* is to them also the way to *Devekuth,* that mystical contact with God which, as we have seen in a previous lecture, is the typical form of *unio mystica* in Kabbalism. Ecstasy is possible here only within the limits imposed by this *Kawwanah;* it is an ecstasy of silent meditation,[103] of a descent of the human will to meet that of God, prayer serving as a kind of balustrade on which the mystic leans, so as not to be plunged suddenly or unprepared into an ecstasy in which the holy waters might drown his consciousness.

8

The doctrine and practice of mystical prayer is the esoteric part of Lurianic Kabbalism, that part of it which is reserved to the elect. Side by side with this doctrine, however, we find ideas of a different character. Above all the doctrine of practical realization of the *Tikkun,* and its combination not only with the aforementioned view of the devotee's task, but also with the doctrine of metempsychosis, secured to all three elements the strongest influence on wide circles of Jewry. The task of man has been defined by Luria in a simple but effective way as the restoration of his primordial spiritual structure or *Gestalt.* That is the task of every one of us, for every soul contains the potentialities of this spiritual appearance, outraged and degraded by the fall of Adam, whose soul contained all souls.[106] From this soul of all souls, sparks have scattered in all directions and become diffused into matter. The problem is to reassemble them, to lift them to their proper place and to restore the spiritual nature of man in its original splendor as God conceived it.

According to Luria the meaning of the acts which the Torah prescribes or forbids is none other than the execution, by and in the individual, of this process of restitution of man's spiritual nature. The Targum already drew a parallel between the 613 commandments and prohibitions of the Torah and the supposed 613 parts of the human body.[106] Now Luria advances the thought that the soul, which represented the original appearance of man before its exile into the body, also has 613 parts. By fulfilling the commandments of the Torah, man restores his own spiritual structure; he carves it out of himself as it were. And since every part corresponds to a commandent, the solution of the task demands the complete fulfilment of all the 613 commandments.

Incidentally, this interrelation of all men through Adam's soul had already moved Cordovero to mystical speculations. To quote his words, "in everyone there is something of his fellow man. Therefore, whoever sins, injures not only himself but also that part of himself which belongs to another." And this, according to Cordovero, is the true reason why the Torah (Lev. xix, 18) could prescribe the commandment "Thou shalt love thy neighbor as thyself," —for the other is really he himself."[107]

At this point I should like to insert a remark. The Gnostical character of this psychology and anthropology is evident. The structure of Luria's anthropology corresponds on the whole to that of his theology and cosmology, with the difference that the point of reference is no longer the mystical light of divine emanation and manifestation, but the soul and its 'sparks.' Man, as he was before his fall, is conceived as a cosmic being which contains the whole world in itself and whose station is superior even to that of Metatron, the first of the angels.[108] *Adam Ha-Rishon*, the Adam of the Bible, corresponds on the anthropological plane to *Adam Kadmon*, the ontological primary man. Evidently the human and the mystical man are closely related to each other; their structure is the same, and to use Vital's own words, the one is the clothing and the veil of the other. Here we have also the explanation for the connection between man's fall and the cosmic process, between morality and physics. Since Adam was truly, and not merely metaphorically, all-embracing, his fall was bound likewise to drag down and affect everything, not merely metaphorically but really. The drama of *Adam Kadmon* on the theosophical plane is repeated, and paralleled by that of *Adam Rishon*. The universe falls, Adam falls, everything is affected and disturbed and enters into a "stage of diminution" as Luria calls it. Original sin repeats the Breaking of the Vessels on a correspondingly lower plane.[109] The effect is again that nothing remained where it should be and as it should be; nothing therefore was from then on its proper place.[110] Everything is in Exile. The spiritual light of the Shekhinah was dragged down into the darkness of the demonic world of evil. The result is the mixture of good and evil which must be dissolved by restoring the element of light to its former position.[111] Adam was a spiritual being whose place was in the world of *Asiyah*[112] which, as we have seen, was also a spiritual realm. When he fell into sin, then and then only did this world, too, fall from its former place and thereby become mixed up with the realm of the *Kelipoth* which originally was placed below it.[113] Thus there came into being the material world in which we live, and the existence of man as a part spiritual, part material being.[114] And whenever we fall into sin we cause a repetition of this process, of the confusion of the holy with the unclean, the 'fall' of the Shekhinah and her exile. "Sparks of the Shekhinah" are scattered in all worlds and "there is no sphere of existence including organic and inorganic nature, that is not full of holy sparks which are mixed up with the Kelipoth and need to be separated from them and lifted up."

To the student of religious history the close affinity of these thoughts to the religious ideas of the Manichaeans must be obvious at once. We have here certain Gnostic elements—especially the theory of the scattered sparks or particles of light—which were either absent from or played no particular part in early Kabbalist thought. As the same time there can be no doubt that this fact is due not to historical connections between the Manichaeans and the new Kabbalah of Safed, but to a profound similarity in outlook and disposition which in its development produced similar results. In spite of this fact, or perhaps rather because of it, students of Gnosticism may have something to learn from the Lurianic system which, in my opinion, is a perfect example of Gnostical thought, both in principle and in detail.

9

But let us go back to where we started. The fulfilment of man's task in this world is connected by Luria, as well as by all the other

Safed Kabbalists, with the doctrine of metempsychosis, or transmigration of the soul. In the later development of the school of Safed, this remarkable doctrine has been elaborated in great detail, and Hayim Vital's *Sefer Ha-Gilgulim,* or "Book of Transmigrations," in which he gave a systematic description of Luria's doctrine of metempsychosis, is the final product of a long and important development in Kabbalistic thought.[115] I do not intend to pursue this point further than to remark that there is a considerable difference between the respective attitudes of the older and the newer school of Kabbalism towards this idea, which as I said found its classis expression in Luria's and Vital's doctrine. As for the motives which prompted both the old and the new Kabbalah to embrace the doctrine of transmigration, they were probably not different at first from those which have always encouraged belief in it, *i. e.* the impression made upon sensitive minds by the sufferings of innocent children, the contentedness of the wicked, and other phenomena which demand a natural explanation in order to conform with the belief in divine justice within the sphere of nature. For it must be admitted that the solution of these apparent contradictions by the conception of divine retribution, and in general by eschatological hopes, has at all times failed to satisfy the mind of many believers in religion. The difference is that the majority of older Kabbalists believed in *Gilgul,* to use the Hebrew term for transmigration, only in connection with certain offences, chiefly sexual. As I have pointed out in the previous lecture, they knew nothing of a universal law of transmigration considered as a system of moral causality—that is to say, a system of moral causes and physical effects—*Karma,* to use the Sanskrit term. It fits into this picture that the whole doctrine, which at first seems to have encountered much opposition, was regarded as a particularly occult mystery and gained no entrance into wider circles. A thirteenth century mystic like Isaac ibn Latif rejected it disdainfully.[116]

Sixteenth century Kabbalism took a totally different view, for meanwhile—as I said at the beginning of this lecture—the doctrine of *Gilgul* had come to express in a new and forcible way the reality of Exile. Its function was, as it were, to lift the experience of the Jew in the *Galuth,* the exile and migration of the body, to the higher plane of a symbol for the exile of the soul.[117] The inner exile, too, owes its existence to the fall. If Adam contained the en-

tire soul of humanity, which is now diffused among the whole genus
in innumerable codifications and individual appearances, all transmigrations of souls are in the last resort only migrations of the one
soul whose exile atones for its fall. In addition, every individual
provides, by his behavior, countless occasions for ever renewed
exile. Altogether we have here a fairly comprehensive conception of
the *Gilgul* as a law of the universe, and the idea of retribution by
punishment in hell is pushed rather far into the background. Obviously a radical theory of retribution in the process of transmigration leaves no room at all for the conception of hell, and it is not
surprising to find that there have indeed been attempts to allegorize
the idea of hell so much as to deprive it of its literal meaning.[113] In
general, however, we find a mixture of both ideas, and the Safed
school in particular was inclined to allot a certain place in its
scheme of transmigratory stages to the old-fashioned hell. The two
ideas intertwine, but the emphasis is undoubtedly on transmigration.

This doctrine now becomes closely involved with the conception
of man's role in the universe. Each individual soul retains its individual existence only until the moment when it has worked out its
own spiritual restoration. Souls which have fulfilled the commandments, be they those of all humanity—of "the sons of Noah"—or,
in the case of the Jews, the 613 of the Torah, are exempted from
the law of transmigration and await, each in its blessed place, their
integration into Adam's soul, when the general restitution of all
things shall take place. As long as the soul has not fulfilled this task
it remains subject to the law of transmigration. Transmigration is
thus no longer mere retribution, it is also at the same time a chance
of fulfilling the commandments which it was not given to the soul
to fulfil before, and of thereby continuing the work of self-emanci-
pation. Pure retribution is indeed implied by the idea of transmigration into other spheres of nature, such as animals, plants and
stones. This banishment into the prison of strange forms of existence, into wild beasts, into plants and stones, is regarded as a particularly dreadful form of exile. How can souls be released from
such an exile? Luria's reply to this question refers to the relationship
between certain souls, in accordance with the place which they
originally occupied in the undivided soul of Adam, the father of
mankind. There are, according to him, relationships between souls,

and even families of souls, which somehow constitute a dynamic whole and react upon one another.[119] These souls have a special aptitude for assisting each other and supplementing each other's actions, and can also by their piety lift up those members of their group or family who have fallen onto a lower plane and can enable them to start on the return journey to higher forms of existence. According to Luria, this mysterious interrelation of souls throws light on many biblical histories. Altogether the true history of the world would seem to be that of the migrations and interrelations of the souls, which is precisely what Hayim Vital tried to describe in the later parts of his *Sefer Ha-Gilgulim*. There, and in similar writings of this kind, we find a characteristic and curious mixture of elements of pure vision, characterological intuitions (including some that are very profound) and purely homiletical ideas and associations of thought.

To recapitulate what we have said, the *Gilgul* is part of the process of restoration, of *Tikkun*. Owing to the power of evil over mankind, the duration of this process is immeasurably extended, but—and here we come to a point in Luria's doctrine which appealed very strongly to the individual consciousness—it can be shortened by certain religious acts, *i. e.* rites, penitential exercises and meditations.[120] Everybody carries the secret trace of the transmigrations of his soul in the lineaments of his forehead and his hands,[121] and in the aura which radiates from his body.[122] And those to whom it is given to decipher this writing of the soul can aid in its wandering. It is true that this power is conceded by Cordovero and Luria only to the great mystics.[123]

Now it is very interesting and significant that this Kabbalistic doctrine of transmigration, the influence of which was originally confined to very small circles, extended its influence with startling rapidity after 1550. The first voluminous book which is based on a most elaborate system of *Gilgul* is the *Galli Razaya*, "The Revealed Mysteries," written in 1552 by an anonymous author.[124] In a short time this doctrine became an integral part of Jewish popular belief and Jewish folklore. This is all the more remarkable as we have here a doctrine which, contrary to many other elements of Jewish popular religious belief, was not generally accepted in the social and cultural environment in which the Jews lived. To repeat what I have already said, I am inclined to believe that the particular

historic situation of the Jews in those generations had as much to do
with its success as did the general popular disposition towards ani-
mism. Primitive belief is animistic in that it is inclined to regard
all things as animated, acting creatures. And the doctrine of the
Gilgul not only appealed to this stratum of primitive thought but
also explained, transfigured and glorified the deepest and most
tragic experience of the Jew in the *Galuth,* in a manner which
appealed most strongly and directly to the imagination. For *Galuth*
here acquires a new meaning. Formerly it had been regarded either
as a punishment for Israel's sins or as a test of Israel's faith. Now it
still is all this, but intrinsically it is a mission: its purpose is to uplift the fallen sparks from all their various locations. "And this is
the secret why Israel is fated to be enslaved by all the Gentiles of
the world: In order that it may uplift those sparks which have also
fallen among them. . . . And therefore it was necessary that Israel
should be scattered to the four winds in order to lift everything
up."[125]

10

The influence of the Lurianic Kabbalah, which from about
1630 onwards became something like the true *theologia mystica* of
Judaism, can hardly be exaggerated. It taught a doctrine of Judaism
which even in its most popular aspects renounced nothing of its
Messianic pathos. The doctrine of *Tikkun* raised every Jew to the
rank of a protagonist in the great process of restitution, in a manner never heard of before. It seems that Luria himself believed the
end to be near and that he "entertained the hope that the year 1575
was the year of Redemption," a hope that was shared by many
other Kabbalists of his generation.[126] It seems to be in the nature of
such doctrines that the tension which they express demands a sudden and dramatic relief. Once the doctrine of *Tikkun* had entered
into the popular consciousness, the eschatological mood was bound
to grow; it could hardly be otherwise. But even after the Messianic
element of the new mysticism had threatened to kindle the flames of
an apocalyptic conflagration in the heart of Jewry, its basic speculative ideas and practical conclusions retained their influence.

Not only the ideas but also a large number of customs and rites
propagated for mystical reasons by the Kabbalists of Safed—by no
means only the followers of Luria—were accepted in all the commu-

nities. To a large extent these rites and customs were connected with the ever growing ascendancy of ascetic principles in communal life, e. g. the fasting of the first born on the day before Passover, the night vigil before *Shevuoth* and *Hoshanah Rabbah*, the transformation of the latter day from a feast of joy into a day of penitence which really concludes the Day of Atonement, the transformation of the last day before every new moon into a so-called "lesser day of atonement" and many other examples of the kind.[127] In place of the rites of penitence prescribed by the old Hasidim of Germany we now find Isaac Luria's prescriptions for penitents.[128] Some spheres of Jewish life become permeated to an extraordinary degree by the new spirit and the mystic restatement of older principles. I would mention three spheres as outstanding in this respect: the celebration of the Sabbath and the other festivals, sexual life and procreation, and, at the other hand, everything pertaining to death and the afterlife. Many of these innovations became extremely popular, e. g. the custom of studying *Mishnah* in remembrance of the deceased (because *Mishnah* has the same consonants as the Hebrew word *Neshamah,* "soul"). But in particular, the liturgy, at all times the clearest mirror of religious feeling, was deeply affected by the influence of the mystics. A multitude of new prayers, for the individual as well as for the community, gradually made their way, at first into the prayer books of private conventicles and later into the generally accepted forms of prayer.[129] Thus the mystics were instrumental in causing the famous hymn *Lekha dodi likrath kallah* of Solomon Alkabez of Safed to be included in the Friday evening liturgy. By far the most beautiful and detailed description of the life of the Kabbalistic devotee all through the year, such as it became under the dominant influence of Lurianic Kabbalism, is to be found in *Hemdath Yamim,*[130] "The Adornment of Days," the work of an anonymous follower of the moderate Sabbatians who remained true to rabbinical tradition. (The old theory that its author was no other than the Sabbatian prophet Nathan of Gaza himself must be discarded.) Written in Jerusalem towards the end of the seventeenth century,[131] this voluminous book remains in my opinion, despite all that strikes us as bizarre, one of the most beautiful and affecting works of Jewish literature.

The Lurianic Kabbalah was the last religious movement in Judaism the influence of which became preponderant among all sections of the Jewish people and in every country of the diaspora, without exception. It was the last movement in the history of rabbinic Judaism which gave expression to a world of religious reality common to the whole people. To the philosopher of Jewish history it may seem surprising that the doctrine which achieved this result was deeply related to Gnosticism, but such are the dialectics of history.

To sum up, the Kabbalah of Isaac Luria may be described as a mystical interpretation of Exile and Redemption, or even as a great myth of Exile. Its substance reflects the deepest religious feelings of the Jews of that age. For them, Exile and Redemption were in the strictest sense great mystical symbols which point to something in the Divine Being. This new doctrine of God and the universe corresponds to the new moral idea of humanity which it propagates: the ideal of the ascetic whose aim is the Messianic reformation, the extinction of the world's blemish, the restitution of all things in God—the man of spiritual action who through the *Tikkun* breaks the exile, the historical exile of the Community of Israel and that inner exile in which all creation groans.

SABBATIANISM AND MYSTICAL HERESY

1

The development of Jewish mysticism from the time of the Spanish exodus onwards has been singularly uniform and free from cross-currents. There is only one main line. The catastrophic events of that period led directly to the rise of the new School of Safed whose thoughts, as we have seen, centered round certain problems created or become visible through that great cataclysm. We have also seen that in dealing with them that school evolved a completely new doctrine. It seems to me that this new doctrine, as it was formulated by Luria and finally adopted by Jewish theology, represents a particularly accurate expression of the outlook which gradually became predominant in Jewry after the turn of the century. These new ideas combine a mystical interpretation of the fact of exile with an equally mystical theory of the path to redemption. The old spirit of mystical contemplation is enriched by the new element of Messianic fervor, with its apocalyptic dream of an end to the period of suffering and degradation. The spread of Lurianic Kabbalism with its doctrine of *Tikkun,* of the restitution of cosmic harmony through the earthly medium of a mystically elevated Judaism, this doctrine could not but lead to an explosive manifestation of all those forces to which it owed its rise and its success. If it be true that the Kabbalah gave expression to the prevalent mood of the age, then nothing seems more natural than that there should have been the closest correspondence between the historical conditions which moulded the fate of the Jewish people in this epoch of Kabbalist ascendancy, and the inner development of Jewish religious thought, including all its new forms. A people which had suffered from all the tribulations which exile and persecution could bring, and which at the same time had developed an extremely sensitive consciousness of life actually lived between the poles of exile and redemption, needed little to take the final step to Messianism. The appearance of Sabbatai Zevi and Nathan of Gaza precipitated this step by liberating the latent energies and potentialities which had gradually accumulated during the generations immediately preceding them. The eruption of the volcano, when it came, was terrific.

It is not my purpose here to describe the swift rise and the sudden collapse of the Sabbatian movement in 1665 and 1666, from Sabbatai Zevi's proclamation of his Messianic mission to his renunciation of Judaism and adoption of Islam when he was led before the Turkish Sultan. I am not primarily concerned with the biography of the Messiah and his prophet, Nathan of Gaza, nor with the details of the tremendous religious mass movement which spread like wild-fire through the entire Diaspora—already prepared, as it were, for such an event by the influence of the new Kabbalism. Suffice it to say that very large numbers of people were swept on a tide of emotion and underwent the most extravagant forms of self-inflicted penance, "the like of which," we are told by the contemporaries, "never were seen before, nor will be again until the true redemption comes."[1] But hand in hand with penitence there also went boundless rejoicing and enthusiasm, for at last there seemed to be visible proof that the sufferings of 1600 years had not been in vain. Before redemption had actually come it was felt by many to have become reality. An emotional upheaval of immense force took place among the mass of the people, and for an entire year, men lived a new life which for many years remained their first glimpse of deeper spiritual reality.

The course which events took is described in every book on Jewish history, though in many details the story still awaits critical revision. My object here is to stress those aspects of the Sabbatian movement which are wholly or partly neglected in the historical literature, and those which through misunderstanding or other causes have remained entirely in the dark. Without a proper appreciation of these aspects of the matter it is impossible to understand the true nature of this grandiose though abortive attempt to revolutionize Judaism from within, its significance for the history of Judaism and for Jewish mysticism in particular.

2

This task, however, cannot be undertaken without saying a few words about the personalities of the two original leaders of the movement and their place in its first outbreak and subsequent development. This is all the more needed because in this, as in so many other matters discussed in the course of these lectures, I am bound to take a view which differs to a considerable extent from the customary one. What then was the basic trait of Sabbatai Zevi's personality and how are we to judge his individual contribution to the movement? In particular, how are we to interpret his relation to Nathan of Gaza, his subsequent prophet? To these questions, the only documents available in print until recent years have not permitted a definite answer. Those which throw most light on the subject have not hitherto been published, and in their absence it has often been impossible to form a correct impression even of published writings. In these circumstances undue weight has been given to the testimony of persons who were not intimately acquainted with the leaders of the movement. It is, therefore, scarcely astonishing that where the scholars had failed, poets, dramatists and other masters of fiction have tried to complete the picture by drawing on the resources of their imagination. Yet there are in our possession not a few highly important documents, some personal and others theological, emanating from the closest circle of Sabbatai Zevi's followers, which throw an entirely unexpected light on all these questions. An analysis of all the sources to which I have had access yields the following main conclusions:

It was not Sabbatai Zevi himself who by his appearance and his constant activity over a number of years finally succeeded, in the teeth of persecution, in founding the movement which bears his name. True, without him it would have been unthinkable in this form, but his own unaided activity would never have sufficed to bring it about. It was the awakening of Nathan of Gaza to his prophetic mission which set the whole train of events in motion. The role of this brilliant and ardent youth, who at the time of the inception of the movement was only twenty years old, has scarcely been understood and now appears in a totally different light.

Even before the critical date of 1665, Sabbatai Zevi (1625-1676) appears to have regarded himself in certain moments as the Messiah and to have made occasional references to this conviction. But no one, literally no one, took this claim seriously. To be precise, nobody, including his admirers in Smyrna, gave the faintest sign between 1648—when there appears to have been for the first time a slight scandal about him—and 1665 of knowing anything about the existence and personality of the true Messiah of God. The explanation of this fact is very simple and provides the key to the understanding of this tragic Messiah: Sabbatai Zevi was physically a sick man. To some extent this truth has of course been suspected before; people have talked of paranoia or hysteria.[2] But a mass of documentary evidence now available shows that his affliction was in fact of a somewhat different nature. he was constitutionally a manic-depressive, that is to say he belonged to a type whose lack of mental balance displays itself in alternate fits of deepest gloom and most uncontrollable exuberance and exaggerated joy. Periods of profound depression and melancholia constantly alternated in him with spasms of maniacal exaltation, enthusiasm and *euphoria,* separated by intervals of a more normal state of mind. What is known of his character does not give the faintest indication of paranoia, but on the other hand it hardly lacks a single trait of manic-depressive psychosis as described in the standard handbooks of psychiatry.[3] The evidence of his biographers permits us to conclude that he showed the first traits of this mental affliction between his sixteenth and his twentieth year.[4] Now it is of special importance for our understanding of his character, that this mental illness is distinguished from all others by the fact that it does not lead to the decomposition and destruction of the human personality and in particular does not affect the intelligence. Actually the term *illness* is used only in a single, a very eloquent testimony, written by one of his most important followers who retained his faith in him to the end: Samuel Gandor, who in the summer of 1665 was sent from Egypt to Gaza in order to investigate the events which had taken place there. This enthusiastic follower of Sabbatai Zevi and travelling companion of Nathan has left us the following description of his master:[5] "It is said of Sabbatai Zevi that for fifteen years he has been bowed down by the following affliction: he is pursued by a sense of depression which leaves him no quiet moment and does not even permit him to read, without his being able to say what is the nature of this sadness which has come upon him. Thus he endures it until the depression departs from the spirit, when he returns with great joy to his studies. And for many years already he has suffered from this illness, and no doctor has found a remedy for it, but it is one of the sufferings which are inflicted by Heaven." The same letter contains a description of an incident during the night before the feast of *Shevuoth* in 1665, when Sabbatai Zevi was suddenly overcome by a profound depression of the kind just described.[6]

Similar clear and incontrovertible evidence exists for the state of manic excitement which alternated with these attacks of depression. The Sabbatians later on no longer refer to these varying states of consciousness as the effects of illness. In their view they represent certain states of mind induced by heavenly power for which they employ theological terms—including novel ones of their own making—corresponding in the closest possible manner to the terms depression and exaltation. Their writings refer to a periodic alternation between a state of "illumination" and one of "fall" or "abandon,"[7] an enthusiastic "stand on the highest steps" and a depth of extreme spiritual "poverty and misery."[8] The accounts of the maniac phase, of which by far the most illuminating comes from Sabbatai Zevi himself, supply the key to the understanding of the role which his mental affliction had in the formation of his character, for they reveal nothing less than the ideational content of his mania. The truth which they lay bare is strange enough, and its importance for the fate of the Sabbatian movement can hardly be overrated: Sabbatai Zevi, the Kabbalistic ascetic and devotee, feels impelled, under the influence of his maniac enthusiasm, to commit acts which run counter to religious law. A latent antinomianism is discernible in these acts—harmless enough at first[9]—to which the Sabbatians gave the restrained but significant name *maasim zarim,* "strange or paradoxical actions."

Only the vaguest of guesses are possible concerning the origin of this irrepressible inclination to commit bizarre and anti-Halakhic acts. It is possible that some light is shed on the matter by the evidence supplied many years later by Moses Pinheiro, one of Sabbatai Zevi's fellow-students in Smyrna, concerning the Kabbalistic books which Sabbatai Zevi had studied at the time. According to Pinheiro, whom it is difficult to credit with wholesale fabrication of the story, Sabbatai Zevi had read in his younger years only the Zohar and the

book *Kanah*.[10] Of the latter, a work written in the fourteenth century, I have already indicated in a previous lecture[11] that it reveals
the same curious combination of pious devotion and mystical reverence for the *Halakhah* with veiled but sometimes very radical
criticism of its precepts, which subsequently was personified as it
were in Sabbatai Zevi. Its various elements may be said to have
come into open conflict in the Sabbatian movement, after the apostasy of the Messiah. It may be, that at the time when his affliction
first began to take possession of him he was under the influence of
this book and that it left its imprint on the ideational content of
his mania. With the doctrine of the Lurianic school he appears to
have concerned himself only at a later date, although from all we
know it seems that his way of life was modelled on the ascetic principles of the Kabbalists of Safed.

Solomon ben Abraham Laniado of Aleppo, an enthusiastic Sabbatian even after the apostasy of the Messiah, relates in a letter to
Kurdistan what he was himself told by Sabbatai Zevi when the latter passed through Aleppo in the late summer of 1665:[12] "Since
1648, the holy spirit and a great 'illumination' had come over him;
it was his practice to pronounce the name of God in accordance
with its letters[13] and to commit various strange acts, because it
seemed to him that to act in this way was right for many reasons
and for purposes of acts of *Tikkun* which he proposed to carry out.
But those who saw him did not understand these matters and he
was like a fool in their eyes.[14] And frequently our teachers in the
holy land punished him for his wicked actions which were far
removed from common-sense, so that he was compelled to part com-
pany with other people and to wander into the desert.... And
sometimes he was overcome by a great depression, but at other
times he saw something of the glory of the Shekhinah. Often, too,
God tried him with great temptations, and he overcame them all."
Laniado even asserts that when the "illumination" had passed from
him, "he was like a normal man and regretted the strange things he
had done, for he no longer understood their reason as he had understood it when he committed them."

Here then we have a clear description of Sabbatai Zevi's state of
mind. Of the temptations to which he was subjected in his fits of
depression a great deal is said, especially in the writings of Nathan
of Gaza, and we are told that they were of a demonic and erotic

character.[15] In brief, we have before us a man who felt himself pursued by demons during periods of melancholy depression which exposed him to a severe physical and mental strain, and who above all was the helpless victim of these forces.[16] On the other hand, he shared with others of the same psychical type who were like him men of a remarkable moral or intellectual level the gift of a strong personal suggestive power over others. This personal magnetism, however, was bound up with his states of exaltation and did not survive them. Incidentally, his intellectual qualities, although fully developed, were by no means out of the ordinary. He has left no writings and, what is more important, he is not credited with a single unforgettable word, epigram, or speech. As a Kabbalist and a scholar he does not appear to have raised himself above mediocrity. The emotional side of his character was more fully developed: he was unusually musical, fond of singing and of listening to song—during his imprisonment in the fortress of Gallipoli, in the summer of 1666, he was almost constantly surrounded by musicians[17]—and the singing of the Psalms, for which he had a special fondness, moved him easily and deeply. But his truly original characteristic is without any doubt to be found in the peculiarity of his mania: the commission of antinomian acts which in his state of exaltation he appears to have regarded as sacramental actions. That was his specific trait and that was also his specific contribution to the Sabbatian movement in which he played on the whole a fairly passive part, for it was this peculiarity which gave its special character to the movement from the moment when he had first been recognized as a religious authority. The law which dominated this development was the law of his own personality, although it was left to Nathan of Gaza to discover it in him and to formulate it in conscious terms. In his state of illumination he was the living archetype of the paradox of the holy sinner, and it may well be that, without his being able to express it, the image of an act of *Tikkun* through the infringement of the holy law was before his eyes in these exalted states of mind. And this and nothing else is the true heritage of Sabbatai Zevi: the quasi-sacramental character of antinomian actions, which here always take the form of a ritual, remained a *shibboleth* of the movement, not least in its more radical offshoots. In his "normal" state, the Sabbatian is anything but an antinomian. The performance of such acts is a *rite,* a festive action of an individual or a whole group, something out of the ordinary, greatly disturbing and born from the deep stirring of emotional forces.

3

Thus Sabbatai Zevi wandered through the world for years, without friends or real followers and without doing anything for the furtherance of the Messianic aspirations which dominated him in rare moments of high exaltation. Had it not been for Nathan of Gaza he would undoubtedly have remained one of the many anonymous enthusiasts of his generation who, in the years after the great catastrophe of the Chmielnitzki persecution in 1648, entertained vague dreams of Messianic vocation, without anybody paying any attention to them. It was a turning-point in his life that he should have settled in Jerusalem in 1662. During the first two years of his stay there, Nathan of Gaza (1644–1680), at that time a young student of the Talmud, cannot have failed to see a good deal of Sabbatai Zevi, already approaching forty and doubtless the subject of much gossip in the small Jewish community of the town. Even in the absence of close personal relations between them, for which there exists no proof, the personality of Sabbatai Zevi must have made a deep impression on the sensitive and susceptible young man who was then between seventeen and nineteen.

In the final and decisive awakening of the prophetic mood in Nathan, Sabbatai Zevi, who was at that time on a mission in Egypt, had no part. Nathan has told the story himself in a hitherto unpublished letter dated in the year 1667, from which I quote the following passage:[18] "I studied the Torah in purity until I was twenty years of age, and I carried out the great *Tikkun* which Isaac Luria prescribes for everyone who has committed great faults. Although, praise be to God, I have not advertently committed any sins, nevertheless I carried it out in case my soul be sullied from an earlier stage of transmigration. When I had attained the age of twenty I began to study the book Zohar and some of the Lurianic writings. But he who comes to purify himself receives the aid of Heaven, and thus He sent me some of His holy angels and blessed spirits and revealed to me many of the mysteries of the Torah. In that same year, my force having been stimulated by the visions of the angels and the blessed souls, I was undergoing a long fast in the week after the feast of *Purim*. Having now locked myself in holiness and purity in a separate room and completed the morning prayer under many tears, the spirit came over me, my hair stood on end and my knees shook and I saw the Merkabah, and I saw visions of God all day long and all night, and I was vouchsafed true prophecy like any other prophet, as the voice spoke to me and began with the words: 'Thus speaks the Lord.' And with the utmost clarity my heart perceived towards whom my prophecy was directed [i. e. towards Sabbatai Zevi], and until this day I have never yet had so great a vision, but it remained hidden in my heart until the Redeemer revealed himself in Gaza and proclaimed himself the Messiah; only then did the angel permit me to proclaim what I had seen."[19]

How then did Sabbatai Zevi come to proclaim himself as the Messiah in Gaza? The answer is as simple as it is startling. When Sabbatai Zevi, who was then in Egypt, learned from a letter sent by Samuel Gandor that an illuminate had appeared in Gaza who disclosed to everyone the secret root of his soul and the particular *Tikkun* of which his soul stood in need, he "abandoned his mission and went also to Gaza in order to find a *Tikkun* and peace for his soul."[20] I consider this to be the most interesting sentence in the history of Sabbatai Zevi. Thus when the story of Nathan's illumination spread, Sabbatai Zevi came to him, not as the Messiah or in accordance with some secret understanding, but "in order to find peace for his soul." To put it plainly: he came as a patient to a doctor of the soul. We know from Laniado's letter that precisely at this time in Egypt he had come into one of his normal periods and was troubled about his transgressions. He sought a cure for his psychosis and only then was he convinced by Nathan—by virtue of the latter's prophetic vision in which, as he discloses in another context,[21] he had also seen the figure of Sabbatai Zevi—of the authenticity of his Messianic mission. It was Nathan who dispelled his doubts and prevailed up him, after they had wandered together for several weeks through the holy places of Palestine, to proclaim himself the Messiah.

Nathan represents a most unusual combination of character traits. If the expression be permitted, he was at once the John the Baptist and the Paul of the new Messiah, surely a very remarkable figure. He had all the qualities which one misses in Sabbatai Zevi: tireless activity, originality of theological thought, and abundant productive power and literary ability. He proclaims the Messiah and blazes the trail for him, and at the same time he is by far the most influential theologian of the movement. He and his successor, the former Marrano Abraham Miguel Cardozo, are the great theologians of classical Sabbatianism, that is to say of a many-colored heretical movement within Jewish mysticism. Nathan does not himself practice antinomianism; he interprets it. He raises an indefinable state of exaltation with its *euphoria,* which manifests itself in absurd, bizarre and sacrilegious actions, to the rank of a "sacred act" in which a sublime reality becomes manifest: the state of the new "world of *Tikkun.*" The meeting of these two personalities made the Sabbatian movement. The great historical force of this new Messianism was born on the day on which Nathan discovered that Sabbatai Zevi, this curious sinner, ascetic and saint who had occasionally dreamed of his Messianic mission, was indeed the Messiah, and having discovered him, made him the symbol of a movement and himself became its standard-bearer.

Thus from the moment of its appearance, long before the apostasy of the Messiah, the theology of Sabbatianism was already conditioned by the need to furnish a mystical interpretation of the personal peculiarities and the strange and paradoxical traits in the character and the actions of Sabbatai Zevi. His manias and depressions receive a Kabbalistic interpretation, and in particular the figure of Job is consistently treated by Nathan from the very beginning as the prototype of the personality of his Messiah. There still exist a few manuscripts of a highly remarkable little book written by Nathan under the title *Derush Ha-Tanninim* "Treatise on the Dragons," in the form of a commentary to a Zoharic passage on the mystery of the "Great Dragon that lieth in the midst of the rivers of Egypt" (Ezekiel xxix, 3).[22] In this treatise, which was written during Sabbatai Zevi's imprisonment in Gallipoli,[23] at a time when no one even dreamed of the apostasy of the Messiah, there are as yet no suggestions of a downright heretical character. The writer develops his ideas in a form which nowhere conflicts with the tenets of traditional religion or with the principles of Lurianic Kabbalism. But already in this book we find him expounding new thoughts in his doctrine of the Messiah for which there is no parallel in Aggadic homiletics or the Lurianic Kabbalists. Luria defines the appearance of the Messiah as the consummation of the *Tikkun,* but in his theory no special place is reserved for the question of the root of the Messiah's soul.[24] He does not raise the problem of the probable fate of his soul before it makes its appearance in the world and fulfils its task. The new step taken by Nathan consists in linking this question with the traditional ideas of Lurianic Kabbalism.

According to Nathan, there exists a certain relationship between the Messiah and the course of all those intrinsic processes of which I have spoken in the last lecture: *Tsimtsum, Shevirah* and *Tikkun.* In the beginning of the cosmic process, *En-Sof* withdrew His light into Himself, and there arose that primal space in the center of *En-Sof* in which all the worlds take birth. This primal space is full of formless, hylic forces, the *Kelipoth.* The process of the world consists in giving shape to these formless forces, in making something out of them. As long as this has not been done, the primal space, and in particular its lower part, is the stronghold of darkness and evil. It is the "depth of the great abyss" in which the demonic powers have their abode. When, following the Breaking of the Vessels, some sparks of the divine light, radiating from *En-Sof* in order to create forms and shapes in the primal space, fell into the abyss, there also fell the soul of the Messiah which was embedded in that original divine light. Since the beginning of Creation, this soul has dwelt in the depth of the great abyss, held in the prison of the *Kelipoth,* the realm of darkness. Together with this most holy soul at the bottom of the abyss there dwell the "serpents" which torment it and try to seduce it. To these "serpents" the "holy serpent" is given over which is the Messiah—for has not the Hebrew word for serpent, *Nahash,* the same numerical value as the word for Messiah, *Mashiah?* Only in the measure in which the process of the *Tikkun* of all the world brings about the selection of good and evil in the depth of the primal space, is the soul of the Messiah freed of its bondage. When the process of perfection, on which this soul is at work in its "prison" and for which it struggles with the "serpents" or "dragons," is completed—which, however, will not be the case before the end of the *Tikkun* generally—the soul of the Messiah will leave its prison and reveal itself to the world in an earthly incarnation. Thus Nathan of Gaza. It is a matter of the deepest interest that one encounters in the writings of a youth from the Ghetto of Jerusalem in the seventeenth century an age-old Gnostical myth of the fate of the Redeemer's soul, built up from Kabbalistic ideas

but nevertheless obviously intended as an apology for Sabbatai
Zevi's pathological state of mind. Were it not for the fact that the
raw material of this Kabbalistic doctrine is actually to be found in
the Zohar and in the Lurianic writings, one would be tempted to
postulate an intrinsic, though to us obscure, connection between
the first Sabbatian myth and that of the ancient Gnostical school
known as Ophites or as Naassenes who placed the mystical symbolism of the serpent in the center of their Gnosis.[25]

The practical application of this new theory is put forward by
Nathan quite frankly and stressed with great frequency. Thus he
says: "All these matters we have only described in order to proclaim the greatness of our master, the King Messiah, how he will
break the power of the serpent the roots of which are deep and
strong. For these serpents always endeavored to allure him, and
whenever he had labored to exact great holiness from the *Kelipoth*,
they were able to take possession of him when the state of illumination had departed from him. Then they showed him that they, too,
had the same power as the Sefirah of 'Beauty' in which he [Sabbatai
Zevi] believed the true God to be represented, just as Pharaoh—
who is the great dragon, the symbol of the *Kelipah*—said: Who is
God? But when the illumination came over him, he used to bend
it [the serpent or dragon which tormented him in his depression]
down. And of this our teachers already said [Baba Bathra 15b]:
"Greater is that which is written of Job than that which is written
of Abraham. For of Abraham it is said only that he feared God, but
of Job that he feared God and eschewed evil. For I have already
explained above that in the Scripture the Redeemer is called Job
because he had fallen under the domination of the *Kelipoth*. And
this refers to the days of darkness which are the days of his depression; but when the illumination came over him, in the days of calm
and rejoicing, then he was in the state of which it is said "and
eschewed evil"; for then he emerged from the realm of the *Kelipoth*
among which he had sunk in the days of darkness."[26]

In this interpretation, therefore, the metaphysical and psychological element are closely intertwined; or to be more exact, they are
one. The metaphysical prehistory of the Messiah's soul is also the
history of those psychical states which for Nathan are precisely the
proof of his divine mission. And it is easy to perceive that the Gnostical idea of an imprisonment of the Messiah in the realm of evil

and impurity, which in this doctrine has as yet no heretical connotations, lent itself without difficulty to such a development after the
apostasy of the Messiah. In a way which strikes one as almost uncanny, the subsequent heretical doctrine of Nathan and the other
Sabbatians concerning the mission of the Messiah, and in particular
concerning his apostasy as a mission, is contained *in nuce* in this
astounding document of early Sabbatianism.[27]

4

It seems to me that the facts which I have briefly outlined thus far
in this lecture throw considerable new light on the origins and the
course of the Sabbatian movement. Having established these facts, I
now propose in speaking of Sabbatianism to give special attention
to the religious movement which developed in consequence of the
tragic apostasy of the new Messiah and both directly and indirectly
deepened the paradoxical nature of his step.[28] I regard it as important to follow the course of this movement, if only because the part
which Sabbatianism played in the spiritual development of Jewry
during the generations that followed, is generally underrated. Sabbatianism represents the first serious revolt in Judaism since the
Middle Ages; it was the first case of mystical ideas leading directly
to the disintegration of the orthodox Judaism of "the believers."
Its heretical mysticism produced an outburst of more or less veiled
nihilistic tendencies among some of its followers. Finally it encouraged a mood of religious anarchism on a mystical basis which,
where it coincided with favorable external circumstances, played a
highly important part in creating a moral and intellectual atmosphere favorable to the reform movement of the nineteenth century.

To trace the history of Sabbatianism through its various stages
objectively, *sine ira et studio,* has been impossible as long as two
distinctly opposed but equally strong emotional currents combined
to prevent the description of this most tragic chapter in later Jewish
religious history. These were on the one hand the very understandable aversion of the orthodox against the antinomian tendencies in
Sabbatianism, and on the other the dread felt by rationalists and
reformers, particularly during the nineteenth century of having
their spiritual ancestry traced back to that despised sect which was
commonly regarded as the incarnation of every conceivable aber-
ration and perversion. Those who felt this way may be said to have

somewhat uncritically adopted the traditional views bequeathed to them by their fathers. In the eighteenth century, to be called a Sabbatian was to all intents and purposes equivalent, so far as the effect on ordinary public opinion was concerned, to being termed an anarchist or a nihilist in the second half of the nineteenth. I could go on telling about my own difficulties in trying to penetrate into this vanished world, difficulties which arise not so much from the supposed obscurity or abstruseness of the Sabbatian doctrine, which is largely a myth, but from the fact that most, if not all, the theological and historical documents which could throw some light upon it have undoubtedly been destroyed. That this should be so is no less understandable from the psychological point of view than it is sad for the historian. The followers of Sabbatai Zevi who persisted in worshipping him as the Messiah, were persecuted during the eighteenth century with all the means at the disposal of the Jewish communities of those days. From the point of view of orthodoxy there is nothing in this that stands in need of being justified. Its representatives could hardly be expected to adopt any other attitude towards a revolutionary sect which kindled the flames of a destructive conflagration and which sometimes, if only darkly and abstrusely, proclaimed a new conception of Judaism. Wherever it was possible, the mystical literature of Sabbatianism was destroyed, and when the movement had been stamped out, everything was done to minimize its importance. It became obligatory to depict it as an affair of a very small minority and to pretend that there had been from the start a sharp division between the orthodox believers and the heretics.

In actual fact things were a little different. There were for instance various moderate forms of Sabbatianism in which orthodox piety and Sabbatian belief existed side by side, and the number of more or less outstanding rabbis who were secret adherents of the new sectarian mysticism was far larger than orthodox apologists have ever been willing to admit. That there should be so much confusion regarding its strength is partly accounted for by the fact that Sabbatianism as a movement was long identified with its more extreme, antinomian and nihilistic aspects, with the result that care was taken to obscure the fact that this or that reputed scholar or well-known family had had anyhing to do with it. Thus stigmatized it became no easy matter to admit one's descent from a Sabbatian family, and only very few men of high standing and untarnished reputation had the courage to do so. For a long time, and particularly during the nineteenth century, descent from Sabbatian ancestors was widely regarded as a shameful thing which might under no condition be publicly mentioned. As late as in the middle of that century, Leopold Loew, the leader of the Jewish reform movement in Hungary who in his youth had come in touch with the Sabbatians in Moravia, wrote that in their circles much was done to propagate and encourage the new rationalist movement.[29] Yet in the whole of Jewish historical literature you will find no reference to this highly important relation between the mystical heretics and the representatives of the new rationalism. It is as though this spiritual and often even ancestral relationship was regarded as something to be ashamed of. In several famous Jewish communities where Sabbatian groups played an important part right up to the beginning of the nineteenth century, care was taken to destroy all documents containing the names of sectarians whose children or grandchildren had risen to influential positions—not infrequently owing to their early attachment to the new world of emancipation.

The important part played by religious and mystical movements in the development of eighteenth century rationalism is today a generally accepted fact so far as the Christian world is concerned, and in England and Germany in particular, much work has been devoted to the task of unravelling these subterranean connections. Thus, to take an example, it has become almost a commonplace that the radical pietists, Anabaptists and Quakers represented such mystical movements the spirit of which, although nourished from the purest of religious motives, created an atmosphere in which the rationalist movement, in spite of its very different origins, was enabled to grow and develop, so that in the end both worked in the same direction. *Mutatis mutandis,* the same applies to Judaism. It is not as though the Sabbatians were a species of Quakers—many of them were anything but that. But here again, the attempt of a minority to maintain, in the face of persecution and vituperation, certain new spiritual values which corresponded to a new religious experience, facilitated the transition to the new world of Judaism in the period of emancipation. Some authors have regarded the eighteenth century Hasidic movement as the trail-blazer for the modern emancipated Jewry of the nineteenth. S. Hurwitz was the first to offer vigorous opposition to this romantic misconception and to stress the fact that this description might with far greater justice be applied to Sabbatianism.[30]

As we have seen, Lurianic Kabbalism had in the seventeenth century become the dominant spiritual influence through the entire Diaspora. It is therefore hardly surprising that the explosion of Sabbatianism, bound up as it was with the preponderant influence of the older school, affected fairly large parts of the community, although it never succeeded in becoming a mass movement. By contrast with its comparatively very limited strength it had a particularly deep and lasting effect upon many of its adherents. Yet even its numerical strength must not be underrated. Immediately after the apostasy of Sabbatai Zevi large groups, particularly among the Sephardic Jews, showed themselves susceptible to the propagation of apostasy as a mystery. In Morocco this tendency was especially marked, but it was also noticeable among many communities in Turkey, particularly in the Balkans, then under Turkish domination.

At first, too, the propaganda for the apostate Messiah was conducted quite openly. It was only later, after a number of years, when the expected triumphant return of Sabbatai Zevi from the spheres of impurity had still not occurred, that Sabbatianism changed its character. From a popular movement it became a sectarian one, whose propagandist work was conducted in secret. The transformation did not take many years. Comparatively soon, Sabbatianism took the form of a more or less loosely organized sect whose adherents met in secret conclave and were at pains to hide their ideas and activities from the outside world in order to avoid persecution. This occurred in spite of the recurrent appearance of prophets who believed that the time was ripe to proclaim the secret of Sabbatai Zevi's Messianic mission, in view of his impending reincarnation as Messiah. As the years went by, the new Kabbalah which purported to correspond to the new Messianic age and to replace the Lurianic doctrine began to occupy a larger place in Sabbatian thought than the doctrine of the Messiah's return. Quite a number of writings which belong undoubtedly to the theological literature of Sabbatianism hardly mention this subject at all, partly out of precaution, but in part also because other problems had come into the foreground. For all this conscious and unconscious dissimulation, however, Sabbatian writings can often easily be recognized from their employment of certain terms and modulations of terms such as *emunah* "belief," *sod ha-elohuth* "the mystery of God," and *Elohe Israel* "The God of Israel."

To turn to its spread as a movement, its first really important strongholds, apart from the Balkans, were to be found in Italy and Lithuania. It is an interesting fact that in Lithuania Sabbatianism never struck firm roots and disappeared more completely than in most other countries inhabited by Ashkenazic Jews. In Lithuania the leaders of the movement were for the most part typical illuminates, including such out-and-out revivalists as Heshel Zoref of Vilna[31] and the prophet Zadok ben Shemaryah of Grodno. In Italy, on the other hand, the men who secretly maintained contact with the movement were educated rabbinical representatives of Kabbalism, above all the disciples of Moses Zakuto: Benjamin Cohen of Reggio and Abraham Rovigo of Modena.[32] Generally speaking, in Italy the influence of the moderates was preponderant, while in the Balkan communities radical and even nihilistic tendencies were soon to gather strength. Owing mainly to the activities of one man, Hayim ben Solomon, better known as Hayim Malakh,[33] who was at first under the influence of the Italian and later of the Turkish "believers,"[34] the sect spread to the southern provinces of Poland of which a large part was at that time under Turkish sovereignty. Eastern Galicia and Podolia in particular became hotbeds of Sabbatianism and remained under its influence for a comparatively long time. In addition, the sect at various times during the eighteenth century gained a foothold in many German communities, including Berlin, Hamburg, Mannheim, Fuerth, and Dresden, but above all in Bohemia and Moravia. It seems that in these latter countries Sabbatianism was particularly strong numerically and that rabbinical circles, large and petty traders and manufacturers were alike under its influence. Some of the most influential Bohemian and Moravian Jews in the reign of Maria Theresa and her successors were secret adherents of the sect. Twice Sabbatianism took the form of organized apostasy by large groups who believed such repetition of the Marranic example to be the way of salvation. The first time in Salonica, where in 1683[35] the sect of the *Doenmeh*—as the Turks called them, the word meaning "apostates" —was founded, its members outwardly professing Islam; and for the second time in Eastern Galicia, where the followers of the sinister prophet Jacob Frank in 1759 entered the Catholic Church in large numbers. The members of both groups continued to call themselves *Maaminim* ("believers," namely in the mission of Sabbatai Zevi), the common name used by all Sabbatians when they speak of themselves. The members of both groups remained in close contact with the extremist wing of Sabbatianism even after their formal apostasy which they regarded of course as purely extrinsic. This was particularly true of the followers of Frank, most of whom remained Jews—almost all in Bohemia and Moravia, and the majority also in Hungary and Rumania. It was the influence of these elements which had not openly cut themselves off from rabbinical Judaism, which, after the French Revolution, became important in fostering the movement towards reform, liberalism and "enlightenment" in many Jewish circles.

Around 1850, a consciousness of this link between Sabbatianism and reform was still alive in some quarters. In circles close to the moderate reform movement, a very remarkable and undoubtedly authentic tradition had it that Aron Chorin, the first pioneer of reformed Jewry in Hungary was in his youth a member of the Sabbatian group in Prague.[36] Prossnitz and Hamburg, both in the eighteenth century centers of Sabbatian propaganda and the scene of bitter struggles between the orthodox and the heretics or their sympathizers, were among the chief strongholds of the reform movement in the beginning of the nineteenth century. The sons of those Frankists in Prague who in 1800 still pilgrimed to Offenbach, near Frankfort, the seat of Frank's successors, and who educated their children in the spirit of this mystical sect, were among the leaders, in 1832, of the first "reform" organization in Prague. The writings of Jonas Wehle himself, the spiritual leader of these Prague mystics around 1800, already display an astonishing mixture of mysticism and rationalism. Of his extensive writings, an extremely interesting commentary to the Talmudic *Aggadoth* is extant in manuscript[37] from which it is clear that his particular pantheon had room for Moses Mendelssohn and Immanuel Kant side by side with Sabbatai Zevi and Isaac Luria.[38] And as late as 1864, his nephew, writing in New York, lengthily praises in his testament his Sabbatian and Frankist ancestors as the standard-bearers of the "true Jewish faith," i. e. of a deeper spiritual understanding of Judaism.[39]

5

The question remains why and how it happened that the Kabbalists who came under the influence of the Sabbatian movement,
became the bearers of ideas which brought them into more or less
open conflict with the tenets of rabbinical Judaism. Let me recall
here what I have said in the last lecture about the doctrine of
redemption through *Tikkun*. The mystical conception and interpretation of exile and deliverance was of course originally based
upon actual experience of the exile and upon the popular ideas of
the way in which Redemption would take place. The very conception of deliverance had a practical and historical connotation: liberation from the yoke, new freedom—these were the enormously
powerful Messianic motivating forces which went into the doctrine
evolved by the Kabbalists of Safed. In their interpretation, the
popular conception of Messianism and national restoration was
transformed into a drama of cosmic importance.

Redemption is no longer primarily a liberation from the yoke of
servitude in exile, but a transformation of the essence of Creation.
It is conceived as a process which runs through all the visible and
the hidden worlds, for it is nothing but *Tikkun*, the restoration
of that great harmony which was shattered by the Breaking of the
Vessels and later by Adam's sin. Redemption implies a radical
change in the structure of the universe. Its significance is seen to be,
not so much the end of that exile which began with the destruction
of the Temple, as rather the end of that inner exile of all creatures
which began when the father of mankind was driven out of paradise. The Kabbalist laid far greater emphasis on the spiritual nature
of Redemption than on its historical and political aspects. These
are by no means denied or discounted, but they tend more and
more to become mere symbols of that mystical and spiritual process
of which I have spoken. "When good and evil are finally separated,
the Messiah will come," as Vital puts it. The historical redemption
is as it were a natural by-product of its cosmic counterpart, and the
Kabbalists never conceived the idea that a conflict might arise between the symbol and the reality which it was supposed to express.
Nobody could foresee the danger inherent in such a shifting of the
emphasis to a sphere of inner reality, as long as the Messianic idea
was not put to the test in a crucial moment of history. In its original form at any rate, Lurianic Kabbalism had as its main purpose

the preparation of men's hearts for that renaissance the scene of which is the human soul. It placed the regeneration of the inner life far above that of the nation as a political entity. At the same time it was convinced that the former was the essential precondition of the latter. Moral improvement was to bring about the delivery of the people from its exile.

With the coming of Sabbatai Zevi and his enthusiastic reception by the masses of the people, this experience of inner freedom, of a pure world, which so far had been experienced only by Kabbalists in rare moments of exaltation, became the common property of the many. Naturally they also expected the complete fulfilment of the external and historical part of the Messianic promise. These hopes were speedily disappointed, but what had taken place in the brief but thorough experience of Messianic uprising could not be taken away again. To many this experience, which the Kabbalists call "the elevation of the Shekhinah from the dust"[40] became a lasting and indestructible part of their consciousness.

Sabbatianism as a mystical heresy dates from the moment when the apostasy of Sabbatai Zevi, which was an entirely unforeseen occurrence, opened a gap between the two spheres in the drama of Redemption, the inner one of the soul and that of history. Inner and outer experience, inner and outer aspects of *Geulah,* of Redemption and Salvation, were suddenly and dramatically torn apart. This conflict, for which nobody was prepared, which nobody had ever dreamt could happen, went to the very root and core of existence. A choice became necessary. Every one had to ask himself whether he was willing to discover the truth about the expected redemption in the distressing course of history or in that inner reality which had revealed itself in the depths of the soul. Sabbatianism as a heresy came into existence when large sections, first of Sephardic and later also of Ashkenazic Jewry, refused to submit the judgment of their soul to that of history. It was argued that God, who does not even place a stumbling-block in the path of the "beast of the righteous,"[41] could not have misled his people and deceived it with the false appearance of Redemption.[42] Doctrines arose which had one thing in common: that they tried to bridge the gap between the inner experience and the external reality which had ceased to function as its symbol. The sudden emergence of a contradiction between the external and the internal

aspects of life imposed upon the new doctrine the task of rationaliz-
ing this conflict, in other words, of making life bearable under the
new conditions. Never before had this task been forced upon the
Kabbalah, whose tendency, as we have seen, had been throughout
to represent the outer world as a symbol of the inner life. Sabbatianism arose out of the awareness of an inherent contradiction,
out of a paradox, and the law of its birth determined its subsequent
development. It is built upon the tragic paradox of an apostate
Savior and it thrives upon paradoxes of which one implies the
other.

Inevitably there is a far-reaching and highly illuminating similarity between the religious characteristics and the development of
Sabbatianism on the one hand, and of Christianity on the other.
In both cases the ancient Jewish paradox of the sufferings of God's
servant is pushed to extremes. In both cases, too, a certain mystical
attitude of belief crystallizes round an historical event which in
turn draws its strength from the very fact of its paradoxality. Both
movements begin by adopting an attitude of intense expectation
towards the *Parousia*, the advent or return of the Savior, be it
from Heaven, be it from the realm of impurity. In both cases the
destruction of the old values in the cataclysm of redemption leads
to an outburst of antinomian tendencies, partly moderate and
veiled and partly radical and violent; in both cases you get a new
conception of "belief" as the realization of the new world of Salvation, and in both this "belief" involves that latent polarity of even
more startling paradoxes. In both cases, finally, you get in the end
a theology of some kind of Trinity and of God's incarnation in the
person of the Savior.

Now the direct and indirect influence of Christian ideas upon
Sabbatianism must not be underrated. It flowed through various
channels, and about one of them, which is of the greatest importance for the understanding of Sabbatianism, the Marranos, I shall
have to say more later on. Yet nothing could be farther from the
truth than the idea that the similarity of which I have just spoken
owes everything to foreign influence or to the imitation of Christian prototypes. The crisis in Judaism came from within and it
would hardly have taken any other course had there been no Christian influence. Moreover, the existence of important historical,

moral and religious differences between Sabbatianism and Christianity must not be overlooked.

In the Sabbatian movement we have a rebellion against the ghetto, but one which never quite succeeded in freeing itself from the very thing against which it rebelled. To this must be added the weakness of Sabbatai Zevi's personality as compared with that of Jesus. It is true that this weakness is somehow in accordance with a certain tendency in later Jewish Messianism. The Jewish conception of the personality of the Messiah is surprisingly colorless, one might also say anonymous, particularly when it is compared with the powerful impact which the personality of Jesus made upon the Christian mind. The picture of the Messiah presented by the two great codifiers of rabbinical Messianism, Isaac Abarbanel among the Sefardim and Jehudah Loewe ben Bezalel of Prague, the so-called "Exalted Rabbi Loew,"[43] is distinctly impersonal. Of classical Lurianism it can be said that it has no interest at all in the *person* of the Messiah. It is therefore not at all surprising that when a Messiah appeared who succeeded in winning general recognition, his comparative lack of personal magnetism, to say nothing of his mental peculiarities, was not regarded as a defect. As I have previously mentioned, there are no unforgettable "words of the master," no "logia," by Sabbatai Zevi, and nobody seems to have expected any. Only towards the end of the Sabbatian movement do you find in Jacob Frank a strong personality whose very words exercise a considerable though sinister fascination. But this Messiah who for once is a personality in every fiber of his being, is also the most hideous and uncanny figure in the whole history of Jewish Messianism.

To return to our comparison, the fate of the Messiahs is entirely different and so is the religious paradox. The paradox of crucifixion and that of apostasy are after all on two altogether different levels. The second leads straight into the bottomless pit; its very idea makes almost anything conceivable. The shock which had to be surmounted in both cases is greater in the case of Sabbatianism. The believer is compelled to furnish even more emotional energy in order to overcome the terrible paradox of an apostate Savior. Death and apostasy cannot possibly evoke the same or similar sentiments, if only because the idea of betrayal contains even less that is positive. Unlike the death of Jesus, the decisive action (or rather, passion) of Sabbatai Zevi furnished no new revolutionary code of values. His betrayal merely destroyed the old. And so it becomes understandable why the deep fascination exercised by the conception of the helpless Messiah who hands himself over to the demons, if driven to its utmost limits, led directly to nihilistic consequences.

As we have seen, the starting point of Sabbatianism is the attempt to defend the mission of Sabbatai Zevi. Perhaps few things could be more paradoxical than the endeavor to glorify the most abominable act known to the Jewish mind—betrayal and apostasy. By implication this fact suggests something of the volcanic nature of the spiritual upheaval which enabled men to maintain such a position.

It seems almost unbelievable that a movement based upon such foundations should have been able to influence so great a number of people. One must, however, take into account the existence of an external factor of crucial importance; and that is the part played in the movement by the Sefardic communities. For generations the Marranos in the Iberian peninsula, the offspring of those Jews who, in their hundreds of thousands, went over to Christianity in the persecutions between 1391 and 1498, had been compelled to lead, as it were, a double life. The religion which they professed was not that in which they believed. This dualism could not but endanger, if it did not indeed destroy the unity of Jewish feeling and thinking, and even those who returned to the fold after they or their children had fled from Spain, particularly in the seventeenth century, retained something of this peculiar spiritual make-up. The idea of an apostate Messiah could be presented to them as the religious glorification of the very act which continued to torment their own conscience. There have been Marranos who tried to find a justification for their apostasy, and it is significant that all the arguments which they were wont to put forward in defense of their crypto-Judaism, recur later on in the ideology of Sabbatianism, above all the frequent reference to the fate of Queen Esther who was supposed to have led a kind of Marranic existence at King Ahasuerus' court "telling not her race nor her birth," yet still faithful to the religion of her fathers."

That the Messiah should by the very nature of his mission be forced into the inescapable tragedy of apostasy was a doctrine ideally made to provide an emotional outlet for the tormented conscience of the Marranos. I doubt whether without this spiritual disposition on the part of numerous Sefardic communities the new doctrine would have taken sufficient root to become an important factor in the disintegration of the ghetto. The similarity between the fate of the Marranos and that of the apostate Messiah was remarked only a short time after Sabbatai Zevi's apostasy, and it is no accident that the leading propagandist of this school, Abraham Miguel Cardozo (died 1706), was himself born as a Marrano and began by studying Christian theology.[45] Cardozo and Nathan of Gaza, the new prophet, are the first in the list of the great Kabbalist heretics, whose doctrines had in common the paradoxical and, to the unsophisticated mind, outrageous character of their basic tenets. Both were men of tireless literary and propagandistic activity and both have taken great pains to develop their new ideas in all their details. Nathan's *magnum opus, Sefer Ha-Beriah,* "The Theory of Creation," was written in 1670, whereas Cardozo wrote a whole literature on the new Sabbatian doctrine of God in the following decades.

6

Taking as their starting point the fate of the Messiah and the question of Redemption in general, these doctrines gradually extend to other spheres fo religious thought, until at last they begin to pervade the whole of theology and ethics. Thus for instance Cardozo taught that in consequence of Israel's sins all of us were originally fated to become Marranos,[46] but that from this awful destiny of having to live as it were in constant denial of one's own inner knowledge and belief, the grace of God has saved us by imposing this supreme sacrifice upon the Messiah; for only the soul of the Messiah is strong enough to bear this fate without loss. It goes without saying that this conception of the Messiah appealed to the unhappy dualism of the Marranic mind. It also happened to recall an idea of entirely different historic origin, namely the Lurianic theory of restitution through "the uplifting of the fallen sparks," which I outlined in the previous lecture. This doctrine was capable of being given a turn of which nobody had thought before Sabbatai Zevi's apostasy, but which from then on quickly became only too fashionable. According to its recognized, orthodox interpretation, Israel has been dispersed among the nations in order that it may gather in from everywhere the sparks of souls and divine light which are themselves dispersed and diffused throughout the world, and through pious acts and prayers "lift them up" from their respective prisons. When this process is more or less complete, the Messiah appears and gathers the last sparks, threby depriving the power of evil of the element through which it acts. The spheres of good and evil, of pure and impure, are from then on separated for all eternity. The heretic version of this doctrine, as expounded with considerable success by Nathan of Gaza,[47] differs from the orthodox mainly in its conclusions: the attraction of saintliness is not always sufficient to liberate the sparks from their prisons, the *Kelipoth* or "shells." There are stages of the great process of *Tikkun,* more particularly its last and most difficult ones, when in order to liberate the hidden sparks from their captivity, or to use another image, in order to force open the prison doors from within, the Messiah himself must descend into the realm of evil. Just as the Shekhinah had to descend to Egypt—the symbol of everything dark and demonic—to gather in the fallen sparks, so the Messiah too at the end of the ages starts on his most difficult journey to the empire of darkness, in order to complete his mission. Not before he has reached the end of his journey will evil disappear and redemption extend to the external world.

It can easily be seen how this doctrine satisfied those who thought they had experienced their own and the world's salvation in their inner consciousness and consequently demanded a solution of the contradiction between their experience and the continuation of Exile. The apostasy of the Messiah is the fulfilment of the most difficult part of his mission, for redemption implies a paradox which becomes visible only at the end, in its actual occurrence. It is not a steady and unhindered progress as it appears in Luria's doctrine, but a tragedy which renders the supreme sacrifice of the Messiah incomprehensible to others. In order to fulfil his mission he must condemn himself through his own acts. An immense amount of religious passion has been lavished on the task of developing this dangerous paradox and letting the believers taste its bitterness to the full.[48]

To this must be added something else. What the Sabbatians call the "strange acts of the Messiah," have not only a negative aspect, from the point of view fo the old order, but also a positive side, in so far as the Messiah acts in accordance with the law of a new world. If the structure of the world is intrinsically changed by the completion of the process of *Tikkun,* the Torah, the true univer- sal law of all things, must also appear from then on under a differ- ent aspect. Its new significance is one that conforms with the pri- mordial state of the world, now happily restored, while as long as the Exile lasts the aspect it presents to the believer naturally con- forms to that particular state of things which is the *Galuth.* The Messiah stands at the crossing of both roads. He realizes in his Mes- sianic freedom a new law, which from the point of view of the old order is purely subversive. It subverts the old order, and all actions which conform to it are therefore in manifest contradiction with the traditional values.•In other words, redemption implies the de- struction of those aspects of the Torah which merely reflect the *Galuth,* the Torah itself remains one and the same, what has changed is its relation to the mind. New vistas are opened up, a new Messianic Judaism takes the place of the Judaism of the *Ga- luth.* The numerous instances of radical phraseology and the hints of a state of the world to come when there will be a new law, in which particularly the *Raya Mehemna* in the Zohar abounds, could be used by the Sabbatians to justify their revolutionary doctrine. Here the ideas of an isolated Jewish "spiritual" around 1300 have at last found a home, so to speak, and begin to exercise an influence among wider circles.⁴⁹

It is amazing how clearly these thoughts were expressed as early as one or two years after Sabbatai Zevi's apostasy. In a treatise written in 1668, Abraham Perez, one of Nathan's pupils in Saloni- ca, sets forth what can only be described as a theory of antinomian- ism:⁵⁰ whoever remained faithful, in the new world, to the "oral Torah," i. e. to the rabbinical tradition, or to put it as plainly as possible, to the real and existing Judaism of the *Galuth,* is to be positively regarded as a sinner.⁵¹ A new understanding of the essen- tially unchangeable Torah, that is to say, a new Judaism, was pro- claimed in the place of the old. And the author shows that he is fully aware of the implications and consequences of this theory. It is true that he has taken precautions against the danger of *pure* antinomianism: the positive law of the new world becomes visible, according to him, only with the complete and final redemption, i. e. after the Messiah will have completed his Calvary through the world of evil and annihilated or transformed its power from within. Until that new epoch, in the early dawn of which we ourselves live, the ancient law retains its force. In this way the facade of orthodoxy is preserved, although there can be no doubt that the emotional relation to its tenets and values has undergone a complete change.

Such theories, in which the antinomian tendencies remain only latent, were put forward in various guises by the moderate schools of Sabbatianism. Not a few Sabbatians achieved the miracle of living in the continuous paradox of devout fulfilment of the law and belief in the impending approach of a new era in which such fulfilment will become meaningless. We know of such enthusiastic Sabbatians, whose devout attachment to the traditional tenets of their religion, within the sphere of rabbinical Judaism, is reflected in documents of the most intimate kind in which they have opened their hearts without reserve. The most astonishing and moving of these documents is the diary of two Sabbatians in Modena, in Northern Italy, of which I have given a detailed account elsewhere.[62] The existence of such a moderate wing of Sabbatianism, in particular until about 1715, is of importance for the understanding of the movement, and the fact that it was ignored has tended to obscure matters. For this reason frequent and unsuccessful attempts have been made to dispute the fact that such men belonged to the Sabbatian movement, which was regarded as nothing but an unholy rebellion against rabbinical Judaism, with an open tendency towards transgressions and sins in theory and practice. A picture which is far from portraying the whole truth.

On the other hand it must be admitted that the mood which speaks from such ideas as were advanced by Abraham Perez had its counterpart in eruptions of real antinomianism. For the first time in the history of mediaeval Jewry, the rigid emotional and intellectual attitude born from the continuity of life under the undisputed dominance of the Mosaic and rabbinic Law gave way to a new mood. The positive influence of this way of life over the Jewish mind had been so great that for centuries no movement, least of all an organized movement, had rebelled against the values linked up with the practical fulfilment of the Law. This is all the more remarkable as orthodox Judaism by its very nature offered much greater scope to antinomian explosions than either Christianity or

Islam, which yet had far oftener to contend with them. For the causes of this apparent contradiction one must go back to certain external historical factors, such as the strong instinct of self-preservation in Jewry which sensed the subversive nature of antinomian tendencies; the historical situation of Jewry was such as to make this danger only too real. One must also take into account the fact that for individuals who rebelled against the Law the obvious course was to seek a way out of the Jewish community and to enter the non-Jewish fold. Only a mystical interpretation of the fundamental categories of the Law and the Redemption was capable of preparing the ground for antinomian tendencies which strove to maintain themselves within the general framework of Judaism. On the other hand, the antinomian rebellion, when it came, was all the wilder while it lasted and engulfed a large part of the Sabbatian movement, its radical wing, to use a modern term.

The motives which came to the surface in the development of extreme antinomianism were of two kinds. There was on the one hand the personality of the Messiah and its paradox, and on the other the attitude and the individual experience of the believer. The point at which moderate and extreme Sabbatianism parted ways was supplied by the question whether the actions of the Messiah serve as an example to the believer or not.[53] The moderate thought not. They held that the paradox of the new religious life is limited to the person of the Messiah. The Messiah alone stands at the crossroads where the old values are no longer binding, and he alone must tread the weary path through the world of evil which is the mark of his mission. His actions are not examples to be followed; on the contrary, it is of their nature to give offense. Already Nathan of Gaza asserted (in 1667) that precisely the "strange actions" of Sabbatai Zevi constituted proof of the authenticity of his Messianic mission: "For if he were not the Redeemer, these deviations would not occur to him; when God lets His light shine over him, he commits many acts which are strange and wonderful in the eyes of the world, and that is proof of his truth."[54] The true acts of Redemption are at the same time those which cause the greatest scandal. In the life of the believers there can be no room for nihilistic tendencies, as long as the completion of the *Tikkun* has not yet transformed the external world and Israel remains in exile. The paradox of the Messiah is a matter purely of belief; if it makes its appearance in the life of the individual it does so only in spheres which lie beyond practicality. Especially Cardozo has taken great pains to defend this stand on the question of mystical apostasy.

7

It was over this point that the split became inevitable. The radicals could not bear the thought of remaining content with passive belief in the paradox of the Messiah's mission. Rather did they hold that as the end draws nearer this paradox necessarily becomes universal. The action of the Messiah sets an example and to follow it is a duty. The consequences which flowed from these religious ideas were purely nihilistic, above all the conception of a voluntary Marranism with the slogan: We must *all* descend into the realm of evil in order to vanquish it from within. In varying theoretical guises the apostles of nihilism preached the doctrine of the existence of spheres in which the process of *Tikkun* can no longer be advanced by pious acts; Evil must be fought with evil.[65] We are thus gradually led to a position which, as the history of religion shows, occurs with a kind of tragic necessity in every great crisis of the religious mind. I am referring to the fatal, yet at the same time deeply fascinating doctrine of the holiness of sin, that doctrine which in a remarkable way reflects a combination of two widely different elements: the world of moral decadence and another, more primitive, region of the soul in which long-slumbering forces are capable of sudden resurrection. That in the religious nihilism of Sabbatianism, which during the eighteenth century proved so dangerous to the most precious possession of Judaism, its moral substance, both these elements had a share, cannot be proved better than by the tragic history of its last phase, the Frankist movement.

The connection postulated by the Torah between the original sin and the sense of shame confronts the Kabbalists concerned with the *Tikkun*, the elimination of the stigma of sin, with the awkward problem of the disappearance of shame in the new Messianic state.[66] The opposite solution, that of seeking redemption by "treading upon the vesture of shame," in the words of a famous phrase ascribed by some Gnostics to Jesus,[67] was openly proclaimed among the radical Sabbatians by Jacob Frank. The ancient and profound word of the Mishnah that it is possible to love God also with the 'evil impulse'[58] now received a meaning of which its author had not thought.

Moses Hagiz distinguishes between two forms of the Sabbatian heresy: "The way of the one sect is to regard every impure person who defiles himself by lighter or heavier transgressions as a saint. They say that what we see with our eyes, how they eat on the days of fast, is not a corporeal but a spiritual meal, and that when they defile themselves before the eyes of the world, that is not an impurity but an act through which they come in contact with the spirit of holiness. And of every evil action which we see them commit, not only in thought but also in reality, they say that this is precisely how it must be, and that there is a mystery in the matter, and a *Tikkun* and a salvaging of holiness from he *Kelipoth*. And thus they are agreed that whoever commits a sin and does evil is good and honest in the eyes of God. But another sect among them turns the heresy to a different purpose. It is their custom to argue that with the arrival of Sabbatai Zevi the sin of Adam has already been corrected and the good selected out of the evil and the 'dross.' Since that time, according to them, a new Torah has become law under which all manner of things formerly prohibited are now permitted, not least the categories of sexual intercourse hitherto prohibited. For since everything is pure, there is no sin or harm in these things. And if before our eyes they nevertheless adhere to the Jewish law, they do so only because it is written: "Do not forsake altogether the Torah of thy mother."[59]

These assertions of a heresy-hunter like Hagiz, which in themselves would perhaps not carry full conviction, are, however, supported by a mass of evidence on the development of Sabbatianism between 1700 and 1760. The doctrine described and condemned by Hagiz in 1714 was practiced in various forms and in widely scattered localities until the end of the century. In the history of Gnosticism, the Carpocratians are regarded as the outstanding representatives of this libertinistic and nihilistic form of gnosis.[60] But nothing that is known of them touches the resolute spirit of the gospel of antinomianism preached by Jacob Frank to his disciples in more than two thousand dogmatic sayings. The ideas he adduced in support of his preachings constitute not so much a theory as a veritable *religious myth of nihilism*.

Generally speaking, it is in the nature of nihilistic doctrines that they are not proclaimed publicly and, even in written tracts, are hardly ever preached without reserve. In the case of Frank, however, the boundless enthusiasm and devotion of his followers led them to preserve this unique document. To them, he was the incarnation of God and his word divine inspiration. For whatever one may think of the character and personality of Jacob Frank, his followers, of whom we have at least two independent writings,[62] were without doubt largely men of pure heart. Deep and genuine religious emotion speaks to us from their words and it is clear that they must have found in those dark sayings of their prophet, on the "abyss into which we must all descend" and on the "burden of silence" which we must bear, a liberation which the rabbinical Torah denied them. Thus it comes about that we possess two or three manuscripts in the Polish language of the *Ksiega Słów Panskich,* the "Book of the Words of the Lord."[63] In this collection of sayings, parables, explanations and 'words of Torah'—if they can be called that—the characteristic mixture of primitive savagery and putrescent morals, which 1 have mentioned, strikes one with its full force. It is only fair to add that a certain vigor of style and élan of thought cannot be denied to this work, perhaps the most remarkable "holy writ" which has ever been produced.

Certain more or less paradoxical utterances from the Talmud and other sources, as well as certain mystical symbols, became after 1700 the slogans of a religious nihilism in which the ideational content of a depraved mysticism comes into open conflict with every tenet of the traditional religion. Talmudic and semi-Talmudic sayings, such as "Great is a sin committed for its own sake,"[64] or "The subversion of the Torah can become its true fulfilment,"[65]—remarks whose meaning was originally by no means antinomistic or nihilistic but which lent themselves to such interpretation—were turned upside down. The Torah, as the radical Sabbatians were fond of putting it,[66] is the seed-corn of Salvation, and just as the seed-corn must rot in the earth in order to sprout and bear fruit, the Torah must be subverted in order to appear in its true Messianic glory. Under the law of organic development, which governs every sphere of existence, the process of Salvation is bound up with the fact of man's actions being, at least in certain respects and at certain times, dark and as it were rotten. The Talmud says: "David's son comes only in an age which is either completely guilty or completely innocent."[67] From this epigram, many Sabbatians drew the moral: since we cannot all be saints, let us all be sinners.

The truth is that this doctrine of the holiness of sin represents a mixture of several ideas. In addition to the belief that certain actions, which are in reality pure and holy, must bear the outward appearance of sin, we also find the idea that that which is really and truly evil is transformed from within by being practiced with, as it were, religious fervor. It is obvious that these conceptions are radically opposed to everything which for centuries had formed the essence of moral teaching and speculation in Judaism. It is as if an anarchist rebellion had taken place within the world of Law. The reaction went so far that in certain radical conventicles acts and rites were practiced which aimed deliberately at the moral degradation of the human personality: he who has sunk to the uttermost depths is the more likely to see the light. In the elaboration of this thesis, the apostles of the radicals who came from Salonica, and above all Jacob Frank, were tireless.

Mere condemnation of this doctrine, however, leads us nowhere. Attention must be given also to its positive side. The religious, and in some cases the moral, nihilism of the radicals is after all only the confused and mistaken expression of their urge towards a fundamental regeneration of Jewish life, which under the historic conditions of those times could not find a normal expression. The feeling of true liberation which "the believers" had experienced in the great upheaval of 1666, sought to find an expression on the moral and religious plane, when historical and political realization was denied to it. Instead of revolutionizing the external circumstances of Jewish life, a thing it could no longer do after the apostasy of the Messiah, it became introverted and encouraged a mood which easily adapted itself to the new spirit of rationalization and reform, once the myth of the Messiah's journey to the gates of impurity had begun to fade.

To this must be added a further motive, also well known from the history of religion and particularly from that of the mystical sects, which almost invariably makes its appearance together with the doctrine of the holiness of sin. That is the idea that the elect are fundamentally different from the crowd and not to be judged by its standards. Standing under a new spiritual law and representing as it were a new kind of reality, they are beyond good and evil.

SABBATIANISM AND MYSTICAL HERESY

It is well known to what dangerous consequences Christian sects in ancient and modern times have been led by the idea that the truly new-born is incapable of committing a sin, and that therefore everything he does must be regarded under a higher aspect. Similar ideas made their appearance very soon in the wake of Sabbatianism especially in Salonica. The inner reality of redemption, which has already been inaugurated in the hidden world, was held to dictate a higher law of conduct to those who experience it.

I do not propose to discuss the various concrete applications of this thesis. The two contentions: it is meritorious to sin in order to overcome the power of evil from within, and: it is impossible for those who already live in the Messianic world of *Tikkun* to sin, because to them evil has already lost its meaning—I say these two contentions appear to conflict with one another, but from a practical point of view their effect is the same. Both have the tendency to make all external action and conduct appear unreal, and to oppose to it an inner secret action which is the counterpart of true belief. The radical Sabbatians, the nihilists, were agreed that just as redemption had so far become only intrinsically real and not yet visible, so the true belief must be held only in secret, while external behavior must conform to the power of evil in the world of the *Galuth*. The belief which one professes can by its very nature no longer coincide with that which one really holds. Everyone must in some way share the fate of the Marranos; one's heart and one's mouth may not be one.[68] This can be done also within the orbit of Judaism, and in fact the great majority even of the radical Sabbatians remained Jews. Here the external world the value of which was denied by the inner and secret rites, was that of rabbinical Jewry, for which the Messianic Judaism of Antinomianism, the secret annihilation of the Torah as its true fulfilment, became the secret substitute. But this external world could also be Mohammedanism, if one followed the example of Sabbatai Zevi, or Catholicism if one followed that of Frank.[69] The blasphemous benediction "Praise be to Thee, O Lord, who permittest the forbidden" came to be considered by these radicals as a true expression of their feeling.[70] For the purpose was not to deny the authority of the Torah, but to oppose a "Torah of the higher world," *Torah de-Atsiluth,* which alone is relevant, to the Torah in its present sensual appearance, *Torah de Beriah.*[71] To the anarchic religious feeling of these new

Jews, all the three great institutional religions have no longer an absolute value. This revolution of the Jewish consciousness was gradually spread by groups who, like the majority of Sabbatian Jews in Germany and in the countries of the Hapsburg Monarchy, remained within the walls of the Ghetto, those who continued to profess rabbinical Judaism but secretly believed themselves to have outgrown it. When the outbreak of the French Revolution again gave a political aspect to their ideas, no great change was needed for them to become the apostles of an unbounded political apocalypse. The urge towards revolutionizing all that existed no longer had to find its expression in desperate theories, like that of the holiness of sin, but assumed an intensely practical aspect in the task of ushering in the new age.

The man of whom it appears to have been thought for some time, that after Frank's death in 1791 he would become his successor as the leader of the sect in Offenbach, was sent to the guillotine in 1794, together with Danton, under the name of Junius Frey.[72] However, these are extreme cases. On the whole, the movement remained within the confines of the Jewish communities. The account given by Moses Porges of Prague of the description of Frankism given to him by his father in 1794 is highly characteristic: "There exists in addition to the Torah a holy book, the Zohar, which has revealed to us the secrets only hinted at in the Torah. It calls upon men to work for their spiritual perfection and shows the way to reach this aim. There are many noble souls who have devoted themselves to the new doctrine. *Their end, their aim is liberation from spiritual and political oppression.* God has revealed Himself in the latter days as He did in days of old. You my son, shall know all about this."[73]

8

In this critical transformation of Judaism in the consciousness of both the moderate and the radical wing of Sabbatianism, the traditional forms of Kabbalism could not but become problematical. As a theory, Sabbatianism had its roots in an extravagant overstressing of certain aspects of Lurianism. It is hardly surprising, therefore, that from now on a multitude of new theories either tried to draw the final consequences from Luria's ideas, or else started from scratch with mystical ideas of their own. In the history of Kabbalism, the emergence of new ideas and systems was almost without exception accompanied by the belief that the last age was drawing near. Again and again we read in Kabbalist documents that the most profound and true mysteries of the Divinity, obscured in the period of Exile, will reveal their true meaning on the eve of the last age. The courage it took to break away from earlier doctrines and substitute new ideas for old ones was grounded in such beliefs, even though the pretence of 'tradition' was maintained. Abulafia, the Zohar, the book *Peliah,* the Kabbalistic systematizers of Safed— they all no less than the Sabbatians and Frankists, plead the coming of the dawn as the justification of what was new in their ideas. Thus, while certain Sabbatians, like Nathan of Gaza, merely gave a new interpretation to the Lurianic ideas without renouncing them, others have more or less radically broken away from them. The Sabbatian Kabbalists, above all during the fifty to sixty years after Sabbatai Zevi's apostasy, spent a great deal of thought on this point.[74] Abraham Cardozo, Samuel Primo, Abraham Rovigo and his disciple Mordecai Ashkenazi, Nehemia Hayun and finally Jonathan Eibeschuetz, are the outstanding representatives of a Sabbatian Kabbalah of more or less definitely heretical character. Their writings and thoughts are now fairly well known,[75] while the details of the more outspokenly nihilistic theories have remained somewhat obscure. In particular we have only indirect knowledge of the teachings of the leading theoretician of the most radical group among the *Doenmeh in Salonica,* Baruch Kunio, better known as Berahya or Barochia.[76] He has undoubtedly inspired the leading ideas of Frank's "theory," probably also important elements of thought found in the esoteric writings of youthful Jonathan Eibeschuetz (1690/1695–1764), one of the last great representatives of rabbinical Judaism, whose secret affinity to Sabbatianism has therefore been denied with particular heat down to our own days.[77] Although Eibeschuetz denied responsibility for these writings when, thirty years later, a scandal broke out in Hamburg because of his alleged Sabbatianism, his authorship can be proved by philological analysis.

On the whole it can be said that the Sabbatian conceptions of God are no whit less paradoxical than the fundamental doctrine of Sabbatianism, namely that the apostasy of Sabbatai Zevi was a sacred mystery. For the rest they are grounded in the thought that

the true "Mystery of the Godhead," *Sod ha-Elohuth*, had been revealed to the Sabbatians, doubtless by Sabbatai Zevi himself, on
the eve of the expected sabbath of the world after remaining obscure during the period of exile alike to scholars and theologians,
philosophers and Kabbalists. The last of the wise at the beginning
of the *Galuth*, Simeon ben Yohai and his friends, knew the secret,
and hints of their wisdom are scattered through the pages of the
Zohar and the Talmudic Aggadah. But these hints and milestones
on the road to true knowledge remained insoluble enigmas as long
as the *Galuth* lasted.[73] They are covered by a veil which even the
Kabbalists were unable to lift. The Sabbatian solution of the dark
riddle, their diagnosis of the true mystery of God and the idea they
offered as the theological content of a Judaism regenerated by the
revelation of the Messiah is so astonishing as to be comparable only
to their paradox of the necessary apostasy of the Messiah. It is
nothing less than a new form of the Gnostic dualism of the hidden
God and the God who is the Creator of the world. This then was
to be the true meaning of Monotheism. The forms under which
these ideas were put forward vary considerably. What they had in
common was their fundamental concept which I should like briefly
to describe.

The ancient Gnostics of the second and third century distinguished between the hidden and benevolent God, the God of the
illuminate whose knowledge they call "gnosis," and the Creator and
Lawgiver whom they also call the Jewish God, and to whom they
attribute the writings of the Old Testament. The term *Jewish God*
or *God of Israel* is abusive and meant to be so. The Gnostics regarded the confusion between the two Gods, the higher loving one,
and the lower who is merely just, as a misfortune for religion. It is
metaphysical antisemitism in its profoundest and most effective form
which has found expression in these ideas and continues to do so.
The same dualism is to be found in Sabbatian theology, but with
a significant difference. The Sabbatians distinguish between the
hidden God, whom they call the "First Cause," and the revealed
God who is the "God of Israel." The existence of a First Cause is
in their opinion evident to every rational being, and its knowledge
forms an elementary part of our consciousness. Every child able to
use its intelligence cannot fail to perceive the necessity of a primary
cause of existence. But this knowledge which we receive through

our reasoning is without religious significance. Religion is in no sense concerned with the First Cause; rather is its essence to be found in the revelation of something which the mind by itself cannot grasp. The First Cause has nothing to do with the world and with creation; it exercises neither providence nor retribution. It is the God of the philosophers, the God of Aristotle, which according to Cardozo even Nimrod, Pharaoh and the pagans have worshipped. The God of religion, on the other hand, is the God of Sinai. The Torah, the documentary evidence of revelation, says nothing about the hidden root of all being, of which we know nothing except that it exists, and which is never and nowhere revealed. Revelation alone has the right to speak, and does speak, of that "God of Israel," *Elohe Israel*, who is the creator of everything, but at the same time Himself the First Effect of the First Cause.

Where the ancient Gnostics disparaged the God of Israel, the Sabbatians disparaged the unknown God. According to them, the error committed by Israel in exile consists in confusing the First Cause and the First Effect, the God of Reason and the God of Revelation. Cardozo and Hayun did not flinch from the awful consequence that, in the martyrdom of exile, Israel had lost the true and pure knowledge of God. The philosophers who tried to bulldoze us into accepting the God of Aristotle as the God of Religion, will one day have to justify themselves, and Israel has little reason to be proud of them.

The object of religion, the goal of our prayers, can only be the "God of Israel" and its unity or union with his Shekhinah. From this original dualism some Sabbatians developed a Trinity of the unknown God, the God of Israel and the Shekhinah, and it did not take long for the idea to develop that the completion of Salvation is dependent upon the separate appearance of a Messiah for each of these three aspects of Trinity, with a female Messiah for the last! The conceptions which the Sabbatians had of this new Trinity, one version of which has been set out at length in Nehemia Hayun's *Oz l'Elohim*, "Power of God,"—the only document of Sabbatian Kabbalism which was ever printed[70]—however interesting they may be, are of no particular importance in this connection. What is more important is the fact that even the moderate Sabbatians tried to evolve a conception of God which conflicted with the fundamental tenets of Judaism. Their passionate insistence in proclaiming a derivative of something else the supreme object of religion has something strange and perturbing. The furious reaction of orthodoxy and also of orthodox Kabbalism against this attempt to tear the God of Reason and the Revealed God asunder, is only too comprehensible.

To the Sabbatians all reality became dialectically unreal and contradictory. Their own experience led them to the idea of an existence in permanent contradiction with itself, and it is not surprising that their God no less than their Messiah bears the mark of such self-contradiction and disintegration.

HASIDISM: THE LATEST PHASE

1

No other phase in the development of Jewish mysticism has been so thoroughly described in literature as its latest, the Hasidic movement. As I have already said towards the end of the third lecture, this Polish and Ukrainian Hasidism of the eighteenth and nineteenth centuries has nothing to do with mediaeval Hasidism in Germany. The new Hasidism was founded shortly before the middle of the eighteenth century by that famous saint and mystic Israel Baal Shem ("Master of the Holy Name") who died in 1760 and who during his life-time impressed the mark of his personality on the movement much as Sabbatai Zevi had shaped the character of Sabbatianism. Large sections of Russian and Polish Jewry were drawn into the orbit of the movement, particularly up to the middle of the nineteenth century, but outside the Slavic countries and Russia this form of mysticism was never able to gain a foothold.

Particularly during the past three decades the literature on Hasidism has grown enormously. Of thoughtful and scholarly writers on the subject there has been no lack. The writings of Martin Buber, Simeon Dubnow, S. A. Horodezky, Jacob Minkin and others[1] have provided us with a deeper insight into the spirit of Hasidism than we have at present of its predecessors. Its history, its quarrels with its opponents, the figures of its great saints and leaders and even its decay into a political instrument of reactionary forces— all this is fairly well known today. That a more scholarly treatment of Jewish mysticism should have taken its starting point from this latest phase, and from there proceeded to the earlier stages, becomes less surprising when it is remembered that Hasidism as a living phenomenon is still with us. For all its decay it remains a living force in the lives of countless thousands of our people. More than that: some open-minded writers, not necessarily all of them so-called scholars, have shown us, as the result of their investigations, that beneath the superficial peculiarities of Hasidic life there sub-sists a stratum of positive values, which were all too easily over-looked in the furious struggle between rationalistic "enlighten-ment" and mysticism during the nineteenth century.

It is a well-known fact that the emotional world of Hasidism exercised a strong fascination upon men who were primarily con-cerned with the spiritual regeneration of Judaism. They soon per-ceived that the writings of the Hasidim contained more fruitful and original ideas than those of their rationalistic opponents, the *Maskilim,* and that the reborn Hebrew culture could find much of value in the heritage of Hasidism. Even so restrained a critic as Ahad Haam wrote around 1900, in a critical essay on modern Hebrew literature:[2] "To our shame we must admit that if today we want to find even a shadow of original Hebrew literature, we must turn to the literature of Hasidism; there, rather than in the litera-ture of the *Haskalah,* one occasionally encounters, in addition to much that is purely fanciful, true profundity of thought which bears the mark of the original Jewish genius."

Among the factors which have made Hasidic writings more easily accessible to the layman than earlier Kabbalistic literature, two must be mentioned above all. One is the comparatively modern style of the more important Hasidic authors, the other their fond-ness for epigrams or aphorisms. In the case of most of the older Kabbalistic authors, the reader must make the effort of transplant-ing himself into a world of strange symbolism; the mind must adapt itself to a complicated and often abstruse mystical vocabulary, and even so understanding often becomes difficult. Hasidism marks an exception. For all their obvious defects in matters of Hebrew gram-mar not a few and not the least important Hasidic treatises are fas-cinatingly written. In general, although it would be very mislead-ing to call it perfect, the style of Hasidic books is easier and more lucid than that of earlier Kabbalistic works of literature. Their mysticism notwithstanding, there is in them what must be called the breath of modernity. We should know more about the older Kabbalah if its representatives had included such masters of inci-sive epigrammatic style as Rabbi Phineas of Koretz, Rabbi Nahman of Brazlav, Rabbi Mendel of Kotzk, and other leaders of Hasidism.

But although, as I said, there are books in all languages which deal with the subject, some of them in a masterly fashion, there is still room for further attempts to interpret Hasidism, particularly in its relation to the whole of Jewish mysticism. I have no wish to compete with the excellent collections of Hasidic anecdotes and epigrams which nowadays enjoy such wide circulation. You will not expect me to add anything to the wealth of Hasidic tales and teachings contained for instance in the writings of Martin Buber or in the voluminous "Hasidic Anthology" which has been compiled by Louis Newman.[3] It is not that I should find any difficulty in adding to it; the range of this literature is enormous. But in this lecture I should like to confine myself to a few points which have a more direct bearing upon our problem.

The fact is that attempts have been made for some time to deny the mystical character of Hasidism.[4] Although I do not agree with these views, it seems to me there is something to be said in their favor; moreover they have a value precisely because they show us that we are dealing with a problem. The problem to my mind is that of the popularization of Kabbalistic thought, or to put it a little differently, we have to consider in this lecture the problem of the social function of mystical ideas. But before going further, let me recall the subject of the last two lectures. Lurianic Kabbalism, Sabbatianism and Hasidism are after all three stages of the same process. As we have seen, a proselytizing tendency was already inherent in the first. The distinguishing feature of Lurianic Kabbalism was the important part played by the Messianic element. Lurianism, as I have said before, appealed to the masses because it gave an expression to their yearning for deliverance by emphasizing the contrast between the broken and imperfect state of our existence and its perfection in the process of *Tikkun*. In the Sabbatian movement this urge for redemption "in our time" became the cause of aberrations. Great as was the influence of Sabbatianism, it was bound to fail as a missionary movement. Its extravagant paradoxicalness, which overstressed the fundamental paradox inherent in every form of mysticism, remained an affair of comparatively small groups. Hasidism, on the other hand, broadly speaking represents an attempt to make the world of Kabbalism, through a certain transformation or re-interpretation, accessible to the masses of the people, and in this it was for a time extraordinarily successful.

I think one can say that after the rise and collapse of Sabbatianism there were only three ways left open to the Kabbalah, in addition to that of accepting the contradictions in which the new believers and adherents of Sabbatai Zevi had become hopelessly muddled. One was to pretend that nothing in particular had happened; that was actually what a good many orthodox Kabbalists tried to do. They continued in the old way without bothering much about new ideas. But the pretence rang hollow; the explosion of the Messianic element contained in Lurianic Kabbalism was a fact which could not well be denied.

Another way was to renounce all attempts to create a mass movement, in order to avoid a repetition of the disastrous consequences which had followed the most recent of these attempts. That was the attitude of some of the most important representatives of later Kabbalism who entirely renounced the more popular aspects of Lurianism and tried to lead the Kabbalah back from the market place to the solitude of the mystic's semi-monastic cell. In Poland, and in particular in those regions where Sabbatianism and Hasidism were at home, a spiritual center was once more formed about the middle of the eighteenth century which came to exercise a strong authority, particularly between 1750 and 1800 in Galicia. Here an orthodox anti-Sabbatian Kabbalism flourished and found enthusiastic followers. This was the great age of the *Klaus,* the "close," in Brody, not a hermitage as the word seems to suggest, but a little room (adjoining the great synagogue) where the Kabbalists studied and prayed. The "close" of Brody, as Aaron Marcus has put it, formed a sort of "paradisical hot-house in which the "Tree of Life" [as the Lurianic *magnum opus* was called] blossomed out and brought forth fruit."⁵ But the classical representative of this tendency has been found in Rabbi Shalom Sharabi, a Yemenite Kabbalist who lived in Jerusalem in the middle of the eighteenth century and founded a center for Kabbalists which exists to this day.⁶ This is Beth-El, now a forlorn spot in the Old City of Jerusalem, where even today as I write these lines, men who are thoroughly "modern" in their thought may draw inspiration from contemplating what Jewish prayer can be in its sublimest form. For here the emphasis was again, and more than ever, laid on the practice of mystical prayer, the mystical contemplation of the elect. "Beth-El," says Ariel Bension, the son of one of its members, "was a community resolved to live in unity and sanctity. Of those who thought to enter its portals it demanded the attainment of the scholar and the self-abnegation of the ascetic. Thus it missed the masses."[7] We are in possession of documents signed by twelve members of this group in the eighteenth century, in which the signatories pledge themselves to build up, through their common life, the mystical body of Israel and to sacrifice themselves for each other "not only in this life but in all lives to come."[8] Kabbalism becomes at the end of its way what it was at the beginning; a genuine esoterism, a kind of mystery-religion which tries to keep the *profanum vulgus* at arm's length. Among the writings of the Sephardic Kabbalists of this school, which has exercised a considerable influence on Oriental Jewry,[9] it would be difficult to find a single one capable of being understood by the laity.

Finally there was a third way, and that is the one which Hasidism took, particularly during its classical period. Here the Kabbalah did not renounce its proselytizing mission; on the contrary, Hasidism—a typical revivalist movement whose founder was innocent of higher rabbinical learning—aimed from the beginning at the widest possible sphere of influence. Later on I shall have to say something about the way in which Hasidism achieved this aim and the price it had to pay for it. But first let us see what distinguishes this movement from the previous ones; this will also give us a starting point for the question, what unites them.

As far as I can see, Hasidism represents an attempt to preserve those elements of Kabbalism which were capable of evoking a popular response, but stripped of their Messianic flavor to which they owed their chief successes during the preceding period. That seems to me the main point. Hasidism tried to eliminate the element of Messianism—with its dazzling but highly dangerous amalgamation of mysticism and the apocalyptic mood—without renouncing the popular appeal of later Kabbalism. Perhaps one should rather speak of a "neutralization" of the Messianic element. I hope I shall not be misunderstood. I am far from suggesting that the Messianic hope and the belief in redemption disappeared from the hearts of the Hasidim. That would be utterly untrue; as we shall see later on, there is no single positive element of Jewish religion which is altogether lacking in Hasidism. But it is one thing to allot a niche to the idea of redemption, and quite another to have placed this concept with all it implies in the center of religious life and thought. This was true of the theory of *Tikkun* in the system of Lurianism and it was equally true of the paradoxical Messianism of the Sabbatians; there is no doubt what idea moved them most deeply, motivated them, explained their success. And this is precisely what Messianism had ceased to do for the Hasidim, although some groups and two or three of their leaders transplanted themselves to Palestine in 1777.[10] It is only typical of this new attitude to Messianism that Rabbi Baer of Meseritz, the disciple of the Baal Shem and the teacher of the aforementioned leaders, used to stress the rather astounding idea that to serve God in Exile was easier and therefore more within the grasp of the devout than to serve him in Palestine. Equally, the old Lurianic doctrine on the "uplifting of the holy sparks" was deprived of its intrinsic Messianic meaning by introducing a differentiation between two aspects of redemption. The one was said to be the individualistic redemption, or rather salvation, of the soul and the second the truly Messianic redemption which is, of course, a phenomenon concerning the whole body of the community of Israel and not the individual soul. The uplifting of the sparks was assumed already by the first theorist of Hasidism, Rabbi Jacob Josef of Polna, to lead up only to the first aspect of redemption, in contradistinction to Messianic redemption which can be wrought by God alone and not by the action of man. This retroversion of the Messianic doctrine of Kabbalism in earlier Hasidic literature has not been sufficiently taken into account by several modern writers on Hasidism.

2

It can hardly be called an accident that the Hasidic movement made its first appearance in the regions where Sabbatianism had taken strongest root, Podolia and Volhynia. Israel Baal Shem, the founder of the movement, began at a time when Sabbatianism, incessantly persecuted by rabbinical orthodoxy, had steadily become more and more nihilistic. Towards the end of his life there occurred the great outburst of antinomianism which found its expression in the Frankist movement. The founder of Hasidism and his first disciples, therefore, must have been fully aware of the destructive power inherent in extreme mystical Messianism, and from this experience they undoubtedly drew certain consequences. They were active among the same people whom Sabbatianism had tried and partly succeeded in converting, and it is by no means impossible that there was at first a certain passing over of members from one movement to the other. Those groups of Polish Jewry which already before and at the time of the first appearance of the Baal Shem called themselves Hasidim[11] included many Sabbatians, if they were not indeed wholly crypto-Sabbatian in character, and it took some time before the difference between the new Hasidim of the "Baal Shem" and the old ones became generally appreciated. During that interval there was time for stock-taking among the followers of either group. What Solomon Maimon tells of one of these "pre-Hasidic" Hasidim, Jossel of Kletzk,[12] shows clearly that there was no difference in principle between "Hasidim" like the aforementioned and the Hasidim of the group of Rabbi Jehudah Hasid who organized a mystical crusade to the Holy Land in the years 1699 and 1700. But with regard to this latter group, we have good reason to believe that the majority of its members were actually Sabbatians.[13]

Moreover, an unexpected find has provided us with a useful hint concerning the relations between these two forms of Hasidism, and therefore between Hasidism and Sabbatianism. Briefly it is this. In the biographical legends concerning the life of the Baal Shem, which were written long after his death, a good deal is said about a mysterious saint, Rabbi Adam Baal Shem, whose mystical writings the Baal Shem was said to have treasured without having known their author personally. The name Rabbi Adam, which was exceedingly unusual among the Jews of that period, seemed to prove that the so-called Rabbi was in reality a legendary figure and I personally am inclined to the view that the whole story of his literary heritage was a figment of the imagination. Only recently, however, we have come to learn of a very curious fact.

As is well known, many of the followers of the Baal Shem's followers, pupils of his pupils, became the founders of Hasidic dynasties in which the leadership of larger or smaller Hasidic groups was and still is more or less automatically passed down from father to son. One of the more important of these dynasties, the descendants of Rabbi Solomon of Karlin,[14] has in its possession a great

many Hasidic manuscripts and other documents which at the end
of the eighteenth century had come into the possession of its
founder and his son. As against the brazen forgeries which in recent
years have been published in great numbers, these documents have
at least the inestimable advantage of being genuine. It is true that
they contain less sensational revelations than the flood of fabrications purporting to be letters written by Israel Baal Shem, or even
the mystical Rabbi Adam Baal Shem himself, which have recently
been offered to a gullible public.[15] The archives of the Zaddikim of
Karlin contain less astounding but more trustworthy documents.
Yet for me they did have something exciting in store, for I learned
to my great surprise that there is among other documents a voluminous manuscript called *Sefer Ha-Tsoref,* written by Rabbi Heshel
Zoref of Vilna who died in 1700, just when the Baal Shem was
born.[36] Its fourteen hundred odd pages deal in the main with Kabbalistic mysteries concerning the *Shema Israel.* The copyist of the
manuscript tells its history in detail and we have no reason to dis-
believe him. We learn then that one of the manuscripts of the book
came after the death of Rabbi Heshel into the hands of the Baal
Shem who guarded it as a most precious mystical treasure. He
must have heard much of Heshel Zoref, who during his closing
years led the secluded life of a saint, in a little room of the *Beth
ha-Midrash* in Cracow. The Baal Shem intended to have the voluminous and partly cryptographic manuscript copied by one of
his friends who was a famous Kabbalist, Rabbi Sabbatai Rashkover,
but nothing came of his plan and the manuscript fell into the possession of the Baal Shem's grandson, Aaron Tutiever, who finally
had it copied. The copy we have is based on that first copy which
became the property of another famous Hasidic leader, Rabbi Mordecai of Czernobyl. So far everything is perfectly straightforward,
and there is an interesting commentary by the copyist in the colo-
phon of the manuscript, where he sings the praise of this profound
Kabbalistic work. What the copyist, however, did not know was
that the author was without doubt one of the outstanding prophets
of moderate Sabbatianism. I mentioned his name in the last lecture.[37] Like many others he seems to have kept his belief in Sabbatai Zevi secret during the latter part of his life, but we know from
trustworthy witnesses that it has found a symbolical expression in
his book[38] of which some contemporary writers speak with the deep-

est veneration. Now all this amounts to no less than the fact that the founder of Hasidism guarded the literary heritage of a leading crypto-Sabbatian and held it in the highest esteem. Apparently we have here the factual basis of the legend of Rabbi Adam Baal Shem. The historical Rabbi Heshel Zoref, who was indeed something like a Baal Shem, was transformed into a mythical figure, when it became known, to the considerable scandal of the Hasidim, that he was "suspected" of Sabbatianism.[19] It seems to me to be a fact of great importance that, between the new Hasidim and the old to whom Rabbi Heshel Zoref belonged, there was a link, if only an unconscious one—assuming that Rabbi Heshel's Sabbatian belief was as little known to the Baal Shem as to his followers, one of whom is even credited with an abortive attempt to have the work printed.

Heshel Zoref, however, was not the only Sabbatian authority on whom the new Hasidim placed much trust. There was also Rabbi Jacob Koppel Lifshitz, a celebrated mystic in his times and the author of a very interesting introduction into what purports to be Lurianic Kabbalah. This book was printed about sixty years after his death by the pupils of Rabbi Baer of Meseritz, the town where the author, too, spent his later years and where he died. Although the book was regarded with some suspicion by orthodox Kabbalists outside the Hasidic camp it enjoyed a wide reputation with the Hasidim. But only recently it has been proved conclusively by Tishby that the author was an outstanding crypto-Sabbatian and based his doctrine to a very considerable extent on the Sabbatian writings of Nathan of Gaza. In his case, too, old Hasidic tradition had it that the Baal Shem had expressed himself with great enthusiasm on his writings when he saw them during a visit to Meseritz some years after the author's death.

There is a further and very important point in which Sabbatianism and Hasidism join in departing from the rabbinical scale of values, namely their conception of the ideal type of man to which they ascribe the function of leadership. For rabbinical Jewry, particularly in those centuries, the ideal type recognized as the spiritual leader of the community is the scholar, the student of the Torah, the learned Rabbi. Of him no inner revival is demanded; what he needs is deeper knowledge of the sources of the Holy Law, in order that he may be able to show the right path to the community and to interpret for it the eternal and immutable word of God. In the place of these teachers of the Law, the new movements gave birth to a new type of leader, the illuminate, the man whose heart has been touched and changed by God, in a word, the prophet. Both movements have also counted scholars among their ranks, and paradoxically the Sabbatians numbered among their adherents a larger number of outstanding minds than the Hasidim, at any rate during the heyday of the Hasidic movement. But for them it was not scholarship and learning that counted; it was rather an irrational quality, the *charisma,* the blessed gift of revival. Ever since the hearts were deeply stirred in 1666 and hidden sources of emotion had begun to flow, one finds many unlettered men among the preachers of the Sabbatian doctrine. Was it not, after all, they who led in the struggle to place faith above knowledge in the scale of values, now that it was necessary to defend an inner reality which in the perspective of reason and knowledge was bound to seem absurd and paradoxical? Inspired preachers, men of the holy spirit, prophets—pneumatics in a word, to employ the term commonly used in the history of religion—led the Sabbatian movement; the Rabbis did not though there was no lack of them in the movement. When, as happened more than once, both types were combined in one person, that was all the better, but it was not considered essential. It is this ideal of pneumatic leadership which Hasidism, likewise a movement born from a deep and original religious impulse, adopted from the Sabbatians, but as we shall have occasion to see, the conception of the ideal was now to undergo a grandiose change.

3

But let us return to our starting point. We know that certain disciples of the Baal Shem's most important follower, Rabbi Baer the *Maggid,* or popular preacher of Meseritz, displayed a behavior which was judged extraordinary by their contemporaries and which seemed to justify the suspicion that they stood for a new form of Sabbatian antinomianism. Abraham Kalisker was the leader of a group of Hasidim who were in the habit—in the words of one of his Hasidic friends, who thoroughly disapproved of the practice—"of pouring scorn on the students of the Torah and the learned, inflicting all manner of ridicule and shame on them, turning somersaults in the streets and market places of Kolusk and Liozna, and generally permitting themselves all sorts of pranks and practical jokes in public."[20] And yet there is an all-important difference between even these radical groups and the Sabbatians: their motives are entirely different. For the followers of the "Great *Maggid*," Messianism as an active force of immediate appeal no longer had any importance. The mood that inspired them and scandalized their opponents was the primitive enthusiasm of mystical "friends of God." I have already mentioned the fact that in its beginnings Hasidism bore a good many revivalist traits. Its founder had evolved a new form of religious consciousness in which rabbinical learning, whatever its intrinsic significance, played no essential part. For the foundations of his immediate experience he went back to the Kabbalistic books which helped him to give expression to his emotional enthusiasm. He follows the ideas of the *Tsimtsum* of God, the uplifting of the fallen sparks, the conception of *Devekuth* as the highest religious value, and other notions of which we have already heard. For the soaring flight of the soul from the worlds created in the act of *Tsimtsum* there are no limits. "He who serves God in the 'great way' assembles all his inner power and rises upwards in his thoughts and *breaks through all skies in one act* and rises higher than the angels and the seraphs and the thrones, and *that* is the perfect worship." And: "In prayer and in the commandment which one keeps, there is a great and a small way . . . but the 'great way' is that of right preparation and enthusiasm through which he unites himself with the upper worlds."[21]

The clearest reflection of this enthusiasm is to be found in the Hasidic prayer which strikes one as an almost complete antithesis of the form of mystical prayer which was developed at about the same time in Jerusalem by the Sefardic Kabbalists of Beth-El. The latter is all restraint, the former all movement. It would be almost possible to speak of a contrast between 'sunken' and 'ecstatic' moods in the literal meaning of the term *ecstatic* "to be out of one's mind"—were it not for the reflection that such extreme opposites are always two sides of the same thing. To the Hasidic mind, *Devekuth* and *Kawwanah* were primarily emotional values, a significance which they had by no means always had before. "That is the meaning of *Devekuth* that when he fulfills the commandments or studies the Torah, the body becomes a throne for the soul . . . and the soul a throne for the light of the Shekhinah which is above his head, and the light as it were flows all round him, and he sits in the midst of the light and rejoices in trembling."[22]

The first fifty years of Hasidism after its founder's death (1760—1810), its truly heroic period, are characterized by this spirit of enthusiasm which expressed and at the same time justified itself by stressing the old idea of the immanence of God in all that exists. But this enthusiasm was anything but Messianic. It was not based on Chiliastic expectations. Here is the explanation of the fact that when it came into conflict, as it could hardly fail to do, with the sober and somewhat pedestrian spirit of rabbinical Orthodoxy, typified by the Lithuanian brand, it more than held its own. We have seen how Sabbatianism centred round the hope of a mystical redemption. On this issue no compromise was possible or even conceivable. With the shelving of the Messianic element an understanding between rabbinical and mystical Judaism was no longer ruled out. From a possibility it became a reality after the Hasidic movement had outgrown its first stormy period of growth and from active revivalism turned to religious organization, if still on a pneumatic and mystical basis. Here and there, an individual became the bearer of Messianic hopes, but the movement as a whole had made its peace with the *Galuth*.

Yet it is this later period of Hasidism, the period of the "Zaddikim" and their dynasties, which in certain important respects is closer to Sabbatianism than the earlier stages of the movement. It is particularly the episode of Frankism which makes for a certain similarity. Sabbatianism as we know, perished, not in a cloud of glory, but in the tragedy of the Frankist movement whose founder incarnates all the hideous potentialities of a corrupted, despotic Messianism. Jacob Frank (1726—1791) is a Messiah with a thirst for power; indeed his greedy lust for power dominated him to the exclusion of every other motive. It is this which makes his personality at once so fascinating and so ignoble. There is a certain demonic grandeur about the man. The quality that set him apart from Sabbatai Zevi is well expressed in a remark attributed to him. "If Sabbatai Zevi," he is reported to have said, " had to taste everything in this world, why did he not taste the sweetness of power?"[23]

This almost sensuous love for power, which Frank possessed in the highest degree, is the stigma of nihilism. To Frank the grand gesture of the ruler is everything.

What matters here is that the development of Zaddikism, after Hasidism had become the religious organization of large masses, took a similar course. True, the unlimited power and authority of the Zaddik over his followers was not purchased at the price of such destructive paradoxes as Frank had to uphold. Zaddikism was able to attain its goal without coming into open confllict with the basic tenets of traditional Judaism. But this fact should not blind us to its doctrinal implications. Lust for power is active even among those profound theoreticians of Zaddikism who developed the doctrine of the Zaddik, the saint and the spiritual leader of the Hasidic community, as the non-Messianic Messiah, and characteristically carried it to its extreme. A man of genius like Rabbi Nahman of Brazlav impresses us by his extravagant references to the power of the Zaddik, but he does so because in his case one senses an obvious concern for the spiritual aspects of Zaddikism. With many others, however, this spiritual character is only faintly or not at all recognizable, and the greatest and most impressive figure of classical Zaddikism, Israel of Rishin, the so-called Rabbi of Sadagora, is to put it bluntly, nothing but another Jacob Frank who has achieved the miracle of remaining an orthodox Jew. All the mysteries of the Torah have disappeared, or rather they are overshadowed and absorbed by the magnificent gesture of the born ruler. He is still witty and quick at repartee, but the secret of his power is the mystery of the magnetic and dominant personality and not that of the fascinating teacher.

4

But I am running ahead of my own thoughts. Let us return for a moment to the question, what Hasidism means and what it does not mean. There are two things about the movement which are particularly remarkable. One is the fact that within a geographically small area and also within a surprisingly short period, the ghetto gave birth to a whole galaxy of saint-mystics, each of them a startling individuality. The incredible intensity of creative religious feeling, which manifested itself in Hasidism between 1750 and 1800, produced a wealth of truly original religious types which, as far as one can judge, surpassed even the harvest of the classical period of Safed. Something like a rebellion of religious energy against petrified religious values must have taken place.

No less surprising, however, is the fact that this burst of mystical energy was unproductive of new religious *ideas,* to say nothing of new theories of mystical knowledge. If you were to ask me: what is the new doctrine of these mystics, whose experience was obviously first hand, more so perhaps than in the case of many of their predecessors? What were their new principles and ideas? I say, if you were to ask me this, I should hardly know what to answer. In the previous lectures it was always possible to lay down a blueprint, so to speak, of the spiritual architecture of the subject-matter and to give a more or less precise definition of its ideational side. In the case of Hasidism, certainly a creative religious movement, we cannot do so without repeating ourselves innumerable times.

It is precisely this fact which makes Hasidism a special problem for our interpretation. The truth is that it is not always possible to distinguish between the revolutionary and the conservative elements of Hasidism: or rather, Hasidism as a whole is as much a reformation of earlier mysticism as it is more or less the same thing. You can say if you like that it depends on how you look at it. The Hasidim were themselves aware of this fact. Even such a novel thing as the rise of the Zaddikim and the doctrine of Zaddikism appeared to them as being, despite its novelty, well in the Kabbalistic tradition. So much seems clear, that the followers of these Hasidim became genuine revivalists. Rabbi Israel of Koznitz, a typical Kabbalist among the Zaddikim, used to say that he had read eight hundred Kabbalistic books before coming to his teacher, the "Great *Maggid* of Meseritz," but that he had really learned nothing from them. If, however, you merely read his books you will not find the slightest doctrinal difference between his teachings and those of the old authors whom he affected to despise. The new element must therefore not be sought on the theoretical and literary plane, but rather in the experience of an inner revival, in the spontaneity of feeling generated in sensitive minds by the encounter with the living incarnations of mysticism.

A good deal of light is thrown on the attitude of the Hasidim to the question of their relationship—or that of their great teachers —to Kabbalism as a whole, by the testimony of Solomon of Luzk who edited the writings of the *Maggid* of Meseritz.[24] On the one hand, he reproves the later Kabbalists for their supercilious attitude towards earlier documents of Kabbalism; but then again he seems to regard the writings of Rabbi Baer of Meseritz as purely Kabbalistic and not at all as a new departure. Speaking generally one does get the impression from reading Hasidic authors that the continuity of Kabbalistic thought was not really interrupted.

Again it would be quite wrong to regard, as the original and novel contribution of Hasidism to religion, the fact that it popularized the Kabbalistic ideas of a mystical life with God and in God. Though it be true that this tendency has celebrated its greatest triumph in the Hasidic movement and its literature, its antecedents go farther back. Too little attention is given to the fact that the popularization of certain mystical ideas had begun long before the rise of Hasidism and that, at about the time of its first appearance, it had already found its most magnificent literary incarnation. I am thinking here of the now almost forgotten writings of Jehudah Loewe ben Bezalel of Prague (about 1520—1609), the "Exalted Rabbi Loew" of the Golem legend. In a sense, one could say that he was the first Hasidic writer. It is certainly no accident that so many Hasidic saints had a penchant for his writings. Some of his more voluminous tracts, such as the great book *Gevuroth Adonai,* "the Mighty Deeds of God",[25] seem to have no other purpose than to express Kabbalistic ideas without making too much use of Kabbalistic terminology.[26] In this he succeeded so well that not a few modern students have failed to perceive the Kabbalistic character of his writings. Some have gone so far as to deny that he occupied himself with Kabbalistic thought at all.

The Hasidim themselves did not go so far in their popularization of Kabbalistic thought as the Exalted Rabbi Loew, who appears to have renounced the Kabbalistic vocabulary only in order to give the widest possible range of influence to Kabbalistic doctrine. They too on occasions depart from the classical terminology of Kabbalism, especially where it had become petrified; there is subtlety and ambiguity in their writings which is not found in earlier authors, but on the whole they stuck fairly close to the old formulae. If one studies the writings of Rabbi Baer of

Meseritz the most important follower of the Baal Shem and the real organizer of the movement, one sees immediately that in them the old ideas and conceptions, all of which duly make their appearance, have lost their stiffness and received a new infusion of life by going through the fiery stream of a truly mystical mind. Even this popularization of the Kabbalistic vocabulary, however, is not a specific product of the Hasidic movement, but one that dates back to the literature of the so-called *Musar*-books (moralizing tracts), particularly those written during the century before the rise of Hasidism. There you get works and pamphlets on moral conduct and Jewish ethics which were written for a broader public. Previously I said that since the period of Safed this kind of literature was for the most part written by men who were under Kabbalistic influence and whose writings propagated doctrines and values peculiar to Kabbalism. Since the Hasidim drew much more on these books than on the metaphysical and theosophical literature of Kabbalism, an analysis of Hasidic doctrines cannot afford to pass them by. Unfortunately no serious attempt has yet been made to establish the true relation between the traditional and the novel elements in Hasidic thought—the one known to me[*] has failed completely. In the absence of a competent scholarly work on the question one is reduced to dangerous generalizations from more or less vague impressions and occasional intuitive glimpses of the situation. The impression one gets is that no element of Hasidic thought is entirely new, while at the same time everything has somehow been transformed; certain ideas are more strongly emphasized than before, while others have been relegated to the background. A consistent attitude inspires these changes, and we have to ask ourselves wherein it is to be found.

If one leaves out of account the lone effort at religious orientation made by Rabbi Shneur Zalman of Ladi and his school, the so-called *Habad*-Hasidism, Hasidism seems to have produced no truly original Kabbalistic thought whatever. However, this interesting attempt to arrive at something like a synthesis of Isaac Luria and the Maggid of Meseritz, despite the fact that it stands alone, provides in fact the best starting point for our investigation. It gives a new emphasis to psychology, instead of theosophy, a fact which must be deemed of the highest importance. To put it as briefly as possible, the distinctive feature of the new school is to be found in the fact that the secrets of the divine realm are presented in the guise of mystical psychology. It is by descending into the depths of his own self that man wanders through all the dimensions of the world; in his own self he lifts the barriers which separate one sphere from the other;[28] in his own self, finally, he transcends the limits of natural existence and at the end of his way, without, as it were, a single step beyond himself, he discovers that God is "all in all" and there is "nothing but Him". With every one of the endless stages of the theosophical world corresponding to a given state of the soul—actual or potential, but at any rate capable of being felt and perceived—Kabbalism becomes an instrument of psychological analysis and self-knowledge, an instrument the precision of which is not infrequently rather astounding. What gives the writings of the *Habad*-school their distinctive feature is that striking mixture of enthusiastic worship of God and pantheistic, or rather acosmistic, interpretation of the universe on the one hand, and intense preoccupation with the human mind and its impulses on the other.

Something of this attitude is indeed common to the whole Hasidic movement, even though the majority of its followers rejected the mood of religious intoxication peculiar to the *Habad* mystics, whose theoretical outlook struck them as being a little too scholastic and strained. This much then can be said: in the Hasidic movement, Kabbalism appears no longer in a theosophical guise, or to be more exact, theosophy with all its complicated theories, if it is not entirely dropped, is at least no longer the focal point of the religious consciousness. Where it continues to play a prominent part, as for instance in the school of Rabbi Zevi Hirsh of Zydaczow (died 1830), it is bound up with some belated offshoot of the older Kabbalah within the framework of Hasidism. What has really become important is the direction, the mysticism of the personal life. Hasidism is practical mysticism at its highest. Almost all the Kabbalistic ideas are now placed in relation to values peculiar to the individual life, and those which are not remain empty and ineffective. Particular emphasis is laid on ideas and concepts concerning the relation of the individual to God. All this centers around the concept of what the Kabbalists call *Devekuth,* the meaning of which I have tried to explain in previous lectures. The comparatively few terms of religious expression which date back to Hasidism, such as *Hithlahavuth*, "enthusiasm," or "ecstasy," or *Hitha-zkuth*, "self-maintenance", are related to this sphere.

There is much truth in Buber's remark in the first of his Hasidic books that Hasidism represents "Kabbalism turned Ethos", but a further ingredient was needed to make Hasidism what it was. Ethical Kabbalism can also be found in the moralizing and propagandist literature of Lurianism which I have mentioned, yet it would be stretching the term too far to call this Hasidic. What gave Hasidism its peculiar note was primarily the foundation of a religious community on the basis of a paradox common to the history of such movements, as the sociology of religious groupings has shown. Briefly, the originality of Hasidism lies in the fact that mystics who had attained their spiritual aim—who, in Kabbalistic parlance, had discovered the secret of true *Devekuth*—turned to the people with their mystical knowledge, their "Kabbalism become Ethos", and, instead of cherishing as a mystery the most personal of all experiences, undertook to teach its secret to all men of good will.

Nothing is further from the truth than the view which regards Zaddikism, that is to say the unlimited religious authority of an individual in a community of believers, as foreign to the nature of Hasidism, and insists that one must distinguish between the "pure" Hasidism of the Baal Shem and the "depraved" Zaddikism of his followers and their followers. This simon-pure Hasidism never existed because anything like it could never have influenced more than a few people. The truth is that the later development of Zaddikism was already implicit in the very start of the Hasidic movement. As soon as the mystic felt the urge to perpetuate his personal and solitary experience in the life of a community, which he addressed not in his language but in its own, a new factor made its appearance round which the mystical movement as a social phenomenon could and did crystallize. The believer no longer needed the Kabbalah; he turned its mysteries into reality by fastening upon certain traits which the saint, or Zaddik, whose example he strove to follow, had placed in the center of his relation to God. Everyone, thus the doctrine ran, must try to become the embodiment of a certain ethical quality. Attributes like piety, service, love, devotion, humility, clemency, trust, even greatness and domination, became in this way enormously real and socially effective.

Already in mediaeval Jewish literature, as we have seen in the third lecture, the radical or extreme practice of a good deed, or *Mitswah,* is mentioned as characteristic of the idea of *Hasiduth.* The modern Hasid certainly showed himself worthy of his name. Certain religious values were pushed so far and became symbolical of so much ardor and piety that their realization sufficed to bring about the mystical experience of *Devekuth.*

All this demanded from the first, and particularly during the most creative and virile period of the movement, the existence of the Zaddik or saint as the actual proof of the possibility of living up to the ideal. The whole energy and subtlety of emotion and thought, which in the case of the orthodox Kabbalist went into the exploration of the theosophical mysteries, was turned about in the quest for the true substance of ethico-religious conceptions and for their mystical glorification. The true originality of Hasidic thought is to be found here and nowhere else. As mystical moralists the Hasidim found a way to social organization. Again we see the ancient paradox of solitude and communion. He who has attained the highest degree of spiritual solitude, who is capable of being alone with God, is the true center of the community, because he has reached the stage at which true communion becomes possible. Hasidism produced a wealth of striking and original formulations of this paradox, formulae which bear the mark of the utmost sincerity, but which with the decay of the movement became only too easily a screen for the more sinister potentialities of saintly existence. To live among ordinary men and yet be alone with God, to speak profane language and yet draw the strength to live from the source of existence, from the "upper root" of the soul[20]—that is a paradox which only the mystical devotee is able to realize in his life and which makes him the center of the community of men.

5

To sum up: the following points are of importance for a characterization of the Hasidic movement:

1. A burst of original religious enthusiasm in a revivalist movement which drew its strength from the people.

2. The relation of the true illuminate, who becomes a popular leader and the center of the community, to the believers whose life

centers round his religious personality. This paradoxical relation led to the growth of Zaddikism.

3. The mystical ideology of the movement is derived from the Kabbalistic heritage, but its ideas are popularized, with an inevitable tendency towards terminological inexactitude.

4. The original contribution of Hasidism to religious thought is bound up with its interpretation of the values of personal and individual existence. General ideas become individual ethical values.

The whole development centers round the personality of the Hasidic saint; this is something entirely new. *Personality* takes the place of *doctrine;* what is lost in rationality by this change is gained in efficacy. The opinions particular to the exalted individual are less important than his character, and mere learning, knowledge of the Torah, no longer occupies the most important place in the scale of religious values. A tale is told of a famous saint who said: "I did not go to the 'Maggid' of Meseritz to learn Torah from him but to watch him tie his boot-laces."[30] This pointed and somewhat extravagant saying, which must not of course be taken literally, at least throws some light on the complete irrationalization of religious values which set in with the cult of the great religious personality. The new ideal of the religious leader, the Zaddik, differs from the traditional ideal of rabbinical Judaism, the *Talmid Hakham* or student of the Torah, mainly in that he himself "has become Torah." It is no longer his knowledge but his life which lends a religious value to his personality. He is the living incarnation of the Torah. Inevitably the original mystical conception of bottomless depths within the Torah was soon transferred to the personality of the saint, and in consequence it quickly appeared that the various groups of Hasidism were developing different characteristics in accordance with the particular type of saint to whom they looked for guidance. To establish a common type becomes not a little difficult. In the development of Hasidism opposing extremes found their place, and the differences between Lithuanian, Polish, Galician and South Russian Jewry were reflected in the personalities of the saints round whom they were grouped; all of which is not to say that the Zaddik was ever completely one with his environment.

The upshot of all this unlimited emotionalism was paradoxically enough a return to rationality. Such paradoxes by the way are not infrequent. In the event the waves went so high that emotion turned against itself. There was a sudden anti-climax. Zaddikim such as Rabbi Mendel of Kotzk, the most important among this group and generally speaking one of the most remarkable personalities—not a "saint", but a true spiritual leader—in Jewish religious history, began to inveigh against the extravagant sentimentalism which the cult of religious emotion had produced, notably among the Jews in Poland. Strict rational discipline suddenly becomes a fetish. The Rabbi of Kotzk had no sympathy for the Hasidic community whose yoke he bore only with the greatest reluctance. He hates emotionalism. In reply to an inquiry about man's way to God he is credited with the frank and laconic answer—in Scriptural language, Numbers xxxi, 53—"The man of war had taken spoil, *every man for himself.*"[31]

After an interval of a hundred years, during which Hasidism as a whole, apart from the solitary figure of Rabbi Shneur Zalman of Ladi, developed independently of the rabbinic tradition, there occured a revival of rabbinic learning, chiefly under the influence of the Rabbi of Kotzk. You find Zaddikim who write rabbinical responsa and works of "Pilpul," that is to say, hair-splitting casuistry. But important as these aspects of later Hasidism no doubt are, they certainly represent a departure from what is new and original in Hasidism. There this sort of learning was of no consequence. Everything was mystery, if not exactly mystery in the Kabbalistic sense, for compared with the peculiar note of Hasidic emotionalism, even the Kabbalistic mystery has a rational character. Now it is dissolved into personality and in this transformation it acquires a new intensity. The miraculous thing about it all is the fact that Hasidism did not conflict much more sharply with orthodox Judaism than it did; and yet everything seemed to move towards a mortal struggle. The personality of the Zaddik, its interpretation by the Hasidic writers, their insistence upon his supreme religious authority, his elevation to the rank of a source of canonical inspiration, of a medium of revelation—all this fairly compelled a clash with the recognized religious authority of rabbinic Judaism.

Such a conflict broke out with great vehemence in many localities. The "Gaon" Elijah of Vilna, the oustanding leader of Lithuian Jewry and an excellent representative of the highest rabbinical learning combined with a strictly theistic, orthodox Kabbalism, took the lead, in 1772, in an organized persecution of the new movement. Nor were the orthodox squeamish about the means that were employed in this struggle. As late as 1800, fanatical opponents of Hasidism tried to induce the Russian Government to take action against it. The history of these organized persecutions and of the Hasidic defence against them has been fully described by Simeon Dubnow. There can be no doubt that the Hasidim cherished a feeling of moral superiority over their contemporaries which has found expression in the writings of some famous Hasidic authors. One could easily make a collection of Hasidic epigrams which breathe a spirit not very far removed from that of Sabbatianism. The Hasidic Zaddik, too, is occasionally compelled to descend to a lower or even dangerous plane in order to rescue the scattered sparks of light, for "every descent of the Zaddik means an elevation of divine light."[32] And yet Hasidism did not go the way of Sabbatianism. Its leaders were far too closely connected with the life of the community to succumb to the danger of sectarianism. Opportunities were not lacking. Yet these men whose utterances not infrequently throw more light on the paradoxical nature of the mystical consciousness than anything before them, became—supreme paradox!—the advocates of the simple and untainted belief of the common man, and this simplicity was even glorified by them as the highest religious value. So profound an intellect as Rabbi Nahman of Brazlav, a man whose Kabbalistic terminology hides an almost hyper-modern sensitiveness to problems, turned all his energy to the task of defending the simplest of all beliefs.

The fact is that from the beginning the Baal Shem, the founder of Hasidism, and his followers were anxious to remain in touch with the life of the community; and to this contact they assigned an especial value. The paradox which they had to defend, that of the mystic in the community of men, was of a different nature than that upon which the Sabbatians took their stand and which inevitably gave a destructive turn to all their endeavors: salvation through betrayal. The greatest saints of Hasidism, the Baal Shem himself, Levi Isaac of Berdiczew, Jacob Isaac the "Seer of Lublin," Moshe Leib of Sassov and others, were also its most popular figures. They loved the Jews and their mystical glorification of this love did not decrease but rather added to its socially effective influence. It is not surprising, rather the contrary, that these men did everything in their power to avoid a conflict with a Judaism they intended to reform from within, and where it could not be avoided, to blunt its edge. Hasidism in fact solved the problem, at least as far as Judaism was concerned, of establishing so close a relation between the pneumatic, that is to say the man who feels himself inspired in every act by a transcendental power, the Pneuma or Spirit, and the religious community, that the inevitable tension between them helps to enrich the religious life of the community instead of destroying it. The fact that this possession of superior faculties, this pneumatic character, became an establishment, as it did in later Zaddikism after the holy fire had burnt down, is merely the reverse side of this positive achievement of Hasidism. Had the typical Zaddik been a sectarian or a hermit and not what he was in fact, namely the center of the community, such an establishment could never have grown up, safeguarding as it did a distinctive form of religious life even after the spirit had departed or, oven worse, been commercialized.

In this connection a further point must be kept in mind. Classical Hasidism was not the product of some theory or other, not even of a Kabbalistic doctrine, but of direct, spontaneous religious experience. Since the men who met with this special experience were for the most part simple and unsophisticated, the form in which they expressed their ideas and feelings was somewhat primitive compared to the older Kabbalah which reflected something of the complicated ambiguity of its subject. This is why we find a far more definite pantheistic tinge in the formulation of the thoughts of the first Hasidic thinkers than ever before. Probably under the influence of this fact, Solomon Schechter defined the doctrine of God's immanence in all things not only as the very root and core of Hasidism, but as its distinguishing characteristic.[33] It is permissible to doubt this; as has been shown in some of the previous lectures, the same doctrine had been expounded long before by some of the great Jewish mystics and Kabbalists. To me not the doctrine seems new, but rather the primitive enthusiasm with which it was expounded and the truly pantheistic exhilaration evoked by the belief that God "surrounds everything and pervades everything." It was this which so deeply shocked the *Gaon* of Vilna who nevertheless was an ardent Kabbalist himself. The Hasidim on their part accused him of having misunderstood the doctrine of *Tsimtsum* and through a misplaced literal interpretation arriving at the false idea of an absolute transcendence of God, a real abyss between God and creation.[34] To the Hasid, at least during the early period of the movement, the *Tsimtsum* is much more a symbol of our natural self than a real occurence in God; in other words, it is nothing real at all. A ray of God's essence is present and perceptible everywhere and at every moment.

Gradually, it is true, with the growth and spread of the movement and in the measure in which it became detached from the primitive environment of Podolia and was joined by more learned and sophisticated minds, the old radicalism began to wane. Compromises were sought and found and gradually Hasidism learned to speak a language which no longer shocked the orthodox. For the rest the Hasidim, for whom it was a commonplace that the Torah is the law of the Jewish people and the cosmic law of the universe, had never by their actions transgressed the limits of orthodox Judaism, at least not in principle. Such apparent heresies as the elimination of fixed hours of prayer, and similar acts which sprang from the unbounded enthusiasm of individual Zaddikim, clashed sharply enough with certain passages of the codes of religious law, but did not amount to anything like a real conflict between the "Torah in the heart" and the written Torah. The fact is that Hasidism represents throughout a curious mixture of conservatism and innovation. Its attitude towards tradition is somewhat dialectical. Thus when a great Zaddik was asked why he did not follow the example of his teacher in living as he did, he replied: "On the contrary, I do follow his example, for I leave him as he left his teacher." The tradition of breaking away from tradition produced such curious paradoxes.

6

Consideration must finally be given to another point. This is the close connection between mysticism and magic throughout the history of the Hasidic movement. It is as though the personality of Israel Baal Shem had been created solely for the purpose of confusing the modern theorists of mysticism. Here you have a mystic

whose authentic utterances permit no doubt as to the mystical
nature of his religious experience and whose earlier and later
followers have resolutely taken the same path. And yet he is also
a true "Baal Shem", that is to say, a master of the great Name of
God, a master of practical Kabbalism, a magician. Unbroken con-
fidence in the power of the holy Names bridges the gap in his
consciousness between the magician's claim to work miracles with
his amulet, or through other magical practices, and the mystical
enthusiasm which seeks no object but God. At the end of the long
history of Jewish mysticism these two tendencies are as closely in-
terwoven as they were in the beginning, and in many of the intermediate states of its development.

The revival of a new mythology in the world of Hasidism, to
which attention has been drawn occasionally, especially by Martin
Buber, draws not the least part of its strength from its connection
between the magical and the mystical faculties of its heroes. When
all is said and done it is this myth which represents the greatest
creative expression of Hasidism. In the place of the theoretical disquisition, or at least side by side with it, you get the Hasidic tale.
Around the lives of the great Zaddikim, the bearers of that irrational something which their mode of life expressed, legends were
spun often in their own lifetime. Triviality and profundity, traditional or borrowed ideas and true originality are indissolubly
mixed in this overwhelming wealth of tales which play an important
part in the social life of the Hasidim. To tell a story of the deeds
of the saints has become a new religious value, and there is something of the celebration of a religious rite about it.[35] Not a few
great Zaddikim, above all Rabbi Israel of Rishin, the founder of
the Eastern Galician Hasidic dynasty, have laid down the whole
treasure of their ideas in such tales. Their Torah took the form of
an inexhaustible fountain of story-telling. Nothing at all has remained theory, everything has become a story.—And so perhaps I
may also be permitted to close these lectures by telling you a story
of which the subject, if you like, is the very history of Hasidism itself. And here it is, as I have heard it told by that great Hebrew
novelist and story-teller, S. J. Agnon:[36]

When the Baal Shem had a difficult task before him, he would
go to a certain place in the woods, light a fire and meditate in
prayer—and what he had set out to perform was done. When a

generation later the "Maggid" of Meseritz was faced with the same task he would go the the same place in the woods and say: We can no longer light the fire, but we can still speak the prayers—and what he wanted done became reality. Again a generation later Rabbi Moshe Leib of Sassov had to perform this task. And he too went into the woods and said: We can no longer light a fire, nor do we know the secret meditations belonging to the prayer, but we do know the place in the woods to which it all belongs—and that must be sufficient; and sufficient it was. But when another generation had passed and Rabbi Israel of Rishin was called upon to perform the task, he sat down on his golden chair in his castle and said: We cannot light the fire, we cannot speak the prayers, we do not know the place, but we can tell the story of how it was done. And, the story-teller adds, the story which he told had the same effect as the actions of the other three.

You can say if you will that this profound little anecdote symbolizes the decay of a great movement. You can also say that it reflects the transformation of all its values, a transformation so profound that in the end all that remained of the mystery was the tale. That is the position in which we find ourselves today, or in which Jewish mysticism finds itself. The story is not ended, it has not yet become history, and the secret life it holds can break out tomorrow in you or in me. Under what aspects this invisible stream of Jewish mysticism will again come to the surface we cannot tell. But I have come here to speak to you of the main tendencies of Jewish mysticism as we know them. To speak of the mystical course which, in the great cataclysm now stirring the Jewish people more deeply than in the entire history of Exile, destiny may still have in store for us—and I for one believe that there is such a course—is the task of prophets, not of professors.

NOTES, BIBLIOGRAPHY, INDEX

GENERAL CHARACTERISTICS OF JEWISH MYSTICISM

1 A. E. Waite, The Secret Doctrine in Israel (London 1913). This book is incorporated in the author's later work, The Holy Kabbalah (1930).

2 Philosophie der Geschichte oder ueber die Tradition. 4 vols. (Münster 1827-1855). The book appeared anonymously. On the philosophy of the author cf. Carl Frankenstein, Molitors metaphysische Geschichtsphilosophie (1928).

3 In my Bibliographia Kabbalistica (1927) p. 94, I have listed the writings of Constant pertinent to the subject of Kabbalism. Eliphas Levi is a Judaization of his Christian names Alphonse Louis. No words need be wasted on the subject of Crowley's "Kabbalistic" writings in his books on what he was pleased to term "Magick," and in his journal, The Equinox.

4 Rufus Jones, Studies in Mystical Religion (1909), p. XV of the Introduction.

5 I owe this quotation from Thomas' Summa Theologiae to Engelbert Krebs' little book, Grundfragen der kirchlichen Mystik (1921) p. 37.

6 Levi Isaac, the "Rabbi" of Berditchev, in his work קדושת לוי at the end of section פקודי:

יש אדם שעובד את הבורא בשכלו שכל אנושי ויש אדם שהוא מסתכל אל האי"ן כביכול וזה אי אפשר בשכל אנושי רק בעזר השם ית'... (וכשזוכה האדם להסתכל אל האי"ן) אז השכל האנושי שלו בטל במציאות ואח"כ כשחוזר אדם על עצמות השכל אז היא מלא שפע.

7 Molitor, Philosophie der Geschichte vol. II (1834) p. 56.

8 מערכת האלהות ascribed sometimes to Perez of Barcelona, Mantua 1558 fol. 82b: דע כי האין סוף אשר זכרנו איננו רמוז לא בתורה ולא בנביאים ולא בכתובים ולא בדברי רז"ל אך קבלו בו בעלי העבודה קצת רמז. In the fixed terminology of this author, the mystics are referred to as בעלי העבודה "the masters of worship."

9 The terms האחדות השוח and המציאות הגדול, שורש כל השרשים (or השואת האחדות) are to be found in particular in the writings of those thirteenth century Kabbalists in Spain who show an outspoken tendency towards Neoplatonism.

10 Hebrew: מה שאין המחשבה משגת which sounds like a paraphrase of a Neoplatonic ἀκατάληπτος. It is to be found, in the place of the term En-Sof, in Isaac's commentary on the "Book of Creation" and in the writings of his disciples.

11 This term עמקי האין is a favorite metaphor of the thirteenth century Kabbalists, cf. my remarks in the Gaster Anniversary Volume (1936) p. 505.

12 Cf. Philo's De vita contemplativa, ed. Conybeare p. 119.

13   Cf. Martin Buber's eloquent dissertation on this point in the introduction to his anthology, Ekstatische Konfessionen (1909).

14   See the first and last sections of the fourth lecture.

15   Simon Ginzburg, ר' משה חיים לוצאטו ובני דורו (Tel Aviv, 1937).

16   J. Bernhart in an essay, Zur Soziologie der Mystik, in Sueddeutsche Monatshefte vol. XXVI (1928) p. 27.

17   Rabbi Kook's great work entitled אורות הקודש, the first two volumes of which were published in Jerusalem in 1938 from papers left by the author, is a veritable *theologia mystica* of Judaism equally distinguished by its originality and the richness of its author's mind. It is the last example of productive Kabbalistic thought of which I know.

18   A bibliography of Jewish mystical literature is still a *pium desiderium* of Kabbalistic research. My "Bibliographia Kabbalistica" (1927) lists only the scholarly literature on the subject of Jewish Mysticism, not the texts themselves.

19   Charles Bennett, A Philosophical Study of Mysticism (1931), p. 31.

20   E. R. Dodds, in his commentary on Proclus' Elements of Theology (1933), p. 219.

21   This thesis is elaborated particularly by Meir ibn Gabbai in עבודת הקודש part III (written in 1531). The idea that the Kabbalah represented the lost tradition of the earliest state of mankind was familiar also to the "Christian Kabbalists" of the late fifteenth and sixteenth centuries, such as Pico della Mirandola and Johannes Reuchlin.

22   הפילוסופים שאתם משבחים חכמתם דעו באמת כי מקום מעמד ראשם מעמד רגלינו, quoted by Isaac of Acre, cf. *Tarbiz* vol. V (1934), p. 318.

23   I have enlarged on this point in my essay, Zur Frage der Enstehung der Kabbala, which appeared in Korrespondenzblatt der Akademie fuer die Wissenschaft des Judentums 1928 p. 4—26. See also Julius Guttmann, Die Philosophie des Judentums (1933), p. 238.

24   David ben Abraham Ha-Laban מסורת הברית (written about 1300), published in קובץ ע"י של חברת מקיצי נרדמים new series vol. I (1936) p. 31. Exactly the same imagery is used by Dionysius the pseudo-Areopagite (quoted by Inge, The Philosophy of Plotinus vol. II p. 112) and by John the Scot, called Erigena, in De divisione naturae, liber III, 19—23.

25   Friedrich Creuzer, Symbolik und Mythologie der alten Voelker. Second edition, first part (1816), p. 70.

26   Alex. Altmann, Was ist juedische Theologie? (Frankfurt-on-Main 1933), p. 15.

27   This analysis is to be found in the third part of the "Guide of the Perplexed." On its importance for the history of religion cf. Julius Guttmann, John Spencers Erklaerung der biblischen Gesetze in ihrer Beziehung zu

Maimonides, in Festskrift af Professor David Simonsen (Copenhagen 1923), p. 258—276.

28 Since the days of the Kabbalistic school of Gerona (about 1230), Kabbalistic writings are full of such mystical interpretations of טעמי המצוות. Specifically Ezra ben Solomon and Jacob ben Sheshet (the true author of the ספר האמונה והבטחון which has later been ascribed to Nahmanides) were the first to treat at considerable length on such questions.

29 Samson Raphael Hirsch, Neunzehn Briefe ueber Judentum. Fourth edition (1911) p. 101.

30 *Gen. Rabba* ed. Theodor p. 68. This conception of primeval worlds also occurs in the "orthodox Gnosticism" of such Fathers of the Church as Clement of Alexandria and Origen, albeit with a difference, in as much as for them these worlds were not simply corrupt but necessary stages in the great cosmic process.

31 To this category belong the prayers grouped under the title תפלת היחוד which are ascribed to Rabbi Nehuniah ben Hakanah and Rabban Gamaliel but the style of which is the enthusiastic one of the Kabbalistic Neoplatonists. Cf. also the great prayer of Jacob ben Jacob Hacohen of Segovia (Castile, about 1265), published by me in מדעי היהדות vol. II (1927) p. 220—226.

32 לקוטי תפלות לנורא תהלות printed first at Brazlav 1822.

33 Zohar II, 63b and III, 69b; cf. also Joseph Gikatila שארי אורה (Offenbach 1715) f. 40b ff.

34 Cf. H. G. Enelow, Kawwana, the Struggle for Inwardness in Judaism, in Studies in Jewish Literature issued in honour of Professor K. Kohler (1913), p. 82—107, and my own exposition Der Begriff der Kawwana in der alten Kabbala, in MGWJ vol. 78 (1934) p. 492—518.

35 See my article Buch Bahir, in EJ vol. III col. 969—979.

36 H. Cohen, Ethik des reinen Willens; second edition (1907) p. 452.

37 Cf. Jacob Lauterbach's studies: The Ritual for the Kapparot-Ceremony, in Jewish Studies in Memory of George A. Kohut (1935) p. 413—422; Tashlik, a Study in Jewish Ceremonies, in Hebrew Union College Annual vol. XI (1936) p. 207—340.

38 The single case of a woman, Hannah Rachel "the Maid of Ludomir," who became the spiritual leader, or Zaddik, of a Hasidic community (in the middle of the nineteenth century), constitutes no convincing evidence of the contrary. Cf. about her S. A. Horodezky, Leaders of Hasidism (1928) p. 113ff.

NOTES TO LECTURE II

MERKABAH MYSTICISM AND JEWISH GNOSTICISM

1 אגרת רב שרירא ed. B. M. Lewin p. 109—110, Graetz vol. V, p. 235.

2 A. Neubauer in REJ vol. XXIII (1893) p. 256—264; D. Kaufmann,

Gesammelte Schriften vol. III (1915) p. 5—11. In the earliest extant text he is described as follows, איש חמודים מארץ בגדים.. ושמו אהרן, סבר בסברון, עוצר חרון מניני ישיני חברון והוא כבני מרון למלך אדירירון.

3   The real Ishmael was still a boy at the time of the destruction of the temple, and it is his father Elisha whom he himself describes as High Priest (*Tosefta Halla* I, 10). Apparently this description was early made to refer to the son. The Babylonian Talmud in two places makes a mystical reference to Ishmael. There is no reason apart from prejudice to follow Zunz and Bacher (Aggada der Tannaiten vol. I p. 267ff) in assuming that these passages are subsequent Gaonic interpolations. The fact that the earliest Hekhaloth texts already make use of this Ishmael legend without troubling to introduce it proves that it was then already an established tradition. This transformation of Ishmael into a High Priest and at the same time a mystic seems likely to have become part of the Talmudic tradition already in the third or fourth century. In *Berakhoth* 7a this already legendary Ishmael is made to say: "Once I entered the holiest of holies in order to burn the incense. Then it happened to me that I saw Akhtariel Jah, the Lord of Hosts, sitting on a high and sublime throne, and he spoke to me thus: Ishmael, my son, give me your praise (or blessing)." While the Hekhaloth tracts visualize Akhtariel on the throne of the Merkabah, Ishmael has a vision of him in the holiest of holies in the Temple. The addition of יה יהוה צבאות to the name entirely accords with the traditional usage of the Greater Hekhaloth. There too we read זהרריאל יהוה אלהי ישראל (chapter III, 2) or טעז"ש יהוה אלהי ישראל (chapter I, 1, according to the Mss.) The archons too, in addition to their angelic names, bear the name יהוה "by the name of their King," cf. Odeberg p. 29, in the commentary to the Hebrew Enoch, chapter 10. Further, *Berakhoth* 51a relates three things which Ishmael heard from the "Prince of the Divine Face" Suriel— not from Metatron, as later Gaonic additions would have it! At an early date Ishmael was already regarded as the "type of the martyr" (Bacher loc. cit.). This may explain his appearance as an apocalyptic visionary in several apocalypses from the Hekhaloth circle. His real position as a disciple of Rabbi Nehuniah ben Hakanah, which however was confined to the Halakhah, received a mystical projection among the members of this circle. Similarly, his controversial attitude toward Akiba in the Halakhic discussions now received a mystic aureole in the Hekhaloth tracts.

4   See Sh. Spiegel, in Journal of Biblical Literature Vol. LIV part III (1935) p. 164-65.

5   According to S. Liebermann, מדרשי תימן (1940) p. 16, this was already attested to in the third century by Origenes in his preface to the Song of Solomon.

6   For this particularly important text see G. H. Box' Introduction and Translation: The Apocalypse of Abraham, London (1919).

7   Baldensperger, Die messianisch-apokalyptischen Hoffnungen des Judentums, p. 68.

8 Thus it is said in Midrash Mishle to Prov. XX, 2 כל מה שברא בעולמו, קבעו
בכסא. Altogether, correspondences such as that between the Throne and
Creation play a large part in the more mystical Midrashim. Instances are
the parallel between the World and Man (macrocosm and microcosm), or
between the Tabernacle and the World. The microcosm motif is most clearly
expressed in the passage in the *Aboth de-Rabbi Nathan,* chapter 31, where
it says כל מה שברא הקב"ה בארץ ברא באדם. The conception of the Tabernacle
as a parallel to Creation, such as it is found in the *Midrash Tadshe,* chap.
II, appears to belong to the later Midrash and to have come from Southern France.

9 Material on the mysticism of the Throne from pseudepigrapha and
Midrashim (but not from the writings of the Merkabah school) is to be
found in Strack and Billerbeck, Kommentar zum Neuen Testament aus
Talmud und Midrasch, Vol. I (1922), p. 974—978.

10 See Ph. Bloch in Festschrift fuer Jakob Guttmann (1915) p. 113—123.
An analysis of the names—not explained by Bloch—of the Roman king
and his wife in the apocalypse which form the second major part of the
Greater Hekhaloth reveals a curious detail: If one reads them as cryptograms according to the א"ת ב"ש alphabet, i.e. if one substitutes for each
letter the corresponding one by counting backward from the end of the
alphabet, one obtains words which, though corrupted, clearly reveal themselves as Germanic names by the end syllables - ich and - ut. And in fact
one also finds cryptograms of awkward words in other parts of the manuscripts of this text. See also the text of this apocalypse derived from such a
manuscript in Naphtali Elhanan Bacharach's *Emek Hamelekh* (1648) f.
39c ff.

11 Important and as yet unedited material on the subject of Merkabah
mysticism is to be found above all in the Hebrew manuscripts of the Bod-
leian Library, Oxford, No. 1531; British Museum 752; Munich State Library 22 and 40; JThS, New York, 828.

12 3 Enoch, or The Hebrew Book of Enoch, edited and translated by
Hugo Odeberg, 1928. Unfortunately the correct text has to be worked out
with the aid of the critical apparatus, since the edition is based on a particularly bad manuscript. The very elaborate commentary, however, is on
the whole valuable.

13 The "Greater Hekhaloth" have been edited as היכלות רבתי in Jellinek's
Beth Ha-Midrash III (1855) p. 83—108, and from a different manuscript
as פרקי היכלות by S. A. Wertheimer, Jerusalem (1889). Both texts are extremely bad. A new edition is being prepared by me on the basis of the
Mss. and the printed material available to me. The "Lesser Hekhaloth",
היכלות זוטרתי are to be found, as Jellinek has already perceived (preface to
Beth Ha-Midrash IV, 44), in the Hebrew manuscript 1531 of the Bodleiana
in Oxford, fol. 38a—46a. Parts therefrom have been printed, without being
recognized as such, from a Ms. of the Musajoff collection in Jerusalem, in

the compilation מרכבה שלמה Jerusalem (1922) fol. 6a—8b. Here again the text is very bad but can be corrected from the manuscripts. Odeberg (Introduction p. 104) mistakenly gives the name of "Lesser Hekhaloth" to a piece which has nothing to do with them but like the former has appeared in the compilation מרכבה שלמה and belongs to the "Mystery of Sandalphon," from a book called *Merkabah Rabba.*

14   In the "lesser Hekhaloth," Enoch-Metatron is not mentioned at all, in the "Greater Hekhaloth" only once, and not in one of the oldest pieces. The fact is that the system of these tracts has no room for him. In the Book of Enoch (ch. X) a belated and somewhat artificial attempt is made to find a place for him at the entrance to the seventh palace, so as to establish a link with the older tracts. These early tracts contain a great deal more truly antique material of somewhat bizarre originality than the Book of Enoch which is more conventional both in subject-matter and style. Their references to the Metatron tradition (for details see further on) are not the source of the corresponding Talmudic passages, as Odeberg seems to have thought, but rather vice versa. The manner in which the legend of Metatron as the celestial scribe, as well as the entire Aggadah on Aher in *Hagigah* and the position of Metatron as the teacher of prematurely dead children in Paradise (*Abodah Zarah* 3b), is transformed in the tracts shows clearly that they belong to a much later phase of development.

15   It is true that here, too, additions were made at the beginning and the end of the main part of the old text, with the result that its antique and very characteristic style has become blurred. The Aramaic of the text is old and genuine, the dialect Babylonian. The hero is Akiba, while the "Greater Hekhaloth" give more prominence to Ishmael.

16   *J. Hagigah* II, 1: *Tosefta* to the same passage. לדרוש בכבוד אבינו שבשמים is employed as a synonym for לדרוש במעשה מרכבה, the term used in *Hagigah* 14b. כבוד as a theosophic term for the one who thrones on the Merkabah is fairly general in second century Rabbinical sources, see Michael Sachs' remarks on the subject in *Kerem Hemed* VII, 275, and Senior Sachs in *Ha-Tehiya* I, 22f. The use of phrases like (משנה) חס על כבוד קונו חגיגה ב׳, א), נושא את הכבוד (ספרא לויקרא א׳ א׳ ס׳ י"ב), התכבד בכבוד חי העולמים (ירושלמי חגיגה ב׳ ב׳). are proof of the existence of a quite definite terminology.

17   *Hagigah* 15b הניחו לזקן זה שראוי להשתמש בכבודי. The verb השתמש in the whole of this literature is a fixed term for "undertaking theurgical practices." אשתמש בתגא is explained already in the *Aboth de-Rabbi Nathan* as signifying "to make magical use of the name of God JHWH."

18   First used in the *Tosefta Megillah* IV, Ed. Zuckermandel p. 228. In *Megillah* 24b the Munich Ms. already reads הרבה צפו למרכבה ולא ראו אותה מימיהם. In the Hekhaloth tracts, mention is always made of צפיית המרכבה. Instead of כבוד one also often finds the term גאוה.

19 Originally probably in the *Aggadath Shir Ha-Shirim*, Ed. Schechter p. 13 הראה אותו חדרים שבמרום.

20 This passage (*Midrash Tanhuma*, Ed. Buber 1, 71a: ראה הקב"ה ואת חדרי המרכבה) has been drawn to my attention by Saul Liebermann. Of still more antique appearance is the formulation of an Aggadah on Simeon ben Azzai, Akiba's collaborator in the Merkabah studies, of which the oldest text is found in Levit. Rabba Par. XVI, 4. Here he is asked אמרו ליה שמא בחדרי המרכבה אתה עסוק. This reading, instead of the corrupted סדרי מרכבה in the prints, is borne out not only by the parallel in *Shir Ha-Shirim Rabba* 1, 10 but, according to Liebermann, by the good Mss. of Levit. Rabba investigated by him.

21 Ms. Oxford 1531f. 39b; מרכבה שלמה f. 6b: א"ר עקיבא באותה שעה שעליתי למרכבה נתתי סימן במבואות של רקיע יותר ממבואות של ביתי... באותה שעה שעליתי למרכבה יצתה בת קול מתחת כסא הכבוד.

22 The names of the archons which must be known in the ascent (which latter is mentioned first!) are, according to ch. XXII (Ed. Jellinek III, 99) different from those which one must know in descending.

23 This interpretation given by Bloch, Ginzberg and Abelson I regret to say I cannot share. Nowhere in all the texts is there ever any suggestion that the visionary himself drives in the Merkabah as though in a chariot. It is true that during the ascent from the sixth to the seventh palace there is a very vivid description of the way in which the celestial traveller passes the gate-keepers in a "chariot of radiance" קרון של נגה on his way to the higher sphere, but this "chariot" has nothing to do with the Merkabah. Also the verb *yarad* is not employed in this context.

24 Of the existence of a heretical Gnosis of a dualistic and antinomian character on the outskirts of Judaism there cannot be any doubt, to my mind. Surely these Gnostics and not the Jewish-Christians are the target of some of the numerous references to "Minim" מינים in the older Rabbinical literature on which, since the appearance of Graetz' Gnosticismus und Judenthum (1846), so many scholars have lavished a profusion of thought. I do not propose to dwell on this controversy which, like the voluminous literature on the subject of the Essenes, has become the happy hunting-ground of those who delight in hypotheses. Any reader can inform himself from the works of such writers as M. Friedlaender: Der vorchristliche juedische Gnosticismus (1898); Die religioesen Bewegungen innerhalb des Judentums im Zeitalter Jesu (1905); M. Joel: Blicke in die Religionsgeschichte (1880); A. Buechler (in Judaica, Festschrift fuer Hermann Cohen, 1912); and the same in MGWJ vol. 76 (1932) p. 412—456.

25 The most remarkable evidence of the author's strictly Halakhic attitude is the very detailed description (Ch. XVIII of the "Greater Hekhaloth") of the procedure by which the adepts recall their master Nehuniah ben Hakanah from his ecstasy to a normal frame of mind. Incidentally,

certain unusual expressions and ways of spelling in this piece are manifestly of Palestinian origin.

26   This is confirmed by a response of Sherira Gaon אוצר הגאונים למס'
חגיגה, חלק התשובות p. 12, and by one of Hai Gaon in שו"ת הגאונים ed.
Lyck no. 31.

27   Ms. Casanatense 179 f. 109; Oxford 1785 f. 281; Brit. Museum 822 f.
270—273. I have found another fragment of this text in the Taylor—
Schechter Collection from the Geniza, at Cambridge, (K 1, 84).

28   This is proved by F. Boll's remarks on the history of chiromancy in
the Graeco-Roman period, cf. Catalogus Codicum Astrologicorum vol. VII
p. 236—237.

29   Jamblichus, De Vita Pythagorica, chapter 17.

30   Cf. *Yebamoth* 120a in an interpretation given by Abbayi. The term
הכרת פנים occurs also in the response quoted in note 26. Harkavy has
questioned its authenticity (*Zikhron Larishonim* vol. IV p. XXVIII and
again in *Ha-Kedem* vol. III (1912) p. 198). His argument may be dismissed. He had of course no knowledge of the fact that a fragment of this
old הכרת פנים still exists.

31   Cf. Anz, Zur Frage nach dem Ursprung des Gnostizismus (1897) p.
9—58.

32   Particularly in chapters 15-23 of the "Greater Hekhaloth."

33   Cf. 14 אוצר הגאונים למס' חגיגה י"ד ע"ב, חלק התשובות עמ'

34   Dennys, The Folklore of China, p. 60—quoted by Otto Stoll, Suggestion und Hypnotismus in der Voelkerpsychologie (1904), p. 49—50.

35   Cf. *Berakhoth* 34b and *Abodah Zarah* 17a.

36   Cf. מרכבה שלמה f. 1b (bottom) שלא אשטף באש ובלחבת ובסופה ובסערה
המתחלכת עמך נורא ונשגב (in a fragment from a book called *Merkabah
Rabba*).

37   היכלות רבתי chapter XVII. Thus Celsus relates (Origenes, Contra Celsum VII, 40) that the members of the Gnostical sect known as Ophites
were compelled to learn the names of the "gate-keepers" laboriously by
heart.

38   אלפא ביתא דר' עקיבא in Jellinek's *Beth Ha-Midrash* vol. III p. 25. Cf.
also my remarks in Zeitschrift fuer die Neutestamentliche Wissenschaft
1931 p. 171—176.

39   We possess no less than four texts of the "Midrash of the Ten Martyrs"
מדרש אלה אזכרה representing four stages of progressive popularization.
Graetz, in a very scholarly article on the subject, has tried to substantiate
the utterly erroneous thesis that the "Alphabet of Rabbi Akiba" was the
chief source of the Hekhaloth literature, cf. MGWJ vol. 8 (1859) p. 67 ff.

40   *Hagigah* 15b: אף רבי עקיבא ביקשו מלאכי חשרת לדוחפו

41   היכלות רבתי chapter III, 4: וחאש חיוצא מן האדם חמסתקל חיא שורפת
אותו.

42   Ms. Oxford 1531 f. 45a (bottom) on the vision of the ruler of the first
door: כשראיתיו נשרפו ידיו (1) והייתי עומד בלא ידים ובלא רגלים

43   Ed. Box chapter XVII "fire came against us round about and a voice
was in the fire... and the high place on which we stood at one moment, rose
upright, but at another rolled downwards."

44   *Hagigah* 14b; *Tosefta* ed. Zuckermandel p. 234 where the decisive (second) sentence is missing.

45   "Paradise," as Joel has pointed out, could well be a Talmudical metaphor for Gnosis, because of the tree of knowledge (Gnosis!) therein, cf.
Manuel Joel, Blicke in die Religionsgeschichte I (1880) p. 163. Origen
(Contra Celsum VI, 33) relates that the Gnostical sect of the Ophites used
the same metaphor.

46   Joel, loc. cit. Graetz, Gnosticismus und Judentum (1846) p. 94—95,
and similar interpretations by other writers. Bacher, Aggada der Tannaiten, vol. I, 2nd edition, p. 333, although he accepts this interpretation
evidently sensed its weakness. A. Hoenig, Die Ophiten (1889) p. 94 has
justly stressed the absurdity of the explanation, but without offering a
better one.

47   Ms. Munich 22 f. 162b, an elaboration of the explanations put forward
in the היכלות זוטרתי (already quoted by Hai Gaon in this connection) and
in the היכלות רבתי chapter. 19. The Hebrew text of the passage reads as
follows: ואת מי שאינו ראוי לראות מלך ביפיו היו נותנין בלבו וכיון שאומרין
לו הכנס היה נכנס. מיד סוחטין אותו ומשליכין אותו לתוך ריגיון גחלין. ופתח
היכל הששי היח נראה כמי שטורדין בו מאה אלף אלפים רבי רבבות גלי מים ואין בו
אפילו מפה אחת של מים אלא מאויר זיו אבני שיש מהור שהיו סלולות בהיכל שהיה
זיו מראיהם גורא ממים והלא המשרתים עומדים כנגדו ואם אמר המים הללו מה טיבן ?
מיד רצין אחריו בסקילה ואומרין : ריקה ממעשיו, אין אתה צופה בעיניך, שמא
מזרעם של מנשקי עגל אתה ואין אתה ראוי לראות מלך ביפיו. אם כן בת קול יוצא
מהיכל השביעי והכרוז יוצא מלפניך (?מלפניו) ותוקע ומריע לומר לחם (למלאכי
החבלה !) : יפה אמרתם בודאי מזרעם של מנשקי עגל הוא ואינו ראוי לראות מלך
ביופיו. ואינו זז משם עד שמפצעין את ראשו במגזרי ברזל (סנהדרין פ"ב, ע"ב).
כסימן הזה יהיה לדורות לא יתעה אדם בפתח ההיכל הששי ויראה זיו אויר האבנים
וישאל ויאמר מים הם שלא יביא עצמו לידי סכנה. מפני שאפילו אינו ראוי לראות
ואינו שואלן על אויר זיו אבני שיש מהור שהיו סלולות בהיכל, ולא היו מכלין
אותו אלא דנין אותו לכף זכות.

48   M. Ninck, Die Bedeutung des Wassers im Kult und Leben der Alten
(1921) p. 112—117, mentions several examples of the fact that it was
possible in a state of ecstasy to experience a feeling of going under or being
drowned in whirling water.

49   Cf. Papyri Graecae Magicae, ed. Preisendanz I (1928) p. 92—96, and
Albrecht Dieterich, Eine Mithraslithurgie, 3rd ed. (1923).

50   The first to recognize the Greek element in an important passage of
the "Greater Hekhaloth" was M. Schwab in the Introduction to his Vocab-
ulaire de l'Angélologie (1897), p. 13. His reading and translating of the
only slightly corrupted Hebrew transcription was, however, quite fantastic.
"L'ange Dumiel portier de l'enfer addresse au survenants ces paroles:
ἀρίστην ἡμέρα[ν] ἀρίστην κανάβινον σεμνό[ν], εἰρήνη אריסמאן ומירא אסמאן
וכנפינן צמנש ערנח... En ce bon jour, à ce squelette vénérable (!!) paix."
Now Domiel, so far from being the gate-keeper of Hell in the Hekhaloth-
tracts is the guardian of the entrance to the sixth palace in the seventh
heaven. The correct reading has been given and interpreted by my colleague Johanan Lewy in Tarbiz vol. XII (1941) p. 164. Domiel says to
the Gnostic: ἀρίστην ἡμέραν, ἀρίστη εὐχήν (or rather, if the text is properly
corrected, τύχην), φῆνον σημεῖον, εἰρήνη. Instead of צמנש one should read
צמיון if the proper graphical changes are made. The phrase now reads:
"Best day, best luck; show [me] your sign [viz. the seal]. Peace!" Thereupon, i. e. after he has seen the seal, Domiel "receives him in the friendliest
manner and sits down next to him on a bench of pure stone" (chapter
XIX, end). Such remains of Greek formulae are to be found also in five
other places in היכלות רבתי. Domiel, another very curious detail, was apparently conceived originally as ruler of the four elements. Chapter XVIII,
6, upon the first mention of Domiel and the seal which is to be shown to
him, asks: "Is he called Domiel? Is not his name אביר גהידרהים?" This is
interpreted by Lewy, rightly as I think, as an only slightly corrupted
transcription of the Greek names of the four elements: ἀήρ, γῆ, ὕδωρ, πῦρ.
אביר is the common Palestinian transcription of אויר ἀήρ, as Saul Liebermann, ירושלמי כפשוטו I p. 221 has shown. הים (thus in the Ms. of the
JThS in New York, instead of the יהם of the Ed. Jellinek) is a graphically
easily explained variation of פיר.

51   This has been justly stressed by G. H. Box in his introduction to
R. H. Charles' Translation of the Ascension of Isaiah (1919) p. XXII: In
4 Ezra VII, 90—98 we find a description of seven "ways" or stages appor-
tioned to souls after death.

52   Hagigah 12b, following a tradition dating from the third century A. D.

53   ראיות יחזקאל published by Jacob Mann in הצופה לחכמת ישראל V (1921)
p. 256—264. Preisendanz has published (in Papyri Graecae Magicae vol.
II (1931) p. 160) the inscription of an amulet from the fifth century which
seems to reflect Jewish ideas. Here we find the names of six heavens and of
their respective archons.

54   In his book (which appeared 1912), Abelson paid no attention to the
kabbalistic conceptions of the Shekhinah.

55   Odeberg, 3 Enoch, Introduction p. 106 quotes היכולת רבתי chapter 26

אתה הר בלבת דינורין ושלהביות is But the correct reading .אתה דר בלב האדם
(Ms. David Kaufmann 238 in Budapest, and Ms. New York J Th S 828).

56 היכלות רבתי chapter 14. In the ברייתא דמעשה בראשית we encounter some
attempts to give a closer description of this "intersection" of the seven
heavens and the seven earths.

57 זהרריאל is quite common in the "Greater Hekhaloth" (corrupted into
זבודיאל and זבוריאל). אכתריאל is to be found already in *Berakhoth* 7a.
אדירירון occurs in the "Lesser Hekhaloth" Ms. Munich 22 f. 163a. Their
meaning is quite obvious. The full formula consists always of the mystical
Name plus י״י אלחי ישראל.

58 מוטרסייא or מטרוסייא is very common in the Hekhaloth texts. It corresponds exactly to names like 'Αρβαθιάω in the Papyri Graecae Magicae.
The Greek magician uses the Hebrew word ארבעת, whereas the Jewish
mystic uses the Greek term τετράς, similar to the predilection for Greek
formulae mentioned in note 50.

59 Cf. שרי גאוה ויראה ורעד ס' 1b, מרכבה שלימה.

60 Cf. especially היכלות רבתי chapters 3—4, 7—10, 24—26, and the
prayers and hymns which are printed at the end of ספר רזיאל Amsterdam
(1701) f. 37—40. Moreover, there is a great deal of unpublished material
of this genre.

61 Rudolf Otto, The Idea of the Holy, translated by John W. Harvey
(1923), chapter VI.

62 Cf. Philipp Bloch in MGWJ vol. 37 (1893) p. 259.

63 Loc. cit. p. 306.

64 Eleazar of Worms calls it שירת המלאכים (in Naftali Treves' commentary on the prayer-book, Thiengen 1560.)

65 היכלות רבתי chapter 26, altered in a few places in accordance with better readings in the Mss.

66 Bloch, loc. cit. p. 259.

67 היכלות רבתי chapter 24.

68 This has been proved in detail particularly by Bloch in his above-
mentioned article on the subject.

69 *Megillah* 18a and *Berakhoth* 33b.

70 Bloch, loc. cit. p. 262ff. He overlooked the passage in *J. Berakoth* V,
end of Halakhah 3, בטיטה אשתתיק באופנייא which, of course, is not a later
addition, as Bloch has contended in his essay, Rom und die Mystiker der
Merkaba (Festschrift fuer J. Guttmann 1915) p. 113. Cf. also *Hullin* 91b
on the prayer of the angels called *Ofannim*.

71 Apocalypse of Abraham, chapters XVII and XVIII. The passage

quoted from the Greater Hekhaloth is from the beginning of chapter 9:
כקול מים ברעש נהרות, כגלי תרשיש שרוח דרומית טורדת בהן.

72 For comparison see the prayers in the so-called Liturgy of Mithras, and the prayer of the primordial man to the "Father of Light", in Ch. Baynes, A Coptic Gnostic Treatise (1933) p. 26—36.

73 Thus for instance the words זיהיון splendour, סיגוב exaltation.

74 Cf. the text in Baer's עבודת ישראל p. 547—552.

75 Moses Taku in כתב תמים quoted by Baer p. 547, contends that the heretics forged it.

76 *Beth Ha-Midrash* vol. III p. 161—163. Ms. 828 of the JThS in New York includes this piece as part of the text of היכלות רבתי.

77 This is not a verse from the Bible, but a formula of the Merkabah mystics, cf. פרקי היכלות ed. Wertheimer ch. 31, where the text is deficient but can be completed from early quotations of this passage, such as Naftali Treves in his commentary to ברכו in the morning prayer.

78 מסכת היכלות § 7, in *Beth Ha-Midrash* vol. II, 45; 3 Enoch chapter 48 (Odeberg p. 155). 955 is the numerical value of the word חשמים, the final *Mem* representing the number 600. Another theory on 390 heavens in *Masekheth Derekh Erets* ed. Higger p. 294; ערוגת הבשם ed. Urbach p. 212; and Azriel פירוש האגדות ed. Tishbi p. 46.

79 היכלות רבתי chapters XVIII, 4 and XXI, 3.

80 האל... שהוא נעלם מעיני כל הבריות Ms. Oxford 1531f. 45b: היכלות זוטרתי ונסתר ממלאכי השרת ונגלה לו לר' עקיבא במעשה מרכבה.

81 The title has frequently been translated "Measure of the Height", קומה being used in the Biblical sense. This is wrong. *Komah* is used here in the sense it has in the Aramaic incantation texts where it simply signifies "body."

82 Cf. Salmon ben Yeruhim in his ס' מלחמות ח' ed. Davidson (1939) p. 114—124. Maimonides' responsum in תשובות הרמב"ם ed. Freimann p. 343; Moses Taku in *Otsar Nehmad* III p. 62.

83 We have the following texts: 1) in מרכבה שלימה f. 30a—33b; 2) ס' רזיאל 1701 f. 37a—38b and, with various different readings, in מרכבה שלימה f. 34a—40a; 3) Ms. Oxford 1791 f. 58—71 ספר הקומה in 12 chapters. Fragments of it are scattered also in the אותיות דר' עקיבא and other works of the Merkabah literature.

84 This formula is an imitation of the ending of the last treatise of the Babylonian Talmud, *Niddah*, where it is said כל השונה הלכות בכל יום מובטח לו שהוא בן העולם הבא.

85 Jehudah Halevi in הכוזרי ס' IV, 3 defends the *Shiur Komah* בעבור שיש בו מהכנס מוראו בנפשות!

86   The verse Psalm CXLV, 5 גדול אדונינו ורב כח was interpreted: The height of our Lord is 236, according to the numerical value of ורב כח.

87   מרכבה שלמה f. 38a.

88   Ibidem f. 37a.

89   Cf. Kropp, Einleitung in die Koptischen Zaubertexte (1930) p. 41. A kind of *Shiur Komah* mysticism is to be found also in the Coptic Gnostic Treatise translated by Charlotte Baynes p. 42: the hair of his head is the number of hidden worlds etc.

90   M. Gaster, Das Shiur Komah, in his Studies and Texts vol. II p. 1330 —1353, particularly p. 1344. Although mistaken in many particulars, Gaster has recognized the true Gnostical connotations of the *Shiur Komah*.

91   The connection between the speculations about the "body of truth" and the idea of the primordial man in Marcus' system is obvious.

92   Ms. Oxford 1531f. 40b: כביכול כמותנו הוא והוא גדול מכל וזהו כבודו שנסתר מפנינו.

93   For this reason, the phrase in some texts reads more fully: ...כל היודע. שבחו של הקב"ה שהוא מכוסה מן הבריות. Cf. also the same meaning of שבח in Gen. Rabba ed. Theodor p. 775.

94   גוף השכינה in אותיות דר' עקיבא on the letter חית; cf. also the quotation in ס' ערוגת הבשם ed. Urbach (1939) p. 127.

95   MGWJ vol. VIII p. 115ff, and similarly in his History of the Jews.

96   "Schahrastani's Religionspartheien und Philosophen-Schulen" translated by Haarbruecker vol. I (1850) p. 116, in his account of the *Mushabbiha*.

97   Ph. Bloch, Geschichte der Entwicklung der Kabbala kurz zusammengefasst (1894) p. 17.

98   3 Enoch ed. Odeberg chapter VII.

99   Ibid. chapter XV.

100   Ms. Oxford 1531 f. 137—145; 1539 f. 1—21; New York JThS Ms. Maggs 419 f. 66—70; Vatican. 228 f. 93—103 (the best manuscript.) Here we find the ideas of 1 Enoch, viz. a) that Azza and Azael betrayed God's secrets to man, b) their fall into the Tartarus (here the "Mountains of Darkness").

101   I have been unable to discover a source in the older literature for the scurrilous legend current in the Middle Ages of Enoch the shoemaker—a mythical Jacob Boehme!—who with every stitch connected the upper and lower world. The legend may or may not have grown out of Hasidic circles in mediaeval Germany. In a Ms. from the year 1458 (Paris, Bibl. Nat. 786 f. 109b) it is already mentioned as מצאתי כתוב. Odeberg, in his extensive study on the Enoch-Metatron legend in the introduction to his 3

Enoch, makes no mention of it. It is quoted by many 16th century Kabbalists.

102   The first writer who seems to have suspected the identity of Metatron and Yahoel is Box (in his introduction to the Apocalypse of Abraham
p. XXV). He has seen deeper than the author of the article on this Apocalypse in the EJ vol. I, 553.

103   In addition to lists given in Odeberg's edition chapter 48 (and in his
note p. 174) mention must be made of the list printed at the end of Abraham Hamoy's ס' בית דין (Livorno 1858) f. 196—201.

104   *Sanhedrin* 38, *Hagigah* 15a and *Abodah Zarah* 3b.

105   Odeberg, Introduction to 3 Enoch p. 189 has analyzed the Gnostic
references to the "little Jao" in the Coptic work Pistis Sophia.

106   The instances quoted from the earlier mystical texts by Odeberg p.
33 could easily be supported by other quotations. Of particular interest in
this connection would be a quotation from an 8th century Christian text in
Syriac which I have found in Bidez et Cumont, Les Mages Hellenisés II p.
115. It reads: בלחוד דין חרא מיתא אנא לעוהדנא אדוני קטן רבחילה דאדוני
גדול טועיי שכירתא דחלתא דבני ישראל. Even the plain spelling אדוני has its
justification in specific passages of the literature on the names of Metatron.
Cf. also J. Mann, Texts and Studies in Jewish History II p. 85 and 88, and
Gruenbaum's quotation from Mas'udi in ZDMG vol. XXX p. 272.

107   The Karaite author Kirkisani (beginning of the 10th century) quotes
the Talmudic passage (obviously *Sanhedrin* 38): קאלו פי אלתלמוד אן
מיטטרון הו י"י קטן. It is well possible that the name י"י קטן was deliberately eliminated from the Talmudic manuscripts because of its heretical
connotations.

108   Ms. British Museum, Margoliouth n. 752 f. 45b:שהיה יהואל על שם שם
רבו של אברהם אבינו והוא למד לאברהם אבינו כל התורה... יהואל הוא המלאך שקרא
למשה רבינו לעלות לשמים במסכת סנהדרין יש ואל משה אמר עלה אל י"י — אלי
מבעי ליה אלא עלה לאותו מלאך ששמו כשם רבו, א"ל יהו"ה, אותיות יהואל.

109   Cf. Odeberg p. 125—142: Origin of the *word* "Metatron", and also
Louis Ginzberg, Legends of the Jews vol. V p. 162.

110   Cf. היכלות רבתי chapter XXII and Odeberg to 3 Enoch ch. XVII,
p. 59.

111   מסכת היכלות ed. Jellinek in *Beth Ha-Midrash* vol. II p. 40—47.

112   *Midrash Mishle* ed. Buber f. 34a ff. In some instances I have corrected
the translation in accordance with the readings of the quotation found in
the Ms. of Azriel's פירוש האגדות in the Hebrew University Library f. 29b.
See also the enumeration of subjects in chapter 13 of the היכלות רבתי.

113 Pistis Sophia, chapter 139, in Carl Schmidt's German translation (1925). The Greek term is καταπετάσματα, whereas the Hebrew texts speak of the פרגוד של מקום or פרגוד.

114 3 Enoch, chapter 45; אותיות דר' עקיבא ed. Wertheimer p. 50; quotation from מדרש אבכי"ר in *Yalkut Shimoni* § 173; cf. also Rashi on *Yebamoth* 63b and *Baba Metsia* 59a.

115 Such apocalypses are: chapters 4—6 of the חושבנא דקצא; היכלות רבתי or פרקי ר' ישמעאל Ms. Enelow Memorial Collection 704 in the JThS in New York (= Parma 541 no. 21 and Oxford 2257), the greater part of which is incorporated in the version of the היכלות רבתי chapters 6—9 in the Ms. New York JThS 828; the entire literature around the figure of Zerubabel; the apocalypse of Simeon ben Yohai, etc.

116 היכלות רבתי chapter XVI.

117 *Midrash Tanhuma* ed. Buber V p. 31.

118 Cf. the Midrash in הלכות גדולות ed. Hildesheimer p. 223 quoted by L. Ginzberg, Legends of the Jews vol. VI p. 438, and Rashi's commentary on Canticles I 2. On the question of מעמי תורה cf. *Pesahim* 119a, *Sanhedrin* 21b, *Shabbath* 120a.

119 Cf. the valuable contribution of N. Glatzer, Untersuchungen zur Geschichtslehre der Tannaiten (Berlin 1932).

120 There are several fragments of the a) ברייתא דמעשה בראשית in בתי מדרשות 1701 f. 35a—36b; b) under the title סדר רבה דבראשית in ס' רזיאל ed. Wertheimer vol. I p. 1—31; c) in the supplement to Chone's רב פעלים (1894) p. 47—50; d) in L. Ginzberg's גנזי שכטר vol. I p. 182—187.

121 Cf. Mishnah *Hagigah* II, 1, and the Excerpta ex Theodoto of Clement of Alexandria ed. Casey (1934), § 78.

122 *Hagigah* 12b.

123 *Aboth de-Rabbi Nathan* chapter 37.

124 See note 35 to lecture I. I have published a German translation (Das Buch Bahir) in 1923.

125 The book is mentioned by Daniel אלקומסי, cf. J. Mann, Texts and Studies in Jewish History vol. II p. 76, 79, and by Hai Gaon, cf. אוצר הגאונים למסכת חגיגה, חלק התשובות p. 21.

126 A pupil of Eleazar of Worms quotes several passages from the ס' סוד הגדול in his commentary on the *Shiur Komah*, which I have discovered in a Ms. of the Angelica in Rome (Capua no. 27) and other Mss. (partly also in New York JThS 844 f. 100a—103a). Another fragment from the סוד הגדול is found in Ms. Milano 57 f. 20 in a piece called סוד המרכבה.

127 There exists a vast literature on this book, cf. my article Jezira in EJ vol. IX col. 104—111 where bibliographical notes are given. The English

translations and commentaries of W. Westcott (1893) and K. Stenring (1923) contain some rather fantastic passages.

128 L. Baeck has tried to show that the Book of Creation is a Jewish adaptation of certain basic ideas of Proclus, much as the books of Dionysius the pseudo-Areopagite are a Christian one, cf. MGWJ vol. 70 (1926) p. 371—376; vol. 78 (1934) p. 448—455. But his reasoning is not convincing, although his thesis looks fascinating enough. Some very remarkable similarities between the Book of Creation and early Islamic gnosticism have been pointed out by Paul Kraus, Jabir ibn Hayyan vol. II (Cairo 1942) p. 266-268.

129 Such words or phrases are גבולי אלכסון, ספירות בלימה, which make no sense in good Hebrew, or the use of עומק in the sense of *principle*. אותיות יסוד seems to imitate the double meaning of the Greek word *stoicheia*, meaning both elements and letters.

130 There is no lack of passages in the old Aggadah in which stress is laid on the link between Creation and the letters of the Torah, as well as on the secret powers of man. Cf. *Berakhoth* 55a, *Sanhedrin* 65b, *Aboth de-Rabbi Nathan* ch. 39 (ed. Schechter p. 116); *Midrash Tehillim* ed. Buber 17a. The ספר יצירה regards the letters and their combinations as cosmical powers—the fundamental hypothesis of every magical application of words and names.

131 The Hebrew phrase לבוש את השם corresponds to the Syriac one, Odes of Solomon XXXIX, 7 לבשו שמה דמרימא. Paul, Rom. XIII, 14 says similarly: put ye on the Lord Jesus Christ. This goes far beyond the corresponding use of לבש in the Hebrew Bible.

132 This rite is described in the ס' המלבוש found in many Mss., e. g. Sassoon 290 f. 311 f.; British Museum 752 (cf. details in Margoliouth's catalouge p. 38). Cf. also note 112 to lecture IV.

133 Cf. היכלות רבתי chapters 27—30 and some very valuable pieces in Ms. Oxford 1531.

134 The book חרבא דמשה has been first published by Gaster (1896). Most of these books are extant in Mss.: הבדלה דר' עקיבא; ס' הישר (cf. note 100); ספר; שמושי תחילים and שמושי תורה (Sassoon 290 p. 302ff); ספר הרזים המעלות שניתנו לאדם הראשון; תפלת רב המנונא סבא—all the latter in many manuscripts. On שמוש תהלים cf. M. Grunwald in Mitteilungen der Gesellschaft für jüdische Volkskunde no. X (1902) p. 81—98, particularly p. 91ff.; Joshua Trachtenberg, Jewish Magic and Superstition (1939) p. 108—113. A full German translation of the שמוש תהלים by G. Selig has appeared in Berlin 1788, an English translation by L. Weber [from Selig] in London s. a. [ca. 1880?].

135 Cf. Aptowitzer in Hebrew Union College Annual vol. VIII/IX p. 397, on *Pesikta Rabbati* ed. Friedmann, 185a.

136   Ms. Oxford 1531 f. 52a: א"ר ישמעאל שאלתי לר' עקיבא כמה שעור בין
גשר לגשר ? א"ל ר"ע ישרות וחסידות בלבביך, וידעת כמה שעור בשמים. אמר לו :
כשעליתי בהיכל ראשון חסיד הייתי, בהיכל ב' טהור הייתי, בהיכל ג' ישר הייתי,
בהיכל ד' תמים הייתי, בהיכל ה' הגעתי קדושה לפני מלכי המלכים ב"ה, בהיכל ו'
אמרתי קדושה לפני מי שאמר ויצר וצוה כל הבריות שלא ישחיתוני מלאכי השרת,
בהיכל ז' עמדתי בכל כחי נרתעתי ונזדעזעתי בכל איברוי ואמרתי : אל חי וקיים
לאשר יצרת שמים וארץ זולתך אין צור לעד, זכרך יפארו גדודי מעלה, מעשה ידיך
בתבל ארצך, האל הגדול יוצר הכל אדיר בגדולה אהוב בגבורה מודים לפניך גבורי כח
שעמלך לפניך באמת וצדק, צדק תעשה בעולמך ובצדקת שמך תציל אותי וברכת כבודך
אגדיל לעד. ברוך אתה י"י אדיר בחדרי גדולה.

137   Jos. Stoffels, Die Mystische Theologie Makarius des Aegypters (1908)
p. 79. The soul is pictured as the Throne of God in Spanish Kabbalism, cf.
Tikkune Zohar (1558) f. 3b: זכאה איהו מאן דאשלים נשמתיה לשריא ביה שם
יהו"ח ועביד ליה כרסיא לגביה.

138   *Gen. Rabba* ed. Theodor p. 475, 793, 983.

NOTES TO LECTURE III

HASIDISM IN MEDIAEVAL GERMANY

1   Cf. A. Epstein ר' שמואל החסיד in *Hagoren* IV (1903) p. 81—101.

2   Cf. M. Guedemann, Geschichte des Erziehungswesens und der Cultur der
Juden im Mittelalter vol. I (1880) p. 153 ff; Jekutiel Kamelhar, ס' חסידים
הראשונים (1917); J. Freimann, מבוא לספר חסידים (1924). Av Aptowitzer,
מבוא לספר ראבי"ה (1938) p. 343—350, who also supplies some interesting
new data on Jehudah the Hasid.

3   Apart from the literature mentioned in the foregoing note, there is a
rather uncritical monograph by Israel Kamelhar, רבינו אלעזר מגרמיזא הרוקח
(1930). Concerning the year of Eleazar's death cf. Aptowitzer p. 317.

4   Cf. Bruell in Jahrbuecher fuer juedische Geschichte vol. IX p. 23.
Kamelhar p. 54 suggests that R. Senior, who transmits this "tradition",
was Jehudah's contemporary in Speyer.

5   There are three versions of these legends: a) a Hebrew one, described
by Bruell, Jahrbuecher vol. IX (1889) p. 20—45; b) מעשה נסים by Juspa
Shamash of Worms (1604—1678) representing the local tradition of
Worms, published (Amsterdam 1696) in Yiddish; c) the מעשה בוך Basle
(1602) no. 158—182, cf. Ma'aseh Book, translated by Moses Gaster (1934),
and Meitlis, Das Ma'assebuch (1933).

6   The *Sefer Hasidim* is extant in two versions, a shorter one published in
print a number of times, and a more detailed one published (1891) by
Wistinetzki. Quotations are from the latter, in accordance with the sequence of paragraphs.

7 Baer, המגמה הדתית והחברתית של ספר חסידים, in *Zion* vol. III (1938) p. 1—50. The objections to this view raised in Urbach's preface to his edition of ערוגת הבשם (1939)—to be found only in some of the copies—have failed to convince me.

8 This question was raised first by Guedemann op. cit. vol. I, who devoted three chapters (V—VII) of his valuable book to the *Sefer Hasidim*.

9 Guedemann, op. cit. p. 158.

10 Cf. note 2 on the second lecture.

11 Published by A. Neubauer, Mediaeval Jewish Chronicles vol. II p. 111—132. A critical edition by B. Klar has recently appeared. (Jerusalem 1945).

12 ס' חכמוני published by D. Castelli, Firenze (1880). On Donnolo cf. Cassuto's article in EJ vol. V.

13 ערוגת הבשם ed. E. Urbach, vol. I, Jerusalem (1939).

14 Cf. A. Marx in *Hatsofeh* vol. V p. 195.

15 Ms. of the Landesbibliothek in Fulda, cf. Weinberg in Jahrbuch der Juedisch-Literarischen Gesellschaft vol. XX p. 283—284.

16 Cf. Scholem in *Tarbiz* II p. 244 and 514; Assaf in *Zion* V p. 117 and 124. Assaf's identification of "the prophet" referred to in the document which I have quoted above with R. Ezra is undoubtedly justified.

17 Cf. Guedemann op. cit., chapter VII. A more recent attempt to analyze these elements has been made by J. Trachtenberg, Jewish Magic and Superstition (New York 1939). The material of this work has been collected chiefly from the literature of the German Hasidim or from that influenced by them.

18 Cf. חכמת הנפש, Lemberg (1876), f. 14c, 17c, 18a, 20c.

19 ברייתא דיוסף בן עוזיאל and a prayer ascribed to him, cf. A. Epstein in *Hahoker* II (1894) p. 41—48.

20 Cf. A. Epstein in MGWJ vol. 37 (1893) p. 75—78, and N. Wieder in Saadya Studies ed. E. Rosenthal (Manchester 1943) p. 256 who quotes a passage from Eleazar of Worms on Saadia as being בקי בסודות הרבה מאד

21 Cf. A. Marx in *Hatsofeh* vol. V p. 198. Mystical commentaries composed by this Rabbi have been preserved also in Ms. Adler 1161 in New York JThS f. 27a and (different content) Oxford 1816 f. 102b.

22 *Sefer Hasidim* § 212 and Wistinetzki's note who quotes the סבוב ר' פתחיה. But § 630 contains Hai Gaon's response on the arrival of the Messiah.

23 In his valuable essay החסידות האשכנזית בימי הבינים which appeared in *Hatsefirah* (1917), especially §§ 10 and 14.

24   *Sefer Hasidim* § 359.

25   Cf. §§ 331, 335, 424, 555, 591, 879—a list which might be lengthened ad libitum. Eleazar's ס' חכמת הנפש abounds in such eschatological material.

26   Cf. especially in ס' חכמת הנפש.

27   *Sefer Hasidim* § 1056.

28   Cf. A. Marx מאמר על שנת הגאולה in *Hatsofeh* vol. V p. 194—202.

29   ס' חכמת הנפש f. 3c: the סוד הייחוד is mentioned in addition to סוד מעשה דע כי כל חיודע סוד חכמת הנפש ידע and בראשית סוד המרכבה. Eleazar says: סוד הייחוד (ibid. f. 3d).

30   Eleazar of Worms in ס' סודי רזייא printed in *Sefer Raziel* (1701) f. 7b speaks on the סוד המצוות as one of the "three mysteries". Cf. *Sefer Hasidim* § 1447 on טעמי תורה. Cf. also note 118 on the second lecture.

31   One can safely say that at least half of the literature of German Hasidism is devoted to Scriptural exegesis.

32   ס' חכמת הנפש f. 24d. Eleazar of Worms makes use of the *Gematria* דורות=קוץ ודרדר. Cf. also *Sefer Hasidim* § 1049.

33   Guedemann op. cit. p. 175.

34   This legend is quoted in ס' עמק המלך (Amsterdam 1648), f. 15a of the preface, from a mystical commentary on Psalm 150 written by Avigdor Kara, a 14th century writer who combined Hasidism and Kabbalism.

35   Cf. L. Gulkowitsch, Die Bildung des Begriffes *Hasid* I (Tartu 1935). where only the Talmudic usage of the term is more closely analyzed. Cf. also Wistinetzki's note to § 975 of the *Sefer Hasidim.*

36   The bulk of the following analysis of *Hasiduth* was written before Baer's article (note 7) was published. Proceeding from different starting points, we often arrived at the same conclusions. I wish to acknowledge my debt to Simhoni's analysis, although I disagree with him on several major points.

37   This is quoted from Eleazar's writings in Menahem Zioni's mystical commentary on the Torah (written about 1460), Cremona (1560) f. 20c.

38   Eleazar's הלכות הכבוד (published under the wrong title סודי רזייא) ed. Kamelhar (1936) p. 39.

39   *Sefer Hasidim* §§ 861, 984, 986.

40   Ibid. §§ 978—980.

41   Ibid. § 975. Cf. also the anecdote in § 860. There may be, perhaps, some connection between these traits of Hasidism and the older Palestinian movement of the אבלי ציון, "the mourners of Zion" of whose adherents similar descriptions are given in the *Pesikta Rabbati* ch. 34.

42   Ibid. § 976.

43   Ibid. § 119.

44   Ibid. § 977.

45   Ibid. §§ 987, 1979.

46   Cf. the passages quoted by Wistinetzki in his note to § 975.

47   On this point, I agree entirely with Baer's views in chapter IV of his essay, and disagree with Urbach's criticism (cf. note 7).

48   Cf. Guedemann op. cit. p. 154.

49   Baer, loc. cit. p. 34; *Sefer Hasidim* § 1005.

50   Baer p. 12.

51   I owe this remark to Simhoni's essay. Aptowitzer maintains that Jehudah wrote גם ספרים בהלכה but there is very meagre proof for this contention. The eight pages on *Shehita* in a Paris Ms. are not a "book", and there is no proof that they contain anything novel from the Halakhic point of view.

52   These הלכות חסידות and the הלכות תשובה following them were also printed separately several times.

53   Cf. *Sefer Raziel* (Ed. 1701) f. 7b and 9a.

54   Eleazar of Worms הלכות חסידות in the paragraph called שורש האהבה.

55   Cf. the passages quoted by Guedemann p. 160.

56   אמונות ודעות 'X,4. Such erotic imagery for Israel's love for God already occurs in a famous passage of the Talmud, Tr. *Yoma* f. 54a.

57   Cf. Rodkinsohn, תולדות בעלי שם טוב (1876) p. 96 from the כתר שם טוב. In ed. Podgorze (1898) f. 6b the passage is given in a much briefer form.

58   Cf. *Sefer Raziel* f. 8b (from Eleazar's סודי רזיא) and *Sefer Hasidim* § 984.

59   A. Jellinek, Beiträge zur Geschichte der Kabbala II p. 45 quotes the Hebrew text. He did not remark that the core of the story is told as a Sufic anecdote in Bahya ibn Pakuda חובות הלבבות ch. V, 5 (ed. Stern 1854 f. 74a/b). Eckhart, Sermones ed. Benz (1937) p. 69 has the same definition of equanimity (aequaliter se habere) as the true perfection of man when he may set out to "unbe" (*longe fieri*, in his German sermons: entwerden).

60   Ms. Vatican. 266 f. 73b. In the Tibbonian translation of Saadia's work (ed. Leipzig p. 88) this point is not brought out clearly, for it refers not to the חסיד but to the עובד. The Ms. reads:

החסיד הוא שנהג כל ימי חייו לעשות מצוה אחת ולקיימה כל ימיו ואעפ"י שהוא
מוסיף ומחסר בשמירת מצוות אחרות אבל המצוה ההיא לא חיסר שמירתה מעודו...
אבל מי שהוא מתהפך בכל יום ממצוה למצוה לעשותה ולשמור אותה ולעבוד אותה
אינו נקרא חסיד.

61 פירוש הרמב"ם למס' אבות, פ"ה, ז'

62 Cf. Baer loc. cit. p. 7.

63 *Sefer Hasidim* § 80. On the Hasid in the brothel cf. *Aboth de-Rabbi Nathan* ed. Schechter f. 19a.

64 All the magical texts of the 13th and 14th centuries are already full of references to Jehudah Hasid as a hero of magic. Cf. also עמק המלך 'ס f. 142a on his magical powers, quoted in the name of Nahmanides!

65 Cf. my article "Golem" in EJ vol. VII col. 501—507. My theory has been accepted and elaborated by B. Rosenfeld, Die Golemsage (1934) p. 1—35.

66 In Eleazar's voluminous work *Sode Razaya* "The Secrets of the Mysteries," preserved in Mss. Brit. Mus. 737, Munich 81 etc., the first part of which is included in the *Sefer Raziel*, (Amsterdam 1701) f. 7b—24a.

67 Cf. the literature quoted in my above-mentioned article col. 503. The purpose of these magical ceremonies comes out very clearly in a recipe which I have found in several Mss. (Casanatense 197 f. 85a; Vatican. 528 f. 71b etc.).

68 Chayim Bloch, The Golem, legends of the Ghetto of Prague, which has appeared also in an English translation (1925), purports to be translated from a manuscript "edited about 300 years ago." As a matter of fact, the book was written by one Y. Rosenberg around the year 1908 and contains not ancient legends but modern fiction.

69 מור אורח חיים סי' קי"ג. The author quotes this in the name of his brother Yehiel.

70 On Gematria and its methods cf. S. A. Horodezky in EJ vol. VII col. 170—179.

71 סוד התפלות by Eleazar of Worms is still extant in several manuscripts, e.g. Paris 772. A considerable part of it has been incorporated, in the form of quotations, in Naftali Treves' commentary on the prayers, Thiengen 1560. This book is a veritable storehouse of Hasidic traditions. In addition, there are quite a number of other writings on the mysticism of prayer.

72 Guedemann, op. cit. p. 160. The simile of the ladder also occurs in Treves' commentary (see last note), signature I ס col. b, in connection with the theory of mystical *Kawwanah*.

73 Cf. Gross in MGWJ vol. 49 (1905) p. 692—700.

74 כתב תמים in *Otsar Nehmad* III (1860) p. 84.

75 שאלות ותשובות מן השמים printed several times (with a commentary, Cracow 1895). Cf. also Steinschneider in Hebraeische Bibliographie vol. XIV (1874) p. 122—124.

76 Many of these recipes are collected in Abraham Hamoy's לדרש אלהים.

77 Eleazar of Worms in his פירוש המרכבה Ms. Paris 850 f. 47b: כן הגיד
לי מורי שפעם אחת עמד בבית הכנסת הוא ואביו והיה צלוחית מלא שמן ומים תלוי
בפניהם והיה החמה זורחת על אותו צלוחית והיה יוצא ממנו זוהר שאין כמותו
ואמר לו אביו : בני תן לבך לזה הזוהר כי כן ענין הזוהר של החשמל.
In a Ms. on קבלה מעשית belonging to the late A. Z. Schwarz, I found:
אלו החרוזים שמע ר' שמואל משפירא בשעה שעלה לרקיע.

78 Cf. H. Tykocinski, Die gaonaeischen Verordnungen (1929) p. 100, 174.

79 Cf. Baer's essay p. 18 and the literature quoted by him.

80 Cf. *Berakhoth* 56a; *Rosh ha-Shanah* 16b; *Sanhedrin* 37b. Jacob Anatoli regarded this form of penitence as unJewish, cf. Enelow's note to his
edition of מנורת המאור III p. 116.

81 Cf. *Sefer Hasidim* §§ 37—53; Eleazar's הלכות תשובה and חטאים יורת 'ס;
Israel Nakawa מנורת המאור ed. Enelow vol. III p. 113—119. Sometimes
these "Halakoth" on penitence are called ספר הכפרות (Ms. Adler 900 f.
128—131, in JThS).

82 *Sefer Hasidim* § 1556.

83 מאירת עינים 'ס Ms. Munich 17 f. 163a.

84 *Responsa* of Jacob Weil No. 12; *Responsa* of Israel Bruna No. 265.

85 We are still in possession of some valuable tracts which represent a
blend of Hasidic and Kabbalistic theology, e. g. in the Mss. British Museum
752 and Adler 1161, dating mostly from the 13th and 14th cent.

86 In particular there is an abundance of new material on angelology in
the writings of the Hasidim.

87 *Sefer Raziel* (1701) f. 8b.

88 Cf. *Sefer Hasidim* § 549 which should be compared with corresponding
formulas in Bahya ben Asher's כד הקמח s. v. אמונה and s. v. השגחה. He
quotes in this connection the poetic formula רחוק רחוק משמי שמים וקרוב
קרוב משארי.

89 הבורא קרוב לכל יותר מגוף p. 9: (1862) 27 כוכבי יצחק in שערי הסוד
לנשמה; cf. also סודי רזייא ed. Kamelhar p. 37.

90 On the שיר הייחוד (printed in every *Siddur*) cf. Baer, עבודת ישראל
p. 133ff.; A. Berliner, Der Einheitsgesang 1910. The passage quoted in the
text is found in this form in Moses Taku's כתב תמים cf. *Otsar Nehmad* III
p. 81. Jehudah's commentary is already quoted in a piece סוד המרכבה
dating from the 13th century, Ms. Ambrosiana 57f. 19a/b.

91 Bloch in MGWJ vol. 19 (1870) p. 451—54;Zunz, Gesammelte Schriften
vol. III p. 233 ff.; Berliner op. cit.

92 De Divisione Naturae, liber V, 8 (Patrol. Latina vol. 122 p. 876): "erit enim Deus omnia in omnibus, quando nihil erit nisi solus Deus." Cf. I Cor. XV, 28.

93 Ms. British Museum 752 f. 78b: והוא באויר העולם אחד שהוא מלא כל אויר העולם והוא בתוך כל דבר שבעולם ואין דבר ממצעו ומתווכו וכל דבר בו והוא רואה כל דבר כי כולו ראייה ואין לו עינים לראות בהם, לפיכך יש לו עצמו בתוך לראות כח. How Xenophanes' famous saying that God οὖλος ὁρᾷ came to the knowledge of the Hasidic author I do not know. Perhaps he found it somewhere in Saadia.

94 Saadya, Commentaire sur le Séfer Yesira... publié et traduit par M. Lambert (1891) p. 19ff, and Jehudah ben Barzilai's פירוש ספר יצירה (1885) p. 340.

95 *Otsar Nehmad* III p. 82: יכולין לומר שעבדו הבורא הנמצא בכל.

96 Berliner op. cit. p. 8, 14.

97 This is to be found in a very interesting explanation of the Sefiroth, in Ms. British Museum 752 f. 41a. God is called נשמה לנשמה for—says the author—מאחר שהנשמה נאצלה מאור ראשונה ודבוקה לבורא ונקראת בינה א"כ אז הקב"ה בנשמה וזהו והוא באחד ומי ישיבנו ונפשו אותה ויעש פי' היה לו לומר והוא אחד ומי ישיבנו. מאי באחד? אלא הוא נשמה לנשמה וזהו כי י"י אלהיך בקרבך אל גדול ונורא—בקרבך ממש והמבין יבין. This last remark proves that the author was fully aware of the implications of his statement!

98 C. Siegfried, Philo von Alexandria als Ausleger des Alten Testaments (1875) p. 223.

99 The chief sources of this theosophy are, apart from the Hasidic books mentioned above, Eleazar's שערי הסוד והיחוד והאמונה published by Jellinek in כוכבי יצחק No. 27 (1862) p. 7—15 and his treatise עשר הוויות in several Mss., e. g. Munich 285.

100 Cf. Aptowitzer מבוא לס' ראבי"ה p. 345 who also corrects Epstein's erroneous interpretation of the subject in *Hahoker* II p. 38—40. Saadia's teaching on the *Kavod* has recently been analysed by Al. Altmann, in Saadya Studies ed. Rosenthal (1943) p. 4—25. He has shown that with Saadia this conception is but a rationalization of the older teaching of Merkabah mysticism on the same subject, and is not borrowed from Islamic sources.

101 Eleazar of Worms שערי הסוד והיחוד p. 9.

102 Cf. *Otsar Nehmad* III p. 65 and Jacob Freimann מבוא לס' חסידים p. 15—16, 49—56 (a collection of quotations).

103 The terms are סודי רזייא in הלכות מלאכים (כבוד פנימי p.6) and רוח הקדש and שכינה, כבוד החסידים (ספר החסידים § 1543). The identity of כבוד החיצון is stressed very often, e. g. in the שערי הסוד and סודי רזייא.

104 סודי רזייא p. 6 uses the expression ידעו דעות שכינה להתחבר עם הכבוד. Such a "communion" with the Shekhinah would have been repulsive to many Talmudic teachers (cf. *Ketuboth* f. 111b where the rhetoric question is asked וכי אפשר לדבוקי בשכינה).

105 Eleazar of Worms שערי הסוד והיחוד p. 9.

106 נקרא חפץ השם ורוח אלהים Ms. Parma Derossi 1390 f. 120b ספר החיים. Of this חפץ השם it is said that it is מודבק בכל חבריות. וכבוד השם ודיבור השם.

107 The same Ms. f. 127a.

108 *Sefer Raziel* f. 12b.

109 שערי הסוד p. 9—10.

110 From the הכבוד 'ס; *Otsar Nehmad* III p. 65.

111 *Sefer Hasidim* § 979.

112 Cf. ערוגת הבשם ed. Urbach p. 201.

113 מסכת היכלות chapter VII (*Beth Ha-Midrash* II p. 45)—but no mention is made there of his appearance on the throne!

114 On the Cherub cf. the passages quoted by Epstein in *Hahoker* II pp. 38—39, 43—44, and those collected by Naftali Treves in his prayerbook, Thiengen 1560 (פתיחה ל,,ברכו") which have escaped Epstein. Much material on the Cherub is found in Elhanan ben Yakar's writings in two Mss. of the JThS in New York.

115 Donnolo, ed. Castelli p. 40; חכמת הנפש f. 7b/c; שערי הסוד והיחוד p. 13.

116 Eleazar of Worms in שערי הסוד והיחוד p. 14.

117 Schreiner in REJ vol. 29 p. 207 (on Malik al-Sejdulani of Ramleh and Benjamin Nahawendi); Schahrastani transl. Haarbruecker vol. I p. 256; Kirkisani transl. Nemoy in HUCA VII p. 386.

118 Poznanski in REJ vol. 50 (1905) p. 10—31. Nemoy seems to have overlooked this important article.

119 Epstein loc. cit.

120 Cf. שערי הסוד והיחוד p. 14 (instead of זהרריאל the reading here is הדריאל); ברייתא דיוסף בן עוזיאל in *Hahoker* II p. 44; Elhanan ben Yakar יסוד היסודות Ms. New York JThS 838 f. 104a.

121 Cf. *Otsar Nehmad* vol. III p. 80—81.

122 I discovered these fragments of the totally unknown book in Ms. Adler 1161 of the JThS in New York f. 70b/71b and 72b/73a. (לשון ר'). שמואל בן ר' קלונימוס מספר שקוד אשר תקן). The "mysterious" title ספר שקוד signifies, as I am informed by S. Liebermann, "Samuel's book", cf. *Ketuboth* 43b. Speaking of the *Kavod* Samuel says f. 73a: והנה חקרתי כי רבים מרבותיי חכמי התלמוד שאינם מכירים באילו הסודות כ"ש המינין הטמאי' שלא עמדו בסוד קדושים, אמנם יש מחכמי המינים שיודעים דוגמא דסודות ולא העיקר.

123 These speculations are found in the שערי הסוד והיחוד p. 13—14 and already in the fragments from ספר שקוד (see last note).

124 *Baba Bathra* 25a.

125 סודי רזייא ed. Kamelhar p. 32.

126 Cf. שערי הסוד והיחוד p. 13; cf. also MGWJ vol. 78 (1934) p. 495.

127 Ms. Adler 1161 f. 71b: הללו יה זה השכינה כי הנבראים מהללים לשכינה שהיא ברואה אבל לעתיד לבוא יהללו להקב"ה בעצמו. This, as far as I am aware, is the earliest reference in Jewish mystical literature to a duality of the two terms הקב"ה and השכינה. It seems to have originated in the later Aggadah, where we find in *Midrash Mishle* ed. Buber 47a a passage such as the following:עמדה שכינה לפני הקב"ה ואמרה לפניו רבונו של עולם וכו'.

128 Epstein in his afore-mentioned article in *Hahoker* vol. II.

129 Cf. my article on this subject in MGWJ 75 (1931) p. 172—190.

130 חכמת הנפש f. 20 a/d and *passim;* ערוגת הבשם p. 39; *Sefer Hasidim* §1514.

131 Cf. note 114 to the second lecture.

132 שערי הסוד והיחוד p. 14.

133 ס' חכמת הנפש f. 23b:

134 Ibid. f. 29c.

135 Ibid f. 28d.

136 סודי רזייא p. 34.

137 חכמת הנפש f. 20d.

138 Ibid f. 20a.

NOTES TO LECTURE IV

ABRAHAM ABULAFIA AND THE DOCTRINE OF PROPHETIC KABBALISM

1 ס' אשל אברהם Fuerth 1701.

2 Cf. my book חלומותיו של השבתאי ר' מרדכי אשכנזי (1938) chapter IV.

3 First published 1831. The best edition of this highly interesting book appeared in Warsaw in 1868 under the title ס' ליקוטי ביאורים.

4 Ms. British Museum 749 f. 10—28; Guenzburg 691 (formerly Coronel 129).

5 An analysis of the idea of דבקות and its development in Judaism is a desideratum. Cf. Ibn Ezra on Psalm I, 3; Nahmanides on Deuter. XI, 22

and on Job XXXI, 7; Ezra ben Solomon (published in my book כתבי יד בקבלה 1930 p. 197ff.). Ezra quotes as a saying of his teacher Isaac the Blind: עיקר עבודת המשכילים וחושבי שמו „ובו תדבקון" וכו' (Pseudo-Nahmanides on שיר השירים, 1763, f. 8d).

6   Cf. the articles on דביקות in ס' (1876) לשון חסידים f. 15 f., and in ס' דרך חסידים (1876) f. 24ff.

7   R. Phineas of Koretz gives a very illuminating paraphrase in Yiddish. He "translates" the words צריך אדם לדבק בה' *mus sich arain gain in Haschem*, cf. ס' ליקוטי שושנים (1876) p. 14.

8   Published in Berlin 1922.

9   The description of the experience of the High Priest in entering the Holy of Holies on the day of Atonement has such an ecstatical character, cf. Zohar III, 67a and 102a; *Zohar Hadash* (1885) f. 19a and 21a.

10   Cf. the bibliography.

11   Jellinek, Philosophie und Kabbala p. 23.

12   I know of some Kabbalists in Jerusalem who copied manuscripts of one of the most difficult of Abulafia's books, not in order to sell them but for the sake of their own work.

13   Jehudah Hayat in the preface to his commentary מנחת יהודה on the book מערכת האלהות Mantua 1558.

14   Moses Cordovero and Hayim Vital quote him more than once as a high authority, not to mention minor Kabbalists. Eliezer Eilenburg, a German Kabbalist (ca. 1555) says of Abulafia's אמרי שפר in rhymed prose כל איש אשר מכחיש ספר אמרי שפר הוא and שכולו עמוק מרחוק חופר איש סכל או איש כופר (Ms. New York JThS 891 f. 101a).

15   The Kabbalists used to quote all sorts of variations on Maimonides' saying (in הלכות יסודי התורה IV, 13): ואני אומר אין ראוי לטייל בפרדס אלא מי שנתמלא כריסו לחם ובשר.

16   Of two great Kabbalists of the 13th century, the brothers Jacob and Isaac Hakohen of Soria, we know on very good authority שלא היו בעלי הוראה בתלמוד cf. *Tarbiz* vol. III p. 261.

17   The following account is based chiefly on the fragment of Ab.'s אוצר עדן גנוז published by Jellinek in *Beth Ha-Midrash* vol. III p. XL ff. of the introduction. Many other details are to be found in his commentaries on his own prophetical writings, cf. Steinschneider's analysis of Ms. Munich 285 in his Catalogue of the Hebrew Mss. in Munich (1895) p. 142—146.

18   Koch, Meister Eckhart und die Juedische Religionsphilosophie des Mittelalters, in Jahresbericht der Schlesischen Gesellschaft fuer vaterlaendische Kultur 1928 (p. 15 of the reprint).

19   Abulafia's commentary on the *Moreh* is extant in two versions: a) חיי הנפש Ms. Munich 408; Erlanger Memorial Collection 96 in JThS; b)

סתרי תורה of which more than 25 manuscripts are known. Some pieces of it were printed (anonymously) in the Kabbalistical collection לקוטי שכחה ופאה (Ferrara 1556) f. 23—31.

20 According to אוצר עדן גנוז Ms. Oxford 1580 f. 17a.

21 The list of these commentaries is printed in *Beth Ha-Midrash* vol. III p. XLII.

22 מפתחות הקבלה Ms. Paris 770¹; JThS 835, cf. my article on the author and the book in EJ III col. 1105.

23 ואני אומר לכתוב ואיני רשאי ואני אומר שלא לכתוב ואיני יכול להניח לגמרי, לכן אני כותב ומניח וחוזר עוד בו במקום אחר וכן דרכי.

24 In 1279 he is full of praise for these pupils, cf. the passage in Jellinek's גנזי חכמת הקבלה German part p. 17 note 4. By 1282 he writes rather coolly about them (ספר החיים Ms. Munich 285f. 21b) and 1285 he says bitterly יצאו לתרבות רעה כי נערים בלי מדע היו ועזבתים (*Beth Ha-Midrash* III p. XLI).

25 Cf. MGWJ vol. 36 (1887) p. 558.

26 Fragments of one of these earlier works מפתחות רעיון ס' are extant in Ms. Vatican 291; of the book גט השמות in Ms. Oxford 1658.

27 A. H. Silver, A History of Messianic Speculation in Israel (1927) p. 146 has been the first to see this connection.

28 The account is published in MGWJ vol. 36 p. 558.

29 ספר האות published by Jellinek in Jubelschrift zum 70. Geburtstage des Prof. H. Graetz (1887) p. 65—85.

30 MGWJ vol. 36 p. 558. Zinberg, The History of Jewish Literature vol. III (1931) p. 52 quotes a poem of one of Abulafia's admirers who complains bitterly of these persecutions. Solomon ben Adreth attacked him for his activities in Sicily as a prophet and quasi-Messiah (cf. שו"ת הרשב"א No. 548).

31 ספר האות p. 76.

32 In his מפתח החכמות on Genesis Ms. Parma Derossi 141 f. 16b and 28b.

33 Ibid f. 16b: ואין ספק שיש מהם קצת חכמים שיודעים זה הסוד ודברו עמי בסוד וגלו לי שזוהי דעתם בלא ספק ואז דנתים אני ג"כ בכלל חסידי אומות העולם ואין לחוש על דברי הפתאים בשום אומה שלא ניתנה תורה אלא לבעלי הדעת.

34 Ibid f. 28b: ומאותו היום והלאה נדר על עצמו לקבל ממני שום דבר מסתרי התורה והתאהב עמי וקבעתי בלבו חץ חשק ידיעת השם עד שהודה ואמר משה אמת ותורתו אמת ואין צורך לגלות מענין הגוי יותר מזה.

35 Cf. Landauer in Literaturblatt des Orients vol. VI (1845) col. 473. He even speaks of Abulafia as a "rationalistic Christian" (!), ibid. col. 590. The same misinterpretation is given by S. Bernfeld.

36 Cf. ספר האות p. 71. The Mss. of his books are full of polemical passages, especially the גן נעול Ms. Munich 58⁴ (partly incorporated into the ס' הפליאה 1784 f. 50—56).

37 Cf. ספר האות p. 71 col. b. He enlarges on such "trinitarian" ideas, especially in the ספר מליץ using the terminology of רוח הקדש and בן אלוה, אלוה for the three aspects of the intellect which are explained in other metaphors in the passage quoted in note 75. In ס' החשק Ms. Enelow Memorial Coll. 858 of the JThS f. 26b he says: ואם יאמר לך אדם שהאלהות שלשה אמור לו שקר וכזב שכן שלשה בגימטריא שק"ר וכז"ב.

38 Cf. גנזי חכמת הקבלה Hebrew part p. 19; Philosophie u. Kabbala p. 38. One of Ab.'s treatises, ס'מצרף לכסף וכור לזהב Ms. Sassoon 56 is written especially against טעות מחשבתו של תלמיד אחד מתלמידיו שהאמין בספירות וכי אין לנו בידיעתם כי אם קריאת שם לכל ספירה בלבד ולא ציור ענין כלל.

39 Cf. his ענין הנבואה, a very illuminating piece (from the ס' חיי הנפש) published by Jellinek in the collectanea following his edition of the ספר האות p. 86.

40 Ms. Enelow Memorial Coll. in the JThS § 702 f. 22b: ויקרא בשמי אברהם אברהם ואומר הנני. וילמדני באורח משפט... ויעירני כאיש אשר יעור משנתו לחבר דבר מחודש לא חובר בזמני דבר ממנו... והכרחתי רצוני והשלחתי ידי במה שהוא למעלה מיכולתי מעט, בראותי דורי קוראים אותי מין ואפיקורוס בעבור שהייתי עובד אלהים באמת ולא כפי דמיון העם ההולכים בחושך. ובעבור היותם הם ודומיהם נשקעים בתהום, היו שמחים כשהיו יכולים להשקיעני גם אני בתהליהם ובמחשך מעשיהם אך חלילה לי מעשות זאת כי לא אעזוב דרכי האמת בעד דרכי השקר. His epistle וזאת ליהודה ed. Jellinek in Auswahl kabbal. Mystik p. 13—28 is one of his refutations of personal attacks. Here he says likewise: כי לא קדמני אדם מקובל להבר בקבלה ספרים מבוארים יותר ממני לפי מיני שני חלקיה הנזכרים, בספירות ובשמות.

41 Cf. the text printed in Philosophie und Kabbala p. 44 to which must be added the introductory part found in my book כתבי יד בקבלה p. 26.

42 In the preface of his ספר החשק Ms. Enelow Memorial Coll. (in JThS) No. 858 f. 2b היודע אמיתת המציאות יהיה יותר עניו ושפל מזולתו.

43 Literaturblatt des Orient vol. VI col. 345. S. Bernfeld (in דעת אלהים) and Guenzig have accepted Landauer's theory without research of their own.

44 Proof of the accuracy of the description now following is to be found in the translation appended to this lecture, and in Abulafia's great systematic manuals, especially the אור השכל and אמרי שפר.

45 He refers to התרת קשרי החותמות cf. גנזי חכמת הקבלה p. 18 (the phrase occurs several times in his unpublished writings).

46 Ibid. p. 20.

47 *Samdhi-nirmocana Sutra* ou Sutra détachant les noeuds, ed. Lamotte, Paris 1935.

48 Thus he parallels the meaning of the metaphor בהגיעי אל השמות
ובהתירי את קשרי החותמות.

49 ס' גן נעול Ms. Munich 58 f. 322b. The text of the passage is printed
in the ס' פליאה (1784) f. 52d/53a.

50 Philosophie und Kabbala p. 15; חכמת הצירוף היא חכמת ההגיון הפנימי
העליון.

51 Cf. אמרי שפר Ms. Munich 285 f. 75b: גם נגזר (מלת אותיות) מלשון ביאת
ענין והוא תרגום בענין העולם העולם הבא שביארוהו עלמא דאתי ופירשו בסוד עולם
האותיות.

52 In his ספר מליץ in the same Ms. he says: כל אות עולם בפני עצמו אצל
הקבלה.

53 Cf. ספר האות p. 71; Philosophie und Kabbala p. 20 where he uses the
phrase צריך להתיך (!) כל הלשונות אל לשון הקדש עד שכל דיבור שיזכירהו
המדבר בפיו ובשפתיו יחשבנו כאלו הוא מחובר מאותיות הקודש שהם כ"ב אותיות.
In his אור השכל part VII, he gives the Gematria האותיות שבעים לשונות-צירוף.

54 חיי עולם הבא (written 1280). I know of about 25 manuscripts. Further details cf. in my book כתבי יד בקבלה p. 24—30.

55 אור השכל (written 1285) extant in no less than fifteen Mss. I have
used Ms. Munich 92. Already Jellinek has justly pointed out that this is an
exceedingly interesting work, cf. Philosophie und Kabbala p. 39.

56 אמרי שפר (written 1291), also extant in about fifteen Mss. I have
used Ms. Munich 285. ספר הצירוף in Ms. Paris Bibl. Nat. 774.

57 Cf. e. g. Philosophie und Kabbala p. 18—20.

58 A full elaboration of the technique of association has been published
by me (from ס' סולם העליה) in Kirjath Sefer vol. XXII (1945) p. 161
—171.

59 Ibid. p. 44—45, from ס' חיי עולם הבא. I have translated several passages in accordance with the better readings of Ms. 8⁰ 540 of the Hebrew
University Library.

60 These seven stages are described by Abulafia in his שבע נתיבות התורה
Philosophie und Kabbala p. 1—4.

61 Cf. כתבי יד בקבלה p. 25.

62 Ibidem. In his אמרי שפר,Abulafia says: דע כי נהר די נור נגיד ונפיק מן
קדמוהי וצריך המצרף לשמור ולהזהר מפחדו לכבוד שמו פן יברח ממנו דמו והיה
הוא הורג את עצמו אבל אם רץ לבו ישוב למקומו כי מפתח השם בידו.

63 ודע שרוב המראות שראה רזיאל כולם נבנו:Ms. Munich 285 f. 37b ספר עדות
על שם המפורש ועל חדוש התגלותו עתה בארץ בימיו אשר לא היה כן מאדם ועדיו.
Cf. also the passage quoted in note 40.

64 חיי הנפש ס' printed at the end of ספר האות p. 85.

65 חיי הנפש ס' Ms. Munich 408 f. 67a: המקובלים הם בני הנביאים ותלמידיהם.

66   Particularly in his commentaries on Maimonides' *Moreh*.

67   Examples of this are to be found in כתבי יד בקבלה p. 27, 29; Philosophie und Kabbala p. 40—41; Moses Cordovero's ס' פרדס רמונים ch. XXI,
1 (from Abulafia's ספר הנקוד).

68   See the sources quoted in the last note.

69   Cf. the passage published in my book כתבי יד בקבלה p. 27.

70   מפתח הספירות ס' Ms. Ambrosiana (Milano) 53 f. 157b: ושכלו צריך
אל מניע מקובל מסתרי התורה מחוץ ואל מעורר פנימי לפתוח לו חשערים הסגורים
לפניו בסוד אמתת הספירות והשמות שהבריאות השכלית היא השגת מדת התפארת
המחייבת הנבואה... והחולי הוא העדר זה.

71   Cf. ס' Ms. Munich 285 f. 90a: אמרי שפר האיש אשר אלה תאריו הוא אשר
ראוי לו הקבלה כולה כאשר היא ומפני שלא יצטרך איש כזה אל רב שימסרנה לו
ויספיק לו מה שימצא כתוב בזה הספר ממנה... ואם ימצא עליו רב מה טוב, ואם לאו
יעבור עם מה שימצא ממנה בזה הספר.

72   ספר עדות Ms. Munich 285 f. 39b Abulafia quotes his own prophecy i.e.
the divine voice speaking to him, and gives his own interpretation. ,,קום
והקם ראש משיחי" — הוא חיי הנפשות; ,,תמשחהו כמלך" — מכח כל השמות;
,,כי אני משחתיהו למלך על ישראל ועל קהלות ישראל"... ,, ו ש מ ו ק ר א ת י
ש ד י ב ש מ י " — שסודו שדי גשמי [sic!] תבין כל הכוונה וכן מאמרו
,, ו ה ו א א נ כ י ו א נ כ י ה ו א " ואי אפשר לגלות בזה מפורש יותר מזה
שסוד השם הגשמ"י הוא משי"ח השם.

73   *Sanhedrin* 38a: שמו כשם רבו. The words מטטרון and שדי have the same
numerical value 314.

74   Cf. כתבי יד בקבלה p. 25; ס' האות p. 70—71.

75   ידיעת המשיח וחכמת הגואל Ms. Munich 285 f. 26b. The Hebrew
text reads: כי זאת החכמה לבדה היא הכלי הקרוב לנבואה יותר משאר חכמות.
ואמתת המציאות כשידענה האדם מתוך מה שלמד מן הספרים המורים עליה, יקרא
חכם. וכשידענה בקבלה שמסר לו מי שידענה על פי השמות או מי שקבלה מפי מקובל,
יקרא מבין. אבל מי שידעה מתוך לבו על פי משא ומתן שנושא ונותן בינו לבין
עצמו על מה שהגיע לידו מן עניני המציאות, יקרא דעתן. ואמנם מי שידע אמתת
המציאות על דרך שנכללהו בלבו אלו הג' עניינים הנזכרים שהם החכמה מרוב למוד
והבינה המקובלת מפי המקובלים האמתיים והדעת מרוב משא ומתן במחשבה, איני
אומר שזה האיש יקרא נביא לבד אלא בכל עת שפעל ומשתכל לא התפעל או התפעל
ולא השיג שממנו התפעל — אבל אם התפעל והשיג שהתפעל (ממנו) דין הוא אצלי
ואצל כל שלם להקרא בשם מורה על היות שמו כשם רבו אם בשם אחד או יותר,
ואם בכל שמותיו, מפני שהוא לא נפרד מרבו והנה הוא רבו ורבו הוא שכבר דבק
בו דבוק שאי איפשר להפרידו ממנו בשום סבה כי הוא הוא (!). וכמו שרבו הנפרד
מכל חומר יקרא תמיד שכל משכיל מושכל אשר שלשתם ענין אחד בו לעולם בפועל,
כן זה המיוחד בעל השם המיוחד יקרא שכל בעת שישיג בפועל ואז יהיה מושכל
משכיל שכל בפועל כרבו. ואין ::ז הבדל ביניהם אלא מפני שרבו תכלית מעלתו בעצמו
ולא בזולתו מן הנבראים כולם, וזה הגיע אל מעלתו על ידי הנבראים ובאמצעותם.

76 This is in accordance with Maimonides' theology and borrowed there-from.

77 מפתח הספירות Ms. Ambrosiana 53 f. 164b: הפוך בה והפוך בה דכולא בה
וכולת בך וכולך בה.

78 Cf. כתבי יד בקבלה p. 225—230.

79 Cf. my article, Eine Kabbalistische Deutung der Prophetie als Selbst-begegnung, in MGWJ vol. 74 (1930) p. 285—290.

80 *Gen. Rabba* ed. Theodor p. 256.

81 Cf. the complete text in the article quoted in note 79.

82 This statement is found in Ibn Ezra's commentary on Daniel X, 21.

83 On the ecstatic sensation of anointment cf. the quotation from Abu-lafia in Johanan Alemanno שער החשק ס' ed. Halberstadt 31a; כתבי יד בקבלה
p. 228. On משיח חשם cf. the passage quoted in note 72.

84 The terms דרך השמות and דרך הספירות occur very often, cf. גנזי חכמה.
הקבלה p. 15, 17.

85 גן נעול ס' Ms. Munich 58 f. 322b.

86 Cf. the passage quoted in note 38.

87 The Sefiroth are עמקי השכל הפועל in the passage from גן נעול (note
85). The שכל הפועל is זיו השכינה Ms. Jerusalem 8⁰ 540 f. 13b.

88 Philosophie und Kabbala p. 11.

89 Ibid. p. 4.

90 Cf. מפתח החכמות Ms. Parma Derossi 141 f. 19a. אין הקבלה מכחשת
מה שגילתה החכמה כי אין בין החכמה ובין הקבלה אלא שהקבלה הוגדה מפי השכל
הפועל ביותר עמוקה ממה שהוגדה החכמה עם היות שתי ההגדות מפיהו א"כ (הקבלה)
הגדה יותר דקה.

91 The same Ms. f. 12b ff. ואמנם הנביא לא יבקש מכל התורה כולה אלא מה
שמספיק להביאו לידי הנבואה. כי מה לו אם העולם קדמון או חדש וקדמותו
לא תוסיף לו מעלה ולא יפחות מדרגתו שאאשר היה כבר היה... ואם כן מה שישלימהו
הוא ענין השמות.

92 He had been attacked for defending the eternity of the world, as re-lated by him in גן נעול Ms. Munich 58 f. 327b. Elsewhere he suggests a solution of his own for the problem.

93 Cf. Jellinek, Auswahl kabbalistischer Mystik, German part p. 20; Steinschneider in Hebr. Bibliographie vol. XIV p. 8 and p. VII (correc-tions).

94 Cf. Philosophie und Kabbala p. 22, 43—44.

95 כתבי יד בקבלה p. 30 and the words of his disciple quoted on p. 150.

96 מפתח רעיון ס' Ms. Vatic. 291 f. 29a in a lengthy passage.

97 אל יעלה במחשבתך שגעון חוקרי ספר 172b .f 10 ס' נר אלהים Ms. Munich
cf. Sanhe-) יצירה כדי לברוא עגלא תליתאה שהמבקשים לעשות כן עגלים הם
drin 65b).

98 מגלת סתרים published in Edelmann's המדה גנוזה (1856) f. 42—45; cf.
my remarks on it in *Tarbiz* vol. VI No. 3 p. 94.

99 ברית מנוחה first edition Amsterdam 1648. In Kabbalistical manuscripts
there still exist a large number of other works of this genre including some
fairly interesting ones in the very valuable Ms. Sassoon 290.

100 These two books are אבן השהם Ms. Jerusalem 8⁰ 416 (cf. כתבי יד
בקבלה p. 89—91) and ס' שארית יוסף Ms. Vienna, Library of the Jewish
Community 260 (Schwarz p. 203—204).

101 Cf. the text published in *Kirjath Sepher* vol. VII (1930/31) p. 153.

102 Cf. כתבי יד בקבלה p. 34 and *Kirjath Sepher* vol. I p. 127—139.

103 Mss. Jerusalem and Columbia University Library X 893—Sh 43.
Several pages of the autobiography have been lost by accident and are not
included in the latter Ms. The two other Mss. are Leiden (Warner 24, 2)
and Gaster 954 (now in the British Museum).

104 The original text was published by me in *Kirjath Sepher* I (1924) p.
130—138. In some places, particularly in the last part, my translation follows the much better readings of Ms. Leiden. Some passages at the beginning and at the end have not been translated as having no direct connection with the subject matter.

105 Hebrew מחיקה. This is indeed the Sufic term *mahw*. Abulafia himself
alludes to this notion when he says, with reference to the Name, that he is
חקיקה שאין לה מחיקה — a play of words on a Talmudic saying concerning ספר האות (after סוד הנבואה cf. his שמות שאינם נמחקים p. 86).

106 This description gives an accurate picture of the actual content of
the bulk of Abulafia's works.

107 This שם בן ע"ב שמות is construed from letters of the three verses
Exodus XIV, 19—21, each of which consists of 72 letters, cf. Blau, Das alt-
juedische Zauberwesen (1898) p. 139. The major part of Abulafia's ס' חיי
עולם הבא is a guide to meditation on these 72 names whose parts and combinations are here inscribed in a large number of circles, each of them
serving for a special meditation.

108 *Kiddushin* 71a.

109 Perhaps the correct translation should be: "For every attainment in
Kabbalah is only an accident in relation to its substance, even if, for us, it
be the substance itself." The Hebrew text reads: שבודאי כל מה שנשיג מן
החכמה הזאת איננה רק במקרה לפי מהותה אע"פ שהיא בעצם לפי מהותינו.

110 Cant. II, 4 ודגלו עלי אהבה. The Midrash reads homiletically ודילוגו
as though God says "and his skipping over me." The Kabbalist gives to
this "skipping" a new meaning.

111   See above p. 139, the passage on self-confrontation.

112   This degree of mystical meditation and perception of the Divine is
mentioned by Moses ben Nahman in his commentary on Genesis XVIII:
הוא כבוד נברא במלאכים יקרא אצל היודעים מלבוש יושג לעיני בשר בזכי
הנפשות כחסידים ובני הנביאים ולא אוכל לפרש.
Abulafia himself mentions it several times in his writings. It seems to be
connected with the ספר המלבוש, cf. note 132 to the second lecture.

NOTES TO LECTURE V

THE ZOHAR I: THE BOOK AND ITS AUTHOR

1   Cf. the manuscript published by M. J. Guttmann under the title תורה
רבינו פנחס מקאערץ (Bilgoraj 1931), § 117 p. 26. The Baal-Shem, the
founder of Hasidism, is credited with the saying: "When I open the book
Zohar, I behold the whole universe," cf. שבחי הבעש"ט f. 6b.

2   מערכת האלחות published Mantua 1558. The book is sometimes ascribed
to R. Perez of Barcelona, cf. my remarks in קרית ספר vol. XXI (1945) p.
284—287. In any event it is certain to have been written by a pupil of
Solomon ben Adreth. An analysis of the book has been attempted with
doubtful success by David Neumark תולדות הפילוסופיה בישראל vol. I
(1921) p. 192—204, 303—322. Neumark proceeds on the false assumption
that the *Maarekheth* is older than the Zohar. He goes so far as to assert
(p. 206) that without the *Maarekheth*, the Zohar would never have been
written.

3   The previous stages of this discussion, which was frequently carried on
without the necessary philological groundwork, are represented by some
books and essays included in the bibliography on this lecture.

4   Cf. Geschichte der Juden vol. VII third ed. (1894) p. 424—442.

5   Cf. e. g. A. Kaminka הרעיונות הסודיים של ר' שמעון בן יוחאי in ספר
קלוזנר (1937) p. 171—180, and by the same author לקדמות ספר הזוהר in
Sinai vol. VII (1940) p. 116—119. These essays are typical of a form of
"scientific" literature with which I do not propose to deal in this book.

6   Cf. my opening lecture at the Hebrew University, מדעי היהדות vol. I
(1926) p. 16—29.

7   Here it may be permissible to mention that I have prepared a special
dictionary of the language of the Zohar which I hope will see the light one
day. The work on this dictionary has done more than anything else to
convince me of the correctness of the views which I have advanced in this
lecture.

8 The usual editions of the Zohar comprise three volumes, the pagination of which is the same as that of the *editio princeps* Mantua 1558—1560. (Only three folio editions include all this material in one volume, Cremona 1560 etc.) I am quoting by volume and folium. To this must be added the volume containing the *Tikkune Zohar* (also printed first in Mantua 1558) and the volume entitled *Zohar Hadash*. This title does not signify that this is a "new Zohar," an imitation of the old one, as some writers have suggested, but that it contains those parts of the Zohar and the *Tikkunim* which were missing in the manuscripts used by the editors of the Mantua versions. The material was collected chiefly by Abraham Halevi Berokhim from Mss. found in Safed and includes some of the most important texts. I am quoting from the ed. Warsaw 1885. All the editions of these three "parts" are enumerated in my Bibliographia Kabbalistica (1927) p. 166 —182.

9 This is simply an Aramaic metaphrase of the Hebrew term מגילת סתרים. צניעו is used Zohar II, 239a in the same sense as in this title.

10 Zohar II, 176b—179a. No scientific value can be attached to Paul Vulliaud's Traduction Intégrale du Siphra di-Tzeniutha (Paris 1930), cf. MGWJ vol. 75 (1931) p. 347—362, 444—448.

11 Zohar III, 127b—145a.

12 In my review of Vulliaud's book (cf. note 10) I have dealt more fully with these links between the two texts.

13 Zohar III, 287b—296b.

14 Ibid. II, 127a—146b. It is quoted or rather alluded to in the *Idra Rabba*, but the later Kabbalists did not know where to look for it. From quotations in an old Kabbalistic work, לבנת הספיר (written 1328) it is clear which part is really meant. In our editions it is simply a part of the section *Terumah*.

15 Ibid. I, 38a—45b and II, 244b—268b (in two parts: a) 244—262b on היכלין דסטרא דקדושא; b) 262b—268b on היכלות הטומאה).

16 Ibid. II, 70a—78a. The continuation of II, 75a is found in *Zohar Hadash* (1885) f. 35b—37c.

17 One text is incorporated in the bulk of the Zohar, the other bears a special title which is clearly an imitation of the pseudo-Aristotelian *secretum secretorum* well known in the Middle Ages, which includes a chapter on physiognomics. The Hebrew translation סוד הסודות of this treatise has been published by Gaster, Studies and Texts vol. III; cf. p. 268—271 שער בהכרת הפרצוף.

18 Zohar II, 94b (bottom) — 114a.

19 Ibid. III, 186a—192a.

20 Cf. ibid. I, 238b ff.; II, 166a; *Zohar Hadash* 9a.

21   Ibid. III, 161b—174a.

22   Ibid. I, 74a—75b, 76b—80b, 88a—90a, 97a—102a, 108a—111a, 146b—
149b. (According to several manuscripts, the piece I, 15a—22b contains
the *Sithre Torah* on פרשת בראשית).

23   Ibid. I, 62, 74, 97, 100b, 107b, 121, 147, 151, 154, 161b, 165, 232,
233b, 251; II, 4a, 12b, 68b, 74, 270b; III, 49, 73b, 270b; *Zohar Hadash* 1d,
3a, 105a, 122b.

24   *Zohar Hadash* f. 61d—75a.

25   Ibid. f. 56d—58d.

26   Ibid. f. 1—9.

27   Ibid. f. 37c—41a.

28   The sections בראשית, נח, לך לך of the *Midrash Ha-Neelam* are printed
in the *Zohar Hadash* f. 2—26; from וירא to תולדות I, 97a—140a; ויצא
in *Zohar Hadash* f. 27—28. Zohar II, 4a—5b, 14a—22a contains the *Midrash Ha-Neelam* to פרשת שמות.

29   *Zohar Hadash* f. 75a—90b. Ibid. f. 90—93 there is also a piece styled
מדרש הנעלם על איכה.

30   The רעיא מהימנא is scattered through vols. II and III of the editions,
although in the manuscripts it is generally found together in separate
copies. The Ms. tradition of this part differs distinctly from that of the
aforementioned ones. The bulk of the R. M. is printed II, 114a—121a, III,
97—104, 108b—112a, 121b—126a, 215a—259b, 270b—283a.

31   There are considerable differences of arrangement between the *editio
princeps* of the *Tikkune Zohar* Mantua 1558 which, it is true, is not to be
relied upon, and later editions.

32   *Zohar Hadash* f. 31a—37c and 93c—122b. To the *Tikkune Zohar* belongs also the passage I, 22a—29b.

33   On the title-page of the Cremona edition of 1560, a מאמר תא חזי
is mentioned as a part incorporated in that edition. Which part this refers
to is not quite clear, but it appears to be col.56—72, where every paragraph
begins with the formula תא חזי. This piece is printed in the vulgata editions as an addition at the end of the first volume, ed. Vilna f. 256a—262a.
Later imitations are: I f. 211b—216a an imitation of the *Midrash Ha-Neelam* (found already in Ms. Vatican. Casa dei Neofiti 23); the so-called
Zohar on Ruth, cf. Bibliographia Kabbalistica p. 183; a chapter called
מאמרי זעירא is mentioned by Azulai and extant in Ms. Paris Bibl. Nat. 782,
as well as in Vital's copies from older Kabbalistic Mss.

34   London 1931—1934. This translation is not always correct but it con-
veys a clear impression of what the Zohar is. It is to be regretted that too
much has been omitted. The innumerable deliberate falsifications of the

French translator, Jean de Pauly, are of course not to be found in this more solid and workmanlike translation.

35 The only attempt to separate "authentic" parts from "interpolations" has been made by Ignaz Stern, Versuch einer umstaendlichen Analyse des Sohar, in Ben Chananja vols. I—V (1858—1862). The argument amounts to a complete *reductio ad absurdum* of the author's own thesis, as I have shown in the case of the ספרא דצניעותא in MGWJ vol. 75 p. 360. Notwithstanding this fact, it is a very interesting essay and much can be learned from it.

36 His preference for sentences with כדין reflects the mediaeval use of Hebrew אז.

37 E. g. למחדי, למיעל, למזכי instead of לחדאה, לאעלאה, לזכאה and vice versa לקרבא, לאשראה, לאחייא instead of למשרי, למקרב etc. Most common is the preposterous אוליפנא for "I have learned."

38 E. g. אסתגי, מתשעריו, אתצריף, אתצייר, אתסדר etc., or אתכאב which is clearly mediaeval Hebrew.

39 אסתמרא in the sense of "to deal with something" is 13th century use of the Hebrew התעורר. אתער. לאתדבקא, לאתזנא, לאתערא מליו, לאסתמרא

40 He frequently uses ב in the sense of "with" e. g. ידור מלכא במטרונגיתא. לגבי appears in the most unlikely places.

41 E. g. גולמא, אמשכותא, עלמא דפירודא (Hyle!), מתמנע, אשגחותא.

42 The author derived this Arabic use of מעו from David Kimhi's ספר השרשים sub voce מעו.

43 Especially in phrases such as גרדיני גליפיו, גרדיני טהיריו, גרדיני נימוסיו meaning always angels of wrath and even demons (=שומרי הדיו).

44 לבסמא דיניו =Spanish *endulzar*. The later Hebrew phrase המתקת הדיו is taken from the Kabbalistic language of the Zohar. Already Simeon Duran תשב"ץ (Part III § 57) endeavoured to explain this highly unMidrashic parlance.

45 Preposterous, too, is the standing expression אוזפוהו תלת פרסי "they accompanied him three miles." The author here confused ליוה and הלות!

46 טייעא— he goads the donkey מעיו חמרא. The author obviously thought that the word had something to do with מעו. The contention of Sh. Pushinski that there was an authentic Aramaic usage of טייעא in the sense employed in the Zohar is baseless. The material collected by him לחקר לשוו הזהר in *Yavneh* vol. II, 1940, p. 140—147 clearly proves the exact contrary of his own thesis.

47 אסקופא (talm. איסקפא) cf. I, 67a כאסקופא דא דאתמליא מכל טובא דעלמא etc. The explanation offered by R. Margulies in ניצוצי זוהר on I, 46b has no philological base.

48   תוקפא based on a misunderstanding of the translation of Numbers XI,
12   שאהו בחיקך in Targum Onkelos בתוקפך.סוברהי The author mistook the
Midrashic *interpretation* for a *literal translation!*

49   He confuses the Aramaic צחותא which never signifies anything but
thirst, with the Hebrew צחות particularly as substitute in the Talmudic
quotation (*Megillah* 28b) שמעתא בעיא צילותא which now becomes צריכנא
מלח דאורייתא בעיא צחותא and צחותא לשמעתא!

50   See note 45.

51   Of this genre are e. g. בוצינא דקרדינותא (a most fantastic development!) מפסא, מהירו, בוסימא.

52   E. g. ואכחיש פומבי דמלכא in the sense of making counterfeit coins — a
very awkward phrase with an interesting "history."

53   קוזפירא, קוזדימא, קירמא, קוספיתא etc.

54   This is the case with סוספיתא "dross" which is not Greek as R. Eisler
assumed MGWJ vol. 69 p. 364 ff. and I believed with him for some time,
but a delicate deformation of the Talmudic כוספא. Of the same kind are
קרופינגוס, מברקא, קוסטורין, קלטופא, (קטרא=) קפטירא etc.

55   This has been pointed out already by Graetz in the first edition vol.
VII p. 503, but the whole paragraph has somehow disappeared in the third
edition!

56   Cf. the literature quoted in note 10.

57   There are more than 125 compounds of this kind in many hundreds of
places.

58   This is not an allusion to Trinitarianism, but refers to the doctrine of
the three parts of the soul, which the author expounds in the following
pages.

59   E. g. בקטפירא דעליתא בקסטייהו (I, 39a), מופסרא דקילמא בחני שכיחי
שכיחי (I, 33a), סיפמא דמופסרא קפטלאי שכיחי (I, 241a) etc. The author has
a predilection for ending such "formulae" with the word שכיחי .

60   אית קץ ואית קץ ; אית מורין ואית מורין etc., in hundreds of places.

61   This was the assumption of the late Dr. H. G. Enelow in the Introduction to part III of his edition of Israel Nakawa's *Menorath Ha-Maor*
(1931) p. 34.

62   Cf. my essay on this question in the yearbook *Zion* vol. I (1926) p.
40—55, to which much could be added.

63   מגדל דצור II, 94b is based, as my late lamented colleague Samuel
Klein has told me, on a misreading of a passage in *Megillah* 6a also found in
En Yaakob.

64   In a note to my essay mentioned in note 62, p. 56. The recent at-

tempt of R. Margulies to "vindicate" the author of the Zohar by pointing to a Talmudical passage which mentions לוד and קפוטקיא together (and according to M.'s interpretation "as neighbouring places") is pure apologetics, cf. his article in *Sinai* vol. V (1941) p. 237—240. The Zohar has clearly misunderstood the *Tosefta* quoted by Margulies in the same way as Margulies himself.

65   Cf. *Sabbath* 33b (חתניה). There is no point in M. Kunitz' "reinterpretation" of the passage, cf. ס' בן יוחאי (1815) § 67.

66   Zohar III, 144b, 200b, 240b.

67   Cf. *Zohar Hadash* f. 22c on יוסי בן שמעון בן לקוניא and the source in *Pesahim* 86b. Cf. also Bacher, Agada der Tannaiten vol. I p. 448.

68   Typical is the case of R. Haggai in Zohar III, 158a who owes his mythical existence to a remark on the Amora of this name in *Abodah Zarah* 68a.

69   Zohar I, 11a and often in מדרש רות הנעלם.

70   Cf. Gaster's article s. v. Zohar in Encyclopedia of Religion and Ethics ed. Hastings vol. XII (1921) p. 858—862. A good many statements in this article do not bear serious investigation.

71   Cf. שער הפרישות, חובות הלבבות chapter 3.

72   חבורא קדמאה often in the R. M. to פרשת פנחס.

73   A list of such passages was compiled as early as 1635 by Aaron Selig ben Moses of Zolkiew in chapter 5 of his חבור עמודי שבע, Cracow 1635.

74   A Tel-Avivian scholar, Reuben Margulies, has begun to publish an annotated edition of the Zohar, in which many of the Rabbinical references are mentioned. It is a very useful book for every student of the Zohar, but the author is careful to avoid any expression of opinion sounding of "criticism" and has in many cases adopted apologetic methods of very doubtful value in order to "explain away" difficulties raised by modern criticism. Yet the "parallels" quoted by him tell the story of the Zohar and its sources to every critical reader, in rather flagrant contradiction to his own apologetic attitude.

75   L'exegèse biblique dans le Zohar, in REJ vol. 22 (1891) p. 33—46, 219—229.

76   Cf. J. L. Zlotnik מאמרים מספר מדרש המליצה העברית; חלק אמרי חכמה (Jerusalem 1939) p. 5—16. As in the case of so many other modern defenders of the "antiquity" of the Zohar, the facts which he presents with much proof of erudition but without critical analysis, prove precisely the opposite of what he infers from them.

77   It is easily forgotten that only the "Zabian" theory of Maimonides made this explanation of the nature of paganism possible. The author has

combined the definitions of הלכות עבודה זרה I, 1—2 with those given in *Moreh Nebukhim* III, 29. This is clearly reflected in passages like Zohar I, 56b, 99b; II 69a, 112a; III, 206b.

78 Cf. on Ezra and Azriel Tishby's introduction to his edition of Azriel's *Perush Ha-Aggadoth* (Jerusalem 1945) and his studies in *Sinai* vol. VIII (1945) p. 159—178 and *Zion* vol. IX (1944) p. 178—185. The Zohar made particular use of Ezra's commentary on the Song of Songs and that of Azriel on the prayers.

79 The author of the Zohar used Nahmanides' תורת האדם, his commentary to the Torah and that to Job. Very illuminating for the manner in which the author read his sources is Zohar III, 23a as compared with its obvious source in Nahmanides to Job XXXVIII, 36.

80 נקודא חדא does not signify "a point" or "one point" but "the centre" I, 15a, 30b, 71b (נקודה חדא דכל עלמא!) 229a; II, 157a, 259a, 268a; III, 250a etc. All this is found in passages which cannot be isolated from their context.

81 The most striking passage is to be found in גנת האגוז (Hanau 1615) f. 55a/b. The Zohar has only added the combination of these ideas and terms with the theory of the Sefiroth of which Gikatila makes no use in this connection. Other Kabbalists before Gikatila have spoken of the divine *Hokhma* as a point, but the term סוד נקודה אחת and the combination with the idea of the primordial Torah is his.

82 Cf. note 74.

83 S. A. Neuhausen (Baltimore) ספריה של מעלה (1937), which is much fuller than the list given by Zunz, Gesammelte Schriften vol. I p. 12—13.

84 Cf. Zohar I, 34b: בספרין קדמאין אשכנחא.

85 An excellent example is provided by the comparison of *Pesahim* 3b and Zohar II, 124a.

86 Very characteristic in this regard is the mythology of the "great dragon" II, 35a and the way it has been connected with the Aggadah on the אור הגנוז in *Hagigah* 12a.

87 An analysis of the commentary on Genes. I (Zohar I, 15a—22a) shows most clearly how these different modes of thought coexist in one context of close literary uniformity.

88 The texts of the Kabbalist brothers of Soria and of Moses of Burgos have been published by me in two studies מדעי היהדות vol. II (1927) and Tarbiz vol. II—V (1931—1934). Todros Abulafia's אוצר הכבוד was printed in a full edition, Warsaw 1879. His שער הרזים (Ms. Munich 209 etc.) still awaits publication.

89 For an example see Bacher in REJ vol. 22 (1891) p. 137—138; vol. 23 p. 133—134.

90   Cf. Karl Preis, Die Medizin im Zohar, MGWJ vol. 72 (1928).

91   D. Neumark's attempt to prove the existence of major doctrinal differences between the "original books," such as the *Sifra Di-Tseniutha* and the *Idras,* and the *Midrash Ha-Zohar* has been unsuccessful; it is based on quite a few unwarranted assumptions, cf. תולדות הפילוסופיה בישראל vol. I p. 204—245.

92   A number of texts bearing on this question are to be found in the studies quoted in note 88.

93   Published Koretz 1784 and in a much better edition Lemberg 1893. This outstanding work still awaits an adequate analysis.

94   Cf. E. Gebhardt, Mystics and Heretics in Italy at the End of the Middle Ages (1923); E. Benz, Ecclesia Spiritualis (1934).

95   Zohar III, 136a in the correct reading preserved by Menahem Recanati טעמי המצות (Basle 1580) f. 21b: ג' אלף שנין דזמין קב"ה לאתבא רוחיה ליה.

96   This idea is mentioned many times in the writings of the *Temunah*-circle, cf. specifically David ibn Zimra's quotation from one of them (in his מגן דוד Amsterdam 1714 f. 49b) כי לסבה זו חסרה אות אחת מן התורה שחיה and Ms. Vatican. 223 f. 197 the far-ראו האלפא ביתא כ"ג אותיות וגו' reaching conclusion (in a text not much later than the Zohar) כי לא תעשה (בתורה) בא מחסרון אותו האות שנחסר שממנו יוצאים הדינים הקשים.

97   Baer has suggested that a strong influence was exercised by the Franciscan followers of Joaquim of Fiore, the so called Spirituals, on the author of the *Raya Mehemna,* cf. his important essay in ציון vol. V (1939) p. 1—44. I would, however, stress the differences between the Zohar and the *R.M.* much more than *Baer* with whose judgment on the historic rôle of the *RM* in Spain I disagree.

98   Cf. passages like II, 42b—43a, III, 257b and the "prayer of Elijah" at the beginning of the *Tikkunim.* Many writers have been led astray by considering these passages as genuine presentations of the theology of the Zohar proper.

99   Cf. Stern's analysis (note 35); Jacob Emden in מטפחת ספרים (1769).

100   Cf. Abraham Zaccuto ספר יוחסין (1857) p. 88, quoting from Isaac of Acre's diary ספר הימים.

101   Most illuminating in this respect are the beginnings of *Idra Rabba* III, 127b using a formula from the *Midr. Ha-N.* in *Zohar Hadash* f. 16a; the beginning of *Idra Zutta* III, 287b quoting a story told in the *Midr. Ha-N.* ibid. 18d ff.; III, 191b quoting *Zohar Hadash* f. 9a—10d.

102   Cf. e. g. *Zohar Hadash* 25c ff. as compared with 1, 89a; *Zohar Hadash* 19a, 21a as compared with III, 67a and 102a; *Zohar Hadash* 80 a/c and 18d as compared with I, 218a/b.

103 The two old-fashioned commentaries to the book show, however, fairly clearly the real state of things, cf. Abraham Mordecai Vernikovski ארחות חיים הנקרא צוואת ר' אליעזר הגדול עם פירוש דמשק אליעזר, and Gershon Enoch Leiner ארחות חיים (Lublin 1903). It is curious that Jellinek who published the second part (סדר גן עדן, in *Beth Ha-Midrash* III p. 131— 140) did not recognize the truth.

104 Moses of Burgos calls the contemporary Kabbalists גאוני המדרש הנעלם cf. *Tarbiz* vol. V, p. 51.

105 Cf. e. g. the beginning of the R. M.-fragment II, 40b—41b and the continuation II, 42—43. Some paragraphs from this part (never from the *Raya Mehemna*) are indubitably quoted by Moses de Leon before 1291.

106 Ms. Cambridge University Library Add. 1023 (written about 1370) f. 8a—11b. I have published it now in the Louis Ginzberg Jubilee Volume (New York 1945), Hebrew Section, p. 425—446.

107 Some unidentified quotations from the Zohar are found in Recanati's commentary on the Torah.

108 Cf. Zohar II, 32a.

109 Cf. Steinschneider, Polemische und apologetische Literatur (1877) p. 360—362.

110 Cf. A. H. Silver, A History of Messianic Speculation p. 90—92. (The date 1608 which he mentions as the year of Redemption is based on a misunderstanding of the text).

111 Zohar II, 9b.

112 He mentions this town in the prefaces of his books until 1290. Isaac of Acre relates that he was known among his contemporaries as "Rabbi Moses of Guadalajara."

113 He cannot have died in 1293 as has sometimes been suggested — cf. מדעי היהדות vol. I p. 20—22 — since we possess a treatise by him which must have been written later, the ס' משכיות כסף Ms. Adler 1577 in JThS. The date given by Isaac of Acre is obviously correct.

114 ס' הנפש החכמה Basle 1608, and ס' שקל הקדש ed. Greenup, London 1911. I know of twenty books and smaller treatises written by him, of which fourteen are, at least in part, still extant.

115 Ms. Cambridge Add. 505,4 and Warsaw, Library of the Jewish Community 50. The lengthy fragment in Ms. Munich 47 which I believed for some time to contain this book, is certainly from a work of Moses de Leon's but not the שושן עדות cf. MGWJ vol. 71 (1927) p. 109—123.

116 No less than six manuscripts are extant. I have used Ms. British Museum 759.

117 Cf. *Tarbiz* vol. III (1932) p. 181—183. Only after having published this article did I find the whole quotation in the Cambridge manuscript of the Zohar mentioned in note 106.

118 Cf. my article in *Kirjath Sefer*, vol. VI (1930) p. 109—118.

119 Isaac of Acre, too, speaks of Moses de Leon's relations with Joseph ben Todros Abulafia.

120 Bahya mentions the מדרש רשב"י only twice, but he uses it in many other places. This has escaped the notice of many modern writers but was recognized already 1589 by Moses Mordecai Margoliouth in חסדי ה' f. 26b.

121 Cf. my essay in *Kirjath Sefer*, vol. IV (1928) p. 311 ff.

122 Some early authors quote parts of the Zohar as עשר ספירות לחכמי המשנה, מעשה בראשית לחכמי המשנה etc. And Moses de Leon himself does the same in quoting Zohar I, 19b with the introduction ראיתי בדברי חכמי המשנה cf. הנפש החכמה ch. 2.

123 Cf. Steinschneider, Gesammelte Schriften I (1925) p. 171—180. St. did not know that the original Arabic text of Ibn Wakkar's voluminous work is still extant in Ms. Vatican. 203, cf. my article in *Kirjath Sefer*, vol. XX (1944) p. 153—162.

124 Ms. Vatican, 203 f. 63b ואמא מה יגד מן ספר הזוהר פינגבי אן יתחדק פמא ואפק למה דכרת פליעזם עליהא ומא האלפה פלא יעזם עליהא אד וקע פיה תגליט כתיר גדא יג'ב אן יתחפט ויתחדד מנה לאן לא יגלט.

"As to what is found of the book Zohar, it is necessary to be careful. To those passages that are in accordance with what I have said he may pay attention, but to those that disagree he should pay no attention, for there occur in the book very many errors. Therefore, it is necessary to be careful and keep within bounds from it in order not to make mistakes." The Hebrew synopsis Ms. Oxford 1627 f. 11a is much shorter וספר הזוהר נפלו בו טעיות רבות מאד יתחייב להשמר מהם (!) כדי שלא יטעו.

125 E. Zeller, Vortraege und Abhandlungen. Erste Sammlung (second edition) 1875 p. 336.

126 The text of this testimony is printed in ספר יוחסין (1857) p. 88f., and better in JQR vol. IV (1892) p. 361 ff. Cf. also Graetz vol. VII (1894) p. 427—430.

127 Ms. Adler 1589 in JThS (in a fragment of Isaac's אוצר החיים) חכמי כתלוניא יסמכו על יסוד חזק הוא ספר הבהיר וחכמי ספרד f. 123b: (Castile =) סמכו על יסוד אמיץ הוא ספר הזוהר והמשכיל יכריע וישים שלום ביניהם.

128 This *epitheton* is found in Graetz vol. IX (1866) p. 451.

129 Ibid. vol. VII (1894) p. 199.

130 It is interesting to note that almost everything that has been said by Jewish rationalistic critics of the author of the Zohar was said in almost identical words by Christian writers of a similar bent about that great Byzantine mystic who wrote about 500 A.D. under the assumed name

of Dionysius the Areopagite, known from the Acts of the Apostles XVII,34. As a matter of fact, the parallel between these two groups of writings goes far beyond these strictures on the genius and the character of their authors (See note 156). The position occupied by them in the history of Christian and Jewish mysticism, respectively, is strikingly similar.

131   Ms. Guenzburg 771, cf. I. Zinberg, The History of Jewish Literature [in Yiddish] vol. III (1931) p. 55.

132   This is especially true of parts of ספר הרמון, of the אור זרוע (Ms. Vatican 212) and of the great fragment without title in Ms. Munich 47 (cf. note 115).

133   Parts of his אור זרוע which are to be found (without title or name of the author) in Ms. Vatican 428 f. 80—90 could easily be taken for writings by Gikatila. On the other hand, it required some critical analysis to ascertain that the important fragment New York JThS 851 f. 62—92 was really written by Gikatila and not by Moses de Leon. This is part of a hitherto unknown commentary on the Torah written in the vein of גנת האגוז and it can be conclusively shown that Moses de Leon has made use of it.

134   Cf. the references given in מדעי היהדות I p. 27.

135   This is borne out by the earliest manuscripts (e. g. Florence, Laurentiana Pl. II Cod. 41, written 1325), although Isaac of Acre quotes the book already as שערי אורה (in his מאירת עינים Cod. Munich 17).

136   Cf. מדעי היהדות I p. 27, note 40.

137   התעורר as a transitive verb; forms like התצייר, התסדר etc.; the gerundival use of the infinitive (נקודה אחת להשתלשל משם כל ההויות ...הוא very common in the Zohar); עלה בשם ; השתדל אחרי in the sense of מסכים מחלוקת ; לחיקרא בשם "to settle a quarrel"(!!), הטא אצלי, and many other wrong constructions with אצל (cf. note 40); חוזר instead of מחזיר — to give only some characteristic examples all of which recur in the Zohar.

138   A. Jellinek, Moses de Leon und sein Verhaeltnis zum Sohar (1851), especially p. 24—36.

139   Thus the parable Zohar I, 170a is used and "edited" in משכן העדות Ms. Berlin Or. 833 f. 59b to serve as a simile for the gradual acclimatization of the soul to the other world.

140   Zohar I, 20a and Zohar Hadash f. 71a as compared with משכן העדות f. 35b.

141   L. Ginzberg has suggested (Legends of the Jews vol. VI p. 123) that Zohar III, 184b made use of Maimonides' explanation of ידוע in his commentary in the Mishnah-Treatise Sanhedrin. It is precisely this passage which Moses de Leon actually quotes in his treatment of אוב וידעוני in the ספר הרמון.

142 *Pesikta de-Rab Kahana* ed. Buber f. 6a. ויהי ביום כלת משה כלת כתיב
ביום דעלת כלתא לגנונא.

143 In his ספר הרמון Ms. Brit. Museum f. 6 he quotes all the *motifs*
and associations of thought which occur in the passage on משה איש
האלהים מאריה דביתא מריה דמטרוניתא in Zohar I, 236b in the name of
the *Pesikta*. In particular, the surprising connection with Num. XXX,14
in both passages is most interesting.

144 This was a favorite idea of Jellinek's and was adopted by Graetz
vol. VII (1894) p. 200. Moses de Leon "quotations" from the Enoch
Book are published in מדרש תלפיות s. v. גן עדן (1860) f. 115a ff. and
partly in Jellinek's *Beth Ha-Midrash* III p. 195—197.

145 Cf. my book כתבי יד בקבלה p. 35.

146 The response in question is to be found in שערי תשובה No. 80. The
סודות on several commandments which constitute the second part of
ס' הנפש החכמה are extant in two versions. One is the printed one in which
Moses de Leon quotes a passage from this response as אמרו רז"ל (§ 12).
But there is another version in manuscript (e. g. in an important codex
which was some years ago in possession of Mr. Jacob Zevi Joskowitz in
Zelow, Poland) and there he quotes R. Hai Gaon! ראיתי בדברי רבינו
האיי גאון ז"ל משל לרועה צאן שכל זמן שהצאן במדבר ודובים ואריות שכיחי אז
הוא צריך שמירה על הצאן : כיון שנכנס לעיר תחת חומה אינו צריך שמירה.

147 David Luria מאמר קדמות ספר הזהר (1856 and 1887), ch. II.

148 Zohar III, 184b quotes a book קדמאה דכשדיאל זיני חרשין. Moses
de Leon has a further legend on this Kasdiel, in his סוד יציאת מצרים
Ms. Schocken f. 82a.

149 The brief allusion in Zohar I, 15b to the three vowel points
חלם שורק חירק ואתכלילו דא בדא ואתעבידו רזא חדא is fully developed in
the ספר הרמון. For another example cf. Jellinek, Moses de Leon, p. 37.

150 שמימים מועטים נתפשט מעין הסוד : (סוד היבום) 12 § ס' הנפש החכמה
בארץ.

151 Ms. Berlin Or. 833 f. 51a/b. The Hebrew text reads as follows:
ואע"פ שתראה שאני מגלה סודות סתורים וגנוזים שהיו בין החכמים הקדושים
קדושים ומסותרים, עמוקים אשר אין להם ראוי לגלותם, למען לא יהיו למטרח
לחץ לכל יבא ממה שעמלו אותם הקדושים כל ימיהם בם והסתירום ולא גלום לכל
ואני באתי עתה לגלותם, על כן יהיו לך לבדך אלא אם תראה ירא השם שמנע (?)
(שומר ?) תורתו ומצוותו... ובראותי אני עניני בני העולם במחשבות זרות ודעות
נפסדות חיצונות בעניינים הללו, ודור הולך ודור בא, והדעת הנפסדת לעולם עומדת
ואין רואה ואין שומע ואין מקיץ כי כלם ישנים כי תרדמת י"י נפלה עליהם לא
לשאול ולא לקרוא ולא לדקדק, הוצרכתי לכתוב ולגנוז ולעיין כדי לגלותי (לגלותו ?)
לכל משכיל ולהודיע כל הדברים האלה אשר החכמים הקדושים הקדמונים עמלו בהם
כל ימותיהם שהם מפוזרים בתלמוד ובדבריהם ובמצפונידהם יקרים וצפונים וטמונים
מפנינים, והשער סגרו עליהם והעלימו כל ספריהם העמוקים וראו שאין לגלותם

ולפרסם אותם. וכבר צונו החכם הידוע ז"ל באומרו באזני כסיל אל תדבר ועל (כן)
העלימו קבלתם והסתירו חכמתם. ועל כי [!sic] ידעתי גם אני כי הוא מצוה להוציא
לאור צלמות ולהודיע דברים הסתומים אשר הם הסתירו ז"ל.

In the same context we read two pages later f. 52b—53a the following
passage (at the beginning of his exposition of the mysteries of Gan
Eden):   בדברים האלה ראיתי בסוד עניני גן עדן ומחלקותיו לחכמים גדולים אשר
אמרו כפי תוכן סברתם וגם הדורות [53a] הבאים אחריהם נמשכו באותן הדברים
ונתבקעו ונתקעו בלבם כמסמרים העניינים האלה. ואינם נשגים מצד אומד הדעת
ולא מצד הסברא זולתי מסוד החכמה הפנימית אשר (היא) קבלה והלכה למשה מסיני
והנחלו חכמים הקדמונים משרתי עליון אשר זכו פנים בפנים נוראות. ויראו את
המלך צבאות בשכלם, המה באו אל מקדשו והמה יקרבו אליו לשרתו ושמרו את משמרתו
וכל דבריהם בהיכל המלך פנימה... מתוקים מדבש ונופת צופים ומסברתם וענייניהם
וסודותיהם שברחו עמהם בהחבא. עכשיו יש עתה להתעורר ולגלות על סוד ענין גן
עדן ומחלקותיו וענייניו וסודותיו. ואקדים לך בתחילה אותם העניינים אשר התעוררו
חכמי עליון הקדמונים ז"ל והצפינו בסתריהם בעומק חכמתם וישאלו איש מאת רעהו
שאלות מעניינים עמוקים ודברים עתיקים וישיבו אותם דבר להעמידם על דת שוכן
שמי ערץ... וסוד החכמה העמוקה לא נגרע מעבודתם דבר אשר לא הגידו וכתבו והעידו.
קבלה נכונה ממרומים כל אלה החכמים אשר אין דרך לנטות ימין ושמאל. ובסבת
עונותינו אשר גרמו אזלת יד בני עמנו ונדדו בגלותם ומרעה אל רעה יצאו אזי נשתכחו
כל החכמות השכליות ומעייני החכמה יבשו ונסעו ודבר ממנה לא ידעו כי אין דורש
ואין מבקש... ועל כן אבדה חכמה מבנים וכלים מכלים שונים ולאחר דורות נמשכו
אחרי דברי הבלי משלי היונים ויהיו לאחור ולא לפנים כאשר אמרתי וסדרתי כל
זה בספר בהקדמת ספר הרמון שעשיתי.

152 Ibid. f. 58b: ואף על פי שעתה אני מגלה סודותם, אל אלהים י"י יודע כי
כוונתי היא לטובה למען רבים יחכמו ויחזיקו יותר באמונתו ית' וישמעו וילמדו
וייראו על נפשותם וישמחו ביודעם האמת והטוב הגנוז לצדיקים כדי שיזכו בו.

153 Jellinek, Moses de Leon, p. 21.

154 The following very interesting passage is found in ספר הרמון Brit.
Mus. f. 107—108a: יומם וראיתי אנשים שהיו משתדלים בתורה ובדברי רז"ל
ולילה והיו עובדים את המקום בטוב לבב כפי הראוי ויהי היום ויבואו בני ספרי
היונים (!) להתיצב על י"י ויבא גם השטן בתוכם ויעזבו מקור מים חיים וישתדלו
באותם הספרים וימשכו דעתם אחריהם עד אשר עזבו דברי התורה והמצוות וישליכום
אחרי גום והיו חושבים (דף ק"ח ע"א) דברי רז"ל לשקר באומד דעתם החצונה.
והנה אין קול ואין עונה כי רחוקים המה מהיונים ועוזריהם ורוח האלהות אין בהם
עד אשר המה נהפכו לאנשים אחרים ויתהו על הראשונות ועל דרכיהם הטובים אשר
הלכו בהם קודם ויתלוצצו וילעגו על דברי ז"ל זולתי שהיו נושאים פנים בפני חרבים
ויאמרו כי דרך חסידות היו עושים שלא היו מדברים רעה ברברים על רז"ל מפני
שהיו מתים לא מפני דבר אחר וחושבים כי טפשות כל דבריהם. עד כי כאשר היו
מתיחדים זה עם זה מליגים ומתלוצצים ומשתעשעים בדברי היונים ועוזריהם
ונושקים דבריהם. ועוד ראיתי להם בימי חג הסוכות שעומדים במקומם בב"ה ורואים
עבדי האלהים סובבים בלולבים סביב ס"ת בתיבה והם שוחקים ומליגים עליהם ואומר
כי סכלים הם חסירי דעת ולהם אין לולב ולא אתרוג ואמרו בטענתם הלא התורה
אמרה שלקיחה זו בשביל שכתוב ושמחתם לפני י"י אלהיכם שבעת ימים אתם חושבים
שיבוא אלו המינים לשמחנו חלא טוב כלי כסף וכלי זהב ושמלות לשמחנו ולענגנגו.

ואמרו הלא חשבתם שאנו צריכים לברך את השם הוא צריך זה ? הכל הבל I עד אשר
לא נראה בראשם תפלין ושאלו להם למה, היו אומרים אין ענין התפילין זולתי כמו
שכתוב ולזכרון בין עיניך הואיל ואין זכרון טוב לנו לזכור לבורא בפינו כמה פעמים
ביום וזהו זכרון שהיא טובה והגונה יותר, ולוקחים אותם הספרים ורואים אותם
הדברים ואומרים כי זו היא תורת אמת. ותופשי התורה היו מתחבאים בדבריהם
ולא היה לבם מלא מלא לדבר אפילו דבר אחד כל שכן דברים אחרים עתיקים שהיה בקבלת
זקנים קדמונים ולא מלאם לבם לדברם ולזכור אותם בפיהם. על סבה זו נשתכחה הרבה
תורה מישראל עד אשר העיר העיר רוח אחרת ולקחו בני אדם עצה טובה לשוב אחר
דעת הבורא האמיתי ית' והבינו דברים בדברי רז"ל בהתעוררות מעט שהתעוררו אבל
עוד העם מזבחים ומקטרים בבמות ולא הניחו דעתם מכל וכל להשתדל אחרי התורה
הקדושה תורה צוה לנו משה מורשה.

155   In his משכן עדות Ms. Berlin f. 32a. The passage is here ascribed
vaguely to מורה צדק perhaps because he did not want to mention Aristotle's name in so sublime a connection.

156   Steinschneider who thought little of Moses de Leon's merits said in
his acid way: "Wie unser gewissenloser Buecherfabrikant ueberhaupt gerne
sich in Moralisation ergeht," cf. his catalogue of the Hebrew manuscripts
in Berlin vol. II (1897) p. 39. This reminds one of the naive exclamation
of John of Scythopolis (about 540) the first Greek commentator of
Dionysius who said of pseudo-Dionysius the Areopagite: "What a desperate human being would a writer have to be who misused the names
of so many sacred persons and things from early Christian times for
such a fabric of lies and who yet proved to be for the rest so pious and
enlightened a writer."

NOTES TO LECTURE VI

THE ZOHAR II: THE THEOSOPHIC DOCTRINE

1   Of Abulafia's commentary to the Torah (written in 1289 in Messina)
we still possess ס' מפתח החכמות to Genesis Ms. Parma 141, New York
JThS 843; ס' מפתח השמות to Exodus Ms. New York 843: ס' מפתח הספירות
to Numbers Ms. Ambrosiana 53; ס' מפתח התוכחה to Deuteron. Ms. Oxford
1805.

2   There can be little doubt in my opinion that the famous stanzas of
the mysterious *Book Dzyan* on which Madame H. P. Blavatsky's *magnum
opus,* The Secret Doctrine, is based owe something, both in title and content, to the pompous pages of the Zoharic writing called *Sifra Di-Tseniutha.*
The first to advance this theory, without further proof, was L. A. Bosman,
a Jewish Theosophist, in his booklet The Mysteries of the Qabalah (1916)
p. 31. This seems to me, indeed, the true "etymology" of the hitherto unexplained title. Madame Blavatsky has drawn heavily upon Knorr von
Rosenroth's Kabbala Denudata (1677—1684), which contains (vol. II

p. 347—385) a Latin translation of the *Sifra Di-Tseniutha*. The solemn
and magniloquent style of these pages may well have impressed her
susceptible mind. As a matter of fact, H. P. B. herself alludes to such a
connection between the two "books" in the very first lines of Isis Unveiled
(vol. I p. 1) where she still refrains from mentioning the *Book Dzyan*
by name. But the transcription used by her for the Aramaic title shows
clearly what she had in mind. She says: "There exists somewhere in this
wide world an old Book . . . It is the only original copy now in existence.
*The most ancient Hebrew document on occult learning — the Siphra
Dzeniuta — was compiled from it.*" The *Book Dzyan* is therefore nothing
but an occultistic hypostasy of the Zoharic title. This "bibliographical"
connection between the fundamental writings of modern and of Jewish
Theosophy seems remarkable enough.

3 See second lecture, section 10.

4 מרכבת המשנה a term used by Todros Abulafia, Moses of Burgos etc.

5 המרכבה הפנימית —a very common term.

6 Particularly the writings centering on the ס' העיון and the ס' מעין
החכמה,   cf. my article in Korrespondenzblatt der Akademie der Wissenschaft des Judentums 1928 p. 18 ff.

7 Fourteenth century Kabbalists (e.g. David ben Jehuda in ספר הגבול
the oldest commentary on the *Idra Rabba* in the Zohar) refer to עשר צחצחות
which are above the Sefiroth. Cf. also Cordovero's פרדס רמונים chapter XI
(שער הצחצחות).

8 See first lecture, section 4. The Zohar uses the Hebrew term אין סוף
without translating it into Aramaic. It was used first by Isaac the Blind
and his disciples.

9 Cf. the anthropomorphic passages in the book *Bahir;* Gikatila's preface
to his *Shaare Orah*. The formula used in the text is found in ibn Latif's
§ 9 רב פעלים and Emanuel Hai Rikki, יושר לבב part one, chapter 3 § 15.

10 Zohar III, 159a, cf. *Tarbiz* vol. III p. 38. The interpretation of the
passage found in the English translation vol. V p. 226 is incorrect.

11 Zohar III, 70a. The phrase itself is taken from the *Sefer Yetsirah* ch.
I, 6.

12 D. H. Joel, Die Religionsphilosophie des Sohar (1849), particularly p.
179 ff.

13 The most important enumeration and analysis of such symbols of the
Sefiroth is contained in Gikatila's ס' שערי אורה. Also very valuable are the
ספר השם by an unknown Rabbi Moses (about 1325)—not written by Moses
de Leon, as has long been thought (cf. *Kirjath Sefer* I p. 45—52)—and
chapter 23 of Moses Cordovero's פרדס רמונים (שער ערכי הכנויים).

14 Cf. my article, Bibel in der Kabbala, in EJ IV, col. 688—692. Very
typical of this attitude is the symbolic aura given to Levit. XVI, 3 בזאת

יבוא אהרן אל הקדש in a large number of passages. It is interpreted as mean‹ ing: Only when the Shekhinah (called זאת) is with a man, shall he enter the holy place!

15. Cf. Bacher's article REJ vol. 22 (1891) p. 37 ff. Only the passage II, 99a/b is from the real Zohar; the passages I, 26b and III, 110a are from the *Tikkunim* and *Raya Mehemna*. Moses de Leon says 1290 that he has composed a *Sefer Pardes* וקראתי שמו פרדס על ענין ידוע שחברתי אותו בסוד ד' דרכים... פ'שט ר'מז ד'רשה ס'וד (Ms. Munich 22 f. 128b).

16 Cf. Bacher loc. cit. p. 41—46, 219—229.

17 Cf. Zohar II, 99a/b and III, 152a.

18 III, 152a.

19 The author calls the Talmudic scholar חמור דמתניתין adding that חמור is an abbreviation of חכם מופלא ורב רבנן (III, 275b). Other examples in Graetz, Geschichte der Juden, vol. VII p. 505—506.

20 See ספר הפליאה ed. Koretz 1784 and better Przemysl 1883; ספר הקנה Porizk 1786. Cf Graetz vol. VIII, note 8; S. A. Horodezky in *Hatekufah* vol. X (1920) p. 283—329; Verus (A. Marcus), Der Chassidismus (1901) p. 244—261. Marcus' views on the authorship of the book, which have been accepted by several recent writers (e. g. by M. Kamelhar ר' אביגדור קרא in *Sinai* vol. III p. 122—148) are entirely mistaken.

21 Many examples are given in the literature quoted in note 20.

22 Cf. Graetz loc. cit. and already Cordovero שעור קומה (1883) f. 79—80.

23 Hibbert Journal vol. 28 (1930) p. 762.

24 There are about ten editions of the book and a Latin translation of large parts of it by Paulus Riccius, Portae Lucis, Augsburg 1516.

25 Waite's Secret Doctrine in Israel, which first appeared 1913, has been incorporated in his Holy Kabbalah (1929) which contains also his earlier book, The Doctrine and Literature of the Kabbalah (1902). The chapters taken from this book are unfortunately of very little value.

26 III, 30b, or simply כתרין עלאין דמלכא קדישא ,כתרי מלכא.

27 Zohar III, 11b, 70a.

28 II, 86a, or אפי מלכא ,אנפין פנימאין.

29 The terms דרגין and נהורין are those employed most frequently. III, 7a speaks of "אינון לבושי יקר דמלכא אתלבש בהו„.

30 Cf. Das Buch Bahir, German transl. by G. Scholem § 85.

31 The term אדם קדמון itself is not used in the main parts of the Zohar but only in the *Tikkunim*. The Zohar speaks of אדם דלעילא. But III, 193b we find the Aramaic term דרגא עלאה דאדם קדמאה טמירא. In the *Idra Rabba* III, 139b we read: כל אינון כתרין קדישין דמלכא כד אתקנו בתקונוי אתקרון אדם, דיוקנא דכליל כלא.

32 This is the expression coined by Cordovero in his פרדס רמונים.

33 The chapter שער עצמות וכלים in Cordovero's *magnum opus* is devoted to the discussion of this problem.

34 Cf. Zohar I, 245a bottom.

35 Cf. Zohar III, 10—11.

36 Zohar I, 16b.

37 Zohar I, 74a. The same symbolism is used I, 15a/b. Moses de Leon expounds its meaning in many passages of his Hebrew books.

38 On הוא and אתה cf. Zohar II, 90a; III, 290a; on אני I, 65b, 204a/b.

39 The tenth Sefirah is the תרעא למיעל ברזא דמהימנותא Zohar I, 11b.

40 Cf. Commentary to the *Sefer Yetsirah* ascribed to R. Abraham ben David, in ed. Warsaw 1884 p. 5 col. a. On the true author of this commentary cf. my essay in *Kirjath Sefer* IV p. 286—302.

41 שערי אורה ס' (Offenbach 1714) f. 108b. The same idea is expressed in the "preface" to *Tikkune Zohar* (Mantua 1558) f. 7a, and in a more developed form in *Peliah* (1883) f. 14c.

42 Zohar I, 2a: Moses de Leon שקל הקדש ס' p. 25. Cf. Isaac Hacohen פירוש המרכבה in *Tarbiz* vol. II p. 195, 206.

43 Jacob ben Shesheth משיב דברים נכוחים ס' Ms. Oxford 1585 f. 28a/b. He does not use the term נקודה but speaks of היוה דקה מאד ממנה מתחיל. His friend Nahmanides uses it in a veiled form קו היושר להמשך ולהתפשט in his (generally misunderstood) commentary on Genesis I, 1.

44 In Moses de Leon's ספר הרמון Ms. British Museum 759 f. 125—230.

45 התחלת הישות a term very common in the writings of the Geronese Kabbalists.

46 Zohar I, 15a. My translation differs considerably from that of the printed English edition, but I cannot go into philological detail here.

47 The author plays on the Talmudic saying (*Megillah* 21b) בראשית נמי מאמר הוא.

48 Zohar I, 15a/b.

49 The Zohar I, 2a says of the divine מחשבה which is identified with wisdom ציור בה כל הציורין, הקק בה כל גליפין. Cf. also III, 43a. Azriel of Gerona states in his פירוש האגדות Ms. Jerusalem f. 42b that חכמה means כח כל מה שאפשר להיות, but he says also (ibid. f. 44a/b) that the essences הויות of everything are contained in חכמה.

50 Cf. Zohar I, 15b.

51 III, 65b כללא דכל פרטא. Azriel of Gerona speaks of *Hokhmah* as כלל כל כלל כל ההויות שיש בהן רשימה and of *Binah* as החויות שאין בהן רשימה in

chapter I of his פירוש ספר יצירה which is found in the printed editions of *Yetsirah*, the name of Nahmanides being given as that of the author.

52　יומין קדמאין Zohar III, 134b, or very often יומין עלאין.

53　Shelley, Adonais LII.

54　Zohar I, 1b—2a, 30a, 85b; II, 126b ff., 138—140b.

55　I, 15b. The same interpretation is given by all the disciples of Isaac the Blind and Nahmanides.

56　Cf. the passages quoted in MGWJ vol. (1927) p. 118—119.

57　One of these pantheists is David ben Abraham Ha-Lavan (about 1300) whose ס' מסורת הברית I have published 1936.

58　Zohar I, 240b.

59　I, 241a.

60　Cf. my analysis of this term in *Tarbiz* III p. 36—39.

61　Zohar I, 241a כד יסתכלון מלי כלא סלקא לחד.Similar expressions are used many times.

62　This idea is advanced as the mystical meaning of Psalm XIX, 5 בכל הארץ יצא קום cf. Zohar II, 137a.

63　These *Hekhaloth* are described at length in the Zohar I, 38—45 and II, 245a—262b.

64　Part of a lengthy passage in Moses de Leon's ספר הרמון Ms. Brit. Museum 759 f. 47b which contains a pantheistic paraphrase of a passage in the *Pesikta Rabbati* ed. Friedmann f. 98b: וחכל נקשר זה בזה עד סוף כל הטבעות אשר מלמטה לחיות אמתת מיצאותו למטה ולמעלה... התבונן העניין ותמצא על כי הוא יתברך אמתת מציאותו נקשרת ומשתלשלת בכל העולמות וכל ההויות נקשרות ונאהזות זה בזו באמתת מציאותו.

65　They speak of השבת כל הדברים להויתם which corresponds exactly to the term *apokatastasis* that played so large a part in the ideas of many Christian mystics.

66　Cf. אין השנויים אלא מצד המקבלים f. 6b מערכת האלהות ; Zohar II, 176a כולי האי לא אתקרי אלא מסטרא דילן; III, 141a/b. The same Neoplatonic formula is used by Christian mystics like Meister Eckhart, cf. A. Dempf, Meister Eckhart (1934) p. 93. Cf. also Gabirol's Fons Vitae ed. Baeumker III, 33 and Jacob Guttmann, Die Philosophie Gabirols, p. 163.

67　Moses de Leon's older contemporary, Isaac ben Jacob Hacohen, has given a vivid description of such an ascent and descent of the Shekhinah in the Sefirotic world in his מאמר על האצילות which I have published in מדעי היהדות vol. II (1927) p. 246.

68　Cordovero's פרדס רמונים (written 1548) appeared 1592 in Cracow, his אלימה רבתי (written 1567—68) in Brody 1881.

69   Elisha Gallico of Safed has a very illuminating passage on this subject
in the preface to his פירוש שיר השירים Venice 1587 f. 2a.

70   Cf. Zohar I, 11b; II, 216a; III, 56a and a long disquisition on the subject at the beginning of Moses de Leon's ספר הרמון.

71   Zohar II, 97a and 146b. These passages have only too frequently been
misinterpreted by modern writers. A very interesting parallel passage is
found in Moses de Leon's משכן העדות Ms. Berlin Or. 833 f. 36a: The
devout may "adhere" to the Shekhinah but solely in her "veiled state" in
which she is called ערפל (Exod. XX, 21). A real mystical union exists
only between the Shekhinah and her Master.

72   Zohar I, 21b—22a: (!) משה שמש ...משה ביה במשה... אזדווגא [מטרוניתא].
בעוד דאיהו בגופא בסיהרא (a symbol of the Shekhinah).

73   A first attempt to analyze this symbolism has been made by Waite in
the chapter on "The Mystery of Sex" in his Secret Doctrine in Israel p.
235—269. But his analysis is built on the incorrect hypothesis that the
Zoharic term רזא דמהימנותא means a sex mystery. As a matter of fact,
this term simply signifies the whole of the ten Sefiroth, the mystical world
of God, without any sexual or erotical connotation.

74   Zohar I, 207b uses the term זווגא קדישא; III, 7a זווגא דמלכא ומטרוניתא.

75   The critics of Kabbalism have fastened on this point as proof of its
essentially pagan character. Cf. in particular the well documented but very
superficial treatise by S. Rubin, Heidenthum und Kabbala, Wien 1893, p.
85—114, and the eloquent polemics of the Yemenite scholar Yahya Kafih
in his work against Kabbalism מלחמות השם ס' Tel-Aviv 1931.

76   Outstanding examples of this symbolism are to be found in Zohar I,
162a; II, 128a/b; III, 5a/b and 26a.

77   M. D. Georg Langer, Die Erotik der Kabbala, Prag 1923.

78   Zohar III, 296a/b, in a mystical interpretation of Psalm CXXXII, 13.
Here ציון is used as a sexual symbol. On the critics of this symbolism cf.
Simeon ibn Labi כתם פז (1795) f. 11b and 185b.

79   Cf. my German translation §§ 36, 43, 44, 52, 90.

80   Ibid. § 90.

81   The terms מטרוניתא, ברתא, and כלולה כלה are employed, particularly the
first.

82   עולמתא שפירתא דלית לה עיינין taken from the Zohar II, 95a where
it symbolizes the Torah. As a symbol of the Shekhinah it is used by the
whole Lurianic school.

83   Cf. ספר חמדת ימים (Venice 1763) vol. II f. 4a/b; Meir Poppers
ספר אור הישר (Amsterdam 1709) f. 7d.

84   Cf. Zohar I, 228b: שכינתא כל נוקבי דעלמא קיימין בסתרהא.

85   See note 73.

86   האדם כלול מכל הדברים הרוחניים — a formula originally employed by
Ezra ben Solomon, fifty years before the Zohar. In the latter's language,
man is דיוקנא דכליל כלא (III, 139b).

87   Ezra says in סוד עץ הדעת Ms. Oxford, Christ Church College 198 f. 7b:
אדם קודם אכילתו היה כולו רוחני ולובש מלאכות כחנוך ואליהו ועל כן היה ראוי
לאכול מפירות גן עדן שהם פירות הנשמה. Cf. Zohar III, 83b.

88   שערי אורה (Offenbach 1715) f. 9a.

89   Zohar II, 41b; 216b; III, 77b.

90   Cf. the interpretation given in Zohar III, 77b of Zechariah XIV, 9 and
III, 260b.

91   Cf. the same passage of the Zohar השתא חייבי עלמא גרמו דלא אשתכח חד.

92   Zohar I, 164a and often.

93   שרשין עלאין cf. II, 34a.

94   The Zohar very often uses the verb אתדבקת במאריה but only seldom
the substantive דבקותא.

95   Nahmanides on Deuteron. XI, 22.

96   Sayings like Hagigah 9b: חזר הקב"ה על כל מדות טובות ליתן לישראל ולא
מצא אלא עניות are exceptional.

97   מאנין תבירין cf. Zohar I, 10b etc., cf. my note in Baer's article in Zion
vol. V p. 30.

98   ספר הרמון Ms. British Museum f. 35b.

99   Cf. Baer's article in Zion vol. V. p. 1—44, and note 97 on the previous
lecture.

100   Zohar I, 249b.

101   Cf. L. Ginzberg, Legends of the Jews vol. V p. 325.

102   Ps.-Nahmanides   אגרת הקדש... בענין חבור האדם אל אשתו,   first
edition Rome 1546. Cf. my article in Kirjath Sefer vol. XXI p. 179—186.

103   Cf. Moses Cordovero פרדס רמונים chapter IV § 9.

104   I have published Moses of Burgos' ס' עמוד השמאלי in Tarbiz vol.
IV p. 208—225, cf. also the analysis ibid. III p. 272—286.

105   These ideas are developed in the numerous סודות of the 13th century
Kabbalists on the question of Adam's sin. The classical formula of the
Zohar is given I, 12b; the essence of sin was: חבר לתתא ואתפרש לעילא . . .
בגין דאצטריך לאפרשא לתתא ולחברא לעילא. The mystical term for this destruc-
tive separation is קצוץ בנטיעות. The term is frequently employed by the
Geronese school. Ezra ben Solomon says in his סוד עץ הדעת Ms. Oxford,
Christ Church College 198 f. 7b—8a that the Tree of Life and the Tree of

Knowledge were separated only by Adam's sin. The other symbolism quoted in the text is used by Meir ibn Abu Sahula, a disciple of Solomon ben Adreth, in ביאור לפירוש הרמב"ן על התורה (1875) p. 5.

106   Cf. Zohar I, 35b and 36b, where the origin of magical knowledge is described as the direct consequence of the קיצוץ בנטיעות. As a matter of fact, Bahya ben Asher (1291) defines כשוף sorcery, as חבור דברים חלוקים זה מזה (in his commentary to Exod. XXII, 17.) Cf. also Zohar III, 86a on כלאים (which is taken from Nahmanides).

107   Zohar III, 15b in a mystical paraphrase of the Talmudic saying עבירה גוררת עבירה.

108   This fundamental thought is alluded to quite often in the Zohar and in Moses de Leon's Hebrew writings. The principal passage where it is expounded at some length in Zohar I, 17a—18a. The world of Satan originates in the hypertrophy of wrath תוקפאדדינא קשיא I, 74b; 148a or תוקפא דיצחק I, 161b.

109   Baader, Vorlesungen zu Jacob Boehme's Lehre (1855) p. 66 tries to sum up Boehme's teachings on the mystical nature in God "in the vein of Angelus Silesius":

Licht und Liebe sich entzuenden
Wo sich Streng' und Milde finden.
Zorn und Finsternis entbrennen
Wo sich Streng' und Milde trennen.

This reads exactly like a versified paraphrase of Zohar I, 17ff.

110   Friedrich Christian Oetinger's Selbstbiographie, edited by Hamberger (1845) p. 46.

111   Cf. Zohar III, 192b. II, 98a describes it as the ענפא מרירא of the cosmic tree. Other frequent similes : מים עכורים, זוהמא דדהבא, שמרים דחמרא דורדיין בישין etc.

112   Zohar I, 19b; II, 69b; 108b; 184b; III, 185a.

113   Gikatila has written a short treatise on this question, סוד הנחש ומשפטו which is found in several manuscripts e. g. Leiden, Cod. Warner 32. Here we find a myth on the origin of evil (f. 155b-156a) : דע כי ביצחק נאחזים ל"ה שרים לשמאל ע"י אדום וע"י עמלק ודע כי עמלק הוא ראש של נחש הקדמוני והוא נאחז בנחש והנחש מרכבתו... ובאותו מקום ("רפידים") נמצאו הנחש ועמלק מזדווגים כאחד וכתיב דרך נחש עלי צור... ודע והאמן כי הנחש בתחלת בריאתו היה צורך גדול בתקון העולם בהיותו עומד במקומו והוא היה שמש גדול נברא לסבול עול הממלכות והשעבוד וראשו עד במתי ארץ וזנבו עד שאול ואבדון כי בכל העולמות כלם היה לו מקום וצורך גדול לתקן כל המרכבות כל אחד במקומו. וזה סוד התל"י תידוע בס' יצירה והוא המניע כל הגלגלים והמהפך אותם ממזרח למערב ומצפון לדרום, ואלמלא הוא — אין לשום בריה מכל העולם שתחת גלגל הירח חיים, זריעה וצמיחה, ואין התעוררות לתולדות כל הנבראים, ומתחלה היה עומד מחוץ

לכתלי מחנות הקדושה והיה מחובר מחוץ לכותל חיצון שבמחברות (1) אחוריו
כי היו דבוקות בכותל ופניו פונות כלפי חוץ ולא היה לו מקום ליכנס לפנים והיה
מקומו לעבוד עבודת הצמיחה והתולדות מבחוץ וזהו סוד עץ הדעת טוב ורע. לפיכך
הזהיר הש"י לאדם הראשון שלא יגע בעץ הדעת בעוד שהטוב והרע שניהם דבוקים
[יחד?] שזה מבפנים וזה מבחוץ עד שימתין להפריד את הערלה שנ' וערלתם ערלתו
את פריו וכתי' ותקח מפריו: הכנים צלם בהיכל ונמצאת הטומאה חיצונה נכנסת
לפנים... דע כי כל מעשה האלהים כשהם מקומם כל אחד באותו מקום שהכינו והעמידו
בבריאתו, הוא טוב... ואם נהפך ויצא ממקומו הוא רע... ולפיכך נאמר עושה שלום
ובורא רע.

114   Zohar II, 69a/b, 216a, 227a; III, 252a.

115   Zohar II, 103a; I, 171a on the "legs" of the serpent, Sammael, who,
according to Gen. III, 14, was left with nothing to stand on, but is provided with "legs on which to stand firm and upright" by Israel's sins.

116   Zohar II, 34b.

117   סטרא דשמאלא and סטרא אחרא are very frequent metaphors for the demonic power.

118   Zohar I, 223b; II, 34b; III, 135b and 292b. Cf. also the תשובה of the
pseudo-Gikatila on the question היאך מהטוב יצא רע in Festschrift Dr. Jakob
Freimann zum 70. Geburtstag (1937), Hebr. part p. 170; מסכת אצילות
ed. Jellinek in גנזי חכמת הקבלה (1853) p. 2.

119   Zohar II, 163a.

120   The Hebrew text of the whole hymn is printed in Michael Sachs, Die
religioese Poesie der Juden in Spanien, 2. Aufl. (1901) p. 50—51.

121   Cf. Sachs, op. cit. p. 328—331; I have given a complete German translation in Almanach des Schocken Verlags auf das Jahr 5696/1936 p. 86—89.

122   Cf. L. Husik, A History of Mediaeval Jewish Philosophy (1918) p.
XLVII.

123   Zohar I, 206a; II, 141b; III, 70b. The original character of this
psychology can still be gauged from the *Midrash Ha-Ne'elam* especially
on the section בראשית (printed in the editions of the *Zohar Hadash*).

124   *Binah* is often called נהר דנגיד ונפיק מן קדמוהי and *Neshamah*
emerges from this stream of light. (The Zohar connects 'stream' נהר with
'light' נהורא). II, 174a hints at an even higher origin of *Neshamah* in the
Sefirah of *Hokhmah*.

125   Moses de Leon puts this question, 1290 in ס' המשקל (Basle 1608)
ch. II, and 1293 in the unpublished ס' משכן העדות. The solution quoted
in the text is that of the latter work.

126   Zohar I, 81b., 226a/b; III, 70b says that *Neshamah* returns immediately after death to its heavenly abode in גן עדן דלעילא. Only one passage
II, 97a mentions a judgment on the נשמתא קדישא; the term, however, is
used there not in the pregnant sense of a special part of the soul but signi-

fies the soul as a whole. Cf. also II, 210a. Moses de Leon says in משכן העדות
Ms. Berlin f. 46a רוח הצדיק נכנס ובא בו [בגיהנם] ושטף ועבר וחלף ויצא בשלום.
The idea that the souls of the just צדיקים גמורים descend to Hell for the
purpose of saving other souls, is alluded to in III, 220b.

127 The theories of the Zohar are further embellished in the pseudepigraphic "Testament of Rabbi Eliezer" (the so-called סדר גן עדן printed
by Jellinek in *Beth Ha-Midrash* III, p. 131—140); cf. note 125.

128 Zohar III, 302b.

129 Ibid. III, 68a/b.

130 Ibid. I, 233b; II, 161b.

131 Ibid. I, 224a.

132 Ibid. II, 209b—212a.

133 Cf. my German translation of the *Bahir*, §§ 86, 104, 126ff., 135. The
term *Gilgul* occurs only after the publication of the book *Bahir*. It is not
generally known that the term was borrowed by the Kabbalists from the
philosophical literature. David Kimhi uses it in his commentary to Psalm
CIV, but the passage is found only in the editio princeps Naples 1487. גלגול
and its synonym העתקה are both translations of the Arabic term for
transmigration, *tanasuh*.

134 On the Catharists cf. Jean Giraud, Histoire de l'Inquisition au Moyen
Age vol. I (1935): Cathares et Vaudois. On metempsychosis p. 59 ff.

135 Zohar I, 186b; III 7a.

136 Ibid. II, 99b; III, 177a.

137 The system of Joseph ben Shalom of Barcelona (ca. 1310), the author of the commentary on *Sefer Yetsirah* ascribed to Abraham ben David,
is based on it, cf. EJ IX col. 708. For Recanati's theory cf. his פירוש על
התורה על דרך האמת in the sections מצורע and קדושים.

NOTES TO LECTURE VII

ISAAC LURIA AND HIS SCHOOL

1 The Marrano Pedro de la Caballeria relates in his Zelus Christi (Venice
1592) f. 34 that the Zohar was found in Castile only in the hands of isolated
Jews, *apud peculiares Judaeos*. This was written about 1450.

2 See above p. 177 and 207—208, 230.

3 ס' קנה בינה (Prague 1610) f. 7a. This text was written by the author of the book *Peliah*.

4 This calculation of the End was based on Job XXXVIII, 7 ברן יחד כוכבי
בקר. The numerical value of בר"ן was variously interpreted as signifying

1490 or 1492, cf. Zunz, Gesammelte Schriften vol. III p. 228. In Ms. Vatican 171 f. 96 b we are told that in 1492 the renovation of the world would begin, יתחדש העולם.

5   This idea is developed in Abraham Halevi's משרא קטרין (Constantinople 1510) and other writings of this kind, especially in the Ms. of ס' כף הקטורת who interpreted ענני במרח"ב יה as alluding to the year 1492.

6   Cf. my essays in *Kirjath Sefer* vol. II (1925) p. 101—141, 269—273 and vol. VII (1930) p. 149—165, 440—456.

7   Regarding the ספר המשיב I have given some details in my כתבי יד בקבלה p. 85—89. The voluminous ס' כף הקטורת is preserved in several manuscripts. I have used Paris, Biblioth. Nationale 845. The book was known to the Mystics of Safed; Vital quotes it in his unpublished book on Magic (Ms. Musajoff f. 69a). Passages from other writings by the same author are found in a Ms. of the Schocken Library in Jerusalem.

8   כף הקטורת on Psalm XXIX.

9   Ibid. חרב חדה בידם של ישראל להרוג ולאבד כל צר ומשטין וכל כח חוצה.

10   Ibid. f. 54b. Their books belong to סמאל ואמון מנוא משנחו and it is they שהאריכו הגלות. These are ideas familiar to us from Joseph Jaabez' polemical writings on the causes of the catastrophe of 1492.

11   *Midrash Ha-Neelam* in *Zohar Hadash* (1885) f. 23d: חייך ! אי יחזרון בתשובה רישי כנישתא או הדא כנישתא, בזכותם יתכנש כל גלותא.

12   Already the author of ס' עמק המלך (1648) f. 148d interpreted this Zoharic saying as a reference to Safed.

13   Very interesting is the quotation in Abraham Azulai's preface to his commentary on the Zohar אור החמה (Jerusalem 1876). He says:
מצאתי כתוב כי מה שנגזר למעלה שלא יתעסקו בחכמת האמת בגלוי היה לזמן קצוב עד תשלום שנת הר"ן (1490 I) ומשם ואילך יקרא דרא בתראה והותרה הגזירה והרשות נתונה להתעסק בספר הזוהר, ומשנת ה"ש ליצירה (1540) מ צ ו ה מ ן המובחר שיתעסקו ברבים גדולים וקטנים... שבזכות זה עתיד לבוא מלך המשיח ולא בזכות אחר.

14   Azikri אזיכרי is the correct spelling of the name usually misspelt Azkari, according to the Mss. written in Palestine at that time, e. g. the autograph of Vital's autobiographical notes (Ms. Toaff in Leghorn).

15   S. A. Horodezky's presentation of the subject is very unsatisfactory, cf. תורת הקבלה של ר' משה קורדוביירו (1924) and תורת האר"י in the yearbook *Keneseth* vol. III (1938) p. 378—415.

16   Schechter, Studies in Judaism, Second Series (1908) p. 202—306.

17   Ibid. p. 258. Cf. Steinschneider's remarks in H. B. vol. VIII p. 147. He finds the Lurianic writings "completely incomprehensible."

18   Cordovero alludes to his experience during meditation in his שעור קומה

(1883) § 93, and in אור נערב end of chapter V. His ספר גירושין (1601) is based on a special mystical technique devised by him and his teacher Solomon Alkabez cf. *Kirjath Sefer* vol. I (1924) p. 164, and vol. XVIII (1942) p. 408.

19 אלימה רבתי (1881) f. 24d: האלוה כל נמצא ואין כל נמצא האלוה. It is perhaps interesting to note that the German philosopher F. W. Schelling employed precisely the same formula to define Spinoza's attitude towards the problem of "pantheism," cf. Schellings Muenchener Vorlesungen zur Geschichte der neueren Philosophie, ed. A. Drews (1902) p. 44. Cf. on this question of Cordovero's "pantheism" MGWJ vol. 75 (1931) p. 452 ff, 76 (1932) p. 167—170.

20 שעור קומה (1883) § 40, p. 98.

21 On Cordovero's works cf. EJ vol. V col. 663—664.

22 Cf. Cordovero's ethical prescriptions published by Schechter op. cit. p. 292—294.

23 שבחי האר"י printed first in תעלומות חכמה (Basle 1629), cf. Schechter p. 323. Another letter of Shlomel's was recently published by S. Assaf קובץ על יד new series vol. III p. 121—133.

24 תעלומות חכמה 37b; לקוטי ש"ס (Livorno 1790) 33c.

25 Published e. g. in Vital's שער מאמרי רשב"י (Jerusalem 1898) f. 22a—30c. The authenticity of the commentary can be proved conclusively; cf. my article on Luria's authentic writings in *Kirjath Sefer* vol. XIX (1943) p. 184—199.

26 The שמונה שערים were printed for the first time in Jerusalem between 1850 and 1898. They contain the version edited by Vital's son Samuel. Another version of Vital's writings is given by Meir Poppers; the best edition of part of which (עץ חיים)appeared in Warsaw 1891. Quotations from the *Ets Hayim* are given in accordance with this edition. The other parts bear separate titles for each volume:

ספר הגלגולים, פרי עץ חיים, שער הייחודים, ס' לקוטי תורה.

27 On Joseph ibn Tabul cf. my essay on Luria's disciples in *Zion* vol. V p. 133—160, especially p. 148 ff.

28 Tabul's book under the title ס' חפצי בה was published at the beginning of שמחת כהן, by Mas'ud Hakohen Al-Haddad (Jerusalem 1921).

29 Many of them are collected in ס' ארחות צדיקים (printed in לקוטי ש"ס Livorno 1790),שער הגלגולים chapter 37ff., and in Jacob Zemah's ס' נגיד ומצוה (1712).

30 Cf. the list of sacred tombs given at the end of שער הגלגולים.

31 Cf. שער הכוונות (1873) f. 50d, which is obviously based on the *Tosafoth* to *Hagigah* 13a.

32 ‫כי לכולם יש רמז וסוד‬ 8d: ‫שער הכוונות‬

33 Ibid. 50d.

34 Cf. *Zion* vol. V p. 125 and 241 ff.

35 Cf. the essay quoted in note 27.

36 On the question of Sarug and his activities cf. my essay in *Zion* vol. V. p. 214—241.

37 Herrera's Puerta del Cielo is found not only in the Royal Library at The Hague, but also in Columbia University Library in New York (X 86—H 42Q).

38 Porta coelorum, at the end of vol. I pars secunda, of Knorr's Kabbala Denudata. This was translated (or rather condensed) from the Hebrew edition which appeared 1655 in Amsterdam.

39 J. G. Wachter, Der Spinozismus im Juedenthumb (!) oder die von dem heutigen Juedenthumb und dessen Kabbala vergoetterte Welt (1699), drew heavily upon Herrera's books.

40 This view, which is entirely unfounded, is taken by Horodezky in a number of books and essays. Cf. note 15.

41 There can be no doubt in my opinion that Luria had read and made use of a treatise written about 1480 by Joseph Alkastiel in Jativa (near Valencia) which is preserved e. g. in Ms. Oxford 1565. Several Lurianic *termini technici* have their origin in this book.

42 Ms. Brit. Museum 711 f. 140b: ‫וזה הלשון שמצאתי בספרי המקובלים...‬
‫כיצד המציא וברא עולמו? כאדם שהוא מקבץ את רוחו ומצמצם את עצמו כדי שיחזיק‬
‫מועט את המרובה, כך צמצם אורו בטפח שלו ונשאר העולם חושך ובאותו חושך קצץ‬
‫צורים וחצב סלעים כדי להוציא מהם הנתיבות הנקראות פליאות חכמה.‬ This explanation leans on Nahmanides' interpretation of the first words of the *Sefer Yetsirah*, cf. *Kirjath Sefer* vol. IV (1930) p. 402.

43 Cf. *Exod. Rabba* to Exod. XXV, 10; *Lev. Rabba* to Levit. XXIII, 24; *Pesikta de-Rab Kahana* ed. Buber 20a; *Midrash Shir Ha-Shirim* ed. Gruenhut (1899), 15b.

44 Vital *Ets Hayim* chapter I, 1—2; ‫מבוא שערים‬ (Jerusalem 1904) f. ‫ו‬; Tabul ‫דרוש חפצי בה‬ chapter I. The images in some manuscript versions of Vital's teaching are highly naturalistic.

45 The formula ‫צמצם עצמו מעצמו אל עצמו‬ is used first by Sarug and the author of the ‫ס׳ שפע טל‬ (Hanau 1618).

46 The parallel between ‫צמצום‬ and ‫שבירה‬ which suggests this interpretation, is hinted at by Vital himself, though in a different context, cf. *Ets Hayim* VI, 5 p. 54 and a veiled allusion in the first chapter of his‫מבוא שערים‬. I am indebted for this remark to Tishby's book quoted in note 68.

47 Vital speaks, therefore, of this first act as צמצום ראשון. The principle is stated *Ets Hayim* p. 71 (all quotations are from ed. 1891) גם תבין כי בכל בחינות הוצאות האורות חדשים היה קודם להם ענין הצמצום.

48 Jacob Emden מטפחת ספרים (Lemberg 1870) p. 82.

49 This was the reason why Joel in "Die Religionsphilosophie des Sohar" attempted to show that the Zohar does not teach emanation.

50 Cf. the discussion on the meaning of *Tsimtsum* in Joseph Ergas' שומר אמונים (part two) and Emanuel Hay Rikki's יושר לבב chapter I.

51 The only attempt in this direction has been made by M. Teitelbaum הרב מלאדי ומפלגת חב"ד vol. II (1913) p. 37—94. Other authors who have written on the question of *Tsimtsum* are Molitor, Philosophie der Geschichte vol. II (1834) p. 132—172; Isaac Misses, Darstellung und kritische Beleuchtung der juedischen Geheimlehre II (1863) p. 44—50.

52 Ms. Jerusalem cf. כתבי יד בקבלה p. 135. The text is published in *Kirjath Sefer* vol. XIX p. 197—199. Its authenticity is beyond doubt.

53 This is emphasized in all the early writings on the doctrine of *Tsimtsum*.

54 This is the course taken by Cordovero's פרדס רמונים in the lengthy chapter VIII מהות והנהגה where he deals chiefly with the question of the meaning of דין. Cf. also ch. V § 4, where Cordovero develops the theory that the primeval worlds were destroyed not because of a hypertrophy of *din* but rather because of its being wanting.

55 This is borne out clearly by the abovementioned fragment written by Luria himself and by Ibn Tabul. The idea is somewhat blurred in Vital's version.

56 *Ets Hayim* p. 57 and particularly p. 59. This fundamental idea has been made the basis of the great Kabbalistic system propounded in Solomon Eliassov's *magnum opus* ס' לשם שבו ואחלמה. The third volume (Jerusalem 1924) is called כללי התפשטות והסתלקות.

57 Vital seems to have had some reason for not mentioning the theory of רשימו in its proper place but only later (e. g. *Ets Hayim* p. 55). Luria and Ibn Tabul stress its importance.

58 Cf. the text quoted in note 52.

59 For Basilides see Hippolytus, *Philosophoumena* VII, 22; cf. Mead, Fragments of a Faith Forgotten, third edition (1931) p. 261. For the Coptic gnostic book Jeou cf. Mead p. 543.

60 Chapter II—VIII (p. 29—78) of the *Ets Hayim* include full details of this process.

61 *Ets Hayim* p. 9 (שער הכללים). The terms עולם הנקודים and עולם העקודים עולם העקודים favored by Vital are based on a *jeu de mots*, cf. Genesis XXX, 39.

62 Cf. the text published in *Zion* vol. V p. 156, and ס' עמק המלך (1648) f. 32d.

63 This process is described in detail in *Ets Hayim* chapter IX.

64 See first lecture, note 30.

65 Zohar III, 128a, 135a/b, 142a/b, 292a/b.

66 Ibid. II, 176b. The Aramaic term is מתקלא.

67 *Ets Hayim* IX, 8 p. 93; XI, 5 p. 103.

68 I am basing myself here on a very thorough analysis of the Lurianic doctrine of שבירת הכלים and the conception of evil, made by my pupil Isaiah Tishby, תורת הרע והקליפה בקבלת האר"י (Jerusalem 1942).

69 Cf. *Ets Hayim* XI, 5 p. 103; שער מאמרי רשב"י (1898) f. 22b (from Luria's authentic writings!) and 33a; מבוא שערים (1904) f. 35d.

70 Vital ספר הלקוטים (Jerusalem 1913) f. 21b.

71 This is, for instance, the objection raised by Moses Hayim Luzzatto at the beginning of his חוקר ומקובל 'ס.

72 Menahem Azariah Fano הקדמה בענין המהירו at the beginning of his עמק המלך (1648); 24b. יונת אלם

73 *Ets Hayim* chapter XVIII, ɪ p. 170.

74 This is described at great length ibid. ch. XI and XVIII. Vital states that the שבירה affected all the worlds, chapter XXXIX, 3.

75 Most of chapters XII—XL of Vital's *Ets Hayim* deal with this subject of *Tikkun.*

76 *Ets Hayim* XI, 7 p. 107 gives the best summary.

77 The following quotation from the German philosopher F. W. Schelling (died 1854) reads like a description of the *Tsimtsum* and its significance for the personality of God. "Alles Bewusstsein ist Konzentration, ist Sammlung, ist Zusammennehmen seiner selbst. Diese verneinende, auf es selbst zurueckgehende Kraft eines Wesens ist die wahre Kraft der Persoenlichkeit in ihm, die Kraft der Selbheit" (Schellings saemtliche Werke, Abteilung I, Band VIII p. 74).

78 Cordovero in אלימה רבתי already speaks of five תמונות in the same sense.

79 Zohar III, 128b.

80 The *Idra Zutta* III, 290 ff. speaks of the symbolism of אבא ואימא (after the chapter on עתיקא קדישא).

81 קצר אפים is taken from Prov. XIV, 17. Gikatila in שערי אורה gives the correct interpretation.

82 *Ets Hayim* chapters XVI—XXIX.

83 These are the mystical stages of זעיר אנפין called עיבור, לידה, יניקה, קטנות וגדלות.

84 חקל תפוחין קדישין Zohar III, 128b and in many other passages (based on a mystical interpretation of a Talmudic passage, *Taanith* 29a).

85 On the development of this theory cf. my essay התפתחות תורת העולמות in *Tarbiz* II p. 415—442; III p. 33—66. Its significance was emphasized by Cordovero, cf. פרדס רמונים chapter XVI.

86 *Ets Hayim* chapters XL ff.

87 *Ets Hayim* chapter XLVI, 1—2, and in many other places. Cf. Molitor, Philosophie der Geschichte vol. I (2nd edition 1857) p. 482. Luria himself (in his שער מאמרי רשב"י, פירוש ספרא דצניעותא f. 23d) states quite bluntly a purely theistic view which seems to have been somewhat blurred in his later oral teachings.

88 Both Ibn Tabul and Vital assert that the theory of the "curtain" holds good only for the אור פנימי but not for the אור מקיף which permeates and surrounds all the worlds in its original substance. In his more popular treatise on morals ס' שערי קדושה Vital deliberately employs a purely theistic terminology.

89 Cf. קונטרס כללי התחלת החכמה (1893) and חוקר ומקובל ed. Freystadt (1840) p. 15—18.

90 This view is taken by Emanuel Hai Rikki in יושר לבב.

91 *Ets Hayim* chapter XXXIX, 1 (vol. II, p. 130).

92 פרי עץ חיים I, 1 (Dubrowno 1804) f. 5a.

93 *Ets Hayim* chapter XXXVI.

94 Cf. the passage quoted in note 91. On Adam's sin cf. also the lengthy passages in ספר הלקוטים (1913) f. 56d and the דרוש חטא אדה"ר   in שער הפסוקים (1912) f. 1d—4b.

95 שער מאמרי רשב"י (1898) f. 37c/d.

96 Cf. *Sefer Ha-Gilgulim* ch. 1—3; שער מאמרי רשב"י loc. cit.

97 לשם יחוד קודשא בריך הוא ושכינתיה בדחילו ורחימו ליחדא שם י"ה בו"ה ביחודא שלים. This formula was generally introduced among the circles influenced by Lurianic Kabbalism, especially with the aid of Nathan Hannover's שערי ציון. Cf. Vital's שער המצוות (1872) f. 3b and 4b.

98 Cf. my essay, Der Begriff der Kawwanah in der alten Kabbala, in MGWJ 78 (1934) p. 492—518.

99 This is the theory of כוונה developed in ס' הכוונות (Venice 1620), ס' פרי עץ חיים (best edition Dubrowno 1804) and שער הכוונות (Jerusalem 1873).

100 *Ets Hayim* chapter I, 5 p. 29.

101 All this was expounded by Vital in a very interesting note printed at

the beginning of the so-called *Siddur Ha-Ari*   סדר התפלה על דרך הסוד
Zolkiew 1781, f. 5c/d.

102   Their prayer-book has been published in Jerusalem 1911—1916. It
is the so-called *Siddur* of R. Shalom Sharabi, concerning whom cf. above
p. 328.

103.   Paulus Berger, Cabalismus Judaeo-Christianus detectus (1707) p.
118, says that he has found the *Kawwanah* called *Sabbatismus ac silentium
sacrum* by the Kabbalists. I have not yet been able to trace the source of
this statement which seems to have been taken from Knorr's Kabbala
Denudata.

104   All this and the following remarks originate from Vital's ספר הגלגולים,
the best and most complete edition of which appeared Przemysl 1875. Cf.
especially ch. 1—4 and 6. A Latin translation in Knorr's Kabbala Denudata
vol. II pars 2 (1684) p. 243—478.

105   This idea is based on the mystical interpretation of an Aggadah on
Adam, cf. *Midrash Tanhuma* פר' כי תשא § 12 and *Exod. Rabba* Par. 40.

106   רמ"ח אברים ושס"ה גידים cf. Targum Jonathan ben Uziel on Gen. I,
27 and Zohar I, 170b.

107   Cordovero, ס' תומר דבורה (Jerusalem 1928) p. 5.

108   Cf. שער הפסוקים f. 3a; ס' הגלגולים ch. XVIII.

109   ספר הלקוטים f. 3b.

110   *Sefer Ha-Gilgulim* chapters XV—XVIII; also   שער מאמרי רשב"י
f. 36b ff.

111   *Sefer Ha-Gilgulim* chapter I.

112   *Ets Hayim* chapter XXVI, 1. In other passages it is stated that his
body was taken from the higher world *Yetsirah*.

113   *Sefer Ha-Gilgulim* chapter XVI and XVIII.

114   *Sefer Ha-Gilgulim* chapter XVIII and ספר הלקוטים f. 8c.

115   Its most important predecessor is a voluminous book, the גלי רזייא
written 1552.

116   Cf. my note on this subject in Gaster Anniversary Volume (1936)
p. 504.

117   The term גלות הנשמה for *Gilgul* was used already in the thirteenth
century by the anonymous author of the ספר תמונה (Lemberg 1892) f. 56b.

118   Cf. EJ vol. IX col. 708 and Festschrift fuer Aron Freimann (1935)
p. 60.

119   *Sefer Ha-Gilgulim* chapter V.

120   Ibid. chapter VIII; Vital's שער תיקוני עונות in שער היחודים (Koretz
1783) f. 30—39; תקוני 21—15 .f (1648) עמק המלך in שער תקוני תשובה

תשובה at the end of ראשית חכמה הקצר and (better) at the end of Menahem
Azariah Fano's מאה קשיטה (1892) f. 58—69.

121   Shemtob ben Shemtob ספר אמונות (Ferrara 1556) f. 78a.

122   Abraham Galante זהרי חמה on Zohar II, 105b. It is said of Isaac
the Blind (about 1200) that he could tell by perception of the aura הרגשת
האויר whether a man's soul was "new" or "old", cf. Recanati פירוש התורה
(sections כי תצא and וישב).

123   Cf. Cordovero שעור קומה f. 83d; Vital שער רוח הקודש (Jerusalem
1912) f. 3a—5b; מדרש תלפיות (1860) f. 108a.

124   The book גלי רזיא was only partly printed (Mohilev 1812) and is
preserved in a more complete version in Ms. Oxford 1820. Cf. *Kirjath Sefer*
II p. 119—124.

125   ספר הלקוטים f. 89b.

126   A. H. Silver, A History of Messianic Speculation in Israel (1927) p.
137—138 has collected the evidence from the legends told by Luria's followers. On the year 1575 as the Messianic year cf. ibid. p. 135—137. The
year 1630 has been marked as the beginning of the *general* spread of Lurianic teaching by the Kabbalist Moses Praeger in ויקהל משה (Dessau 1699)
f. 58a: תלמידי האר"י ז"ל היו מכסין דבריו משנת של"ה (1575) עד שנת ש"ץ
(1630).

127   Most of these rites are explained in the שער הכוונות at their proper
place. See also A. Abeles, Der kleine Versoehnungstag (1911), and מקיץ
רדומים (Mantova 1648) on הושענא רבה.

128   See the literature quoted in note 120.

129   Cf. A. Berliner, Randbemerkungen zum taeglichen Gebetbuche vol. I
(1909) p. 30—47; Abr. I. Schechter, Lectures on Jewish Liturgy (1933) p.
39—60. This important subject still requires a more exhaustive study.

130   חמדת ימים printed first at Izmir 1731.

131   Cf. Rosanes קורות היהודים בתורקיה vol. IV (1935) p. 445—449; M.
Heilprin כבוד חכמים (Jerusalem 1896) which has given rise to a good deal
of polemical discussion; Jehuda M. Fetaya מנחת יהודה (Bagdad 1933)
f. 37—39.

NOTES TO LECTURE VIII

SABBATIANISM AND MYSTICAL HERESY

1 Jacob ben Abraham de Botton שו"ת עדות ביעקב (1720) f. 42a, reprinted by Rosanes vol. IV p. 473.

2 S. Trivush in the Russian monthly Voschod 1900 No. 7 p. 99.

3 Bleuler, Lehrbuch der Psychiatrie, sechste Auflage, p. 321 ff; J. Lange in Handbuch der Geisteskrankheiten vol. VI (1928) p. 93 ff.

4 Thomas Coenen, Ydele Verwachtinge der Joden getoont in den Persoon van Sabethai Zevi (Amsterdam 1669) p. 9.

5 This has now been published by A. M. Habermann חברת של יד על קובץ מקיצי נרדמים   new series vol. III (1940) p. 209.

6 Ibid. p. 208.

7 הארח and הסתר פנים   in the account given by Baruch of Arezzo (עניני שבתי צבי) ed. Freimann p. 64, 67); הארה and נפילה in a letter by Nathan published in REJ vol. 104 (1938) p. 120, where he plays on the Talmudic name of the Messiah בר נפלי (Sanhedrin 96b).

8 Nathan of Gaza in his ספר הבריאה Ms. Berlin Or. oct. 3075 f. 6b: וכן יש דוגמא יותר פרטית לאמונה הקדושה מעניני האמיר"ה [= S. Zevi] שפעם דרוש התנינים Nathan in. עומד ברום המעלות ופעם בתכלית הדלות והשפלות Ms. Halberstamm 40 f. 92a says: הביאו הקב"ה בנסיונות גדולות כמה פעמים אחר שהיה עומד ברום שמים היה נופל לעומקא דתהומא רבה והיו מפתין אותו הנחשים לומר לו איה אלהיך בראיות גדולות בדרך שאין השכל המעשי יכול לסובלו.

9 Cf. the interesting account given by Tobias Cohen מעשה טוביה I, 6: ועם כל חכמתו ולימודו היה מנעוריו נוהג ועושה מעשה נערות ואומרים כי לפעמים נכנסה בו רוח שטות ועושה כמעשה הכסילים עד שהבריות היו מרנגין אחריו והיו קורין אותו שוטה וכסיל.

10 עניני שבתי צבי p. 95.

11 See above p. 207—208.

12 The Hebrew text is found in Ms. 2223 of the Enelow Memorial Collection in the JTh Seminary in New York f. 228: כשעבר מכאן בארם צובא, ספר לנו את כל ענייניו שמשנת הזא"ת (ת"ח) נחה עליו רוח ה' בלכתו לילה א' חוץ לעיר רחוק מן היישוב כשתי שעות מופשט ומתבודד עד ששמע קול אלהים מדבר עמו: אתה מושיע ישראל משיח בן דוד משיח אלהי יעקב ואתה עתיד לגאול את ישראל לקבצם מד' כנפות הארץ בתוככי ירושלים ונשבע אני בימיני ובזרוע עוזי שאתה הגואל האמתי ואין זולתך גואל. ובכן מאותה שעה נתלבש ברוח הקודש ובהארה גדולה והיה הוגה את ה' באותיותיו ועושה מעשים זרים כפי מה שנראה לו שכן ראוי לעשות מפני כמה סבות ותקונים אשר הוא היה מתקן. הרואים לא היו מבינים ענייניו והיה בעיניהם כמתעתע וכמה פעמים לקו עליהם רבותינו שבארץ

ישראל על רוב (צ"ל רוע?) מעשיו שהיו רחוקים מהשכל עד שהיה מוכרח לפרוש מבני
אדם אל המדברות ובכל פעם שהיה מתראה היה גדל והולך ומתרבה ורואה מה שאין
הפה יכולה לדבר ולפעמים היה מצטער בצער גדול ולפעמים נהנה מזיו השכינה ולפעמים
השם נסתן בנסיונות גדולים קשים ממות ועמד בכולם עד שבשנת התכ"ה בהיותו
במצרים נסתן הקב"ה נסיון גדול שלי"ת עמד בנסיון ואח"כ עשה השבעה גדולה
בכמה תפלות ותחנונים שעוד לא ינסהו ויהי היום באותו העת אשר עשה ההשבעה
ההיא נסתלק מעליו כל רוח הקודש ההוא וכל ההארה והיה כאחד העם והיה מתנחם
על מעשיו הזרים אשר עשה כי לא היה מבין עוד טעם שלהם כמו שהיה מבין בשעת
עשייתם.

13 From the important Sabbatian manuscript Kaufmann 255 (now in the
Hungarian Academy in Budapest) f. 30a we know that this transgression
was practised by him precisely in the hours of maniac exaltation:
ידעתי שאמיר"ה קודם שנתפרסמה מלכותו היה לפעמים כשהיה בהארה היה מזכיר
את השם בברכותיו.

14 Cf. note 9.

15 Nathan's apocalypse on Sabbatai Zevi — ascribed to Abraham Yakhini by modern historians without justification, as has been shown by
Rosanes — mentions them in the spring of 1665: ...יתחברו אליו בני זנונים
Cf. עניני שבתי צבי .איגון בני נעמה נגעי בני אדם ותמיד ירדפוהו להטעינתו
p. 99. The meaning of the expression בני נעמה is that of demons born of
concupiscence, cf. Zohar I, 19b; III, 76b.

16 Cf. Nathan's דרוש התנינים Ms. Halberstamm 40 f. 90b: וכל היסורים
שנאמרו באיוב אינם כי אם עליו שסבל כמה יסורים קשים ע"י כל מיני קליפות,
and f. 102b: וכן הוצרך אמיר"ה להיות ז' שנים בבית האסורים של הקליפות
ואז סבל יסורים קשים גדולים וחזקים.

17 Relation de la véritable imposture du faux Messie des Juifs nommé
Sabbatay Sevi (Avignon 1667) p. 37.

18 The original text is found in a Sabbatian notebook preserved in the
Columbia University Library in New York (X 893—Z 8 vol. ı No. 29)
f. 16b—17a. This is the full text of the passage:
הנה מי שהכיר אותי יכול להעיד עדות אמת כי מקטנותי עד היום הזה לא נמצא בי
שמץ פיסול וקיימתי התורה מעוני והגיתי בה יומם ולילה, תודה לאל, ומעולם לא
רדפתי אחר תאוות גשמיות ובכל יום הייתי מוסיף סיגופים ועינויים בכל מאמצי
כחי ולא נהניתי כלל הנאה גשמית מסיבת בשורתי זאת... ולמדתי תורה בטהרת
עד היותי בן עשרים שנה ועשיתי התיקון הכללי שאמר האר"י ז"ל על כל מי שהרבה
לפשוע אעפ"י שת"ל לא נמצא בי עון במזיד עשיתיו באם ואולי נפשי מלגלכת
מגלגול אחר ח"ו. ובשנת העשרים התחלתי ללמוד ספר הזהר ומעט מכתבי האר"י
ז"ל והבא ליטהר מסייעין אותו מן השמים ושלח ממלאכיו הקדושים ונשמותיו
הטהורות והודיעוני הרבה מסודות התורה. ובאותה שנה אהר שנתעורר כהי במראות
מלאכים ונשמות קדושות בהיותי בהפסקה בפרשת ויקהל ואני סגור בחדר מיוחד
בקדושה ובטהרה אחר שהתפללתי תפילת לחש בבכי גדול בהיותי עוסק בתהנונים הנח
רוח על פני יהלוף תסמר שערת בשרי וארכובותי דא לדא נקשן צפיתי במרכבה וראיתי
מראות אלהים כל היום ההוא וכל הלילה ואז נבאתי נבואה גמורה כאחד מן הנביאים
כה אמר ה' ונחקק בלבי בבירור גמור על מי היתה נבואתי... ושוב לא ראיתי מראה

גדולה כזאת עד היום ונשאר הדבר כמוס בלבי עד שהגואל פרסם עצמו בעזה וחתם
בשם משיח ואז הורשיתי ע"י מלאך הברית לפרסם מה שראיתי ונודע לי אמיתותו.

19 This autobiographical statement is confirmed by Nathan's account of
his ecstasy to Moses Pinheiro in Livorno, cf. ‏ענייני שבתי צבי‎ p. 95, where
the text is corrupt, and the original manuscript in the JThS reads: ‏וראה כל‎
‏הדברים כסדרן והמרכבה ופרצוף אמיר"ה.‎

20 In the letter published by Habermann — cf. note 5 — p. 208: ‏הניח‎
‏השליחות באשר הוא והלך לעזה למצוא תיקון ומנוח לנפשו.‎

21 Cf. note 19.

22 Ms. Halberstamm 40 (Jews' College, London); British Museum 856,ı;
Beth Ha-Midrash in London (Catalogue by Neubauer 1886) 123,3; Badhab
83 in Jerusalem (erroneously ascribed to Isaac Luria!)

23 Nathan speaks of the year ‏תכ"ז‎ in terms of a future event, but he
mentions Sabbatai Zevi's imprisonment.

24 Vital says of the soul of the Messiah in his ‏ספר הגלגולים‎ ch. 19:
‏דע כי הנשמה לנשמה מזיהרא עלאה לא זכה אליה עדיין שום נברא שבעולם והמלך‎
‏המשיח עתיד ליטלה.‎ Nathan makes no use of this passage.

25 On the symbolism of the serpent cf. Mead, Fragment of a Faith Forgotten, third edition (1931) p. 182 ff.

26 Ms. Halberstamm 40 f. 99b. The full text of the passage reads:
‏כל הדברים אלו לא נתגלגלו אלא להודיע גדולת אדונינו ירום הודו איך יבטל כח‎
‏הנחש המשתרש בשרשין עלאין תקיפין שתמיד היו מפתין אותו, ואחר שהיה טורח‎
‏להוציא קדושה גדולה מתוך הקליפות היו יכולים להתאחז בו כשהיתה נסתמת הארתו‎
‏והיו מראים לו שהיה להם שליטה ואמונתו שהיא תפארת היו מראים שכחם ככחו‎
‏ויש להם מרכבה כמוהו כמו שאמר פרעה מי ה'. ובעת הארתו הית חוזר ומכניעהו‎
‏וכל זה רמוז במה שכתבו רז"ל גדול הנאמר באיוב ממה שנאמר באברהם דאלו באברהם‎
‏כתיב ירא אלהים לבד ובאיוב ירא אלהים וסר מרע ‚וכבר אמרתי שאמר הכתוב איוב‎
‏שמו שהיה מושקע בין הקליפות וזה היה בימי החשך שהם ימי צער וכשהיה בא לו‎
‏הארה שהם ימי מנוחה ושמחה כי לוה אמר והיה האיש ההוא תם וישר וגו' כי אין‎
‏והיה אלא לשון שמחה ואז היה „וסר מרע" יוצא מתוך הקליפות, לא כן בימי החושך‎
‏שהיה מושקע בין הקליפות, ויש לו יתרון מאברהם שאפילו שהיה לו ענויים ומושקע‎
‏ביניהם היה איש תם, לא כן אברהם כי כאשר [יצא] מהם שוב לא חזר.‎

27 This is the major point in which the views taken in this lecture differ
from the presentation of the subject in my essay ‏מצוה הבאה בעבירה‎ published in Keneseth II (1937) p. 346—392.

28 It is not impossible that his apostasy itself was brought about by this
illness, for it appears that at the time of it he was once more in a state of
depression and utter passivity, cf. my note in ‏קובץ הוצאת שוקן לדברי ספרות‎
pp. 165—166.

29 Leopold Loew, Gesammelte Schriften, vol. II p. 171 and IV p. 449.

30 S. Hurwitz (‏ש"י איש הורוויץ‎) ‏מאין ולאין‎ (1914) pp. 181—285.

31   Cf. W. Rabinowitsch in *Zion* vol. V p. 127—132.

32   Cf. G. Scholem חלומותיו של השבתאי ר' מרדכי אשכנזי (1938) and *Zion* vol. VI p. 94—96.

33   His full name is mentioned in a document published by Israel Halperin in *Haolam* (1930) No. 36. This disposes of the suggestions advanced by Rosanes IV p. 478.

34   מאמרים לזכרון ר' צבי פרץ חיות (Vienna 1933) p. 333.

35   The exact date has been settled by Cardozo's account of the event, cf. Bernheimer in JQR (1927) p. 102 and my article in *Zion* vol. VII p. 12 ff.

36   Leopold Loew, Gesammelte Schriften vol. II, p. 255 and Adolf Jellinek's letter ibid. vol. V p. 193 who says very characteristically: "Ueber den Sab-bataeismus Chorins habe ich einen Zeugen, der merkwuerdige Beweise gibt: es ist aber die Frage, ob es klug ist, jetzt diesen Punkt zu diskutieren."

37   פירוש לעין יעקב Ms. in the Schocken Library in Jerusalem.

38   Cf. also my essay מצוה הבאה בעבירה in *Keneseth* vol. II (1937) p. 392. A very interesting light on this connection between the late Sabbatian-ism and the "enlightenment" is shed in the documents published by V. Zacek in Jahrbuch fuer Geschichte der Juden in der Czechoslovakischen Republik vol. IX (1938) pp. 343—410.

39   I am very much indebted to Miss Pauline Goldmark of New York, who has been kind enough to present me with a copy of this very remark-able document written by her grandfather, Gottlieb Wehle.

40   לאקמא שכינתא מעפרא   cf. the long disquisition of the "Maggid," one of the holy souls, addressed to Mordecai Ashkenazi, in my חלומותיו של השבתאי ר' מרדכי אשכנזי pp. 79—100.

41   *Hullin* 7a.

42   Cf. the aforementioned discourse p. 80.

43   Far too little account has been taken in the literature on Messianism of his great book נצח ישראל (Prague 1599).

44   Cf. Cecil Roth, The Religion of the Marranos, in JQR n. s. vol. 22 (1931) p. 26.

45   Cf. מאמרים לזכרון ר' צבי פרץ חיות (1933) p. 344.

46   Cf. Cardozo's great epistle in עניני שבתי צבי ed. Freimann (1913) p. 87—92, especially 88 and 90.

47   Cf. Ch. Wirszubski's Hebrew essay on the Sabbatian view of the Apos-tasy of the Messiah, in *Zion* III (1938) pp. 215—245.

48   There exists an extensive Sabbatian literature on the reasons for the apostasy of the Messiah. We still have some of Nathan's epistles on the subject, his disciple Abraham Perez' אגרת מגן אברהם (cf. note 50), and the

Ms. David Kaufmann 255 in Budapest, the author of which interprets many Psalms as foreshadowing the fate of the new Messiah.

49 Cf. p. 175—177 on the books *Temunah* and *Raya Mehemna.*

50 אגרת מגן אברהם published by me in קובץ על יד n. s. vol. II (1938) pp. 121—155. There I made the erroneous assumption that its author was Cardozo. The real author is mentioned in Ms. Guenzburg 517,4. Cf. Wirszubski (see note 47) pp. 235—245 on the doctrine of the book.

51 אגרת מגן אברהם p. 135.

52 Cf. my book חלומותיו של השבתאי ר' מרדכי אשכנזי (1938).

53 The author of Ms. David Kaufmann 255 (of which a photostate is extant in the Schocken Library in Jerusalem) mentions with much indignation that some scholars among "the believers" refused to become Moslems when called up to do so by Sabbatai Zevi.

54 Cf. *Zion* vol. III p. 228.

55 Cf. לחישת שרף (Hanau 1726) f. 2b: באמרם חשכינה כבר עלתה ונתקנה ולא נשאר לקליפות אחיזה כי אם אחורי הזעיר ושאי אפשר לתקן את הזעיה מצד הקדושה רק ע"י דברים שלא כדרכן. Cf. on this theory my remarks in *Zion* vol. VI (1941) p. 136—141.

56 Cf. Ps.-Nahmanides in אגרת הקדש chapter II; Is. Horovitz in שני לוחות הברית (1698) f. 293a; Nehemyah Hayun in עוז לאלהים (1713) f. 20d; אגרת מגן אברהם p. 150.

57 This phrase, quoted by Clement of Alexandria, *Stromata* III 13, 92 from the "Gospel according to the Egyptians," originally had a radically ascetic meaning.

58 Mishnah, *Berakhoth* IX, 5.

59 שבר פושעים (London 1714) f. 33b (the book has no pagination).

60 Cf. Eugéne de Faye, Gnostiques et Gnosticisme (1925) pp. 413—428; L. Fendt, Gnostische Mysterien (1922); H. Liboron, Die karpokratianische Gnosis (1938).

61 I have given a detailed account of this mythology of nihilism in *Keneseth* II (1937) pp. 381—387. Cf. also Joseph Kleinmann's valuable essay (in Russian) *Moral i poezia Frankizma,* in *Yevreiski Almanach* (Petrograd 1923) pp. 195—227, which came to my knowledge only after my aforementioned article had appeared in print.

62 These writings are (a) a "rewriting" of the prophecy of Isaiah in the spirit of Frankism, a very curious document fragments of which have been published by A. Kraushar, Frank i Frankisci Polscy, vol. II (1895) pp. 183—218; (b) the commentary on *En Yaakob* Ms. Schocken, in Jerusalem.

63 A considerable part is included in scattered form throughout Kraushar's book (see the aforegoing note) and particularly in the annexes vol. I pp. 378—429; vol. II pp. 304—392.

64 *Nazir* 23b גדולה עבירה לשמה ממצוה שלא לשמה.

65 בצולה של תורה זהו קיומה. The saying is found in *Menahoth* 99b with the reading זהו יסודה. The reading of the Sabbatian formula is the same as in Wistinetzki's edition of the *Sefer Hasidim* § 1313.

66 Cf. לחישת שרף (1726) f. 2a/b.

67 *Sanhedrin* 98a.

68 This is the doctrine of משא דומה expounded in hundreds of Frank's sayings, but mentioned already 1713 by Hayun in דברי נחמיה f. 81 ff., who describes it (polemically) by using other symbols.

69 It must be borne in mind that only a small part of Frank's followers actually went over to Catholicism.

70 This formula is attested to by several writers dealing with the antinomianists of Salonica who used to ascribe it to Sabbatai Zevi himself. It is based on a pun, מתיר אסורים for מתיר איסורים "who frees those who are imprisoned." Cf. *Midrash Tehillim* ed. Buber f. 268 and Buber's notes.

71 Cf. *Keneseth* II pp. 370—371.

72 Cf. Zacek in his essay quoted in note 38 p. 404. A monograph on Moses Dobrushka — Thomas Edler von Schoenfeld — Junius Frey is still a *desideratum*. He was certainly one of the leading Frankists.

73 היסטאריושע שריפטען די זכרונות פון מאועם פארגעם in published by the Yiddish Scientific Institute, vol. I (1929) col. 266. The original German text (of which only a translation has been published by Dr. N. Gelber), reads "Die Erloesung aus geistigem und politischem Druck ist ihr Zweck, ist ihr Ziel."

74 Some of them, such as Israel Jaffe in אור ישראל (1702) and Zevi Chotsh represent the Lurianic school of Sabbatianism. It is scarcely an accident that the author of the first attempt to popularize parts of the Zohar in the vernacular Yiddish was a Sabbatian, Zevi Chotsh in נחלת צבי (1711). But the most interesting among this group is undoubtedly Jacob Koppel Lifshitz, the author of an exposition of Kabbalistic doctrine שערי גן עדן which was held in high esteem by the later Hasidim. Tishby has proved his intimate connection with the heresy beyond doubt, cf. *Keneseth* vol. IX (1945) p. 238—268.

75 Of these Sabbatian authorities Samuel Primo's ideas are known only indirectly, through lengthy polemics against them in Cardozo's writings. By far the most voluminous tracts on Sabbatian theology are those of Cardozo of which we have several volumes in manuscript.

76 My study on this important Sabbatian leader has appeared in *Zion* vol. VI (1941) p. 119—147, 181—202.

77 Cf. Mortimer Cohen's apology of Eibeschuetz in his book Jacob Emden, a Man of Controversy (1937) and my critical remarks on it in *Kirjath Sefer*

vol. XVI (1939) pp. 320—338. The whole question has now been re-examined by M. A. Perlmutter in his comprehensive analysis of Eibeschuetz' Kabbalistical writings which leaves no further doubt as to his Sabbatian belief, cf. his book ר' יהונתן אייבשיץ ויחסו אל השבתאות (Jerusalem 1946).

78   Cf. Cardozo's account of these ideas published by Bernheimer in JQR n. s. vol. XVIII (1927) p. 122. In several of his unpublished tracts he is still much more outspoken about this "philosophy of Jewish History." Cf. also Cardozo's treatise מכתב בסוד האלהות published in Weiss' *Beth Ha-Midrash* (1864) pp. 63—71, 100—103, 139—142.

79   עוז לאלהים Berlin 1713. This book has in its day given rise to bitter and protracted polemics, cf. Graetz vol. X (1897) p. 468—495; D. Kaufmann in REJ vol. 36 (1897) pp. 256—282, vol. 37 pp. 274—283; G. Levi in Rivista Israelitica vol. VIII (1911) p. 169—185; vol. IX p. 5—29; J. Sonne in קובץ על יד n. s. vol. II (1938) p. 157—196. Graetz' interpretation of Hayun's teachings is incorrect insofar as he ascribes to him the theory of incarnation accepted by the most radical wing of the Sabbatian movement, but rejected by many Sabbatians. On the real history of the Sabbatian ideas on Sabbatai Zevi's apotheosis and their transformation into a theology of incarnation cf. chapter V of my essay on Baruchiah, in *Zion* vol. VI (1941) p. 181—191.

NOTES TO LECTURE IX

HASIDISM: THE LATEST PHASE

1   See the bibliography.

2   Ahad Haam תחית הרוח, in על פרשת דרכים vol. II p. 129.

3   See the bibliography.

4   This was the view taken by M. Loehr, Beitraege zur Geschichte des Hasidismus, Heft I (Leipzig 1925) and Lazar Gulkowitsch, Der Hasidismus religionswissenschaftlich untersucht (1927) p. 68.

5   Verus (i. e. Aaron Marcus), Der Chassidismus (1901) p. 286.

6   Cf. Ariel Bension שר שלום שרעבי (Jerusalem 1930).

7   Ariel Bension, The Zohar in Moslem and Christian Spain (1932) p. 242.

8   Several of these documents have been published, cf. e. g. Ar. Bension, שר שלום שרעבי pp. 89—90 and especially E. Tcherikover's essay די קאמונע פון ירושלימער מקובלים "אהבת שלום" אין מיטן 18-טען יאהרהונדערטס in YIVO Studies in History (in Yiddish) vol. II (1937) pp. 115—139.

9   The members of this congregation of Kabbalists were recruited from among the Jews of North Africa, Turkey, the Balkans, Persia and Yemen.

10   There is a vast literature on the "Palestinian movement" in early Hasidism most of which is calculated to obscure the real issue of Hasidism and Messianism, e. g. Isaac Werfel החסידות וארץ ישראל (Jerusalem
1940). A historical analysis of the movement in less romantic colors has
been given by Israel Halperin in his study העליות הראשונות של החסידים
לארץ ישראל (Jerusalem 1946).

11   Even the legendary שבחי הבעש"ט still remember the existence of such
Hasidim, and we are informed that two of the Baal Shem's earliest disciples
belong to them, cf. שבחי הבעש"ט ed. S. A. Horodezky (1922) p. 25.

12   Salomon Maimon's Lebensgeschichte ed. J. Fromer (1911) p. 170.

13   The nephew of Jehudah Hasid who was later converted to Lutheranism
tells us that he and his comrades made the journey to Jerusalem "because
of the false Messiah," cf. A. Fuerst, Christen und Juden (1892) p. 260.

14   Cf. Wolf Rabinowitsch, Der Karliner Chassidismus (1935).

15   The most complete collection of these fabrications has appeared in the
Quarterly of the *Habad* Hasidim התמים 1935—1938. The motive of the authors was obviously to prove the historicity of everything told in the שבחי
הבעש"ט.

16   Cf. now the texts published by Wolf Z. Rabinowitsch in *Zion* vol. V
(1940) pp. 126—131.

17   Cf. the details concerning his personality in the article quoted in the
preceding note.

18   Cf. *Zion* vol. VI (1941) pp. 80—84.

19   Cf. my note on this subject in *Zion* VI pp. 89—93.

20   Cf. Dubnow תולדות החסידות (1930) p. 112.

21   צוואת הריב"ש (1913) p. 27, 30.

22   אור הגנוז (Zolkiew 1800), section בראשית.

23   Kraushar, Frank i Frankisci Polscy vol. I (1895) p. 30.

24   Cf. his foreword to his teacher's ס' לקוטי אמרים (1781).

25   ס' גבורות ה' Cracow 1592.

26   Cf. A. Gottesdiener, הארי שבחכמי פרג (1938) p. 38—52: המהר"ל
בתור מקובל, who has collected some Kabbalistic material from his writings
without attempting anything like a real analysis.

27   Torsten Ysander, Studien zum Bescht'schen Hassidismus in seiner re-
ligionsgeschichtlichen Sonderart, (Uppsala 1933).

28   Cf. עבודת הלוי by Rabbi Aaron Halevi of Staroselje vol. II (Lemberg
1862) f. 62 d.

29   All the writings of the "Maggid" of Meseritz and his disciples abound
in references to this basic paradox of Zaddikism.

30　Cf. סדר הדורות החדש　p. 35.

31　Verus, Der Chassidismus (1901) p. 308.

32　Cf. S. A. Horodezky, Religioese Stroemungen im Judentum (1920) p. 95.

33　S. Schechter, Studies in Judaism vol. I (1896) p. 19—21.

34　Cf. M. Teitelbaum הרב מלאדי ומפלגת חב"ד vol. I (1913) p. 87 ff.

35　Cf. שבחי הבעש"ט (1815) f. 28a in a passage remarkable for its radicalism: מי שמספר בשבחי צדיקים, כאילו עוסק במעשה מרכבה. Rabbi Nahman of Brazlav goes so far as to say that by telling ספורי מעשיות של צדיקים one draws the light of the Messiah into the world and expells much of the darkness, cf. his ספר המדות s. v. צדיק.

36　The core of this story is to be found already in a Hasidic collection on Rabbi Israel of Rishin, *Keneseth Israel*, Warsaw 1906 p. 23.

BIBLIOGRAPHY TO LECTURE I

GENERAL CHARACTERISTICS OF JEWISH MYSTICISM

(a) *On Mysticism in General*:

Charles A. Bennett, A Philosophical Study of Mysticism. New Haven 1931.

Martin Buber, Ekstatische Konfessionen. Jena 1909.

Henri Delacroix, Etudes d'Histoire et de Psychologie du Mysticisme. Paris 1908.

Friedrich von Huegel, The Mystical Element of Religion, [especially:] Second Volume, Critical Studies. London 1908.

William Ralph Inge, Christian Mysticism, Considered in Eight Lectures. Second Edition. London 1912.

Rufus M. Jones, Studies in Mystical Religion. London 1909.

Rudolf Otto, Mysticism East and West. A comparative Analysis of the Nature of Mysticism. New York 1932.

E. Récéjac, Essay on the Bases of the Mystic Knowledge. London 1899.

Evelyn Underhill, Mysticism, A Study in the Nature and Development of Man's Spiritual Consciousness. London 1926.

(b) *On Jewish Mysticism in General*:

Franz Joseph Molitor, Philosophie der Geschichte oder ueber die Tradition. Vol. I—IV. Muenster 1827—1857.

G. Scholem, Bibliographia Kabbalistica. Leipzig 1927.

Idem, Kabbala, in Encyclopaedia Judaica vol. IX col. 630—732 (1932).

J. Abelson, Jewish Mysticism. London 1913.

Arthur Edward Waite, The Holy Kabbalah, A Study of the Secret Tradition in Israel. London 1929.

BIBLIOGRAPHY TO LECTURE II

MERKABAH MYSTICISM

(a) *On Gnosticism in General*:

Wilhelm Anz, Zur Frage nach dem Ursprung des Gnostizismus. Leipzig 1897.

Ernesto Buonaiuti, Gnostic Fragments. London 1924.

F. C. Burkitt, Church and Gnosis. Cambridge 1932.

Eugène de Faye, Gnostiques et Gnosticisme. 2nd Edition. Paris 1925.

A. Hilgenfeld, Die Ketzergeschichte des Urchristentums. Leipzig 1884.

Hans Jonas, Gnosis und spaetantiker Geist. Goettingen 1934.

G. R. S. Mead, Fragments of a Faith Forgotten. Third Edition. London 1931.

Carl Schmidt, Koptisch-Gnostische Schriften. Erster Band. Leipzig 1905.

(b)   *On Merkabah Mysticism and related subjects*:

J. Abelson, The Immanence of God in Rabbinical Literature. London 1912.

Avigdor Aptowitzer, בית המקדש שלמעלה על פי האגדה in *Tarbiz* vol. II (1931) pp. 137—153, 257—287.

L. Blau, Altjuedisches Zauberwesen. Budapest 1898.

Philipp Bloch, Die יורדי מרכבה, die Mystiker der Gaonenzeit, und ihr Einfluss auf die Liturgie. In MGWJ vol. 37 (1893) pp. 18—25, 69—74, 257—266, 305—311.

Idem, Geschichte der Entwicklung der Kabbala und der Juedischen Religionsphilosophie kurz zusammengefasst. Trier 1894 pp. 5—36.

Moritz Friedlaender, Der vorchristliche juedische Gnosticismus. Goettingen 1898.

H. Graetz, Gnosticismus und Judenthum. Krotoschin 1846.

Idem, Die mystische Literatur in der gaonaeischen Epoche. In MGWJ vol. VIII (1859) pp. 67—78, 103—118, 140—152.

D. H. Joel, Der Aberglaube und die Stellung des Judenthums zu demselben. Fascicle I—II. Breslau 1881—83.

J. Lewy, שרידי משפטים ושמות יונים בס' היכלות רבתי in *Tarbiz* vol. XII (1941) pp. 163—167.

Hugo Odeberg, 3 Enoch or the Hebrew Book of Enoch, edited and translated for the first time with Introduction, Commentary and critical Notes. Cambridge 1928.

G. Scholem, Zur Frage der Entstehung der Kabbala. In Korrespondenzblatt des Vereins zur Gruendung und Erhaltung einer Akademie fuer die Wissenschaft des Judentums IX (1928) pp. 4—26.

Idem, Ueber eine Formel in den koptisch-gnostischen Schriften und ihren juedischen Ursprung, in Zeitschrift fuer Neutestamentliche Wissenschaft vol. XXX (1931) pp. 170—176.

(c) Texts:

היכלות אותיות דרבי עקיבא השלם ed. S. A. Wertheimer, Jerusalem 1914. רבתי ed. Jellinek, in בית המדרש vol. III (1855) pp. 83—108, 161—163.

חרבא דמשה ed. M. Gaster, London 1896.

מסכת היכלות ed. Jellinek, in בית המדרש vol. II (1853) pp. 40—47; ed. Wertheimer in בתי מדרשות vol. II (1894) pp. 15—22.

מרכבה שלמה ed. S. Mussajoff. Jerusalem 1922.

סדר רבה דבראשית ed. Wertheimer, in בתי מדרשות vol. I (1893) pp. 1—31.

פרקי היכלות רבתי ed. S. A. Wertheimer, Jerusalem 1889.

ראיות יחזקאל ed. J. Mann, in הצופה לחכמת ישראל vol. V (1921) pp. 256—264.

(d) On Sefer Yetsirah:

ספר יצירה המיוחס לאברהם אבינו Mantua 1562; Warsaw 1884.

Jehudah ben Barzilai of Barzelona פירוש ספר יצירה ed. S. Z. H. Halber-stamm. Berlin 1885.

David Castelli, II Commento di Sabbatai Donnolo sul Libro della Creazione. Firenze 1880.

Translations: Isidor Kalish, A Book on Creation, New York 1877.

Lazarus Goldschmidt, Das Buch der Schoepfung. Frankfort on the Main 1894.

Knut Stenring, The Book of Formation. London 1923.

Leo Baeck, Zum Sepher Jezira, in MGWJ vol. 70 (1926) pp. 371—376.

Idem, Die Zehn Sephiroth im Sepher Jezira, in MGWJ vol. 78 (1934) pp. 448—455.

Abraham Epstein, Recherches sur le Séfer Yecira. Versailles 1894.

Louis Ginzberg, Book Yezirah, in Jewish Encyclopedia vol. XII col. 606—612.

BIBLIOGRAPHY TO LECTURE III

HASIDISM IN MEDIAEVAL GERMANY

(a) Texts:

ספר חסידים ed. Wistinetzki. Berlin 1891.

ספר חסידים [vulgata]. Lwów 1926.

Eleazar of Worms, ס' חכמת הנפש Lwów 1876.

Idem, שערי חסוד וחיחוד והאמונח ed. Jellinek, in כוכבי יצחק No. 27 (1867) pp. 7—15.

Idem, סודי רזיא ed. Kamelhar. Bilgoraj 1936.

Idem, הלכות תשובה and הלכות חסידות in his ספר רוקח.

ספר רזיאל Amsterdam 1701.

Moses Taku, כתב תמים ed. R. Kirchheim in אוצר נחמד III pp. 54—99.

Abraham ben Azriel, ערוגת הבשם 'ס ed. E. Urbach. Vol. I Jerusalem 1939.

Naftali H. Treves, תפלה מכל חשנה עם פירוש ע"ד הקבלה. Thiengen 1560.

(b) *Studies:*

Av. Aptowitzer, מבוא לספר ראבי"ח Jerusalem 1938, pp. 316—318; 343—350.

I. F. Baer, המגמה הדתית-חברתית של ס' חסידים in *Zion* vol. III (1938) pp. 1—50.

A. Berliner, Der Einheitsgesang (שיר היחוד) eine literar-historische Studie. Berlin 1910.

Abr. Epstein, לקורות הקבלה האשכנזית, in החוקר vol. II (1892) pp. 1—11; 37—48.

Idem, ר' שמואל החסיד, in הגורן vol. IV (1904) pp. 81—101.

Jakob Freimann, מבוא לספר חסידים. Frankfort on the Main 1924.

M. Gaster, The Maaseh Book, translated. 2 vols. Philadelphia 1934.

M. Guedemann, Geschichte des Erziehungswesens und der Kultur der Juden in Frankreich und Deutschland, vol. I. Vienna 1880. Chapters V—VIII.

Israel Kamelhar, רבינו אלעזר מגרמיזא בעל ה"רוקח". 1930.

Jekutiel Kamelhar, חסידים הראשונים Waitzen 1917.

Adolf Neubauer, Abou Ahron le Babylonien, in REJ vol. 23 (1891) pp. 256—264.

Beate Rosenfeld, Die Golemsage. Breslau 1934.

G. Scholem, Reste neuplatonischer Spekulation bei den Deutschen Chassidim, in MGWJ vol. 75 (1931) pp. 172—191.

Idem, Golem, in EJ vol. VII col. 501—507.

I. N. Simhoni, החסידות האשכנזית בימי הבינים, in הצפירה 1917 in continuations.

Joshua Trachtenberg, Jewish Magic and Superstition. New York 1939.

BIBLIOGRAPHY TO LECTURE IV

ABRAHAM ABULAFIA AND THE DOCTRINE OF PROPHETIC KABBALISM

Dov Baer ben Shneur Zalman, קונטרס ההתפעלות, best edition Warsaw 1868 under the title ס' ליקוטי ביאורים.

Joseph Gikatila, גנת אגוז. Hanau 1614.

Adolph Jellinek. גנזי חכמת הקבלה. Title of the German part: Auswahl kabbalistischer Mystik. Leipzig 1853.

Idem, Philosophie und Kabbala, Erstes Heft, enthaelt Abraham Abulafia's Sendschreiben ueber Philosophie und Kabbala. Leipzig 1854.

Idem, *Sefer Ha-Oth*, Apokalypse des Pseudo-Propheten und Pseudo-Messias Abraham Abulafia. Published in Jubelschrift zum siebzigsten Geburtstage des Prof. Dr. H. Graetz. Breslau 1887 pp. 65—88 of the Hebrew section.

Idem, Bet Ha-Midrash vol. III (1855) pp. XL-XLIII of the Introduction.

M. H. Landauer, Vorlaeufiger Bericht in Ansehung des Sohar, in Literaturblatt des Orient vol. VI (1845), in twelve issues. [On Abulafia as author of the Zohar.]

G. Scholem, כתבי יד בקבלה הנמצאים בבית הספרים הלאומי והאוניברסיטאי בירושלים. Jerusalem 1930 pp. 24—30; 89—91; 225—236.

Idem, „שערי צדק" מאמר בקבלה מאסכולת ר' אברהם אבולעפיה *in Kirjath Sefer* vol. I (1924) pp. 127—139.

Idem, פרקים מס' סולם העליה לר' יהודה אלבוטיני in *Kirjath Sefer* vol. XXII (1945) pp. 161—171.

Idem, Eine kabbalistische Deutung der Prophetie als Selbstbegegnung, in MGWJ vol. 74 (1930) pp. 285—290.

Moritz Steinschneider, Die Hebraeischen Handschriften der Hof- und Staatsbibliothek in Muenchen. 1895, pp. 142—146. [On Abulafia's prophetical writings].

Simon Bernfeld, בני עליה Tel Aviv 1931, pp. 68—90; [sic!] אברהם אבועלפיא.

I. Guenzig, המקובל ר' אברהם אבולאפיא in *Ha-Eshkol* vol. V (1904) pp. 85—112.

On the theory of meditation on the Holy Names:

Pseudo-Abraham of Granada, ברית מנוחה Amsterdam 1648.

Moses Cordovero, פרדס רמונים Cracow 1592, chapters XX, XXI and XXX.

BIBLIOGRAPHY TO LECTURES V AND VI

THE ZOHAR. THE BOOK AND ITS AUTHOR. THE THEOSOPHIC DOCTRINE
OF THE ZOHAR

(a) *Texts*:

ספר הזהר 3 vols. Vilna 1882.

זהר חדש Warsaw 1885.

תיקוני זהר Mantua 1558; Amsterdam 1718.

ספר הזהר vol. I-II (Genesis and Exodus) with Rabbinic parallels ניצוצי זהר
by Reuben Margulies. Jerusalem 1940—1944.

ס' ארחות חיים הנקרא צוואת ר' אליעזר הגדול with the commentary דמשק
אליעזר by Abraham M. Vernikovski. Warsaw 1888

Moses de Leon, הנפש החכמה Basle 1608.

Idem, שקל הקדש London 1911.

Joseph Gikatila, שערי אורה Offenbach 1715.

Meir ibn Gabbai, דרך אמונה Berlin 1850.

Perez[?], מערכת האלהות Mantua 1558.

Abraham Azulai, אור החמה 4 vols. Przemysl 1896—98.

Simeon ibn Labi, כתם פז 2 vols. Livorno 1795.

[The last two works are the most valuable commentaries on the Zohar yet
produced. A complete list of these commentaries is given in my Bibliographia Kabbalistica, pp. 183—210]

Menahem Recanati, פירוש על התורה על דרך האמת Venice 1523.

ספר הפליאה Koretz 1784.

ספר הקנה Poritzk 1786.

ספר התמונה Lemberg 1892.

The Zohar. Translated by Harry Sperling and Maurice Simon. 5 vols.
London 1931—34.

Der Sohar. Das heilige Buch der Kabbala. Nach dem Urtext herausgegeben
von Ernst Mueller. Vienna 1932.

Die Geheimnisse der Schoepfung. Ein Kapitel aus dem Sohar von G.
Scholem. Berlin 1935.

Das Buch Bahir, ins Deutsche uebersetzt und kommentiert von G. Scholem.
Leipzig 1923.

(b) Studies:

W. Bacher, L'exegèse biblique dans le Zohar, in REJ vol. XXII (1891) pp. 33—46, 219—229.

I. Baer, "רעיא מהימנא" של ה„רעיא מהימנא הרקע ההיסטורי in *Zion* vol. V (1940) pp. 1—44.

Ariel Bension, The Zohar in Moslem and Christian Spain. London 1932.

Jacob Emden, מטפחת ספרים Altona 1768.

A. Franck, The Kabbalah or the Religious Philosophy of the Hebrews. Enlarged Translation by Dr. I. Sossnitz. New York 1926.

M. Gaster, Zohar, in Hastings' Encyclopedia of Religion and Ethics, vol. XII (1921), pp. 452—469.

H. Graetz, Geschichte der Juden, vol. VII note 12: Autorschaft des Sohar.

A. Jellinek, Moses de Leon und sein Verhaeltnis zum Sohar, Leipzig 1851.

Idem, Beitraege zur Geschichte der Kabbala, vols. I—II. Leipzig 1852.

D. H. Joel, Die Religionsphilosophie des Sohar und ihr Verhaeltnis zur allgemeinen juedischen Theologie. Leipzig 1849.

S. Karppe, Etude sur les origines et la nature du Zohar. Paris 1901.

Moses Kunitz, ספר בן יוחאי Vienna 1815.

M. D. G. Langer, Die Erotik der Kabbala. Prague 1923.

David Luria, מאמר קדמות ספר הזהר Warsaw 1887.

Isaac Myer, Qabbalah. The Philosophical Writings of Solomon Ibn Gabirol... and their connection with the Hebrew Qabbalah and Sepher ha-Zohar, etc. Philadelphia 1888.

David Neumark, תולדות הפילוסופיה בישראל על פי סדר המחקרים vol. I New York - Warsaw 1921, pp. 166—354.

Karl Preis, Die Medizin im Sohar, in MGWJ vol. LXXII (1928) pp. 167—184.

S. Rubin, Heidenthum und Kabbala. Vienna 1893.

G. Scholem, האם חבר ר' משה די ליאון את ספר הזהר ? in מדעי היהדות I (1926), pp. 16—29.

Idem, Alchemie und Kabbala, in MGWJ LXIX (1925) pp. 13—30, 95—110, 371—374.

Idem, שאלות בבקורת הזהר מתוך ידיעותיו על ארץ-ישראל with a note by Samuel Klein in the yearbook *Zion* vol. I (1925) pp. 40—56.

Idem, פרקים לתולדות ספרות הקבלה chapters I, II, VI, VIII, in *Kirjath Sefer* vol. IV (1928) pp. 286—327, vol. VI (1930) pp. 109—118, 385—419.

Idem, פרשה חדשה מן המדרש הנעלם שבזוהר in Louis Ginzberg Jubilee Volume (New York 1946), Hebrew Section, pp. 425—446.

vol. II   מדעי היהדות in קבלות ר' יעקב ור' יצחק בני ר' יעקב הכהן ,*Idem*
(1927) pp. 163—293.

Idem, לחקר קבלת ר' יצחק הכהן in *Tarbiz* vol. II—V (1931—1934).

pp. (1940)   מאסף סופרי ארץ ישראל in עקבותיו של גבירול בקבלה ,*Idem*
160—178.

Idem, Eine unbekannte mystische Schrift des Mose de Leon, in MGWJ
vol. LXXI (1927) pp. 109—123.

Idem, Vulliauds Uebersetzung des Sifra de-Zeniutha aus dem Sohar, in
MGWJ vol. LXXV (1931) pp. 347—362.

Ignaz Stern, Versuch einer umstaendlichen Analyse des Sohar, in Ben
Chananja I—V (1858—1862).

A. E. Waite, The Secret Doctrine in Israel. A Study of the Zohar and its
Connections. London 1913.

Hillel Zeitlin,"זהר„ח לספר מפתח in התקופה VI (1920) pp. 314—334; VII,
pp. 353—368; IX (1921), pp. 265—330.

J. L. Zlotnik, מאמרים מספר מדרש המליצה העברית. חלק אמרי חכמה Jerusalem
1939.

BIBLIOGRAPHY TO LECTURE VII

ISAAC LURIA AND HIS SCHOOL

(a) *Texts*:

Moses Cordovero פרדס רמונים 'ס   Cracow 1592; Munkacs 1906.

Idem, שיעור קומה 'ס Warsaw 1883.

Idem, אלימה רבתי 'ס Brody 1881.

Idem, תומר דבורה 'ס Jerusalem 1928.

Elijah de Vidas, ראשית חכמה 'ס Venice 1593.

Abraham Halevi Berukhim [?] גלי רזייא 'ס Mohilev 1812.

Joseph ibn Tabul,בה חפצי in שמחת כהן 'ס Jerusalem 1921 [ascribed erroneously to Vital].

Hayim Vital, עץ חיים 'ס Warsaw 1891.

Idem, פרי עץ חיים 'ס Dubrowno 1804.

Idem, שער הקדמות I: שמונה שערים Jerusalem 1850 (better edition 1909);
II/III שער מאמרי רז"ל and שער מאמרי רשב"י Jerusalem 1898; IV
שער הכוונות Jerusalem 1872; VI שער המצוות Jerusalem 1864; V שער הפסוקים
Jerusalem 1873; VII שער רוח הקודש Jerusalem 1874; VIII שער הגלגולים
Jerusalem 1863.

Idem, ספר הגלגולים complete edition, Przemysl 1875.

Idem, מבוא שערים Jerusalem 1904.

Idem, שערי קדושה Jerusalem 1926.

Israel Saruk, למודי אצילות Munkacs 1897 [ascribed eroneously to Vital.]

Shlomel Dresnitz, ס' שבחי האר"י Livorno 1790.

Isaiah Horovitz, ס' שני לוחות הברית Amsterdam 1648.

Naftali ben Jacob Elhanan Bacharach, ס' עמק המלך Amsterdam 1648.

Abraham Herrera, ס' בית אלהים ושער השמים Amsterdam 1655.

Joseph Ergas, ס' שומר אמונים Amsterdam 1736.

Emanuel Hay Rikki, ס' יושר לבב Amsterdam 1737.

Moses Hayim Luzzatto, קל"ח פתחי חכמה Koretz 1785.

ס' חמדת ימים 4 vols. Venice 1763.

Solomon Eliassov, ס' לשם שבו ואחלמה 5 vols. 1911—1935.

Christian Knorr von Rosenroth, Kabbala Denudata. Sulzbach 1677—1684.
[Copious Latin translations from Lurianic writings]

(b) Studies:

Ph. Bloch, Die Kabbala auf ihrem Hoehepunkt und ihre Meister. Pressburg 1905.

A. Berliner, Randbemerkungen zum taeglichen Gebetbuch (Siddur) Vol. I, Berlin 1909.

S. A. Horodezky, תורת הקבלה של ר' משה קורדוברירו Berlin 1924.

Idem, האר"י in מאזנים 1934 pp. 277—293.

Idem, תורת האר"י in כנסת III (1938) pp. 378—415.

Idem, מאה שנים של פרישות ומוסר in התקופה vol. XXII (1924) pp. 290—323; vol. XXIV (1928) pp. 389—415.

Idem, ר' משה חיים לוצאטו כמקובל in כנסת vol. V (1940) pp. 303—328.

Isaac Misses, צפנת פענח Darstellung und kritische Beleuchtung der juedischen Geheimlehre. Two fascicles, Cracow 1862/63.

Abraham Schechter, Lectures on Jewish Liturgy. Philadelphia 1933.

Solomon Schechter, Safed in the sixteenth century, in Studies in Judaism, second series (Philadelphia 1908) pp. 202—306, 317—328.

G. Scholem, שטר ההתקשרות של תלמידי האר"י in *Zion* vol. V (1940) pp. 133—160.

Idem, ישראל סרוג — תלמיד האר"י? in *Zion* vol. V (1940) pp. 214—243.

Idem, בקבלה האר"י של האמתיים כתביו in *Kirjath Sefer* vol. XIX (1943) pp. 184—199.

Idem, הלוי אליעזר בן אברהם ר' המקובל in *Kirjath Sefer* vol. II (1925) pp. 101—141, 269—273; vol. VII (1931) pp. 149—165, 440—456.

Idem, Lyrik der Kabbala? in Der Jude vol. VI (1921), pp. 55—69.

Idem, Der Begriff der Kawwanah in der alten Kabbala, in MGWJ vol. 78 (1934) pp. 492—518.

M. Teitelbaum חב"ד ומפלגת מלאדי הרב vol. II (1913) pp. 3—94 [on the *Tsimtsum* doctrine].

Isaiah Tishby, האר"י בקבלת והקליפה הרע תורת Jerusalem 1942.

J. G. Wachter, Der Spinozismus im Juedenthumb oder die von dem heutigen Juedenthumb und dessen geheimen Kabbala vergoetterte Welt. Amsterdam 1699.

M. Wiener, Die Lyrik der Kabbalah. Wien—Leipzig 1920.

BIBLIOGRAPHY TO LECTURE VIII

SABBATIANISM AND MYSTICAL HERESY

(a) *Texts*:

Abraham Miguel Cordozo, האלהות בסוד מכתב ed. Bruell, in המדרש בית ed. I. H. Weiss vol. I (1865) pp. 63—71, 100—103, 139—142.

Jonathan Eibeschuetz, עולם שם ed. Weissmann. Vienna 1891.

Jacob Emden, הקנאות תורת Altona 1752; Lwów 1877.

Idem, התאבקות Altona 1769: Lwów 1877.

Aron Freimann [editor], צבי שבתי ענייני Berlin 1913.

A. M. Habermann [editor], השבתאות נגד הפולמוס לתולדות in יד על קובץ new series vol. III, Jerusalem 1940, pp. 187—215.

Nehemiah Hayun, לאלהים עוז Berlin 1713.

Idem, צבי הצד Amsterdam 1714.

Moses Hagiz, פושעים שבר London 1714.

Idem, שרף לחישת Hanau 1726.

S. Ginzburg [editor], דורו ובני לוצאטו חיים משה ר' 2 vols. Tel Aviv 1937.

Jehuda Loewe ben Bezalel, ישראל נצח Prague 1599.

Nathan of Gaza, משיח בעקבות ed. G. Scholem. Jerusalem 1944 [a collection of some of his tracts on Sabbatian theology].

Abraham Perez, אגרת מגן אברהם ed. G. Scholem in קובץ על יד new series vol. II, Jerusalem 1938, pp. 123—155 [there erroneously ascribed to Cardozo].

Moses Porges, די זכרונות פון מאזעס פאראגעס ed. N. Gelber, in Historische Schriften, published by the Yiddish Scientific Institute, vol. I (1929) col. 253—296.

Jacob Sasportas, קצור ציצת נובל צבי Altona 1757, Odessa 1867.

(b) *Studies*:

M. Balaban, לתולדות חתנועה הפראנקית vol. I—II Tel Aviv 1934-35.

C. Bernheimer, Some new contributions to Abraham Cardoso's Biography, in JQR n. s. XVIII (1927) pp. 97—129.

Mortimer Cohen, Jacob Emden, A Man of Controversy. Philadelphia 1937.

H. Graetz, Geschichte der Juden, vol. X.

S. I. Hurwitz, מאין ולאן Berlin 1914. pp. 259—286.

David Kahana, תולדות המקובלים השבתאים והחסידים 2 vols. Odessa 1913/14.

Joseph Kleinmann, Moral i poezia Frankizma, in *Yevreiski Almanach*. Petrograd 1923 pp. 195—227 (in Russian).

A. Kraushar, Frank i Frankisci Polscy, 2 vols. Cracow 1895.

G. Levi, La lotta contro N. Ch. Chajjun a Firenze, in Rivista Israelitica vol. VIII (1911), pp. 169—185; IX (1912) pp. 5—29.

D. Kaufmann, La lutte de Rabbi Naftali Cohen contre Hayyoun, in REJ vol. XXXVI (1897), pp. 256—282; XXXVII (1898) pp. 274—283.

M. Perlmutter, ר' יונתן אייבשיץ ויחסו אל השבתאות Jerusalem 1947.

W. Rabinowitsch, מן הגניזה הסטוליניאית in *Zion* vol. V (1940) pp. 126—132. על ספר הצורף in *Zion* vol. VI (1941) pp. 80—84.

S. Rosanes, דברי ימי ישראל בתוגרמה vol. IV. Sofia 1935.

I. Sonne, ספר היובל לכבוד אלכסנדר מארכס in לתולדות השבתאות באיטליה New York 1943 pp. 89—104.

G. Scholem, מצוה הבאה בעברה in כנסת vol. II (1937) pp. 437—392.

Idem, חלומותיו של השבתאי ר' מרדכי אשכנזי Tel Aviv 1938.

Idem, מאמרים לזכרון ר' צבי פרץ חיות in חדשות לידיעת אברהם קארדושו Vienna 1933, pp. 323—350.

Idem, קובץ הוצאת שוקן לדברי ספרות Tel Aviv in שבתי צבי ונתן העזתי 1940, pp. 150—166.

Idem, פרשיות בחקר התנועה השבתאית in *Zion* vol. VI (1941) pp. 85—100.

Idem, ברוכיה ראש השבתאים בשאלוניקי ibid. pp. 119—147, 181—201.

Idem, Review of M. Cohen's Jacob Emden, in *Kirjath Sefer* vol. XVI (1939) pp. 320—338.

Idem.   לקט מרגליות (להערכת הסנגוריה החדשה על ר' יונתן אייבשיץ)   Tel Aviv 1941.

Idem,   לידיעת השבתאות מתוך כתבי קארדוזו   in *Zion* vol. VII (1942) pp. 12—28.

Idem, תעודות שבתאיות חדשות   מס' תועי רוח   in *Zion* vol. VII pp. 172—196.

Idem,   סדר תפלות של ה„דונמה"   in *Kirjath Sefer* vol. XVIII (1941—1942) pp. 298—312, 394—408; XIX pp. 58—64.

Is. Tishby, בין שבתאות לחסידות   in כנסת vol. IX (1945) pp. 238—268.

Ch. Wirszubski, האידיאולוגיה השבתאית של המרת המשיח in *Zion* vol. III (1938) pp. 215—245.

Idem, התיאולוגיה השבתאית של נתן העזתי in כנסת vol. VIII (1944) pp. 210—246.

Idem, השבתאי ר' משה דוד מפודהייץ   in *Zion* vol. VII pp. 73—93.

V. Zacek, Zwei Beitraege zur Geschichte des Frankismus in den boehmischen Ländern, in Jahrbuch fuer Geschichte der Juden in der Czechoslovakischen Republik vol. IX (1938) pp. 343—410.

BIBLIOGRAPHY TO LECTURE IX

HASIDISM: THE LAST PHASE

(a) *Texts:*

ס' צוואת הריב"ש   Warsaw 1913.

ס' כתר שם טוב   Podgorze 1898.

ס' בעל שם טוב   [A collection of all sayings of Israel Baal Shem, quoted in Hasidic literature] vols. I—II. Lodz 1938.

שבחי הבעש"ט   ed. Horodezky. Berlin 1922.

Dov Baer, the Maggid of Meseritz,   ס' מגיד דבריו ליעקב or ליקוטי אמרים   Koretz 1781.

Jacob Joseph of Pollenoji, ס' תולדות יעקב יוסף   Koretz 1780.

Elimelech of Lizensk, נועם אלימלך   Lwów 1788.

Phineas Shapira of Koretz, מדרש פנחס   Lwów 1872. נופת צופים   Piotrkow 1911;   תורת רבינו פנחס מקאריץ   ed. M.J. Gutman, Bilgorai 1931.

Nahman of Brazlav, ליקוטי מוהר"ן   1808—1811.

Idem, ספר המדות   Lwów 1872.

Nathan of Niemirov, ליקוטי תפילות Zolkiew 1872.

Idem, ס' שבחי הר"ן ושיחות הר"ן Lwów 1864.

Shneur Zalman of Ladi, ס' תניא or לקוטי אמרים Vilna 1912.

H. I. Bunin, ס' משנת חבד Warsaw 1936.

Aaron Halevi of Starosselye, ס' עבודת הלוי 1862—1866.

Israel Araten, ס' אמת ואמונה [A collection of the sayings of R. Mendel of Kotzk] Jerusalem 1940.

דרך חסידים and לשון חסידים [Two very valuable anthologies from Hasidic writings]. Lwów 1876.

(b) *Studies:*

A. Z. Aeshcoli-Weintraub, Le Hassidisme. Essai Critique, Paris 1928.

Martin Buber, Die chassidischen Buecher. Hellerau 1928.

Idem, Des Baal-Schem-Tow Unterweisung im Umgang mit Gott. Berlin 1927.

Idem, Jewish Mysticism and the Legend of Baal Shem. London 1931.

Idem, Deutung des Chassidismus. Berlin 1935.

Idem, מפרדס החסידות Jerusalem 1945.

H. Bunin, החסידות החב"דית in השלח vol. XXVIII (1913) pp. 250—258, 348—359; XXIX (1913) pp. 217—227; XXXI (1914/15) pp. 44—52, 242—252.

Benzion Dinaburg, ראשיתה של החסידות ויסודותיה הסוציאליים והמשיחיים in *Zion* vol. VIII (1934) pp. 107—115, 117—134, 179—200; IX pp. 39—45, 89—108, 186—197; X (1945) pp. 67—77, 149—196.

Simon Dubnow, תולדות החסידות Tel Aviv 1930/32.

Idem, Geschichte des Chassidismus, 2 vols. Berlin 1931.

Lazar Gulkowitsch, Der Hassidismus, religionswissenschaftlich untersucht. Leipzig 1927.

Idem, Die Grundgedanken des Chassidismus als Quelle seines Schicksals. Tartu 1938.

Idem, Das kulturhistorische Bild des Chassidismus. Tartu 1938.

S. A. Horodezky, החסידות והחסידים 4 vols. Berlin 1922.

Idem, Leaders of Hassidism. London 1928.

A. Marcus [Pseudon. Verus], Der Chassidismus. Pleschen 1901.

Jacob S. Minkin, The Romance of Hassidism. New York 1935.

Mordecai ben Jeheskel, למהות החסידות in השלח vol. XVII (1907) pp. 219—230; XX (1909) pp. 38—46, 161—171; XXII (1910) pp. 251—261, 339—350; XXV (1912) pp. 434—452.

Louis Newman, The Hasidic Anthology. Tales and Teachings of the Hasidim. Translated from the Hebrew, Yiddish and German. New York 1934.

Wolf Rabinowitsch, Der Karliner Chassidismus, seine Geschichte und Lehre. Tel Aviv 1935.

S. Schechter, The Chassidim, in Studies in Judaism vol. I, Philadelphia 1896, pp. 1—46.

G. Scholem ר' אדם בעל שם in Zion vol. VI (1941) pp. 89—93.

M. Teitelbaum, הרב מלאדי ומפלגת חב"ד 2 vols. Warsaw 1910/13.

Is. Tishby, בין שבתאות לחסידות in כנסת vol. IX (1945) p. 238—268.

Isaac Werfel, החסידות וארץ ישראל Jerusalem 1940.

Torsten Ysander, Studien zum Bescht'schen Hassidismus. Upsala 1933.

E. Z. Zweifel, שלום על ישראל... והוא ציור כללי ומושג הקפי מענין הבעש"ט ותלמידיו 4 vols. Shitomir 1868—1873.

SUPPLEMENT TO THE BIBLIOGRAPHY

LECTURE I. GENERAL CHARACTERISTICS OF JEWISH MYSTICISM

Jacob Agus, Le-Heker Hegion Ha-Kabbalah. In Sefer Ha-Shanah li-Yehudei Amerika, vol. VIII-IX (1946) pp. 254—279.

Ernst Benz, Die christliche Kabbala, ein Stiefkind der Theologie. Zürich 1958.

R. Edelmann, Jodisk mystik. Kopenhagen 1954.

Louis Gardet, Thèmes et textes mystiques; recherche de critères en mystique comparée. Paris 1958.

Christian D. Ginsburg, The Essenes, Their History and Doctrines. The Kabbalah, its Doctrines, Development and Literature. New York 1956. (Photostat of the 1863 edition).

Abraham J. Heschel, The Mystical Element in Judaism. In The Jews, edited by Louis Finkelstein. New York 1949. Vol. II, ch. XIII.

Jean René Legrand, Méditations cabbalistiques sur des symboles traditionels. Paris 1955.

Solange Lemaitre, ed., Textes mystiques d'Orient et d'Occident. Préface de Louis Massignon. Paris 1955.

G. Scholem, Kabbala und Mythus. In Eranos Jahrbuch XVII (1949) pp. 287—334.

Idem, Zur Entwicklungsgeschichte der kabbalistischen Konzeption der Sche-chinah. In *Eranos Jahrbuch* XXI (1952) pp. 45-107.

Idem, Collectanea to the Bibliography of the Kabbalah [Hebrew]. In *Kirjath Sepher* XXX (1954-1955) pp. 412-416.

Idem, Zehn unhistorische Sätze über Kabbala. Zürich 1958. (Reprint from Geist und Werk ... Zum 75. Geburtstag von Daniel Brody. Zürich 1958).

Idem, Die Lehre vom "Gerechten" in der jüdischen Mystik. Reprint from *Eranos-Jahrbuch* XXVII. Zürich 1959.

Georges Vajda, Recherches recents sur l'esoterisme juive (1947-1953). In *Revue de l'Histoire des Religions*, 1955.

LECTURE II. MERKABAH MYSTICISM AND JEWISH GNOSTICISM

Alexander Altmann, Shirei Kedushah be-Sifruth ha-Hekhaloth ha-Kedumah. In *Melilah: A Volume of Studies* II. Manchester 1946.

Robert Ambelain, La notion gnostique du démiurge dans les Ecritures et les traditions judéo-chrétiennes. Paris 1959.

Jean Doresse, Les livres secrets des gnostiques d'Egypte. Paris 1958.

G. Scholem, Reshith Ha-Kabbalah. Jerusalem-Tel Aviv 1948.

Idem, Hakkarath Panim ve-Sidre Shartutin. In S. *Assaf Jubilee Volume*. Jerusalem 1943, pp. 459—495.

Idem, Die Vorstellung vom Golem in ihren tellurgischen und magischen Beziehungen. In *Eranos Jahrbuch* XXII (1953) pp. 235-289.

Idem, Isaac of Acco's Commentary to the First Chapter of the Book of Creation [Hebrew]. In *Kirjath Sepher* XXXI (1955-1956) pp. 379-396.

Idem, Jewish Gnosticism, Merkabah Mysticism, and Talmudic Tradition. New York 1960.

Georges Vajda, Le Commentaire Kairouanais sur le "Livre de la Création." In REJ VII, pp. 97-156; X (1949-1950) pp. 67-92; XII (1953) pp. 5-33.

Idem, Nouveaux fragments arabes du commentaire de Dunash b. Tamim sur le "Livre de la Création." In REJ XIII (1954) pp. 37-61.

Idem, "Une citation kabbalistique de Juda ben Nissim." In REJ XVI (1957) pp. 89-92.

Idem, Saadya commentateur du "Livre de la Création." In *Annaire Ecole Pratique des Hautes Etudes, Section de Sciences Religieuses*. 1959-60.

LECTURE III. HASIDISM IN MEDIAEVAL GERMANY

G. Scholem, Magische und tellurische Elemente in der Vorstellung vom Golem. In *Eranos Jahrbuch* XXII (1953), pp. 235—289.

LECTURES V AND VI. THE ZOHAR

Alexander Altmann, A Note on the Rabbinic Doctrine of Creation. In *Journal of Jewish Studies* VII (1956) pp. 195-206.

Idem, The Motif of the "Shells" (Qelipoth) in Azriel of Gerona. *Ibid.* IX (1958) pp. 73-80.

Idem, Ha-Eschatologia shel R. Moshe de Leon be-Sefer Mishkan ha-Eduth. In *Otzar Yehudei Sefarad* II. Jerusalem, 1959.

Reuben Margalioth, Malachei Elyon. Jerusalem 1947.

Menahem Zevi Qaddari, The First Zohar Manuscript [Hebrew]. In *Tarbiz* XXVII (1957-1958) pp. 265-277.

Francois Secret, Le Zôhar chez les kabbalists chrétiens de la Renaissance. Paris 1958.

Gershom G. Scholem [editor], Zohar: the Book of Splendor. New York 1949.

Idem, Zur Entwicklungsgeschichte der kabbalistischen Konzeption der Schechinah. In *Eranos Jahrbuch* XXI (1952) pp. 45—107.

Isaiah Tishby, Mishnath Ha-Zohar. Vol. I, Jerusalem 1949.

Georges Vajda, "La conciliation de la philosophie et de la loi religieuse" de Joseph b. Abraham ibn Waqar. In *Sefarad* IX-X (1950).

Z. Werblowsky, Philo and the Zohar, part one. *Journal of Jewish Studies* X (1959) pp. 25-44.

LECTURE VII. ISAAC LURIA AND HIS SCHOOL

Moses Cordovero, The Palm Tree of Deborah. Transl. by Louis Jacobs. London 1960.

H. L. Gordon, The Maggid of Caro. New York 1949.

S. A. Horodetzky, Torath Ha-Kabbalah shel R. Moshe Cordovero (New Edition). Jerusalem 1950.

Idem, Torath Ha-Kabbalah shel R. Yizhak Luria. Tel Aviv 1947.

Yael Nadav, An Epistle of the Qabbalist R. Isaac Mar Hayyim Concerning the Doctrine of "Supernal Lights" [Hebrew]. In *Tarbiz* XXVI (1956-1957) pp. 440-458.

G. Scholem, Tradition und Neuschoepfung im Ritus der Kabbalisten. In *Eranos Jahrbuch* XIX (1950) pp. 121—180.

Idem, Derush al ha-Geulah le Rabbi Shelomo le-Beth Turiel. In *Sefunoth* I (1956) pp. 62-79.

Idem, Mekorotav shel Maase Gadiel ha-Tinok be-Sifruth ha-Kabbalah. Reprint from *Le-Agnon Shay*, Jerusalem 1958.

Idem, New Contributions to the Biography of R. Joseph Ashkenazi of Safed [Hebrew]. In *Tarbiz* XXVIII (1958-1959) pp. 59-89.

David Tamar, Safed Miscellany [Hebrew]. In *Tarbiz* XXVII (1957-1958) pp. 105-118.

Isaiah Tishby, Torath ha-Ra veha-Kelipah be-Kabbalath ha-Ari. Jerusalem 1952.

Idem, Gnostic Doctrines in Sixteenth Century Jewish Mysticism. *Journal of Jewish Studies* VI (1955) pp. 146-152.

Idem, The Sources of Hemdath Yamim [Hebrew]. In *Tarbiz* XXIV (1954-1955) pp. 441-455, and XXV, 1955-1956, pp. 66-92.

Idem, Early 18th Century Sources in Hemdath Yamim [Hebrew]. In *Tarbiz* XXV (1955-1956) pp. 202-230.

R. J. Zevi Werblowsky, The Character of R. Joseph Qaro's Maggid [Hebrew]. In *Tarbiz* XXVII (1957-1958) pp. 310-321.

LECTURE VIII. SABBATIANISM

A. Z. Aescoly, "Iton" Flandri al odot Tenuath Shabbatai Zevi. In *Sefer Dinaburg*. Jerusalem 1949. Pp. 215—236.

Y. Ben-Zvi, Sabbatai Zevi's Burial Place and the Sabbatian Community in Albania [Hebrew]. In *Zion* XVII (1952) pp. 75-78, 174.

Ben Zion Bokser, From the World of the Cabbalah: the Philosophy of Rabbi Judah Loew of Prague. New York 1954.

S. D. Goitein, On What Day Did Shabbetai Zevi Die? [Hebrew]. In *Tarbiz* XXVII (1957-1958) p. 104.

U. Heyd, A Turkish Document Concerning Sabbatai Zevi [Hebrew]. In *Tarbiz* XXV (1955-1956) pp. 337-339.

Jacob Leveen, An Autograph letter of the Pseudo-Messiah Mordecai ben Hayyim of Eisenstadt. In *Ignace Goldziher Memorial Volume*. Budapest 1948. Part I, pp. 393—399.

Jacob Sasportas, Sefer Tzitzath Novel Zevi, ed. I. Tishby. Jerusalem 1954.

Gershom Scholem, Regarding the attitude of Jewish Rabbis to Sabbatianism [Hebrew]. In *Zion* XIII—XIV (1948—49) pp. 47—62.

Idem, A Poem by Israel Najara as a Sabbatian Hymn (Hebrew). In *Ignace Goldziher Memorial Volume*. Budapest 1948. Part I, pp. 41—44.

Idem, A Sabbathian Will from New York. In *Miscellanies of the Jewish Historical Society of England*. Part V (1948) pp. 193—211.

Idem, R. Elijah Ha-cohen Ha-itamari and the Sabbathaism [Hebrew]. In *Alexander Marx Jubilee Volume*. New York 1950. Hebrew Section, pp. 451—470.

Idem, Where Did Sabbatai Zevi Die? [Hebrew]. In *Zion* XVII (1952) pp. 79-83.

Idem, Perush Mizmorei Tehillim mi-Hugo shel Shabbatai Zevi be-Adrianopel. In *Alei Ayin:* The Salman Schocken Jubilee Volume. Jerusalem 1953.

Idem, Le mouvement sabbataiste en Pologne. In *Revue de l'histoire des religions* CLXIII (1953) pp. 30—90, 209—232; CLXIV (1953) pp. 42—47.

Idem, A Letter of Abraham Cardozo to the Rabbis of Smyrna [Hebrew]. In *Zion* XIX (1954) pp. 1-22.

Idem, Parshath ha-Shabtauth. Jerusalem 1955 [mimeographed].

Idem, Shabbetai Zevi veha-Tenuah ha-shabtaith biymei Hayyav. 2 vols. Tel-Aviv 1956-57.

Idem, A New Document on the Early Sabbatian Movement [Hebrew]. In *Kirjath Sepher* XXXIII (1957-1958) pp. 532-540.

Isaiah Tishby, Teudoth al Nathan ha-Azati etc. In *Sefunoth* I (1956) pp. 80ff.

Idem, The First Sabbatian "Maggid" in the Bet-Midrash of R. Abraham Rovigo [Hebrew]. In *Zion* XXII (1957) pp. 21-55.

Idem, M. H. Luzzatto's Attitude to Sabbatian Doctrines [Hebrew]. In *Tarbiz* XXVII (1957-1958) pp. 334-357.

Idem, On the Teachings of Gershom Scholem in the Field of Sabbatian Studies [Hebrew]. In *Tarbiz* XXVIII (1958-1959) pp. 101-133.

Mordecai Wilensky, Four English Pamphlets on the Sabbatian Movement published in 1665-1666 [Hebrew]. In *Zion* XVII (1952) pp. 157-172.

K. Wilhelm and G. Scholem, The Proclamations against the Sabbatian Sect [Hebrew]. In *Kirjath Sepher* XXX (1954-1955) pp. 99-104.

Abraham Yaari, Taalumath Sefer (al Sefer Hemdath Yamim). Jerusalem 1954.

Solomon Zeitlin, The Sabbatians and the Plague of Mysticism. JQR XLIX (1958-1959) pp. 145-155.

LECTURE IX. HASIDISM

Isaac Alfassi, Toledoth ha-Hasiduth. Tel Aviv 1958.

Martin Buber, Or Ha-Ganuz. Jerusalem-Tel Aviv 1947.

Idem, Tales of the Hasidim. Two volumes. New York 1947—48.

Idem, Hasidism. New York 1948.

Idem, Die chassidische Botschaft. Heidelberg 1952.

Idem, The Way of Man According to the Teachings of the Hasidim. London 1950, Chicago 1951.

Idem, For the Sake of Heaven. A chronicle. New York 1953.

Idem, Christus, Chassidismus und Gnosis. In *Merkur,* Munich, October 1954.

Idem, The Legend of the Baal-Shem. Transl. by M. Friedman. New York 1955.

Idem, Hasidism and Modern Man. Ed. M. Friedman. New York 1958.

Idem, The Origin and Meaning of Hasidism. Ed. M. Friedman. New York 1960.

Samuel H. Dresner, The Zaddik: The Doctrine of the Zaddik According to the Writings of R. Yaakov Yosef of Polnoy. London-New York-Toronto 1960.

A. M. Haberman, Shaarei Habad. In *Alei Ayin,* The Salman Schocken Jubilee Volume. Jerusalem 1953. Pp. 293—370.

I. Halpern, Ha-Aliyoth ha-Rishonoth shel ha-Hasidim le-Eretz Yisrael. Jerusalem-Tel Aviv 1946.

Idem, The Attitude of R. Aaron of Karlin to the Kehilah System [Hebrew]. In *Zion* XX (1957) pp. 86-92.

Idem, Associations for the Study of the Torah and for Good Deeds and the Spread of the Hassidic Movement [Hebrew]. In *Zion* XXII (1957) pp. 195-213.

Idem, R. Levi Yizhaq of Berdichew and the Edicts of his Times [Hebrew]. In *Tarbiz* XXVIII (1958-1959) pp. 90-98.

A. J. Heschel, R. Gershon Kotover [Hebrew]. *The Hebrew Union College Annual* XXIII (1950—51), Part Two, pp. 17—71.

Idem, Umbekante Dokumenten zu der Geschichte fun Hasidus. In *Yivo Bleter* XXXVI (1952) pp. 113—135.

Idem, Le-Toledeth R. Pinhas mi-Koretz. In *Alei Ayin,* The Salman Schocken Jubilee Volume. Jerusalem 1953. Pp. 213—244.

Sigmund Hurwitz, Archetypische Motive in der chassidischen Mystik. In *Zeitlose Dokumente der Seele,* Zuerich 1952. Vol. III, pp. 121—212.

Judaism: A Quarterly Journal, Hasidism Issue. IX, Summer 1960.

Kitvei Rabbi Nahman, edited by Eliezer Steinman. Tel Aviv 1951.

Gershom Scholem, The Two First Testimonies on the Relations between Chassidic Groups and Baal-Shem-Tov [Hebrew]. In *Tarbiz* XX (1949) pp. 228—240.

Idem, Devekuth, the Communion with God in Early Hasidic Doctrine. In *Review of Religion* XV (1950).

Idem, The Polemic against Hassidism and its leaders in the Book Nezed ha-Dema [Hebrew]. In *Zion* XX (1955) pp. 73-81.

Idem, New Material on Israel Loebel and his anti-Hassidic Polemics [Hebrew]. In *Zion* XX (1955) pp. 153-162.

Joseph Yizhak Shneersohn, Sefer ha-Zikhronoth. Brooklyn, N.Y. 1955.

A. Shochat, On Joy in Hassidism [Hebrew]. In *Zion* XVI (1951) pp. 30—43.

Eliezer Steinman, Sefer Beer ha-Hasiduth. Tel Aviv 1954-1958.

Idem, Sefer Mishnath Habad. 2 vols. Tel Aviv 1956.

Idem, Sefer ha-Besht. Tel Aviv 1957.

Jochanan Twersky, Ha-Baal Shem Tov. Tel Aviv 1959.

Joseph Weiss, Beginnings of Hassidism [Hebrew]. In *Zion* XVI (1951) pp. 46—105.

Idem, R. Abraham Kalisker's Concept of Communion with God and Men. *Journal of Jewish Studies* VI (1955) pp. 87-99.

Idem, A Circle of Pneumatics in Pre-Hasidism. *Journal of Jewish Studies* VIII (1957) pp. 199-213.

Idem, Some Aspects of R. Nahman of Braslav's Allegorical Self-Interpretation [Hebrew]. In *Tarbiz* XXVII (1957-1958) pp. 358-371.

Mordecai L. Wilensky, The Polemic of R. David of Makow Against Hasidism. *Proceedings of the American Academy of Jewish Research* XXV (1956).

INDEX

Aaron ben Samuel of
  Baghdad, 41, 84
Aaron Halevi of Starosselje, 123, 423
Aaron Selig ben Moses, 390
Aaron Tutiever, 332
Abarbanel, Isaac, 247, 308
Abba, 270
Abbahu, 32
Abbayi, 360
Abeles, A., 415
Abelson, J., 55, 229, 359, 362
Abner, 97
Abraham, 26, 68 f., 366
Abraham Azulai, 408
Abraham bar Hiya, 86, 115, 117
Abraham ben Azriel of
  Bohemia, 85
Abraham ben David, 401, 407
Abraham ben Eliezer Halevi, 146,
  247, 408
Abraham Galante, 415
Abraham Halevi Berokhim, 230, 386
Abraham Hamoi, 374
Abraham ibn Ezra, 86, 142, 377, 383
Abraham Kalisker, 334
Abraham Perez, 312, 419
Abraham Yakhini, 417
Abulafia, Abraham, 17, 100, 120-
  145, 194, 205, 277, 321, 398
Abulafia, Joseph ben Todros, 394
Abulafia, Todros, 175, 187, 391,
  398 f.
Active intellect, see *Intellectus agens*
Acosmism, 123, 341
Adam, 21, 22, 232, 279, 281, 404 f.,
  413 f.
Adam Baal Shem, 331 ff.
Adam Kadmon, 215, 265, 267, **279**,
  400
Adam's Fall, 90, 91, 224, 231, 236 ff.,
  275, 278, 280, 282, 305, 316
Adam's soul, 278, 282
Adiriron, 55, 69, 114, 363

Aeons, 71 ff., 178, 179, 230
Aggadah, 19, 28, 31 ff.
Agnon, S. J., 349
Aha ben Jacob, 40
Ahad Haam, 326, 422
Aher, 358
Akhtariel, 56, 114, 356, 363
Akiba ben Joseph, 18, 42, 45f., 57,
  63 f., 66, 78, 356, 358, 359, 361,
  364, 369
Albertus Magnus, 126
Albottini, Jehudah, 141
Alfarabi, 26
Alkabez, Solomon, 285, 409
Allegory and Allegorization, 26 ff.,
  31
Alma de-peruda, 222
Alma de-yihuda 213
Altmann, Alexander, 28, 354, 375
Alphabet, 75, 132-138, 143, 147 f.,
  153 ff., 368; *see also* Language
"Alphabet of ben Sira," 87, 174
"Alphabet of Rabbi Akiba," 51, 66,
  360 f., 364 f., 367
Amitai ben Shefatiah, 84
Amora, Rabbi, 157
Anabaptism, 10, 301
Anamnesis, 92
Anafiel, 70
Angelology, 42, 272
Angelus Silesius, 405
Anthropomorphism, 63, 65 f., 111,
  114, 268
Antinomianism, 211, 291, 293, 296,
  299, 307, 312 f., 316, 319, 330, 334,
  359
Anz, W., 360
Apocalypse (Apocalyptic), 72, 87 f.,
  246, 248, 356, 367
Apocalypse of Abraham, 43, 52, 61,
  68 f., 72, 356, 363, 365
Apocalypse of Simeon of Yohai, 367

Apocrypha, 41
Apokatastasis, 402
Apostasy of the Messiah, 296, 299, 302, 306 f., 308-311, 321
Aptowitzer, V., 369, 372, 375
Archetypes, 117 f.
Archons, 49 f., 56, 356
Arikh Anpin, 270
Aristocratic character of Kabbalism, 81, 152
Aristotle, 26, 32, 80, 240, 249, 323, 398
Arugath Ha-Bosem, 364, 365, 370, 376 f.
Ascension of Isaiah, 54, 362
Asceticism, 49, 92, 96, 106, 235
Asiyah, 272, 282
Assaf, S., 370, 409
Association, technique of, 135
Astrology, 48, 117
Ataraxy, 96 f.
Atsiluth, 272
Attika Kaddisha, 270
Attributes of God, 11 ff., 74, 107 f., 114, 116, 143, 208, 213 f., 224
Augustine, 108, 126
Autobiography of mystics, 15, 38, 147 ff.
Avicenna, 26
Avodath Ha-Kodesh, 354
Avodath Ha-Levi, 423
Azikri, Eliezer, 251, 408
Azriel of Gerona, 173, 364 ff., 391, 401
Azulai, A., 408
Azza and *Azael*, 365

Baader, Franz von, 238, 405
Bacharach, Naphtali ben Jacob, 258, 357
Bacher, W., 173, 356, 361, 390 f., 400
Baeck, L., 368
Baer the *Maggid* of Meseritz, 334 f., 338 ff., 344, 350, 423
Baer S., 364, 370

Baer, Yitzhak Fritz, 83, 94, 234, 369, 371-374, 392, 404
Bahir, 35, 74 f., 157, 170, 175, 177, 191, 207, 214, 229 f., 242, 355, 367, 399 f., 407
Bahya ben Asher, 188, 374, 394, 405
Bahya ibn Pakuda, 170, 372
Balance, 266
Baldensperger, W., 356
"Baraitha on the Work of Creation," 73, 363, 367
Barochia, *see* Kunio, Baruch
Baruch of Arezzo, 416
Baruch Togarmi, 127
Basilides, 264, 269, 411
Baynes, Ch., 364
Belief, 303, 307
Benjamin Cohen, 303
Bennett, Charles, 20, 354
Bension, Ariel, 329, 422
Benz, E., 392
Berahya, *see* Kunio, Baruch
Berger, Paulus, 414
Beriah, 272
Berith Menuhah, 146, 255, 384
Berliner, A., 374 f., 415
Bernard of Clairvaux, 226
Bernfeld, S., 380
Bernhart, Joseph, 18, 354
Bernheimer, C., 419, 422
Bible, 10-12, 14, 19, 26, 28, 33, 71, 77, 90, 91, 105, 111, 248
Biblical exegesis, 46, 90, 210
Billerbeck, 357
Binah, 213, 219 f., 270
Black Magic, 144
Blake, William, 206
Blau, L., 384
Blavatsky, H. P., 398
Bleuler, 416
Bloch, Chayim, 373
Bloch, Philipp, 58 f., 61, 67, 108, 357, 359, 363, 365, 374
Boehme, Jacob, 190, 206, 237 f., 365
Boll, F., 360
Bonaventura, 253

"Book of Archetypes," 118
"Book of Combination," see Sefer Ha-Tseruf
"Book of Creation," see Sefer Yetsirah
"Book of Eternal Life," see Haye Olam Ha-Ba
Book of Ezekiel, 42
"Book of the Devout," see Sefer Hasidim
"Book of the Glory," 112
"Book of Life," 112, 376
"Book on Untying the Knots," 131, 380
"Book of Testimony," 128
"Book of the Wars of the Lord," 364
Books of Enoch, 40, 43-46, 52, 68 ff., 72, 89, 174, 200, 356 ff., 364 ff., 389, 376
Bosman, L. A., 398
Box, G. H., 61, 356, 361 f., 366
Breaking of the Vessels, 261, 265-268, 271, 280, 297, 305
Brody, H., 328
Bruell, N., 365
Buber, Martin, 325, 327, 342, 349, 354
Buechler, A., 359

Cardozo, Abraham Miguel, 296, 310, 315, 321, 323, 419-422
Carpocratians, 316
Cassuto, U., 370
Castilian and Catalan Kabbalism, 191
Catharists, 242
Catholic mysticism, 10, 277
Celsus, 360
Charles, R. H., 362
Cherub (on the throne), 110, 113 f., 116, 376
Cherubim, 67
Chiromancy, 48, 360
Chorin, Aron, 304, 419
Chotsh, Zevi, 421
Christian influence: on Sefer Hasi-

dim, 97 f.; on practice of penitence, 104; on Sabbatianism, 307
Christian mysticism and mystics, 5, 10, 44, 79, 84, 96, 103, 108, 132, 226, 319, 354
Christianity, 10, 19, 27, 43, 90, 307 f., 314
"Chronicle of Ahimaaz of Oria," 84
Clement of Alexandria, 355, 367, 420
Coenen, Th., 416
Cohen, Hermann, 36, 38, 355
Cohen, Mortimer, 421
Cohen, Tobias, 416
Combination of letters, see Hokhmath ha-Tseruf
Commandments, see Mitswoth
Community of Israel, 233
Constant, Alphonse Louis, 2, 353
Contemplation, 14, 16, 116, 122, 132, 137 f., 155, 287; see also Meditation
Coptic Gnostic Treatise, 365
Cordovero, Moses, 225, 251-255, 259 f., 265, 271 f., 279, 283, 378, 382, 399-402, 404, 408 f., 411-414
Corpus symbolicum, 28
Cosmogony, 20, 73-76, 222, 245, 260
Cosmology, 73, 75
Creation: 9, 10, 12, 17 ff., 27, 85, 111, 114, 133, 216-224, 245, 357, 368; out of God, 25; out of nothing, 25, 223, 262
Creator, 13, 16, 18, 27, 63-66, 70, 111, 322; see also Demiurge
Creuzer, F., 27, 354
Crowley, Aleister, 2, 353
Crusades, 80
Cryptography, 357
Curtain (Veil), 72, 74, 117, 273
Cynicism, 96 f.

Daniel Al-Kumisi, 367
Danton, 320
David ben Abraham, 354, 402
David ben Jehudah, 188, 399

David ibn Zimra, 392
Death, 249
De Divisione Naturae, 375
Demiurge, 12, 65, 114; *see also* Creator
Dempf, A., 402
Demuth, 117
Dennys, 360
Derush Ha-Tanninim, 296, 416 f.
Deus absconditus, 11, 12, 110 f., 271; *see also* God, hidden
Devekuth, 96, 123, 140 f., 233 f., 278, 335, 341 ff., 377
Dialectics, 218, 252
Dieterich, A., 362
Dillug, 135
Din, 213, 263, 267
Din shamayim, 94
Dionysius the pseudo-Areopagite, 354, 368, 395, 398
Divre Nehemiah, 421
Dobrushka, Moses, 421
Dodds, E. R., 354
Doenmeh, 303, 321
Domiel, archon, 53, 362
Donnolo, Sabbatai, 84, 370, 376
Dov Baer ben Shneur Zalman, 121
Dualism, 11-14, 65, 322
Dubnow, Simon, 325, 346, 423
Dzyan, 398

Eckhart, Meister, 126, 372, 378, 402
Ecstasy, Ecstaticism, Ecstatics, and Ecstatic experience, 5, 15, 50-60, 78, 86, 102, 119-123, 130 ff., 136-142, 278
Ecstatic Kabbalism, 123, 130-142
Eduth Be-Yaakov, 416
Effacement, 147, 149
Eibeschuetz, Jonathan, 321, 421
Eilenburg, Eliezer, 378
Eisler, R., 389
Eleazar ben Jehudah of Worms, 82, 85 f., 89 f., 92, 95 f., 99, 101-104, 108, 112, 116 f., 226, 239, 363, 367, 369-377

Eleazar ben Simeon, 157
Elements, 76 f., 362
Elhanan ben Yakar of London, 85, 376
Eliassov, S., 411
Eliezer ben Hyrkanus, 42, 182
Eliezer Kalir, 62, 255
Elijah, the prophet, 49
Elijah, the Gaon of Vilna, 109, 345, 348
Elimah Rabbati, 402, 409, 412
Elisha Gallico, 403
Elisha, the High Priest, 356
Elohim, 221
Emanation, 25, 209, 252, 261
Emden, *see* Jacob Emden
Emek Ha-Melekh, 258, 358, 371, 373, 408, 411 f., 414
Emotionalism, 345
Emunoth, 415
Emunoth We-Deoth, 86, 372
Enelow, H. G., 355, 389
Enlightenment, 23, 203, 301-304
Enoch and Enoch books, *see* Books of Enoch
Enoch the shoemaker, 365
En-Sof, 12, 208 f., 214-217, 218 f., 252, 261, 263 ff., 269-273, 297, 353
Epstein, A., 369 f., 375 ff.
Ergas, Joseph, 411
Eschatology and eschatological, 20, 88 f., 92, 241
Eshel Abraham, 121, 377
Esoteric character of Kabbalism, 21, 244, 329
Essenes, 43, 359
Ethics of Kabbalism, 233 ff., 342
Ets Hayim, 254, 409-414
Even Ha-Shoham, 384
Evil, 13, 35 f., 235-239, 263, 267 f., 311
Exile, 248 ff., 261, 274, 280 f., 284, 286, 288, 305, 312, 321 f., 336
Exile of the Shekhinah, 232, 250, 275
Exodus from Spain, 23, 244-247, 249

Ezra ben Solomon, 173, 355, 377, 391, 404
Ezra of Montcontour, 85, 370

Fano, see Menahem Azariah Fano
Faye, E. de, 420
Fendt, L., 420
Fetaya, Jehuda M., 415
First Cause, 322
Fourth Book of Ezra, 40, 54, 63, 362
Francis of Assisi, 83
Franciscans, 234
Franckenberg, Abraham von, 238
Frank, Jacob, 304, 308, 315-318, 319 ff., 336 f., 420 f.
Frankenstein, Carl, 353
Frankist movement, 315, 320 f., 330, 336, 420
Freimann, Jacob, 369, 375
French Revolution, 304, 320
Frey, Junius, 320, 421
Friedlaender, M., 359
Fuerst, A., 423

Galgalim, 71
Gali Razaya, 283, 414 f.
Galuth, see Exile
Gamaliel, 355
Gan Naul, 381, 383
Gandor, Samuel, 290, 295
Gaster, M., 65, 82, 170, 353, 365, 368, 386, 390
Gatekeepers, 50
Gebhardt, E., 392
Geiger, A., 1, 251
Gematria, 100, 127, 135, 373, 381
Gerona, 173, 251, 354
Geronese school of Kabbalism, 173, 176, 218, 354, 401, 404
Geulah, see Redemption
Gevurah, 213, 266
Gevuroth Adonai, 339, 423
Gikatila, Joseph, 127, 173, 194 ff., 212, 218, 222, 231, 236, 239, 355, 391, 395, 399, 405, 412

Gilgul, 242, 281-284, 407, 414; see also Metempsychosis
Ginnath Egoz, 173, 194 f., 391, 395
Ginzberg, Louis, 359, 366 f., 395, 404
Ginzburg, Simon, 17, 354
Glatzer, N., 367
Glory of God, 46, 66, 207; see also Kavod
Gnosis, Gnosticism and Gnostics, 13, 32, 35, 44, 49, 55, 65, 73 ff., 117, 166, 175, 229 f., 235 f., 238, 260, 267, 269, 279 f., 298, 316, 322 f., 355, 359, 420; see also Jewish Gnosticism
Gnostical school of Kabbalism, 175, 177
God: as absolute Becoming, 13; as absolute Being, 11, 13, 15; as Holy Being, 61; as indifferent unity, 12; as infinite Being, 11; as King, 55 f., 64, 107, 116; as an organism, 215; as prime mover, 108; as soul of the soul, 110; as union of contradictions, 13; G.'s conception in the Hekhaloth, 55; G. the Creator, see Creator; G. the Demiurge, see Demiurge; G.'s glory, see Glory and Kavod; experience of G., 4-5, see also ecstatic experience; hidden G., 12, 13, 108, 207, 322, see also deus absconditus; G.'s immanence, see Immanence; impersonal G., 12; living G., 13; manifestation of G., 11, 12; G.'s holiness, see Holiness; G.'s measurement, see Measurement and Shiur Komah; G. of Israel, 322 f., G.'s name, see Name; G.'s omnipresence, 108, 112; personal G., 12, 269, 271; presence of G., 7; quest for G., 10; relation with G., 6-9, 11, 226, 231, 341; transcendence of G., 347; unity of G., 10, 13, 231; voice of G., 7-8, 115
Goerres, Josef, 103

Golem, 99
Gottesdiener, A., 423
Graetz, Heinrich, 1, 22 f., 55, 61, 66, 159, 191, 203, 228, 251, 355, 359 f., 389, 394, 396, 400, 422
Greatness of God, see Holiness of God
Greek formulae, 53, 362
Greek mysticism, 6, 61, 277
Gross, 373
Gruenbaum, 366
Grunwald, M., 368
Guedemann, M., 84, 91, 369 f., 372 f.
Guenzig, I., 380
"Guide of the Perplexed," see Moreh Nebukhim
Guiraud, Jean, 407
Gulkowitsch, L., 371, 422
Guru, 140
Guttmann, Jacob, 402
Guttmann, Julius, 354
Guttmann, M. J., 385

Habad-Hasidism, 121, 340 f.
Habermann, A. M., 416, 418
Haggai, 390
Hagiz, Moses, 316
Ha-Hoker We-Ha-Mekubbal, 412 f.
Hai Gaon, 49, 200, 360 f., 367, 370, 396
Hakhmoni, 365
Hakkarath Panim, 48
Halakhah, 19, 28 ff., 47, 94 f., 98, 356 f.
Halakhoth Gedoloth, 367
Halperin, Israel, 419, 423
Hamoy, A., 366, 374
Hanina ben Dossa, 50, 60
Hannah Rachel, 355
Harba de-Moshe, 78, 368
Harkavy, A., 360
Hasde Hashem, 394
Hashmal, 71, 73, 103
Hasid, 91-95, 97-99
Hasidism (Hasidim), German, 37, 80-118, 144, 173, 226, 365

Hasidism, Polish, 1, 2, 10, 16, 19, 118, 325-350
Hasiduth, 91 ff., 95 f., 104, 343
Havdalah of Rabbi Akiba, 68, 78, 368
Haye Ha-Nefesh, 378-381
Haye Olam Ha-Ba, 135, 381, 384
Hayim Malakh, 303
Hayoth, 42, 73, 76
Hayun, Nehemiah, 321, 323, 420 ff.
Heavens, seven, 50, 54
Hebrew language, 17, 62, 134
Hecht, Koppel, 238
Heftsi Bah, 409
Heilprin, M., 415
Hekhaloth tracts, 20, 45-79, 114, 117, 160, 207, 356-368, 376
Hell, 243, 282, 362, 407
Hemdath Yamim, 285, 403, 415
Heresy and Heretics, 9, 10, 47, 65, 114 f., 125, 299, 306, 311
Herford R. T., 211
Herrera, Abraham Cohen, 257, 410
Hesed, 213
Heshel Zoref, 303, 332 f.,
Hibbut Ha-Kever, 89
Hibbur Ammude Sheva, 390
Hilkhoth Ha-Kavod, 371
Hippolytus, 411
Hirsch, S. R., 30, 351
History, 8, 19 ff., 90, 245, 274
Hithazkuth, 342
Hithlahavuth, 342
Hod, 213
Hoenig, A., 361
Hokhmah, 213, 219, 270
Hokhmath Ha-Nefesh, 370 f., 376 f.
Hokhmath ha-Tseruf, 133 f., 143, 145, 149, 153 f.
Holiness of God, 111, 115 f.
Holiness of sin, 315, 317, 319
Holy Spirit, 111 f.
Holy union in God, 228
Homiletics, 157 f.
Horedezky, S. A., 325, 355, 373, 400, 408, 410, 424

Horovitz, Isaiah, 251, 420
Hovoth Ha-Levavoth, 372, 390
Hurwitz, S., 302, 418
Husik, L., 406
Hymns, 57-62, 248

Idra di-be-Mashkana, 160
Idra Rabba, 160, 166, 181, 185, 215, 266, 386, 399
Idra Zutta, 160, 166, 181, 266, 392
Iggereth Ha-Kodesh, 404, 420
Iggereth Magen Abraham, 420
Iggereth Rav Sherira, 355
Imma, 270
Immanence of God, 55, 108 ff., 112, 216, 347
Imre Shefer, 135, 380 ff.
Incarnation, 307
Inge, 354
Initiation in *Merkabah* mysticism, 48
Intellectus agens, 131, 139 f., 143
Intention, *see Kawwanah*
Intuition, 10, 21, 120
Isaac ben Moses of Vienna, 94
Isaac ibn Abu Sahulah, 187
Isaac ibn Latif, 281
Isaac Hacohen, 120, 175, 178, 236, 378, 391, 401 f.
Isaac of Acre, 96, 106, 190 f., 354, 392-395
Isaac of Dampierre, 85
Isaac the Blind, 12, 353, 378, 399, 402, 415
Ishmael, 369
Ishmael the "High Priest," 42, 45, 48, 52, 64, 67, 71, 78, 356, 358
Islam and Moslem, 10, 37, 44, 66, 314
Israel, angel, 62
Israel Baal Shem, 96, 325, 330-334, 340, 346, 348 f., 385
Israel Bruna, 106, 374
Israel of Koznitz, 338
Israel of Rishin, 337, 349 f., 424

Israel Sarug, 257 f., 410
Italy, 47, 102

Jacob Anatoli, 374
Jacob ben Abraham de Botton, 416
Jacob ben Asher, 100
Jacob Emden, 392, 411
Jacob ben Jacob Hacohen, 100, 120, 175, 355, 378, 391
Jacob ben Sheshet, 120, 355, 401
Jacob Halevi of Marvège, 103
Jacob Isaac of Lublin, 346
Jacob Koppel Lifshitz, 333, 421
Jacob Weil, 374
Jacob Zemah, 409
Jaffe, Israel, 421
Jamblichus, 48, 360
James, William, 19
Jehudah ben Barzilai, 375
Jehudah Halevi, 24, 33, 173, 364
Jehudah Hasid (17th century), 331, 423
Jehudah the Hasid, 82 f., 88 f., 94, 98 f., 101, 103, 107 f., 112 f., 369, 372
Jehudah Hayat, 124, 378
Jehudah Loewe ben Bezalel, 308 f.
Jehudai Gaon, 78
Jellinek, Adolph, 124, 130, 199, 203, 372, 375, 378 f., 381, 383, 393, 395 ff., 419
Jerome, St., 42
Jerusalem, 278, 297
Jesus, 19, 308, 315, 368
Jewish Gnosticism and Gnostics, 5, 41, 50, 55, 65 f., 74, 115, 355, 357
Jewish mysticism, definition of and characteristics, 3, 6, 10, 13, 18-21
Jewish philosophy and philosophers, 23 ff., 28 ff., 35
Jewish theology, 28, 38, 63
Joaquin of Fiore, 179, 392
Job, 296, 298
Joel, D. H., 209, 399, 411
Joel, M., 359, 361
Johanan Alemanno, 383

Johanan ben Zakkai, 41 f., 47
John the Baptist, 295
John the Scot, 109, 354, 375
John of Scythopolis, 398
Jones, Rufus, 3, 4, 6, 353
Joseph, 235
Joseph Alkastiel, 410
Joseph ben Abba, 41
Joseph ben Shalom of Barcelona
    (Pseudo-Abraham ben David),
    217, 255, 401, 407
Joseph ben Uziel, 87, 370
Joseph de Avila, 190
Joseph ibn Sayah, 146
Joseph ibn Tabul, 254, 257, 263,
    409 ff., 413
Joseph ibn Wakkar, 189, 394
Joseph Jaabez, 408
Joskowitz, J. Z., 396
Jossel of Kletzk, 331
Juliana of Norwich, 37
Juspa Shamash of Worms, 369

Kabbalah, meaning of the term, 18,
    20, 197
Kabbalism, origins of, 75; popu-
    larity of, 250; popularization of,
    327 f., 339 f., 342
Kabbalistic Neoplatonists, 353, 355
Kabbalists as outstanding rabbis, 125
Kad Ha-Kemah, 374
Kaf Ha-Ketoreth, 248, 408
Kalonymides, 82, 84, 102
Kamelhar, Israel, 369
Kamelhar, Jekutiel, 369
Kamelhar, M., 400
Kaminka, A., 385
Kanah, 211, 255, 292, 400
Kant, Immanuel, 304
Kapotkia, 169
Kara, Avigdor, 371
Karma, 281
Kasdiel, 396
Katspiel, archon, 53
Kaufmann, D., 355, 422
Kav Ha-Middah, 161

Kav Ha-Yashar, 251
Kavod, 110-115, 358, 375
Kawwanah, 34, 101, 116, 275-278,
    335, 353, 373, 413
Kedushah, 60
Kedushath Levi, 353
Kelipah, 239, 267, 280, 297 f., 311
Keneseth Israel, 213
Kethav Tamim, 373, 374
Kethem Paz, 403
Kether Elyon, 213, 217
"Keys to Kabbalah," 127, 379
Kimhi, David, 388, 407
Kirkisani, 366, 376
Kithve Ha-Ari, 254
Klar, B., 370
Klein, Samuel, 169, 389
Kleinmann, Joseph, 420
Kne Binah, 407
Knorr von Rosenroth, 398, 410, 414
Knowledge, the unity of knower,
    knowledge, and the known, 141
Koch, Josef, 126, 378
Kook, Abraham Isaac, 18, 354
Kraus, Paul, 368
Kraushar, A., 420, 423
Krebs, Engelbert, 353
Kropp, 365
Kunio, Baruch, 321
Kunitz, M., 390
Kuntras Ha-Hitpaaluth, 121
Kuzari, 364

Landauer, M. H., 130, 379
Lange, J., 416
Langer, G., 403
Language, 14, 17, 75, 133 f.
Laniado, Solomon, 292, 295
Lauterbach, Jacob, 355
Left emanation, 177
Left side, 239
Lehishath Saraf, 420 f.
Leiner, G. E., 393
Letters, see Alphabet
Levi, Eliphas, see Constant, Al-
    phonse Louis

Levi, G., 422
Levi Isaac of Berdichev, 346, 353
Lewy, Johanan, 362
Liboron, H., 420
Liebermann, Saul, 356, 359, 362, 376
Lifshitz, J. K., 333, 421
"Light of Intellect," *see Or Ha-Sekhel*
Likkute Amarim, 423
Likkute Shas, 409
Likkute Torah, 409
Lilith, 174
Limmude Atsiluth, 257
Liturgy, 33 f., 57, 60 f., 100, 176, 285
Liturgy of Mithras, 53, 364
Livnath Ha-Sapir, 386
Loehr, M., 422
Loew, Leopold, 301, 418 f.
Logos, 107, 112, 114 ff.
Lot, 26
Love of God, 55, 95, 138, 226
Luria, David, 200, 396
Luria, Isaac, 17, 22, 82, 210, 251-266, 269-287, 294, 296, 304, 320, 340, 409 ff., 413, 418
Luria, Solomon, 109
Lurianic Kabbalism, 22, 251, 256-287, 292, 295-98, 302, 305, 308, 310, 320, 327 f., 330
Luzzatto Moses Hayim, 17, 251, 272 f., 412
Luzzatto, Samuel David, 1, 29

Maaminim (Sabbatians), 304
Maarekheth Ha-Elohuth, 158, 232, 353, 378, 385, 402
Maase Buch, 82, 369
Maaseh Bereshith, 20, 42, 55, 73, 75
Maaseh Merkabah, 143
Maayan Ha-Hokhmah, 399
Macarius the Egyptian, 79, 369
Macro-anthropos, 269
Mafteah Ha-Sefiroth, 382 f.
Magen David, 392
Maggid of Meseritz, see Baer the Maggid

Magic, 30, 33, 36, 49 f., 61, 77 f., 102, 144 ff., 153, 237, 277, 348 f.
Mahshav, 135
Maimonides, *see* Moses Maimonides
Maimon, Solomon, 331, 423
Malbush, 155
Malebranche, 252
Malik al-Sejdulani, 376
Malkhuth, 213
Man, 231, 233, 238, 273
Mani, Manichaeism, 243, 269, 280
Mann, Jacob, 362, 366 f.
Marcus, Aaron, 328, 400, 422 ff.
Margoliouth, M. M., 387
Margulies, Reuben, 388, 390
Markos, the Gnostic, 65, 365
Maroth Ha-Tsoveoth, 188
Marranos, 307-310, 319
Marriage, 235
Martyrdom, 146, 356
Marx, A., 370 f.
Mashal Ha-Kadmoni, 187
Masoreth Ha-Berith, 354, 402
Masekheth Atsiluth, 406
Mas'ud Hakohen Al-Haddad, 409
Mas'udi, 366
Mathematical mysticism, 76
Mathnithin, 161
Mead, 411, 418
Meah Kesitah, 415
Measurement of God, 71
Mechthild of Magdeburg, 37
Meditation, 5, 7, 10, 23, 34, 122, 125, 132-138, 143, 145 f., 150-153, 155, 221; *see also* Contemplation
Megillath Setharim, 384
Meirath Eynayim, 374, 395
Meir ibn Gabbai, 354
Meir ibn Abu Sahula, 405
Meitlis, 369
Menahem of Recanati, 243, 392, 393, 407, 415
Menahem Azariah Fano, 412, 415
Menahem Zioni, 367
Mendel of Kotzk, 345
Mendelssohn, Moses, 304

Menorath Ha-Maor, 374, 389

Meorer penimi, 139

Merkabah, 42, 46, 103, 223, 272, 295, 356, 358

Merkabah mysticism, 37, 40-79, 84 f., 89 f., 96, 102, 107, 110, 183, 206 f., 357, 359 f., 363 f.

Merkabah Rabba, 358, 360

Merkabah, second, 207

Merkabah Shelemah, 358, 360, 363 ff.

Meshare Kitrin, 408

Mesilath Yesharim, 251

Messiah, 72, 88, 274, 296-299, 308-312, 314 f., 318, 324

Messianic: — age, 302; — calculation, 87, 246; — end, 87, 89, 245 ff.; — tendencies, 244 f.; — world, 224, 319

Messianism, 245-248, 250, 284-288, 296, 305, 308, 329 f., 335 f.

Metatron, 67-70, 72, 140, 279, 356, 358, 366

Metempsychosis, 243, 250, 278, 281 ff.; *see also Gilgul*

Mevo Shearim, 410

Micro-cosmos, 269, 353

Middoth, 74

Midrash Ha-Neelam, 162, 166, 169, 181-188, 191, 193, 200, 204, 232, 239, 387, 406, 408

"Midrash of Rabbi Simeon ben Yohai," 188, 394

"Midrash of the Ten Martyrs," 51, 360

"Midrash on the Creation of the Child," 92

Midrash Rabba, 173

"Midrash to the Proverbs," 71, 377

"Midrash to the Psalms," 173

Midrash Talpiyoth, 396, 415

Midrash Ha-Zohar, 392

Miktav, 135

Minhath Yehudah, 378

Minim, 359

Minkin, Jacob, 325

Mishkan Ha-Eduth, 192, 195, 199, 201, 395, 398, 403, 406 f.

Mishnah, study of in remembrance of the deceased, 285

"Mishnah of the Hasidim," 94

Mishneh Torah, 29

Misses, Isaac, 411

Mitpahath Sefarim, 392, 411

Mitswoth, 28 f., 90, 149, 233, 242, 343

Mivta, 135

Molitor, Franz Josef, 2, 353, 411, 413

Monotheism, 11, 22, 38, 225, 322

Moralizing mystical literature, 250 f., 340, 342

Mordecai Ashkenazi, 121, 321, 377, 419

Mordecai of Czernobyl, 332

Moreh Nebukhim, 194, 251, 354, 378, 382, 391

Moses, 6, 170, 199 f., 226 f., 366

Moses Azriel, 109

Moses of Burgos, 24, 175, 178, 236, 391, 393, 399, 404

Moses Leib of Sassov, 346, 350

Moses de Leon, 159, 186-204, 218, 221, 223, 226 f., 231, 234, 236, 241, 243, 393-396, 398, 400-403, 405 ff.

Moses Maimonides, 11, 29, 38, 95, 97, 126 f., 138, 145, 148, 173, 183, 194, 203, 240, 251, 354, 364, 378, 383, 390, 395

Moses Nahmanides, 28, 125, 128, 173, 233, 235, 240 f., 255, 355, 373, 377, 385, 391, 401 f., 404 f., 410, 420

Moses Taku, 101, 109, 114, 364, 374

Moslem ascetics, 147

Moslem mysticism, 144; *cf.* also *Islam*

"Mourners of Zion," 371

*Musar-*books, 340

Mystical moralism, 118

Mystical Union, *see unio mystica*

Mysticism, definition of, 3, 4 ff.; *see also* Jewish mysticism
Mysticism of prayer, *see* Prayer mysticism
Myth, mythology, and mythical, 7 f., 13, 22, 29, 31, 34 37 f., 68, 87, 113, 117, 157, 174, 178, 225-230, 265, 269, 271, 297, 349

Nagid Umetsawweh 409
Nahawendi, 376
Nahlath Zevi, 421
Nahmanides, *see* Moses Nahmanides
Nahman of Brazlav, 20, 326 f., 337, 346, 424
Name of God, 56, 133, 137, 210, 213
Nathan Hannover, 413
Nathan of Gaza, 285, 288 ff., 292-298, 310 ff., 314, 321, 416-419
Nathan of Nemirov, 33
Natural forms, 131, 147
Nature, 7, 8
Nefesh, 240 f.
Nefesh Ha-Hokhmah, 393, 396
Negation of negation, 11
Nehuniah ben Hakanah, 355, 359
Nemoy, 376
Neoplatonism, 20, 48, 86, 115 f., 166, 175, 184, 203, 208, 257, 260, 353, 402
Neshamah, 240 f.
Netsah, 213
Netsah Yisrael, 419
Neubauer, A., 355, 369
Neuhausen, S. A., 391
Neumark, David, 158, 385, 392
Newman, Louis, 327
Nihilism, mystical, 299, 303, 309, 314-318
Ninck, M., 361
Notarikon, 99, 127
Nothing, the mystical experience of, 5, 25, 217 f., 221

Occultism, 86
Odeberg, Hugo, 45, 356, 357, 362, 365 f.

Odes of Solomon, 368
Oetinger, F. C., 238, 405
Ofannim, 67, 71, 73, 363
Olam Ha-Nekudoth, 265
Olam Ha-Tohu, 265
Ophites, 298, 360
Or Ha-Ganuz, 423
Or Ha-Hamah, 408, 415
Or Ha-Sekhel, 135, 379, 381
Or Ha-Yashar, 403
Orhoth Hayim, 393
Orhoth Zaddikim, 409
Origenes, 355 f., 360 f.
Original Sin, *see* Adam's Fall
Oroth Ha-Kodesh, 354
Or Yisrael, 421
Or Zarua, 94, 395
Otsar Ha-Kavod, 188, 391
Otto, Rudolf, 57, 363
Oz Lelohim, 420, 422

Pablo Christiani, 128
Palaces, heavenly, 49, 78
Palestine, 250
Pantheism, 38, 107, 109 f., 123, 141, 216, 222 ff., 241, 251 f., 258, 262, 272, 341, 347, 409
Paradise, 89
Pardes, 400
Pardes Rimonim, 382, 399, 401 f., 404, 411, 413
Partsuf, 269-273
Path of the Names, 143 f., 150
Path of the Sefiroth, 143
Paul, the Apostle, 295, 368
Pauly, Jean de, 212, 388
Pedro de la Caballeria, 407
Peliah, 211, 244, 321, 400 f., 407
Penitence, 78, 104 f.; *see also Te-shuvah*
Perek Shirah, 62
Perez of Barcelona, 353, 385
Peri Ets Hayim, 408, 413
Perlmutter, M. A., 422
Perush Al Ha-Torah, 407, 415
Perush Shir Ha-Shirim, 403

Pesiktoth, 173, 199 f., 371, 402
Petahyah of Regensburg, 88
Petrus Olivi, 234
Philo of Alexandria, 14, 110, 112, 114, 353
Philosophy, 22-28, 143 f., 323
Phineas ben Yair, 169
Phineas of Koretz, 156, 326, 378
Physiognomics, 48, 386
Pico della Mirandola, 354
Pinheiro, Moses, 292, 418
Pirke Rabbi Eliezer, 170, 173, 182
Pistis Sophia, 72, 366
Piyut, 57
Plato, 80, 117, 240
Platonism, 257
Pleroma, 44, 73, 207, 230, 265, 268
Plotinus, 203, 224, 272
Pneumatics 334, 347
Poppers, Meir, 397, 409
Porges, Moses, 320
Poverty as religious value, 234
Poznanski, Sam., 114, 376
Practical Kabbalism, 144,259
Practical mysticism, 125, 341
Praeger, Moses, 415
Prayer: 8, 33 f., 62, 100 f., 116, 233, 274-277, 285, 334, 355, 415; mysticism of, 100 ff., 116, 373
Preis, Karl, 392
Preisendanz, 362
Primo, Samuel, 321, 421
Primordial man, 65, 365
Primordial point, 173, 218 ff.
Proclus, 354, 368
Prophecy, 102, 111, 113, 116, 118, 138-142, 144
Prophetic Kabbalism, 125, 130-155, 193, 205
Prophets, 6
Provence, 33, 75
Psychology, mystical, 90, 239-242, 282, 341
Pushinski, Sh., 388

Quakers, 301

Rabia, 37
Rabbinical Judaism, 47
Rabinowitsch, W., 419, 423
Rachel, 270, 275
Radical Sabbatianism, 314 ff., 317 ff.
Rahamim, 213
Rashi, 93, 173, 366 f.
Rationalism, 23, 301, 345
Rav, 74
Rava, 41
Rav Methivtha, 161
Rav Pealim, 399
Raya Mehemna, 162, 168, 170, 176, 180, 185, 188, 191, 211, 234, 244, 312, 387, 392 400, 420
Raza de-mehemanutha, 230
Raza de-Razin, 160
Raza Rabba, 75, 367
Raziel, 127, 138
Raziel, 363 f., 367, 371-374, 376
Rebirth, 249
Recanati, *see* Menahem of Recanati
Recejac, E., 225
Redeemer, *see* Messiah
Redemption, 9 f., 49, 72 f., 89, 142, 224, 231, 245-248, 250, 274, 286, 288, 305 f., 311, 314, 330
Rehumai, Rabbi, 157, 170
Reincarnation of Sabbatai Zevi, 302
Religion, the function of, 7
Religion, mystical, 10
Religious anarchism, 299
Repentance, 249
"Responses from Heaven," 103, 373
Restoration, *see Tikkun*
Reshimu, 264, 267
Reshith Hokhmah Ha-Katser, 251, 415
Resurrection, 89
Reuchlin, Johannes, 354
Revelation, 9-13, 17, 22, 111, 217 f., 261, 323
Revival and revivalism, 334, 336, 338, 343
Riccius, Paulus, 400
Rikki, Emanuel Hai, 399, 411, 413

Rodkinsohn, 372
Rokeah, 82, 95
Root of all Roots, 12
Rosanes, S. A., 408 f., 411, 415, 417, 419
Rosenfeld, B., 373
Rosenberg, Y., 373
Roth, Cecil, 419
Rovigo, Abraham, 303, 321
Ruah, 110, 240f.
Rubin, S., 403

Saadia Gaon, 28, 38, 86 f., 96 f., 107 f., 111-114, 116f., 372, 375
Sabbatai Rashkover, 332
Sabbatai Zevi, 211, 287-296, 298, 300, 302-306, 308 ff., 312, 316, 319-322, 325, 328, 332, 336, 418-422
Sabbatianism, 10, 247, 288-324, 327, 328, 330-336, 346; *see also* Radical Sabbatianism
Sachs, Michael, 358, 406
Sachs, Senior, 358
Safed, 81, 247, 250 f.
Safed school of Kabbalism, 19, 226, 249, 259 f., 272, 281 f., 292, 305, 321, 338
Salmon ben Yeruhim, 364
Salvation, 245, 268, 274, 306 f., 323
Sammael, 239, 406
Samuel ben Kalonymus the Hasid, 82, 102, 115 f., 376
Samuel ben Vital, 409
Samuel of Niniveh, 88
Sandalphon, 358
Sar Torah, 77
Sarah, 26
Sarug, *see* Israel Sarug
Satan, 177, 237, 405
Sava, 161
"Sayings of the Fathers," 93, 141
Schechter, Abr. I., 415
Schechter, Sol., 252, 347, 408, 424
Schelling, F. W., 409, 412
Schneerson, F., 123
Schopenhauer, Arthur, 134

Schreiner, 376
Schwab, M., 362
Schwarz, A. Z., 374
Sefer Eduth, 381 f.
Sefer Ha-Beriah, 310, 416
Sefer Ha-Emunah We-Ha-Bitahon, 355
Sefer Ha-Gevul, 399
Sefer Ha-Gilgulim, 281, 283, 402, 406 f., 409, 413 f., 418
Sefer Ha-Hayim, see "Book of Life"
Sefer Ha-Iyyun, 399
Sefer Ha-Kavod, 376
Sefer Ha-Kawwanoth, 413
Sefer Ha-Likkutim, 412-415
Sefer Ha-Malbush, 368
Sefer..Ha-Meshiv, 248, 408
Sefer Ha-Middoth, 424
Sefer Ha-Mishkal, 406
Sefer Ha-Oth, 128, 379-382
Sefer Haredim, 251
Sefer Ha-Rimmon, 187, 198, 203, 395 ff., 402 ff.
Sefer Ha-Shem, 399
Sefer Ha-Shorashim, 388
Sefer Hasidim, 83, 88 f., 92 ff., 97 f., 105 f., 117, 234, 369-377, 421
Sefer Ha-Tseruf, 135, 332
Sefer Ha-Yamim, 392
Sefer Melits, 379, 381
Sefer Yetsirah, 69, 75, 77, 84 f., 88, 99, 112, 126 f., 138, 145, 149, 153, 206, 353, 367 f., 399
Sefer Yuhasin, 392, 394
Sefiroth, 11, 13, 76 f., 112 f., 143, 177 f., 197, 206-209, 213-222, 224 f., 227 f., 233, 252, 265 ff., 269, 271
Self-knowledge, 18, 341
Senior, 369
Seraphim, 67, 73
Serpent, 297 f., 406
"Seventy Names of Metatron," 68
Sexual symbolism, 225-228, 235, 372
Shaar Ha-Heshek, 383
Shaar Ha-Mitswoth, 413
Shaar Ha-Yihudim, 409, 414

Shaar Ruah Ha-Kodesh, 415
Shaare Gan Eden, 421
Shaare Ha-Sod, 375 ff.
Shaare Kedushah, 122, 251, 413
Shaare Orah, 195, 212, 355, 395, 399,
    401, 404, 412
Shaare Teshuvah, 396
Shaare Tsedek, 146
Shaare Zion, 413
Shaddai, 140
Shahrastani, 66, 361, 371, 376
Sharabi, Shalom, 328, 414
Sheerith Yosef, 384
Shekel Ha-Kodesh, 393, 401
Shekhinah, 38, 66, 111 ff., 116, 192 f.,
    216, 220, 223, 226 f., 229-233, 235,
    270 f., 276, 323, 362, 376 f., 400, 403
Shemitah, 178 f.
Shelley, Percy, 220, 402
Shemonah Shearim, 254, 409
Shemtob ben Shemtob, 415
Shemuiel, 62
Shene Luhoth Ha-Berith, 251, 420
Sherira Gaon, 360
Shever Posheim, 420
Shevirath Ha-Kelim, see Breaking
    of the Vessels
Shimmushe Tehillim, 78
Shinanim, 67
Shiur Komah: the conception of,
    63-67, 70, 85, 113, 365, 367; the
    book, 400, 408, 415
Shivhe Ha-Ari, 409
Shivhe Ha-Besht, 423 f.
Shlomel Dresnitz, 253, 409
Shneur Zalman of Ladi, 340, 345
Shomer Emunim, 411
Shushan Eduth, 187, 393
Siddur Ha-Ari, 414
Siegfried, C., 375
Sifra di-Tseniutha, 160, 166, 185,
    254, 392, 398 f.
Silver, A. H., 379, 393, 415
Simeon ben Azai, 359
Simeon ben Lakish, 79
Simeon ben Yohai, 157, 159-163,
    169 f., 182, 188, 190, 228, 322

Simeon Duran, 388
Simeon ibn Labi, 403
Simhoni, J. N., 88 f., 371 ff.
Simon, Maurice, 162
Sin, 231, 236, 239, 241, 404, 406, 413
Sithre Othioth, 162
Sithre Torah (part of the *Zohar*),
    161, 184
Sithre Torah (commentary on the
    Moreh), 379
Sitra ahra, 178
Skipping, 154
Sode Razaya, 371-377
Solomon ben Adret, 125, 379, 385,
    405
Solomon ibn Gabirol, 33, 402
Solomon of Karlin, 332
Solomon of Luzk, 339
Song of Unity, 108, 374
Sonne, J., 422
Soul: 130 ff., 135, 153, 239-243, 250,
    278, 279; as throne of God's glory,
    77; the ascent of, 48-53, 62, 77,
    122, 154, 226, 276
Spaeth, Johann Jacob, 238
Spanish Kabbalism and Kabbalists,
    12, 19, 81, 111, 117, 124, 175, 177,
    226, 233, 259
Sparks: of the holy light, 268, 311;
    of the Shekhinah, 280
Sperling, Harry, 162
Spiegel, Sh., 356
Spinoza, 252, 409
Spinozism, 258
Spiritualization, the ways to it, 146-
    150, 153 ff.
Steinschneider, M., 1, 374, 378, 383,
    393 f., 398, 408
Stenring, K., 368
Stern, Ignaz, 388, 392
Stoffels, J., 369
Stoics, 96
Stoll, Otto, 360
Strack, 357
Stratton, G., 5
Sufism, 10, 96, 384

Sullam Ha-Aliyah, 141
Suriel, angel, 356
Suriyah, angel, 48
Symbol, symbolism, and symbolical, 25-28, 33 f., 36 f., 209-212, 214-218, 220 f., 225, 269
Synagogal poetry, 85
Syncretism: Graeco-Oriental, 40, 51; Jewish-Hellenistic, 68

Taalumoth Hokhmah, 409
Taame Ha-Mitsvoth, 392
Tabernacle, 357
Tabul, *see* Joseph ibn Tabul
Talmud, 18, 42 f., 50, 68, 71, 80, 111, 115, 164, 317
Targum, 164
Tcherikover, E., 422
Teitelbaum, M., 411, 424
Temunah, 178, 414, 420
Temurah, 100, 127
Teshuvah, 105; *see also* Penitence
Testament of Rabbi Eliezer, 183, 200, 407
Tetrassiyah, 56, 359
Theism, 181, 222, 252, 262, 272 f.
Theogony, 222 f.
Theology and theologians, 35, 249
Theology of Aristotle, 203
Theosophy and theosophical, 12, 30, 90, 205, 206 (definition), 236, 341; of German Hasidism, 107, 111-118; of Kabbalists, 75, 225, 268
Therapeutae, 14
Theresa de Jesus, 37
Theurgy, 56, 77, 145 f.
Thomas Aquinas, 4, 126, 253, 353
Throne, 5, 44, 46, 67, 74, 356
Throne-mysticism, 44, 68, 70, 73, 90
Tibbonides, 165
Tifereth, 213, 298
Tikkun, 233, 246, 265, 268 ff., 273-278, 283-287, 292-298, 305, 311-315, 327, 412

Tikkune Zohar, 162, 168, 170 f., 176, 180, 188, 191, 368, 387, 392, 400 f.
Tishby, Isaiah, 267, 391, 410, 412, 421
Tomer Devorah, 251, 414
Torah, 10, 14, 19, 28, 72, 141, 178 ff., 209 f., 233, 274 f., 279, 312, 323
Torah de-Atsiluth, 319
Torah de-Beriah, 319
Torath Ha-Adam, 391
Tosefta, 43
Totrossiyah, 56, 363
Trachtenberg, J., 368, 370
Tradition, 21, 23
Transmigration, *see Gilgul* and Metempsychosis
Tree of God, 214
"Tree of life," 180
Treves, Naftali, 363 f., 373, 376
Trinitarianism, 129, 307, 323, 380, 389
Trivush, S., 416
Troestlin the Prophet, 88, 370
Tsawaath Ha-Ribash, 423
Tsimtsum, 260-265, 271, 273, 297, 335, 348, 411 f.
Tykocinski, H., 374
Typological interpretation, 26

Underhill, Evelyn, 3, 6, 252
Unio mystica, 5, 55, 123, 226, 278
Union with God, 123, 249 f.
Union of contradictions, 13
Urbach, E., 370, 372

Valentinus, 269
Veil, *see* Curtain
Vernikovski, A. M., 393
Verus, *see* Marcus, Aaron
Vessels, 252, 266
Vidas, Elijah de, 251
Visions of Ezekiel, 54, 362
Vital, Hayim, 121, 251, 254 ff., 266, 272, 277, 279, 281, 283, 305, 378, 408-414, 418
Vulliaud, Paul, 386

Wachter, J. G., 410
Waite, Arthur Edward, 2, 212, 353, 400, 403
Way to God, 20, 34, 153, 345
Wehle, Gottlieb, 419
Wehle, Jonas, 304
Weil, Jacob, 106, 374
Weinberg, 370
Werfel, Isaac, 423
Westcott, W., 368
Wieder, N., 371
Wirszubski, Ch., 419 f.
Wistinetzki, J., 369-372
Women's place in Kabbalism, 37
"Words of Beauty," see Imre Shefer
Worlds, 117; 272

Xenophanes, 375

Yahya Kafih, 403
Yalkut Reubeni, 31 f.
Yalkut Shim'oni, 31
Yahoel, angel, 68 f., 366
Yehiel ben Asher, 373
Yenuka, 161
Yesod, 213, 228
Yesod Ha-Yesodoth, 376

Yetsirah, 272
Yihud, 230
Yoel, 68
Yoga, 139, 144, 146
Yonath Elem, 412
Yorde Merkabah, 47, 56, 61
Yoreh Hataim, 374
Yosher Levav, 399, 413
Yotser Bereshith, 65
Ysander, Torsten, 423
Yuhasin, 386, 388

Zacek, V., 419, 421
Zaddik, 344
Zadok ben Shemaryah, 303
Zaccuto, Abraham, 392
Zakuto, Moses, 303
Zeller, Edward, 189, 394
Zerubabel, 367
Zevi Hirsch of Zydaczow, 341
Zinberg, I., 379, 395
Zlotnik, J. L., 390
Zohar, 22, 33, 123 f., 129 f., 156-244, 246, 252-256, 260, 262, 266 f., 270-273, 296, 312, 320 ff., 355, 378, 408, 411 f., 417
Zoharariel, 56, 59, 69, 114, 356, 363, 376
Zunz, L., 1, 61, 356, 374, 391, 408